INTRODUCTION
TO THE NEW TESTAMENT

Founded by

PAUL FEINE AND JOHANNES BEHM

Completely reedited by

WERNER GEORG KÜMMEL

Professor of New Testament at Marburg University

14th Revised Edition

Translated by

A. J. Mattill, Jr.

NASHVILLE ABINGDON PRESS NEW YORK

EINLEITUNG IN DAS NEUE TESTAMENT

Copyright © 1965 Quelle & Meyer, Heidelberg

INTRODUCTION TO THE NEW TESTAMENT

Translation © 1966 by Abingdon Press

*Library of Congress
Catalog Card Number: 66-11944*

ISBN 0-687-19574-8

SET UP, PRINTED, AND BOUND BY THE
PARTHENON PRESS, AT NASHVILLE,
TENNESSEE, UNITED STATES OF AMERICA

FOREWORD

When I completely rewrote Paul Feine's and Johannes Behm's time-tested handbook of New Testament Introduction, it was my aim not only to bring the book up-to-date quite generally but especially to help French and English New Testament scholarship, which has won increasing importance in recent decades, to take the part it merits. It was, therefore, with great pleasure that I greeted the wish expressed in several quarters that an English translation of this book be published to make it accessible to those interested in the subject who do not read German. And I am very grateful to Dr. A. J. Mattill, Jr., who in a remarkable way has mastered the difficult task of transforming a complicated German original into a clear and readable English. I personally have examined the translation and am convinced that it reproduces the sense of the German text as correctly as possible. Some small slips in the German text have been corrected, without notation, and in the bibliographies care has been taken to mention English translations of German and French books and articles wherever possible. An English translation of Latin quotations is also given.

Marburg/Lahn, November 11, 1964.   WERNER GEORG KÜMMEL

PREFACE TO THE TWELFTH EDITION

In the year 1826 Martin Leberecht de Wette began the preface to his *Textbook of Historical-Critical Introduction to the Canonical Books of the New Testament* with the words:

If, with the joyous feeling which the completion of a long protracted work instills, I give to the public this Introduction to the N. T. which was announced long ago, I cannot, on the other hand, conceal that I fear not to fulfill the expectations which one appears to entertain concerning this work. The friends of critical investigations will not be satisfied with most of the indefinite results; those, on the other hand, who regard our Holy Scriptures only with the eye of pious devotion, will feel offended because of the freedom of the investigation.

I cannot better express my own thoughts towards this new edition of the "Feine-Behm." Quite some time ago when, after considerable deliberation, I assumed the task of bringing the "much used study book" (J. Behm) abreast of present-day research, I well perceived what a difficult and extensive task I had thereby assumed. Yet the more deeply I plunged into the work, the clearer it became to me that the book must be largely rewritten, though the structure and methodological aim of the book would be retained. My intention was to bring the new edition in a comprehensive manner abreast with international scholarship and at the same time to reach clear decisions in debatable cases. Nevertheless, I have not hesitated to leave open those questions to which no fairly certain answers can be given.

From the older literature (up to about 1940) which was mentioned in earlier editions, only those titles were taken over which today are still indispensable. Even to list completely the almost overwhelming amount of literature of the last twenty-five years was impossible for reason of space, and all specifically theological investigations had to remain out of consideration. Yet I have striven for completeness insofar that nothing really essential for introductory questions should be missing. Where possible, it is noted where further literature can be found. Literature which appeared after January 1, 1963, could not be taken into consideration. The titles, however, which came to be known to me up to the end of April, 1963, are mentioned in the bibliographical supplement.

For excellent help in procuring the extensive literature, in completing the manuscript and index, and for proofreading, I am greatly indebted to my assistants, Otto Merk and Adolf Fritz. My hearty thanks are also due to the kind helpfulness of Father Béda Rigaux, O.F.M., Brussels, who proofread the French titles and thereby contributed considerably to the trustworthiness of the bibliographical data.

Marburg, April, 1963   *Werner Georg Kümmel*

PREFACE TO THE THIRTEENTH EDITION

The completely reedited twelfth edition of the "Feine-Behm," which appeared in August, 1963, found such an unexpectedly favorable reception that already at the beginning of 1964 a new edition became necessary. In view of the short time since the conclusion of the manuscript of the twelfth edition, the incorporation of the literature published since then and thus a completely new edition of the book seemed impracticable. I have therefore limited myself to the correction of several small oversights and misprints and to the addition on pp. 392 ff. of the new literature which has appeared since 1963, without incorporating it into the text. The bibliographical supplement of the twelfth edition was combined with the supplement of the thirteenth edition.

Marburg, February, 1964 *Werner Georg Kümmel*

PREFACE TO THE FOURTEENTH EDITION

Contrary to all expectation, the thirteenth edition of the "Feine-Behm," which appeared at the beginning of 1964, was sold out already within a year. Hence in this fourteenth edition, as in the previous one, I have been able to correct only misprints and minor mistakes. The literature which has appeared from the beginning of 1963 to the end of January, 1965, has been added in an appendix. I am deeply grateful to a number of my colleagues and students for pointing out various inadvertencies and typographical errors.

Marburg, February, 1965 *Werner Georg Kümmel*

CONTENTS

Part I

The Origin of the New Testament Writings
A. THE NARRATIVE BOOKS
I. The Synoptic Gospels and the Acts of the Apostles

II

Explanation of Bibliographical Data

In the indexes to literature at the beginning of the individual sections and paragraphs
the titles are cited in chronological order, though the works of the same author are
grouped together. The names of authors cited within the text without titles of books
or articles refer either to the "Introductions to the New Testament" listed on pp. 27 ff.,
or to the commentaries on the respective books of the New Testament cited on pp.
387 ff., or to the literature given at the head of each section. All other works are cited
with titles or references. Monographs which appear in series are, as a rule, mentioned together with the name of the series (but when frequently cited only with the first
reference). In view of the numerous "new editions" whose texts are not changed at
all, only the last revised edition of a work is cited (especially in the index of commentaries), so far as it can be determined. Only in special cases is reference made to a
reprint or to an unchanged new edition.

LIST OF ABBREVIATIONS

AB .... *The Anchor Bible*
ad loc. .... *ad locum*
ägypt. .... ägyptisch
AGGW .... *Abhandlungen der Gesellschaft der Wissenschaften zu Göttingen, philosophisch-historische Klasse*
AKG .... *Arbeiten zur Kirchengeschichte*
ALBO .... *Analecta Lovanensia Biblica et Orientalia*
Anm. .... Anmerkung
Apg. .... Apostelgeschichte
Apk. .... Apokalypse
apost. .... apostolisch
aram. .... aramäisch
arm. .... armenisch
art. .... article
ASNU .... *Acta Seminarii Neotestamentici Upsaliensis* (formerly: *Arbeiten und Mitteilungen aus dem Ntl. Seminar zu Uppsala*)
AT .... Altes Testament
AThANT .... *Abhandlungen zur Theologie des Alten und Neuen Testaments*
AThR .... *Anglican Theological Review*
atl. .... alttestamentlich

Barn. .... Barnabasbrief, Epistle of Barnabas
Bauer, Wb .... W. Bauer, *Griechisch-deutsches Wörterbuch zu den Schriften des Neuen Testaments* . . . ,[5] 1958
Bb .... *Biblica*
BBB .... *Bonner Biblische Beiträge*
Bd. .... Band
BdJ .... *Bible de Jérusalem*
bearb. .... bearbeitet
Beginnings .... Foakes-Jackson, Lake, *The Beginnings of Christianity* I, *The Acts of the Apostles*, Vols. 1-5, 1920-33
Beih. .... Beiheft
BeO .... *Biblica et Orientalia*
bes. .... besonders
Bespr. .... Besprechung
BeTh .... *Beiträge zur evangelischen Theologie*
BFTh .... *Beiträge zur Förderung christlicher Theologie*
BhHw .... *Biblisch-historisches Handwörterbuch*
BhTh .... *Beiträge zur historischen Theologie*
bibl. .... bibliography
BJRL .... *Bulletin of the John Rylands Library*
Blass-Debrunner .... Blass-Debrunner, *Grammatik des NTl. Griechisch*, [7] 1943
BNTC .... *Black's NT Commentaries*
BR .... *Biblical Research*
BSt .... *Biblische Studien*
BWANT .... *Beiträge zur Wissenschaft vom Alten und Neuen Testament*

13

BZ .... *Biblische Zeitschrift*
bzw. .... beziehungsweise

c. .... *circa*
cath. .... catholic
CBL .... *Calwer Bibellexikon,* [5] 1959
CBQ .... *Catholic Biblical Quarterly*
CGTC .... *Cambridge Greek Testament Commentary*
ch. .... chapter
chaps. .... chapters
(I II) Chron. .... Chronik, Chronicles
(I II) Clem. .... I II Epistle(s) of Clement
CNT .... *Commentaire du NT*
Col. .... Epistle to the Colossians
Comm. .... Commentary
(I II) Cor. .... Epistle(s) to the Corinthians
CSCO .... *Corpus Scriptorum Christianorum Orientalium*
CSEL .... *Corpus Scriptorum Ecclesiasticorum Latinorum,* hrsg. v.
der Wiener Akademie der Wissenschaften

Dan. .... Daniel
DBS .... *Dictionnaire de la Bible,* Supplément
Did. .... Didache
Diss. .... Dissertation
DLZ .... *Deutsche Literaturzeitung*
Dt. .... Deuteronomium, Deuteronomy
Dt.-Jes. (Is.) .... Deuterojesaja, Deutero-Isaiah

ed. .... *edidit,* edited
e.g. .... *exempli gratia*
EH .... *Ecclesiastical History*
Einl. .... Einleitung
EKL .... *Evangelisches Kirchenlexikon*
engl. .... englisch
Ep., ep. .... *epistula(e)*
Eph. .... Epheserbrief, Epistle to the Ephesians
EphThL .... *Ephemerides Theologicae Lovanienses*
Erg. Bd. .... Ergänzungsband
Esr. .... Esra
Esth. .... Esther
Ét. bibl. .... *Études bibliques*
Eus. .... Eusebius
EH .... *Ecclesiastical History*
Ev., Evv. .... Evangelium, Evangelien
EvTh .... *Evangelische Theologie*
ExpT .... *Expository Times*
Ez. .... Ezechiel, Ezekiel

f., ff. .... following
Festschr. .... Festschrift
fr. .... fragmentum
FRLANT .... *Forschungen zur Religion und Literatur des Alten und
Neuen Testaments*
FuF .... *Forschungen und Fortschritte*

Gal. ....Galaterbrief, Epistle to the Galatians
GCS ....*Die griechischen christlichen Schriftsteller*, hrsg. v. der
Berliner Akademie der Wissenschaften
Gen. ....Genesis
GGA ....*Göttinger gelehrte Anzeigen*
Gn ....*Gnomon*
griech. ....griechisch

Hab. ....Habakuk, Habakkuk
HarvThR ....*Harvard Theological Review*
HarvThSt ....Harvard Theological Studies
Hb. ....Hebräerbrief, Epistle to the Hebrews
Hdb. ....*Handbuch zum Neuen Testament* (or only "Handbuch")
hebr. ....hebräisch
hellen. ....hellenistisch
Herm. ....Hirt des Hermas, Shepherd of Hermas
  m. ....   *mandata*
  s. ....   *similitudines*
  v. ....   *visiones*
Hier. ....Hieronymus
  vir. ill. ....   *de viris illustribus*
hrsg. ....herausgegeben
HThK ....*Herders Theologischer Kommentar zum NT*

i.a. ....im allgemeinen
ibid. ....*ibidem*
ICC ....*The International Critical Commentary*
i.e. ....*id est*
Ign. ....Ignatius
  Philad. ....   To the Philadelphians
  Smyrn. ....   To the Smyrnans
Int. ....*Interpretation*
IntB ....*The Interpreter's Bible*
Intr. ....Introductio, Introduction
Iren. ....Irenaeus
  Haer. ....   *Adversus Haereses* (cited according to Harvey's edition)
Isa. ....Isaiah

Jas. ....Epistle of James
Jbch. ....Jahrbuch, Jahrbücher
JBL ....*Journal of Biblical Literature*
Jer. ....Jeremia(h)
Jes. ....Jesaja
Jhdt. ....Jahrhundert
Jk. ....Jakobusbrief
Jn. ....Epistle(s) of John, Gospel of John
Joh. ....Johannesevangelium
joh. ....johanneisch
Johbr. (or I II III Joh.) ....Johannesbriefe (or 1. Johannesbrief, 2. Johannesbrief, 3.
Johannesbrief)
Jos. ....Josephus (cited according to the ¶¶ of Niese's edition)
  Ant. ....   *Antiquitates*
  Ap. ....   *Contra Apionem*
  Bell. ....   *Bellum Judaicum*
  Vit. ....   *Vita*

JR .... *Journal of Religion*
JThSt .... *Journal of Theological Studies*
Jub. .... Buch der Jubiläen, Book of Jubilees
Jud. .... Judasbrief, Epistle of Jude
Just. .... Justin
　Apol. .... *Apologie, Apology*
　Dial. .... *Dialog, Dialogue*

Kap. (p) .... Kapitel
kath. .... katholisch
Kath. Br. .... Katholische Briefe
KG .... Kirchengeschichte
(I II) Klem. .... 1. Klemensbrief, 2. Klemensbrief
Klem. Al. .... Klemens Alexandrinus
Kol. .... Kolosserbrief
Komm. .... Kommentar
kopt. .... koptisch
(I II) Kor. .... 1. Korintherbrief, 2. Korintherbrief
kor. .... korinthisch

lat. .... lateinisch
lit. .... literature
Lk. .... Lukasevangelium (or "Lukas" in sense of Lukasevan-
　　　　　　　　　　　　　gelium), Gospel of Luke
loc. cit. .... *loco citato*
LThK .... *Lexikon für Theologie und Kirche*, 2. Auflage
LXX .... Septuagint

Mal. .... Maleachi, Malachi
Manson, St. .... T. W. Manson, *Studies in the Gospels and Epistles*, 1962
MBE .... *Monumenta biblica et ecclesiastica*
Meyer .... *Krit-exeget. Komm. über das NT*, begründet v. H. A.
　　　　　　　　　　　　　W. Meyer
Mk. .... Markusevangelium (or "Markus" in sense of Markus-
　　　　　　　　　　　　　evangelium), Gospel of Mark
Moffatt .... *The Moffatt NT Commentary*
MP .... *Monatsschrift für Pastoraltheologie*
Mt. .... Matthäusevangelium (or "Matthäus" in sense of Mat-
　　　　　　　　　　　　　thäusevangelium), Gospel of Matthew
MThSt .... *Münchener Theologische Studien*
MThZ .... *Münchener Theologische Zeitschrift*

n. Chr. .... nach Christus
Ndr. .... Nachdruck or Neudruck (= reprint)
N.F. .... Neue Folge
NGGW .... *Nachrichten der Göttinger Gesellschaft der Wissen-
　　　　　　　　　　　　　schaften*
NIC .... *The New International Commentary on the NT* (=
　　　　　　　　　　　　　The New London Commentary*)
NovT .... *Novum Testamentum* (periodical)
Nr. .... Nummer, number
NRTh .... *Nouvelle Revue Théologique*
N.S. .... New Series, Nova Series
NT .... Neues Testament or Novum Testamentum, New Testa-
　　　　　　　　　　　　　ment, Nouveau Testament, Nuovo Testamento

NTA .... *Neutestamentliche Abhandlungen*
NTD .... *Das Neue Testament Deutsch. Neues Göttinger Bibelwerk*
NTF .... *Neutestamentliche Forschungen*
ntl. .... neutestamentlich
NTSt .... *New Testament Studies*
NTTS .... *New Testament Tools and Studies*
Num. .... Numeri, Numbers
NZSTh .... *Neue Zeitschrift für systematische Theologie*

o. ä. .... oder ähnlich
OC .... *Oriens Christianus*
OCA .... *Orientalia Christiana Analecta*
OLZ .... *Orientalistische Literaturzeitung*
OT .... Old Testament

p., pp. .... page(s)
Pap. .... Papyrus
par. .... parallel
Past. .... Pastoralbriefe, Pastoral epistles
(I II) Pet. .... 1. Petrusbrief, 2. Petrusbrief, I II Epistle(s) of Peter
Phil. .... Philipperbrief, Epistle to the Philippians
Phlm. .... Philemonbrief, Epistle to Philemon
Plsbr. .... Paulusbriefe
Plur. .... Plural
Pol. .... Polycarp of Smyrna
PRE .... *Realenzyklopädie für protestantische Theologie und Kirche*, 3. Auflage
Preuschen, *Analecta* .... E. Preuschen, *Analecta* II, ² 1910 (= Sammlung ausgewählter kirchen- und dogmengeschichtlicher Quellenschriften I, 8)
Prov. .... Proverbien
Prvbs. .... Proverbs
Ps. .... Psalm, Psalms
PW .... Pauly-Wissowa, *Realencyklopädie der klassischen Altertumswissenschaft*

RAC .... *Reallexikon für Antike und Christentum*
RB .... *Revue Biblique*
RBd .... *Revue Bénédictine*
RdQ .... *Revue de Qumran*
RechB .... *Recherches Bibliques*
Reg. .... Register
Rev. .... Revelation
RGG ² .... *Die Religion in Geschichte und Gegenwart*, 2. Auflage
RGG ³ .... *Die Religion in Geschichte und Gegenwart*, 3. Auflage
RHPR .... *Revue d'Histoire et de Philosophie religieuses*
RHR .... *Revue de l'Histoire des Religions*
RNT .... *Das NT übersetzt und kurz erklärt*, hrsg. v. Wikenhauser und Kuss (Regensburger NT)
Rom., Röm. .... Epistle to the Romans, Römerbrief
RQ .... *Römische Quartalschrift*
RScR .... *Recherches de Science Religieuse*
RThPh .... *Revue de théologie et de philosophie*
RVV .... *Religionsgeschichtliche Versuche und Vorarbeiten*

S. ....Seite
s. .... siehe
Sach. ....Sacharja
SaD ....Studies and Documents
(I II) Sam. ....1. und 2. Samuelbuch, I and II Samuel
Sap. Sal. ....Sapientia Salomonis
SBA ....*Sitzungsberichte der Berliner Akademie der Wissenschaf-*
                                ten, philosophisch-historische Klasse
SBU ....*Symbolae Biblicae Upsalienses*
SGV ....*Sammlung gemeinverständlicher Vorträge*
SHA ....*Sitzungsberichte der Heidelberger Akademie der Wis-*
                                senschaften, philosophisch-historische Klasse
Sir. ....Jesus Sirach
SNTSB ....*Studiorum Novi Testamenti Societas Bulletin*
SPIB ....Scripta Pontificii Instituti Biblici
Spr. ....Sprüche
SStW ....*Synoptische Studien für A. Wikenhauser*
StBTh ....*Studies in Biblical Theology*
StEv ....*Studia Evangelica,* TU 73, 1959
StG ....*Studies in the Gospels, Essays in Memory of R. H.*
                                Lightfoot, 1955
StTh ....*Studia Theologica*
Suppl. ....Supplement-Band (-Bände)
s. v. ....*sub voce*
Synpt. ....Synoptiker
synpt. ....synoptisch
syr. ....syrisch

Taf. ....Tafel
Tert. ....Tertullian
  de pud. ....*de pudicitia*
  adv. Marc. ....*adversus Marcionem*
  praescr. haer. ....*de praescriptione haereticorum*
Test. XII ....Testaments of the Twelve Patriarchs
ThBl ....*Theologische Blätter*
ThEh ....*Theologische Existenz heute*
(I II) Thess. ....1. Thessalonicherbrief, 2. Thessalonicherbrief, I II
                                Epistle(s) to the Thessalonians
ThHK ....*Theologischer Hand-Komm. zum NT*
ThJ ....*Theologische Jahrbücher*
ThLZ ....*Theologische Literaturzeitung*
ThRdsch ....*Theologische Rundschau*
ThRv ....*Theologische Revue*
ThSt ....*Theologische Studien*
Thv ....*Theologia viatorum*
ThWB ....*Theologisches Wörterbuch zum NT*
ThZ ....*Theologische Zeitschrift* (Basel)
(I II) Tim. ....1. Timotheusbrief, 2. Timotheusbrief, I II Epistle(s) to
                                Timothy
Tit. ....Titusbrief, Epistle to Titus
Torch ....*Torch Bible Commentaries*
tr. ....translated
TSt ....Texts and Studies
t.t. ....*terminus technicus*

TU .... *Texte und Untersuchungen zur Geschichte der altchrist-*
lichen Literatur
Ty .... *Tyndale NT Commentaries*
TZTh .... *Tübinger Zeitschrift für Theologie*

u.a. .... unter anderen (m)
u.A. .... und andere
u.ä. .... und ähnlich
u.o. .... und oft
u.ö. .... und öfter
UB .... *Die urchristliche Botschaft*
UNT .... *Untersuchungen zum NT*
usw .... und so weiter

v. .... von
V. .... Vers
VC .... *Vigiliae Christianae*
v. Chr. .... vor Christus
VE .... *Vox Evangelica. Biblical and Historical Essays by Mem-*
bers of the London Bible College, 1962
Verf. .... Verfasser
vgl. .... vergleiche
v.l. .... *varia lectio*
vol(s). .... volume(s)
VuF .... *Verkündigung und Forschung*

W. A. .... Weimarer Ausgabe
WGK, NT .... W. G. Kümmel, *Das Neue Testament. Geschichte der*
Erforschung seiner Probleme, 1958
WMANT .... *Wissenschaftliche Monographien zum Alten und Neuen*
Testament
WUNT .... *Wissenschaftliche Untersuchungen zum NT*

Zahn .... *Komm. zum NT*, hrsg. von Th. Zahn
ZAW .... *Zeitschrift für die atl. Wissenschaft*
ZKG .... *Zeitschrift für Kirchengeschichte*
ZkTh .... *Zeitschrift für katholische Theologie*
ZNW .... *Zeitschrift für die ntl. Wissenschaft und die Kunde der*
älteren Kirche
ZRGG .... *Zeitschrift für Religions- und Geistesgeschichte*
ZsystTh .... *Zeitschrift für systematische Theologie*
z.T. .... zum Teil
ZThK .... *Zeitschrift für Theologie und Kirche*
ZüB .... *Zürcher Bibelkommentare* (formerly *Prophezei*)

INTRODUCTION

§1. The Most Important Tools for the Study of the New Testament

Editions of the Greek NT

Most useful pocket-editions: Eberhard Nestle, *Novum Testamentum Graece*, 1898, reedited by Erwin Nestle ([13]1927) [24]1960 (together with K. Aland). Further B. F. Westcott-F. J. A. Hort, *The New Testament in the Original Greek*, 1886; A. Souter, *Novum Testamentum Graece*, (1910) [2]1947; Herm. v. Soden, *Griech. NT, Text mit kurzem Apparat* (pocket-edition), 1913; H. J. Vogels, *Novum Testamentum Graece* (1920) [4]1955 (cath.); A. Merk, *Novum Testamentum Graece* (1933) [7]1951 (SPIB; cath.); J. M. Bover, *Novi Testamenti Biblia Graeca et Latina*, (1943) [3]1953 (cath.; cf. thereto B. M. Metzger, JBL 66, 1947, 415 ff.); H ΚΑΙΝΗ ΔΙΑΘΗΚΗ, 2nd Ed. *with Revised Critical Apparatus*, edited by D. Kilpatrick and E. Nestle, 1958.

Critical Editions of the NT for specialized scholarly studies: C. v. Tischendorf, *Novum Testamentum Graece, ad antiquissimos testes denuo recensuit* . . . Editio octava major I 1869, II 1872, III (*Prolegomena, scripsit* C. R. Gregory) 1894; B. F. Westcott-F. J. A. Hort, *The New Testament in the Original Greek* I (1881) [2]1898, II (1882) [2]1896; Herm. v. Soden, *Die Schriften des NT in ihrer ältesten erreichbaren Textgestalt hergestellt auf Grund ihrer Textgeschichte* I, 1-3 (Untersuchungen) 1902-1910, II (Text mit Apparat) 1913; *Novum Testamentum Graece secundum textum Westcotto-Hortianum: Ev. secundum Marcum cum apparatu critico novo plenissimo* . . . edidit S. C. E. Legg, 1935; *Ev. secundum Matthaeum* . . . edidit S. C. E. Legg, 1940 (the edition is inadequate; see thereto H. J. Vogels, ThRv 34, 1935, 305 ff.; T. W. Manson, JThSt 43, 1942, 83 ff. Therefore it has not been continued).

Dictionaries, Concordances, Biblical Lexicons

Dictionaries and concordances to the Greek NT: W. Bauer, *Griechisch-Deutsches Wörterbuch zu den Schriften des NT und der übrigen urchristlichen Literatur*, ([2]1928) [5]1958; *A Greek-English Lexicon of the NT and Other Early Christian Literature*. Tr. Wm. F. Arndt and F. Wilbur Gingrich from 4th ed., 1952, 1957; F. Zorell, *Lexicon Graecum Novi Testamenti*, (1911) [3]1961; H. Cremer, *Biblisch-theologisches Wörterbuch der NTl. Gräzität* (1867); 11th., completely revised edition by J. Kögel, 1923; *Biblico-Theological Lexicon of NT Greek*. Tr. William Urwick from 2nd ed., 1878. Supplement to BThL, based on 3rd and 4th eds., 1886; G. Kittel-G. Friedrich, *Theologisches Wörterbuch zum NT* I-VI, 1933-1959; VII, 1960 ff.; *Theological Dictionary of the NT*. Tr. and edited by Geoffrey W. Bromiley, 1964 (only Vol. 1 complete); J. H. Moulton-G. Milligan, *The Vocabulary of the Greek Testament Illustrated from the Papyri and Other Non-Literary Sources*, 1914-1929; R. C. Trench, *Synonyms of the NT*, 1854, and often; tr. into German by H. Werner, 1907. —C. H. Bruder, *TAMIEION* . . . *sive Concordantiae omnium vocum NiTi Graeci*, (1842) [7]1913; A. Schmoller, *Handkonkordanz zum griech. NT*, (1869) [10]1953; W. F. Moulton-A. S. Geden, *A Concordance to the Greek Testament According to the*

Texts of Westcott and Hort, Tischendorf and the English Revisers, (1897) [8]1953;
R. MORGENTHALER, *Statistik des NTl. Wortschatzes,* 1958. German concordances, see
RGG[3] I, 1957, 1184.
 On the Greek OT: E. HATCH-H. A. REDPATH, *A Concordance to the Septuagint
and the Other Greek Versions of the Old Testament,* 1892-97, Suppl. 1906 (reprint
1954). On the earliest patristic lit.: E. J. GOODSPEED, *Index Patristicus sive Clavis
Patrum Apostolicorum operum,* 1907; *idem, Index Apologeticus sive Clavis Justini
Martyris operum aliorumque Apologetarum pristinorum,* 1912.
 Historical and theological dictionaries of the Bible:
 Calwer Bibellexikon, edited by TH. SCHLATTER (1893) [5]1959; *Stuttgarter Biblisches
Nachschlagewerk.* Anhang zur Stuttgarter Jubiläumsbibel, 1932; H. GUTHE, *Kurzes
Bibelwörterbuch,* 1903; T. R. CHEYNE-J. S. BLACK, *Encylopaedia Biblica,* 1899-1903;
J. HASTINGS, *A Dictionary of the Bible* (1898) [4/9]1909 ff.; *idem, A Dictionary of
Christ and the Gospels,* 1906-8; *idem, Dictionary of the Apostolic Church,* 1915-18;
F. VIGOUROUX, *Dictionnaire de la Bible,* 5 tomes, 1905-12, Suppl. I-VI, 1928-62 ff.
(cath.); E. KALT, *Biblisches Reallexikon* (1931) [2]1937-39 (cath.); K. GALLING, *Biblisches Reallexikon,* Hdb. zum AT, I, 1, 1937; E. OSTERLOH und H. ENGELLAND, *Biblisch-
theologisches Handwörterbuch zur Lutherbibel,* 1954; *Vocabulaire Biblique,* publié sous
la direction de J.-J. VON ALLMEN, 1954; *A Companion to the Bible.* Tr. P. J. Allcock
from 2nd ed. (1956), 1958. Published in England as *Vocabulary of the Bible,* 1958;
J. B. BAUER, *Bibeltheologisches Wörterbuch,* (1958) [2]1962 (cath.); *Deutsches Wörterbuch zum NT,* nach dem griech. Urtext bearbeitet von G. RICHTER, RNT 10, 1962
(cath.); *Vocabulaire de Théologie Biblique,* publié sous la direction de X. LÉON-
DUFOUR, 1962 (cath.); *Biblisch-historisches Handwörterbuch,* edited by B. REICKE and
L. ROST, I, 1962.

Grammars

 G. B. WINER, *Grammatik des NTl. Sprachidioms,* (1822) 8th ed. (1894) since
reedited by P. W. SCHMIEDEL (uncompleted); *A Grammar of the Idiom of the NT.*
Tr. W. F. Draper from the 7th ed. [1881?]; F. BLASS, *Grammatik des NTl. Griechisch,*
(1896), since the 4th ed. (1913) revised by A. DEBRUNNER, [10]1959 (the English
translation by R. W. FUNK [*A Greek Grammar of the NT and Other Early Christian
Literature,* 1961] also contains the emendations prepared by Debrunner for a new
edition); L. RADERMACHER, *NTl. Grammatik. Das Griechisch des NT im Zusammen-
hang mit der Volkssprache dargestellt* (1911) [2]1925 (= Hdb. 1); A. T. ROBERTSON,
A Grammar of the Greek NT in the Light of Historical Research, (1914) [4]1923; *idem,
Kurzgefasste Grammatik des NTl. Griechisch.* Deutsche Ausgabe von H. STOCKS, 1911;
J. H. MOULTON, *A Grammar of NT Greek I* (Prolegomena), (1906) [8]1908, II
(Accidence and Word-Formation, ed. by W. F. HOWARD), 1929; *idem, Einleitung in
die Sprache des NT.* Auf Grund der vom Verf. neu bearbeiteten 3. engl. Aufl. übersetzte
deutsche Ausgabe, 1911; F.-M. ABEL, *Grammaire du grec biblique, suivie d'un choix
de Papyrus,* [2]1927 (= Ét. bibl.); M. ZERWICK, *Graecitas Biblica,* [3]1955 (SPIB 92);
C. F. D. MOULE, *An Idiom Book of NT Greek,* (1953) [2]1959; K. BEYER, *Semitische
Syntax im NT* I, I, Studien zur Umwelt des NT I, 1962.

Hermeneutics

 F. SCHLEIERMACHER, *Hermeneutik und Kritik mit besonderer Beziehung auf das
NT,* edited by F. LÜCKE, 1838; J. C. K. v. HOFMANN, *Biblische Hermeneutik,* edited

by W. VOLCK, 1880; E. v. DOBSCHÜTZ, *Vom Auslegen des NT*, 1927; J. WACH, *Das Verstehen* I, 1926; II, 1929; III, 1933; E. FASCHER, *Vom Verstehen des NT*, 1930; F. TORM, *Hermeneutik des NT*, 1930; R. BULTMANN, "Das Problem der Hermeneutik," ZThK 47, 1950, 47 ff. (= Glauben und Verstehen II, 1952, 211 ff.); "The Problem of Hermeneutics," *Essays Philosophical and Theological* (Glauben & Verstehen, II), pp. 234-61. Tr. James C. G. Greig, [1955]; E. LERLE, *Voraussetzungen der ntl. Exegese*, 1951; E. FUCHS, *Hermeneutik* (1954) ²1958; G. EBELING, Art. "Hermeneutik," RGG³ III, 1959, 242 ff. (lit.); A. N. WILDER, "NT Hermeneutics Today," *Current Issues in NT Interpretation, Essays in honor of O. A. Piper*, 1962, 38 ff.

Complete NT Commentaries

From German evangelical theology of recent generations the following scientific commentaries on the entire NT are worthy of mention:

Kritisch exegetischer Kommentar über das NT, founded by H. A. W. Meyer; since 1832, sixteen divisions, whose up to sixteen editions have a strictly scientific character and thus reflect the changes in methods of NT exegesis (cited: Meyer I¹⁰, 1, etc.). *Critical and Exegetical Hand-Book to the NT.* Tr. by various people from the 3rd-6th eds., 1884-89.

Die heilige Schrift NTs zusammenhängend untersucht, by J. C. K. v. Hofmann, 1862 ff., 11 vols.; a masterpiece of ingenious expository skill ("Heilsgeschichte"), with much arbitrariness.

Kurzgefasster Kommentar zu den heiligen Schriften A und NTs, edited by H. L. Strack-O. Zöckler, 1886 ff.; conservatively oriented; now completely antiquated.

Hand-Commentar zum NT, edited by H. J. Holtzmann, 1889 ff.; brief explanation from the viewpoint of rigorous historical criticism; now thoroughly outmoded.

Kommentar zum NT, edited by Th. Zahn, 1903 ff.; seventeen volumes appeared; a large, important work of conservative exposition, with several distinguished essays, especially on textual criticism and the history of exegesis (cited: Zahn ⁴1, etc.).

Handbuch zum NT, edited by H. Lietzmann, 1906 ff., by G. Bornkamm, 1949 ff.; exegetically meager; theologically inadequate in the earlier editions; distinguished by its abundance of comparative material in contemporary history and in the history of religions and of languages (cited: Hdb.).

Kommentar zum NT aus Talmud und Midrasch by (H. L. Strack-) P. Billerbeck, 1922-61; a comprehensive, excellent collection of comparative rabbinic material, but no detailed commentary.

Das NT nach dem Stuttgarter griech. Text übersetzt und erklärt by O. Holtzmann, 1926; a quite scanty, eclectic exposition, scientifically unsatisfactory.

Theologischer Hand-Kommentar zum NT mit Text und Paraphrase, 7 vols., 1928-39; new revision edited by E. Fascher, 1957 ff.; written from the conservative point of view, but open to all problems of modern criticism; seeks to present the religious content of the NT (cited: ThHK).

Popular studies for educated persons, on a scientific basis:

Erläuterungen zum NT, by A. Schlatter, (1887 ff.) ⁴1928 (reprint); simple interpretations of the Scriptures.

Die Schriften des NTs übersetzt und für die Gegenwart erklärt (so-called "Göttinger Bibelwerk"), edited by J. Weiss (then by W. Bousset and W. Heitmüller), (1906) ³1917-18 (= ⁴1929); the biblical work of the "religionsgeschichtlichen Schule."

Das NT Deutsch. Neues Göttinger Bibelwerk, edited by P. Althaus and J. Behm, 1932 ff.; [7-9]1957 ff., edited by P. Althaus and G. Friedrich; aims to give expression to the present state of the scientific, historical investigation of the NT, but at the same time to make it relevant as a living authority for Christians of today (cited: NTD).

Die urchristliche Botschaft; an introduction to the literature of the NT, edited by O. Schmitz, (1929 ff.) [2-7]1951 ff.; seeks to set forth the original meaning of the primitive Christian message in its uniqueness and matchlessness (cited: UB).

Prophezei, Schweizerisches Bibelwerk für die Gemeinde, 1943 ff.; since 1960 *Zürcher Bibelkommentare;* within everybody's grasp; partly a strictly scientific, partly a more devotional, orientation (cited: ZüB).

The most significant English commentary is *The International Critical Commentary on the Holy Scriptures of the Old and New Testament,* edited by S. R. Driver, A. Plummer, and C. A. Briggs, 1895 ff.; a counterpart to Meyer's commentary, and of equal rank with it (cited: ICC).

Of conservative bent is *The New International Commentary* (in the English edition, *The New London Commentary*), 1951 ff.; very painstaking; intended for wider circles (cited: NIC).

The *Cambridge Greek Testament Commentary,* 1957 ff., offers a concise, very careful exposition of the Greek text (cited: CGTC).

Black's NT Commentaries, 1957 ff., contain detailed, strictly scientific exposition, yet are also directed to wider circles (cited: BNTC).

The Interpreter's Bible, 1951 ff., presents scientific and homiletic exposition side by side (cited: IntB).

The Moffatt NT Commentary, 1928 ff., is a biblical work for the educated (cited: Moffatt).

Tyndale NT Commentaries, 1956 ff., are conservative, with a strong theological slant, and have detailed historical introductions (cited: Ty).

Torch Bible Commentaries, 1949 ff., give full introductions and a brief commentary, with emphasis upon the religious significance (cited: Torch).

Commentaire du NT, 1949 ff., the series of commentaries of French-speaking Protestantism, is very independent and valuable (cited: CNT).

The most important Catholic series of commentaries to the NT:
Cursus Scripturae Sacrae, Sectio Tertia: Commentarii in NT, 1890 ff.

The commentaries of the French school of Dominicans in the *Études bibliques,* 1907 ff., are extensive and, for the most part, very solid interpretations, with full bibliographies (cited: Ét. bibl.).

Herder's Theologischer Kommentar zum NT, edited by A. Wikenhauser, 1953 ff., presents strictly scientific expositions (cited: HThK).

Intended for broader circles:
Die Heilige Schrift des NTs übersetzt und erklärt, edited by F. Tillmann, (1913 ff.) [2]1931 ff.; now superseded by

Das NT übersetzt und kurz erklärt, edited by A. Wikenhauser and O. Kuss, (1938 ff.) [3]1959 ff., so-called "Regensburger NT" (cited: RNT).

Le NT traduit en français sous la direction de l'École biblique de Jérusalem, 1958 (cited: BdJ). Also detailed separate editions under the title: *La sainte Bible traduit en français sous la direction . . . ,* 1948 ff.

Bibliographies

Biblica, the journal of the Papal Biblical Institute, regularly offers a systematic bibliography of all new publications, articles, and reviews in the area of NT studies. The *Internationale Zeitschriftenschau für Bibelwissenschaft und Grenzgebiete,* 1951 ff., and *NT Abstracts,* 1956 ff., contain summaries of periodical articles in all languages. Cf. also B. M. Metzger, *Index of Articles on the NT and the Early Church Published in Festschriften,* 1951, and his *Suppl. to Index . . . ,* 1955. NTTS, edited by B. M. Metzger, includes extensive bibliographies of NT literature: B. M. Metzger, *Index to Periodical Literature on the Apostle Paul,* NTTS 1, 1960; *idem, Index to Periodical Literature on Christ and the Gospels,* NTTS 6, 1966; A. J. and M. B. Mattill, *A Classified Bibliography of Literature on the Acts of the Apostles,* NTTS 7, 1966.

§2. CONCEPTION AND DIVISION OF THE INTRODUCTION TO THE NEW TESTAMENT

F. C. BAUR, "Die Einleitung ins NT als theologische Wissenschaft. Ihr Begriff und ihre Aufgabe, ihr Entwicklungsgang und ihr innerer Organismus," ThJ 9, 1850, 462 ff.; 10, 1851, 291 ff. (extracts in WGK, NT, 156 ff. 172 f.); TH. ZAHN, art. "Einleitung in das NT," PRE³ V, 1898, 261 ff.; W. G. KÜMMEL, "'Einleitung in das NT' als theologische Aufgabe," EvTh 19, 1959, 4 ff.; W. MARXSEN, "Die Bedeutung der Einleitungswissenschaft für die Predigtarbeit," MP 49, 1960, 1 ff. Cf. also, the introductory paragraphs of the NT introductions.

The scientific discipline of "introduction to the NT" treats the historical questions of the origin of the NT writings, their collection, and the textual tradition of this collection. It presupposes the existence of the NT canon, in which the church of the second to fourth centuries collected those writings which were supposed to serve as the norm for the church's preaching and to be read in worship. The science of introduction is, accordingly, a strict historical discipline. Through the clarification of the historical circumstances connected with the origin of the individual writings, it furnishes to exposition the necessary presuppositions for the understanding of the writings in their historical individuality. Through the study of the origin and the contents of the collection, it provides the secure historical basis for the question about the doctrinal contents of the NT. As a historical science, the science of introduction makes use of the methods of historical research, and for that reason it is a thoroughly justified goal of such research to treat the investigation of the circumstances surrounding the origin and of the literary connections of the individual writings as the oldest part of a "history of primitive Christian literature," and the elucidation of the origin of the canon as part of church history and of the history of dogma (cf. H. Jordan, *Geschichte der altchristlichen Literatur,* 1911, 69 ff.; P. Wendland, *Die urchristlichen Literaturformen,* Hdb. I, 3²,³, 1912; O. Stählin, *Christliche Schriftsteller* in: W. v. Christ, *Geschichte der griechischen Literatur,* revised by W. Schmid and O. Stählin II, 2, ⁶1924, 1105 ff.; M. Dibelius, *Geschichte der urchristlichen Literatur* I II, Sammlung Göschen 934 + 935, 1926; D. W. Riddle–H. H. Hutson, *NT Life and Literature*, 1946, and works on the history of dogma). The separate investigation of the twenty-seven writings collected in the NT canon as "introduction to the NT" has been objected to on historical grounds by G. Krüger, *Das Dogma vom NT*, 1896, and W. Wrede, *Über Aufgabe und Methode der sog. NTl. Theologie*, 1897. But in spite of these objections this special investigation is to be preserved, because the writings which have been collected in the NT have, through their belonging to the canon delimited by the early church, their special character recognized by Christians in faith. The laying of a secure historical foundation for the exposition of these writings is, therefore, an especially important task for the Christian theologian. Also, without a clear insight into the process and the motives behind the formation of the canon, theological reflection about the limit of the dogmatic validity of the norm of the canon cannot be properly undertaken. Not because of its scientific method, but only because of the peculiar nature of its subject matter, is, therefore, "introduction to the NT" a theological discipline. Corresponding to its historical character, the investigation proceeds appropriately from 1) the origin of the individual writings, to 2) the origin of the collection, and to 3) the preservation of the text of the collection.

§3. History and Literature of the Introduction to the New Testament

W. G. Kümmel, *Das NT. Geschichte der Erforschung seiner Probleme*, Orbis academicus III, 3, 1958 (abbreviated WGK, NT). Further, the relevant sections in the NT introductions by H. J. Holtzmann, A. Jülicher (also in English as *An Introduction to the NT*. Tr. Janet Penrose Ward, 1904), M. Meinertz.

Not until after the Age of Enlightenment has there been a science of introduction in the modern sense. Its development has taken place in the following chief periods:

1. The early church and the Middle Ages only seldom showed interest in the circumstances of the composition of the NT books in connection with the question of the canon (prologues to the Pauline epistles and Gospels, Muratorian canon, Origen, Dionysius of Alexandria). The *introductores scripturae divinae* (Tyconius, Augustine, Adrianos, who c. 450 wrote an *Introduction to the Divine Writings*, Eucherius, Junilius Africanus), which were combined by Cassiodorus, treat questions of exposition rather than of introduction.

2. Since the time of the Reformation there have come into use out of dogmatic and polemic interests—especially in the Roman Catholic Church—studies about the origin of the canonical books of the NT.

3. Proceeding from studies in textual criticism, the Oratorian Richard Simon, with his three books concerning the *Histoire critique* of the NT (1689-93), paved the way for NT introduction as a scientific discipline. In order to push on to the original text of the NT, he raised the question about the manuscript tradition and the origin of individual writings. Rationalism produced the first

great introductory work in which the problems of the origin of the individual writings and of the canon were consciously treated historically, though still with the interest of defending the canon: J. D. Michaelis, *Einleitung in die göttlichen Schriften des Neuen Bundes*, (1750) ⁴1788 (*Introduction to the NT*. Tr. Herbert Marsh from 4th ed. [1788], 1793; 2nd English ed., 1802), stimulated by R. Simon. At the same time J. S. Semler, in his *Abhandlung von freier Untersuchung des Canon* (1771-75), established the historical origin of the NT canon. J. G. Eichhorn's five volume *Einl. in das NT* (1804-27) provided the first really free investigation of the origin of the writings of the canon and of the text of the NT. There followed, with diverse handling of similar critical standards, the works of de Wette, Schleiermacher, Credner, Reuss, Hug (Roman Catholic), and others.

4. F. C. Baur, with his Tübingen School (A. Schwegler, E. Zeller, A. Hilgenfeld, A. Ritschl [in his beginnings]), gave a new direction to the science of introduction. Baur defined introduction as criticism of the canon or as the science whose task is to investigate the provenance and the original character of the canonical writings. The origin of the individual NT writings should be understood in respect to the great context of the spiritual conflicts of the apostolic and postapostolic ages and their settlement in the unity of early Catholicism. The basis of Baur's view of history is the scheme borrowed from the Hegelian logic: thesis, antithesis, synthesis. Baur thinks that the apostolic age was governed by the opposition between the narrow-minded Judaizing Christianity of the primitive apostles and the law-free, universalistic gospel of Paul. In the postapostolic age the opposition was mollified: Through concessions and compromises the parties came nearer to one another and united in a middle position over against the Gnosticism and Montanism of the second century. The ambiguous term, "tendency criticism" [Tendenzkritik], indicates, for the Tübingen critics, that each NT writing was written out of a definite tendency. Galatians, I and II Corinthians, and Romans are witnesses of the pure Pauline gospel. The Apocalypse is a document of the rigid Ebionitism of the primitive apostles. Only these five writings are authentic. In the Synoptic Gospels and Acts the unionistic tendency comes to light—they belong to the time of adjustment and settlement of the opposition. The synthesis and peaceful conclusion is complete in John. Baur's *Church History of the First Three Centuries* (Tr. and edited by Allan Menzies from 3rd ed. [1863], 1878-79) offers a comprehensive presentation of his theory. This constructive and comprehensive view, already frequently modified by Baur's pupils, proved a failure; likewise the majority of the literary-critical hypotheses, which only the so-called "radical criticism," with its opposition to the Pauline origin even of the chief epistles (at least in their traditional form), sought to outdo (cf. thereto A. Jülicher, *Introduction*, 1904, 28 ff.). From the work of Baur remains the fundamental recognition that the history of primitive Christian literature can be investigated only in closest connection with the external and internal history of primitive Christianity.

5. The development of the Protestant science of introduction in the German language until now reveals the following works, some critical, some conservative:

H. J. HOLTZMANN, *Lehrbuch der historisch-kritischen Einleitung in das NT*, (1885) ³1892 (summary of the entire work of the 19th century); A. JÜLI-CHER, *Einleitung in das NT*, (1894) ⁷1931 (reedited in collaboration with E. Fascher); *An Introduction to the NT.* Tr. Janet Penrose Ward, 1904; R. KNOPF, *Einführung in das NT*, (1919) ⁵1949, edited by H. WEINEL-H. LIETZMANN; O. PFLEIDERER, *Das Urchristentum, seine Schriften und Lehren* (1886) ²1902; *Primitive Christianity; Its Writings and Teachings in Their Historical Connections.* Tr. W. Montgomery, 1906-11; A. HARNACK, *Geschichte der altchristlichen Literatur* I, 1893; II, 1897; B. WEISS, *Lehrbuch der Einleitung in das NT*, (1886) ³1897; *A Manual of Introduction to the NT.* Tr. A. J. K. Davidson, 1889; TH. ZAHN, *Einleitung in das NT*, (1897-99) ³1906-07 (= ⁴1924); *Introduction to the NT.* Tr. John Moore Trout, *et al.*, from 3rd ed., 1909; *idem, Grundriss der Einleitung in das NT*, 1928; C. R. GREGORY, *Einleitung in das NT*, 1909; F. BARTH, *Einleitung in das NT*, (1908) ⁴/⁵1921; P. FEINE, *Einleitung in das NT* (1913) ⁷1935, since ⁸1936 revised by J. BEHM, ⁹1950 (= ¹¹1956); H. APPEL, *Einleitung in das NT*, 1922; W. MICHAELIS, *Einleitung in das NT*, (1946) ³1961 (with supplement); M. ALBERTZ, *Die Botschaft des NTs* I, 1, 1947; I, 2, 1952.

Semi-popular studies: A. SCHLATTER, *Einleitung in die Bibel* (1889) ⁴1923; HERM. V. SODEN, *Urchristliche Literaturgeschichte*, 1905; *The History of Early Christian Literature: The Writings of the NT.* Tr. J. R. Wilkinson, 1906. Also published as: *Books of the NT: Contributions to Early Christian Literature*, 1907; C. CLEMEN, *Die Entstehung des NT*, 1907; M. DIBELIUS, *Geschichte der urchristlichen Literatur*, I II, 1926; F. HAUCK, *Die Entstehung des NTs*, 1949.

Of English and American works the following are cited: B. W. BACON, *An Introduction to the NT*, 1900; *idem, The Making of the NT*, 1912; J. MOF-FATT, *An Introduction to the Literature of the NT*, (1911) ³1918; G. MILLI-GAN, *The NT Documents, Their Origin and Early History*, 1913; M. JONES, *The NT in the 20ᵗʰ Century*, 1914; A. H. McNEILE, *An Introduction to the Study of the NT* (1927) ²1953, edited by C. S. C. WILLIAMS; E. F. SCOTT, *The Literature of the NT*, 1932; E. J. GOODSPEED, *An Introduction to the NT*, 1937; *idem, New Chapters in NT Study*, 1937; K. and S. LAKE, *An Introduction to the NT*, 1937; F. B. CLOGG, *An Introduction to the NT*, 1937; M. S. ENSLIN, *Christian Beginnings*, 1938; semi-popular: D. W. RIDDLE-H. H. HUT-SON, *NT Life and Literature*, 1946; R. HEARD, *An Introduction to the NT*, 1950; T. HENSHAW, *NT Literature in the Light of Modern Scholarship*, (1952) ²1957; H. F. D. SPARKS, *The Formation of the NT*, 1952; D. GUTHRIE, *The Pauline Epistles. NT Introduction*, 1961; *idem, Hebrews to Revelation. NT Introduction*, 1962.—French works: F. GODET, *Introduction au NT*, 1893 ff.; *Introduction to the NT.* Tr. W. Affleck, 1894, 1899; M. GOGUEL, *Introduction au NT* I-IV, 1/2, 1922-26 (uncompleted);—Dutch works: J. DE ZWAAN, *Inleiding tot het Nieuwe Testament* I-III, (1941-42) ²1948; A. F. J. KLIJN, *Inleiding tot het NT*, 1961.—Italian works: F. LO BUE, *Che cosa è il NT?*, 1954.

Cath. Literature: R. CORNELY, *Introductionis in S. Scripturam compendium . . . novis curis retractavit* A. MERK II: *Introductio specialis in singulos*

NiTi libros, [12]1940; A. Schaefer, *Einleitung in das NT,* (1898) [3]1921, edited by M. Meinertz; in place of that reedited by M. Meinertz, ([4]1933) [5]1950; F. Gutjahr, *Einleitung zu den heiligen Schriften des NT,* [6/7]1923; J. Belser, *Einleitung in das NT,* [2]1905; E. Jacquier, *Histoire des livres du NT* I-IV, [6-11]1928-35; *History of the Books of the NT.* Tr. J. Duggan, 1907; J. Sickenberger, *Kurzgefasste Einleitung in das NT,* (1916) [5/6]1939; H. J. Vogels, *Grundriss der Einleitung in das NT,* 1925; H. Höpfl-B. Gut, *Introductionis in s. utriusque Testamenti libros compendium,* Vol. III: *Introductio specialis in NT,* ([4]1938) [6]1962, curavit A. Metzinger; P. Gaechter, *Summa Introductionis in NT,* 1938; K. Th. Schäfer, *Grundriss der Einleitung in das NT,* (1938) [2]1952; A. Wikenhauser, *Einleitung in das NT,* (1953) [4]1961, revised by A. Vögtle; *NT Introduction.* Tr. Joseph Cunningham from 2nd ed. (1956), 1958; *Introduction à la Bible* II, *NT,* edited by A. Robert and A. Feuillet, 1959.

6. The literary-critical [literarkritische] way of thinking, with its questions about the sources and literary connections of the NT writings, largely dominated the research of the nineteenth century. Recently, however, there has appeared another way of thinking which in a special sense is a history-of-literature [literaturgeschichtliche] way of thinking, which is connected with the thought of Herder and OT research, and which above all dedicates its interest to the literary forms and style categories [Stilgattungen] in the NT. According to this form-critical [formgeschichtlichen] or history-of-tradition [traditionsgeschichtlichen] formulation of the problem, we do not have to do with the literary output of individual authors, but with the prehistory of the form of the material which came to them. We have to do with the preliterary origin of the primitive Christian tradition after the analogy of the growth of folk tradition generally (Sitz im Leben), with the setting down of traditional forms in primitive Christian literature. The new history-of-literature work in NT has been influenced not only by the OT scholar H. Gunkel (see RGG[3] II, 1958, 1908 f., WGK, NT, 423, 550, note 388) but also by theologians such as G. Heinrici (*Der literarische Charakter der NTl. Schriften,* 1908), A. Deissmann (*Light from the Ancient East.* Tr. Lionel R. M. Strachan, 1910), and scholars of antiquity such as U. v. Wilamowitz (*Die griech. Literatur des Altertums,* in *Die Kultur der Gegenwart* I 8, [1905] [4]1924), and E. Norden (*Die antike Kunstprosa* [1898] [2]1909-15; also *Agnostos Theos* [1913] [2]1926). This approach is still in flux; complete works are still inadequate (see the literary data in §2). The history-of-tradition or form-critical view is important for its recognition of the primitive Christian literature as an expression of the life of primitive Christianity and for insight into its religious motives. But form criticism [die Formgeschichte] will never make the history of literature [die Literaturgeschichte] superfluous as a historical-critical science whose subject is the entire history of the origin of a literature.

To present the history of the individual writings of the NT in chronological sequence and to begin with the Pauline epistles (thus, e.g., A. Jülicher, M. Meinertz) would be practical in and of itself and suitable to the historical-critical method, which alone is valid for the science of introduction. But since a certain dating for almost all other writings of the NT is not possible, it is advisable on grounds of objectivity to retain, upon the whole, the sequence of the NT canon, taking up together only Luke and Acts, and proceeding chronologically with the authentic Pauline epistles.

PART I

The Origin of the New Testament Writings

A. THE NARRATIVE BOOKS

I. The Synoptic Gospels and the Acts of the Apostles

§4. GOSPEL AND GOSPELS

Concerning this concept cf. J. SCHNIEWIND, *Euangelion. Ursprung und erste Gestalt des Begriffs Ev.*, BFTh II, 13, 25, I, 1927, II, 1931; G. FRIEDRICH, ThWB II, 1935, 718 ff.; R. ASTING, *Die Verkündigung des Wortes im Urchristentum*, 1939, 300 ff.; J. HUBY-H. LÉON-DUFOUR, *L'Évangile et les Évangiles*, 1954; W. MARXSEN, *Der Evangelist Markus*, FRLANT, N.F. 49, 1956, 77 ff.; H. KÖSTER, *Synoptische Überlieferung bei den Apostolischen Vätern*, TU 65, 1957, 6 ff.; BAUER, Wb, 628 ff.; BAUER-ARNDT-GINGRICH, *Lexicon*, p. 318; W. SCHMAUCH, EKL II, 1956, 1213 ff.; J. SCHMID, LThK III, 1959, 1255 ff.; P. BONNARD, BhHw I, 449 ff.—Concerning the literary form cf. K. L. SCHMIDT, "Die Stellung der Evv. in der allgemeinen Literaturgeschichte," in: Εὐχαριστήριον, Studien H. Gunkel dargebracht, 1923, II, 50 ff.; ALBERTZ, *Botschaft* (see p. 28) I, 1947, 165 ff.; G. BORNKAMM, art. "Evangelien, formgeschichtlich," RGG³ II, 1958, 749 ff. (bibl.).

Gospel (τὸ εὐαγγέλιον, also plural τὰ εὐαγγέλια) means in Greek "reward for the transmission of good news," but also "the good news" itself. "Euangelion" had acquired religious significance in antique oracular cults, but chiefly in the cult of the emperor: The appearance of the divine world ruler, his accession to the throne, and his decrees are glad tidings (see ThWB II, 721 f.). On the calendar inscription from Priene in Asia Minor (c. 9 B.C.), it is said of Augustus' birthday: ἦρξεν δὲ τῷ κόσμῳ τῶν δι' αὐτὸν εὐαγγελί[ων ἡ γενέθλιος] τοῦ θεοῦ—"The birthday of the god was for the world the beginning of glad tidings, which have gone forth for his sake."

In the NT, "gospel" has the special meaning "news of salvation." At its basis lies the verb εὐαγγελίζεσθαι, Hebrew "bissar," "to proclaim news of salvation" (Isa. 40:9; 52:7; 61:1; Ps. 96:2, etc.). This act of proclaiming the news of salvation was firmly connected by Second Isaiah with the messenger of God who proclaims the eschatological glad tidings concerning the breaking-in of God's sovereign lordship. In Jesus' saying (Matt. 11:5), which is directly connected with Third Isaiah, "gospel" is the news of salvation, which he himself brings. Otherwise in the NT, and above all in Paul, "gospel" means the proclamation about Christ and the salvation which has come in him (Rom. 1:1 ff.; I Cor. 15:1 ff., etc.). And so "gospel" in the NT is always the living word of the sermon. Accordingly, "evangelist" is a designation of the wandering preacher

31

Quellenanalyse, FRLANT, N.F. 35, 1937; E. HIRSCH, *Frühgeschichte des Ev. 1: Das Werden des Mk.*, (1940) [2]1951, II: *Die Vorlagen des Lk. und das Sondergut des Mt.*, 1941 (thereto E. HAENCHEN, ThLZ 67, 1942, 129 ff. and E. HIRSCH, "Fragestellung und Verfahren meiner Frühgeschichte des Ev.," ZNW 41, 1942, 106 ff.); B. H. THROCKMORTON, "Did Mark Know Q?" JBL 67, 1948, 319 ff.; B. P. W. STATHER HUNT, *Primitive Gospel Sources*, 1951; B. C. BUTLER, *The Originality of St. Matthew*, 1951; P. PARKER, *The Gospel before Mark*, 1953; H. HELMBOLD, *Vorsynpt. Evv.*, 1953 (thereto P. WINTER, ZRGG 6, 1954, 355 ff. and P. VIELHAUER, Gn 26, 1954, 460 ff.); V. TAYLOR, "The Order of Q," JThSt, N. S. 4, 1953, 27 ff.; *idem*, "The Proto-Luke Hypothesis," ExpT 67, 1955-56, 12 ff.; *idem*, "Methods of Gospel Criticism," ExpT 71, 1959-60, 68 ff.; *idem*, "The Original Order of Q," *NT Essays in Memory of T. W. Manson*, 1959, 246 ff.; J. SCHMID, "Mk. und der aram. Mt.," SStW 1953, 148 ff.; H. G. WOOD, "The Priority of Mark," ExpT 65, 1953-54, 17 ff.; F. BUSSBY, "Is Q an Aramaic Document?", *ibid.*, 272 ff.; J. LEVIE, "L'évangile araméen de S. Matthieu est-il la source de l'évangile de S. Marc?", NRTh 76, 1954, 689 ff., 812 ff.; L. VAGANAY, *Le problème synoptique*, 1954 (thereto J. SCHMID, ThRv 52, 1956, 56 ff. and P. VIELHAUER, ThLZ 80, 1955, 647 ff.); E. L. BRADBY, "In Defence of Q," ExpT 68, 1956-57, 315 ff.; A. M. FARRER, "On Dispensing with Q," StG 1957, 55 ff.; *La formation des évangiles*, RechB II, 1957 (contains essays by L. CERFAUX, J. LEVIE, J. W. DOEVE, X. LÉON-DUFOUR, N. VAN BOHEMEN); F. C. GRANT, *The Gospels. Their Origin and Their Growth*, 1957; W. L. KNOX, *The Sources of the Synoptic Gospels I, St. Mark*, 1953; II, *St. Luke and St. Matthew*, 1957 (thereto R. BULTMANN, Gn 30, 1958, 274 ff.); G. BORNKAMM, art. "Evangelien, synpt.," RGG [3] II, 1958, 753 ff. (bibl.); H. E. TÖDT, *Der Menschensohn in der synpt. Überlieferung*, 1959, 215 ff. (on Q); CASSIAN, "The Interrelation of the Gospels: Matthew-Luke-John," StEv, 1959, 129 ff.; N. TURNER, "The Minor Verbal Agreements of Mt. and Lk. against Mark," *ibid.*, 223 ff.; S. PETRIE, " 'Q' is Only What You Make It," NovT 3, 1959, 28 ff.; J. P. BROWN, "An Early Revision of the Gospel of Mark," JBL 78, 1959, 215 ff.; T. R. ROSCHÉ, "The Words of Jesus and the Future of the 'Q' Hypothesis," JBL 79, 1960, 210 ff.; H. SCHÜRMANN, "Sprachliche Reminiszenzen an abgeänderte oder ausgelassene Bestandteile der Spruchsammlung im Lk. und Mt.," NTSt 6, 1959-60, 193 ff.; W. R. FARMER, "A 'Skeleton in the Closet' of Gospel Research," BR 6, 1961, 18 ff.; *idem*, "Notes on a Literary and Form-Critical Analysis of Some of the Synoptic Material Peculiar to Luke," NTSt 8, 1961-62, 301 ff.; J. P. BROWN, "Mark as Witness to an Edited Form of Q," JBL 80, 1961, 29 ff.; A. W. ARGYLE, "Agreements Between Matthew and Luke," ExpT 73, 1961-62, 19 ff.; R. NORTH, "Chenoboskion and Q," CBQ 24, 1962, 154 ff.; F. W. BEARE, *The Earliest Records of Jesus*, 1962; R. S. CHERRY, "Agreements Between Matthew and Luke," ExpT 74, 1962-63, 63. On the problems of oral tradition and form criticism: Reports of the literature and bibliographies: E. FASCHER, *Die formgeschichtliche Methode*, Beih. ZNW 2, 1924; P. BENOIT, "Réflexions sur la 'Formgeschichtliche Methode,' " RB 53, 1946, 481 ff. = Exégèse et théologie I, 1961, 25 ff.; G. BORNKAMM, see to §4; G. IBER, "Zur Formgeschichte der Evv.," ThRdsch, N.F. 24, 1956-57, 283 ff.; J. HEUSCHEN, see above.—Most important lit.: TH. SOIRON, "Die Logia Jesu," NTA 6, 4, 1916; M. DIBELIUS, *Die Formgeschichte des Ev.* (1919) [2]1933 = [4]1961; *From Tradition to Gospel.* Tr. Bertram Lee Woolf from 2nd ed. (1933), 1935; *idem*, "Zur Formgeschichte der Evv.," ThRdsch, N. F. 1, 1929, 185 ff.; K. L. SCHMIDT, *Der Rahmen der Geschichte Jesu*, 1919; R. BULTMANN, *Die Geschichte der synpt. Tradition* (1921) [2]1931 = [5]1961, Ergänzungsheft, [2]1962; *The History of the Synoptic Tradition.* Tr. John Marsh, 1963; *idem, Die Erforschung der synpt. Evv.* (1925), Aus der

Welt der Religion, N. F. 1, [8]1960; *The Study of the Synoptic Gospels in Form Criticism: A New Method of NT Research*. Tr. Frederick C. Grant, 1934; M. ALBERTZ, *Die synpt. Streitgespräche*, 1921; G. BERTRAM, *Die Leidensgeschichte Jesu und der Christuskult*, FRLANT, N. F. 15, 1922; O. PERELS, *Die Wunderüberlieferung der Synpt. in ihrem Verhältnis zur Wortüberlieferung*, 1934; V. TAYLOR, *The Formation of the Gospel Tradition*, 1933; R. H. LIGHTFOOT, *History and Interpretation in the Gospels*, 1935; E. B. REDLICH, *Form Criticism*, 1939; L. J. McGINLEY, *Form Criticism of the Synoptic Healing Narratives*, 1944; G. SCHILLE, "Bemerkungen zur Formgeschichte des Ev.," NTSt 4, 1957-58, 1 ff., 101 ff.; 5, 1958-59, 1 ff.; H. RIESENFELD, *The Gospel Tradition and its Beginnings. A Study in the Limits of "Formgeschichte,"* 1957; D. E. NINEHAM, "Eye-Witness Testimony and the Gospel Tradition," JThSt, N. S. 9, 1958, 13 ff., 243 ff.; N. S. 11, 1960, 253 ff.; C. F. D. MOULE, "The Intention of the Evangelists," *NT Essays in Memory of T. W. Manson*, 1959, 165 ff.; B. GERHARDSSON, *Memory and Manuscript*, ASNU 22, 1961, 253 ff.; A. WILDER, "Form-History and the Oldest Tradition," *Neotestamentica et Patristica, Freundesgabe O. Cullmann*, NovTSuppl. 6, 1962, 3 ff.; W. D. DAVIES, "Reflections on a Scandinavian Approach to 'The Gospel Tradition,' " *ibid.*, 14 ff.; E. JÜNGEL, "Paulus und Jesus," *Hermeneutische Untersuchungen zur Theologie* 2, 1962, 290 ff.

Commentaries on the Synoptic Gospels, see p. 387.

The synoptic problem is the question about the literary relationship of the first three Gospels to one another: How is the remarkable, complex commingling of agreements and disagreements among Matthew, Mark, and Luke to be explained? The state of affairs is all the more striking in that John has no share in the matter at all.

1. The Problem

1. The contents and the arrangement of the material of the Synoptics are closely related. The course of Jesus' activity is represented in similar manner. To the appearance of the Baptist are joined Jesus' baptism and temptation and his appearance in public. Jesus works until his passion almost only in Galilee, and on the whole his appearance takes place according to all in the same sequence. Jesus' journey to Jerusalem, his appearance there, and his trial are quite similarly recounted. All three reports close with the Crucifixion and Resurrection.

Matthew and Luke have much richer material than Mark, but again and again all three coincide in their portrayal of the course of Jesus' activity. Thereby they offer no biography in continuous representation. Neither do they seek to depict Jesus' personality but report in popular speech concerning his deeds and discourses and the impression which they made. The synoptic representation is somewhat anecdotical; it consists of a multitude of separate units of narrative and discourse which are complete in themselves, and which very often are placed next to one another without any temporal or spatial connection. Yet there are also homogeneous sections, in which material of similar content is placed together, e.g., the three controversy discourses (concerning the forgiveness of sins, association with sinners, and fasting; Mk. 2:1-22 par.), the Sabbath stories (Mk. 2:23–3:6 par.), and the chapter of parables (Mk. 4 par.). Also, the language of Jesus is the same throughout the Synoptics, in distinction from John: no long discussions, but separate, sharp, characteristic sayings, short discourses and fragments of discourses, and therewith the predilection for parables.

2. The relationship extends even to the particulars of style and language. In the pericope about the authority of Jesus (Mk. 11:27 ff. par.), in the narrative about the healing of the leper (Mk. 1:40 ff. par.), and in the eschatological discourse (Mk. 13:5-8, 14-17, 28-32 par.), large parts are similar even to the wording. Further examples: Mk. 8:34-36 par.; Mk. 9:1 par.; Mk. 10:13-15 par. The same is true for texts of which there are parallels in only two of the Gospels (e.g., Mt. 4:18-21 par. Mk. 1:16-19; Mk. 1:21-25 par. Lk. 4:31-35), and above all in the discourse sections which only Matthew and Luke have (e.g., Mt. 3:7b-10, 12 par. Lk. 3:7b-9, 17; Mt. 23:37-39 par. Lk. 13:34-35; Mt. 11:4 ff. par. Lk. 7:22 ff.). In many sections which are found in all three Gospels, two Gospels agree extensively, whereas the third Gospel diverges (e.g., Mt. 20:24-28 par. Mk. 10:41-45 against Lk. 22:24-27; Mk. 12:38-40 par. Lk. 20:46 f. against Mt. 23:6-13).

3. Out of these agreements the compelling conclusion appears to follow that the Synoptics somehow are literarily dependent upon one another. The state of affairs is, however, complicated in that the three Gospels also differ strikingly from one another in content and form. The infancy narratives of Matthew and Luke contradict each other in essential features: In Matthew the birth story is told from the standpoint of Joseph, in Luke from that of Mary; in Matthew Bethlehem is the home of Jesus' family, in Luke, Nazareth; the flight to Egypt (Mt. 2:13 ff.) cannot be accommodated to Luke, likewise the visit of the Magi (Mt. 2:1 ff.). The entirely different genealogies (Mt. 1:1 ff.; Lk. 3:23 ff.) are irreconcilable. Even the reports of the Resurrection present no uniform tradition: Luke 24 knows only appearances of Jesus in Jerusalem, Matthew 28 in Jerusalem and Galilee, and Mark has no report of appearances at all. And in the material out of the public activity of Jesus, of which Matthew has twenty-five chapters, Luke twenty-one, and Mark only fifteen, there are differences at every turn. From Mark the great discourse sections (Sermon on the Mount, the discourse sending out the twelve, and the discourse to the Pharisees), and even a portion of the parables, are missing almost entirely. But in material for parables Matthew and Luke also differ from each other. Matthew presents the discourse material in various places in his Gospel in the form of discourse compositions: 5-7, Sermon on the Mount; 10, discourse sending out the twelve; 12, first discourse to the Pharisees; 13, discourse of parables concerning the kingdom of God; 18, church discourse; 23, second discourse to the Pharisees; 24-25, eschatological discourse. Luke, on the contrary, collects the great mass of discourse material, mingled, however, with narrative material, in the sections 6:2-8:3; 9:51—18:14. Part of the Sermon on the Mount in Matthew is found in Luke in other places and in other connections, but still again in quite similar setting. The Lukan field discourse (Lk. 6:20 ff.) is, in comparison to Matthew 5-7, strikingly short. Finally, each of the three Synoptics has special material which is peculiar to it, Matthew and Luke much more than Mark, who indeed is silent even about

the childhood of Jesus and the appearances of the Risen One. The special material of Matthew and Luke, however, is not seldom closely bound with materials which both have in common; cf. Luke's passion story or the Sermon on the Mount in Matthew and Luke. In the pieces which all three Gospels have, occasionally all three agree, often Matthew, Mark against Luke, often Mark, Luke against Matthew, and sometimes, however, also Matthew, Luke against Mark.

How are these strange findings to be explained?

2. History of the Synoptic Problem

The problem was not actually recognized until the second half of the eighteenth century. Already discrepancies and contradictions had attracted the attention of the early church and its opponents, but exposition remained fixed upon particulars. Augustine was the first to consider seriously the literary relationships among the different Gospels. In *On the Harmony of the Evangelists* [*De consensu evangelistarum*] I, 2 are found historical remarks about the Gospels: Augustine thinks that the Gospels originated in the sequence in which they stand in the canon, and that the later Gospels were written not without knowledge of the earlier, even if each independently formed the course of his narrative. His view that Mark is an abridgment of Matthew ("Mark follows him [Matthew] closely and looks as if he were his servant and epitomist" [Marcus eum, sc. Matthaeum, subsecutus tamquam pedisequus et breviator eius videtur]) anticipated the synoptic criticism of the eighteenth century.

1. The Primitive Gospel Hypothesis. J. D. Michaelis had been able to explain the agreements among the Synoptics only through common use "of several apocryphal Gospels" (*Introduction*, see above, p. 27; III, i, 94). Lessing was the first who sketched hastily the hypothesis that our Gospels are different translations and abridgments of a very old Aramaic apostolic writing, the Gospel of the Nazarenes, which still in the fourth century Hieronymus had seen among the sect of the Nazarenes (*Theses aus der Kirchengeschichte*, 1776; "New Hypothesis Concerning the Evangelists as Merely Human Historians." Tr. Henry Chadwick. *Lessing's Theological Writings*, pp. 65-81; cf. WGK, NT, 90 f.). To this conception J. G. Eichhorn gave scientific form. At first in his writing *Über die drei ersten Evv.* (1794), he assumed that each evangelist had used the primitive gospel in a different form, but in his *Einl. in das NT* I (1804) he developed the hypothesis anew and independently (see WGK, NT, 92 ff.). He assumed an Aramaic primitive gospel, and from this primitive writing he derived nine different gospel writings, which, among other sources, were supposed to lie at the basis of our Gospels. Eichhorn's hypothesis was too artificial and worked with too many unknown quantities to be able to win, as it was presented, permanent approval. But it paved the way for the recognition that our canonical Gospels represent the culmination of a literary process, and the supposition of a common source for Matthew and Luke was the first insight into the necessity of the hypothesis of a sayings source.

2. The Fragment or "Diegesen" Hypothesis. Already H. E. G. Paulus had

assumed that Matthew and Luke had grown out of sketches (memorabilia) of single days of Jesus' activity. Schleiermacher accepted these views (*Über die Schriften des Lk., ein kritischer Versuch*, 1817). He conjectured that the original narrators, therefore the apostles, as well as their hearers, had already noted down isolated sayings and deeds of Jesus. Outside of Palestine a strong demand made itself felt for such sketches ("Diegesen" [from διηγήσεις, Lk. 1:1], as Schleiermacher said), especially as the first generation began to die out. Thus the recorders soon became collectors. The one compiled miracle stories, the other discourses, and a third perhaps narratives out of the stories of the Passion and Resurrection. From these collections our Gospels arose. Here flashed the important recognition that the Synoptics contain edited, collected materials of different origin, whose origin was connected with the practical needs of the primitive Christian churches. But Schleiermacher's hypothesis does not explain the agreement of the Gospels in their sequence and wording. It is on this account, also, that W. Knox's attempt to prove as the foundation of the Synoptics a large number of "tracts" arranged according to content is in no wise convincing (see Bultmann's criticism). It was still more important that Schleiermacher in his investigation, *Über die Zeugnisse des Papias von unsern ersten beiden Evv.* (1832), expressed the conjecture that in our Matthew a collection of Jesus' sayings going back to the apostle Matthew was embodied, whereby the hypothesis of a sayings source appeared again in the field of vision.

3. The Tradition Hypothesis. If Eichhorn had derived a literary hypothesis from Lessing's idea of a primitive gospel, so Herder, following Lessing, supposed an oral primitive gospel which arose out of isolated pieces (*Vom Erlöser der Menschen. Nach unsern drei ersten Evv. . . . Nebst einer Regel der Zusammenstimmung unserer Evv. aus ihrer Entstehung und Ordnung*, 1796-97; see WGK NT, 94 ff.). Then J. C. L. Gieseler gave a firm form to this hypothesis (*Historisch-kritischer Versuch über die Entstehung und die frühesten Schicksale der schriftlichen Evv.*, 1818). According to Gieseler, very soon a uniform oral gospel developed spontaneously among the apostles in Jerusalem for the purpose of preaching. This primitive type of oral gospel tradition was transmitted in Aramaic but then also received two different Greek forms, upon which the Synoptics were dependent. To this hypothesis is still related J. W. Doeve's theory that behind our Gospels lies the single narrative which was handed down in connection with the exegesis of OT texts (in the RechB II, 1957). Also Stather Hunt places at the beginning of the gospel formation the connection of Jesus-reports with OT prophecy. Gieseler's hypothesis does represent a correct conception: Doubtless a period of oral tradition did precede the writing down of the Gospels, within which the transition from the Aramaic to the Greek language took place. But the supposition of oral tradition alone cannot solve the complicated problem of the parallels and contradictions in the Synoptics, all the less since Luke explicitly speaks of predecessors in the sphere of written reports (1:1).

4. The Utilization Hypothesis. The three theories depicted above presuppose that the Synoptics arose without direct literary connection with one another.

But the contacts among the three Gospels are so close that the hypothesis of a literary dependence, which Augustine had already advocated, has also been repeatedly defended. Although all theoretically possible combinations have found their supporters (see the account by Höpfl-Gut, *Intr.*, 172), only three views have been able seriously to hold their ground.

a) The sequence accepted by Augustine, Matthew-Mark-Luke, is advocated until this day (Zahn, Schlatter, Butler, Farmer), mostly, however, in a modified form, which views Mark as dependent upon a preliminary stage of Matthew (see below, p. 40).

b) The supposition of the sequence Matthew-Luke-Mark, the so-called Griesbach hypothesis, was established by J. J. Griesbach (*Treatise in Which the Entire Gospel of Mark Is Shown to Be Extracted from the Works of Matthew and Luke* [*Commentatio qua Marci evangelium totum e Matthaei et Lucae commentariis decerptum esse monstratur*], 1789). Here Mark, as by Augustine, is considered as the epitomist of Matthew, but also Luke is regarded as the "Vorlage" of Mark. As the most notable evidence for this view, F. Bleek in his *An Introduction to the NT* (Tr. William Urwick from 2nd ed. [1866], 1869, I, 259, with reference to lectures of 1822) cites Mk. 1:32 par.: Mark: ὀψίας δὲ γενομένης, ὅτε ἔδυσεν ὁ ἥλιος is composed out of Mt. 8:16, ὀψίας δὲ γενομένης and Lk. 4:40, δύνοντος δὲ τοῦ ἡλίου. De Wette, Bleek, and Baur's School followed this hypothesis; but the hypothesis must assume too many improbabilities and fails to recognize the literary independence of Mark.

c) The sequence Mark—Matthew + Luke, that is, the priority of Mark to Matthew and Luke, was already occasionally advocated in the eighteenth century (J. B. Koppe, 1782; G. C. Storr, 1786). Later on the philologian C. Lachmann made the observation during his work on the primitive text of the NT (see below, p. 380) that Matthew and Luke agree with each other in sequence only when they have the same sequence as Mark. From that he concluded that Mark reproduced the tradition closest to the original. Further, Matthew combined with the Markan material a collection of sayings ("Concerning the Sequence of the Narratives in the Synoptic Gospels" ["De ordine narrationum in evangeliis synopticis"], ThStKr 8, 1835, 570 ff.; see WGK, NT, 180 f.). Shortly thereafter C. G. Wilke and H. Weisse at the same time (1838), but independently of each other, pointed out that Mark represents the common source for the narrative material of Matthew and Luke. Weisse supplemented this statement through the hypothesis that Matthew and Luke combined with Mark a source of Jesus' sayings which was common to them (see WGK, NT, 181 ff.). The two-source theory, which was thereby established, then found in H. J. Holtzmann its most active defender (cf. WGK, NT, 185 ff.). Like many advocates of the two-source theory after him, Holtzmann originally assumed a primitive Mark [Urmarkus] as a source for Matthew and Luke. This primitive Mark, however, was different from our Mark.

The two-source theory has obtained wide recognition in the last hundred years (even among Catholic scholars); cf. recently, e.g., Jülicher, Albertz, Feine-Behm, Michaelis, McNeile-Williams, Henshaw, Heard, Klijn, Johnson, Filson,

Schniewind, Geldenhuys, Perry, Bornkamm, Vielhauer, Schmid, Grant, De Solages, Bradby, Beare, and others. Nonetheless, two facts have frequently caused the correctness of this hypothesis to be questioned by many scholars.

a) Luke offers not only extensive special material but also often diverges strikingly from Mark in the texts which are common with Mark, above all in the passion story. It has therefore been supposed that Luke took up, in addition to Mark and the sayings source, an additional narrative source (Schlatter, Rengstorf, Grundmann), or at least a special passion report (Klijn, Schürmann, Rehkopf, Tyson; see the lit. to §8), or that Luke incorporated the Markan material into a Proto-Luke which had already been combined with the sayings source (Streeter, Taylor, J. Jeremias, Evans, De Zwaan, Perry, Henshaw, Grant; see the lit. to §8).

b) Papias declares in his notice concerning the Gospel of Matthew that Matthew joined together the Logia in the Hebrew language and each person translated them as best he could (Eus., EH III, 39, 16; see below, pp. 43, 85). From this statement it was concluded that there must have been an Aramaic gospel of apostolic origin, and it was firmly maintained that also the agreements between Matthew and Luke against Mark in the Markan material led back to a common source for all three Synoptics. Benoit and Vaganay therefore advocated the thesis that a Matthew which was translated into Greek in different ways was used by all three Synoptics. Matthew and Luke besides that used the Greek Mark and a special source which was composed as a supplement to the Aramaic Matthew. The canonical Matthew, however, is the best witness for the Aramaic Matthew, whereas Mark abbreviated the Aramaic Matthew and added to it particulars from the Roman preaching of Peter. Parker set forth a similar hypothesis, according to which Mark also is thought to be dependent upon the primitive Aramaic gospel which is best reproduced by Matthew. Whereas Vaganay's form of the hypothesis of an Aramaic primitive Matthew is widely rejected (e.g., by Levie in RechB II, Schmid, Léon-Dufour, Wikenhauser, Vielhauer, Bornkamm), other scholars, too, have postulated a written or oral Aramaic gospel lying behind the three Synoptics (Cerfaux in RechB II, Léon-Dufour, Levie).

Besides these two forms of a modified two-source theory, Streeter, Bussmann, Hirsch, Helmbold, Grant, and others have advocated various "multiple source theories" (Grant), which have met with no broader approval, above all not the especially arbitrary views of Hirsch and Helmbold. In §§6-8 we shall speak of the sources which are peculiar to each of the Synoptic Gospels.

5. The Prehistory of the Gospel Material. In addition to this literary-critical [literarkritisch] view of the Synoptics, which prevailed above all in the nineteenth century, but which up to the present again and again has assumed new forms, scholarship also since the end of the eighteenth century was paying attention to the history of the oral tradition of the gospel material (see above, p. 38 for the Tradition Hypothesis, and cf. the ideas of C. Weizäcker and F. Overbeck in WGK, NT, 208 ff., 256 ff.). At the beginning of our century, especially W. Wrede, *Das Messiasgeheimnis in den Evv.* (1901), and J. Well-

hausen in his commentaries on the Synoptic Gospels (1903-04), called attention to the influence of the community's faith upon the formation and transformation of the synoptic tradition and to the theology of the individual evangelists (see WGK, NT, 362 ff., 359 ff.). But a methodical investigation of the gospel tradition was first undertaken after World War I by the so-called form-critical [formgeschichtlich] approach to the Gospels (see WGK, NT, 419 ff.). It carried over to the synoptic tradition observations which had been made by the history-of-literature [literargeschichtlichen] investigation in other areas, above all in the OT literature (H. Gunkel, H. Gressmann). Folk tradition follows strict laws in the reproduction and formation of its materials, materials which differ according to literary category [Gattung]: fairy tale, saga, historical narrative, song, saying with this or that object in view, etc. That holds true also for the single, small units of tradition out of which the Gospels or their literary predecessors coalesced. To analyze units form-critically and to classify them correctly means at the same time to find criteria for their historical origin, for the individual form or category is no creation of accident or free invention, but arises under certain historical conditions—it has a "Sitz im Leben" (Gunkel). K. L. Schmidt prepared the way for the form-critical investigation of the synoptic material through his proof that in Mark the framework of the narrative is the work of the author. Therefore, no original continuous narrative lies at its basis, but a loosely joined-together collection of separate stories and separate sayings, which previously had circulated independently. Dibelius and Bultmann, and their followers Albertz, Bertram, Taylor, Grant, Lightfoot, J. Jeremias, and others, have carried out in detail the form-critical approach to the traditional materials of the Gospels. The basic results were the classification of these materials by Dibelius into parables and sayings of various forms, paradigms [pronouncement stories—Taylor], Novellen [tales or miracle stories], cult and personal legends; by Bultmann into apophthegmata (i.e., units whose point constitutes a Jesus-saying set in a brief frame), unframed sayings of the Lord, parables, miracle stories, historical narratives, and legends. Only the passion narrative was shaped early as a connected account. The first impetus to the formation and transmission of the evangelical tradition arose from the primitive Christian preaching and not from interest in a biography of Jesus. The oldest traditional material was variously modified through motives of dogma and apologetics, of exhortation and church discipline, within the Palestinian or the Hellenistic church, and also through acceptance of strange material out of the surrounding world, which originally had nothing to do with Jesus, as well as through incorporation of geographical and chronological data. The collection of this separate material into (possible) preliterary groupings and their incorporation according to the peculiar theological motives of each evangelist into the literary form of the Gospel (a form created by Mark) represents, therefore, the second stage of the history of the synoptic tradition.

The form-critical view of the Gospels has gained wide acceptance in its basic features, but has also met with opposition in principle and with widespread repudiation of the historical judgments which are connected with it (see the report by Iber). Very recently Riesenfeld and Gerhardsson have wanted to prove false the presupposition of form criticism that the formation of the tradition took place within the community. They contend, on the contrary, that the narrative- and sayings-tradition goes back to Jesus himself. In analogy to the rabbinic teacher-pupil relationship, Jesus delivered to his disciples in fixed formulation material which they in turn were to hand down. Against that, Nineham, Wilder, and Davies have rightly objected that neither was Jesus a rabbi nor was the primitive church the bearer of a "holy Word." Rather, before the Gospels were formed, the traditional material was doubtless shaped and reshaped by the community. This does not mean, however, that the tradition, or a part of it, could not, in its primary stages, rest upon the testimony of eyewitnesses. The correctness of the starting point of the form-critical investigation is, therefore, in no way proved false.

On the other hand, the research of the last decade has correctly and newly raised the question about the theological and literary presuppositions and tendencies controlling the formation of each individual Gospel ("Redaktionsgeschichte"). We must, however, consider this problem in connection with our discussion of the individual Synoptic Gospels.

The way to the form-critical view of the gospel material can only be traversed backward, because first of all we must raise the literary-critical questions about the connection of the Synoptics among themselves and about the possible sources behind our Gospels. Not until then can we put the query about the material worked up in these sources.

3. Attempt at a Solution of the Synoptic Problem

We shall most easily find the way to a solution of the synoptic problem if we proceed from the results which have been assured to some extent by tradition and research, and then attempt to press forward through the region of the probable to the borders of the recognizable. First of all, there are three negative statements to make.

1. The original wording of the Synoptic Gospels is not for certain preserved. Their text in the first two centuries had not yet been established as sacrosanct. In connection with their dissemination by means of practical use in worship, instruction, and missions, no importance was laid upon literally exact reproduction. For that reason the Gospels not only underwent various changes spontaneously, but also intentional expansions, cuts, or assimilation of the one Gospel to the other. Thus the Lukan text used by Marcion appears already to have been assimilated to the Matthean and Markan texts. Also dogmatic corrections can be followed back into the second century, e.g., in Mt. 1:16; 11:27. Since the text of the Synoptics consequently cannot be restored with certainty in respect to each word, it often cannot be determined in particular where agreements and variations between two or three Synoptics are original or only the consequence of a textual revision.

2. The oldest tradition about the origin of Matthew and Mark is the reports of Papias handed down by Eus., EH III, 39,15 f. Now certainly the interpretation of the terms used by Papias to characterize Matthew and Mark, and thus the translation of the text, is extremely controversial. It is, therefore, method-ologically improper in connection with the elucidation of the literary relations of the Synoptics to one another, and the origin of Matthew and Mark, to begin with the data of Papias, as is so often done even today. For it can easily be shown that Papias had no clear knowledge which allows us to understand more cer-tainly the origin of Matthew or Mark than does the investigation of the Gospels themselves. Papias, whose dates even are disputed (see the lit. in B. Altaner-A. Stuiber, *Patrology*. Tr. Hilda C. Grael from 5th ed. [1958], 1960, 113, and E. Bammel, RGG[3] V, 1961, 47 f.), stated in the introduction to his writing, "Λογίων κυριακῶν ἐξήγησις," presumably written in the first quarter of the second century, that he above all had investigated the oral tradition of the Lord, and had ascertained what the presbyters (enumerated by name) and the disciples of the Lord had said, "and what Aristion and the presbyter John, the Lord's disci-ples, were saying" (Eus., EH III, 39,3 f.). Later we shall go into this *prooimion* more exactly (see §10,6; §32,3). Here the statement will suffice that Papias appeals to a John with the title ὁ πρεσβύτερος, and this authority is probably meant (see Eus., EH III, 39,14) when he introduces the statements about Mark and Matthew with the phrase, "καὶ τοῦθ᾽ ὁ πρεσβύτερος ἔλεγεν":

Mark was the interpreter (ἑρμηνευτής) of Peter and wrote down accurately, though not in order (τάξει), that which he remembered of what was said or done by the Lord. He had, of course, neither heard the Lord nor did he follow him, but later, as I said, Peter. The latter adapted his teaching to the needs of the moment (πρὸς τὰς χρείας), but not as if he wanted to make a compilation of the Lord's sayings (κυριακῶν λογίων), so that Mark made no mistake when he wrote down some things as he remembered them. He intended only one thing, to omit or falsify nothing which he had heard. . . . Matthew compiled the reports in the Hebrew language ('Εβραΐδι διαλέκτῳ), and each one interpreted (ἡρμήνευσεν) them as best he could.

In the notice concerning Mark it is clear that Papias allows himself to add his own interpretation to the one sentence taken over from the presbyter. What the presbyter had said about Mark is twofold: 1) Mark as ἑρμηνευτής of Peter wrote down Peter's statements from memory; 2) in spite of his care, this record does not correspond to the τάξις of the sayings and deeds of Jesus. The presbyter, therefore, knows that Mark has written his Gospel as a pupil of Peter and that this Gospel is reproached because of its lack of order. Papias excuses Mark by the unsystematic manner of teaching of Peter, his authority, and attests Mark's care in the reproduction of that which he has heard. In con-nection with the interpretation of the presbyter's sentence there are at least two things questionable: a) how the relation between Peter and Mark is conceived (what is the meaning of ἑρμηνευτής?); and b) why Mark is charged with lack of τάξις. That Peter made use of an interpreter for his preaching is improbable. Therefore, attempts have frequently been made to interpret ἑρμηνευτής as "middleman" (e.g., J. Behm, ThWB II, 1935, 659, note 3; J. Kürzinger, "Das Papiaszeugnis und die Erstgestalt des Mt.," BZ, N.F. 4, 1960, 27). But, in view of the formulation of the sentence about Matthew, that is hardly possible. Whether the presbyter was, therefore, correctly instructed concerning the relationship of Mark to Peter is at the least an open question (see below, p. 68). The missing τάξις of Mark in relation to the story of Jesus, however, compares Mark either with the course of Jesus' life known to the presbyter from another quarter or with another Gospel (that τάξις is supposed to indicate the "literary artistic form" [Kürzinger, loc. cit.] is extremely improbable in view of the reference to sayings and deeds of Jesus). Since the presbyter hardly could have had an independent knowledge of the sequence of Jesus' work, Mark is probably compared with another Gospel, most probably with the Gospel most influential at the end of the first century, with Matthew (hardly with Luke; so J. Munck, "Das Mt. bei Papias," Neotestamentica et Patristica, Freundesgabe O. Cullmann, NovT Suppl.6, 1962, 250). But from that it does not follow that Matthew really offers a chronologically better order, and the notice of the presbyter is also hardly helpful at this point. All the more the attached defense of Mark by Papias betrays no better knowledge of the literary relations, and we cannot avoid this judgment by making Papias speak, against the clear sense of the text, not of Mark, but of the sayings source Q (R. G. Heard, NTSt 2, 1955-56, 114 ff.), or of Markan additions to a report written by Peter (T. Y. Mullins, "Papias on Mark's Gospel," VC 14, 1960, 216 ff.).

And it stands no better with the notice about Matthew. Because our Matthew doubtless is no translation out of the Aramaic, the statement of Papias has often been referred, since Schleiermacher (see above, p. 38), to the hypothetical sayings source Q, or recently to an Aramaic primitive gospel. But there can be no serious doubt that Papias (or the presbyter, that is unclear) means the canonical Matthew (τὰ λόγια designates the Jesus-reports; see most recently J. Munck, "Presbyters and Disciples of the Lord in Papias," HarvThR 52, 1959, 228, and Kürzinger, loc. cit., 37 f.), and on grounds unknown to us assumes behind it an Aramaic primitive text. If this understanding proves true (and the proposal of Kürzinger to make Papias speak, not of Matthew's Aramaic language, but of Matthew's Jewish manner of representation, is hardly acceptable), then likewise this notice does not correspond to the literary facts of the case. But Papias as "the first Christian man of letters" (M. Dibelius, art. "Papias," RGG[2] IV, 1930, 892 f.) applies in any event false standards to the Gospels. It is therefore advisable to leave Papias' notices, in spite of their great age, out of consideration with respect to the investigation of the literary connections of the Synoptic Gospels.

3. Aramaic predecessors of the Greek gospel writings. It is indisputable that originally there was only oral transmission of the narratives and sayings of Jesus. The primitive language of this oral tradition was Aramaic. Yet our Gospels written in Greek show clearly the foundation of Aramaic tradition. According to all probability, the stream of oral tradition, first the Aramaic, then also the Greek, remained long in circulation, even after it had come to a

fixed written tradition. It is therefore extremely probable that material out of the oral tradition has flowed in even to the Synoptic Gospels and that therefore even in the later Gospels must be recognized influences out of the Aramaic oral tradition or from the translation variants which go back to this tradition.

On the other hand, there is no reason to hold Eichhorn's hypothesis, which Torrey renewed, that the Synoptics are all translations of Aramaic primitive writings, because the numerous alleged mistakes in translation are only partly convincing and can be no proof for the translation of entire Gospels out of the Aramaic. But above all, the literary relationship of the Synoptics to one another can be made understandable only as a relationship among Greek texts, and for Mark nothing points to a translation out of the Aramaic (cf. the dependence upon the Greek OT in Mk. 7:6 ff., and E. J. Goodspeed, "Greek Idiom in the Gospels," JBL 63, 1944, 87 ff.). Papias' notice about Matthew, however, cannot secure the hypothesis of an Aramaic gospel source (see above, p. 44). Aramaic predecessors of our Gospels are, therefore, only to be accepted with certainty for the oral tradition (see the account of research by F. Rosenthal, *Die aramaistische Forschung seit Th. Nöldeke's Veröffentlichungen*, 1939, 111 ff., the lit. in J. Schmid, LThK I, 1957, 798 f., and the comprehensive presentation by M. Black, *An Aramaic Approach to the Gospels and Acts,* ²1954).

4. A comparison of all three Synoptics with one another is astonishing chiefly because of the extensive agreement in the range of material between Matthew-Mark and Luke-Mark. Only three short reports (Mk. 4:26-29, parable of the self-growing seed; 7:31-37, healing of a deaf mute; 8:22-26, the blind man of Bethsaida) and three very short texts (3:20 f., the relatives regard Jesus as beside himself; 9:49, salt with fire; 14:51 f., the fleeing youth) of Mark are found neither in Matthew nor in Luke, which signifies that the material of Mark is encountered almost completely either in Matthew + Luke or in Matthew or in Luke. This observation, which is based solely upon an examination of the pericopes, is confirmed by vocabulary statistics: In the sections which are common to Matthew and/or Luke, 8,189 of the 10,650 words of Mark are found in the two other Gospels also (7,040 in Luke and 7,768 in Matthew; see De Solages, 1049-52). Matthew and Luke, therefore, coincide extensively with Mark in the material which is common to all three.

If, moreover, Mark were the source for Matthew and Luke, then one can completely understand the omission by Matthew and Luke of the small pieces of the Markan special material: the two healings (because of their magical manipulations) and the attitude of Jesus' relatives are offensive; Mk. 9:49 is incomprehensible; the notice of 14:51 f. is no longer of interest; only the omission of the parable of the seed is inexplicable; nevertheless, Mt. 13:24 ff. has for it in this place of the Markan framework the parable of the weeds among the wheat. That Matthew and Luke must have had a source very similar to Mark surely follows from the comparison of the range of material. For the dependence of Mark upon Matthew or Luke, or of Matthew upon Luke, or of Luke upon Matthew, is unthinkable, since the extensive omissions, which then must be admitted, cannot be explained.

5. The comparison of the sequence of the narratives in the Gospels is decisive: Within the material common with Mark, Matthew and Luke agree in sequence only so far as they agree with Mark; where they diverge from Mark each goes his own way.

E.g., Mk. 2, 3 par., all three accounts first of all go together (Mk. 2:1-22; Mt. 9:1-17; Lk. 5:17-39). With 9:18, however, Matthew digresses, and presents several healings, the sending-out discourse (9:35–10:42), sections about Jesus and the Baptist, exclamations of woe, joy, and salvation (ch. 11), all pieces which Luke has also, but in various other places. Mk. 2:23–3:6 agrees again basically with Mt. 12:1-14 and Lk. 6:1-11; but now Luke diverges with his Sermon of the Plain (6:20-49) and the material of 7:1–8:3, whereas the two others, apart from Mk. 3:13-19 and Mt. 12:33-45, remain together. Not until 8:4 does Luke return to the pericope succession of Matthew and Mark.

This fact, that Mark in respect to sequence represents the common ground for Matthew and Luke, was first recognized by Lachmann (see above, p. 39), who, upon that basis, postulated a primitive gospel best preserved by Mark. If, from Lachmann's correct observation, later scholars drew the conclusion that Mark itself is this common ground, that is no "Lachmann-fallacy" (Butler, Farmer), provided that the divergence of Matthew and Luke from Mark in sequence can be made understandable, but not the divergence of Mark from Matthew and Luke.

But such is the case. Since from Mk. 6:7 on, Matthew and Luke seldom ever diverge from the Markan sequence, though in completely different places of the Markan sequence they show striking additions over against Mark (exception Lk. 22:21-23, 56-66), only the sequence of the sections of Matthew and Luke which are parallel to Mk. 1:1–6:6 is to be tested.

There it follows easily that Luke shows only four divergences from the Markan sequence:

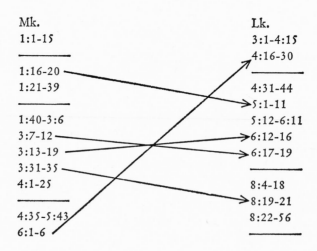

Mk.	Lk.
1:1-15	3:1-4:15
	4:16-30
1:16-20	
1:21-39	4:31-44
	5:1-11
1:40-3:6	5:12-6:11
3:7-12	6:12-16
3:13-19	6:17-19
3:31-35	
4:1-25	8:4-18
	8:19-21
4:35-5:43	8:22-56
6:1-6	

a) The rejection of Jesus in Nazareth (Mk. 6:1-6) is made into a program-matic scene at the beginning of Jesus' activity; b) the call of the disciples (Mk. 1:16-20) is placed after Jesus' activity because here the reaction of those called is so much more plausible; c) the call of the twelve (Mk. 3:13-19) is placed before the report about the rush to Jesus (Mk. 3:7-12), because thus the hearers are obtained for the Sermon on the Plain (Lk. 6:20 ff.), which Luke has added; d) the change of position of the rejection of Jesus' family (Mk. 3:31-35) after the discourse of parables creates the necessary multitude for the scene. In all four cases, therefore, Luke's changes in Mark's sequence are easily explicable. Moreover, particular features show that Luke had before him Mark's sequence: Lk. 4:23 speaks of miracles which took place in Capernaum, about which Luke, however, does not report until 4:31 ff., because Mk. 6:1 ff. is placed before Mk. 1:21 ff. par. Lk. 4:31 ff. In Lk. 4:38 Simon is named, whose call-ing Luke does not relate until 5:1 ff. (put in a different place from Mk. 1:16 ff.).

Basically, Matthew diverges from the Markan sequence only in two ways:

Mk.	Mt.
1:1-20	3:1-4:22
1:29-34	———
1:39	4:23-25
1:40-45	8:1-4
———	8:14-17
———	8:23-34
2:1-22	9:1-17
———	9:18-26
———	10:1-4
2:23-3:12	12:1-21
3:13-19	———
3:22-4:34	12:22-13:35
4:35-5:20	———
5:21-43	———
6:1-6	13:53-58

a) Matthew makes a series of Jesus' ten miraculous healings follow the conclusion to the first great discourse of Jesus (Mt. 5-7), and on that account he collected together in chapters 8 and 9 the miracles which are scattered in the first half of Mark (Mk. 1:29 ff.; 4:35 ff.; 5:21 ff.). b) Matthew joins to these miracle chapters a sending-out discourse (10:5 ff.), to whose introduction he brought forward the call of the twelve (Mk. 3:13 ff.). Here, too, the change of Mark's sequence may be recognized in particular features: Both contro-versy discourses (Mt. 9:9-17) are out of place in the miracle cycle of Matthew and are to be explained only by the fact that these pericopes in Mark followed here. Very significant also is the comparison of the parable chapter, Mk. 4:1-34, with Mt. 13:1-52, because the insertion of Mt. 13:36-52 into the Markan text, while maintaining the Markan sequence, has the consequence that the interpretation of the parable of the weeds (Mt. 13:36 ff.) is separated from the text of the parable (Mt. 13:24-30) by the parables in Mt. 13:31-33 and a discourse conclusion (Mt. 13:34 f.); and in Mt. 13:51 f. a second discourse conclusion follows.

The reverse hypothesis that Mark has changed the sequence of Matthew or Luke cannot be made intelligible in any of the cases enumerated (Wood adduces other examples). Hence, not only Griesbach's hypothesis, according to which Mark made excerpts from both of the other Synoptics, but also the supposition that Mark used and abridged either Matthew or Luke, are refuted.

6. Decisive for the recognition of Mark's priority over Matthew and Luke, however, is the comparison of language and subject matter. For the strong agreement in wording among the Synoptics in the text which is common with Mark (see above, p. 36) indeed proves in the first instance only that there must be a literary connection. But if we compare in particular the linguistic usage of Matthew and Luke with that of Mark, we see that Matthew and Luke often change, in similar or different manner, the folk- and Semitically colored text of Mark to better Greek, or also that only Matthew or Luke undertakes such a change (cf. the substitution for κράβατος Mk. 2:4 ff. of κλίνη [Mt.] or κλινίδιον [Lk.], or the change of the difficult construction τί οὗτος οὕτως λαλεῖ; βλασφημεῖ [Mk. 2:7] in differing manner by Matthew and Luke; lists of such changes in Wernle [see lit. to §5], 11 ff., 18 ff., 131 f., 146 ff.; Hawkins [see lit. to §5], 131 ff.). That in all of these instances Mark is primary cannot be doubted, and already, therefore, is Vaganay's thesis untenable: Mark expanded, by means of details out of Peter's oral preaching, the text which Matthew better preserves of the Aramaic Matthew which lies at the basis of Matthew and Mark.

More decisive than these purely linguistic changes of the Markan text are, however, the indications of changes in subject matter. In Mt. 3:16 εὐθύς before ἀνέβη ἀπὸ τοῦ ὕδατος is not understandable, but is easily explained by Mk. 1:10 εὐθὺς ἀναβαίνων . . . εἶδεν. In Mt. 9:2 the reason for the remark, "Jesus saw their faith," is not to be recognized, but Mk. 2:4 reports about the completely unusual undertaking of bringing the sick one to Jesus through the dug-up roof, a feature which Matthew has obviously omitted. In Mt. 14:1 we read the correct title τετραάρχης for Antipas instead of the popular βασιλεύς (Mk. 6:14), in spite of which Mt. 14:9 uses βασιλεύς = Mk. 6:26, which is understandable only as an oversight in connection with the taking over of the Markan text. Yet more striking is the substitution for Mk. 10:18 τί με λέγεις ἀγαθόν of the inoffensive τί με ἐρωτᾷς περὶ τοῦ ἀγαθοῦ in Mt. 19:17, and the strengthening of the ἐθεράπευσεν πολλούς (Mk. 1:34) by πάντας (Mt. 8:16) and ἑνὶ ἑκάστῳ (Lk. 4:40). And, as here, so Luke appears also in other places as secondary: Instead of the unclear statement of the subject, "And as he sat at table in his house" (Mk. 2:15), Lk. 5:29 offers the elucidation, "And Levi made him a great feast in his house." In Lk. 23:18 it is not understandable why the crowd suddenly asks for the release of Barabbas (his person is not identified until in the following verse), but from Luke even the allusion to Pilate's custom of releasing a prisoner is missing (Mk. 15:6 f.).

Upon the basis of all these facts it follows from a comparison of the material common to all three Synoptics that Mark was used as a source by Matthew and Luke.

7. But is it really Mark and not a source which also lay before Mark which Matthew and Luke as well as Mark used? Lachmann and H. J. Holtzmann had indeed supposed the dependence of Matthew and Mark upon a preliminary stage of Mark, and the hypothesis of a "primitive Mark" [Urmarkus] which underlay Matthew and Luke in different form has since often been advocated (see older advocates in Taylor, Comm., 67 ff.; further, Hauck, Feine-Behm, Bornkamm), but especially the hypothesis that Mark, like Matthew and Luke, was dependent upon an Aramaic Matthew (see above, p. 40). As proof is cited: a) the absence of Mk. 6:45–8:26 from Luke (the so-called "great omission") is only explicable if Luke had not read this section in his Markan "Vorlage"; b) the negative and positive agreements of Matthew and Luke against Mark in the texts which are common with Mark force the acceptance of a common "Vorlage" different from Mark; c) the cases in which Matthew, in the material common with Mark, offers an older form of the tradition lead to the same conclusion.

But none of these arguments is convincing (cf. against the "Urmarkus" or "Grundschrift" hypothesis Michaelis, Streeter, Johnson, Grant, Taylor, Heuschen, Schnackenburg, SStW, 205, Schürmann, NTSt, 1959-60, 196; above all Schmid, *Mt. und Lk.*, 70 ff., 170 f. and SStW, 159 ff.). a) From Luke numerous pericopes of Mark are missing, and in many cases the omission of a Markan text, or the replacement of a Markan text by the taking up of a parallel text, can be objectively accounted for (cf. H. Schürmann, "Die Dublettenvermeidungen im Lk.," ZkTh 76, 1954, 83 ff.). The omission of Mk. 6:45–8:26 is, however, puzzling; at times Luke offers indications that he has read the section (Schürmann). Therefore, the hypothesis that Luke had before him a mutilated copy of Mark (Streeter) explains the facts just as little as any sort of "Urmarkus" hypothesis. b) The agreements of Matthew and Luke against Mark in the Markan material are very dissimilar. i) Some of these agreements are only the result of textual corruption, and disappear with an improved form of the text (thus probably κύριε in Mk. 1:40 is to be read and τοῦ κρασπέδου in Lk. 8:44 to be rejected; cf. Streeter, 306 ff.). But because of the uncertainty of the wording in the Synoptics this explanation remains also uncertain in many cases. ii) By far the greatest part of the agreements have to do with grammatical and stylistic improvements over against Mark (see the lists of De Solages, 1055 ff.), by which a coincidence is either inevitable or easily explainable. In addition, at least quite as often such variations are found only in Matthew *or* Luke or are undertaken in differing ways in Matthew and Luke (lists by Hawkins, 129 f., 135 f., 139 ff., and Schmid, *Mt. und Lk.*, 38 f., 41 f., 66 f.). These agreements cannot, therefore, be used as a foundation for a "Vorlage" of Matthew and Luke which diverges from Mark. iii) Finally, there are a small number of agreements which hardly can be designated as accidental (see the lists in Hawkins, 210 f.; e.g., Mt. 13:11 par. Lk. 8:10 ὑμῖν δέδοται γνῶναι τὰ μυστήρια against ὑμῖν τὸ μυστήριον δέδοται Mk. 4:11; Mt. 26:68 par. Lk. 22:64 τίς ἐστιν ὁ παίσας σε; which Mk. 14:65 lacks). These few cases can be explained through the influence of the oral tradition and are not sufficient to justify the hypothesis of an "Urmarkus" (also not the hypothesis that Matthew and Luke used an edited form of our Mark which was preserved in the "Caesarean" text [so Brown]). c) There remain the cases in which Matthew is supposed to have used an older form of the tradition than Mark. In behalf of this point are cited especially Mk. 7:1 ff., 24 ff.; 10:1 ff. and par., because here Matthew exhibits a Jewish setting. Schmid, however, demonstrated convincingly that in all these texts Matthew Judaized the texts of Mark which are radically critical of the Law (SStW, 171 ff.; cf. also W. G. Kümmel, ZNW 33, 1934, 122 ff.)

Since none of the arguments cited for an "Urmarkus" or for a basic writing [Grundschrift] is convincing, the hypothesis remains by far the most likely that Mark in the form handed down to us served as a source for Matthew and Luke.

8. Eichhorn was the first to postulate a common source for Matthew and Luke. From Papias' Matthew notice, Schleiermacher inferred a sayings source, and Weisse connected this hypothesis to the thesis of Mark's priority (see above, p. 39). The two-source hypothesis, according to which Matthew and Luke used as sources Mark and a second common source, usually called Q, proceeds from the insight that Matthew and Luke have an extensive amount of common material that neither Luke could have taken directly out of Matthew nor Matthew directly out of Luke. The dependence of Matthew upon Luke is today no more defended and may be left out of consideration. On the other hand, it is advocated again and again that Luke took over directly from Matthew his material common with Matthew (Schlatter, Ropes, Butler, Farrer, Rengstorf, Cassian, Turner, Farmer, Argyle). Yet this hypothesis is completely untenable. For example, what could have moved Luke to break up Matthew's Sermon on the Mount and to embody part of it in his Sermon on the Plain, to distribute part over the various chapters of his Gospel, and to omit part? How is the fact to be explained that Luke not a single time brings the texts common to Matthew (naturally apart from the baptism text [Lk. 3:7-9, 17] and the temptation story) to the same place in the Markan plan as Matthew, if he took them over out of Matthew and thus in dependence upon the Markan sequence which is also encountered in Matthew (the facts are given vividly in the colored tables by J. Weiss-R. Schütz and De Solages, 1089 ff.)? Is it conceivable that Luke would have taken over none of the Matthean additions to the Markan text (see Schmid, Mt. und Lk., 25 ff., Bradby)? Schmid (loc. cit., 183 ff.) and Vaganay (293 ff.) have shown in addition that Matthew or Luke alternately offers the original setting in the common material. Thus on the basis of all these arguments the hypothesis of a direct dependence of Luke upon Matthew must be designated as untenable.

If, therefore, for the common material of Matthew and Luke a source common to both must be supposed, the hypothesis of a written source Q is disputed from various aspects, and it is usually supposed that we have rather to do with a common oral tradition (J. Jeremias, Höpfl-Gut, W. Knox, Vaganay, Rosché, North, Petrie, Argyle). This contention is substantiated by indicating that the supposed source can be imagined only arbitrarily and cannot be reconstructed with certainty, that the verbal agreements in the Jesus-sayings are less than in the text which has been taken over from Mark, that a sayings source without a passion narrative is inconceivable, and that, on the other hand, the catchword connections point to oral tradition. But the indications of the use of a common written source are nevertheless so clear that the majority of scholars regard this hypothesis as inescapable (recently besides the advocates of the two-source hypothesis named on pp. 39 f., e.g., Taylor, Leaney, Gilmour, Grundmann, Cole, Wikenhauser, Riddle-Hutson, Sparks, Evans, Throckmorton, Hirsch, Helmbold, Bussby, Schürmann, Tödt, Brown, Cherry, and others). The following facts are decisive:

a) The agreements in wording in the texts common to Matthew and Luke are in part very extensive (e.g., Mt. 3:7-10; 7:7-11; 11:4-6; 12:43-45; 24:45-51 par.), so that the supposition of a common textual "Vorlage" urges itself upon us; in part these agreements are certainly inconsiderable (e.g., Mt. 10:26-33; 25:14-30 par.). Still, the common vocabulary in all the relevant sections is over 50 percent (De Solages, 1047), which would hardly be explicable by pure oral tradition.

b) Matthew and Luke inserted the discourse materials which are additions to Mark into the Markan framework in a completely different manner. Matthew offers great discourse sections in chaps. 5–7; 10; 11; 18:10 ff.; 23; 24:37 ff.; 25; and, if one excludes these sections, there remains, on the whole, the material of Mark. Luke offers the material which is additional to Mark for the most part in 6:20–8:3 and 9:51–18:14, the so-called small and great insertions. In view of this so differing manner of arranging the common material in Matthew and Luke, it would now be expected that no common sequence of these texts in Matthew and Luke could be observed. But the opposite is the case. If one counts in their Lukan sequence the sections of Luke which have in Matthew a parallel which more or less agrees, and places the Matthean parallels with the numbers of the Matthean sequence next to it, there results (with omission of single sayings) the picture shown on the following page (cf. the tables in Appel, 251 f.; Taylor, JThSt 1952, 29 f.). The underlined texts have in Matthew and Luke, in spite of the different methods of composition, the same sequence. Taylor has shown that that also holds true for numerous smaller units, if one does not compare the entire sequence of Matthew but single discourses of Matthew with the Lukan sequence. Such agreements can be no accident, and point to a common, written source.

c) The doublets and double traditions, however, furnish the decisive proof for a common, written source of Matthew and Luke (double traditions are texts which are encountered in divergent form in two evangelists; doublets are texts which one evangelist has twice). Strange to say, Luke reports the sending out of the disciples twice, ch. 9 and ch. 10, the one time in the main parallel

	Lk.		Mt.	
1	3:7–9:16 f.	John's Preaching	3:7-12	1
2	4:2-13	Jesus' Temptation	4:2-11	2
3	6:20-23, 27-30, 32-36	Sermon on the Plain I	5:3-6, 11 f., 39- 42, 45-48	3
4	6:37 f., 41-49	Sermon on the Plain II	7:1-5, 16-21, 24-27	7
5	7:1-10	Centurion from Capernaum	8:5-13	9
6	7:18-35	John's Question; Jesus' Reply	11:2-19	13
7	9:57-60	Nature of Discipleship	8:19-22	10
8	10:1-12	Sending Out Discourse	9:37–10:15	11
9	10:13-15, 21 f.	Cries of Woe and Joy	11:21-23, 25 f.	14
10	11:1-4	Lord's Prayer	6:9-13	5
11	11:9-13	Concerning Prayer	7:7-11	8
12	11:14-23	Beelzebub Controversy	12:22-30	15
13	11:24-26	Return of the Evil Spirit	12:43-45	17
14	11:29-32	Against Sign Seeking	12:38-42	16
15	11:33-35	Saying on Light	5:15; 6:22 f.	4
16	11:39-52	Against the Pharisees	23:4, 23-25, 29-36	19
17	12:2-10	Exhortation to Confession	10:26-33	12
18	12:22-34	Anxiety and Possessions	6:25-33, 19-21	6
19	12:39-46	Watchfulness	24:43-51	22
20	13:18-21	Mustard Seed and Leaven	13:31-33	18
21	13:34 f.	Lament over Jerusalem	23:37-39	20
22	17:22-37	Parousia Discourse	24:26-28, 37-41	21
23	19:11-28	Parable of the Talents	25:14-30	23

with Mk. 6:7-13, the other time with Mt. 10. Lk. 10:1 is, to be sure, directed to the seventy disciples, but 10:4 was, according to 22:35, originally intended for the twelve disciples. But Mt. 10:1-16 alternately parallels Mk. 6:7-13 and Lk. 10:1-12. Similar doublets in Matthew, of which the one goes together with Mark, the other with discourse material, are, e.g., Mt. 18:8 f. and 5:29 f., 19:9, and 5:32.

Further, there is a series of Jesus' sayings in Matthew and Luke in two places, once in a connection which Mark also has; a second time in discourse pieces, which only Matthew and Luke have. Most important examples:

a) "For to him who has will more be given" (Mt. 13:12; Mk. 4:25; Lk. 8:18; on the other side, Mt. 25:29; Lk. 19:26).

b) "If any man would come after me, let him deny himself," etc. (Mt. 16:24 f.; Mk. 8:34 f.; Lk. 9:23 f.; on the other side, Mt. 10:38 f.; Lk. 14:27; 17:33).

c) The eschatological retaliation for the rejection of Jesus (Mt. 16:27; Mk. 8:38; Lk. 9:26; on the other side, Mt. 10:32 f.; Lk. 12:8 f.)

d) Persecutions of the disciples for Jesus' sake (Mt. 24:9, 13; Mk. 13:9, 13; Lk. 21:12, 17, 19; on the other side, Mt. 10:19 f., 22; Lk. 12:11 f.).

e) Mk. 3:23-30 is missing from Luke; for it Lk. 11:17-23 offers a varying form of Jesus' defense against the charge of the demonic covenant. Mt. 12:25-31 nevertheless alternates again between Mark 3 and Luke 11 (cf. the complete lists of doublets in Hawkins, 80 ff., and De Solages, 928 ff.).

If one places these facts of the doublets and double traditions in Matthew and Luke alongside the fact that Mark exhibits one sole doublet (Mk. 9:35; 10:43 f., cf. De Solages, 1069), it follows indisputably that Matthew and Luke must have used a second source in addition to Mark. That this source lay before Matthew and Luke in writing is, in view of the extensive common sequence and of the doublets or their mixture in Matthew, not to be doubted. And the linguistic agreement proves that this source was composed in Greek. If, in the Jesus-sayings which have been transmitted in Q, we encounter doubtless Aramaisms or variants in translation, we cannot conclude therefrom that the Greek source Q was translated out of the Aramaic (so Bussby), since this transition from Aramaic to Greek could very well already have taken place within the oral tradition.

Attempts have often been made to restore the source Q (cf., e.g., Harnack, Streeter, Bussmann, Hirsch), but without any certain, harmonious results. This state of affairs only confirms the fact that we can know with certainty as little concerning the exact extent of the text of the source as about the wording in particular. For if we can decide about the existence of Q only from the concurrence of Matthew and Luke in materials not encountered in Mark, then only what agrees extensively in wording can be proved as belonging to Q. But does that indicate that texts like the Beatitudes, which have been transmitted in the same context (Mt. 5:3 ff. and Lk. 6:20 ff.), or the parable of the talents or minas (Mt. 25:14 ff. and Lk. 19:11 ff.), which one encounters in Matthew and Luke at the end of the Q material, do not stem from Q, because even though these texts have similar construction yet in wording they agree only very sporadically? And if we know from the editing of Mark by Matthew and Luke that Matthew as well as Luke omitted a series of Markan texts, could not then also Matthew or Luke have preserved Q texts in their special material, especially if this special material has to do with components of a text which in other respects is related in both Gospels (cf., e.g., Mt. 11:28-30 or Lk. 9:61 f.)? Because an unequivocal answer to these questions cannot in any way be given, possibilities of proof have been sought. Schürmann, e.g., has attempted to show by the appearance of words which otherwise in Matthew or Luke are not met, or met only seldom, that Matthew or Luke read certain texts in Q but omitted them. But that is all much too hypothetical to lead to a sure statement about the extent of Q. And if we, with arguments based upon style, language, or content, can disclose an original text which lay behind Matthew and Luke (e.g., for Mt. 13:16 f. par. Lk. 10:23 f.; cf. W. G. Kümmel, *Promise and Fulfillment.* Tr. Dorothea M. Barton, 1957, 112; [2]1961, 112, note 27), it would still remain uncertain whether this wording was in Q or is to be accepted as prior to it. If the exact extent and wording of Q are thus unattainable for us, we may nevertheless advance some conjectures about the literary character of Q. Inspection of the material which certainly is to be claimed for Q shows that it has to do mostly with discourse material, but that Q also must have contained narratives (cf. Lk. 4:2-13; 7:1-10; 7:18-23; 11:29-32). Yet the contention that Q was a complete gospel (Hirsch, Helmbold) is an unprovable postulate. That a certain subject-matter principle held sway from the beginning over the arrangement of material in Q is probable, because this "gospel writing" was created for the practical use of the church. We already know from the Pauline epistles that the sayings of the Lord had decisive ecclesiastical authority in the apostolic age (cf. I Thess. 4:15; I Cor. 7:10, 12, 25; 9:14; 11:23 ff.). Hence we must conclude that the need for a fixation of Jesus' sayings made itself felt very soon. The beginnings of such fixation certainly reach back into the Palestinian primitive church, probably into its early period. During the process of fixing the Lord's sayings, the material was arranged from the viewpoint of subject matter (as is shown by the arrangement of the sayings into groups of sayings in Q), because such arrangement corresponded best to the need which this "gospel writing" was intended to serve. Beyond that, no subject-matter principle for the arrangement of the entire writing can be recognized, outside of the fact that also in Q, as in Mark, the Baptist seems to have been spoken of at the beginning, and parousia and judgment at the end, of the writing. If we now observe the different methods by which Matthew and Luke have inserted the Q material into the Markan framework, then we find in Matthew the Q material scattered over the entire Gospel, but in Luke chiefly in two great blocks (6:20–7:35; 9:57–13:34). Thus the conjecture is obvious that Luke has preserved the sequence of Q better than Matthew. And Taylor's investigation of the sequence of the Q material in the discourses of Matthew strengthens the conjecture that Luke, on the whole, followed the sequence from Q, whereas Matthew, corresponding to his systematic transformation of his "Vorlage," departed repeatedly from this sequence.

If, on these grounds, a hypothesis regarding the complete material can be advanced in respect to the sequence of Q, nothing generally valid can be said about the wording, because the original tradition is to be recognized sometimes in Matthew (e.g., Mt. 4:2 ff.), sometimes in Luke (e.g., Lk. 6:20 ff.). This state of affairs, together with the presence of variations in translation in Matthew and Luke (cf. M. Black; see above, pp. 45, 274 ff.) and with the strong difference in wording in many common texts (e.g., Mt. 25:14 ff. par. Lk. 19:11 ff.), leads to the often expressed conjecture that Q lay before Matthew and Luke in somewhat different form. If this conjecture is stated to the effect that Q has to do only with a growing stratum of tradition (Dibelius, *From Tradition to Gospel.* Tr. Bertram Lee Woolf from 2nd ed. [1933], 1935, p. 235; Meinertz, Bornkamm, Klijn, Fascher, *Textgeschichte,* see below, p. 359, 76), that certainly would not be sufficient to explain the facts mentioned on pp. 50 ff. If by this conjecture is meant that the written source Q developed in different directions, perhaps even at some time the Greek form of one or other of the texts was replaced by a divergent form out of the oral tradition, then this hypothesis may correspond best to the observations about the common text of Matthew and Luke.

If now we seek to analyze this hypothetical source Q historically and form-critically, we need not stress that the author is completely unknown to us. For the oft-repeated hypothesis that the apostle Matthew was the author (e.g., La-grange, Michaelis, Albertz, McNeile-Williams, Cole) rests exclusively upon Schleiermacher's problematic interpretation of Papias' testimony about Matthew (see above, p. 38). That Q originated in Palestine is probable because ob-viously it is a collection which was influenced by the oral tradition of Jesus' sayings, even after it was written down for the first time. In order to determine the time of Q's origin, it has been asked whether Q is earlier or later than Mark, and whether there exists a literary connection between both gospel writings. Since the detailed comparison of the texts which one encounters in Mark and Q (double traditions; see the list in Grant, *Gospels*, 108 f.) shows that often Mark (e.g., 3:28 f.; 6:7 ff.), but also occasionally Q (e.g., Lk. 3:16; Mt. 7:2 par.), offers the earlier tradition, it cannot be proved from this comparison whether in general Mark or Q is the earlier writing. That there is a connection of tradition between the texts preserved in Mark *and* Q is indisputable, but there is nothing to compel us to accept the hypothesis that this connection, which in-deed has to do with only an infinitely small part of the material of Mark and Q, is to be explained by a literary relationship between these two writings (accord-ing to Wellhausen, Jülicher, Q is dependent upon Mark; according to Goguel, Grant, Brown [1961] Mark upon Q; a literary dependence is denied by, e.g., Bussmann, Goodspeed, Streeter, Feine-Behm, Michaelis, Albertz, Throckmorton). The hypothesis of a literary dependence, which in view of the strong linguistic difference between Mark and Q in the double traditions (cf., e.g., Mk. 4:30-32 with Lk. 13:18 f.) is not probable at all, is rather the consequence of the erroneous presupposition that parallels between the materials of tradition can be explained only by literary dependence. We shall have to visualize the rela-tionship of the gospel writings to one another and to the oral tradition as essen-tially freer (see below, p. 60).

Since a literary connection between Mark and Q is very improbable, the time of Q's origin cannot be determined in this way. Some have claimed to find a *terminus a quo* in Mt. 23:35 par. Lk. 11:50 f., where reference is made to "all the righteous blood shed on earth, from the blood of innocent Abel to the blood of Zechariah [Mt.: + the son of Barachiah], whom you murdered [Luke: who perished] between the sanctuary and the altar." Following Wellhausen, numerous scholars assumed that by this Zechariah, son of Barachiah, is meant a Ζαχαρίας υἱὸς Βαρισκαίου, who, according to Jos., *Bell.*, IV, 335 (to be sure, only according to a part of the manuscripts!), was killed in the temple in the year 68. If this Zechariah were meant, the Jesus-saying in its Matthean form could not have been formulated until after 68. Certainly it is thoroughly possible that Matthew first added the father's name, Barachiah. In that case, the saying trans-mitted in Q could originally have referred to the prophet who, according to II Chron. 24:20 ff., under Joash was killed in the temple. Then Matthew either erroneously connected the father's name, Barachiah, father of the literary prophet Zechariah (Zech. 1:1), to the prophet's name out of II Chronicles, or likewise erroneously exchanged the prophet out of II Chronicles spoken of by Jesus with the Zechariah of the Jewish war. For none of these possibilities can a compelling argument be adduced, and therefore Mt. 23:35 cannot be utilized in the dating of Q (cf. on this text H.-J. Schoeps, *Aus frühchristlicher Zeit*, 1950, 138 ff.).

Thus every possibility for an exact dating of Q is missing; yet it is improbable that this work was written later than about 50-70.

But in what historical context are we to think this source arose? Since the material of Q is mostly discourse material arranged according to subject grouping, and any indication of the passion story is completely lacking in the Q material known to us, the opinion has been advocated already, in connection with a purely literary-critical consideration of the Gospels, that the source Q shows a didactical or catechetical character, and was therefore written for the instruction of the Christians on questions of religious, moral, and congregational life, and follows no missionary aim (Wernle, Goguel, Jülicher; T. W. Manson, *The Sayings of Jesus*, 1949, 15 f. calls attention to the almost complete lack of polemic). And even the form-critical view has been satisfied with the statement that the collection of Jesus' sayings was undertaken in interests of exhortation. But since in the meanwhile the fundamental significance of the Easter faith had been recognized, this collection of Jesus' sayings could be thought of as originating for a hortatory purpose only as a consequence of a progressed development of the primitive church (Dibelius). With some justification the opponents of the hypothesis of a Q source have objected (see above, pp. 50 f.) that a source of such a nature has nowhere been attested, and that one cannot conceive in early Christendom a collection of Jesus' sayings without the passion story. On the other hand, Bornkamm and Tödt have proposed another historical understanding of Q: A not inconsiderable part of Q cannot be proved as hortatory but serves an avowed Christological need (cf. only Lk. 10:21 f.!), but does not yet presuppose the passion kerygma. Rather, Jesus' sayings were collected with the aim of the continuing proclamation of Jesus' preaching of the coming of God's reign and of the Son of man. This thesis is doubtless correct in that the sayings of Jesus were collected with the aim of continuing proclamation and in the faith of their abiding worth, and that therefore the taking up into Q of Jesus' statements about himself [Selbstaussagen] (e.g., Mt. 12:32; 13:16 f. par.) serves the same kerygmatic goal as in Mark. It is questionable, however, whether the lack of a proclamation of Jesus' passion and of a passion story of any kind may be explained by saying that Q did not *yet* presuppose the passion kerygma. For even if the *argumentum e silentio* is permitted to be of value here (to be sure, in actuality we know nothing certain about the original extent of Q), we must bear in mind that already very early in the Palestinian Church, in which Q must have originated, the passion kerygma which was handed down by Paul (I Cor. 15:3 ff.) was formulated, a formulation which indicates the significance for salvation of Jesus' death. Then the collection of Jesus' sayings also could not have taken place with conscious neglect of this fundamental confession (cf. also I Cor. 11:25). Why, then, did the church which stood behind the Q collection "not make passion and resurrection into content of proclamation" (Tödt)? This question, which derives from the lack of statements about the passion and resurrection of Jesus in the material which is recognizable to us certainly as Q text, and appraises this lack as a certain hint to the original content of Q, and is therefore problematic in and of itself, can after all, be answered only hypothetically. One can in any case answer that Q obviously was compiled for the need of the Christian churches themselves, for whom the primitive ecclesiastical kerygma was the presupposition of their existence, and that beyond this we do not know whether the gospel's first tangible literary form (which for us is Mark) did not originate in the same churches at the same time. But in any case the Q source owes its existence to the need of the Christian community, which was separating from Judaism, to strengthen, by going back to the transmitted sayings of the the risen Jesus, its faith in his first advent and in the expected consummation of God's kingdom, and to get in this way direction for life in the present.

If the origin of a collection of Jesus-sayings and Jesus-reports without a passion narrative can thus be made comprehensible, then there is the further objection that a collection of such a nature without narrative framework has no parallel at all. Very recently attempts have been made to refute this objection by referring to the Coptic Gospel of Thomas, which belongs to the Gnostic papyrus find at Nag Hamadi (German translation by J. Leipoldt in J. Leipoldt-H. M. Schenke, "Koptisch-gnostische Schriften aus den Papyrus-Codices von Nag Hamadi," *Theologische Forschung* 20, 1960, 10 ff., and H. Quecke in W. C. van Unnik, *Evangelien aus dem Nilsand,* 1960, 161 ff.; R. M. Grant and D. N. Freedman, *The Secret Sayings of Jesus* [with an English translation of the Gospel of Thomas, translated by W. R. Schoedel], 1960; *The Gospel According to Thomas,* Coptic text established and tr. by A. Guillaumont, H.-Ch. Puech, G. Quispel, W. Till, and Yassah 'Abd Al Masih, 1959; literature report by E. Haenchen, ThRdsch, N.F. 27, 1961, 147 ff., 306 ff.). The text, which in the subscription is designated as "The Gospel According to Thomas," consists of about 114 disconnected sayings of Jesus placed side by side, the majority of which are introduced with the words, "Jesus said." Occasionally these sayings answer a disciple's question, or, in rare cases, are joined by means of details about the circumstances. The sequence reveals no organizing principle outside of catchword connections. A part of the sayings are pure Gnostic, but a greater part agree more or less with synoptic Jesus-sayings or strongly resemble the type of synoptic Jesus-sayings. It has been repeatedly asserted that through this find the possibility of the existence of a sayings source like Q has been proved. Some have even claimed to see used in the Gospel of Thomas a sayings collection which represents a parallel to Q, a parallel which was independent of the synoptic Gospels (so, e.g., C.-H. Hunzinger, "Aussersynpt. Traditionsgut im Thomas-Ev.," ThLZ 85, 1960, 843 f.; O. Cullmann, "Das Thomasev. und die Frage nach dem Alter der in ihm enthaltenen Tradition," ThLZ 85, 1960, 330; H. K. McArthur, "The Gospel According to Thomas," *NT Sidelights, Essays in Honor of A. C. Purdy,* 1960, 44; F. V. Filson, "New Greek and Coptic Gospel Manuscripts," *Biblical Archaeologist* 24, 1961, 17; R. Haardt, "Das kopt. Thomasev.

und die ausserbiblischen Herrenworte," in *Der historische Jesus und der Christus unseres Glaubens,* 1962, 277). Now in the discussion up to this date it certainly has not been proved at all convincingly that the Gospel of Thomas used, in addition to the Gospels or exclusive of the Gospels, a tradition of Jesus' sayings which leads back to the early time of Christendom and which is independent of the Synoptics (so Hunzinger, Cullmann, Haardt, *loc. cit.;* further, J. Leipoldt, *loc. cit.,* 28; G. Quispel, "Some Remarks on the Gospel of Thomas," NTSt 5, 1958-59, 277; R. McL. Wilson, " 'Thomas' and the Growth of the Gospels," HarvThR 53, 1960, 231 ff.; H. Montefiore in Montefiore and H. E. W. Turner, "Thomas and the Evangelists," StBTh 35, 1962, 78). Rather, much may be said for the view that the Gospel of Thomas cites and freely changes the canonical Gospels according to the oral tradition, whereby additional non-Gnostic Jesus-sayings also could be taken up out of the free tradition (cf. E. Haenchen, ThRdsch, N.F. 27, 1961, 314; H. E. W. Turner, *loc. cit.,* 39). But now whether or not a very old tradition parallel to the synoptic tradition lies at the basis of the Gospel of Thomas, the writing as such is doubtless no late form of the same literary category as Q, but a different, later stage of development in the tradition of Jesus' sayings (thus rightly E. Haenchen, *loc. cit.,* 316; R. McL. Wilson, *Studies in the Gospel of Thomas,* 1960, 143; B. Gärtner, *The Theology of the Gospel According to Thomas,* 1961, 30; J. B. Bauer in R. M. Grant and D. N. Freedman, *Geheime Worte Jesu. Das Thomasev.,* 1960, 200). This conclusion follows not only from the lack of any narrative and any subject arrangement, but above all from the lack of any Christology and therefore any connection with the gospel development which emerged first in Mark. The Gospel of Thomas presupposes the meaning of Jesus' person in the role of the Gnostic revealer, and thereby shows itself as a literary form of a later time.

Thus if the Gospel of Thomas can teach us nothing concerning the origin and literary character of Q, it nevertheless does show us, in the paralleling and mingling of modified synoptic texts and of texts taken up out of the tradition, a phenomenon which is of great importance for the understanding of the synoptic problem.

9. If it may be considered as certain that Mark and the hypothetical source Q served the two great Gospels, Matthew and Luke, as a foundation, there remains unexplained the origin of something more than a fifth of Matthew and of more than a third of Luke. Various sources have been postulated out of which this material was taken, but a critical examination of these hypotheses (see §§7 and 8) shows that there is little probability that Matthew and Luke used yet additional written sources: "The source-critical work on the Synoptics as a matter of fact reached its end with the two-source theory" (Vielhauer, ThLZ 80, 1955, 652). The special material of Matthew and Luke is much too dissimilar for the use of one or more written sources to be proved as probable. Only by the thoroughgoing consideration of the insights of the form-critical method can the origin of the Synoptics be completely understood.

This method has achieved two fundamental insights:

a) Our Gospels, or perhaps the written sources utilized in them, were collected out of isolated traditions, which were secondarily joined together in a connected narrative or a connected order arranged according to subject matter. Through synoptic comparison and stylistic analysis we can have considerable success in separating out the original units of tradition from the transmitted compositions, and in this manner we can push on to the forms of the text which existed in the oral tradition. These individual texts, however, are distinguished from one another by their literary form. That applies not only to the sayings tradition, in which parables, words of wisdom, prophetic sayings, legal interpretations, and Christological sayings can be distinguished, but above all to the narratives. Here are found, on the one hand, reports useful strictly for proclamation (e.g., Mk. 2:1-12; 10:13-16); on the other hand, pure miracle stories (Mk. 8:22-26); also narratives reproduced in legendary style (Mk. 9:2-8); and finally the connected complex of the passion narrative. Concerning the designations of these categories, the belonging of individual texts to this or that category, and the exact limits of this or that individual text, opinions of the scholars often diverge widely. This diversity, however, changes nothing in connection with the common conviction that there are individual texts of various kinds, which are characteristically distinguished from one another, and through the type of their literary form allow us to recognize their origin and their tendency.

b) For there is the other insight of form criticism which is yet more important for the synoptic question: The "form" of the individual tradition which was shaped in the oral tradition points back to the historical context in which the tradition took its form, to the "Sitz im Leben." "Form and style are a function of the life of the community, a moment of its history" (Iber). Therefore, from the "form" of a Gospel text we are able to reason a posteriori to the community which formed it, and to the interests which were prevailing in this connection. Above all, the transformation of the tradition in the oral transmission and in the written copy reveals the missionary, catechetical, and hortatory ecclesiastical interests of the early Christians. Very recently the thesis that "the process of tradition formation really got moving into action through the needs of preaching" (Iber after Dibelius) has been fundamentally questioned. Instead of this position, some have emphasized as the "Sitz im Leben" of the gospel tradition a Christian school activity (Stendahl, see lit. to §7), preaching *and* doctrine (Schille), the mission (Moule), and the reign of God as becoming language in the proclamation of Jesus (Jüngel). Whereas Jüngel's thesis is untenable because it declares an object of faith to be a step in historical development, the remaining theses rest upon correct observations, which show that the concept of "preaching" must be comprehended more broadly. But that changes nothing of the fact that in connection with the oral tradition of the Gospel texts the various interests of the community influenced the formation and transformation of the tradition.

Naturally there arise from this statement two questions: What role in this formation of the tradition did eyewitness reports of Jesus' works and the handing on of Jesus' sayings by his hearers play? And, how far does the history of the synoptic tradition help us to understand the history of primitive Christianity? But here these two questions are not up for discussion. Yet the form-critical view teaches us that the oral tradition not only was the decisive source for the first fixation of the gospel material in written forms, but that also in connection with the further transformation of the earliest gospel writings the oral tradition played a decisive role. For the use of the earlier sources by the later evangelists doubtless did not so proceed that the written sources were simply copied or were always consciously changed. Free reproduction of sources was already self-evident in Greek historical writing (see H. J. Cadbury, *The Making of Luke-Acts*, 1927, 155 ff.). And in the Christian churches the written Gospels were known above all through reading in worship, so that the reproduction or alteration of the written sources which were used doubtless took place extensively upon the basis of memory (cf. Schniewind, ThRdsch, N.F. 2, 1930, 141 f.). Hence the incorporation of the still living oral tradition into the composition of the great Gospels, Matthew and Luke, almost necessarily resulted. J. Jeremias has already referred to this fact apropos of the discovery of the "Unknown Gospel" in Papyrus Egerton 2: The four canonical Gospels which were known to this gospel could have been used only out of memory, in view of the constant change of allusions (ThBl 15, 1936, 43 f.; see also E. Hennecke-W. Schneemelcher, *NT Apocrypha, I. Gospels and Related Writings*. Tr. R. McL. Wilson, *et al.*, from 3rd ed. [1959], 1963, 941 f.). Likewise the Gospel of Thomas shows this fact together with the further influence of oral tradition.

If this supposition proves true also for the literary contacts among the three Synoptic Gospels, then these Gospels are to a certain degree fixations of a certain stage of oral tradition. But beyond that, in the manner of the reception and modification of this tradition, and in the altered taking-over of their written "Vorlagen," they are the work of purposive authors who shaped the tradition theologically. To be sure, the peculiarity of the individual Synoptic Gospels can first of all be understood against the background of the synoptic problem. Yet the history-of-redaction view and with it the history-of-theology [theologiegeschichtliche] view of each Gospel must be added, if we indeed want to understand the Synoptics in their individuality.

§6. THE GOSPEL OF MARK

Commentaries, see p. 387. Studies: cf. besides the lit. to §5 M. WERNER, *Der Einfluss paulinischer Theologie im Mk.*, Beih. ZNW 1, 1923; B. W. BACON, *The Gospel of Mark: Its Composition and Date*, 1925; E. VON DOBSCHÜTZ, "Zur Erzählerkunst des Mk.," ZNW 27, 1928, 193 ff.; C. H. DODD, "The Framework of the Gospel Narrative," ExpT 43, 1932, 396 ff. (= NT Studies, 1953, 1 ff.); J. SUNDWALL, *Die Zusammensetzung des Mk.*, Acta Academiae Aboensis, Humaniora 9, 1934; R. THIEL, *Drei Markus-Evv.*, Arbeiten zur Kirchengeschichte 26, 1938 (thereto W. G. KÜMMEL, ThLZ 64, 1939, 118 ff.); C. C. TORREY, "The Date of Mark," in *Documents of the Primitive Church*, 1941, 1 ff.; F. C. GRANT, *The Earliest Gospel*, 1943; T. W. MANSON, "The Foundation of the Synoptic Tradition: The Gospel of Mark," BJRL 28,

1944, 119 ff. (= Manson, St., 28 ff.); D. F. Robinson, "The Sources of Mark," JBL 66, 1947, 153 ff.; R. H. Lightfoot, *The Gospel Message of St. Mark,* 1950; A. Farrer, *A Study in St. Mark,* 1951; P. Carrington, *The Primitive Christian Calendar,* 1952 (thereto W. D. Davies, "Reflections on Archbishop Carrington's *The Primitive Christian Calendar,*" in *The Background of the NT and Its Eschatology,* 1956, 124 ff.); G. H. Boobyer, "Galilee and Galileans in St. Mark's Gospel," BJRL 35, 1953, 334 ff.; idem, "The Secrecy Motif in St. Mark's Gospel," NTSt 6, 1959-60, 225 ff.; H. A. Guy, *The Origin of the Gospel of Mark,* 1954; H. Riesenfeld, "Tradition und Redaktion im Mk.," *Ntl. Studien für R. Bultmann,* Beih. ZNW 21, 1954, 157 ff.; W. Marxsen, *Der Evangelist Markus,* FRLANT 67, 1956 (thereto G. Strecker, ZKG 72, 1961, 141 ff.); D. E. Nineham, "The Order of Events in St. Mark's Gospel—an Examination of Dr. Dodd's Hypothesis," StG, 1957, 223 ff.; J.-B. Colon, DBS V, 1957, 935 ff.; A. Kuby, "Zur Konzeption des Mk.," ZNW 49, 1958, 52 ff.; O. Michel, CBL, 1959, 848 ff.; T. A. Burkill, "Anti-Semitism in St. Mark's Gospel," NovT 3, 1959, 34 ff.; idem, "Strain on the Secret: An Examination of Mark 11:1–13:37," ZNW 51, 1960, 31 ff.; idem, "The Hidden Son of Man in St. Mark's Gospel," ZNW 52, 1961, 189 ff.; C. Beach, *The Gospel of Mark. Its Making and Meaning,* 1959; H. E. W. Turner, "The Tradition of Mark's Dependence upon Peter," ExpT 71, 1959-60, 260 ff.; S. F. G. Brandon, "The Date of the Markan Gospel," NTSt 7, 1960-61, 126 ff.; J. B. Tyson, "The Blindness of the Disciples in Mark," JBL 80, 1961, 261 ff.; M. Karnetzki, "Die galiläische Redaktion im Mk.," ZNW 52, 1961, 238 ff.; J. Schreiber, "Die Christologie des Mk.," ZThK 58, 1961, 154 ff.; S. Schulz, "Mk. und das AT," ibid., 184 ff.; E. Schweizer, "Amerkungen zur Theologie des Mk.," *Neotestamentica et Patristica, Freundesgabe O. Cullmann,* NovT Suppl. 6, 1962, 34 ff.; J. Blinzler, LThK VII, 1962, 95 ff. (bibl.).

1. Contents

Introduction (1:1-13): the message of the Baptist, Jesus' baptism and temptation.

First Part: Jesus in Galilee (1:14–5:43): 1:14-45: Jesus in and around Capernaum (Jesus' message, first disciples, preaching and exorcism in the synagogue, healings, departure for itinerant preaching in Galilee, healing a leper); 2:1–3:35: controversy discourses, scenes of conflict (a paralytic and the forgiveness of sins, Jesus and the publican, the question of fasting, two Sabbath conflicts, Jesus and his relatives, parrying of the scribes' charge that Jesus is in league with Beelzebub) (in the midst of which is inserted the choice of the twelve [3:13-19], after a description of the pressure of the multitude [3:7-12]); 4:1-34: preaching in parables (four kinds of soil with interpretation, purpose of speaking in veiled form, self-growing seed, mustard seed); 4:35–5:43: miracles by the Sea of Gennesaret (stilling of the storm at sea, Gerasene demoniac, daughter of Jairus, and the woman with an issue of blood).

Second Part: Jesus' journeyings inside and outside of Galilee (6:1–9:50): rejection at Nazareth (6:1-6); sending out of the disciples (6:7-13); Herod and Jesus (6:14-16) (joined to it the execution of the Baptist by Herod, 6:17-29); feeding of the 5,000 (6:30-44); Jesus walking on the sea (6:45-52); short stay in Gennesaret (6:53-56); discourse about clean and unclean (7:1-23); the Syrophoenician woman (7:24-30); healing of a deaf and dumb man (7:31-37); feeding of the 4,000 (8:1-10); demand for a sign (8:11 f.); discourse concerning the need for bread and the feedings (8:13-21); healing of a blind man at Bethsaida (8:22-26); Peter's confession at Caesarea Philippi and the first passion announcement (8:27-33); the disciples' way of suffering and the coming of God's kingdom (8:34–9:1); the Transfiguration and discourse while descending (9:2-13); healing of an epileptic boy (9:14-29); second passion announcement (9:30-32); discourse to the disciples (9:33-50).

Third Part: Jesus' journey to Jerusalem (10:1-52): Jesus' attitude toward marriage (10:1-12), toward the children (10:13-16), toward riches (10:17-31); third passion announcement (10:32-34); Jesus and the sons of Zebedee (10:35-45); healing of a blind man at Jericho (10:46-52).

Fourth Part: Jesus in Jerusalem (11:1–13:37): Messianic entry (11:1-10); return to Bethany (11:11); cursing of the fig tree and the discourse in reference to it (11:12-14, 20-25; in between, cleansing the temple [11:15-19]); controversy and doctrinal discourses (question of authority, parable of the wicked husbandmen, tribute-money, Resurrection, the Great Commandment, Davidic sonship of the Messiah, warning against the scribes) (11:27–12:40); the widow's mite (12:41-44); eschatological discourse (13:1-37).

Fifth Part: passion and resurrection narrative (14:1–16:8): the conspiracy of death (14:1 f.); anointing in Bethany (14:3-9); betrayal by Judas (14:10 f.); the last meal (preparation, prediction of the betrayal, institution of the Last Supper) (14:12-25); the way to the Mount of Olives, prediction of Peter's denial (14:26-31); Gethsemane (14:32-42); Jesus' arrest (14:43-52); Jesus before the Sanhedrin (14:53-65); Peter's denial (14:66-72); Jesus before Pilate (15:1-5); condemnation (15:6-15); mocking (15:16-20); way to Golgotha and Crucifixion (15:21-32); Jesus' death (15:33-41) and burial (15:42-47); the empty tomb and the news of Resurrection (16:1-8).

2. Literary Character and Theological Purpose of Mark

If it follows from the literary comparison of the Synoptics that Mark as a source underlies the two other Gospels, then Mark is for us the earliest directly accessible form of a "Gospel." From this conclusion, "liberal" theology confidently inferred that in Mark we must meet the most original form of the Jesus tradition (see WGK, NT, 185 ff., 216, 220 f.). But this confidence was shaken when W. Wrede (1901) demonstrated that Mark was shaped by the dogmatic theory of the messianic secret. And then this liberal inference became completely untenable when K. L. Schmidt (1919) showed that "the framework of the history of Jesus" in Mark is the links connecting the separate units of tradition, and that these connecting links were freely created by the evangelist. Behind Mark are recognizable only separately transmitted units of tradition or small groups of oral units of tradition already joined together (e.g., the controversy discourses [2:1–3:35], the parables [4:1-32], the miracles by the sea [4:35–5:43], the passion narrative). This view, which was achieved by the work of form-critical investigation, certainly is by no means recognized on all sides. In the most varied manner scholars think that they are able to establish sources of Mark: Thiel finds three complete gospels taken up, one of which goes back to Peter. Hirsch thinks of a Petrine gospel expanded by means of a source of the twelve. D. F. Robinson postulates a short Mark (composed of two sources), plus three additional sources, and the redactor's additions. W. Knox accepts at least nine "tracts" as sources. Parker claims that there must have been an Aramaic Jewish-Christian gospel which was reedited by Mark from a Gentile-Christian viewpoint. According to Karnetzki, a Galilean redactor expanded a historical source which was also used by Matthew and Luke, and a second redactor produced the final Mark. And Guy sees in Mark a compilation of individual papyrus pages, out of which a redactor made a connected book. But none of these hypotheses is convincing because neither is there an objective criterion for arranging the various pieces of Mark into one or more previously existing written sources, nor can objectionable passages in the text sufficiently substantiate the hypothesis of a secondary redaction. We cannot go beyond the statement that probably no extensive written sources underlie Mark; rather, the evangelist combined small collections of separate traditions and single units of tradition into a more or less connected presentation (so finally, e.g., Taylor, Johnson, J. Jeremias, *The Eucharistic Words of Jesus*. Tr. Arnold Ehrhardt from 2nd ed., 1955, 61 ff.; against the source hypotheses see also, e.g., Michaelis, Grant, Cranfield, Cole).

What conception guided the evangelist as he joined together these isolated units? This question is exceedingly difficult to answer, since it must be answered exclusively upon the basis of the analysis of Mark itself, and accordingly the answers vary widely. That a biographical-chronological interest was not under consideration by Mark is shown by the loose linkage of the separate texts by καί, πάλιν, ἐκεῖθεν, ἐν ἐκείναις ταῖς ἡμέραις, ἐξελθών, etc. (see R. Bultmann, *History* [see lit. §5], 339 ff.), and the lack of any clear geographical or pragmatic connection (see finally Guy). To be sure, Dodd has wanted to show that the arrangement of the accounts in Mark is essentially based upon the transmitted sequence of the history of Jesus, which also is recognizable in Acts 10:37-41, and he has found much agreement (e.g., T. W. Manson, Taylor, Riesenfeld). But Nineham has demonstrated that neither the existence of such a chronological framework nor the insertion of the detached tradition into such a framework can be established convincingly.

For that reason others have sought to show literary schemes as the organization principle for the construction of Mark. According to Farrer, the reports in Mark are arranged in conformity with a theological pattern that repeatedly recurs in the sense of a typological fulfillment of OT texts. Carrington sees the sequence in Mark determined by the liturgical calendar, according to which the individual pericopes are supposed to be read on certain Sundays of the year in worship. Carrington thinks that he has discovered traces of such liturgical allo-

14-16). But not until after 8:27 is the question about the nature of this Jesus put directly and answered, and at the same time reference made to the necessity for salvation of his death and resurrection (8:27-31, 38; 9:2 ff., 12, 31, 41; 10:33 f., 45; 11:1 ff., 27 ff.; 12:6 ff., 35 ff.; 13:26 f., 32 and the passion narrative). This concentration of the Christological and soteriological material in the second half of the Gospel is doubtless the conscious construction of the evangelist: "Now for the first time the Gospel, as the apostles proclaimed it, actually begins; previously one notices little of it" (J. Wellhausen, *Das Ev. Marci*, [2]1909, 62). Therefore, it becomes evident in this editorial concentration of the Christological material that "Mark is fully conceived according to the post-Easter kerygma" (so finally with methodical, convincing proof, Schweizer; see also Burkill, ZNW 1961, 197 f.). This fact is all the more revealed by a motif which is utilized in this composition, namely, the motif of the "messianic secret." Wrede first established this idea as characteristic for Mark by reference to the commands to silence (1:34, 44; 3:12; 5:43; 7:36; 8:26, 30; 9:9), to the instruction of the disciples alone (7:17 f.; 9:30 f., 33; 10:10), and to the veiled meaning of the discourse of parables (4:10 ff., 34*b*). In this idea of the "messianic secret" Wrede saw a dogmatic harmonization (which was already taken over by Mark) between the nonmessianic actuality of the historical Jesus and the messianic faith of the primitive community since the Resurrection (see WGK, NT, 362 ff.). This explanation of the facts (taken over by Bultmann) doubtless does not prove true for Mark (and then also not for the tradition taken over by Mark, if his "messianic" claim belonged to the reality of the historical Jesus; cf. W. G. Kümmel, "Das Problem des geschichtlichen Jesus in der gegenwärtigen Forschungslage," in *Der historische Jesus und der kerygmatische Christus*, edited by H. Ristow and K. Matthiae, 1960, 51 f.). For Mark knows nothing of a nonmessianic Jesus. On the contrary, his presentation of the required secrecy about the office of Jesus meets again and again with the breaking through of this secret as reported by Mark himself through the demons (1:24; 3:11), through the sick (10:47), and through Jesus himself (2:19; 9:2 ff.; 11:1 ff., 27 f.; 14:62; cf. Burkill). But above all, the extensive discussion about the problem of the messianic secret since Wrede has shown that the presentation used by Mark is more differentiated (see besides the lit. in §6: H. J. Ebeling, *Das Messiasgeheimnis und die Botschaft des Marcus-Evangelisten*, Beih. ZNW 19, 1939; E. Percy, *Die Botschaft Jesu*, Lunds Universitets Aarsskrift, N. S. 1, Vol. 49 Nr. 5, 1953, 271 ff.; E. Sjöberg, *Der verborgene Menschensohn in den Evv.*, Skrifter utgivna av Kungl. Humanistiska Vetenskapssamfundet i Lund 53, 1955, 100 ff.). On the one hand, the disciples appear as a chosen group to whom the secret is announced, and therefore it is not entirely concealed (already 4:11 f., 34; cf. Percy, Schweizer.). On the other hand, there appears before 8:26 a different relation of Jesus and his disciples to the secret than after 8:26 (Sjöberg, Kuby, Burkill, Schweizer): Up to 8:26 Jesus does not speak of the necessity of his passion and of his resurrection, and the disciples do not comprehend who Jesus is, but after 8:27 they misunderstand the secret disclosed to them about the suffering Messiah. It is, therefore, still clearer that Mark's presentation of the messianic secret has to do with a dogmatic theory which shaped the recital of the traditional material; yet the evangelist's goal intended in connection with this theory is by no means clearly recognizable. Hence attempts have been made to explain the secret with the contention that *"the union of the Hellenistic kerygma about Christ*, whose essential content consists of the Christ myth as we learn of it in Paul (esp. Phil. 2:6 ff.; Rom. 3:24) with the *tradition of the story of Jesus"* (Bultmann, *History* [see above, p. 34], 347 f.) necessarily brings with itself the concealment of the Redeemer (Schreiber). But the joining of the myth about the concealed Redeemer with the Palestinian Jesus tradition (so also Marxsen, Schulz) doubtless is not present in Mark, since Mark knows neither the preexistence of Jesus nor the ascent of the Redeemer from the cross. The intentional concealment of the Messiah has also been understood as a form of expression for the divine rejection of the unfaithful Jews (Boobyer), but then it must be objected that the Messiah's dignity now and then breaks through. Some (Percy, Boobyer, Schweizer) have claimed to find in the messianic secret the form of expression for the knowledge that faith in the man Jesus as the Son of God was first possible on the basis of faith in the act of God in the crucifixion and resurrection of Jesus. But this view cannot explain the change in the relation of Jesus to his disciples after 8:27. According to Sjöberg, the concealment of the Messiah corresponds with the apocalyptic idea of the Son of man who is not revealed until the parousia; but the concealment in Mark is only very limited. And according to Dibelius, Lightfoot, Grant, and Burkill, the theory about the Messiah who wishes to be concealed is a theory forced upon the material with the intention of explaining the puzzling unbelief of the Jews as a consequence of divine predestination. But this interpretation does not explain why even the chosen disciples do not understand the secret made known to them. And the contention that the messianic secret has to do only with a literary means of the evangelist which was supposed to call special attention to the significance of Jesus' person (Ebeling), is even more unconvincing because it then remains unexplained why Mark again and again allows the command to be violated. Consequently, a *clear* explanation of the Christological purpose of the evangelist does not follow from the text. Yet we most easily will determine correctly the intention of the evangelist if we understand the portrait of the Son of man who wants to be concealed but who cannot remain concealed as an expression of faith. This faith recognizes already in the earthly life of Jesus the concealed dignity of the Son of God who goes through death to resurrection. In contrast to this faith, the unbelief of the Jews and the misunderstanding of the disciples can be explained only by intentional concealment. But even if the theological purpose of Mark can be explained only hypothetically, it is nevertheless clear that Mark wrote a book which shaped theologically the Palestinian Jesus tradition. It is also evident that Mark intended his "book of secret epiphanies" (Dibelius) for Gentile-Christian readers. In this way the puzzle of Jewish unbelief and the grace of the call of the Gentiles was supposed to be made understandable to Gentile Christians through the portrayal of the earthly way of the Risen One.

As a result of the preceding investigation, two frequently advocated theses turn out to be false:

a) Since Papias maintained that Mark is based upon the preaching of Peter (see above, p. 43), attempts have often been made to show that in Mark Peter is prominent in a special manner or at least to trace back to Peter a part of the material taken up by Mark (thus recently, e.g., Albertz, Höpfl-Gut, Klijn, Schäfer, Meinertz, Michaelis, Wikenhauser, Sparks, Heard, Cranfield, Cole, Johnson, Grundmann, Michel, Vaganay, Léon-Dufour, Colon, Grant, Guy, T. W. Manson, Turner, and others). But neither the mention of the blameworthy features in the portrait of Peter (8:33; 9:5; 14:30 f., 66 ff.) nor the references to the role of Peter as spokesman of the disciples (1:36; 5:37; 8:29; 9:2; 11:21; 13:3; 14:33; 16:7) can establish the contention that these data can go back only to the narrative of Peter, since nothing speaks against the fact that all is simply taken over from the tradition. And that which must be recognized concerning the material lying at the basis of Mark and its composition leads in no wise to an eyewitness as chief transmitter of the tradition. "Without the suggestion by Papias we would hardly have claimed Peter as authority for the material of the Markan report" (Jülicher-Fascher). Hence there was hardly a special connection of Mark with Peter (cf. Riddle-Hutson, Beare, Bornkamm, Nineham, JThSt 1958, 20 f.).

b) Since G. Volkmar (1857) the thesis has been advocated, at first in opposition to the Tübingen school, that Mark stands under the influence of Pauline theology (for the history of this thesis see Werner, 1 ff.). But after Werner demonstrated that Mark rather was dependent upon the Gentile-Christian tradition, this thesis was reconstructed so that one assumes that Mark joins "the Pauline Kerygma and the (so-called) synoptic tradition" (Marxsen, similarly Bultmann, Percy [see p. 66], 295 f., Schreiber, Tyson). But so little as it is demonstrable that Mark was influenced by the Hellenistic Christ myth (see above, p. 67), so little is there any basis for the hypothesis that Mark, under Paul's influence, regarded the death of Jesus as redemptive. According to I Cor. 15:3, this evaluation of Jesus' death was already the view of the primitive community. And the concept κύριος, which is especially characteristic of Paul, is lacking in Mark, as well as the Pauline conception of the humiliation of God's Son. Just as it is clear that Mark molded theologically the Palestinian Jesus-tradition according to Gentile-Christian presuppositions, so it is equally evident that we cannot demonstrate any direct connection with Paul or with the Pauline form of Gentile Christianity (so also Feine-Behm, Grant, Guy).

3. Author

The author of Mark reveals his identity nowhere in his Gospel. For that he, by mentioning the youth who fled naked in connection with Jesus' arrest (14:51 f.), recounts a "personal experience" (so Zahn, Wohlenberg, Höpfl-Gut, Feine-Behm, Albertz, Meinertz, Michaelis, Henshaw, Grundmann, Schniewind), is a strange and completely improbable conjecture, and, even if it proves true, discloses no name. But the oldest tradition, which we find attested by Papias, mentions Μᾶρκος as author of this Gospel, who wrote down the reports of Peter from memory (see above, p. 43). We have already seen that a special relation of Mark to the Petrine tradition cannot be proved, and that Papias, or the presbyter cited by him, had no trustworthy knowledge concerning the relation of the author of Mark to Peter. Neither can we shore up the remark of Papias about Mark by conjecturing τάχει for τάξει and then translating: ". . . as much as he (Peter) remembered . . . , he (Mark) set down in writing accurately, indeed not at all hastily—in a slipshod manner. . . ." For the hypothesis of a change in subject from "as much as he (Peter) remembered" to "he (Mark) set down in writing" is just as arbitrary as the hypothesis that the τάξει of Papias was erroneously heard as τάχει (against H. A. Rigg, "Papias on Mark," NovT 1, 1956, 161 ff.). But even if the report of Papias about the relation of the author of Mark to Peter is untrustworthy, his statement could yet prove right in that the author of Mark was called Mark. Papias is, of course, the only independent witness, for the other reports concerning Mark as "Peter's Memoirs" (Just., *Dial.* 106, 3) and about the circumstances which induced Mark to write down the preaching of Peter (Irenaeus, Clement, Origen, Hieronymus; texts in Huck-Lietzmann, *Synopse* [9] VIII ff.), are all dependent upon Papias and have no independent value as evidence. And the great age of the Latin prologue to Mark, according to which Mark wrote his Gospel in Italy after the death of Peter, has become completely uncertain (see below, p. 343).

The Mark whom Papias named as the author of Mark is certainly identical with the John Mark mentioned more than once in Acts (and not with an unknown Roman Christian named "Marcus" [so Grant]). He was the son of a Mary, in whose house in Jerusalem a part of the primitive congregation came together (Acts 12:12). His cousin (Col. 4:10) Barnabas and Paul took him with them to Antioch after the collection journey (Acts 12:25) and on the so-called first missionary journey (Acts 13:5), yet John Mark soon returned to Jerusalem (Acts 13:13). On Mark's account Barnabas later separated from Paul in Antioch and went with Mark to Cyprus (Acts 15:37 ff.). Later Mark again belonged to the circle of Paul. Paul (Phlm. 24) names him among his fellow workers. In Col. 4:10 Paul commends him to the congregation at Colossae for a hospitable reception. According to II Tim. 4:11, Timothy is supposed to bring Mark to Rome with him. I Pet. 5:13 refers to Mark as "Μᾶρκος ὁ υἱός μου." In view of the pseudonomity of I Pet. (see §28, 4) we cannot say how this notice in I Pet. is related to these reports concerning the temporary working together of Mark with Paul. On the other hand, the ending of the sentence about Mark which is preserved at the beginning of the Muratorian Canon ("at which he nevertheless was present and thus set them down" [quibus tamen interfuit et ita posuit]) can well be understood to mean that Mark was present at some of the events which he narrates. Even if Mark was not a follower of Jesus, he presumably grew up in Jerusalem and witnessed the time when Jesus appeared there and died.

For the correctness of the tradition first attested by Papias that this John Mark was the author of Mark, we may adduce the fact that apparently early the tendency existed of ascribing the Gospels to the personal disciples of Jesus, even if we can establish this fact for the time of Papias only for Matthew (see below, pp. 84 f.). Consequently, it was not natural to ascribe Mark secondarily to a nonapostle and nondisciple. Hence the great majority of scholars regard the composition of Mark by John Mark as certain. Nevertheless there are still some difficulties not easily eliminated (cf. Heard, Grant, Johnson, Beach): The author does not appear to know the Palestinian geography clearly (cf. 7:31); he writes for Gentile Christians with a sharp rejection of the unbelieving Jews; he does not know that the report about the Baptist's death (6:17 ff.) does not correspond with Palestinian practice. Of these objections the reference to the polemic tendency of Mark weighs the most heavily, but it can also be said that it was entirely possible for a Jewish Christian living in a Gentile-Christian environment to adopt such an attitude. That John Mark wrote Mark is therefore thoroughly possible, even if the question can hardly be answered unequivocally.

4. Place and Time of Composition

From Eusebius (EH II, 15, 2) we can only infer with much uncertainty that Papias already advocated the composition of Mark in Rome. On the other hand, Clement of Alexandria (in Eus., EH VI, 14, 6) clearly testifies to this tradition, with which the great majority of modern scholars agree. In support of this tradition the use of numerous Latin loan-words has been referred to, e.g.: μόδιος (4:21), λεγιών (5:9, 15), σπεκουλάτωρ (6:27), δηνάριον (6:37), ξέστης = sextarius, jug (7:4), κῆνσος = census (12:14), φραγελλοῦν = flagellare (15:15), κεντυρίων (15:39, 44 ff.); the explanations λεπτὰ δύο, ὅ ἐστιν κοδράντης (quadrans) (12:42), αὐλῆς, ὅ ἐστιν πραιτώριον (15:16); phrases like τὸ ἱκανὸν ποιῆσαι = satisfacere (15:15) or ῥαπίσμασιν αὐτὸν ἔλαβον = verberibus eum acceperunt (14:65). But here Mark has to do largely with technical military terms, and Luke-Acts likewise has numerous Latinisms (see Moule, Idiom-Book [see above, p. 22], 192).—If the right of the wife to dissolve the marriage mentioned in 10:12 (which, in accordance with Jewish regulations, is missing from Mt. 5:32; 19:9) is an amplification of Mark with regard to his Gentile readers, then he just as well could have had the Hellenistic as the Roman legal situation in mind. And the argument that Mark, in competition with Matthew and Luke, could have found general ecclesiastical recognition only if an important congregation stood behind it, can be cited for any larger Christian congregation, if the argument has cogency at all. In other respects nothing points directly to Rome, and a Gentile-Christian congregation of the East is very probable (e.g., Syria, so Karnetzki, Schreiber; less probably, Galilee, so Marxsen; Ropes thinks of a region where Alexander and Rufus were known).

The time of Mark's composition is difficult to determine. An early origin (c. 40: Torrey; about 50-60: Meinertz, Albertz, Höpfl-Gut) is improbable, because the development of the evangelical tradition is already far advanced, and in Mk. 13 at least the threatening nearness of the Jewish war can probably be perceived. But inasmuch as there is no clear reference to the destruction of Jerusalem in the year 70, most scholars date Mark in the years 64-70. Certain scholars, however, regard composition after 70 as more probable (Johnson, Beach, Brandon). Brandon claims to see reflected in Mk. 13 the situation of the Roman Christians in the year 71, but his proof is hardly convincing. Since no effective argument for a year before or after 70 can be cited, we must be satisfied with the conclusion that Mark was written around 70.

5. The Ending of Mark

Today it is generally recognized that the report of the Resurrection and Ascension (16:9-20) found in the majority of the manuscripts and versions was not a part of the original Mark. In support of that is not only the lack of this report in the oldest tradition ($\aleph$ B k sy^{sin} and the testimony of Eusebius and Hieronymus), but also the divergent character of the text in respect to the other Gospels (lit. to the question of the Markan ending is indicated in J. Duplacy, *Où en est* . . . [see p. 359], 44; R. Bultmann, *History* [see p. 34], 437; W. G. Kümmel, ThRdsch 17, 1948-49, 9 note 2; 18, 1950, 23 note 1. Also E. Helzle, "Der Schluss des Mk. und das Freer-Logion," ThLZ 85, 1960, 470 ff. [Diss. Tübingen]). This section, which represents a rounded-off composition strongly dependent upon Luke, must have originated in the second century, since Tatian and Irenaeus know it (Iren. already as Markan ending), but before the fifth century (Codex W) it is not attested in Greek manuscripts of the NT. The so-called "Freer-Logion" also probably arose in the second century as a supplement to the secondary Markan ending. The "Freer-Logion," which in W is interpolated between 16:14 and 16:15, is a defense of the twelve with reference to the power of Satan, and an answer of Christ (English in S. E. Johnson, *Mark*, p. 265). And the "shorter Markan ending" attested in some manuscripts (L Ψ etc.) and later versions between 16:8 and 16:9 (in k instead of 16:9-20) is all the more a secondary supplement to 16:1-8.

From these various attempts to bring Mark to an end after 16:8, we must clearly recognize that the feeling arose very early that Mark could not have ended with 16:8. Matthew and Luke must also have had the same feeling, for their divergence after Mk. 16:8 shows that the Mark which was expanded by them already concluded with 16:8. But was that the original conclusion of Mark? Till today that is disputed by many, mainly because it is thought that the predicted appearance of the Risen One in Galilee (14:28; 16:7) must have been reported. To be sure, no one has yet been able to make really clear how the originally existing ending was lost. One could hardly have remained satisfied with a loss which arose because of the breaking off of a page; and no one can say why the conclusion would have been intentionally removed (that would have had to happen before Matthew and Luke!). Consequently, scholarship in increasing measure is inclining toward the view that Mark reached his intended end with 16:8 (e.g., Michaelis, Lightfoot, Lohmeyer, Grant, Grundmann, Carrington, Farrer, Klijn, Marxsen, Heard, Schreiber, Guy, Tyson, W. C. Allen, JThSt 47, 1946, 46 ff.; 48, 1947, 201 ff.; L. J. D. Richardson, JThSt 49, 1948, 144 ff., and others). In this connection, especially, the two following questions must be answered: Could a book have ended with γάρ? What meaning has the abrupt ending ἐφοβοῦντο γάρ? The stylistic possibility of a γάρ at the end of a book has been established (cf. Richardson, *loc. cit.*). The reference to the fear of the women means the awe in view of the message of the Resurrection. Such a reference is an appropriate conclusion as emphasis upon the message of the angel (16:6), a message which is crucial for Mark. Moreover, Mark through his composition of 16:6-8 created a contradiction between the command of the angel (16:7) and the silence of the women (16:8) (see thereto most recently H. Grass, *Ostergeschehen und Osterberichte*, ²1962, 16 ff., 289). This contradiction permits no continuation at all. Thus there is some probability that the εὐαγγέλιον, which Mark according to 1:1 wanted to proclaim, reached its goal with 16:7 f., and that therefore we have Mark entirely preserved.

§7. The Gospel of Matthew

Commentaries, see p. 387. Studies: cf. besides the lit. to §5 E. VON DOBSCHÜTZ, "Mt. als Rabbi und Katechet," ZNW 27, 1928, 338 ff.; B. W. BACON, *Studies in Matthew*, 1930 (thereto W. G. KÜMMEL, ThLZ 57, 1932, 29 ff.); C. C. TORREY, *The Biblical Quotations in Matthew*, Documents of the Primitive Church, 1941, 41 ff.; S. E. JOHNSON, "The Biblical Quotations in Matthew," HarvThR 36, 1943, 135 ff.; T. W. MANSON, "The Gospel According to St. Matthew," BJRL 29, 1945-46, 392 ff. (= Manson, St. 68 ff.); K. W. CLARK, "The Gentile Bias in Matthew," JBL 66, 1947, 165 ff.; C. H. DODD, "Matthew and Paul," ExpT 58, 1946-47, 293 ff. (= NT Studies, 1953, 53 ff.); J. S. KENNARD, "The Place of Origin of Matthew's Gospel," AThR 31, 1949, 243 ff.; G. D. KILPATRICK, *The Origins of the Gospel According to St. Matthew*, ²1950; S. G. F. BRANDON, *The Fall of Jerusalem and the Christian Church*, 1951, 217 ff.; K. STENDAHL, *The School of St. Matthew*, ASNU 20, 1954 (see thereto P. VIELHAUER, ThLZ 81, 1956, 39 ff.); *idem*, "Quis et unde? An Analysis of Mt.1-2," *Judentum, Urchristentum, Kirche, Festschr. für J. Jeremias*, Beih. ZNW 26, 1960, 94 ff.; B. GÄRTNER, "The Habakkuk Commentary (DSH) and the Gospel of Matthew," StTh 8, 1954, 1 ff.; N.A. DAHL, "Die Passionsgeschichte bei Matthäus," NTSt 2, 1955-56, 17 ff.; F. V. FILSON, "Broken Patterns in the Gospel of Matthew," JBL 75, 1956, 227 ff.; L. VAGANAY, DBS V, 1957, 940 ff.; C. U. WOLF, "The Gospel to the Essenes," BR 3, 1958, 28 ff.; P. NEPPER-CHRISTENSEN, *Das Mt., ein judenchristliches Ev.?*, Acta Theologica Danica I, 1958 (bibl.); O. MICHEL, CBL, 1959, 857 ff.; J. JEREMIAS, "Die Muttersprache des Evangelisten Matthäus," ZNW 50, 1959, 270 ff.; H.-W. BARTSCH, "Die Passions- und Ostergeschichten bei Matthäus," *Basileia, W. Freitag zum 60. Geburtstag*, 1959, 28 ff. (= "Entmythologisierende Auslegung," *Theologische Forschung* 26, 1962, 80 ff.); W. TRILLING, *Das wahre Israel. Studien zur Theologie des Mt.*, Erfurter Theologische Studien 7, 1959 (thereto G. BARTH, ThLZ 86, 1961, 756 ff.); J. C. FENTON, "Inclusio and Chiasmus in Matthew," StEv, 1959, 174 ff.; E. P. BLAIR, *Jesus in the Gospel of Matthew*, 1960; G. BORNKAMM, G. BARTH, H. J.

HELD, *Überlieferung und Auslegung im Mt.*, WMANT 1, 1960 (bibl.); *Tradition and Interpretation in Matthew.* Tr. Percy Scott, 1963; G. HEBERT, "The Problem of the Gospel According to Matthew," *Scottish Journal of Theology* 14, 1961, 403 ff.; C. H. LOHR, "Oral Techniques in the Gospel of Matthew," CBQ 23, 1961, 403 ff.; J. P. BROWN, "The Form of 'Q' Known to Matthew," NTSt 8, 1961-62, 27 ff.; G. STRECKER, *Der Weg der Gerechtigkeit. Untersuchung zur Theologie des Mt.*, FRLANT 82, 1962; J. SCHMID, LThK VII, 1962, 176 ff.; X. LÉON-DUFOUR, "Théologie de Matthieu" (lit. report), RScR 50, 1962, 90 ff.

1. Contents

Chaps. 1, 2: *Jesus' names and places of origin* (see Stendahl, Jeremias-Festschr.): Genealogy of Jesus (1:1-17); birth and naming of Jesus (1:18-25); homage of the Magi in Bethlehem (2:1-12); flight to Egypt (2:13-15); slaughter of the innocents in Bethlehem (2:16-18); return from Egypt and taking up residence in Nazareth (2:19-23). 3:1–4:11: *Preparation for Jesus' appearance:* John the Baptist (3:1-12); Jesus' baptism (3:13-17); temptation (4:1-11).

First Principal Part (4:12–13:58): Jesus in Galilee. After an introductory description of Jesus' first appearance (4:12-17), the call of his first disciples (4:18-22), and his first teaching and healing activity (3:23-25), there is a description of his activity through word (Chaps. 5–7: Sermon on the Mount) and deed (Chaps. 8, 9: ten miracles, interrupted by discourses [8:18-22; 9:9-17], namely: healing of a leper [8:1-4], of the servant of the centurion from Capernaum [8:5-13], of Peter's mother-in-law and of many sick [8:14-17], rejection of unfit followers [8:18-22], stilling the storm at sea [8:23-27], healing of Gadarene demoniacs [8:28-34], of a paralytic [9:1-8], call of Matthew the publican and the banquet at his house [9:9-13], question about fasting [9:14-17], healing of Jairus' daughter and of the woman with the issue of blood [9:18-26], of two blind men [9:27-31], and of a dumb demoniac [9:32-34]). Discussions follow (11, 12), framed by discourses (10, 13), and introduced by a new description of the teaching and healing activity of Jesus (9:35-38): sending out of the twelve disciples and discourse to the disciples (directions for the mission, sayings on the destiny of the disciples, exhortation to fearless confession and suffering) (10:1–11:1); Jesus and the Baptist (11:2-19); woes on the cities of Galilee (11:20-24); cry of joy and call of the Savior (11:25-30); controversy discourses with the Pharisees (Sabbath conflicts, wrongful accusation of Jesus as ally of Beelzebub, demand for a sign) (12:1-45); Jesus' true relatives (12:46-50); seven parables on the kingdom of heaven (sower and interpretation, purpose of the discourse in parables, weeds among the wheat and interpretation, mustard seed, leaven, treasure, pearl, drag-net) (13:1-52); rejection at Nazareth (13:53-58).

Second Principal Part (14:1–20:34): Jesus' journeys through Galilee, neighboring regions, and to Jerusalem: Herod and Jesus (14:1-2); execution of the Baptist (14:3-12); feeding of the 5,000 (14:13-21); Jesus' walking on the sea and Peter's sinking (14:22-33); healings at Gennesaret (14:34-46); discourse concerning clean and unclean (15:1-20); Jesus and the Canaanite woman (15:21-28); healing of the sick (15:29-31); feeding of the 4,000 (15:32-39); demand for a sign (16:1-4); warning against the leaven of the Pharisees (16:5-12); Peter's confession at Caesarea Philippi (16:13-20); first announcement of the Passion (16:21-23); sayings concerning suffering of the disciples and the coming of the Son of man (16:24-28); Transfiguration and discourse about the return of Elijah (17:1-13); healing of an epileptic boy (17:14-21); second announcement of the Passion (17:22-23); question with regard to the temple tax (17:24-27); the discourse to the disciples (sayings concerning relation to children, concerning offenses, concerning relations in the church, parable of the unmerciful servant) (18:1-35); discourse concerning marriage and divorce (19:1-12); blessing of the children (19:13-15); the rich young man (19:16-26); reward for following Jesus (19:27-30); parable of the laborers in the vineyard (20:1-16); third announcement of the Passion (20:17-19); Jesus and the sons of Zebedee (20:20-28); healing of two blind men before Jericho (20:29-34).

Third Principal Part (21:1–27:66): Jesus in Jerusalem: entrance into Jerusalem (21:1-11); cleansing of the temple (21:12 f.); homage of the children in the temple (21:14-17); cursing of the fig tree (21:18-22); question about authority (21:23-27); parables of the dissimilar sons (21:28-32); of the wicked husbandmen (21:33-46), and of the royal marriage (22:1-14); question of the Pharisees about tribute money (22:15-22); question of the Sadducees concerning the Resurrection (22:23-33); question of the Pharisees about the Great Commandment (22:34-40); Jesus' question to the Pharisees concerning the Davidic sonship of the Messiah (22:41-46); discourse against the scribes and Pharisees (seven cries of woe) (23:1-36); lament over Jerusalem (23:37-39); eschatological discourse (chaps. 24, 25) (destruction of the temple [24:1 f.]; signs of the end [24:3-14]; the great tribulation [24:15-28]; the parousia of the Son of man [24:29-31]; the time of the end [24:32-36]; parables of the flood, the watchful householder, the faithful and the wicked servant, the ten virgins, the entrusted talents [24:37–25:30]; prophecy of the Son of man's world judgment [25:31-46]).

26:1–27:56: passion narrative: decision of death (26:1-5); anointing at Bethany (26:6-13); betrayal by Judas (26:14-16); preparation for the Passover meal (26:17-19); designation of the traitor and institution of the Lord's Supper (26:20-30); prophecy of the denial, Gethsemane, arrest of Jesus, trial before the Sanhedrin, Peter's denial (26:31-75); deliverance of Jesus to Pilate, death of Judas, trial before Pilate and death sentence, mocking, way to Golgotha, crucifixion and death of Jesus (27:1-56); burial (27:57-61); guard at the tomb (27:62-66). Resurrection report (28:1-20): news of the Resurrection at the empty tomb (28:1-8); appearance of the Risen One before the women (28:9 f.); the Jewish lie about the theft of Jesus' corpse (28:11-15); last words of the Risen One to his disciples on a mountain in Galilee (command to baptize and to disciple the nations) (28:16-20).

2. Literary Character and Theological Purpose of Matthew

The question about the organization of Matthew in the purport of the evangelist cannot be answered with certainty. The organization reproduced under 1., which corresponds with that in many commentaries and NT introductions, is basically oriented toward Mark and indicates that Matthew only up to 13:35 diverges from the Markan sequence, and even there only to a very limited extent (see above, pp. 47 f.), and therefore essentially follows the geographical organization of Mark. But because this intention is not positively demonstrable, various other organizations have been proposed: according to the number seven (Albertz, Lohmeyer); according to thematic viewpoints (Léon-Dufour in Robert-Feuillet). Many have accepted Bacon's proposal that Matthew, by means of the uniform endings of the discourses in 7:28; 11:1; 13:53; 19:1; 26:1 (καὶ ἐγένετο ὅτε ἐτέλεσεν ὁ Ἰησοῦς τοὺς λόγους τούτους or similar), wishes to indicate that the five discourses in chaps. 5–7; 10; 13; 18; 24–25, together with the narratives which precede each discourse, form five books corresponding to the five books of Moses (so also Kilpatrick, Stendahl, Johnson, Dahl, Höpfl-Gut, Benoit, BdJ, Grant, Brown). But this view has rightly been opposed for the following reasons: 1) the acceptance of this fivefold division of the discourses leaves ch. 23 out of consideration; 2) chaps. 1, 2 must be designated incorrectly as prologue and chaps. 26–28 as epilogue; 3) after all, we need not even consider the idea that Matthew wants to picture Jesus as the "new Moses"; 4) Matthew in no wise points out to his readers that he is presenting five identical discourse endings; 5) nor does Matthew suggest that the narratives which precede the discourses are supposed to be paired with the discourses (cf. Bornkamm, Barth, Blair, Lohr, Trilling, Strecker). We must be satisfied to state that basically Matthew took over the Markan framework of the reports and placed it at the basis of his expanded presentation, since Mark's framework apparently appeared suitable to him for the purpose he had in view.

Matthew fundamentally transformed Mark's report by means of scattered rearrangements, by means of considerable abbreviation and reformulation, but, above all, by means of inserting extensive material. We have already alluded to the fact that the rearrangements which Matthew undertook in respect to Mk. 1–5 assisted in the systematic collection of similar material (see above, pp. 47 f.). This systematization becomes further evident in that in the discourse compositions inserted by Matthew the material was arranged together from the topical point of view (cf. the six antitheses [5:21-48], the three texts about the correct cultic behavior [6:1-18], the eschatological parables [24:37–25:46], etc.), even though the material, as the parallels out of Q which are present in Luke show, had not yet had such arrangement in the tradition. This systematization, which is recognizable through a comparison with Mark and Q, is in accord with Matthew's fondness for the repetition of similar formulations (4:23, 9:35, 10:1; 9:13, 12:7; 8:12, 13:42, 50, 22:13, 24:51, 25:30; 3:7, 12:34, 23:33; the introductory formulas of the so-called "formula quotations", see below p. 78, etc.), the use of schematic numbers (seven parables [ch. 13], ten miracle stories [chaps. 8, 9], seven woes against the Pharisees [ch. 23], etc.), the stereotyped formulation of the beginning and ending of the miracle stories, and generally the easily remembered presentation (see the lists in von Dobschütz, Held, 214 ff. and the lists in Lohr that are to be sifted critically). Moreover, Matthew considerably improved Mark's Greek (cf. Wernle [see lit. to §5], 146 ff.), substantially abbreviated Mark's reports, and assimilated the miracles of healing to the controversy discourses [Streitgespräche] and the teaching discourses [Schulgespräche] (Held). Furthermore, Matthew augmented Mark's loose connectives of the separate traditions, thereby creating a stronger impression of a temporal or spatial connection (cf., e.g., 12:46; 13:1; 14:1), without actually changing the juxtaposition of the reports. The secondary character of such connectives over against Mark appears in 14:12, where Matthew failed to note that the report of the Baptist's death (Mk. 6:17-29) is a supplement reaching back chronologically, and therefore he falsely joined the end of this report to the following narrative about the feeding of the 5,000 (Mk. 6:30 ff. par. Mt. 14:13 ff.) (cf. on these changes R. Bultmann, *History* [see above, p. 34], 350 ff.).

Matthew also undertook changes in content in his Markan "Vorlage" (but almost never in the *sayings* of Jesus taken over from Mark! Cf. Rosché [see lit. to §5], 214). We have already indicated that he assimilated through abbreviation the miracles of healing to the controversy discourses and to the teaching discourses: By means of elimination of the concrete, individual features the emphasis falls more clearly upon the figure of Jesus, who healed "every disease and every infirmity among the people" (4:23; 9:35), and upon faith as the presupposition for the reception of Jesus' help ("O woman, great is your faith! Be it done for you as you desire" [15:28 against Mk. 7:29]). Held (pp. 207 ff.) therefore probably conjectures correctly that Matthew omitted two healings (Mk. 7:31 ff.; 8:22 ff.) because he found in them no point of contact for this theological interpretation. Moreover, Matthew to a greater degree than Mark assimilated the figure of Jesus to the faith in the exalted Lord by removing or changing Jesus' emotions (ὀργισθείς Mk. 1:41 par. Mt. 8:3; ἠγανάκτησεν Mk. 10:14 par. Mt. 19:14) and offensive features of reports about Jesus (ἐξέστη Mk. 3:21; οὐκ ἐδύνατο ἐκεῖ ποιῆσαι οὐδεμίαν δύναμιν Mk. 6:5 par. Mt. 13:58 οὐκ ἐποίησεν ἐκεῖ δυνάμεις πολλάς) (cf. also the examples mentioned above, p. 48, and Strecker, 120 f.). Correspondingly, Matthew more strongly idealized the disciples by expunging reproof or reference to their failures (the censure of Mk. 4:13 is replaced by the beatitude of Mt. 13:16 f.; "for they did not understand about the loaves, but their hearts were hardened" [Mk. 6:52] becomes they "worshiped him, saying, 'Truly you are the Son of God'" [Mt. 14:33]; cf. Trilling, 72 f., Strecker, 193 f.). The denial of this state of affairs by referring to the fact (which is correct in and of itself) that Matthew more than once rebuked the disciples for lack of faith and obedience (Barth, 110 ff.; cf., e.g., ὀλιγόπιστοι [16:8] against Mk. 8:17 or σκάνδαλον εἶ ἐμοῦ said to Peter [16:23] in contrast to Mk. 8:33) overlooks the other fact that Matthew did not proceed consistently, but now and then took over features of the tradition which were unfavorable to the disciples and then intensified them to emphasize Jesus' saving power (cf. 14:30-33).

Matthew's real theological aim in taking over and transforming Mark first becomes recognizable, however, when we fix our eyes upon Matthew's extensive expansion of Mark. Approximately half of Matthew has no parallel in Mark. Of this half about five ninths is also found in Luke. The remaining four ninths is special material (according to the word-count in De Solages [see lit. to §5], 1049). If, according to the hypothesis established in §5, the material common with Luke is taken over from Q, then the question remains to be answered, What is the origin of the special material? Even if we refuse to let Matthew and Mark be dependent upon a common primitive Matthew and thus do not seek to derive the special material from this source (see against that, pp. 40, 49 f.), we may wish to explain the origin of the special material in two different ways by the use of one or more written sources. According to the one hypothesis, Matthew used the source Q in an expanded form in contrast to the "Vorlage" of Luke, and therefore took over the entire amount of material which exceeds that of Mark, or at least the greatest part of it, from the same source Q ^{Mt} (Bacon, Brown, Strecker). Obviously there is the possibility that this or that text which is encountered only in Matthew was in Q. But one cannot establish this hypothesis by claiming that the Gentile-Christian author of Matthew could not have inserted into his Gospel Jewish-Christian texts like 5:20; 10:23 without a "Vorlage," or that the expansion of Lk. 17:3 f. par. Mt. 18:15, 21 f. by means of a rule for church discipline (Mt. 18:16-20) must have already been effected in Q before in Matthew (Strecker). For if Matthew's use of Mark and Q must be pictured, not as pure literary revision, but as more or less orally mediated dependence (see above, p. 60), then there is by all means the possibility that the evangelist took up separate material of varying origin and inserted it in places which appeared appropriate to him, even in a Q context. And Filson (see lit. to §7) has demonstrated convincingly that Matthew does not shrink from destroying formally, by means of insertions, the traditional literary grouping (cf. only the dovetailing of 6:7-15 into 6:1-18 or the scattering of Mk. 4 in Mt. 13). The thesis of the origin of Matthew's special material out of Q becomes still more questionable when its defenders see themselves forced to derive a part of the special material (Brown: the parables; Strecker: the formula quotations) from additional sources, because Q seems to offer no place for it. It is therefore very improbable that the Matthean special material is taken over entirely, or in part, from Q.

More widespread, therefore, is the hypothesis that Matthew, in addition to Mark and Q, used yet a third source, "M" (above all Streeter, then T. W. Manson, *The Sayings of Jesus,* 1949, 21 ff., Hirsch, Henshaw, Kilpatrick, Johnson, Taylor, *NT Essays in Memory of T. W. Manson,* 246 ff., and others). In favor of this hypothesis there is basically only one presupposition, which is regarded as self-evident: Extensive material must be derived from a written source. But if we consider the form-critical and theological disparity of Matthew's special material, then its unity in written form before Matthew cannot in any way be made intelligible. Furthermore, if Mt. 1–2 proves to be the composition of the evangelist, which claims to point to Jesus' names and places of origin (Stendahl), and in the passion narrative no written source besides Mark becomes visible (Dahl), then only the special material in chaps. 3–25 can be derived from the postulated source M, and no one can form a judicious opinion of the literary character which this source was supposed to have had.

Thus the most probable hypothesis is that Matthew, besides Mark and Q, used only oral tradition (Albertz, Michaelis, Heard, Grant, Dahl, Beare). That even before Matthew a part of this tradition was arranged in formal groups, or groups connected together by subject matter, is thoroughly probable but hardly verifiable in detail. For one complex, the so-called "Reflexionszitate," some think they can prove that Matthew must have quoted from an oral or written source. Traditionally, the "Reflexionszitate" comprise those OT quotations which are encountered only in Matthew (1:23; 2:6 f., 15, 17 f., 23; 4:14-16; 8:17; 12:17-21; 13:35; 21:4 f.; 27:9 f.) and are introduced by introductory formulas, such as ἵνα πληρωθῇ τὸ ῥηθὲν ὑπὸ κυρίου διὰ τοῦ προφήτου λέγοντος (2:15) or the like, and thus are contrasted with all other quotations. Hence the English designation, "formula quotations," is preferable to the German "Reflexionszitate." These quotations are differentiated from the other quotations in Matthew not only through their introductory formulas but also through their text. This state of affairs and its explanation is unusually controversial. Torrey's thesis that Matthew inserted his OT quotations in the Hebrew language into his Aramaic text and that in our Greek text the quotations are a translation which accidentally or through dependence upon Mark now and then coincides with the LXX certainly misconstrues the facts (cf. Johnson). As for the quotations which are common to Matthew, Mark, and Luke—all more recent investigations are agreed that Matthew took them up in the Greek language from his sources, and in occasional details assimilated them to the LXX (cf. Mt. 3:3 par. Mk. 1:3, verbatim = LXX; Mt. 4:6 f. par. Lk. 4:10 f., verbatim = LXX). Also in the quotations which are offered by Matthew alone, so far as they are not introduced by the introductory formula of the formula quotations, Matthew as a rule follows the LXX (Mt. 21:16 = LXX, whose text is useful exclusively in this context). Yet no doubt there are exceptions here: Mt. 11:29 εὑρήσετε ἀνάπαυσιν ταῖς ψυχαῖς ὑμῶν follows Jer. 6:16 in the Hebrew text against the LXX and may, of course, have been taken over with the "logion" 11:28-30; 16:27 f., however, is Mk. 8:38 expanded by means of Prvbs. 24:12 according to the Hebrew text and against the LXX; and in 27:43 (against Mk. 15:32) Ps. 22:8 (in correspondence with the Hebrew text) is put into the mouth of the Jewish leaders. If it cannot be inferred from these isolated examples that the evangelist knew the Hebrew text itself, then they show he could have found OT citations in the tradition which was at his disposal, citations which were derived, not from the LXX, but from other versions of the Hebrew text.

As for the formula quotations already mentioned, the investigation of their text form shows that their Greek stands essentially nearer to the Hebrew text than that of the other quotations, but that also an influence of the LXX is not to be denied. E.g., Isa. 53:4 is reproduced in Mt. 8:17 exactly according to the Hebrew text, but in complete divergence from the LXX and every other Greek version. On the other hand, Mt. 1:23, in the quotation from Isa. 7:14, follows the LXX in translating hā'almāh as ἡ παρθένος, but in other respects assimilates the quotation to the context by means of καλέσουσιν against qārā't of the Hebrew text *and* of καλέσεις of the LXX: indeed, it is not the parents who give the name "Immanuel" to the child! Because of the divergent character of the text and of the special introductory formulas of these quotations it is assumed that Matthew took over these quotations from a written (Bacon, Lohmeyer, Strecker) or oral (Kilpatrick, guardedly Nepper-Christensen) source. But Stendahl, contending that these quotations are not derived from a source, rather traces them back to the exegetical activity of a Christian "school," which carried on an exegesis similar to that of the Habakkuk commentary of the find at Qumran (1QpHab). On the other hand, Gärtner denies this similarity of exegetical method and assumes that the formula quotations grew out of the endeavor of early Christians to have at their disposal suitable scriptural proofs for preaching against the Jews, and out of this tradition Matthew took up the quotations. Strecker (p. 50), however, has made it quite probable that the introductory formulas of these quotations originated with the evangelist. If that is true, then it becomes very questionable whether the quotations so introduced are taken over from a source. Doubtless the quotation from Zechariah in Mt. 21:5 caused the peculiar misunderstanding that Jesus sat upon the ass *and* the foal (21:7), so conversely the context clearly caused the change of the quotation in 1:23 (see above; similarly in 2:6). On the other hand, it is also improbable that Matthew himself created all the formula quotations, as the few Matthean linguistic characteristics in them prove. Neither is there any trace of the activity of an exegetical school. Therefore, Gärtner's hypothesis that these quotations owe their origin to the missionary preaching tradition comes closest to the truth. In any case, these quotations do not point to a written or to a continuous oral source, which Matthew used in addition to Mark and Q. If, in taking up these quotations, Matthew is not dependent upon a specially composed source, then it is no longer necessary to expunge the quotation in 13:14 f. as a later interpolation, on the grounds that the introductory formula diverges from that of the formula quotations and the quotation is pure LXX text (against Torrey, Johnson, Stendahl, Strecker).

If Matthew does not follow a source for these quotations which are characteristic of his Gospel, but consciously takes these quotations from the tradition just as the other special material and inserts it together with the Q material into the transformed Mark, then the question arises: In expanding and transforming Mark, what is Matthew's aim? Since the formula quotations emphasize the "fulfillment" of the scriptural sayings in the person of Jesus and therefore obviously want to prove Jesus as the goal of the OT revelation of God, they have often been seen in connection with related phenomena in Matthew: a) He does not explain Jewish usages, ordinances, and expressions: 15:2 par. Mk. 7:2 f. (hand washing); 23:5 (φυλακτήρια and tassels); 23:24 (straining at a gnat); 23:27 (whitewashed tombs); he does not translate Hebrew expressions (5:22; 27:6). b) He recasts reports in the direction of a specifically rabbinic formulation of a question: Instead of the general question, "Is it lawful for a man to divorce his wife?" (Mk. 10:2), Mt. 19:3 has the Pharisees ask, "Is it lawful to divorce one's wife κατὰ πᾶσαν αἰτίαν?" and therewith assimilates the fundamental question to the casuistic discussion about the permissible grounds of divorce. Correspondingly, he inserts the so-called "fornication clause" μὴ ἐπὶ πορνείᾳ (19:9; similarly, 5:32) into the unconditional statement of Jesus, "Whoever divorces his wife and marries another, commits adultery against her" (Mk. 10:11), and thus has Jesus advocate the strict, yet conditional, view of Shammai's school (see J. Dupont, Marriage et divorce dans l'évangile, 1959, 27 ff., 85 ff.). c) He brings forth a series of sayings which support the unconditional validity of the Law: "Whoever then relaxes one of the least of these commandments . . . shall be called least in the kingdom of heaven" (5:19) (and in connection with that the saying that "not an iota, not a dot, will pass from the law," receives against Lk. 16:17 an intensification, though Mt. 5:18 is not certain of interpretation); "So practice and observe whatever they [the scribes and the Pharisees] tell you" (23:3). d) Matthew brings forth Jesus' sayings which expressly limit the activity of Jesus to Israel: "Go nowhere among the Gentiles, and enter no town of the Samaritans" (10:5); "I was sent only to the lost sheep of the house of Israel" (15:24; cf. 10:6), addition to Mk. 7:24 ff.; "You will not have gone through all the towns of Israel, before the Son of man comes" (10:23). e) Matthew assimilates the speech of Jesus to the Jewish speech formulas: Except in 12:28; 19:24; 21:31, 43 Matthew always has ἡ βασιλεία τῶν οὐρανῶν instead of ἡ βασιλεία τοῦ θεοῦ which is exclusively encountered in Mark and Luke; whereas Mark only in 11:25 offers the designation of God ὁ πατὴρ ὑμῶν ὁ ἐν τοῖς οὐρανοῖς and Luke does not offer it at all, it (or a corresponding designation) appears fifteen times in Matthew (6:9; 7:11; 10:32 f.; 12:50 in divergence from the synoptic parallels); the conduct demanded of the disciples is designated as δικαιοσύνη only by Matthew (5:6, 10, 20; 6:1, 33; 21:32); Matthew takes up the Lord's Prayer in a form which approximates Jewish liturgical usage by means of its address, the sevenfold petition, and the formulation of the plea for forgiveness (6:12 ὀφειλήματα instead of ἁμαρτίας Lk. 11:4).

On the basis of these considerations it has been concluded that Matthew, with the help of the tradition taken up by him, transformed Mark from a Jewish-Christian standpoint, in order to defend Christianity and to make it acceptable to Jewish-Christian readers and to prove Jesus as the Jewish Messiah. The author is said to be a Jewish Christian, who also had at his disposal rabbinic knowledge (so in varying ways, Ropes, Schmid, Schlatter, von Dobschütz, Michaelis, Feine-Behm, Meinertz, Heard, McNeile-Williams, Wikenhauser, Kilpatrick, Stendahl, Blair, Gärtner, Wolf). Another hypothesis goes even further. The congregation whose view Matthew advocated still found itself in association with Judaism and interpreted the Law in a Jewish manner: in 12:1 the addition to the pericope about plucking ears of grain on the Sabbath, "his disciples were hungry" (against Mk. 2:23), shows that the Sabbath is still observed; the transformation of Lk. 16:16a, "The law and the prophets were until John," into Mt. 11:13, "All the prophets and the law prophesied until John," indicates that the Law is still regarded as valid; and when 24:9 against Mk. 13:13 reads, "You will be hated by all nations," it shows that according to Matthew the disciples must suffer as Jews (so Bornkamm, Held). This latter hypothesis originates in a violent and hardly convincing exegesis. That the church of Matthew knows itself as standing opposed to Judaism, is signified by the fact that Matthew again and again speaks of "their scribes, their synagogues, your synagogues," etc. (7:29; 9:35; 23:34; cf. Kilpatrick, 110 f.).

But other scholars recently have generally denied the hypothesis that Matthew exhibits a Jewish-Christian character and is intended for Jewish Christians, and they have sought to demonstrate that the author of Matthew was not a born Jew and did not write for Jewish Christians. Rather, the author is thought to be a Gentile who addressed himself to the Gentile-Christian church, which in his time was in the majority (so in various ways Clark, Nepper-Christensen, Hebert, Trilling, Strecker). The arguments which are brought forth for this view are, to be sure, of very different weight. That Matthew does not reproduce some Semitic words from Mark (Mk. 3:17; 5:41; 7:11, 34; 10:46, 51; 14:36) does not prove that he does not understand them, since he generally abbreviates texts, and takes over (Mt. 6:24; 10:4, 25; 27:33) or inserts other Semitic words (Ἐμμανουήλ 1:23; ῥακά 5:22; κορβανᾶν 27:6). That he, instead of the correct Semitic Ἰσκαριώθ (Mk. 3:19; 14:10) uses the Greek form Ἰσκαριώτης (10:4; 26:14), shows only that he is writing in a society which speaks Greek. If it cannot thus be demonstrated that the author of Matthew understood no Semitic language, then hardly also the opposite: Jeremias has inferred that the evangelist's mother tongue was Aramaic because he combines ὡσαννά (21:9, 15) with the dative; but there is no evidence against the fact that that was not already Greek-Jewish linguistic usage. Also the theory that Matthew had to write in the language of the Jews, and therefore Hebrew or Aramaic if he wrote for ex-Jews (Nepper-Christensen), is not established if the readers spoke Greek. And that only a Gentile Christian who confused the "tefillin," the phylacteries of the Jews, with amulets could have written πλατύνουσι τὰ φυλακτήρια (23:5; Clark), is an erroneous argument, since it is probable that Jesus in this text indeed controverted the show of wearing amulets (see J. Bowman, "Phylacteries," StEv, 523 ff.).

If all these arguments for or against a Gentile-Christian origin of Matthew are not convincing, then, on the other hand, the contention proves completely true that Matthew's attitude is in no wise particularistic, but rather that, according to Matthew, Jesus' message is intended for all peoples. That follows not only from the command of the Risen One to disciple all the nations (28:19), but also from the interpreting sentence, ὁ ἀγρός ἐστιν ὁ κόσμος (13:38), from the prophecy that "this gospel of the kingdom will be preached ἐν ὅλῃ τῇ οἰκουμένῃ εἰς μαρτύριον πᾶσιν τοῖς ἔθνεσιν" (24:14), and from the expansion of the parable of the wedding feast πορεύεσθε οὖν ἐπὶ τὰς διεξόδους τῶν ὁδῶν (22:9) (additional examples in Trilling, 101 ff.). Matthew by no means, therefore, advocates the view that the gospel above all or exclusively was intended for the Jews, as one could assume in view of Jesus' sayings mentioned above on p. 80 (10:5 f., 23; 15:24). On the contrary, we may refer to some texts which are supposed to prove that for Matthew Christianity has supplanted Judaism, that, according to Matthew, the Jews have been finally rejected: "The sons of the kingdom will be thrown into the outer darkness" (8:12); "The kingdom of God will be taken away from you" (21:43); the Jews pronounce upon themselves the final judgment: "His blood be on us and on our children!" (27:25); "the Jews" stand over against the church (28:15). The features in Matthew which are contradictory to Matthew's alleged harsh anti-Jewish standpoint, the features which speak of a preference for the Jews and seek to prove Jesus as the Messiah of the Jews (see above, pp. 79 f.), are explained by the advocates of this view as tradition taken over and not assimilated to Matthew's own standpoint (cf. especially Strecker, 16 ff.). This view surely is completely untenable. For one thing, it does not prove correct that according to Matthew the Jews have been finally rejected: πάντα τὰ ἔθνη in the missionary command (28:19) includes the Jews just as much as does πάντα τὰ ἔθνη in connection with the world judgment (25:32); if, according to the parable in 21:33 ff., the vineyard is taken away because of the murder of the vinedresser's son, then that means, according to 21:43, that the kingdom will be given, not to the unbelieving Jews who lay in ambush for Jesus and before that against the Baptist (21: 23, 31 f., 45 f.), but to ἔθνει ποιοῦντι τοὺς καρποὺς αὐτῆς, i.e., in place of the unbelieving Jews steps the eschatological people of God, who are characterized by their productivity, without the distinction between Jew and Gentile playing any further role; and if 23:39 ("You will not see me again, until you say, 'Blessed be he who comes in the name of the Lord.' ") does not promise the eschatological conversion of Israel, then it is nevertheless presupposed here that there will be Jews who will welcome with praises the Risen One when he appears at the parousia. Thus if the Jews, according to the view of Matthew, are by no means already finally rejected, we can on the other side only in a very forced argumentation trace back all texts which manifest an outspoken Jewish-Christian tendency to the tradition which the evangelist had not assimilated to his view. For the stricter Jewish formulation of the material taken over, the accented taking up of the formula quotations, and the insertion of the texts which advocate the continuing validity of the Law and Israel's special role, indeed belong together, and show that the author not only lives in a Jewish-Christian tradition but also wishes to offer to his readers the message about the omnipotence of the risen Jesus, and salvation through baptism, and keeping of his commandments (28:17 ff.) in a form which will reveal to them as Jewish Christians Jesus Christ as "the son of David, the son of Abraham" (1:1), whose "gospel of the kingdom will be preached throughout the whole world, as a testimony to all nations; and then the end will come" (24:14).

It must be admitted that this intention of the evangelist could be carried out but not without contradictions, and that from these contradictions the contradictory interpretations followed, of which we have been speaking. But if one makes this intention of the evangelist clear and seriously accepts the probability that Jesus' sayings like 10:5, 23; 15:24 (see above, p. 80) go back to Jesus (see J. Jeremias, *Jesus' Promise to the Nations*. Tr. S. H. Hooke, 1958, 19 ff.), and therefore belong to the oldest Palestinian Jesus tradition, then it follows that Matthew did not belong to a Jewish Christianity which called the Gentile church into question, but probably to a Jewish Christianity which, in connection with total recognition of the sending of Jesus as intended for all peoples, had softened Jesus' radical criticism of the Law by emphasizing the Law's abiding value (cf. 5:18 f.; 23:3). This criticism is well illustrated by the antitheses of 5:21-48, which in part were taken up by Matthew, and in part first formulated by him (see W. G. Kümmel, ZNW, 33, 1934, 125). But Jesus' opponent according to this understanding of Jesus' attitude toward the Law (an understanding which is approximating the traditional Jewish understanding of the Law) is not the Gentile-Christian interpretation of the Law (a polemic against antinomianism, as Barth, 75 ff., 159 ff., and Hebert assume, is out of the question; see Strecker, 137 f.), but the pharisaical, that is, the casuistic Jewish interpretation of the Law (15:3 ff., 13 f.; 23:3 f., 13, 23 f.): "Matthew feels that the Pharisees have missed altogether the true meaning of the Scriptures" (Blair, 141).

But even if our attempt to point to the historical position of Matthew and his individuality in relation to Mark and Luke has forced us to clarify more precisely the attitude of the evangelist to Jewish Christianity and to Gentile Christianity, we must not deceive ourselves about the fact that the actual interest of Matthew is to be found not in this attitude, but on the one hand in the proof that Jesus is "the Christ, the Son of the living God" (16:16), promised by God from time immemorial, who "will save his people from their sins" (1:21), and, on the other hand, in the constantly repeated emphasis of the fact that such salvation is to be obtained only in the ἐκκλησία of Christ (16:18 f.; 18: 17 f.), and as a member of that people that produces its fruits (21:43). Scholars erroneously have disputed about Matthew's "Sitz im Leben" and have claimed to make its origin intelligible in the context of liturgical reading (Kilpatrick), catechetical instruction (von Dobschütz), or scholastic scriptural research (Stendahl). But for each of these theses only a part of the material can be cited, and Trilling (p. 197) has, therefore, correctly stated "that an all-around satisfactory answer to the question about the 'Sitz im Leben' has till today not been found." Matthew writes his expanded new draft of Mark as a "congregational book" (A. Harnack, *The Acts of The Apostles* [NT Studies III]. Tr. J. R. Wilkinson, 1909, p. xv, note 1) and thus for the needs of specific Christian congregations, which should receive strengthening in the recognition of Jesus as the Christ for controversy with contemporary Judaism (10:17), and which should receive direction through Jesus' word for the reality of church life (18: 15 ff.) and for ethical decision (19:1 ff.). To deny in spite of 4:17; 16:28; 24:33 f. that Matthew held fast to an imminent expectation (so finally Strecker, 41 ff.) is unjustified. Yet even so the indispensable waiting (24:42 ff.) demanded directions for the church and the individual Christians in the interim ἕως τῆς συντελείας τοῦ αἰῶνος (28:20) (see E. Grässer, "Das Problem der Parusieverzögerung in den synpt. Evv. und in der Apg.," Beih. ZNW 22, 1957, 200 ff.), and the church book of Matthew seeks to meet this need. Now we have only to ask for which congregations Matthew wrote.

3. Place and Time of Composition

It follows with certainty from the previous discussions that the author of Matthew was at home in a Greek-speaking environment, and wrote for Greek-speaking Christians, of whom the majority were of Jewish origin (nothing speaks in favor of the origin of the readers out of the sect of Qumran, against Wolf). Composition in Palestine (Schlatter, Albertz, Michaelis) is, therefore, hardly to be accepted. And from the report of the flight of Jesus' parents to Egypt (2:13 ff.), we cannot seriously infer the composition of Matthew in Alexandria (against Brandon). Most scholars, in agreement with Streeter, presume that Matthew was written in Antioch or in Syria in general, and in support of this position the fact can be cited that the oldest witness for the knowledge of Matthew is Ignatius (cf. Ign., Smyrn. 1:1; Pol. 1:2, 3). As for Phoenicia, which is conjectured now and then (Kilpatrick, Blair), nothing speaks for it.

For the time of composition the starting point is the dependence upon Mark, and therefore a dating before about 70 is excluded (Höpfl-Gut, Meinertz: 50-60; Michaelis, Cassian: 60-70). The addition to the parable of the marriage feast (22:7) certainly points to an origin after 70: "The king was angry, and he sent his troops and destroyed those murderers and burned their city," for here is obviously an allusion to the destruction of Jerusalem; and even if here a fixed description is used which characterizes ancient expeditions of punishment, the author of Matthew could hardly have inserted it as an expansion into the parable (it is missing in Lk. 14:16 ff.) without thinking of the destruction of Jerusalem, which was interpreted as God's punishment for the unbelief of the Jews (against K. H. Rengstorf, "Die Stadt der Mörder," *Judentum, Urchristentum, Kirche, Festschr. J. Jeremias*, Beih. ZNW 26, 1960, 106 ff., especially 125 f.). And even if Mark and Matthew originated in different regions, Matthew nevertheless shows in his revision of Mark such a clear development of the ecclesiastical situation and of theological reflection (cf. only 18:15 ff. and 28:19) that a time of composition shortly after Mark (e.g., Wikenhauser, Tasker, Michel, Schmid, Ropes, Klijn think of c. 75) is less probable than the time between 80 and 100 (so, e.g., Henshaw, Heard, McNeile-Williams, Riddle-Hutson, Johnson, Feine-Behm, Bornkamm, Kilpatrick, Blair, Strecker). An origin after 100 is excluded because of Ignatius' use of Matthew.

4. Author

Since Matthew contains no direct reference to its author, we must refer to the external tradition for designation of the author. Its oldest witness is the report of Papias: Ματθαῖος . . . Ἑβραΐδι διαλέκτῳ τὰ λόγια συνετάξατο, ἡρμήνευσεν δ'αὐτὰ ὡς ἦν δυνατὸς ἕκαστος (Eus., EH III, 39, 16; see above, pp. 43 f.). That Papias in this notice means the canonical Matthew has been denied only since Schleiermacher, because our Matthew is no translation from a Semitic language, but (in dependence upon the Greek Mark) was written in the Greek language. Papias, however, doubtless means our Matthew, yet he, just as little as the later witnesses of the early church who were dependent upon him, ever saw a Matthew in Semitic language, as finally Nepper-Christensen established (pp. 37 ff.; there pp. 210 f. the witnesses of the early church). The thesis, which has been advocated again and again, that Matthew was the author of a chief source of Matthew (the "Logia source" or of an Aramaic Matthew) and from that the entire Matthew *a parte potiore* was named Κατὰ Ματθαῖον (so recently Vaganay, Léon-Dufour, Meinertz, Wikenhauser, Sparks, Feine-Behm), is, therefore, a completely unfounded hypothesis. We must admit that the report about the Matthew composed by Matthew "in the Hebrew language" is false, however it may have originated (J. Munck, "Die Tradition über das Mt. bei Papias," *Neotestamentica et Patristica, Freundesgabe O. Cullmann*, NovTSuppl. 6, 1962, 249 ff., raised for discussion the noteworthy possibility that the hypothesis of a "Hebrew" Matthew arose in connection with the formation of the canon in order to clarify the differences among the Synoptics).

Of the tradition which Papias took over, only the name "Matthew" may possibly prove to be correct. The Ματθαῖος must be meant who is found in all lists of the "twelve" (Mt. 10:3; Mk. 3:18; Lk. 6:15; Acts 1:13), but who is designated as "tax collector" only in Mt. 10:3. It must also be noted that the tax collector called "Levi" in Mk. 2:14 par. Lk. 5:27 (Mark: "son of Alphaeus"), whom Jesus called, bears in Mt. 9:9 the name Matthew. How this difference in names is to be explained is fully unknown, and concerning the Matthew of the circle of the twelve we otherwise know nothing at all. Could the Gospel of Matthew have stemmed from Matthew, the member of the circle of the twelve, and thus from an eyewitness and member of the first circle of Jesus' disciples? The dependence of Matthew upon the Greek gospel of a nondisciple, the systematic (and that means nonbiographic) manner of Matthew's outline, the late-apostolic theological attitude, and the Greek language of Matthew, make this hypothesis completely impossible, and it is, therefore, no longer advocated by most scholars (e.g., Michaelis, Henshaw, Heard, Johnson, Tasker, Filson, Michel, Schmid, T. W. Manson, Bornkamm, Blair, Clark, and those named above, p. 40, who claim the name for a source of Matthew). But if the apostle Matthew, one of the twelve, is not the author of Matthew, then he is unknown to us, and we do not know how the tradition arose that this Matthew composed our Matthew. Only this much is probable: The change of the name of the tax collector who was called and the addition of the professional designation, "the tax collector," to the name "Matthew" in Matthew perhaps has something to do with this tradition. The author of Matthew, whose name is unknown to us, was a Greek-speaking Jewish Christian, who possibly had rabbinic knowledge, and in any case was bound to a form of the Jesus tradition which had strongly assimilated the sayings of Jesus to Jewish views. To be sure, he himself endeavored to proclaim the meaning of Jesus as Israel's Messiah for the church of all nations. In this way Matthew became in the truest sense the ecclesiastical Gospel.

§8. THE GOSPEL OF LUKE

Commentaries, see p. 387. Studies: cf. besides the lit. to §5 W. K. HOBART, *The Medical Language of St. Luke*, 1892; A. HARNACK, *Lukas der Arzt*, Beiträge zur Einl. in das NT I, 1907; *Luke the Physician* (NT Studies I). Tr. J. R. Wilkinson, 1907; H. J. CADBURY, *The Style and Literary Method of Luke*, HarvThSt 6, 1920; *idem, The Making of Luke-Acts*, 1927 (reprint 1958); V. TAYLOR, *Behind the Third Gospel*, 1926; *idem,* "The Proto-Luke Hypothesis," ExpT 67, 1955-56, 12 ff.; *idem,* "Methods of Gospel Criticism," ExpT 71, 1959-60, 68 ff.; *idem,* "The Narrative of the Crucifixion," NTSt 8, 1961-62, 333 f.; *idem,* "Theologians of Our Time: H. Schürmann," ExpT 74, 1962-63, 77 ff.; M. DIBELIUS, *Jungfrauensohn und Krippenkind. Untersuchungen zur Geburtsgeschichte Jesu im Lk.*, SHA 1932, 4 (= Botschaft und Geschichte I, 1953, 1 ff.); M. GOGUEL, "Luke and Mark," HarvThR 26, 1933, 1 ff.; G. D. KILPATRICK, "A Theme of the Lucan Passion Story and Luke 23:47," JThSt 43, 1942, 34 ff.; H. SPARKS, "The Semitisms of St. Luke's Gospel," JThSt 44, 1943, 129 ff.; T. E. BLEIBEN, "The Gospel of Luke and the Gospel of Paul," JThSt 45, 1944, 134 ff.; T. W. MANSON, "The Work of St. Luke," BJRL 28, 1944, 382 ff. (= Manson, St., 60 ff.); H. SAHLIN, *Der Messias und das Gottesvolk*, ASNU 12, 1945; *idem, Studien zum 3. Kap. des Lk.*, Uppsala Universitets Aarsskrift 1949, 2; S. M. GILMOUR, "A Critical Re-examination of Proto-Luke," JBL 67, 1948, 143 ff.; R. MORGENTHALER, *Die lukanische Geschichtsschreibung als Zeugnis I. II*, AThANT 14.15, 1948 (thereto W. G. KÜMMEL, ThRdsch, N. F. 22, 1954, 197 ff.); E. SCHWEIZER, "Eine hebraisierende Sonderquelle des Lk.?," ThZ 6, 1950, 161 ff.; L. GIRARD, *L'évangile des voyages de Jésus*, 1951; P. VIELHAUER, "Das Benedictus des Zacharias (Lk.1:68-79)," ZThK 49, 1952, 255 ff.; R. KOH, *The Writings of St. Luke*, 1953; J. BLINZLER, "Die literarische Eigenart des sog. Reiseberichts im Lk.," SStW 1953, 20 ff. (lit.); J. SCHNEIDER, "Zur Analyse des lukanischen Reiseberichts," SStW 1953, 207 ff.; H. SCHÜRMANN, "Die Dubletten im Lk.," ZkTh 75, 1953, 338 ff.; *idem,* "Die Dublettenvermeidungen im Lk.," ZkTh 76, 1954, 83 ff.; *idem, Der Paschamahlbericht Lk.22: (7-14.) 15-18*, NTA 19,5, 1953; *idem, Der Einsetzungsbericht Lk.22:19-20*, NTA 20,4, 1955; *idem, Jesu Abschiedsrede Lk.22:21-38*, NTA 20,5, 1957; *idem,* "Protolukanische Spracheigentümlichkeiten?," BZ, N. F. 5, 1961, 266 ff.; E. LOHSE, "Lukas als Theologe der Heilsgeschichte," EvTh 14, 1954, 256 ff.; P. SCHUBERT, "The Structure and Significance of Luke 24," *Ntl. Studien für R. Bultmann*, Beih. ZNW 21, 1954, 165 ff.; P. WINTER, "Some Observations on the Language in the Birth and Infancy Stories of the Third Gospel," NTSt 1, 1954-55, 111 ff.; *idem,* "Magnificat and Benedictus-Maccabaean Psalms?," BJRL 37, 1954, 328 ff.; *idem,* "The Treatment of His Sources by the Third Evangelist in Luke XXI–XXIV," StTh 8, 1955, 138 ff.; *idem,* "The Proto-Source of Luke I," NovT 1, 1956, 184 ff.; *idem,* "On Luke and Lucan Sources," ZNW 47, 1956, 217 ff.; *idem,* "The Main Literary Problem of the Lucan Infancy Story," AThR 40, 1958, 257 ff.; H. RUSSELL, "Which was Written First, Luke or Acts?," HarvThR 48, 1955, 167 ff.; C. F. EVANS, "The Central Section of St. Luke's Gospel," StG 1955, 37 ff.; N. TURNER, "The Relation of Lk. I and II to Hebraic Sources and to the Rest of Luke-

Acts," NTSt 2, 1955-56, 100 ff.; P. BENOIT, "L'enfance de Jean-Baptiste selon Luc I," NTSt 3, 1956-57, 169 ff.; H. F. D. SPARKS, "St. Luke's Transpositions," NTSt 3, 1956-57, 219 ff.; E. GRÄSSER, *Das Problem der Parusieverzögerung in den synpt. Evv. und in der Apg.*, Beih. ZNW 22, 1957 (= ²1960 with supplement), 178 ff., 204 ff.; L. CERFAUX et J. CAMBIER, DBS 5, 1957, 545 ff. (bibl.); R. LAURENTIN, *Structure et théologie de Luc I–II*, Ét. Bibl., 1957 (bibl.); J. JEREMIAS, "Perikopen-Umstellungen bei Lukas?," NTSt 4, 1957-58, 115 ff.; *idem, Die Abendmahlsworte Jesu*, ³1960, 91 ff.; *The Eucharistic Words of Jesus*. Tr. Arnold Ehrhardt from 2nd ed., 1955; A. STROBEL, "Lukas der Antiochener," ZNW 49, 1958, 131 ff.; A. HASTINGS, *Prophet and Witness in Jerusalem. A Study of the Teaching of Saint Luke*, 1958; O. MICHEL, CBL, 1959, 819 ff.; J. C. O'NEILL, "The Six Amen Sayings in Luke," JThSt, N.S. 10, 1959, 1 ff.; *idem, The Theology of Acts in Its Historical Settings*, 1961 (thereto H. CONZELMANN, ThLZ 87, 1962, 753 ff.); B. REICKE, "Instruction and Discussion in the Travel Narrative," StEv, 1959, 206 ff.; R. M. WILSON, "Some Recent Studies in the Lucan Infancy Narratives," StEv, 1959, 235 ff.; J. TYSON, "The Lucan Version of the Trial of Jesus," NovT 3, 1959, 249 ff.; W. GRUNDMANN, "Fragen der Komposition des lukanischen Reiseberichts," ZNW 50, 1959, 252 ff.; F. REHKOPF, *Die lukanische Sonderquelle*, WUNT, 5, 1959 (thereto H. CONZELMANN, Gn. 32, 1960, 470 f.); H. CONZELMANN, *Die Mitte der Zeit. Studien zur Theologie des Lukas*, BhTh 17, (1954) ³1960 (= ⁴1962); *The Theology of St. Luke*. Tr. Geoffrey Buswell, 1960 (thereto P. WINTER, ThLZ 81, 1956, 36 ff.; 85, 1960, 929 ff.); L. GASTON, "Sondergut und Markusstoff in Lk.21," ThZ 16, 1960, 161 ff.; U. LUCK, "Kerygma, Tradition und Geschichte Jesu bei Lukas," ZThK 57, 1960, 51 ff.; H. C. SNAPE, "The Composition of the Lucan Writings: A Re-Assessment," HarvThR 53, 1960, 27 ff.; W. C. ROBINSON, "The Theological Context for Interpreting Luke's Travel Narrative (9:51 ff.)," JBL 79, 1960, 20 ff.; J. SCHMID, LThK VI, 1961, 1207 ff. (lit.); H. W. MONTEFIORE, "Does 'L' Hold Water?," JThSt, N. S. 12, 1961; 59 f.; C. K. BARRETT, *Luke the Historian in Recent Study*, 1961; C. S. C. WILLIAMS, "Luke-Acts in Recent Study," ExpT 73, 1961-62, 133 ff.; R. LEANEY, "The Birth Narratives in St Luke and St Matthew," NTSt 8, 1961-62, 158 ff.; J. GNILKA, "Der Hymnus des Zacharias," BZ, N. F. 6, 1962, 215 ff.

1. Contents

The structure of Luke diverges from that of Mark (and Matthew), for in the place of the section, "Jesus' journeyings inside and outside of Galilee" (Mk. 6:1–9:50 par. Mt. 14:1–20:34; this section continues Jesus' activity in Galilee in a form which varies only slightly with respect to geography), appears the extensive section, Lk. 9:51–19:27, which shows Jesus journeying to Jerusalem, and at its end in 18:15-43 takes up into itself the great part of Mk. 10 (par. Mt. 20: "Jesus' journey to Jerusalem"). It is disputed whether Luke offers any kind of a hint as to a subdivision of this extensive so-called "travel document" (see on this below, p. 99), yet with good reason we may refer to the fact that the intention of Jesus (9:51) to go to Jerusalem is emphasized anew in 13:31-35, so that in 14:1 (or better in 13:31) a new section begins (Reicke, O'Neill). If that proves to be correct, then we can carefully divide Luke into five chief parts (1:5–4:13: early history and preparation for Jesus' appearance; 4:14–9:50: Jesus' activity in Galilee; 9:51–13:30 and 13:31–19:27: Jesus on the way to

Jerusalem; 19:28–24:53: Jesus in Jerusalem), before which is placed a prologue. As a result, then, we have the following detailed sequence of the Lukan account:

The First Principal Part (1:5–4:13), which follows the prologue (1:1-4), begins with the infancy narrative: announcement of the birth of John (1:5-25); announcement of the birth of Jesus (1:26-38); Mary's visit to Elizabeth (1:39-56, including Mary's hymn of praise, the "Magnificat," 1:46-55); birth of John (1:57-80, including Zechariah's hymn of praise, the "Benedictus," 1:68-79); birth of Jesus (2:1-20); circumcision and presentation of Jesus in the temple (2:21-40, including Simeon's hymn of praise, the "Nunc dimittis," 2:29-32); Jesus at twelve years in the temple (2:41-52). The preparation for Jesus' appearance includes the appearance of the Baptist and his preaching (3:1-18), his imprisonment by Herod (3:19 f.), Jesus' baptism (3:21 f.), Jesus' genealogy, traced back from Joseph to Adam and God (3:23-38), and Jesus' temptations (4:1-13).

The Second Principal Part (4:14–9:50) (Jesus' activity in Galilee) begins, after a short description of Jesus' appearance in Galilee (4:14 f.), with his inaugural sermon in Nazareth (4:16-30). Lk. 4:31–6:19 follows Mark (healings in Capernaum, preaching in Judea [4:31-44]; the first disciples [5:1-11]; healing of a leper, a paralytic, forgiveness of sins, Jesus and the tax collector, questions about fasting [5:12-39]; plucking ears of grain and healing on the Sabbath [6:1-11]; choice of the apostles and press of the multitude [6:12-19]). In 6:20-49 follows the Sermon on the Plain, which to some extent corresponds to Matthew's Sermon on the Mount, and there follow additional pieces out of another tradition: centurion from Capernaum (7:1-10); young man from Nain (7:11-17); the Baptist and Jesus (7:18-35); the anointing of Jesus by a sinful woman (7:36-50); the women in Jesus' company (8:1-3). The following two pieces (the parable of the four kinds of soil, with interpretation and attached discourses [8:4-18], and the true relatives of Jesus [8:19-21]) stand against Mark in reverse sequence; 8:22–9:50, however, again corresponds to the Markan sequence (4:35–9:41), yet the following are missing from Luke: Mk. 6:1-6, 17-29; 9:9-13 and the entire section Mk. 6:45–8:26. Lk. 8:22–9:50: storm at sea, Gerasene demoniac, daughter of Jairus, and the woman with the hemorrhage (8:22-56); sending out of the twelve, Herod's opinion, feeding of the 5,000 (9:1-17); Peter's confession with prediction of the Passion and discipleship sayings (9:18-27); Transfiguration and healing of the epileptic boy (9:28-43a); second prediction of the Passion, dispute for precedence; and rejection of a strange exorcist (9:43b-50).

The Third Principal Part (9:51–13:30) (beginning of the journey to Jerusalem) contains chiefly texts common with Matthew, but also special material: At the beginning is the narrative about the village in Samaria that refused to receive Jesus because Jerusalem was the goal of his journey (9:51-56). There follow discourses concerning discipleship (9:57-62); sending out of the seventy (10:1-20); cry of joy and blessedness of the eyewitnesses (10:21-24); question about the attainment of eternal life and parable of the good Samaritan (10:25-37); Mary and Martha (10:38-42); Lord's Prayer (11:1-4); sayings about prayer (before them the parable of the importunate friend) (11:5-13); controversy discourses (Jesus' defense against the reproach of a covenant with Beelzebub, blessedness of Jesus' mother, demand for a sign, sayings about light, discourse against the Pharisees (11:14-54); exhortations to the disciples (fearless confession, no anxiety, heavenly treasure, vigilance, faithfulness, the time of division—joined together with the discourse about the controversy over the inheritance and the parable of the rich fool [12:13-21]) (12:1-53); warnings to the people to repent (signs of the time, necessity of repentance, parable of the unfruitful fig tree, Jewish offense at the healing of a bent woman on the Sabbath, parables of the mustard seed and leaven, threatening judgment upon the Jews) (12:54-13:30).

The Fourth Principal Part (13:31-19:27) (renewed beginning of the journey to Jerusalem) presents till 18:14 mostly special material, but also some parallel material with Matthew; from 18:15-43 again follows Mk. 10:13-52 and closes with special material and with material common to Matthew: By way of introduction to this section, Jesus stresses the necessity of going to Jerusalem and threatens with judgment (13:31-35). Dinner discourses follow (healing of a man with the dropsy on the Sabbath, exhortation to humility and unselfishness, parable of the great supper) (14:1-24); to that are joined sayings about discipleship, parables of the tower and conduct of war (14:25-35); parables of the lost sheep, coin, and son (ch. 15); doctrinal discourses concerning the attitude toward worldly possessions (parable of the unjust steward and appended sayings concerning the pride of the Pharisees, law and the kingdom of God, parable of the rich man and poor Lazarus) (ch. 16); instructions for the disciples (offenses, forgiveness, faith, duty of servants, the thankful Samaritan among the ten lepers) (17:1-19); little eschatological discourse (the coming of the kingdom of God, the advent of the Son of man) (17:20-37); parables of the judge and the widow (18:1-8) and of the Pharisee and the tax collector (18:9-14). 18:15-43 follows Mk. 10:13-52 (blessing of the children, question about eternal life, third prediction of the Passion, healing of a blind man); the story of Zacchaeus (19:1-10) and the parable of the pounds (19:11-27) are added from another tradition.

The Fifth Principal Part (19:28-24:53) (Jesus in Jerusalem) essentially follows the sequence of Mark until 22:53, but diverges from the Markan sequence more than once in the following passion narrative, and from 24:13 on offers special material: entry into the temple and cleansing of the temple (19:28-48); to that are joined the question concerning authority, the parable of the wicked husbandmen, question concerning tribute, question of the Sadducees, question about David's son, warning about the scribes, the widow's mites (20:1-21:4); eschatological discourse (21:5-36); conclusion of activity in Jerusalem (21:37, 38). In the passion narrative (22:1-23:56) follow the betrayal of Judas (22:1-6); Last Supper with farewell discourse (22:7-38); Jesus on the Mount of Olives and Jesus taken captive (22:39-53); Peter's denial, mockery of Jesus, hearing before the Sanhedrin (22:54-71); hearing before Pilate (23:1-25) (in the midst of which is the sending of Jesus to Herod Antipas, 23:6-16); the

road to Golgotha and sayings to the women of Jerusalem (23:26-32); crucifixion and death of Jesus (23:33-49); burial (23:50-56). Following the Easter
message at the empty tomb (24:1-11 [12?]) are: disciples on the road to
Emmaus (24:13-35); the appearance of the Risen One before the eleven in
Jerusalem (24:36-49); parting from the disciples and Ascension (24:50-53).

2. The Literary Purpose of the Gospel of Luke According to Its Own Data

Luke is the only one of the evangelists who, according to the literary usage
of the time, placed at the beginning of his Gospel a prologue, in which he spoke
his mind about his sources and the principles which guided him in composition
(cf. thereto in addition to the commentaries H. J. Cadbury, "Commentary on
the Preface of Luke," *Beginnings* I, 2, 1922, 489 ff., Lohse, see lit. to §8,
E. Haenchen, ZThK 1961, 362 ff.). The prologue, which was composed in good
Greek and according to literary usage, is first of all recognizable as the preface
only of Luke. But not only the probability that the author from the beginning
had his mind on continuing the narrative past the death of Jesus into the history
of the church, but also his reference to "the things which have been accomplished among us" (1:1) indicate that Lk. 1:1-4 is intended to be the prologue
to both books of Luke (e.g., Cadbury, *loc. cit.*, Feine-Behm, Ropes, Grundmann, Lohse, Luck, Russell, O'Neill; otherwise, Conzelmann, Michaelis, E. Haenchen, Meyer III[13] on Acts 1:1 and pp. 672 f. and ZThK, *loc. cit.*). If we read
through Lk. 1:1-4 with this supposition in mind and with regard to literary
usage, then the author says to us the following about his sources and his purpose:

1. Luke, like all Gospel writings before it, is based upon the tradition of
"those who from the beginning were eyewitnesses and ministers of the word."

"From the beginning" obviously cannot include the infancy narratives, but
extends to the beginning of Jesus' public activity. In preparation for the appearances of the Baptist and of Jesus, Luke furnishes his great synchronistic summary (3:1). What Luke and his predecessors report is derived from men who
witnessed the things in part from the beginning, and who were the first messengers of the gospel. Whether this tradition was passed on orally or in writing
he does not say. But Luke, according to the manner in which he distinguishes
between the tradition of the primitive witnesses (1:2) and the gospel writings
known to him (1:1), obviously does not presuppose the existence of a complete Gospel from the hand of an apostle.

2. Upon the basis of the tradition of the eyewitnesses, "many" already before
Luke have undertaken to give a description of the "things" which "have been
accomplished among us" (ἐν ἡμῖν). With this expression, which is more con-
cealing than revealing, Luke points to the facts associated with the life, death,
and resurrection of Jesus, which were concluded with the resurrection and which
yet continued working in the "preaching of the kingdom of God" and in the
"teaching about the Lord Jesus Christ" (Acts 28:31), and which were repro-

duced in the gospel writings known to him. Luke, who himself was not an eyewitness from the beginning, adds his historical work to them, without, by means of the traditional ἐπεχείρησαν (v.1), designating his predecessors as inadequate attempts. The likewise traditional πολλοί reveals nothing about the number of the predecessors known to Luke.

3. Luke's goal in his work was to awaken in Theophilus (and in the readers generally), by means of trustworthy reproduction of the narratives, complete trust in the contents of Christian teaching. Toward this end, he investigated "from the beginning" (ἄνωθεν) the divinely guided history, and strove for complete (πᾶσιν) and accurate (ἀκριβῶς) information (see below, p. 127), so that he could "write an orderly account" (καθεξῆς).

4. By means of the dedication to the κράτιστος Θεόφιλος, the book receives a still stronger literary character, since the addressee had the obligation to tend to the dissemination of the book. Κράτιστος, to be sure, can be the title of a high official, but it is also used as a polite form of address (see Bauer-Arndt-Gingrich, *Lexicon*, 450, and Cadbury, *loc. cit.*, 505 ff.). Hence concerning the position of Theophilus, who is completely unknown to us, we learn nothing from this address. Κατηχήθης also is ambiguous, so that we cannot decide whether Theophilus was a Christian or only had heard something about Jesus and the Christians.

From all of this it follows that Luke knows himself as a man of the second generation of the Christian tradition. He pursues his purpose of giving, upon the basis of the tradition of the first generation which he has examined, a trustworthy representation of that which has taken place, because according to his opinion certain knowledge of "the things which have been accomplished (by God) among us" is necessary for the evaluation of the Christian λόγοι. Luke claims, with this information, to create a work which can lay claim to literary quality, and he gives expression to this claim by means of the prologue and dedication. It remains to be asked in which manner Luke carried out this intention.

3. Literary Character and Theological Purpose of the Gospel of Luke

If Luke wants to report καθεξῆς = in good order, in succession (1:3; on καθεξῆς cf. 8:1; Acts 3:24; 11:4; 18:23), then, so far as we are able to determine that does not mean that he presents the transmitted material in a sequence which is essentially different from the sequence he found in his sources. This statement, of course, can be checked clearly only in relation to Mark, but it does prove true in respect to Mark over against Lk. 1:1–22:53, with the exceptions named above on pp. 46 f. (removal of Mk. 6:1-6 forward to Lk. 4:16-30; removal of Mk. 1:16-20 backward to Lk. 5:1-11; reversal of Mk. 3:7-12 and 3:13-19; removal of Mk. 3:31-35 backward to Lk. 8:19-21). Lk. 22:54–23:49, however, offers an essentially different sequence from Mk. 14:53–15:41. For the relation of Luke to Q, only the well-grounded conjecture can be advanced that Luke also retained in the main the sequence of this source (see above, p. 54).

Nevertheless, the correctness of this proposition depends upon how one generally views Luke's use of sources, and here the opinions diverge widely.

The facts of the case are as follows: Luke follows Mark's sequence extensively, except in the passion story, but he reproduces only about seven tenths of Mark's material in three great blocks (3:1–6:19; 8:4–9:50; 18:15–24:11). In between stands tradition not derived from Mark (6:20–8:3, the so-called "small interpolation"; 9:51–18:14, the so-called "great interpolation"). Material not derived from Mark is also found within the Markan blocks (larger pieces are Lk. 3:23–4:13; 4:16-30; 5:1-11; 19:1-27; 22:14-18, 24-38; 23:6-16, 27-31, 39-43). The infancy and post-resurrection narratives (Lk. 1, 2 and 24:12-53) contain special material exclusively. The material of Luke which is not also encountered in Mark comprises approximately three fifths of the entire Gospel. More than one third of Luke also has no parallel in Matthew, and is, therefore, special material (according to De Solages' vocabulary statistics [see lit. to §5], 1049; similar ratios upon the basis of counting entire pericopes in Goguel, *Intr.* I, 494). The great extent of the special material, the lack of about three tenths of the Markan material in Luke, the substantial difference of the Lukan passion narrative over against Mark, and the considerable linguistic divergence of some Lukan parallels from Mark (e.g., Lk. 21:12-26 par. Mk. 13:9-25), have led to the thesis, first advocated by Streeter, that we should reverse the hypothesis that Mark lies at the basis of Luke and was expanded by means of material from Q and special material. Rather the author of Luke first of all created from Q + L (= special material) a Gospel beginning with 3:1, the so-called "Proto-Luke." Into "Proto-Luke" he subsequently inserted parts of Mark, and before 3:1 he later placed chaps. 1 and 2. By some scholars (in the main part already by Streeter) this thesis is expounded even more precisely in that "Proto-Luke" was composed by the Pauline pupil Luke upon the basis of inquiries made of eyewitnesses during Paul's imprisonment in Caesarea (Acts 23:35–27:1). Later, after Luke had come to Rome with Paul, he expanded his "Proto-Luke" upon the basis of the Roman Mark (thus or similarly Taylor, Perry, Grant, de Zwaan, Henshaw, T. W. Manson, Evans, Koh, Lohse, Rehkopf, Gaston, Williams; Jeremias, Winter would like to distinguish between the author of "Proto-Luke" and of Luke). Other scholars hold that only for the passion narrative can it be demonstrated that a special source lies at the basis of the account (Tyson, Klijn, Schürmann). Some advocate the kindred view that the entire special material of Luke is derived from an apostolic narrative source, but do not regard this special source as the *foundation* of Luke (so in various ways Schlatter, Bussmann, Rengstorf, Grundmann; earlier advocates of views of that kind in Schürmann, ZkTh 1954, 90 note 64; Schweizer supposes a Hebrew special source, Sahlin a Hebrew-Aramaic "Proto-Luke" extending from Lk. 1:5–Acts 15). Yet many have generally rejected the hypothesis of a "Proto-Luke" (Goguel, Dibelius, Gilmour, Kilpatrick, Michaelis, Grobel, Leaney, Conzelmann, Schürmann, Hastings, O'Neill, Montefiore, Klijn, Beare) or at least have designated the proof of a special source for the passion narrative as not successful (Iber, R. H. Lightfoot, *History and Interpretation in the Gospels*, 1935, 164 ff., J. Finegan, *Die*

Überlieferung der Leidens- und Auferstehungsgeschichte Jesu, Beih. ZNW 15, 1934, 35 ff., Bultmann, *History* [see lit. to §5], 266, 431, J. Blinzler, *The Trial of Jesus*. Tr. Isabel and Florence McHugh from 2nd ed., 1959, 115 ff.). Indeed, the hypothesis of a Lukan special source or even a "Proto-Luke" is just as questionable as that of a special source for the Lukan passion narrative. a) If, first of all, we leave aside the infancy narrative (Lk. 1, 2), then the comparison of Luke with Mark shows that Luke certainly follows on the whole the sequence of Mark, but now and then does not shrink from changes of sequence (see above, pp. 46 f.). The contention that Luke knows no pericope inversions over against Mark outside the passion narrative (Schürmann, Jeremias, Rehkopf) can be maintained only if it is denied without sufficient reason that the events narrated in Lk. 4:16-30 and 5:1-11 (rejection in Nazareth, call of the first disciples) have received in Luke another position within the narrative (it makes no difference whether these pericopes were taken over by Luke already formulated or more probably were newly shaped in dependence upon Mark with the help of other traditions), and if one refers to the transposition of Mk. 3:7 ff. and 3:31 ff. by Luke without any reason as appendices (even less can the moving forward of the Baptist's imprisonment to Lk. 3:19 f. instead of parallel to Mk. 6:17 f. be called an "appendix"!). There is no adequate reason on this basis to deny the possibility of transpositions by Luke in the passion narrative (cf. Sparks).

b) The hypothesis that Luke secondarily inserted the Markan material in four blocks (Mk. 1:21–3:6; 4:1–9:40; 10:13–52; 11:1–14:16) into his special source (see tables in Jeremias, *Abendmahlsworte³*, 92) runs aground on two facts: i) From the places where the small (Lk. 6:17–8:3) and where the large (9:51–18:14) "interpolations" interrupt the sequence of the Markan material which Luke took over, is missing both times a section from Mark (3:20-30; 9:42–10:12); that can be explained only if, in connection with the insertion of other material in the Markan course, a section of Mark was always omitted (see Schürmann, ZkTh 1954, 83 f.). ii) When Luke presents doublets of another origin besides Markan material of the same contents or instead of an omitted Markan pericope another form of the same pericope, then the Markan pericope of the doublet or the position of the omitted Markan pericope always *precedes* the other form (see Schürmann, ZkTh 1953, 341 f.; the only exception would be Lk. 5:1-11 instead of the omitted Mk. 1:16-20, if Luke here did not change the position of the Markan pericope and therewith expanded it through another tradition). That is explicable only if Mark lies at the basis of the composition.

c) The so-called "travel narrative" (9:51–19:27) is, as the recent works on it have shown (see below, p. 99), a creation of Luke, who inserted didactical material of various origin into the framework of a journey to Jerusalem (a framework not really carried out). In this "central section" there is not just a primitive tradition taken over by Luke, but a composition of the evangelist, who has widened the situation advanced in Mk. 10:1; 11:1 for the insertion of his disparate material.

d) Rehkopf has not succeeded in demonstrating, by means of isolating non-Lukan linguistic materials, the presence of a connected special tradition in

Luke, or even the working together of this special tradition with Q before the insertion of the Markan material (cf. Conzelmann, Gn 1960, and Schürmann, BZ 1961). And just as little have Tyson, Schürmann, Winter, Rehkopf, and others been able to show that the diverse pieces and little pieces of special tradition in the Lukan passion narrative represent a primitive connected source in which Luke later inserted particular verses from Mark. For, on the one hand, the reasons which are cited for a primitive connected narrative of the individual pieces of the Lukan special material (e.g., 22:15-20 and 22:24-32) are altogether other than obvious; and, on the other hand, there is by no means only the alternative of "connected written source" or "free invention" by Luke (so Schürmann, *Jesu Abschiedsrede*, 140, note 476). Rather, we must seriously consider the possibility that Luke enriched Mark's passion narrative by orally transmitted features or accounts, or transformed it on the basis of such tradition, so long as no really compelling reasons for the dependence of Luke upon a connected special source in the passion narrative are adduced. And it is significant that V. Taylor very recently saw himself forced to admit that Mark presumably furnishes the framework of the Lukan passion narrative (see ExpT 1959-60, 69).

e) Winter and Gaston seek to show that in the apocalyptic discourse (Lk. 21) in the same way as in the passion narrative Mark does not form the foundation, but particular verses from Mk. 13 were inserted into a previously existing connected source. The foundation for this hypothesis is, on the one hand, that a clear coherence results after removal of the sentences which plainly correspond with Mark, a coherence which can only be original, and, on the other hand, that the contradictions in the Lukan text (e.g., 21:20 compared with 21:21 and 21:27 compared with 21:28) can be explained only by means of an insertion of verses corresponding with Mark (therefore 21:20, 21a and 21:27) into a coherent account which without these verses is meaningful. We, however, reject the Winter-Gaston hypothesis for three reasons: 1) The connected account which arises when we eliminate the Markan verses is by no means always more intelligible (e.g., 21:20, 21b, 22). 2) Contradictions between combined apocalyptic traditions can be explained at least as well through expansion of Mark through other traditions as through insertion of particular Markan verses into the postulated connected account of a special source. 3) Luke has extensively transformed the wording of Mark (in the sense of a considerable extension of the time until the parousia) precisely where a dependence upon Mk. 13 cannot be denied (cf., e.g., Lk. 21:8 with Mk. 13:5 f.). In view of all these points, the hypothesis is basically more obvious for Lk. 21 also that Luke placed the text of Mk. 13 at the basis of his composition in connection with the use of additional pieces of tradition (cf. Grässer, 152 ff., Schmid, LThK VI, 1209, Barrett).

f) That Luke placed Mark at the basis of his report is shown conclusively by the disarrangement of the Markan construction by Luke's expansion. Especially striking is Luke's separation of the passion predictions which in Mark are inserted at like intervals (Mk. 8:31 f.; 9:30 ff. par. Lk. 9:22, 43 ff., but Mk. 10:32 ff. par. Lk. 18:31 ff., because the "great interpolation" [Lk. 9:51–18:14] is shoved in between). But also the insertion of the genealogy (Lk. 3:23 ff.) between Jesus' baptism and temptation (Mk. 1:9-11, 12 f.) secondarily separates material belonging together. And the "brackets" which Luke has placed around the public activity of Jesus, the "brackets" of the temporary departure of the devil from the time of Jesus' temptation until the beginning of the passion narrative, which in 4:13 are inserted into Q material and in 22:3 into Markan material, show that the evangelist produces from Mark and Q a deliberate unity (cf. Conzelmann, 16, 28, 76).

From this discussion it follows that the hypotheses of a Lukan special source or of a "Proto-Luke" composed of Q and special material are not tenable and also that a connected special tradition hardly lies at the basis of Luke's passion narrative. And the great age, or at least the Palestinian origin, of the Lukan special material is not to be ensured by means of the unproved hypothesis of a Lukan special source or of a "Proto-Luke" (Montefiore wants to strengthen this position by pointing to the fact that the alleged "Proto-Luke" could not at all have been brought by Luke to Rome, because the papyrus manuscript must have perished in the shipwreck at Malta [Acts 27:41 ff.]!). If, therefore, Luke probably did not take over from a connected source the extensive material in chaps. 3–24 which is not found in Mark and Q, then the possibility is not excluded that he, as has also been conjectured for Mark, found and took over some special traditions already arranged together in oral or even written form, but that can hardly be established with any kind of certainty. Farmer would like, e.g., to trace back 13:1-9 and 15:1-32 to the same source, but his arguments lack cogency. In view of Luke's undoubted conscious LXX style (Sparks), the hypothesis of Hebraic or Hebraicized sources (Sahlin, Schweizer; against that, Michaelis, *Einl.*, 71 ff.) is in no case convincing. It is also futile to seek after various sources of tradition (Albertz: women's tradition, relative's tradition, Hellenistic tradition) or transmitters of tradition (Hastings: The evangelist Philip, Symeon of Cyrene; Joanna, the wife of Chuza [8:3; 24:10], who supplied reports about Herod!). We can only attempt to ascertain the historical origin of the individual units of tradition and the manner of their revision and arrangement by Luke.

The infancy narratives in Lk. 1 and 2, however, pose a special problem in connection with the question of Luke's sources. This problem follows not only from Luke's chronological synchronism (3:1 f.), which shows that the actual reporting first begins here, but also from the unmistakable fact that, after the literary, stylized prologue (1:1-4), the narratives and songs of 1:5–2:52 abruptly change to a Greek which is strongly reminiscent of the Semitized LXX language. The supporters of the "Proto-Luke" hypothesis have drawn the conclusion from these observations that it was not until the final composition of Luke that Luke's infancy narratives based upon written sources were placed before "Proto-Luke," which originally began with 3:1. Related to this is the statement that the strongly Semitized language of these chapters can be made comprehensible only through the hypothesis that Hebrew sources were translated and enlarged by the author of Luke, or at least were taken over by him from Greek sources translated from the Hebrew. There are various views as to whether the hymns

(1:46 ff., 68 ff.; 2:29 ff.) were taken over with these sources or were inserted out of another tradition (cf., e.g., in various ways Winter, Sahlin, Laurentin, Hastings, Wilson). Others are of the opinion that Luke himself composed these narratives upon the basis of ancient oral or written traditions in conscious adaptation to the language of the LXX (Sparks, Dibelius, Bultmann, Turner, Benoit). Furthermore, in numerous works (completely enumerated AThR 1958, 260, note 6), Winter has sought to prove that the greater part of Lk. 1, 2 originated in the circles of the Baptist's disciples and only secondarily was transferred to Jesus. In the hymns (1:46 ff., 68 ff.) he purports to see Maccabean war-hymns, sung before and after battle, which only by means of the link in 1:76-79 were connected to the Baptist. Especially concerning the original character of the "Benedictus" (1:68 ff.), opinions diverge considerably, in that some claim to see in the entire hymn a baptismal song (Vielhauer, Bultmann), others a Christian poem with reference to the Baptist (Benoit) or to Jesus (Sahlin, Leaney), or a combination of a messianic psalm with a birth hymn about John from Jewish-Christian circles (Gnilka). Now the linguistic observations of Sparks, Benoit, and Turner show that the hypothesis of a translation of both chapters out of the Hebrew is hardly tenable. Yet it cannot be dienied that the birth stories of the Baptist could hardly have originated in Christian circles (cf. above all 1:16 ff.). And there are some reasons for the supposition that the "Benedictus" originated in circles of the Baptist. On the other hand, the remaining parts of chaps. 1 and 2 are doubtless of a Christian origin, with considerable utilization of OT language and conceptions. But above all the observation is important that in 1:26-37 and 2:1-10 two completely different conceptions of Jesus' birth are encountered (Dibelius, Leaney), which only secondarily were placed in a context which was not free of contradictions. At the present time a sure judgment about the origin and the unity of the single units of tradition in Lk. 1, 2 can hardly be passed. Yet the observations mentioned speak strongly against the hypothesis that in Lk. 1, 2 larger connected sources were taken up. Rather, the probability is that Luke revised at least three diverse traditions, which already in part had attained a certain linguistic firmness, and placed them before his representation of Jesus' public activity. If the slight linguistic variations in Lk. 1, 2 in comparison with Lk. 3–24 demand an explanation at all, they presumably can be traced back to the fact that the infancy narrative was written later than the remainder of the Gospel (so Benoit, NTSt 1956-57, 175 f.).

If, therefore, it must probably be thought to be true that Luke originated by means of the insertion of material from Q and from special tradition into the sequence of Mark (a sequence which was essentially retained), then the proposition is confirmed (see above, p. 91) that "Luke offers no order which reproduces the historical course of events more accurately than Mark, and that, therefore, his program 'to write an orderly account' ($\kappa\alpha\theta\epsilon\xi\tilde{\eta}s$) cannot indicate a strict chronological order which his sources would not have allowed him" (J. Schmid, LThK VI, 1208). Therefore, Luke obviously seeks to attain the goal toward which he strives ($\kappa\alpha\theta\epsilon\xi\tilde{\eta}s\ \gamma\rho\acute{\alpha}\psi\alpha\iota$), not by means of a sequence which is chronologically more reliable, but through revision of Mark done in a different way and through the insertion of extensive other tradition.

1) The revision of Mark (and, what can only be inferred, also of Q and the special tradition) was done first of all, similarly as in Matthew, by means of a closer linkage of the separate accounts with one another, and by means of occasional preparation of greater connecting links in the course of the narrative (ties through expressions like μετὰ ταῦτα, καὶ ἐγένετο ἐν μιᾷ τῶν ἡμερῶν, ἀναστὰς δέ [5:27, 17; 4:38]; 5:27-39, in contrast to Mk. 2:13 ff., 18 ff., becomes one report by equating the partners in conversation [5:30, 33 as opposed to Mk. 2:16, 18]; 19:11 places the parable of the pounds into the biographical context by referring to the nearness of Jerusalem and the false expectation of the multitude [cf. Mt. 25:14]; 4:13, the remark about the temporary departure of the devil, points in advance to 22:3; 8:2 f., by way of preparation, names the women who are present at the Crucifixion and the discovery of the empty tomb [23:49, 55; 24:10]; cf. to these features Bultmann, *History* [see lit. to §5], 307 f., 334 ff.). This repeated drawing together of two reports speaks, in addition to other reasons, against Morgenthaler's hypothesis that Luke composes consistently according to the principle of doubling.

2) Luke considerably changes the wording of Mark and probably also of his other tradition, in that he replaces vulgar words and turns of expression and forms better Greek sentences (cf. Klostermann, Hdb., 243 ff.; Wernle, *Synpt. Frage* [see lit. to §5], 10 ff.). It is especially significant that Luke deletes all foreign words with the exception of ἀμήν; even this word Luke more than once expunges or replaces by Greek words; he uses it, however, six times in sayings which indicate direct instructions for the life of the Christian (4:24; 12:37; 18:17, 29; 21:32; 23:43; see O'Neill, JThSt 1959). Luke doubtless writes a more elevated speech than his sources; yet this tendency works against his connection with the biblical Greek of the LXX (see Sparks). Luke also does not apply this new linguistic formation of the tradition to the entire material in the same manner: In the narrative material, above all in the introductions to the pericopes, we encounter the Lukan linguistic peculiarities four times as often as in the Jesus-sayings, and correspondingly the number of words which agree with Mark in the Jesus-sayings exceeds those in the narrative sections (Schürmann, *Paschamahlbericht*, 2; Rosché, JBL 1960 [see lit. to §5], 212). And in the early history Luke follows the LXX style more closely than in the remainder of the Gospel. From all of this it follows that Luke very consciously shaped anew the tradition for Greek-speaking readers, but in doing so imposed upon himself narrower limits for the reproduction of the Lord's sayings.

3) Like Matthew, Luke also removed offenses which the Markan text offers: the healing of "many" in Mk. 1:34; 3:10 becomes the healing of "all" in Lk. 4:40; 6:19; emotional states of Jesus are omitted (6:10; 18:22 against Mk. 3:5; 10:21); likewise the explanation of Jesus' kin that he is beside himself (Mk. 3:21), and healing through touching (Lk. 4:39; 9:42 against Mk. 1:31; 9:27) are left unmentioned; Jesus' cry, "My God, my God, why hast thou forsaken me?" (Mk. 15:34) is replaced by "Father, into thy hands I commit my spirit!"

(Lk. 23:46). Correspondingly, Jesus from the beginning acknowledges himself as the Messiah (4:21), and thus already the earthly Jesus is addressed as κύριε by Peter (5:8), and frequently in the narrative is called ὁ κύριος by the evangelist (7:13; 10:1, 41; 22:61 and often), because in Jesus' activity the time of salvation has broken in (σήμερον σωτηρία τῷ οἴκῳ τούτῳ ἐγένετο 19:9, said to Zacchaeus). This accentuation of the Messiahship and Lordship of the earthly Jesus in no way prevents Luke from gladly stressing Jesus' feelings of sympathy: Jesus converses with the women on the way to the cross (23:27 ff.), and with one of those crucified with him (23:40 ff.); he heals the ear of a high priest's slave cut off by a disciple (22:51); and he looks out of the high priest's house at Peter, who has denied him (22:61).

4) With this emphasis upon Jesus' feelings of sympathy is to be taken the fact that Jesus, in Luke more so than in Mark and Matthew, expresses God's love for the despised through his conduct and his message: to sinners (5:1 ff. [ἀνὴρ ἁμαρτωλός εἰμι says Peter, 5:8]; 7:36 ff.; 15:1 ff., 18:9 ff.; 19:1 ff. ["For the Son of man came to seek and to save," 19:10]; 22:31 f.); to the Samaritans (10:30 ff.; 17:11 ff.); the women (7:12, 15; 8:2 f.; 10:38 ff.; 23:27 ff.). Here belongs also the more strongly stressed rejection of riches (12:15 ff.; 16:19 ff.), the warning of the μαμωνᾶς τῆς ἀδικίας (16:9, 11), the woe upon "the rich" and those "that are full now" (6:24 f.), and the beatitude of the "poor" and "those that hunger now" (6:20 f.). It has been supposed that Luke, with this emphasis upon poverty, "gave to the preaching of Jesus a light Ebionitic coloring" (Feine-Behm). But in view of the totality of the features enumerated above this supposition turns out to be false: Luke more strongly emphasized the influence on Jesus of the late Jewish "poverty piety," just as he rejected the religious scorn of certain groups of men, only from the presupposition that in Jesus the divine love for the lost in the eyes of men had really become salvation in the present (cf. Grundmann, ThHK on Lk. 6:20 f. [lit.]).

5) It is still more significant that Luke in three ways places the history of Jesus in clearly recognizable connection with the history of his time: a) Through the reference to the connection of Jesus' birth in Bethlehem with the census command of Emperor Augustus under Quirinius (2:1 f.), and through the chronological fixing of the Baptist's appearance on the basis of dates of the Roman and Jewish history (3:1 f.), the history of Jesus is made recognizable as part of the general course of history. Correspondingly, in the NT the names of Roman emperors appear only in Luke (cf. also Acts 11:28; 18:2). Likewise Luke expressly stresses: "This (the history of Christ as fulfillment of the prophetic promises) was not done in a corner" (Acts 26:26). The history of Jesus Christ belongs, acording to Luke, to world history. b) Luke was probably the first to represent the history of Jesus as the beginning of the still continuing church history (Lk. 19:11; 21:8), in that he has Acts follow Luke as the second book of a connected historical report. In that way the history of Jesus becomes past history and the report of this history becomes the "first life of Jesus" (E. Käsemann, ZThK 51, 1954, 137 = Essays on New Testament Themes, 1964, 28 f.; likewise Conzelmann, Barrett, Haenchen, Apg., Meyer

III [13], 86 f.). Jesus' journey to Jerusalem first reached its actual goal when Paul in Rome preached τὰ περὶ τοῦ κυρίου Ἰησοῦ (Acts 28:31, cf. O'Neill, *Theology*, 6). c) Luke endeavors to demonstrate the political innocence of Jesus in the eyes of the Romans, above all of Pilate (Lk. 23:4, 14, 20, 22; 23:47 ["Certainly this man was innocent!"]), whereas the Jews appear as those who approve of insurrection and seek unjustly to accuse Jesus as a political agitator (20:20, 26; 23:2, 5, 18 f., 23, 25). There is no doubt that there is a political apologetic here which fully absolves the Romans of the guilt in Jesus' crucifixion (Pilate does not condemn Jesus [23:25 against Mk. 15:15 par. Mt. 27:26]) and therewith prepares the defense of the Christians against political accusation in Acts (e.g., Acts 17:7, see below, p. 114; Kilpatrick, Manson, St., 60 f.; Conzelmann, 90, 138 ff.). Also in connection with this political defense the relation of Jesus' history with general history appears.

6) The decisive motive in Luke's new form of Mark is, however, the theological. That becomes evident in the change of Mark's geographical design. The author of Luke obviously has no accurate conception of the geography of Palestine (cf. Conzelmann, 18 ff., who, however, describes Luke's conceptions with too much certainty). He also knows nothing of several journeys of Jesus to Jerusalem (so Girard); rather he expanded the report handed down to him by Mark of Jesus' journey to Jerusalem after conclusion of his activity in Galilee and its environs (Mk. 10:1 ff.), so that Jesus now is frequently represented in 9:51–19:27 as being on the way to Jerusalem (9:51; 13:22, 33; 17:11; 18:31; there are general references to Jesus' travels in 9:57; 10:1, 38; 14:25. The data in 17:11 διήρχετο διὰ μέσον Σαμαρείας καὶ Γαλιλαίας is unintelligible, but needs no conjecture as in Blinzler). Into the connected account of this journey to Jerusalem Luke inserted material from Q, special material, and material from the Jerusalem journey of Mk. 10. These materials for the most part have no recognizable connection to this biographical situation (Blinzler, Reicke). This emphatic change of the Markan "Vorlage" allows us to conjecture that Luke in this report of the journey to Jerusalem did more than create a framework in order to accommodate additional material out of his tradition.

Therefore, the more recent works on the "travel narrative" have sought to find the leading viewpoint of this composition (Schneider: doctrine for the disciples, with directions for the life and work of the disciples and the future missionary work of the community of the disciples; Evans: material arranged in connection with Dt.; Reicke: instruction of the apostles and discussion with opponents; Conzelmann: Jesus' consciousness of suffering is expressed as a journey [likewise O'Neill]; Grundmann: journey to the Passion united with Jesus' activity as prophetic teacher destined to be the Messiah; W. C. Robinson: the advance of salvation history represented as the "Way," and preparation for the apostolic witness). But their diversity shows that such viewpoints do not stand out clearly, and we must be satisfied with the insight that in 9:51–19:27 the Lord, who goes to suffer according to God's will, equips his disciples for the mission of preaching after his death (9:60; 10:3,16; 17:22-25). The extent and the position of this composition before the actual passion narrative confers upon this section of Jesus' activity a special importance, and thus it becomes clear in connection with this formal change of the Markan design that Luke wishes to describe the history of Jesus as the preparation for the activity of the disciples after Easter.

And here we touch the ruling theological viewpoint for the shaping of the history of Jesus in the Lukan work: The place of Jesus' life in God's *salvation* history. It has long been observed that the "eschatology in the preaching of Jesus in Luke is not so prominent as in Mark and Matthew," and that "the expectation of the imminent End seems subdued in comparison with Mark and Matthew (19:11; 9:27; 22:69)" (Feine-Behm). But only the more recent investigations of Luke's theology (Lohse, Conzelmann, Grässer, Luck, O'Neill, Haenchen, *Apg.*, Meyer III [13]) have shown that this receding of the imminent expectation is merely an especially striking reference to the fact that Luke "outlines a Christian view of history which comprehends the activity of Jesus, his death and resurrection as fulfillment of the divine promises, beyond these events extends the line farther away, and lets the salvation history continue in the course of the church till the end of the times" (Lohse, 265). There are three basic thoughts with which Luke, from this fundamental theological view, gives a new direction to the history of Jesus.

a) The imminent expectation is displaced from its controlling position: The summary of Jesus' preaching, "The kingdom of God is at hand" (Mk. 1:15), is replaced by Jesus' inaugural sermon in Nazareth (Lk. 4:21), "Today this scripture (about the eschatological sending of the Spirit upon Jesus) has been fulfilled in your hearing"; from the promise, "there are some standing here who will not taste death before they see the kingdom of God come with power" (Mk. 9:1), there develops Lk. 9:27, "there are some standing here who will not taste of death before they see the kingdom of God"; the parable of the entrusted pounds is, according to Lk. 19:11, spoken "because they supposed that the kingdom of God was to appear immediately"; and the warning, "Many will come in my name, saying, 'I am he!' and they will lead many astray" (Mk. 13:6) is expanded to Lk. 21:8, "Many will come in my name, saying, 'I am he!' and, 'The time is at hand!' Do not go after them." Indeed, the question, "When does the kingdom of God come?" is rejected, because there are no signs upon the basis of which it can be answered, and because "the kingdom of God is in the midst of you" (Lk. 17:20 f.) (cf. on the translation of this puzzling saying, W. G. Kümmel, *Promise* [see above, p. 53], 32 ff. and F. Mussner, "Wann kommt das Reich Gottes?," BZ, N.F. 6, 1962, 107 ff.). But did this rejection of the question about the moment take place because "this moment indeed lies in the far distance" (Grässer, 194), because "Luke resolutely renounced his adherence to the imminent expectation" (Conzelmann, 122)? These answers are contradicted by several texts which proclaim the nearness of the judgment (3:9, 17 in the mouth of the Baptist), the nearness of the kingdom of God (10:9, 11 as commission to the seventy), the early judgment of God (18:7 f.), and in 21:32 it is said as in Mk. 13:30 that "this generation will not pass away till all has taken place." These texts cannot be explained away with the contention that Luke "simply took over" these sayings, and that the total sense decides over the individual saying (Grässer, 190). For in 10:11 Luke obviously added ἤγγικεν ἡ βασιλεία τοῦ θεοῦ (cf. Mt. 10:14), and the reference to the fate of Sodom "on that day," i.e., on the day of judgment, in the following verse (10:12), proves that Luke must have understood the nearness of the kingdom of God not as present, but as threatening future. It is, therefore, hardly correct to say that for Luke the imminent expectation is completely given up, but it has lost its urgent character, and the present is emphasized more strongly as the time of salvation.

b) If, therefore, it does not prove correct that Luke *replaces* the imminent expectation with his conception of salvation history (e.g., Conzelmann, Grässer, Barrett, Haenchen, *Apg.*, Meyer III [13], 86, U. Wilckens, *Missionsreden* [see lit. to §9], 93), there can be no doubt that he depicts the history of Jesus as the decisive period *in the course* of salvation history and not as *the* eschatological event. In behalf of that Lk. 16:16 is especially characteristic. Mt. 11:12 preserves a Jesus-saying probably in its original form: "From the days of John the Baptist until now the kingdom of heaven has suffered violence." In Lk. 16:16 this saying becomes: "The law and the prophets were until John; since then the good news of the kingdom of God is preached, and every one enters it violently" (for the critical problem, see W. G. Kümmel, *Promise* [see above, p. 53], 121 ff.). Conzelmann, chiefly upon the basis of this saying, has advocated the thesis that Luke depicts the history of Jesus as the "middle of time," which is preceded by the time of the law and prophets and followed by the time of the church (pp. 16, 112 f., 160 f., 185 ff.). In behalf of his view that salvation history steps into the place of eschatology, he cites the growing consciousness of the nonappearance of the parousia (122, 131; thus also Grässer, Barrett, O'Neill). There is no doubt that first in Luke the problem of the delay of the parousia consciously influenced the reproduction of Jesus' message. That becomes evident not only in the already mentioned repression of the imminent expectation (cf. also οὐκ εὐθέως τὸ τέλος, 21:9) but is especially striking in the separation of the firmly held eschatological expectation from events within history: the persecution of the disciples and the destruction of Jerusalem (21:12 ff., 20 ff.) as events within history are clearly distinguished (over against Mk. 13:9 ff., 14 ff.) from the signs of the parousia and from the parousia itself (21:25 ff. par. Mk. 13:24 ff.) (the signs of the parousia are not placed in any clear chronological connection with the events within history) (cf. πρὸ δὲ τούτων πάντων 21:12 and with respect to the revision of Mark by Luke in Lk. 21:12 ff.: Grässer, 158 ff.). The growing consciousness of the delay of the parousia does bring about the fact that "in place of the short, limited time has appeared the elongated time of the church" (Grässer, 197), but not so that first in Luke the conception of salvation history appears as a substitute for realistic eschatology. For, on the one hand, it must be said that there are good reasons for presuming that Luke does differentiate between the time of Jesus' activity and the time of the church. Yet "the salvation history design" "even in Luke is only to be inferred and is not explicitly made into the theme" (Luck, 53).

Luke, too, emphasizes only the contrast of the time of the law and prophets to the time from John the Baptist until the parousia (Lk. 16:16; 21:27 f.). And, on the other hand, it must be said that Luke by no means was the first who introduced the conception of salvation history into the reproduction of the evangelical tradition, because the proclamation of the presence in Jesus of the eschatological salvation which remains future formed the basic view of the evangelical proclamation since the preaching of Jesus himself (see W. G. Kümmel, *Promise* [see above, p. 53], *passim; idem,* "Futurische und präsentische Eschatologie im ältesten Urchristentum," NTSt 5, 1958-59, 113 ff.; O. Cullmann, *Christ and Time,* 1964, 1 ff.). But to be sure, Luke, from the experience of extended time which yet is always impending short time, placed the presence of the still expected consummation so strongly in the foreground that the history of Jesus has become the ἀρχή of "the things which have been accomplished among us" (1:1 f.).

c) Hence the fact that Luke reports the "life of Jesus" as the beginning of a still continuing church history (see above, pp. 98 f.) turns out to be a theological necessity. For the experience of the Spirit as the power of the time of the end in the church of the present (Acts 1:8; 2:1 ff, 38; 5:32; 10:44 ff.; 15:28) makes it possible to see the history of Jesus governed by the Spirit of God, who σωματικῷ εἴδει (Lk. 3:22) descended upon Jesus and controlled him until the cry of prayer (23:46) (cf. 4:1, 18 and δύναμις 4:14, 36; 5:17). For the Gentile-Christian church, which has experienced the Spirit, "the apostolic teaching about Jesus is proved only by the work of the Spirit as activity of God" (Luck, 59). The history of Jesus is, therefore, consciously reported by Luke retrospectively from the present church (Acts 10:36 ff.). In spite of that it must be asked whether Luke can be designated as the "first representative of the developing primitive catholicism" (E. Käsemann, "Ntl. Fragen von heute," ZThK 54, 1957, 20) since we encounter neither the church as an institution of salvation nor the sacraments as ecclesiastical means of salvation (thus rightly Barrett, 70 ff.; Conzelmann, 211, note 1).

Thus it may have become clear that Luke so sought to reach his goal καθεξῆς γράψαι the tradition of the eyewitnesses that he represented Jesus' history controlled by the Spirit of God as the basis for the witness of the apostles "in Jerusalem and in all Judea and Samaria and to the end of the earth" (Acts 1:8), in order to offer to faith the ἀσφάλεια (Lk. 1:4) which for him was indispensable.

4. The Author

Luke and Acts manifest themselves through the dedication to the same Theophilus and through the reference of Acts 1:1 to "the first book" as the work of one author. Also they doubtless belong together according to language, style, and theological attitude. Neither Luke nor Acts, directly or indirectly, allows us to recognize who their author was. Since the testimony of Papias is lacking, and the great age of the Lukan prologue, falsely designated as "anti-

Marcionite," is very questionable (see below, p. 343), we first encounter the early ecclesiastical tradition in the Muratorian Canon:

The third Gospel book, that according to Luke. This physician Luke after Christ's ascension (resurrection?), since Paul had taken him with him as an expert in the way (of the teaching) [reading *itineris* instead of *iuris*], composed it in his own name according to (his) thinking. Yet neither did he himself see the Lord in the flesh; and therefore, as he was able to discern it, so he begins to tell the story from the birth of John. (Hennecke-Schneemelcher [see above, p. 60], I, 43).

The more recent tradition (printed in *Beginnings* II, 210 ff.) was able to add nothing to the old report. For the contention that Luke originated in Antioch (most recently defended by Strobel) is encountered first for certain in Eus., EH II, 4, 6, since the so-called anti-Marcionite prologue is no useful source (see above). And the "we" in one part of the "Western" textual tradition of Acts 11:28, which probably also presupposes this tradition, is not even demonstrable as ancient in the Western text (see below, p. 124 f.). Thus there remains as going back to the second century only the report that Luke the physician was the author of Luke-Acts. This reference can only be to "Luke the beloved physician" (Col. 4:14; Phlm. 24; II Tim. 4:11), who must have been born a Gentile, because in Col. 4:14 Paul expressly excludes him from his "fellow workers of the circumcision." An identification with the "Lucius" of Rom. 16:21 (Michaelis) is extremely improbable, since this Lucius is probably designated as Paul's fellow countryman, i.e., as a Jew. According to the references in Colossians and Philemon, Luke must have been in the place of imprisonment from which these epistles originated. Since this place cannot be fixed with certainty (Caesarea? see §21, 5), no significant biographical information can be inferred from these verses. Whether the "we-report" of Acts enables us to recognize something about the participation of Luke in Paul's missionary journeys, will be questioned in §9.

First of all, in respect to this tradition which appears at the end of the second century about Luke the physician as the author of Luke-Acts, we must ask whether here there really is an early tradition. For H. J. Cadbury (*Beginnings* II, 250 ff.) has pointed out that already at the end of the second century it could have been *inferred* that Luke was the author by reasoning from the presupposition that a canonical Gospel must have an apostolic author (Tert., *adv. Marc.* IV, 2), and by comparing the "we" in Acts with the data concerning the associates of Paul during his imprisonment (Col. 4:10-12; Phlm. 23 f.; II Tim. 4:9-12). So little as that can be established, so little is it certain that any early information lies at the basis of the tradition from the end of the second century. So much the more, then, must we ask whether the hypothesis (inferred or handed down) that Luke the physician was the author of Luke-Acts can be brought into harmony with the evidence of Luke (and then also of Acts).

The question has been much discussed whether the books of Luke in language and mental horizon allow us to recognize a physician as author. Especially Hobart, upon the basis of an extensive comparison of the Lukan vocabulary with the language and style of Greek physicians, came to the conclusion that throughout both Lukan writings there sounds clearly a familiarity with technical medical language which leaves no doubt as to the vocation of the author. Zahn, Harnack, Moffatt, Höpfl-Gut, Meinertz, Albertz, Michaelis, Wikenhauser, Geldenhuys, Feine-Behm, and others agreed with more or less certainty to this argumentation. Cadbury, however, exposed the methodological untenability of this thesis by showing that almost all alleged purely medical expressions in Luke are also found, e.g., in LXX, Josephus, Plutarch, and Lucian, and that the style of Luke exhibits no more medical resources of language and interest than the style of contemporary writers who were not medical men. The presence of individual words and phrases, which principally have their parallels in the medical literature of the Greeks, e.g., συνεχομένη πυρετῷ μεγάλῳ Lk. 4:38 (πυρέσσουσα Mk. 1:30), ἀνὴρ πλήρης λέπρας Lk. 5:12 (λεπρός Mk. 1:40), ἔστη ἡ ῥύσις τοῦ αἵματος αὐτῆς Lk. 8:44 (ἐξηράνθη ἡ πηγὴ τοῦ αἵματος αὐτῆς Mk. 5:29), ἐκψύχω Acts 5:5, 10; 12:23, ἀνακαθίζω Lk. 7:15; Acts 9:40, shows only that Luke writes a more cultured Greek than Mark, especially since all of these expressions are also otherwise attested (cf. Bauer-Arndt-Gingrich, Lexicon, for the particular words). And still less is proved by descriptions of sickness such as Lk. 4:35 (different from Mark) and 13:11; or the depiction of the care of the wounded man (Lk. 10:34 f.); or the blotting out of the harsh judgment upon the medical profession (Mk. 5:26; Lk. 8:43); or even the addition of δεξιός in Lk. 6:6; 22:50. In short, Luke's style and language establish nothing for or against a physician as author.

It has also been maintained that Luke shows a remarkable affinity for the theology of Paul and therefore must have originated from a pupil of Paul (cf., e.g., Léon-Dufour in Robert-Feuillet, Feine-Behm, especially Höpfl-Gut). Those who hold this view point to Luke's universalism (4:27; 24:47), to the emphasis upon faith (8:12; 18:8), upon God's love for sinners (15:1 ff.), upon the gospel of joy (2:10; 10:20), and to common concepts (σωτηρία 19:9; κύριος for the earthly Jesus [see above, p. 98], δικαιόω 18:14), etc. But in all of these cases it is a matter of general Gentile-Christian concepts and words, and specifically Pauline theologoumena are completely lacking. Even if we leave the picture of Paul in Acts entirely out of consideration for the moment, it becomes evident even in Luke that its author is altogether unfamiliar with the Pauline theology (cf. Bleiben). This unfamiliarity can most clearly be recognized in the author's conception of Jesus' death. Although he understands it as corresponding to the divine necessity (9:22; 24:26), he makes no clear reference to an expiatory death. Mk. 10:45 is wanting. Lk. 22:19 f. is carried out no further. Likewise, the cry of the God-forsaken One on the cross (Mk. 15:34) is missing (see Conzelmann, 197, 201; Barrett, 59; E. Lohse, Märtyrer und Gottesknecht, FRLANT 64, 1955, 187 ff.; U. Wilckens [see lit. to §9], 184, 200 f.). Since it is simply unthinkable to regard the character of the Gospel of Luke as standing close to the theology of Paul, from here on the tradition of Luke as the author of the third Gospel can only be questioned.

Upon the basis of the Gospel of Luke, only one thing can be said with certainty about its author—he was a Gentile Christian. This deduction is supported by the above mentioned facts that the author has no knowledge of the geography of Palestine and, except for ἀμήν, avoids Semitic words. That he writes for Gentile Christians follows also from the observation that in Luke characteristic traditions concerning Jesus' battle against the Pharisaical understanding of the Law are lacking, just as Palestinian features are changed to Hellenistic ones (these passages are missing: Mt. 5:17, 20; the antitheses of Mt. 5:21-48; the sayings against false cultic piety [Mt. 6:1-8, 16-18]; the argument concerning clean and unclean [Mk. 7:1-23]; the narrative of the Canaanite woman [Mk. 7:24 ff.], etc.; Lk. 5:19 par. Mk. 2:4 and Lk. 7:36 ff. presuppose Hellenistic situations). Yet this insight into the Gentile-Christian origin of the author of Luke cannot decide the question whether the author was really Luke the physician; and if decisive arguments speak against a pupil of Paul this possibility can be denied with certainty only upon the basis of Acts (see §9, 4).

5. Time and Place of Composition

Again and again the proposition has been advanced that Luke and Acts were written at the beginning of the sixties, before the end of Paul's trial (e.g., Harnack, Höpfl-Gut, Meinertz, Michaelis, Schäfer, Albertz, Cerfaux-Cambier, Sahlin, Koh, Hastings, Geldenhuys). But Lk. 1:1 ff. is hardly compatible with this dating, for according to the Lukan prologue there must have existed in this case already about the year 60 many gospel writings, among them Mark. Yet decisive against such an early date is the fact that Luke looks back upon the fall of Jerusalem (A.D. 70). Jesus' prophecy of judgment upon Jerusalem must be regarded as historical (Mk. 13:2 par.; Lk. 13:34 f. par.). But in Lk. 21:20, 24 the apocalyptic prophecy concerning "the desolating sacrilege" (Mk. 13:14 ff.) appears to have been transformed into a prophecy of judgment upon Jerusalem which was shaped *ex eventu:* The events of the year 70, with the siege and destruction of the city by the Romans, the massacre of countless Jews, and the conveyance of the survivors into Gentile captivity, are presupposed. The same thing holds true for the description of 19:43 f.: The wall which the enemies will cast up around the city, the siege and blockade, the surrender of the conquered city and its inhabitants to the victors, and the complete destruction of the city, correspond exactly with descriptions which contemporary reports give about Titus' march upon Jerusalem. Luke in any case, then, was written after 70. How far down the date must be brought cannot be clearly decided upon the basis of Luke. On the other hand, the composition of Acts doubtless forms the *terminus ad quem*, since Acts 1:1 looks back upon Luke as the πρῶτος λόγος. The hypothesis that Acts was written before "Proto-Luke," and Luke then after Acts (Koh, C. S. C. Williams, BNTC on Acts, 12 f.), falls with the hypothesis of a Proto-Luke. Russell certainly has shown that for Luke, but not for Acts, there is a clear witness for its composition after 70, but he has not been able to cite any reasons for the composition of Acts before Luke. O'Neill's attempt to date Luke between 115-135 shatters upon the date of Acts (see below, pp. 132 f.). We may regard the period between 70 and 90 as probable for the composition of Luke.

Concerning the place of composition, there is no early tradition. Scholars have conjectured about Caesarea (Michel, Klijn), Achaea (T. W. Manson), the Decapolis (Koh), and, above all, Rome (Michaelis, Geldenhuys, Hastings, and others). But for none of these conjectures can any conclusive arguments be adduced, and we can say only that Luke was surely written outside of Palestine.

§9. The Acts of the Apostles

Commentaries, see p. 388. Research reports: W. G. Kümmel, ThRdsch, N.F. 14, 1942, 162 ff.; 18, 1950, 16 ff.; 22, 1954, 194 ff.; J. Dupont, *Les problèmes du Livre des Actes d'après les travaux récents*, Analecta Lovanensia Biblica et Orientalia II, 17, 1950; *idem, Les sources du Livre des Actes. État de la question*, 1960; A. J. Mattill, Jr., "Luke as a Historian in Criticism since 1840," diss., Vanderbilt University, 1959; W. Bieder, *Die Apg. in der Historie. Ein Beitrag zur Auslegungsgeschichte des Missionsbuches der Kirche*, ThSt 61, 1960; E. Grässer, ThRdsch, N.F. 26, 1960, 93 ff.; E. Haenchen, *Apg.*, Meyer III[13], 1961, 13 ff. 670 ff.— Studies: J. Weiss, *Über die Absicht und den literarischen Charakter der Apg.*, 1897; A. Harnack, *Die Apg.*, Beiträge zur Einl. in das NT III, 1908; *The Acts of the Apostles* (NT Studies III). Tr. J. R. Wilkinson, 1909; C. C. Torrey, *The Composition and Date of Acts*, HarvThSt I, 1916; F. J. Foakes-Jackson-K. Lake *el al.*, *Prolegomena and Criticism* in: *Beginnings* I, 1, 1920; I, 2, 1922; A. Wikenhauser, *Die Apg. und ihr Geschichtswert*, NTA 8,3–5, 1921; *idem*, LThK I, 1957, 743 ff.; M. Dibelius, "Zur Formgeschichte der Apg.," ThRdsch, N.F. 3, 1931, 233 ff.; *idem, Aufsätze zur Apg.*, FRLANT 60, 1951 (cf. thereto A. D. Nock, Gn 25, 1953, 497 ff.); *Studies in the Acts of the Apostles*. Tr. Mary Ling, 1956; B. S. Easton, *The Purpose of Acts*, 1936 (= *Early Christianity*, 1955, 33 ff.); J. Jeremias, "Untersuchungen zum Quellenproblem der Apg.," ZNW 36, 1937, 205 ff.; M. H. Shepherd, "A Venture in the Source Analysis of Acts," *Munera Studiosa*, Festschr. W. H. P. Hatch, 1946, 91 ff.; W. L. Knox, *The Acts of the Apostles*, 1948; P. Benoit, "Remarques sur les 'sommaires' des Actes II, IV et V," *Aux sources de la tradition chrétienne*, Festschr. M. Goguel, 1950, 1 ff. (= *Exégèse et théologie* II, 1961, 181 ff.); *idem*, "La deuxième visite de Saint Paul à Jérusalem," Bb 40, 1959, 778 ff.; H. F. D. Sparks, "The Semitisms of Acts," JThSt, N.S. 1, 1950, 16 ff.; Ph. Vielhauer, "Zum 'Paulinismus' der Apg.," EvTh 10, 1950-51, 1 ff.; E. Hirsch, *Frühgeschichte des Ev.* I, [2]1951, XXX ff.; A. W. Argyle, "The Theory of an Aramaic Source in Acts 2:14-40," JThSt, N.S. 3, 1952, 213 f.; A. Vögeli, "Lukas und Euripides," ThZ 9, 1953, 415 ff.; Ph. H. Menoud, "Remarques sur les textes de l'ascension dans Luc-Actes," *NTl. Studien für R. Bultmann*, Beih. ZNW 21, 1954, 148 ff.; *idem*, "Le plan des Actes des apôtres," NTSt 1, 1954-55, 44 ff.; *idem*, "Pendant quarante jours (Actes 1,3)," *Neotestamentica et Patristica, Freundesgabe O. Cullmann*, NovT Suppl. 6, 1962, 148 ff.; O. Bauernfeind, "Zur Frage nach der Entscheidung zwischen Paulus und Lukas," ZsystTh 23, 1954, 59 ff.; E. Haenchen, "Tradition und Komposition in der Apg.," ZThK 52, 1955, 205 ff.; *idem*, RGG[3] I, 1957, 501 ff.; *idem*, "Quellenanalyse und Kompositionsanalyse in Act 15," *Judentum, Urchristentum, Kirche, Festschr. J. Jeremias*, Beih. ZNW 26, 1960, 153 ff.; *idem*, "Das 'Wir' in der Apg. und das Itinerar," ZThK 58, 1961, 329 ff.; H. J. Cadbury, *The Book of Acts in History*, 1955; *idem*, "Acts and Eschatology," *The Background of the NT and Its Eschatology, Festschr. C. H. Dodd*, 1956, 300 ff.; *idem*, " 'We' and 'I' Passages in Luke-Acts," NTSt 3, 1956-57, 128 ff.; C. F. Evans, "The Kerygma," JThSt, N.S. 7, 1956, 25 ff.; B. Reicke, *Glauben und Leben der Urgemeinde. Bemerkungen zu Apg. 1-7*, AThANT 32, 1957; *idem*, "The Risen Lord and His Church. The Theology of Acts," Int 13, 1959, 157 ff.; E. Käse-mann, "Ntl. Fragen von heute," ZThK 54, 1957, 20 f.; E. Schweizer, "Zu den Reden der Apg.," ThZ 13, 1957, 1 ff.; E. Trocmé, *Le "Livre des Actes" et l'histoire*, Études d'histoire et de philosophie religieuses 45, 1957; G. Klein, review of E. Haenchen, *Apg.*, Meyer III[10], 1956 und Meyer III[13], 1961, ZKG 68, 1957, 362 ff., 73, 1962, 358 ff.; *idem*, *Die zwölf Apostel*, FRLANT 77, 1961, 115 ff.; A. Ehrhardt, "The Construction and Purpose of the Acts of Apostles," StTh 12, 1958, 45 ff.; A. E. Haefner, "The Bridge between Mark and Acts," JBL 77, 1958, 69 ff.; U. Wilckens, "Kerygma und Ev. bei Lukas (Beobachtungen zu Acta 10,34-43)," ZNW 49, 1958, 223 ff.; *idem*, *Die Missionsreden der Apg. Form- und traditionsgeschichtliche Unter-suchungen*, WMANT 5, 1961 (lit.; cf. thereto J. Dupont, RB 69, 1962, 37 ff.); G. Schille, "Die Fragwürdigkeit eines Itinerars der Paulusreisen," ThLZ 84, 1959, 165 ff.; O. Michel, CBL, 1959, 71 ff.; R. Bultmann, "Zur Frage nach den Quellen der Apg.," *NT Essays in Memory of T. W. Manson*, 1959, 68 ff.; J. Dupont, "Le salut des gentils et la signification théologique du livre des Actes," NTSt 6, 1959-60, 132 ff.; W. C. van Unnik, "The 'Book of Acts' the Confirmation of the Gospel," NovT 4, 1960, 26 ff.; J. T. Townsend, "The Speeches in Acts," AThR 42, 1960, 150 ff.; H. Conzelmann, review of E. Haenchen, *Apg.*, Meyer III[12], 1959, ThLZ 85, 1960, 241 ff.; H. Zimmermann, "Die Sammelberichte der Apg.," BZ, N. F. 5, 1961, 71 ff.; W. Eltester, "Lukas und Paulus," *Eranion, Festschr. H. Hommel*, 1961, 1 ff.; J. Cambier, "Le voyage de S. Paul à Jérusalem en Act. 9, 26 ff. et le schéma mis-sionaire théologique de S. Luc," NTSt 8, 1961-62, 249 ff.; S. S. Smalley, "The Chris-tology of Acts," ExpT 73, 1961-62, 358 ff.; G. Strecker, "Die sogenannte zweite Jerusalemreise des Paulus," ZNW 53, 1962, 67 ff.—On the text of Acts: Th. Zahn, *Die Urausgabe der Apg. des Lukas*, Forschungen zur Geschichte des ntl. Kanons IX, 1916; J. H. Ropes, *The Text of Acts, Beginnings* I, 3, 1926; A. C. Clark, *The Acts of the Apostles*, 1933; W. G. Kümmel, ThRdsch, N. F. 11, 1939, 96 ff.; *idem*, "Die älteste Form des Aposteldekrets," *Spiritus et veritas, Festschr. K. Kundsin*, 1953, 83 ff.; M. Dibelius, "The Text of Acts. An Urgent Critical Task," JR 21, 1941, 421 ff. (also in *Studies*, 84 ff.); L. Cerfaux, "Citations scripturaires et tradition textuelle dans le Livre des Actes," *Aux sources de la tradition Chrétienne, Festschr. M. Goguel*, 1950, 43 ff. (= *Recueil Lucien Cerfaux* II, 1954, 93 ff.). Ph.-H. Menoud, "The Western Text and the Theology of Acts," *Studiorum Novi Testamenti Societas, Bulletin* II, 1951, 19 ff.; C. C. Williams, *Alterations* [see below, p. 359], 54 ff.; E. Haenchen, "Schrift-zitate und Textüberlieferung in der Apg.," ZThK 51, 1954, 153 ff.; *idem*, "Zum Text der Apg.," ZThK 54, 1957, 22 ff.; *idem*, *Apg.*, Meyer III[10], 1956, 41 ff., Meyer III[13], 1961, 47 ff., 657 f. (lit.), 667 ff.; A. F. J. Klijn, *Western Text* [see below, p. 385], NovT 3, 1959, 169 ff.; H. C. Snape, "The Composition" [see lit. to §8], 34 ff.; E. J. Epp, "The 'Ignorance Motif' in Acts and Anti-Judaic Tendencies in Codex Bezae," HarvThR 55, 1962, 51 ff.

1. Contents

The widespread division of Acts into two unequal principal parts (1-12: From Jerusalem to Antioch, Petrine part; 13-28: From Antioch to Rome,

Pauline part; so also Feine-Behm) is hardly according to the understanding of the author, who follows no biographical purpose. Preferably, we can accept a twofold division of the book at 15:35-36 (1:15–15:35: expansion from Jerusalem until the securing of the Gentile mission; 15:36–28:31: expansion to Rome; so Menoud). Or we may attempt a division into five geographically determined sections in accordance with the missionary commission (1:8): 1:15–8:3: Jerusalem; 8:4–11:18: Samaria and coastal region; 11:19–15:35: Antioch and Antiochian mission; 15:36–19:20: lands around the Aegean Sea; 19:21–28:31: from Jerusalem to Rome (thus O'Neill, *Theology* [see lit. to §8], 67; similarly Dupont, NTSt 1959-60, 135). The following summary is based upon the latter division that is naturally hypothetical also.

After the prologue and the account of the Ascension (1:1-14) the First Principal Part (1:15–8:3) treats the spread of the gospel in Jerusalem. 1:15-26: restoration of the circle of the twelve through the choice of Matthias; 2:1-41: Pentecost (outpouring of the Holy Spirit, 1-13; Peter's sermon, 14-36, and its success, 37-41); 2:42-47: first summary account; 3:1–4:22: healing of a lame man by Peter, Peter's preaching in the temple, Peter and John before the Sanhedrin; 4:23-31: prayer of the community for release of the apostles; 4:32-35: second summary account, to which is added the example of Barnabas (4:36, 37) and the counterexample, Ananias and Sapphira (5:1-11); 5:12-16: third summary account; 5:17-42: the apostles before the Sanhedrin; 6:1–8:3: Stephen and the first persecution (6:1-7: choice of the "seven"; 6:8-15: accusation of Stephen; 7:1-53: speech of Stephen; 7:54–8:3: martyrdom of Stephen and persecution of the Hellenistic Christians in Jerusalem).

The Second Principal Part (8:4–11:18) reports the spread of the gospel in Samaria and the coastal regions. 8:4-25: preaching in Samaria; 8:26-40: Philip and the Ethiopian court official; 9:1-9: conversion of Paul; 9:10-30: Paul in Damascus and Jerusalem; 9:31-43: Peter in Lydda and Joppa; 10:1–11:18: Peter in Caesarea: conversion of the Gentile Cornelius.

The Third Principal Part (11:19–15:35) recounts the spread of the gospel to Antioch and then out from Antioch. 11:19-26: the first Christians in Antioch (name Χριστιανοί); 11:27-30; 12:25: collection journey of Barnabas and Paul from Antioch to Jerusalem, in the midst of which is the persecution of the primitive church by Herod Agrippa I (12:1-19: martyrdom of James, the son of Zebedee, and the rescue of Peter) and the death of Herod (12:20-24); 13:1–14:28: mission, commencing at Antioch (13:1-3: sending out of Barnabas and Paul; 13:4-12: preaching in Cyprus; 13:13-52: journey to Antioch in Pisidia, speech of Paul, and expulsion of the missionaries; 14:1-6*a*: preaching in Iconium and flight; 14:6*b*-20*a*: preaching and miracle of healing in Lystra, and persecution; 14:20*b*-28: return from Derbe to Antioch); 15:1-35: apostolic council (1-2: controversy in Antioch; 3-21: proceedings in Jerusalem; 22-29: apostolic decree; 30-35: return of the emissaries to Antioch).

The Fourth Principal Part (15:36–19:20) depicts the spread of the gospel in the lands around the Aegean Sea. 15:36-40: separation of Barnabas and Paul; 15:41–16:10: journey of Paul through Asia Minor to Troas; 16:11–17:14:

Paul in Macedonia (16:11-40: Philippi; 17:1-9: Thessalonica; 17:10-14: Berea); 17:15–18:17: Paul in Greece (17:15-34: Athens; 18:1-17: Corinth); 18:18-22: return to Antioch via Ephesus; 18:23–19:20: repeated journey of Paul to Asia Minor (18:23: Galatia and Phrygia; 18:24-28: Apollos in Ephesus; 19:1-20: Paul in Ephesus [1-7: disciples of John; 8-20: preaching and miracles of Paul]).

The Fifth Principal Part (19:21–28:31) represents the spread of the gospel from Jerusalem to Rome. 19:21, 22: resolve to make the journey via Jerusalem to Rome; 19:23-40: riot of Demetrius in Ephesus; 20:1-6: journey to Macedonia, Greece, and back to Troas; 20:7-12: Troas; 20:13-16: journey from Troas to Miletus; 20:17-38: farewell to the elders from Ephesus and Miletus; 21:1-14: journey from Miletus to Caesarea; 21:15-26: arrival in Jerusalem; 21:27-39: imprisonment of Paul; 21:40–22:21: Paul's speech from the steps of the temple site; 22:22-29: hearing by the Roman officer; 22:30–23:11: Paul before the Sanhedrin; 23:12-22: Jewish attempt on Paul's life; 23:23-35: transfer of Paul to Caesarea; 24:1–26:32: Paul's imprisonment in Caesarea (24:1-26: accusation and defense of Paul before Felix the procurator; 24:27: Festus, successor of Felix; 25:1-12: Paul's appeal to Caesar; 25:13-27: visit of Herod Agrippa II with Festus in Caesarea; 26:1-32: Paul before Agrippa); 27:1–28:16: Paul's voyage to Rome (27:1-12: voyage to Crete; 27:13-26: stormy journey; 27:27-44: shipwreck; 28:1-10: stay at Malta; 28:11-16: journey to Rome); 28:17-31: confinement of Paul in Rome.

2. The Acts as the Second Part of the Lukan Historical Work

Acts is no isolated literary work. As the dedication to the same Theophilus (Acts 1:1; Lk. 1:3) shows, it forms the continuation of Luke and belongs with it as the second part of a complete historical work. The prologue of Acts in its transmitted text refers to Luke as "the first book" (1:1), joins to Luke's conclusion the appearances of the risen Lord before the apostles and his farewell (1:2 ff.), and then tells of his last meeting with them and his ascension again in more detail (1:6 ff.).

This reference back to Luke and this repetition are certainly not without difficulties: No ὁ δὲ δεύτερος λόγος or the like corresponds to τὸν μὲν πρῶτον λόγον (1:1), and thus is lacking the expected summary of the second volume introduced by these words. The sentence in 1:2 is hardly translatable. The account of the Ascension attached in 1:9 ff. refers back to the period of the first volume, which, according to Acts 1:2, had already been terminated by the Ascension. According to Lk. 24:50 f., the Ascension took place on the day of the Resurrection near Bethany, but according to Acts 1:3, 12 after forty days on the Mount of Olives (in Lk. 24:51, καὶ ἀνεφέρετο εἰς τὸν οὐρανόν is to be left in the text with 𝔓75 and the "Egyptian" witnesses; see J. Jeremias, The Eucharistic Words of Jesus, 1955, 99, and Haenchen, Apg., Meyer III [13], 668). Therefore, various conjectures have been made regarding a secondary alteration of the beginning of Acts. According to one hypothesis, the lack of a summary of the contents of the second volume and the repetition of the account of the Ascension can be explained only if the statements about the forty-day period before the Ascension and the new account of the Ascension (therefore, Acts 1:3-14 or the greater part of it) are interpolated (so W. G. Kümmel, ThRdsch, N.F. 17, 1948, 9, note 1, and the scholars cited there; Clark, 407 f., regards 1:1-11 as added). Related to this view is the less far-reaching hypothesis that at least the first verses of Acts 1 were disrupted by an interpolation, but this interpolation did not include the account of the Ascension (1:6 ff.) (E. Norden, *Agnostos Theos*, 1913, 310 ff.; Feine-Behm, Bauernfeind, Albertz). According to the other hypothesis, Lk. 24:50-53 proves to be linguistically and factually in contradiction with Luke even as Acts 1:1-5 is with Acts. On the other hand, Lk. 24:49 connects well with Acts 1:6, so that it must be assumed that Luke and Acts originally formed a connected work which was not divided until canonization, when Lk. 24:50-53 and Acts 1:1-5 were attached (Lake, *Beginnings* V, 1 ff.; A. N. Wilder, "Variant Traditions of the Resurrection in Acts," JBL 62, 1943, 311; Sahlin, *Messias* [see lit. to §8], 11 ff.; Menoud, *Bultmann-Festschr.*; Trocmé, 31 ff.; Conzelmann [see lit. to §8], 94, 203, note 4, regards only Lk. 24:50-53 as secondary). But this latter hypothesis concerning an original unity of Luke-Acts is in any case untenable. On the one hand, there is no sufficient reason for the hypothesis of a secondary attachment of Lk. 24:50-53. On the other hand, we know nothing about Luke and Acts coming as a connected work into the canon, where both books are never found together, whereas all the evidence points to the conclusion that Luke was regarded as canonical considerably earlier than Acts. But three facts speak decisively against this hypothesis: a) If Lk. 24:50-53 and Acts 1:1-5 were first affixed as the conclusion of the separated first half and as the beginning of the separated second half of the complete work, Luke-Acts, then it would be incomprehensible that precisely the originator of these two additions would have occasioned the very contradictions whose presence is supposed to be explained by this hypothesis. b) At the time of the composition of Luke the literary form of the "Gospel" was already so firmly fixed that the author of Luke could hardly have included the spread of the Christian message to Rome in his Gospel. Moreover, according to the standard technique of bookmaking, the complete work, Luke-Acts, would have been too long, whereas Luke and Acts are almost of the same length and of normal size (Cadbury, *Book of Acts*, 138 f.). c) Acts 1:6 ff. does not at all connect smoothly with Lk. 24:49, since the disciples, according to Lk. 24:33, are in a house in Jerusalem, which Jesus enters (24:36). But according to Acts 1:12 the Ascension occurs without change of place in the open on the Mount of Olives. Also, the οἱ μὲν οὖν συνελθόντες (Acts 1:6) collides with εὗρον ἠθροισμένους τοὺς ἕνδεκα (Lk. 24:33). The hypothesis that Acts 1:1-5 is an addition because Lk. 24:49 originally connected with Acts 1:6 must, therefore, be rejected as impossible (so also Conzelmann, Barrett, Haenchen, van Unnik, Wilckens, 57, note 1, Dupont, *Les sources*, 24, note 2, Menoud, Cullmann-Festschr.).

But also the hypothesis that Acts 1:3-14 (or a part of it) is interpolated is lacking in probative force. 1:8 formulates the theme of Acts so suitably that this statement of the theme could hardly be derived from a strange hand. If an interpolator had wished to reproduce a divergent tradition, he would scarcely have mentioned in such an unemphasized manner the period of forty days between Resurrection and Ascension (1:3), a period which diverges from Lk. 24. But, above all, one would expect from an interpolator that he, according to literary convention, would have attached the summary of the second volume which corresponds to the recapitulation in 1:1, 2. Moreover, we meet precisely in 1:1-5 some unobtrusive stylistic peculiarities of Luke which an interpolator could hardly have noticed and copied (see the evidence in Haenchen, *loc. cit.*). The hypothesis that the beginning of Acts, in spite of its stylistic offenses, stems from the author of Acts offers, therefore, the fewest difficulties. The fact that the chronological reference for the Ascension in Luke is different from that in Acts cannot simply be put out of the way, certainly not with the contention that the round number "forty" has nothing to do with the time of the Ascension but only is supposed to characterize the unique authority of the witnesses of the Resurrection (so Menoud, Cullmann-Festschr.). But this divergence becomes quite understandable if it is made clear that Luke obviously pictured the Ascension in Lk. 24 as the conclusion of Jesus' life and in Acts, together with the forty days of instruction and with the message of the angel (1:11), as the beginning of the time of the church (cf. Barrett [see lit. to §8], 56; Haenchen, *Apg.*, Meyer III[13], 114).

If the author of Acts gave to Acts a title or a superscription, of which we know nothing, then it is not preserved. The name πράξεις (τῶν) ἀποστόλων or, briefly, πράξεις, *acta* or *actus apostolorum*, has been attested since Irenaeus and Clement of Alexandria (Muratorian Canon: *acta omnium apostolorum*) (cf. Höpfl-Gut, 257), but is hardly original, and does not coincide with the contents of the book (otherwise Wendland, *Literaturformen*, see above, p. 25, Meinertz, Schäfer, Höpfl-Gut; Wikenhauser is uncertain). For Luke, apostles are always the twelve (except 14:4, 14), but of them only Peter is prominent in Acts, and from 13:4 on, Paul plays the chief role, who, with the exception of 14:4, 14, is not called an apostle. Moreover, the author has no biographical interests. The name, "Acts of the Apostles," which must have come into use in connection with the formation of the NT canon in the second century, corresponds much more to the interests of the early church in Peter and Paul as the two chief apostles and to the misunderstanding of Acts as a literary work in the age of the apologists. The changing designations of the book in Irenaeus (*Haer.* III 31,3: *Lucae de apostolis testificatio*) and Tertullian (*De jejunio* 10: *commentarius Lucae*) also show that an authentic title was wanting.

Because Acts apparently abruptly breaks off with a notice about the two-year preaching activity of the imprisoned Paul in Rome, it has been conjectured that the ending was accidentally or intentionally broken off, or that Luke wanted to write yet a third book (so Zahn, de Zwaan, Goguel, W. L. Knox, J. Jeremias, NTD IX, [6]1953, 2). But since no indication can be found anywhere that such a third book had been planned or existed (τὸν πρῶτον λόγον [1:1] refers to no more than two volumes [see Bauer-Arndt-Gingrich, *Lexicon*, 733], and since 28:30 can be understood as a meaningful conclusion to the book, these conjectures are unsuccessful (cf. Trocmé, 34 ff.).

3. Literary Peculiarity and Theological Character of Acts

The investigation of the literary character and purpose of Acts (for its history cf. Goguel, *Intr*. III, 37 ff.; A. C. McGiffert and J. W. Hunkin, *Beginnings* I, 2, 363 ff.; Trocmé, 1 ff.; Haenchen, *Apg.*, Meyer III [13], 13 ff.; for the most recent investigations cf. the works cited below, p. 115) received, after sundry disparate attempts, its decisive impetus from F. C. Baur, who in 1838 first proposed the thesis that Acts stems from the late period of primitive Christianity and arises from the intention of softening the opposition (recognizable in the genuine Pauline epistles) between Jewish Christians and Gentile Christians through reconciliation of both parties (see WGK, NT, 162 f.). Following out these thoughts, M. Schneckenburger, *Über den Zweck der Apg.* (1841), saw in Acts an apology for Paul against the Judaizers: Luke consciously omits everything which would call to mind the real opposition of the Jewish Christians against Paul and intentionally stresses everything which places Paul on the same level as Peter. Baur himself, in his book which laid the foundation for his entire interpretation of history, *Paulus, der Apostel Jesus Christi* (1845) (Tr. A. Menzies from 2nd ed. [1867], 1873-76), went a decisive step further: Whereas Schneckenburger found no objectively incorrect features in Acts' picture of Paul and regarded Luke as the author of the book, Baur interpreted the book as a creation of the second century, which, in the interest of settling the opposition between Paul and Peter, falsified the history, and consequently in contrast to the genuine Pauline epistles offers no trustworthy historical source (see WGK, NT, 164 ff.). This view, that the author of Acts followed a conciliatory "tendency" which falsified the facts, was further sharpened by Baur's pupils, E. Zeller and A. Schwegler (see WGK, NT, 177 f.). This Tübingen position not only met with the opposition of the conservative theologians, but also was questioned by scholars of a fundamentally critical orientation (especially E. Reuss and A. Ritschl) on the basis of their proof that the primitive period of Christianity in no wise exhibited only the opposition between Jewish Christianity and Gentile Christianity as maintained by Baur (see WGK, NT, 191 ff., 201 ff.). Even though the hypothesis of a conciliatory tendency and of a conscious falsification of history by Acts appeared unfounded, the recognition that between the Pauline epistles and Acts numerous contradictions exist which cannot be harmonized readily could not be laid. Some scholars then explained these contradictions with the hypothesis that Acts delineated the unionistic image of primitive Christian history as held by Gentile Christianity of the early postapostolic age: "Paul was not judaised nor Peter Paulinised, but both Paul and Peter were 'Lucanised,' i.e., Catholicised" (A. Jülicher, *An Introduction*

to the NT. Tr. Janet Penrose Ward, 1904, p. 438; see WGK, NT, 217 ff.).
Already in 1870 F. Overbeck had similarly characterized the historical position
of Acts and also ascribed to Acts the intention of defending Christianity against
political inculpation (see Haenchen, *Apg.*, Meyer III [13], 21). Also J. Weiss
(1897) found no inner Christian tendencies of any sort in Acts, and interpreted
it as an apology for Christianity, addressed to the Gentile public, against Jewish
accusations, with the goal of showing that the world mission of Christianity
had supplanted Judaism.

If the "tendency criticism" of the "Tübingen School" was recognized as the
wrong way, the task still remained of ascertaining the aim which the author of
Acts pursued and, at the same time, of determining the theological standpoint
of the book, for only thus could the historical value and the message of the book
be certainly recognized. And although scholarship at the beginning of the twentieth century devoted itself chiefly to the question of the sources of Acts (see
below, pp. 123 f.), P. Wendland (see above, p. 25, 321, 325), already in 1912,
sought to understand Acts as the "natural expression of developing ecclesiastical
relations and the concomitant changed concept of history," and to point out that
literarily it is a "mid position between history and a collection of heroic poems
[Heldenbuch]." But the question about the literary character and the share of
the author in the composition of Acts was first methodically set about by M. Dibelius in his essay, "Style Criticism of the Book of Acts" (1923; = *Studies*,
1 ff.). The result of this and other investigations by Dibelius was not only the
separation of small units and of a travel journal [Reisetagebuch] from the
continuous account of Acts, but above all the proof of the methods employed
by the author in the revision of the tradition, and his intention "to present the
meaning of events" (*Studies*, 125). This question concerning the literary purpose of the author of Acts in the shaping of the separate scenes of his account
has been studied especially by E. Haenchen and U. Wilckens. And at the same
time the questions about the author's theological point of departure and accom-
panying aim in his revision of the tradition have been taken up anew through
the investigation of his actual relation to Paul and his conception of salvation
history (Vielhauer, Käsemann, and others). This investigation is by no means
concluded.

At the outset three views of the literary intention of Acts must doubtless
be rejected as false. a) Although the author shows himself conversant with the
literary usage of his time, and makes use of a literary method of ancient historians by inserting speeches, Acts is not "a genuine historical work" (E. Meyer,
Ursprung und Anfänge des Christentums III, 1923, 7), and its author is not
"the first Christian historian" (Dibelius, *Studies*, 123 ff.; cf. Vielhauer, 14;
Wilckens, *Missionsreden*, 92). The fact that Luke precedes Acts as the first
volume of a twofold work speaks against such a hypothesis. Further, so many
of the characteristics of actual historical writing are missing—completeness of
material, precision in historical details, a complete chronology, biographical
interest—that reporting as such, or reporting with a definite tendency, cannot
be the aim of Acts (see van Unnik, 44).

b) The contention that Acts was written with the goal of being submitted as a defense of Paul in his trial in Rome (so most recently Sahlin, Koh; earlier advocates in Sahlin, 35 f.) is untenable. It presupposes an impossibly early origin of Acts (about 62; see below, p. 132). It cannot explain the greatest part of the material in Acts nor the manner of its presentation (chaps. 1–12; threefold report of the conversion of Paul in chaps. 9; 22; 26; etc.). It overlooks the fact that Acts is Luke's second volume.

c) In a double manner recent attempts have been made to view Acts as the document of an intraecclesiastical controversy. i) According to Trocmé (52 ff.), Acts seeks to defend Pauline Christianity from Jewish contentions that the Pauline form of Christianity is a threat to the state and signifies an apostasy from primitive Christianity. But we do not know whether there still was such an anti-Pauline Judaizing polemic at the end of the first century in Gentile-Christian regions (the reference to Alexandria after Brandon [see lit. to §7] is fantastic). Nor does there appear in Acts more than one solitary echo (21:20 ff.) of Jewish charges against Paul, so that such a defense is out of the question. ii) According to Barrett ([see lit. to §8], 62 f.) and Klein, Acts seeks to rescue Paul from the Gnostics, in that he is proved to be orthodox (Barrett), or dependent upon the primitive apostles (Klein). Against this view we may say, first of all, that a polemic against Gnosticism in Acts is found only in 20:29 f., but there Paul in no wise must differentiate himself from the Gnostics. Above all, it does not prove true in any manner that in Acts the significance of Paul is consciously diminished in favor of the twelve apostles (Klein). And even if it is correct that "Luke studiously avoids gnostic thought and language" (Barrett), that happens altogether implicitly and without any direct rejection of Gnostic thought. An anti-Gnostic defense of Paul is, therefore, certainly not the aim of the author of Acts (see Trocmé, 56 f.; Haenchen, *Apg.*, Meyer III [13], 676 ff.).

If in Acts there appears no inner Christian apologetic, we still cannot fail to recognize the purpose of defending the Christians against the charge of hostility toward the state Placed over against the charge of the Jews: "They are all acting against the decrees of Caesar, saying that there is another king, Jesus" (17:7; cf. 17:6; 24:5) is the defense of Paul: "Neither against the law of the Jews, nor against the temple, nor against Caesar have I offended at all" (25:8). And thus Luke repeatedly shows that the Roman officials must testify to the complete innocence of the Christians and above all of Paul (16:39; 18:15 f.; 19:37; 23:29; 25:25; 26:32). Luke also makes it plain that they did not hinder Paul from preaching during his Roman detention pending investigation (28:30 f.). The apologetic intent of these and related texts is even more undeniable than the same apologetic feature observed in Luke (see above, p. 99). But such apologetics would have been purposeless in respect to Christians and could only have had Gentile readers in mind (so, in addition to the scholars named by Dupont, NTSt 1959-60, 133, e.g., C. T. Craig, *The Beginnings of Christianity*, 1943, 321; van Unnik, 40 f.; O'Neill, 171 f., Haenchen, *Apg.*, Meyer III [13], 513, 552, 620). We have already seen that this apology was not intended to reach Paul's judges in Rome: "No Roman official would ever have filtered out so much of what to him would be theological and ecclesiastical rubbish in order to reach so tiny a grain of relevant apology" (Barrett, 63). Hardly at all did the author intend to address the public (against J. Weiss). Rather, the author obviously hoped to reach particular Gentile readers and to win them for the cause of the Christians. But thereby it was not his aspiration to demonstrate the unity of Judaism and Christianity in order to bring Christianity into the enjoyment of the political recognition granted to the Jewish religion (so Easton, Haenchen). Rather, the Christians are placed over against the Jews and are pictured, in spite of the calumnies of the Jews, as politically innocuous (25:7 f.) and as the true heirs of the OT revelation of God (26:6, 22 f.; 28:28; cf. Conzelmann, ThLZ, 1960, 244 f.; O'Neill, 172 f.).

But this apologetic purpose is, for Luke, only a secondary, though certainly not an unimportant, aim. The greatest part of the material of Acts, especially the speeches, is proclamation and has Christian readers in view. Acts doubtless, therefore, has a twofold purpose: It "tells about the age of the apostles in order to edify the Christians and to woo the Gentiles" (Haenchen, RGG; similarly, O'Neill). There has been much disagreement concerning what is the actual theme of this edifying narrative about the apostolic age (see the summary in van Unnik, 39 ff.). But the large number of well-grounded proposals concerning the purpose of the book make it questionable whether an unequivocal answer to this question is possible (recently, e.g., Feine-Behm, Wikenhauser: victorious course of the gospel to the capital of the Empire; Stagg: breakthrough of religious, racial, and national limitations to the unhindered preaching of the gospel; Trocmé, Eltester: the entire work of Luke-Acts is gospel; Ehrhardt: gospel of the Holy Spirit; O'Neill: the chief object is preaching of the gospel for unbelievers; van Unnik: testimony for God's own saving activity in relation to the world). From most of these answers it follows that the geographical organization of the account in Acts in the sense of broadening of mission territory (see above, p. 108) includes the gradual broadening of subject matter: from the preaching to the Jews in Jerusalem to the final self-exclusion of the Jews from God's salvation and to the unhindered proclamation before the Gentiles in Rome: "They will listen" (28:28-31). And Dupont (NTSt 1959-60, 139 ff.) has correctly pointed out that already in Lk. 24:46 f. the Risen One designates as the meaning of the Scriptures not only the suffering and the resurrection of the Christ but also preaching "to all nations, beginning from Jerusalem," and that the same Risen One in Acts 1:8 has imparted to them precisely the charge: "You shall be my witnesses in Jerusalem and in all Judea and Samaria and to the end of the earth" (cf. also Cambier, NTSt 1961-62). The theme of 1:8 is carried out in Acts, and the statement of 28:30 f. that Paul in Rome "welcomed all who came to him, preaching the kingdom of God and teaching about the Lord Jesus Christ μετὰ πάσης παρρησίας ἀκωλύτως," strikes a "triumphant note" (Nock), which corresponds exactly to the author's goal in Acts. Acts 28:30 f. thus turns out to be the intended end of the book: "In fact, the two-volume work, Luke-Acts, is brought to a dramatic close and epitomized in an adverb" (namely, ἀκωλύτως Stagg, 1).

In order to accomplish his aim of describing God's saving activity in Christ which first reached its goal with the preaching to Gentiles in Rome, the author of Acts created a literary form which had no real prototype either in the Christian or in the pagan world, and which also has found no successors of any sort (the apocryphal Acts of the second century are of a completely different literary nature; cf. the survey by J. Michl, LThK I, 1957, 747 ff.). Scholars have called our attention to the claim that Acts has formal parallels with Hellenistic representations of divine men (Barrett), but these parallels concern only individual accounts and features, since Acts purports to offer no sort of religious biography. Others have been more nearly correct in pointing to the relationship which Acts shows in the manner of its missionary narrative with the missionary literature of Hellenistic Judaism. But it is hardly his acquaintance with this literature which has caused the author to choose the form of a historical report for his work (O'Neill). This form resulted rather from the author's basic theological view that Jesus' history was the beginning of the still continuing history of the church (see above, pp. 98 f.). The decisive question is, however, with which literary methods the author represents this history and what theological meaning he has stamped upon it.

It must first of all be stated that the author found himself in a different position in respect to the composition of Luke than in respect to the composition of Acts. In the case of Luke, as is indicated by his own statement (Lk. 1:1-4) and confirmed by literary criticism, he had predecessors, to whose works he could join his to a great extent. In the case of Acts, however, he confronted a completely new task. For even if the author used sources of some size (we shall see that that is quite improbable), still none of these sources, according to the generally accepted view, included the entire period described by the author. In any case, the joining of the history of the primitive church with that of the Pauline Gentile mission as far as Rome was first accomplished by the author of Acts. But he did not strive for any kind of completeness. He would rather give individual pictures than a continuous narrative in a larger context. In his presentation he intermingles the deeds and speeches of the chief persons. He does not enter into the conflicts between Paul and his opponents, which are known to us from the Pauline epistles. In his depiction of the activity of Peter and the development of the primitive church, and even in the history of the Pauline mission, there are great gaps between the characteristic, instructive, separate narratives, so that open questions remain in abundance. What we learn about the community in Jerusalem—its community life, its worship, its relation to Judaism, its groups (Hebrews and Hellenists), its mission, concerning the deeds and fate of the apostles, etc.—is very scanty. Important events, such as the action of Herod Agrippa I against the Christians (12:1 ff.), or the beginning of Christianity in Antioch (11:19 ff.), are only touched upon. Again, for other subjects, such as the two similar scenes before the Sanhedrin (4:1 ff.; 5:17 ff.) and the story of Cornelius (10:1–11:18), there is the largest amount of space.

We do not learn the historically significant things about Paul. Concerning Paul's chief places of working, Corinth and Ephesus, where he sojourned for years, we are informed only of petty individual features. On the other hand, the experiences of the imprisoned Paul from his arrest in Jerusalem to his hearing by Felix, Festus, and Agrippa, the voyage until arrival in Rome, and the discussions with the leaders of the Roman Jews, are told in the greatest detail. The author obviously omits what to him does not seem suited for the attainment of his literary and missionary goal, and repeats with significant variation what he wants to make especially impressive (cf. the twofold narration of Peter's vision [10:9 ff.; 11:5 ff.] and the threefold report of Paul's conversion [9:3 ff.; 22:5 ff.; 26:12 ff.]). Both in the selection of the accounts and in the brevity or length of the accounts, his narrative is dependent not only upon the tradition which is available, but at least as much upon his purpose.

This purpose, however, appears above all in the sections whose shaping by the author is most certain: the summary accounts and the speeches.

Already in Luke, the author took over the literary device of the summary accounts from Mark (Lk. 4:40 f.; 6:17 ff.). If we disregard particular, generalized sentences such as 9:31 and 16:5, then we see that in Acts the author used summary accounts only in connection with his representation of the primitive church (2:42 ff.; 4:32 ff.; 5:12 ff.). These three comprehensive, parallel descriptions of the life of public worship, the renunciation of property, and the miraculous deeds of the apostles, are strikingly repetitious. Since these summaries furnish us with no clear reconstruction of events, it has been postulated in various ways that these summary accounts were secondarily expanded (J. Jeremias: During the final redaction of Acts, a shorter summary account was enlarged each time by utilization of the other summary accounts; Benoit: An unknown reviser expanded all three accounts at their center on the basis of the other summary accounts; Zimmermann: The author of Acts enriched and idealized the separate accounts handed down to him). But none of these hypotheses is convincing, for nothing points either to the taking over and revision of separate accounts or to an unknown reviser. Rather, the summary accounts originate as a whole from the author of Acts. This fact explains the linguistic relationship of these texts. They follow the purpose of generalizing, starting from transmitted separate accounts, which explains the slight logical construction of these texts (see Haenchen, Apg., Meyer III [13] to 2:42 ff.; Conzelmann, ThLZ 1960, 245). If that proves right, then these summary accounts may use transmitted separate accounts. But primarily they attest the author's conception of the primitive community as the ideal community, which leads its life of prayer and table fellowship with complete unity and common property, respected by everyone, and esteemed for the sake of its miraculous deeds. This conception was not the result of conscious idealization, but it is the picture of the primitive Christian period, as it was seen at the time of the author.

The question about the origin of the speeches in Acts is basically more difficult to answer (for the history of criticism, cf. Wilckens, *Missionsreden*, 7 ff.; Grässer, ThRdsch 1961, 133 ff.). According to Haenchen's calculations, the speeches constitute "300 of the approximately 1,000 verses of the book" (*Apg.*, Meyer III [13], 93). Their significance in the mind of the author is indicated by the fact that speeches are found at all decisive turning points, and the facts which, according to the author's opinion, are important facts are more than once recited in speeches. This interest of the author in speeches does not by itself show that he had no kind of sources or reliable reports available when he formulated the speeches. Since Stephen's speech (Acts 7), the missionary sermons of Peter (2:14 ff.; 3:12 ff.; 4:9 ff.; 5:30 ff.; 10:34 ff.) and of Paul (13: 16 ff.) before Jews, the speeches of Paul before Gentiles (14:15 ff.; 17:22 ff.) and Christians (20:18 ff.), the speeches of defense (22:1 ff.; 26:2 ff.), and the aggressive speech (28:25 ff.) of Paul represent completely different types of speeches, it has been concluded that the speeches in Acts mediate to us basically correct information about what was said in the particular situations (cf., e.g., Feine-Behm, Bruce, Williams). Those who are of the opinion that it is not possible to go so far have followed Dibelius (*From Tradition to Gospel* [see lit. to §5], 15 ff.) and C. H. Dodd (*The Apostolic Preaching and Its Developments,* 1936, 29 ff.). In the missionary sermons in Acts 2–13 these scholars see the utilization of the kerygmatic formulations of the primitive community (most recently Smalley). In Stephen's speech, especially 7:44 ff., they infer the views of Stephen and of the Hellenists (e.g., M. Simon, *St. Stephen and the Hellenists in the Primitive Church,* 1958), and in the Areopagus speech (17:22 ff.) they discover Paul's theology of missions (see below, p. 130).

But several general observations call this view into question. Schweizer and Wilckens have demonstrated that, in spite of the different situations involved, the same pattern lies at the basis of the missionary speeches of both Peter and Paul in Acts. This consideration points to the molding hand of the same writer. Further, Townsend has shown that the speeches of Acts turn out to be the creations of the author, which are dependent upon one another: The reader does not notice gaps in the course of argument of the speeches because he unconsciously expands them out of other speeches in the same book (thus the connection of the quotation from Ps. 13:35 to David, which is presupposed in 13:36, is not understandable in this context, but it is understandable for those who already know the train of thought in 2:15 ff.). And finally Evans has called attention to another consideration: Quite in contrast to the transmission of the tradition about Jesus, no "Sitz im Leben" can be recognized for the repetition and preservation of the apostolic discourses up to the late apostolic period. "One does not remember the argument of a speech twenty, thirty, or forty years afterward unless it has been constantly repeated in the meanwhile. But why should it be repeated?" (Evans, 28). When these speeches were delivered no one thought of preserving apostolic speeches for future times. Still less stenographic notes were taken (in spite of Bruce), and the idea that Paul probably had his speeches in manuscript (Blaiklock) is an audacious proposition.

Of more importance in this connection are two fundamental statements: a) Dibelius has shown in his essay, "The Speeches in Acts and Ancient Historiography" (1949, see *Studies*, 138 ff.), that the author followed the literary custom of ancient historical writers who at the turning points of the narrative put speeches into the mouths of the participating persons to indicate to the reader the meaning of the events (cf. already H. J. Cadbury, "The Speeches in Acts," *Beginnings* I, 5, 402 ff.). An exact analysis of all the longer speeches shows that they are primarily intended for the readers, and, therefore, only to a limited degree take into consideration the special situation of the hearers at the scene in question (cf. e.g., the designation of the Christians as "the saints" [26:10], the reference to the collection [24:17], the enumeration of the nations [2:9 ff.], the historical midrash [7:2 ff.]). The repetition of certain facts and thoughts in several speeches, the literary device of interrupting the speeches at an effective place in the train of thought (7:53 f.; 17:31 f.; 19:27 f.; 23:6 f.; 26:23 f.), and the Hellenistic coloring of the Areopagus speech and the speech before Agrippa II (optative [17:27; 26:29], secular quotations [17:28; 26:14]), reveal the shaping activity of the writer in formulating the speeches. Therefore, the speeches of Acts originate with the author, even if in one or the other instance he has worked up reports or units of tradition. Dibelius, however, correctly emphasized that the author of Acts does not express his personal opinions in the speeches, but he wants to preach:

He has found a new method of presenting material which has not yet been dealt with in literature; in doing so he has made new use of the traditional art of composing speeches, an art which had already been employed in many different ways. He used this device not only to illuminate the situation but also to make clear the ways of God; he did not desire to testify to the capabilities either of the speaker or of the author, but to proclaim the gospel (Martin Dibelius. *Studies in the Acts of the Apostles*. Edited by Heinrich Greeven. Tr. Mary Ling, 1956, p. 183).

b) Wilckens, through his investigation of the missionary speeches of Acts, has confirmed and continued Dibelius' results. Wilckens points out that the missionary speeches in Acts 2–13 indeed exhibit a common pattern (cf. also Schweizer). But he also shows that the traditional character and, therefore, the great age of these patterns cannot be proved. He further demonstrates that these speeches as a whole were not inserted secondarily into the connected narrative, but were formed by the author together with the connected narrative. From that it follows that "the apostolic speeches of Acts . . . are to be evaluated, not as witnesses of early or even the earliest primitive Christian theology, but of the Lukan theology at the end of the first century" (p. 186). When Wilckens seeks to establish in addition that the particular material of these speeches is not based upon early tradition but is derived from the theology of the author's time, then various objections can be raised, especially if one keeps his eye upon the other speeches of Acts (e.g., Stephen's speech [7:1 ff.] is not understandable without the hypothesis of a tradition, even if it is uncertain whether this tradition goes back to the primitive community; likewise, the παῖς-title for Jesus is not the result of a Lukan scriptural exegesis). But that the speeches of Acts are the decisive literary means by which the author of Acts stamps his theological interpretation upon the traditional narrative which he took over may be regarded as indisputable.

We may now ask whether the author of Acts, by means of his fashioning of the narratives and by means of his selection of the material reported by him, has not expressed his theological views. The answer to this question is especially difficult, for, in contrast to Luke, there is preserved none of the sources or traditions which the author probably used. Only occasionally can a comparison be made with the Pauline epistles. Since the author was not acquainted with the Pauline epistles (see below, pp. 132 f.), we can in no case know whether the author was cognizant at all of a fact known to us from Paul, if he does not report it. Hence, conclusions based upon the lack of certain facts in the report of Acts are very problematic. For example, Barrett's view (pp. 60 f.) that the author *consciously* passed over in silence the opposition of the primitive church against the Gentile mission, which may be inferred from Paul, because only in this way could he visibly connect the Gentile mission with Jesus, is very questionable. And as necessary as it is to the understanding of the theological meaning of the reports to attempt to discover the motives which control the composition of the individual narratives (cf. above all Haenchen's commentary), so it is dangerous also here to attempt to know these motives too precisely. Thus Haenchen has hardly interpreted correctly the origin and the Lukan meaning of the report about the attempted worship of Barnabas and Paul in Lystra (14:11 ff.), when he assumes that in this narrative the author wanted to create "a high point in the development of apostolic power," which is supposed to outshine the following passion of Paul (14:19 f.). And the proposition that the author named Paul and Barnabas as apostles in 14:4, 14, contrary to his usual linguistic usage, in order to conceal the fact from the reader that otherwise he denies to Paul the title of apostle (Klein, *Zwölf Apostel*, 212), ascribes to the author of Acts without any grounds a refined duplicity with the readers. Therefore, in order to establish with methodical certainty the theological conceptions of the author of Acts which control his account, we must restrict ourselves to the summary accounts and the speeches.

We have already seen in connection with the question about theological motives governing the Gospel of Luke that it interpreted the history of Jesus as the beginning of salvation history, which moves forward via the present until the end of the times (see above, p. 98). Naturally, this conception likewise governs Acts. Correspondingly, it has also been assumed for Acts that its salvation-history conception results from the nonarrival of the parousia: "The imminent expectation has vanished, the parousia which did not take place is no more a problem, . . . the time between Pentecost and parousia is the time of the Spirit and of the progressive evangelization of the world, therefore increasing salvation history" (Vielhauer, EvTh 1950-51, 13; similarly, the scholars cited above, p. 100, and R. Bultmann, *Theology of the NT* [Tr. Kendrick Grobel, 1951-55], II, 116 ff.). The existence of Acts itself has been cited as evidence for the correctness of this hypothesis. Moreover, there is the fundamental rejection of the question about the time of the parousia (1:7); the substitution of

the command for world mission for the imminent expectation of the parousia
(1:8); thinking in terms of long periods of time (26:29); and the conception
of the Holy Spirit as substitute for the coming of the kingdom of God (1:8)
(cf. the summary in Grässer, *Das Problem* [see lit. to §8], 204 ff.). It certainly
is true for Acts, too, that the imminent expectation does not stand in the center
of things, but we must also affirm that for the author of Acts eschatology is
more than a mere *locus de novissimis* (dogmatic pattern of last things) (Vielhauer, 12). That comes to light already in the fact that Acts 2:17, in the
quotation from Joel 3:1, instead of καὶ ἔσται μετὰ ταῦτα (thus according to the
Hebrew text and LXX and also the NT MSS B˙ 076), offers the form καὶ ἔσται
ἐν ταῖς ἐσχάταις ἡμέραις (so ℵ A 096, 81; D Tert. Iren.; also 096 and 81 are
"Egyptian" witnesses; therefore it is not a matter of a specifically "Western"
reading!). This change of the OT text makes it clear that the gift of the Spirit
signifies for the author the beginning of the eschatological time of salvation
(the approval of the reading from B 076, which agrees with the LXX, by Ropes,
ad loc., and Haenchen, *ad loc.*, and ZThK 1954, 162 is methodologically untenable; see F. Mussner, "In den letzten Tagen" (Apg. 2:17a), BZ, N. F. 5,
1961, 263 ff.). If this early speech in Acts thus shows the eschatological significance of the present, there is found in the next speech (3:19-21) an even
clearer reference to the parousia: "Repent therefore . . . that times of refresh-
ing may come from the . . . Lord, and that he may send the Christ appointed
for you, Jesus, whom heaven must receive until the time for establishing all
that God spoke by the mouth of his holy prophets from of old." It is, then,
completely unfounded to interpret the speech of the taking up of Jesus into
heaven (1:7-8) as an expression of the delay of the parousia (Bultmann,
Haenchen, Grässer). It also does not prove correct that the eschatological conception in 3:20 f. interrupts an otherwise good train of thought. It is, therefore,
improbable that an eschatological Elijah speculation was taken over from the
circles of the Baptist, transferred to Jesus, and by means of the following scriptural proof (3:22 ff.) for the past appearance of Jesus was made ineffective
(Bauernfeind, Schweizer, Wilckens). For the Jewish expectation of the restoration of all things at the end of days, which in Mal. 3 is connected to Elijah, is
also used and reinterpreted in Acts 1:6 ff.; 15:16 f. (cf. F. Mussner, "Die Idee
der Apokatastasis in der Apg.," *Lex tua veritas, Festschr. H. Junker*, 1961,
293 ff.), and thus it becomes evident that the author saw as well the eschatalogi-
cal consummation fulfilled in the present, beginning with the sending and
exaltation of Jesus, as he expected its final fulfillment by the parousia of Jesus.
This insight is confirmed by the connection which is established in 1:11 between Ascension and parousia; through the reference to the sovereign appearance of the Risen One as world judge in the central places of 10:42 and 17:31;
and through the statement that "through many tribulations we must enter the
kingdom of God" (14:22; the denial of the eschatological sense of this connection of θλῖψις and βασιλεία τοῦ θεοῦ [Conzelmann, Haenchen] rests upon a
circulus vitiosus; cf. in addition to the commentaries, Cadbury, Dodd-Festschr.,
311, and R. Schnackenburg, *Gottes Herrschaft und Reich*, 1959, 183 f.). It

is correct, then, that the concept of the βασιλεία is "no longer the center of proclamation" (Schnackenburg, *loc. cit.*; Acts 1:3; 8:12; 19:8; 20:25; 28:23, 31, especially 24:25, do not permit the precise meaning of "preaching the kingdom of God" or the "future judgment" to be recognized). It is also true that the imminent expectation is not to be found *expressis verbis*. But just as clearly Acts reports about the proclamation of Jesus Christ spreading to Rome, always conscious of the approaching end and of the expectation of the parousia and of the breaking in of the kingdom of God, an expectation which remains alive through faith in the Risen One who was exalted for this purpose (cf. Cadbury, Dodd-Festschr., van Unnik, 45 f.). And also the existence of Acts itself does not speak against this statement, because this report is not at all intended to be a historical writing for later generations, but proclamation and propaganda for the present in connection with the Gospel of Luke and for the confirmation of it.

Therefore, it hardly proves true that Luke describes as his real theme the period of the church as the middle of time, and thus is the first representative of the developing primitive catholicism [Frühkatholizismus] (so Käsemann, ZThK, 1957, 20 = *Essays on New Testament Themes*, 1964, 89 ff.; Acts is also designated as "primitive catholic" by Vielhauer, 15; Klein, ZKG, 1957, 371; O'Neill, *Theology* [see lit. to §8], 168). Whether Acts can be associated with "primitive catholicism" is very questionable, because firmly established ecclesiastical officials, apostolic succession, sacramental priesthood, in short, the church as an institution dispensing salvation, are still completely lacking (cf. Michaelis, *Einl.*, 141, and supplement, 21 f.; Barrett [see lit. to §8], 70 ff.; Conzelmann, *Theology of St. Luke* [see lit. to §8], 211, note 1 and ThLZ 1962, 755; Haenchen, *Apg.*, Meyer III [13], 46, 84, 678 [otherwise 202]; Eltester, 7 f.). In Acts as in Luke there are found typical conceptions of the late period of primitive Christianity (Ascension in addition to Resurrection, meal of the Risen One, punitive miracles, magical healings, mediation of the Spirit through laying on of the hands of the apostles [1:9 ff.; 1:4; 10:41; 5:1 ff.; 13:9 ff.; 5:15; 19:11 f.; 8:7; 19:6, and frequently]). Yet for the author of Acts, too, the time of the church is not the middle of time (so also Luck [see lit. to §8], 66), but the present of the church is the time of the end, which has been proclaimed since the beginning of the coming kingdom of God in Jesus and which has been present in the Spirit since Pentecost. Upon the consummation of the kingdom through the appearance of the Christ now tarrying in heaven, the faithful wait, no longer ardently, but nonetheless certainly. Thus we can by all means say that the theological problem for the author to solve was "the problem of the historical time of Christianity, which meanwhile had been effective everywhere, and which, therefore, had plainly become evident" (Wilckens, *Missionsreden,* 200). But it by no means proves true that for the author of Acts salvation was present in the past history of Jesus, whereas Christian faith is directed backward to the past life of Jesus and "participation in salvation in the Christian present . . . [is understood] consistently as a historically mediated participation in a definite past" (Wilckens, *ibid.*, 202, 205 ff.). For thereby it is completely overlooked that the author not only has the Risen One intervene directly again and again in the spread of the gospel (9:4 ff.; 18:9 f.; 22:18 ff.; 23:11), but also knows that the experience of the Spirit who was bestowed by Christ upon the Christians at Pentecost as the power of the time of the end (1:8; 2:3 f., 33) is often bestowed upon the faithful (2:38; 5:32; 10:44 ff.; 15:8 f.) and also shows itself to be evident in the life of the Christian congregations (4:8, 31; 6:3; 7:55; 9:31; 11:24, 28; 13:4, 9; 15:28; 20:28; cf. E. Schweizer, ThWB VI, 1959, 401 ff.). From faith in the presence of the Spirit bestowed by the exalted Lord, the author of Acts forms the history of the eschatological salvation which is spreading in the preaching, and intends thus to make ready for the expected coming of the promised Christ. If the author is the theologian of salvation history which began with Christ, he, with his hope in the consummation begun in Christ, still stands in the framework of the primitive Christian view of history, even though he has taken theologically seriously the historical reality of the Christendom of his time by including in his narrative "of the things which have been accomplished among us" (Lk. 1:1) the Christ who continues to work in the spread of the gospel.

But where did he obtain the information for this report, and in what time did he write?

4. The Sources and the Author of Acts

That the author of Acts in the composition of his work used written sources has been conjectured primarily upon the basis of a "we" which appears in the account only now and then, but the use of written sources has also been inferred from the prologue of Luke, according to which the author was not among those "who from the beginning were eyewitnesses" (for the history of research see, above all, Dupont, Sources). At the outset three hypotheses can be rejected. a) At the end of the nineteenth and beginning of the twentieth centuries scholars accepted in the most varied ways either a thorough revision of an original writing by a redactor (finally Loisy), or the composition of Acts from several sources (finally Shepherd: a Petrine source, an Antiochene source, Acts of Paul; Macgregor: 3 sources for chaps. 1–15), but none of these theories has succeeded. b) Just as little convincing evidence can be adduced for the hypothesis that a special source used in Lk. 24 continues in Acts 1:15 ff. (Hirsch), or that a source beginning in Acts 3 originally was connected via the "bridge" of Acts 1:13 f. with Mk. 16:8 (Haefner). c) The hypothesis advocated by Torrey that the author of Acts 15:36 ff. placed before his report his translation of an Aramaic source which he took over (Acts 1:1b–15:35), and Sahlin's similar hypothesis that Acts 1:6–15:35 is the ending of an Aramaic "Proto-Luke," which the author of Acts translated and expanded, run aground on the composite character of Acts 1–15, but chiefly on the fact that several OT quotations were useful in the context only in the wording of the LXX (e.g., 2:17 ff.; 15:17), and that in this section extensive LXX language is found (cf. Sparks,

Argyle, Townsend; further, W. G. Kümmel, ThRdsch 1942, 168, note 1; 1950, 17 f., and Dupont, *Sources,* 29 ff.).

On the other hand, three source theories have found numerous supporters until the present. a) Harnack found in Acts 2–5 two parallel sources, of which the one (3:1–5:16) is the beginning of the Jerusalem-Caesarean account (8:5–40; 9:31–11:18; 12:1-23) and is historically valuable, whereas the other (2:1-47 and 5:17-42) represents a worthless doublet (the remainder of the account to 15:35 [i.e., 6:1–8:4, 11:19-30; 12:25–15:35] Harnack ascribed to an "Antiochene" source; see under b). This division of Acts 2–5 into two sources was modified in various ways (cf. W. G. Kümmel, ThRdsch 1942, 168 f., and Dupont, *Sources,* 37 ff.). Reicke and Trocmé have offered new forms of this theory. According to Reicke, 2:42–4:31 and 4:32–5:42 are two sources from the primitive church, placed next to each other; they are parallel even in details. Trocmé sees a written account used in 3:1–5:42, which the author of Acts expanded with speeches, summary accounts, and the separate account, 5:1-11. Against Reicke's construction speak not only its artificiality but also Jeremias' proof that the two trial reports (4:1 ff.; 5:17 ff.) are by no means parallels, but describe materially different proceedings. Moreover, the summary accounts in 2:42 ff. and 4:32 ff. stem from the same author. And against Trocmé we may say that the report which he assumes lies at the basis of Acts 3–5 in no wise is differentiated linguistically from the alleged additions of the author. Furthermore, we cannot conceive of a "Sitz im Leben" in the primitive community for a pure trial account which has been divested of all kerygmatic components.

b) The hypothesis of an Antiochene source in Acts 6–15 is essentially better grounded. Harnack based his thesis of an Antiochene source upon the argument of unity in respect to content. Jeremias established this thesis anew upon the contention that in the account in Acts 6:1–15:35 the sections 8:5-40; 9:31–11:18; 12:1-24; 15:1-33 turn out to be interpolations in a connected account, and that this mission-history which lies at the basis of the account can also be observed up to the end of Acts (for criticism see W. G. Kümmel, ThRdsch 1942, 170). In 1959, independently of each other, Bultmann and Benoit took up this hypothesis. According to Bultmann, there lies at the basis of Acts an Antiochene source originally written in "we-style," and recognizable in 6:1-12a; 7:54–8:4; 11:19-26; 12:25. In addition, there is a travel account composed in "we-style" and beginning in 11:28 (where the "we" is original) and 13:2 (where the "we" has been changed by the author into the third person). Moreover, the author's interpolations also show that he took up written sources (in 15:1-35, Paul and Barnabas are inserted; 2:14-21, 24-31, 33-35, e.g., are also such interpolations). Benoit postulates an Antiochene account which originally connected 11:27-30 with 15:3 ff., but the narrative was interrupted by the insertion of a Palestinian tradition (12:1-23) and a Pauline tradition (chaps. 13–14). 12:25 and 15:1, 2 are then redactional! It follows that Paul's Jerusalem journey of 11:27 ff. is identical with the journey of 15:3 ff., and that in the source thus recognized there are agreements with the account in Galatians.

But Bultmann's hypothesis of an original "we" in 11:28 and 13:2 is untenable. Already in 1899 Harnack demonstrated the secondary character of the "we" in 11:28 (see A. v. Harnack, *Studien zur Geschichte des NT und der Alten Kirche*, I, AKG 19, 1931, 33 ff.). In 13:2 λειτουργούντων cannot have the community for a subject (see Dupont, *Sources*, 66, note 1). As for the disturbance of an original literary connection, e.g., between 6:12*a* and 7:54, or 11:26 and 12:25, there is as little evidence as for the change from the first to the third person plural in the alleged Antiochene source in chaps. 6–12. Also the proof of interpolations in Peter's speech (2:14 ff.) and in the account in 15:1 ff. has hardly succeeded (for ch. 15., cf. Haenchen, Jeremias-Festschr.). Benoit's reconstruction of the sources is untenable also, for 11:27-30 cannot have originated from a source, but represents the author's combination (see M. Dibelius, *Wochenschrift für klassische Philologie* 36, 1919, 5 ff., and the convincing proof from Strecker). Benoit's theory also cannot make understandable why the author, by means of the redactional links (12:25; 15:1, 2) in connection with the interpolation of chaps. 12 and 13 f., should have created an additional Pauline journey to Jerusalem contrary to his basic source. Hence the supposition of an Antiochene source is improbable.

c) The hypothesis which has attracted to itself the most supporters is the one which holds that the author used a written source in the second half of his book. In any case, to this source are supposed to belong the texts which narrate in the first person plural, the so-called "we-sections": 16:10-17 (journey from Troas to Philippi); 20:5-15 (journey from Philippi to Miletus); 21:1-18 (journey from Miletus to Jerusalem); 27:1–28:16 (journey from Caesarea to Rome). From time to time these we-sections begin altogether unexpectedly and end just as abruptly. Each section reports exclusively about journeys at sea, and has its beginning and ending on land. The "we" usually indicates Paul and his companions, including the reporter. But in 16:17 and 21:18, before the transition to the third person, Paul is distinguished from the ἡμεῖς (28:16 *can* be understood likewise; see Cadbury, NTSt 1956-57, 129). Since antiquity the view has been repeatedly advocated that the author wanted to indicate with this "we" that in the sections thus characterized he was a personal participant; therefore, the "we" is simply a redactional, stylistic device of the author. Yet the author nowhere indicates that directly, and this supposition became problematic the moment scholars began to entertain doubts that Acts could have originated from a travel companion of Paul. Thus, since the beginning of the nineteenth century the hypothesis has been advocated in various forms that a we-source was taken up by the author of Acts. As a rule, and in conformity with the tradition of the early church, Luke was assumed to be the author of the we-source, but other companions of Paul were also proposed (see the summary in Dupont, *Sources*, 77, note 2). On the other hand, those scholars who were of the opinion that they were able to retain the traditional hypothesis of the composition of Acts as well as of Luke by Luke the physician (see above, p. 103-4), very often gave the hypothesis of a we-source a new twist whereby Luke in these sections took up his own records (so recently, e.g., Meinertz, Michaelis,

Wikenhauser, McNeile-Williams, Henshaw, Feine-Behm, Cerfaux in Robert-Feuillet, Macgregor, Blaiklock, W. L. Knox, Dupont). Most of these investigators point to the fact that the accounts in the first person plural are quite fragmentary and cannot be distinguished stylistically from the surrounding accounts in the third person. Hence they raise the question as to whether to these reports stemming from the author of Acts could not also have belonged additional accounts not originally narrated in we-form. With this consideration coincides the hypothesis first established by Dibelius, following Norden, that at the basis of his account in chaps. 13–21 the author of Acts placed an "itinerary," to which the we-sections also belonged. As evidence, Dibelius noted the references to sundry stations about which nothing at all is reported (e.g., 14:24-26; 17:1; 20:13-15), and that more than once the insertion of speeches and separate accounts into a travel report can be recognized by unevennesses of the account (cf. the double mention of Derbe in 14:6, 20b). Dibelius assumed that the "we" did not stand in the travel journal kept by one of Paul's companions, but that Luke the physician as the author of Acts took up this travel journal and indicated by means of the "we" where he personally participated. Dibelius' thesis as a whole has hardly been accepted. Trocmé modified it so that a diary was kept by several companions of Paul, but by Luke, the author of Acts, only where the "we" is encountered. Nock prefers to speak of several diaries. On the other hand, a series of scholars, following Dibelius' hypothesis of an itinerary, have not identified the author of the itinerary (Luke?) with the author of Acts (Beyer, Haenchen, ZThK 1955, 220 ff., and *Apg.* Meyer III [10], 1956; Grässer, ThRdsch 1960, 126 f.; Klein, ZKG 1957, 365 f.; 1962, 359 f.). Recently the hypothesis of an itinerary also has met with energetic opposition. Ehrhardt (78, note 3) regards the existence of such a document as impossible, because papyrus was too expensive; Paul could not have carried such a list around with him, and no parallels to it exist. Schille regards the proof for the use of an itinerary by the author of Acts as altogether unconvincing, and the knowledge of such an eyewitness account by the author as impossible, since the author has a completely false picture of Paul's missionary activity. Also, in view of Paul's imminent expectation, the keeping of a diary is unthinkable. And Haenchen (*Apg.*, Meyer III [13], 1961, and ZThK 1961) has now given up the hypothesis of an itinerary and discusses fancifully the possibilities through which the author of Acts could have obtained his information: visits to churches, making inquiries, the diary of one of the men who accompanied Paul from Philippi on the last journey to Jerusalem.

The question of the sources lying at the basis of Acts 13–28 is, therefore, completely open. It cannot, however, be separated from the question of authorship (in spite of Dupont's protestations, *Sources*, 161). For it follows from the investigation of the we-sections that they are very fragmentary and cannot be distinguished stylistically from the surrounding sections. Whether the author speaks in these we-sections can be established in a literary way only if it can be shown that the reader can perceive the meaning of the "we" (to which he is not referred in the context) because he was prepared for it in the prologue.

Otherwise, the only possible way to decide the correctness of the supposition that in the "we" the author wishes to make perceptible his participation in events is through discussion of the problem of authorship.

As a matter of fact, recently Cadbury (NTSt 1956-57) and Dupont (*Sources*, 99 ff.; cf. also Nock, 502 f.; Trocmé, 126 f.) have sought to demonstrate that the prologue (Lk. 1:1-4) does prepare for the "we" in Acts 16 ff. Whereas the author with οἱ ἀπ' ἀρχῆς αὐτόπται (1:2) refers to the men who could witness to Jesus' activity from its beginning, a fact not true for him, he says of himself in 1:3: "I, for my part, since I have accurately [soigneusement; sorgfältig] participated in all events for some time past, decided to write an orderly account for you, most excellent Theophilus." This translation (Dupont) is based upon the contention that παρακολουθέω never means "to investigate something," but always "to participate in something," and that ἄνωθεν (1:3) means "for some time past," in contrast to ἀπ' ἀρχῆς (1:2) = "from the beginning." The author of the double work, Luke-Acts, explains here, therefore, that he personally participated in a part of the events he reports, and thus points beforehand to the "we" in Acts 16 ff. This translation of Lk. 1:3 is, however, doubtless incorrect (cf. Haenchen, ZThK 1961, 362 ff.; *idem*, ThLZ 87, 1962, 43). Against this view is, first of all, the fact that πᾶσιν ἀκριβῶς is a qualification of παρηκολουθηκότι: One cannot participate in events "accurately" [sorgfältig], and if the "we" reaches back to this παρηκολουθηκότι in the sense of "participate," the author of Acts by no means participated in "all events." Furthermore, in Acts 26:4 f. the author places ἀπ' ἀρχῆς and ἄνωθεν in the same way next to each other, without making any distinction in meaning (see Haenchen), and the reader cannot recognize at all any change in meaning from 1:2 to 1:3, since the meaning, "from the beginning," is quite familiar for ἄνωθεν (Philo, *vita Mosis* II, 48: the author of the book of Moses ἠρχαιολόγησεν ἄνωθεν ἀρξάμενος ἀπὸ τῆς τοῦ παντὸς γενέσεως, i.e., "he narrated all things from the beginning"). But above all παρακολουθέω can by all means mean "to investigate a thing" (see Bauer-Arndt-Gingrich, *Lexicon*, 624, and the examples cited there from Demosthenes; thus the *vetus Latina* also understood it: "having investigated all things accurately from the beginning" ["adsecuto a principio omnibus diligenter"]), and in connection with ἄνωθεν πᾶσιν ἀκριβῶς no reader could give to the word another meaning. Lk. 1:3 is, therefore, to be translated: "I, since I from the beginning investigated all things accurately, decided. . . ." Thus there is no reference to a participation by the author of Luke-Acts in a part of the events nor any preparation for the "we" in Acts 16 ff.

This "we," therefore, remains unexplained for the reader, and whether the author of Acts wished to refer, or could have referred, to his participation in a part of Paul's journeys, can be settled only by an answer to the question whether Acts could actually have been written by a companion of Paul. Since Vielhauer sought to show that "the author of Acts is pre-Pauline in his Christology, and post-Pauline in his natural theology, conception of the Law, and eschatology," and, therefore, he finds himself at an "obvious factual distance from Paul" (p. 15), the question of the relation of the theology of Acts to that of Paul has been much discussed. But as important as this question is in this connection, it must be broadened through the other question: How is the report of Acts to be related to what we can infer from the Pauline epistles about the activity of Paul? These questions cannot be discussed fully here, but for the purpose of deciding the question about the author of Acts reference to a few essential facts will suffice.

a) Let us commence with the report of Paul's activity. We have already referred (p. 125) to the conclusion that the account of Paul's second journey to Jerusalem (Acts 11:27 ff.) originated as a combination of the author of Acts, and that, therefore, Acts is wrong in depicting Paul as having been in Jerusalem twice before the "apostolic council" (Acts 15 = Gal. 2). In Gal. 2:1, however, Paul places the greatest importance on his claim that his journey to the apostolic council was only his second journey to Jerusalem.

b) According to the account of Acts 10:1–11:18, Peter, through his preaching, effected the first conversion of a Gentile, and through his report in Jerusalem obtained the approval of the "apostles and the brethren" there for table fellowship with these Gentiles called by God. And when Paul is indicted in Jerusalem because of his law-free Gentile mission, Peter and James, according to 15:7 ff., tend to the defense of the Gentile mission. But Paul reports in Gal. 2:1 ff. that he had to defend his Gentile mission before the δοκοῦντες, and that he finally worked out an agreement with the "pillars," James, Peter, and John, whereby the work was divided into a mission to the Gentiles and a mission to the circumcised.

c) From the report about the apostolic council in Acts 15 this settlement concerning the division of the mission is missing. Instead of this settlement, 15:22 ff. tells that the assembly in Jerusalem, with the participation of Paul and Barnabas, decided to make an injunction for the Gentile Christians in Antioch, Syria, and Cilicia, to the effect that they should "abstain from what has been sacrificed to idols and from blood and from what is strangled and from unchastity." In Gal. 2 Paul says nothing of this so-called apostolic decree; indeed, he clearly excludes it through οὐδὲν προσανέθεντο (2:6). Moreover, in his discussion in I Cor. 8–10 of the right of Christians to eat meat sacrificed to idols, Paul shows no knowledge at all of these regulations. Attempts have, of course, been made to elude this clear state of affairs. Some scholars have emphasized that the regulation was intended only for the special problems of the churches in Antioch, Syria, and Cilicia, so that Paul did not need to mention the decree to the Corinthians (e.g., Höpfl-Gut). Others contend that the nonritualistic form of the apostolic decree found in the "Western" text (without καὶ πνικτῶν) is the primitive text of Acts 15:20, 29; 21:25. This moral regulation concerning abstinence from idolatry, murder, and unchastity, was no "injunction" which Paul was obliged to mention to the Corinthians (so Feine-Behm). But even if it were certain that the formulation of the letter (15:22 ff.) and the address was taken over verbatim by the author (which is most questionable), there can be no doubt that the regulation proposed in 15:19-21 and transmitted in 15:28 f. has in mind Gentile Christians in general. And it can be clearly demonstrated that as a starting point for the complicated textual development of the clauses of the apostolic decree only the fourfold ritualistic form can be accepted (see W. G. Kümmel, *Aposteldekret*, see above, p. 107; Williams, *Alterations* [see below, p. 359], 72 ff.). The apostolic decree, in the form reported in Acts, cannot have been adopted at the apostolic council, with the participation of Paul, irrespective of how its origin is to be explained historically (cf. the surveys in W. G. Kümmel, ThRdsch, N.F. 17, 1948, 32 ff.; 18, 1950, 28; Haenchen, *Apg.*, Meyer III [13], 410 ff.).

There can be no doubt, then, that in the above-mentioned three basic points of the report about Paul's activity the author of Acts has such an erroneous acquaintanceship with the historical facts that he could hardly have been a companion of Paul on his missionary journeys. And we find additional support for this conclusion when we examine the representation of the Pauline theology in Acts. Certainly it is not altogether astonishing that in the book of Acts there "is found no single, specific Pauline conception" (Vielhauer, 15, in agreement with Bauernfeind, ZsystTh 1954, 74), since we cannot know to what extent Paul was understood by his companions in his specific theology. And also we may not simply assume as self-evident that the author of Acts himself thinks in terms of Pauline theology. But it is well to ask whether he so represents Paul and his message that we can recognize in this representation whether or not he has knowledge of the most significant features of the historical Paul. We cannot affirm that, even if we keep in mind only the following three points.

a) In the "address" of most of his epistles Paul emphatically calls himself ἀπόστολος Χριστοῦ Ἰησοῦ or similarly. He insists that he can claim this title because he has seen the Lord, and that the Corinthians must recognize this, his dignity, even if it is denied him by opponents (I Cor. 9:1 f.; 15:9; II Cor. 12: 11 f.; Rom. 11:13). But in Acts Paul receives the title of apostle only together with Barnabas in 14:4, 14, where it is completely unemphasized. Otherwise, the author designates the twelve as apostles and very clearly places Paul to one side (1:26; 15:2, 6, 22 f.; 16:4). It is difficult to say why it is that the author as a rule does not consider Paul among the apostles and yet this view breaks through in 14:4, 14. This exception can most nearly be traced back to a report taken over by the author; certainly it was not intentional (see above, p. 126). This avoidance of the title of apostle for Paul does not originate in the intention to make Paul appear as subordinate in respect to the twelve (Klein), for the entire plan of Acts speaks against that. But however this fact is to be explained, it shows in any case that the author of Acts does not know the claim to the title of apostle which Paul emphasized and held fast.

b) Paul's preaching about God's sin-redeeming, life-giving, saving act in Christ has as a presupposition the conviction that "all men sin." Since they have rejected the work of the Law and the knowledge of God which is possible for them, they have lost their share in the divine glory (Rom. 3:23; 1:19-21; 2:14 f.). Therefore, neither Jew nor Gentile by himself can attain salvation (Rom. 1:22 ff.; 2:17 ff.; 9:31 f.). Only the sending of Christ makes possible salvation for him who has faith (Rom. 3:21 f., 25; II Cor. 5:18 ff.; Gal. 4:4 f.;

I Thess. 1:9 f.). But the Areopagus address (Acts 17:22 ff.), with reference to a quotation from a pagan poem, speaks of men as God's offspring, not far from God, whom they should seek. Correspondingly, Christ's role is that of world judge, whose significance has been made understandable through the raising of Jesus from the dead by God. Although it has been denied again and again, there can be no doubt that the author here has placed in Paul's mouth a characteristic example of a missionary sermon before Gentiles, in the main *"a hellenistic* speech about the true knowledge of God" (Dibelius, *Studies*, 57; see the lit. on the Areopagus speech in B. Gärtner, *The Areopagus Speech and Natural Revelation*, ASNU 21, 1955, and Dupont, NTSt 1959-60, 152, note 4; also W. G. Kümmel, *Man in the NT*, 1963, 87 ff.). Even if we must grant the possibility that Paul in a missionary sermon before Gentiles sought to make contact with their conceptual world, still it is inconceivable that he would have substituted the Stoic doctrine of God's relation to man for the eschatological preaching of salvation which was so fundamental for him. And it is likewise unthinkable that a missionary companion of Paul could have ascribed to him these radically different views of God and salvation.

   c) In the center of the Pauline theology is the message that God has effected salvation through Christ's death for us (Rom. 3:24 ff.; 5:6 ff.; I Cor. 1:18 ff.; 15:3; II Cor. 5:18 ff.; Gal. 3:13). In the Pauline speeches of Acts, however, there is only one reference to the killing of Jesus according to the prophecy of Scripture (13:27-29), and one to "the church of the Lord which he obtained [for himself] with his own blood" (20:28). Even in the latter passage there is no reference to the saving significance of Jesus' death for the believer. This state of affairs, which corresponds to our findings in Luke (see above, p. 104), shows that the author at best knows about the center of the Pauline doctrine of salvation only through hearsay, and could not have become acquainted with it through personal contact.

   From these facts it is sufficiently clear that the author of Acts was not a missionary companion of Paul. Hence in the "we" of Acts 16 ff. he cannot express his participation in these sections of Paul's missionary journeys. We cannot avoid this judgment by alleging that the Luke who speaks in the we-sections was with Paul only for a short time and, therefore, knew him insufficiently (Nock, Trocmé, 143 ff.). For the above-mentioned deviations from historical reality and the central features of the Pauline theology cannot be traced back to an insufficient relation to Paul but only to a complete lack of relationship. Moreover, the author should have been with Paul during the long period of the journey from Jerusalem to Rome and in Rome itself. Nor can we, as Eltester wants to do, explain the misinterpretation of the Pauline theology by Luke the companion of Paul on the grounds that Luke as a Greek could not at all understand Paul's Jewish-based theology. Neither can we accept Eltester's explanation that Luke's concept of apostleship is based upon the fact that Luke also wrote the Gospel of Luke and, therefore, could see the surety of the evangelical tradition only in the disciples of Jesus. For even a Greek, if he had ever been a personal pupil of Paul at all, must have known that at the apostolic council Paul accepted no obligations. And the Third Evangelist, as a pupil of Paul, must have known Paul's claim to the apostleship and his understanding of Jesus' death. Moreover, a third argument that Acts must have originated with Luke the physician proves nothing. According to Goodspeed, Dibelius, and Dupont, Acts from the first must have carried the name of the author, because through its dedication (1:1) it was designated as appointed for the book market. But Nock (501 f.) and Haenchen (ZThK 1961, 335 f.) have shown that the dedication does not mean anything more than that the addressee was supposed to care for the circulation of the book. Besides, there are examples from the ancient world of anonymous writings with a dedication. We must, then, in spite of the contrary view of very many scholars, hold to the statement that Acts was not composed by a companion of Paul, and, therefore, not by Luke the physician, to whom the tradition refers (see above, p. 103) (so also H. H. Wendt, *Apg.*, Meyer III ⁹, 1913, H. Windisch, *Beginnings* I, 2, 298 ff., Beyer, Conzelmann, Haenchen, Vielhauer, Klein, Evans, O'Neill).

For the explanation of the we-sections there remain only two possibilities: Either the author of Acts (who is unknown to us) took over the "we" from a source, or he himself inserted the "we" into the report. The second hypothesis is very improbable, since the author hardly would have inserted the "we" so sporadically if he intended by these insertions to give his account the appearance of an eyewitness report. Basically more probable is the view that he found this "we" in a source which he used. It is especially probable, if (in spite of the objections by Ehrhardt, Schille, and Haenchen [see above, p. 126]) the hypothesis is well grounded that a travel account in some kind of form lies at the basis of Acts 13–28. But that is the case. The general arguments against this hypothesis prove little, because we really know nothing about the necessity and possibility of making memoranda of travel stations. And naturally we cannot say whether the thread lying at the basis of the narrative consists of one or more sources. But the observations will probably endure that there are numerous data concerning places about which nothing important is reported, and that the continuation of the report is interrupted more than once by clearly inserted independent accounts. The probability is, therefore, great that in Acts 13–28, or in any case in the greatest part of this division of Acts, one or more travel accounts, diaries, itineraries [Stationenverzeichnisse] or the like were used, even though we cannot with precision disentangle the thread lying at the basis of the narrative. According to all probability, the we-sections belong to this thread of the narrative. The conjecture that Luke the physician is speaking through the we-sections can be supported by the argument that without such a state of affairs no one later would have chanced upon Luke, a nonapostle, as author of Luke-Acts. Yet that argument is not compelling, for this name could have been found through conjectures (see above, p. 103). Norden (316 ff.) and Nock (500 ff.) have demonstrated that there were such travel descriptions and reports, which narrated partly in the first, partly in the third, person. It is often assumed that the account of the sea voyage (27:1–28:14) did not belong to this thread of narrative, because the references to Paul can easily be separated from a secular account of a shipwreck taken over by the author (so Dibelius, Bultmann, Klein, ZKG 1956, 366; 1962, 360, Grässer, Conzelmann, ThLZ 1960, 248 f.). Nock (499) and Haenchen (ZThK 1961, 358 ff.) have objected to this idea and have urged that the account lying at the basis already spoke of a shipment of prisoners. Thus it is more probable that also in 27:1–28:16 a travel account from the associates of Paul was used, and that the "we" also here belonged to the "Vorlage."

Sources other than the travel account (or travel accounts) in 13–28 cannot be ascertained in Acts. This circumstance is accompanied by the fact often repeated since Harnack that Acts represents a linguistic unity (so most recently Dupont, *Sources*, 85). That is not to say that here and there separate texts taken over verbatim were not used (perhaps in the speech of Stephen [7:1 ff.] or of Tertullus [24:2 ff.], or in parts of the Areopagus speech, or the letter from the apostolic council). But we cannot go beyond such unprovable conjectures (Vögeli has demonstrated that neither in the maxim of 26:14 nor otherwise is the author directly dependent upon Euripides). The popular guessing game of determining from which persons of primitive Christianity the author could have obtained reports (cf. Michaelis, Wikenhauser, Albertz, Schäfer, Höpfl-Gut, Reicke, Stagg, Feine-Behm, even Haenchen, *Apg.*, Meyer III [13], 77 f.) is fruitless.

5. Time and Place of Composition

Since Acts, as the second part of the Lukan double work, must have been written later than Luke, which was written after 70 (see above, p. 105), a date before 80 is out of the question. For the linguistic differences between Luke and Acts (cf. Hawkins [see lit. to §5], 177 ff., and Clark, 396 ff.) demand a certain linguistic interval between the two writings by the same author. The attempts to place Acts at the beginning of the sixties before the death of Paul (see besides those cited above on p. 114 Clark, Bruce, Blaiklock) or to have it written around 70 (Michaelis, Wikenhauser, Williams, Michel, Benoit, BdJ, Stagg, T. W. Manson) are, therefore, untenable. On the other hand, the dependence of Acts upon Josephus, which formerly was often assumed, has rightly been given up (see finally Ehrhardt, 64 f.); therefore, a date after 95 can no longer be substantiated. Klein (ZKG 1957, 371) would like to fix a date for Acts in the second century, and bases his contention upon the book's primitive catholicism. That is certainly not convincing, for this characterization of Acts' theology is problematic (see above, p. 122), and does not indicate any exact possibility of dating. O'Neill seeks to establish the period between 115 and 130 as the time of composition, by pointing to Justin as the theologian with whom Acts exhibits the most relationship. But his denial that Justin knew Luke-Acts is much forced (the texts cited on p. 30 are not taken seriously), and his early dating of Justin is arbitrary. Besides, the alleged parallels between the theology of Acts and Justin are by no means convincing. A decisive consideration against

Klein's and O'Neill's dating of Acts in the second century is the almost universal opinion that the author of Acts did not know the Pauline epistles, which according to all appearances were assembled after the end of the first century (see below, p. 338; Klein's contention [*Zwölf Apostel,* 189 ff.] that the author of Acts knew the Pauline epistles but did not want to use them is purely arbitrary). Therefore, the dating of Acts between 80 and 90 is the most probable hypothesis (though Goodspeed's dating between 90 and 100 is not excluded).

Where the author wrote can no longer be established. Upon the basis of the traditional interpretation of the "we," many have conjectured Rome, but Ephesus (Goodspeed), or a Pauline church in Macedonia, Achaia, or Asia Minor (Trocmé), are also proposed.

6. The Text of Acts

The text of Acts in all of the critical editions of the NT is that of the earliest uncials (B ℵ A C $\mathfrak{P}$ 74) and of the Alexandrian church fathers, which $\mathfrak{P}$ 45 attests already for the early third century. At the same time there exists a considerably divergent text form in "Western" witnesses like D e.a, the Old Latin, the *vetus Syra,* so far as can be inferred from Ephraem's commentary on Acts, which is preserved only in an Armenian translation; further, by the Latin church fathers like Irenaeus, Cyprian, Augustine; also in the marginal notes of *Syra Charklensis;* and even in the papyri $\mathfrak{P}$ 48 and $\mathfrak{P}$ 38 (concerning this fragment of the fourth century which was published by H. A. Sanders in HarvThR 20, 1927, 1 ff., cf. W. G. Kümmel, ThRdsch, N.F. 10, 1938, 297). The great majority of the Greek manuscripts for Acts also represent the Koine text (cf. to all of these data below, pp. 363 ff.; Ropes, in his edition of the text, offers on opposite pages the text from B and D with the other pertinent witnesses from time to time, so far as they were known up to 1925). Since the great number of the variations of the "Western" text cannot simply be traced back to corruption of the primitive text, the question has been raised whether the Western text form is a recasting of the "Egyptian" or its presupposition, or whether both text forms developed from an original text which we may assume was prior to them. Certainly Zahn's thesis (revised by A. J. Wensinck, *Bulletin of the Bezan Club,* 12, 1937, 11 ff.) that the Western text is Luke's original edition, and the Egyptian text a second edition by the same author, cannot be maintained, for the differences between both text forms have to do with partly contradictory statements (cf. only the clauses of the apostolic decree; see above, pp. 128 f.). But that the Western text of Acts stands closest to the primitive text has often been assumed (e.g., by Clark, Glaue [see below, p. 384], Snape; for the LXX quotations, by Cerfaux). Today, in view of papyrus $\mathfrak{P}$ 48, there can be no more doubt that the Western text of Acts is as old as the Egyptian, and also it may be established as fact that the Western text is not simply a text which grew wild. For it can be shown that a large number of the additions and variations of the Western text over against the Egyptian can be explained only as adjustments of difficulties or changes in content (cf. the "we" in 11:28; the ritualistic form of the apostolic decree, and the addition to this form of the decree of the Golden Rule [15:29]; the motivation for the authorities' change of mind [16:35], and the journey of Apollos to Corinth [18:27]). Other variations serve to strengthen the divine guidance (19:1), the activity of the missionaries (14:25), the theological statements (28:31), but also the intensification of the guilt of the Jews (cf. 13:27 with 17:30 and the works of Menoud and Epp cited above, p. 107). Thus there can be no doubt that the larger part of the variations of the Western text in Acts originated in a conscious revision of the text, a process which doubtless was favored by the fact that Acts received canonical recognition later than the Gospels, with the result that its text was less protected (Dibelius; but cf. also Haenchen's proof that the Lukan text of 𝔓 75 shows several readings of the Western text of Luke as secondary). This fact does not exclude the possibility that also in Acts the Western text preserves readings which can hardly be understood as secondary changes and, therefore, come into question as original text (cf. the geographical data [12:10; 20:15], the indications of time [19:9; 27:5], Δουβ[ε]ριος [20:4] as the place of origin of the Macedonian Gaius). But on the whole the Egyptian text form offers the more original text, and thus there remains for the determination of the sporadic, original readings in the Western text only an eclectic method (cf. Williams and Klijn, see above, p. 107), which occasionally must fall back to an individual witness (τοῖς ψαλμοῖς 𝔓 45 in 13:33) or must make a conjecture (to 4:25, cf. Haenchen, ZThK 1954, 156 f.).

§10. The Gospel of John

Commentaries, see p. 388. Research reports: W. BAUER, ThRdsch, N. F. 1, 1929, 135 ff.; L. SCHMID, "Joh. und Religionsgeschichte," Diss. Tübingen 1933; PH.-H. MENOUD, L'évangile de Jean d'après les recherches récentes, Cahiers théologiques de l'actualité protestante 3, ²1947; idem, "Les études johanniques de Bultmann à Barrett," in RechB III, 1958 (see below), 11 ff.; J. BEHM, ThLZ 73, 1948, 21 ff.; E. HAENCHEN, ThRdsch, N. F., 23, 1955, 295 ff.; W. F. HOWARD, The Fourth Gospel in Recent Criticism and Interpretation. Revised by C. K. BARRETT, 1955; J. A. T. ROBINSON, "The New Look on the Fourth Gospel," StEv, 1959, 338 ff.; A. M. HUNTER, "Recent Trends in NT Studies," ExpT 71, 1959-60, 164 ff., 219 ff.; C. L. MITTON, "The Provenance of the Fourth Gospel," ibid., 337 ff.; R. SCHNACKENBURG, La théologie du NT. État de la question, Studia Neotestamentica, Subsidia I, 1961, 79 ff.; New Testament Theology Today. Tr. David Askew, 1963. Studies: W. BALDENSPERGER, Der Prolog des 4. Ev., 1898; A. SCHLATTER, Die Sprache und Heimat des 4. Evangelisten, BFTh VI, 4, 1902; W. WREDE, Charakter und Tendenz des Joh., SGV 37, 1903 (= ²1933); E. SCHWARTZ, Über den Tod der Söhne Zebedäi, AGGW, N. F. 7, 5, 1904; idem, "Aporien im 4. Ev.," NGGW 1907, 341 ff.; 1908, 115 ff., 149 ff., 497 ff.; J. WELLHAUSEN, Erweiterungen und Änderungen im 4. Ev., 1907; W. HEITMÜLLER, "Zur Johannes-Tradition," ZNW 13, 1914, 189 ff.; C. F. BURNEY, The Aramaic Origin of the Fourth Gospel, 1922; C. C. TORREY, "The Aramaic Origin of the Gospel of John," HarvThR 16, 1923, 305 ff.; H. WINDISCH, "Der joh. Erzählungsstil," ΕΥΧΑΡΙΣΤΗΡΙΟΝ, Festschr. H.

Gunkel II, FRLANT, N. F. 19, 1923, 174 ff.; *idem, Johannes und die Synpt.*, UNT 12, 1926; *idem*, "Die Absolutheit des Joh.," ZsystTh 5, 1928, 3 ff.; K. KUNDSIN, *Topologische Überlieferungsstücke im Joh.*, 1925; *idem, Charakter und Ursprung der joh. Reden*, Acta Universitatis Latviensis, Series theologica I, 4, 1939; R. BULTMANN, "Die Bedeutung der neuerschlossenen mandäischen und manichäischen Quellen für das Verständnis des Joh.," ZNW 24, 1925, 100 ff.; *idem*, RGG[3] III, 1959, 840 ff.; B. W. BACON, "The Elder John in Jerusalem," ZNW 26, 1927, 187 ff.; *idem*, "John and the Pseudo-Johns," ZNW 31, 1932, 132 ff.; *idem, The Gospel of the Hellenists,* 1933; M. DIBELIUS, "Joh. 15, 13. Eine Studie zum Traditionsproblem des Joh.," *Festgabe A. Deissmann,* 1927, 168 ff. (= Botschaft und Geschichte I, 1953, 204 ff.); *idem*, RGG[2] III, 1929, 349 ff.; E. LOHMEYER, "Aufbau und Gliederung des vierten Ev.," ZNW 27, 1928, 11 ff.; F. BÜCHSEL, *Johannes und der hellen. Synkretismus,* BFTh, 2. Reihe 16, 1928; E. C. COLWELL, *The Greek of the Fourth Gospel,* 1931; W. VON LOEWENICH, *Das Johannesverständnis im zweiten Jhdt.,* Beih. ZNW 13, 1932; G. HOFFMANN, *Das Joh. als Alterswerk,* NTF IV, 1, 1933; T. SIGGE, *Das Joh. und die Synpt.,* NTA 16, 2-3, 1935; E. HIRSCH, *Studien zum vierten Ev.,* BhTh 11, 1936; *idem, Das vierte Ev. in seiner ursprünglichen Gestalt verdeutscht und erklärt,* 1936; *idem*, "Stilkritik und Literaranalyse im vierten Ev.," ZNW 43, 1950-51, 129 ff.; L. VAGANAY, "La finale du quatrième évangile," RB 45, 1936, 512 ff.; H. PREISKER, "Das Ev. des Johannes als erster Teil eines apokalyptischen Doppelwerkes," ThBl 15, 1936, 185 ff.; *idem*, "Jüdische Apokalyptik und hellen. Synkretismus im Joh., dargelegt an dem Begriff 'Licht,'" ThLZ 77, 1952, 673 ff.; P. GARDNER-SMITH, *Saint John and the Synoptic Gospels,* 1938; *idem*, "St. John's Knowledge of Matthew, JThSt, N. S. 4, 1953, 31 ff.; E. SCHWEIZER, *Ego eimi . . . ,* FRLANT, N. F. 38, 1939; E. PERCY, *Untersuchungen über den Ursprung der joh. Theologie,* 1939 (thereto R. BULTMANN, OLZ 43, 1940, 150 ff.; M. DIBELIUS, DLZ 61, 1940, 1 ff.); J. JEREMIAS, "Joh. Literar-Kritik," ThBl 20, 1941, 33 ff.; R. M. GRANT, "The Fourth Gospel and the Church," HarvThR 35, 1942, 95 ff.; *idem*, "The Odes of Solomon and the Church of Antioch," JBL 63, 1944, 363 ff.; *idem*, "The Origin of the Fourth Gospel," JBL 69, 1950, 305 ff.; E. C. BROOME, "The Sources of the Fourth Gospel," JBL 63, 1944, 107 ff.; H. A. FISCHEL, "Jewish Gnosticism in the Fourth Gospel," JBL 65, 1946, 157 ff.; T. W. MANSON, "The Fourth Gospel," BJRL 30, 1946-47, 312 ff. (= Manson, St., 105 ff.); E. KÄSEMANN, Review of Bultmann, Komm., VuF 1942-46, 1946-47, 182 ff.; *idem*, Review of Howard, Fourth Gospel, and Barrett, Comm., GGA 211, 1957, 145 ff.; M.-E. BOISMARD, "Le chapitre XXI de saint Jean," RB 54, 1947, 473 ff.; *idem*, "Clément de Rome et l'Évangile de Jean," RB 55, 1948, 376 ff.; *idem*, "L'évolution du thème eschatologique dans les traditions johanniques," RB 68, 1961, 507 ff.; C. M. CONNICK, "The Dramatic Character of the Fourth Gospel," JBL 67, 1948, 159 ff.; W. G. WILSON, "The Original Text of the Fourth Gospel," JThSt 50, 1949, 59 ff.; J. BONSIRVEN, "Les aramaïsmes de saint Jean l'évangéliste," Bb 30, 1949, 405 ff.; C. MAURER, *Ignatius von Antiochien und das Joh.,* AThANT 18, 1949; N. URICCHIO, "La teoria delle trasposizioni nel vangelo di S. Giovanni," Bb 31, 1950, 129 ff.; E. RUCKSTUHL, *Die literarische Einheit des Joh.,* Studia Friburgensia, N.F. 1, 1951; S. MENDNER, "Joh. Literarkritik," ThZ 8, 1952, 418 ff.; *idem*, "Die Tempelreinigung," ZNW 47, 1956, 93 ff.; *idem*, "Zum Problem 'Joh. und die Synpt.,'" NTSt 4, 1957-58, 282 ff.; *idem*, "Nikodemus," JBL 77, 1958, 293 ff.; H. P. V. NUNN, *The Authorship of the Fourth Gospel,* 1952; H. F. D. SPARKS, "St. John's Knowledge of Matthew: The Evidence of John 13,16 and 15,20," JThSt, N.S. 3, 1952, 58 ff.; C. H. DODD, *The Interpretation of the Fourth Gospel,* 1953 (thereto R. BULTMANN, NTSt 1, 1954-55, 77 ff.; P. WINTER,

ThLZ 80, 1955, 141 ff.); *idem*, "Some Johannine 'Herrnworte' with Parallels in the Synoptic Gospels," NTSt 2, 1955-56, 75 ff.; C. K. BARRETT, "Zweck des 4. Ev.," ZsystTh 22, 1953, 257 ff.; *idem*, "The Theological Vocabulary of the Fourth Gospel and the Gospel of Truth," *Current Issues in NT Interpretation, Festschr. O. Piper*, 1962, 210 ff.; B. NOACK, *Zur joh. Tradition*, Publications de la Société des Sciences et des Lettres d'Aarhus, Série de Théologie 3, 1954 (thereto R. BULTMANN, ThLZ 80, 1955, 521 ff.); R. A. EDWARDS, *The Gospel According to St. John. Its Criticism and Interpretation*, 1954; R. GYLLENBERG, "Die Anfänge der joh. Tradition," *Ntl. Studien für R. Bultmann*, Beih. ZNW 21, 1954, 144 ff.; L. MOWRY, "The Dead Sea Scrolls and the Background for the Gospel of John," *The Biblical Archaeologist* 17, 1954, 78 ff.; C. GOODWIN, "How Did John Treat His Sources?" JBL 73, 1954, 61 ff.; H. C. SNAPE, "The Fourth Gospel, Ephesus and Alexandria," HarvThR 47, 1954, 1 ff.; J. N. SANDERS, " 'Those whom Jesus Loved': St. John XI.5," NTSt 1, 1954-55, 29 ff.; I. BUSE, "John V.8 and Johannine-Marcan Relationship," NTSt 1, 1954-55, 134 ff.; *idem*, "St. John and the Marcan Passion Narrative," NTSt 4, 1957-58, 215 ff.; *idem*, "St. John and the Passion Narratives of St. Matthew and St. Luke," NTSt 7, 1960-61, 65 ff.; K. ALAND, "Der Montanismus und die kleinasiatische Theologie," ZNW 46, 1955, 114 ff.; K. WEISS, "Der westliche Text von Lc. 7:46 und sein Wert," ZNW 46, 1955, 241 ff.; F.-M. BRAUN, "L'arrière-fond judaïque du Quatrième Évangile et la Communauté de l'Alliance," RB 62, 1955, 1 ff.; *idem*, "Hermétisme et Johannisme," *Revue Thomiste* 55, 1955, 22 ff. 259 ff.; *idem*, "La 'Lettre de Barnabé' et l'Évangile de saint Jean," NTSt 4, 1957-58, 119 ff.; *idem*, *Jean, le théologien, et son évangile dans l'église ancienne*, Ét. bibl., 1959 (thereto M.-E. BOISMARD, RB 67, 1960, 592 ff.); *idem*, "Saint Jean, la sagesse et l'histoire," *Neotestamentica et Patristica, Freundesgabe O. Cullmann*, Suppl. NovT 6, 1962, 123 ff.; R. M. WILSON, "The Fourth Gospel and Hellenistic Thought," NovT 1, 1956, 225 ff.; E. STAUFFER, "Probleme der Priestertradition," ThLZ 81, 1956, 135 ff.; *idem*, "Historische Elemente im vierten Ev.," in *Bekenntnis zur Kirche, Festschr. E. Sommerlath*, 1960, 33 ff.; H. BECKER, *Die Reden des Joh. und der Stil der gnostischen Offenbarungsrede*, hrsg. von R. BULTMANN, FRLANT 68, 1956 (thereto C. K. BARRETT, ThLZ 82, 1957, 911 f.); P. PARKER, "Two Editions of John," JBL 75, 1956, 303 ff.; *idem*, "John and John Mark," JBL 79, 1960, 97 ff.; *idem*, "John the Son of Zebedee and the Fourth Gospel," JBL 81, 1962, 35 ff.; W. F. ALBRIGHT, "Recent Discoveries in Palestine and the Gospel of St. John," *The Background of the NT and Its Eschatology, Festschr. C. H. Dodd*, 1956, 153 ff.; E. K. LEE, "St. Mark and the Fourth Gospel," NTSt 3, 1956-57, 50 ff.; CASSIAN, "John XXI," NTSt 3, 1956-57, 132 ff.; R. E. BROWN, "The Qumran Scrolls and the Johannine Gospels and Epistles," in *The Scrolls and the NT*, edited by K. STENDAHL, 1957, 183 ff.; G. D. KILPATRICK, "The Religious Background of the Fourth Gospel," in *Studies in the Fourth Gospel*, edited by F. L. CROSS, 1957, 36 ff.; S. SCHULZ, *Untersuchungen zur Menschensohn-Christologie im Joh.*, 1957 (bibl.); *idem, Komposition und Herkunft der Joh. Reden*, BWANT, 5. Folge 1, 1960 (bibl.); H. STRATHMANN, EKL II, 1958, 357 ff.; R. SCHNACKENBURG, "Das vierte Ev. und die Johannesjünger," *Historisches Jahrbuch* 77, 1958, 21 ff.; *idem*, LThK V, 1960, 1101 ff.; G. BAUMBACH, *Qumran und das Joh.*, Aufsätze und Vorträge zur Theologie und Religionswissenschaft 6, 1958; *L'Évangile de Jean. Études et Problèmes*, RechB III, 1958 (contains essays by M.-E. BOISMARD, H. VAN DEN BUSSCHE, F.-M. BRAUN, G. QUISPEL); W. WILKENS, *Die Entstehungsgeschichte des vierten Ev.*, 1958 (thereto J. M. ROBINSON, JBL 78, 1959, 242 ff.; C. K. BARRETT, ThLZ 84, 1959, 828 f.); *idem*, "Evangelist und Tradition im Joh.," ThZ 16, 1960, 81 ff.; P. BORGEN, "John and the Synoptics in the Passion Narrative," NTSt 5, 1958-59, 246 ff.; O. MICHEL, CBL, 1959, 658 ff.; E. HAENCHEN, "Joh. Probleme," ZThK 56, 1959, 19 ff.; A. KRAGERUD, *Der Lieblingsjünger im Joh.*, 1959 (thereto W. MICHAELIS, ThLZ 85, 1960, 667 ff. and M.-E. BOISMARD, RB 67, 1960, 405 ff.); R. D. POTTER, "Topography and Archaeology in the Fourth Gospel," StEv, 1959, 328 ff.; W. C. VAN UNNIK, "The Purpose of St. John's Gospel," StEv, 1959, 382 ff.; T. C. SMITH, *Jesus in the Gospel of John*, 1959; J. A. T. ROBINSON, "The Destination and Purpose of St. John's Gospel," NTSt 6, 1959-60, 117 ff.; A. GUILDING, *The Fourth Gospel and Jewish Worship*, 1960 (thereto E. HAENCHEN, ThLZ 86, 1961, 670 ff.); A. J. B. HIGGINS, *The Historicity of the Fourth Gospel*, 1960; W. GRUND-MANN, *Zeugnis und Gestalt des Joh.*, Arbeiten zur Theologie 7, 1960; H. M. TEEPLE, "Qumran and the Origin of the Fourth Gospel," NovT 4, 1960, 6 ff.; *idem*, "Methodology in Source Analysis of the Fourth Gospel," JBL, 81, 1962, 279 ff.; S. TEMPLE, "The Two Traditions of the Last Supper, Betrayal, and Arrest," NTSt 7, 1960-61, 77 ff.; *idem*, "A Key to the Composition of the Fourth Gospel," JBL 80, 1961, 220 ff.; *idem*, "The Two Signs in the Fourth Gospel," JBL 81, 1962, 175 ff.; K. A. ECKHARDT, *Der Tod des Johannes als Schlüssel zum Vertändnis der joh. Schriften*, 1961; G. H. C. MAC-GREGOR and A. Q. MORTON, *The Structure of the Fourth Gospel*, 1961 (thereto E. HAENCHEN, ThLZ 87, 1962, 487 ff.); O. MERLIER, *Le Quatrième Évangile. La question johannique*, 1961; H. BRAUN, "Qumran und das NT," ThRdsch, N.F. 28, 1962, 192 ff.; K. G. KUHN, "Joh. und Qumrantexte," *Neotestamentica et Patristica, Freundesgabe O. Cullmann*, Suppl. NovT 6, 1962, 111 ff.; M.-E. BOISMARD, "Saint Luc et la rédaction du quatrième évangile," RB 69, 1962, 185 ff.

1. Contents

The Gospel of John is divided into two principal parts: 1. Jesus' work in the world (1:19–12:50); 2. his return to the Father (13:1–20:29). A prologue (1:1-18) is placed at the beginning, and a supplement (ch. 21) is appended to the conclusion (20:30 f.). Whereas this division is evident, the further organization of John is very uncertain. Although in the opinion of numerous scholars John has not been transmitted in its original form, others have wished to show an artistic arrangement in the transmitted text according to the numbers 7, 3, and 5 (thus in various ways Albertz, Lohmeyer, Dodd [for chaps. 2–12], Hirsch [for the reconstructed "Grundschrift"], Grundmann, van der Bussche in RechB III, 108 f.; cf. also F.-M. Braun, *Jean*, 13 ff.). But none of these artistic arrangements can be made intelligible on the basis of the text (cf. also Haenchen, ThRdsch 1955, 311 ff.), and it may be fitting to renounce such an arrangement.

The Prologue (1:1-18) proclaims the incarnation in Jesus Christ of the divine Logos who existed "in the beginning." Jesus brought grace and truth, and as the unique one, God by nature, made God known. In the midst of the prologue (1:6–8,15), John the Baptist is spoken of.

The First Principal Part is introduced through the Baptist's testimony to Jesus (1:19-34), and reports about the gathering of the first disciples around Jesus (1:35-51). At the wedding in Cana Jesus manifests his glory by means of the first sign, the changing of water to wine (2:1-11). Via Capernaum he goes to the festival of the Passover at Jerusalem. By cleansing the temple he demonstrates his authority (2:12-22). On the basis of his signs, he finds faith among many of the people (2:23-25). In a nocturnal discourse, he instructs Nicodemus, the Pharisee, concerning the conditions of entry into the kingdom of God (3:1-21), in the course of which Nicodemus is lost sight of after 3:11. Jesus baptizes in the Jordan; second testimony of the Baptist concerning him (3:22-30), which in 3:31-36 can no more be clearly characterized as a discourse of the Baptist. On the way to Galilee Jesus reveals himself to a Samaritan woman at the well as the giver of "living water" and as Messiah, but only from the people of her region does he find belief because of his word (4:1-42). Then Jesus does his second sign in Galilee (4:43-54), the healing of the son of the royal official in Capernaum. In connection with a feast in Jerusalem there ensues, as the result of his healing on the Sabbath at the pool of Bethesda a man who had been lame for thirty-eight years, the first great argument of Jesus with the Jews about the authority of the Son (5:1-18, 19-47). Before the Passover (6:4) Jesus is again in Galilee. He feeds the five thousand on the east bank of the sea, and avoids the enthusiasm of those who had been fed (6:1-13). Walking on the sea, he appears to the disciples and on the next day is sought out by the crowd (6:14-24). In the synagogue at Capernaum he disputes with the Jews about the "bread of life" and eating the flesh and drinking the blood of the Son of man (6:25-59). Then the mass of the disciples forsake him (6:60-66), but the twelve, through the mouth of Peter, confess him as "the Holy One of God," while Jesus prophesies Judas' betrayal (6:67-71). Again Jesus goes to Jerusalem, for the feast of Tabernacles (7:1-13), and discusses his mission with the Jews (7:14-30). The Sanhedrin seeks to arrest him (7:31-36); on the last day of the feast Jesus summons men to believe in him (7:37-44); the arrest fails, yet the Jewish leaders reject him as a Galilean (7:45-52). In additional controversy discourses (light and darkness, existence above and below, freedom and slavery, children of God and childen of the devil, Abraham and Jesus) the opposition between Jesus and the Jews reaches its peak (8:12-59) (7:53-8:11 is interpolated: Jesus and the adulteress). The healing on the Sabbath of the man born blind brings the delusion of the Pharisees to light (9:1-41). In the figurative discourse about the shepherd and his flock Jesus designates himself as the true Shepherd, whereupon some of the Jews declare him to be possessed of demons (10:1-21). At the feast of Dedication he openly declares himself to be the Messiah, who is one with the Father. But when he is threatened with stoning, he withdraws to Perea (10:22-42). In connection with the raising of Lazarus Jesus reveals himself as "the resurrection and the life" (11:1-44). Then follows the death decision of the Sanhedrin against him (11:45-53). Before Passover Jesus once more withdraws into solitude with his disciples (11:54-57) and is then anointed by Mary in Bethany (12:1-11). Upon his arrival in Jerusalem he is greeted by the people as "King of Israel" (12:12-19). But when the Greeks want to see him, he speaks about his glorification through the death which he is going to meet (12:20-36a). The report that Jesus has again hidden himself is followed by an explanation of the unbelief of most of the people as the fulfillment of Israel's prophecy (12:36b-43). The first principal part concludes with a situationless synopsis of Jesus' preaching (12:44-50).

The Second Principal Part (chaps. 13–20) pictures the departure of Jesus from his disciples: the footwashing in connection with the meal as a symbol of purification and of serving love (13:1-20), designation of the betrayer (13:21-30), farewell discourses (13:31–16:33) (his departure from the disciples, love commandment, reference to the denial of Peter [13:31-38], comfort for his own: he is going to the Father, but will come anew to them through the Spirit [ch. 14]; Jesus the vine [15:1-17], the hate of the world [15:18–16:4a], the coming of the Spirit [16:4b-15], Jesus comes to his own in full fellowship [16:16-33]), Jesus' farewell prayer (the high-priestly prayer, ch. 17: petition for glorification [17:1-5], intercession for the disciples [17:6-19], and for those who come to believe through their word [17:20-23], prayer for their unification with him, the Glorified One [17:24-26]). Chaps. 18–20 show the perfecting of Jesus. Passion narrative (chaps. 18, 19): arrest (18:1-11), Jesus in the house of Annas and Peter's denial (18:12-27), hearing before Pilate (18:28-40), scourging, crowning with thorns, Pilate's surrender of Jesus for crucifixion (19:1-16a), crucifixion and death (19:16b-30), piercing of his side with a spear, and reference to the witness (19:31-37), removal from the cross and burial (19:38-42). Manifestations of the Risen One (20:1-29): discovery of the empty tomb (20:1-10), encounter of Jesus with Mary Magdalene (20:11-18), the Risen One with the disciples, without Thomas (20:19-23), and with Thomas (20:24-29).

Conclusion (20:30 f.): the purpose of the book.

Supplement (ch. 21): revelation of the Risen One by the Sea of Tiberias (21:1-14), the Risen One with Peter and the Beloved Disciple (21:15-23), equating of the Beloved Disciple with the author, and a second conclusion (21:24, 25).

2. The History of the Johannine Problem

Since the beginning of the third century it was not denied that the Gospel of John stems from John, the son of Zebedee, and thus from a member of the circle of the twelve, and, therefore, like Matthew, has an eyewitness of Jesus' life as its author. But this view, which was first established at the end of the second century (see below, pp. 168 ff.), was at first not undisputed. Irenaeus (Haer. III, 11, 12) knew of people who denied the Johannine promise of a Spirit-Paraclete (Jn. 14:16 f.; 15:26; 16:7 ff.), and therefore "repudiated the Gospel [= John] as well as the prophetic spirit." The Roman presbyter Gaius, who wrote at the beginning of the third century, obviously had the same intention of eliminating the scriptural foundation used by the Montanists for their teaching about the presence of the Paraclete. Gaius designated John and the Apocalypse as the works of the Gnostic, Cerinthus, and in doing so used the divergence of John from the Synoptics as an argument (cf. F.-M. Braun, Jean, 147 f.).

A group of ecclesiastical anti-Montanists, whom Epiphanius (*Panarion* 51) nicknamed "Alogoi" (see Goguel, *Intr.* II, 158 ff., and A. Grillmeyer, art. "Aloger," LThK I, 1957, 363 f.), advocated the same derivation of John. This criticism of the apostolic composition of John, which originated in the polemics of and against heretics, remained largely ineffective, but it shows that the text of John certainly permits such a criticism and that the comparison of John with the Synoptics has decisive significance. Not until the eighteenth century were isolated voices again raised against the apostolic origin of John. At the beginning of the nineteenth century several theologians agreed with this view. In addition to the divergence of John from the Synoptics, they also referred to the contradictions in the text of John, which point to the use of sources or to a secondary revision (see WGK, NT, 101). K. G. Bretschneider, General Superintendent of Gotha, was the first to attract attention with his writing which appeared in 1820, *Probabilities concerning the Nature and Origin of the Gospel and the Epistles of the Apostle John* [*Probabilia de evangelii et epistularum Joannis, apostoli, indole et origine*]. As arguments against the apostolic origin of John, Bretschneider cited not only the divergence of Jesus' teaching in John from that of the Synoptics, but also the non-Jewish character of John and the late testimony to John. The strong opposition aroused against his contentions caused Bretschneider to withdraw his criticism four years later (see WGK, NT, 101 f.). But in spite of the great influence of Schleiermacher, who, upon the basis of the spiritual content of John, decided in favor of an eyewitness as author, the critical objections could no longer be entirely silenced. D. F. Strauss, in his *Leben Jesu* (1835-36) (*The Life of Jesus.* Tr. George Eliot from 4th ed. [1840], 1846), sought to show that in John, in comparison with the Synoptics, there is a more highly developed form of the "myth," so that generally speaking John is out of the question as a source for the historical understanding of Jesus (cf. WGK, NT, 152 ff.). Strauss's criticism, which by and large was felt to be purely negative, was methodically secured by F. C. Baur's *Kritische Untersuchungen über die kanonischen Evv.* (1847). Baur adhered to the view that John, written in the late second century, possesses no historically valuable traditions about Jesus, but at the same time stressed that John was not intended to be a historical account at all but the presentation of an idea (see WGK, NT, 157 f., 169 ff.). If mere criticism of the tradition was thus replaced by the real historical problem concerning the purpose of John and the circumstances of its origin, the discussion nevertheless concentrated first of all upon the question of the authenticity and historical worth of John. Although Baur's late dating of John found little approval in the second half of the nineteenth century, his denial of its apostolic origin and his assertion of the slight value of its sources in comparison with the Synoptics convinced many (cf., e.g., Weizsäcker, Jülicher; see WGK, NT, 214 f., 221). On the other hand, conservative scholarship defended John as the work of an eyewitness and insisted upon its apostolic origin (e.g., B. Weiss, Schlatter, Zahn).

This discussion about the authenticity and historical value of John has continued to the present. But since the middle of the nineteenth century other problems, which the critics had already begun to discuss in part at the beginning of the nineteenth century, have also come to the fore (cf. the somewhat too much differentiated history of methods in Schulz, *Menschensohn*, 39 ff.). In order to explain, or even to remove, the numerous difficulties which the progress of the narrative as well as the train of thought of the discourses in John present, four basic hypotheses, or combinations of them, have been proposed: a) Since 1871 the view which was occasionally advocated already in the Middle Ages has won many supporters. According to this view, the text of John which has been transmitted to us has fallen into disorder through displacement of pages, or was left behind by the author unfinished and was incorrectly arranged by his pupils. The attempt to restore the sequence which was originally intended by the author is then the task of present-day investigators, and the indispensable presupposition of proper exposition (cf. the history of such theories in Uricchio; Howard, 111 ff., 303; F.-M. Braun, *Jean*, 23). b) According to a view often advocated since the beginning of the nineteenth century, the transmitted text of John has come about through the weaving together of several written sources or through extensive expansion of an apostolic "Grundschrift" by an editor (see Schulz, *Menschensohn*, 48 ff.). Since these partition hypotheses have proved to be inadequately grounded in respect to methodology and therefore have essentially been abandoned for a long time, we need not go into them more thoroughly here. c) Methodologically related to the partition hypotheses is the supposition advocated in various forms since the works of Schwartz and Wellhausen (1907) that a redactor (or redactors) expanded the original Gospel, rearranged it, and adapted it to the ecclesiastical situation. The starting points for such theories are literary and doctrinal difficulties (see the survey in Howard, 95 ff., 297 ff.; Schweizer, 84 ff.; Schulz, *Menschensohn*, 62 ff.). d) The juxtaposition of narratives and extensive discourses and the occasional but not frequent parallels of John with the Synoptics have frequently led, since the beginning of the nineteenth century, on the one hand, to the question whether John is dependent upon the Synoptics and, on the other hand, to the conjecture that the author of John not only used isolated traditions but also larger connected sources (cf. Menoud, *L'évangile*, 16 ff.; Ruckstuhl, 10 ff.; Haenchen, ThRdsch 1955, 302 ff.). Recently, to be sure, the tenability of such source theories has been fundamentally disputed with the help of vocabulary statistics (especially Schweizer, Menoud, Ruckstuhl).

In addition to the methods of historical and literary criticism as applied to John, the method of the history of religions has arisen since the beginning of our century. Besides the constantly posed alternative of "Jewish or Greek background" for the conceptual world of John (cf. for the Jewish thesis Büchsel and F.-M. Braun; for the Greek, Goodspeed and Hirsch), there has appeared in the twentieth century the supposition that John belongs in the spiritual milieu of Near Eastern Gnosticism (cf. chiefly Bauer and Bultmann). Since the discovery of the community at Qumran, the influence upon John of the Qumran world of thought has been maintained with more or less certainty (cf. the reports by L. Schmid, Menoud, *L'évangile*, 30 ff., and RechB III 26 ff., Haenchen, ThRdsch 1955, 313 ff., Schulz, *Menschensohn*, 43 ff.).

Upon the answer to these history-of-religion questions largely depends the solution to a problem which likewise has much occupied the investigation of John in the last half century, and which points to the problem which is theological in the narrower sense, namely, the question about the aim of John and about the readers for whom it was written. This question has also often been put as an alternative question (Jewish or Hellenistic readers?). Furthermore, since the time of Baldensperger, who was the first to refer to the polemic recognizable in John against the disciples of the Baptist, attempts have been made to prove that John has a polemical aim in respect to various fronts. In connection with that such scholars as Dodd, Stauffer, Smith, van Unnik, and J. A. T. Robinson have recently advocated again the long-abandoned supposition of a missionary intention of John. Moreover, we should refer, if only in passing, to the intensive occupation of scholarship of recent decades with the Johannine theology, for which chiefly the commentaries of Bultmann and Barrett and Dodd's book about the interpretation of the Fourth Gospel are significant (cf. the accounts by Menoud, *L'évangile*, 51 ff., Haenchen, ThRdsch 1955, 326 ff., Schnackenburg, *New Testament Theology Today*).

3. The Literary Character and the Sources of the Gospel of John

John belongs to the same literary category of "Gospel" as the Synoptics, in so far as all four Gospels narrate the activity of Jesus from the time of his contact with John the Baptist until his death and attach the account of Jesus' resurrection as conclusion. And also in John, as in the Synoptics, we find reports both of Jesus' miracles and his teaching activity. In spite of these similarities, John is differentiated from the Synoptics in purely external aspects in a threefold way: a) Whereas the Synoptics terminate Jesus' activity in Galilee and surrounding regions with the one journey to Jerusalem which ends with his crucifixion, according to John's account, Jesus sets out three times from Galilee to Jerusalem (2:13; 5:1; 7:10); and whereas according to Mk. 11–15, Jesus' stay in Jerusalem continues for about a week, according to John, Jesus stays in Jerusalem and Judea from 7:10 on. b) This stay in Jerusalem continues from a feast of Tabernacles (7:2) through a feast of Dedication (10:22) to the Passover of his death (11:55; 12:1; 18:28), therefore about half a year. In addition, Jn. 2:13 mentions a Passover, and 6:4 the approach of a Passover. To be sure, 5:1, according to the best attested text, mentions only "a feast," so that we cannot decide whether a Passover is meant. But even if we leave 5:1 out of consideration, the activity of Jesus according to Jn. 2–19 comprises more than two years, of which the last half year is in Jerusalem and Judea. The chronological inferences in Mk. 2:23 (fully developed grain between Passover and Pentecost) and Mk. 14:1, however, point to an activity of Jesus of not more than one year. The chronological and topographical framework of Jesus' activity in John is, therefore, different from that of the Synoptics. c) The account of the work and teaching of Jesus in the Synoptics is pieced together from separate accounts and isolated sayings or groups of sayings, which are combined into a series of accounts and discourses; only the passion narrative offers a larger connected account (cf. above, pp. 40 f.). John, of course, also contains single, separate accounts (e.g., 2:1-10, 13-21; 4:46-53; 12:1-9, 12-15; 13:36-38), and also the Johannine passion narrative forms a larger connected narrative. But on the whole John consists of larger discourse compositions, which more than once grow out of a preceding narrative (chaps. 4, 5, 6, 9, 11). And these discourse compositions are not pieced together from separate sayings, but revolve about one or even more themes, in part in the form of a dialogue, so that with a certain correctness we may speak of the "dramatic" character of the Johannine account (Windisch, Connick, Noack, 116 f.).

John, therefore, diverges considerably from the Synoptics not only in the framework of its account and in the manner of its presentation, but also in material. John has only a few narratives in common with the Synoptics: call of the disciples (1:35 ff.), the healing of the royal official's son (4:46 ff.), the feeding of the five thousand and walking on the sea (6:1 ff., 16 ff.), Peter's confession (6:66 ff.), the entry into Jerusalem (12:12 ff.), the last meal, with the prophecy of the betrayal (13:1 ff.), and several sections of the passion narrative. The cleansing of the temple (2:13 ff.) and the anointing in Bethany (12:1 ff.) also correspond to synoptic pericopes, but stand in other contexts. On the other hand, John offers several miracle stories not transmitted by the Synoptics: the wedding at Cana (2:1 ff.), the healing of the lame man at the pool of Bethesda (5:1 ff.), the healing of the man born blind (9:1 ff.), and the raising of Lazarus (11:1 ff.). The narratives of Nicodemus (3:1 ff.) and of the Samaritan woman (4:5 ff.) are also found only in John. Often John presupposes as known some circumstances reported in the Synoptics, without narrating them: the baptismal work of the Baptist (1:25), the baptism of Jesus (1:32), the imprisonment of the Baptist (3:24), the circle of the twelve (6:67 ff.; 20:24), and the scene in Gethsemane (12:27). And occasionally Johannine sayings are reminiscent of the synoptic Jesus: cf. Jn. 2:19 = Mk. 14:58 par.; 3:3 = Mt. 18:3; 3:35 = Mt. 11:27 par.; 4:44 = Mk. 6:4 par.; 5:23b; 13:20 = Lk. 10:16 par. Mt. 10:40; 12:35 = Mk. 8:35 par.; 13:16; 15:20 = Mt. 10:24; 15:7b = Mk. 11:24 par.; 16:23 = Mt. 7:7 par.; 16:32 = Mk. 14:27 par.; 18:11 = Mk. 14:36 par.; 20:23 = Mt. 18:18; yet these sayings are hardly ever found in the same context as in the Synoptics. The large part of the Johannine Jesus discourses, however, have no parallels in the Synoptics, and the language of the Johannine Jesus discourses is altogether different from that of the synoptic Jesus.

In view of these occasional parallels of John with the Synoptics, side by side with the extensive difference of the Johannine account, the question arises as to whether there is a literary connection between John and the Synoptics. For a long time the opinion prevailed that John knew and presupposed the Synoptics, but since Gardner-Smith's investigation (1938), the view that John knew none of the Synoptic Gospels and drew upon a completely independent tradition has won many supporters (e.g., Michaelis, Manson, Menoud, J. A. T. Robinson,

Sanders, Wilkens, Higgins). Still more widespread is the view that John knew none of our Synoptic Gospels, but he did know the tradition reproduced by these Gospels (e.g., Feine-Behm, Connick, Noack, Mendner, Feuillet in Robert-Feuillet, Klijn, Heard, F. C. Grant, *The Gospels* [see above, p. 34], Bultmann, Dodd, Hunter, Käsemann, Borgen, Haenchen, Grundmann; Buse and Temple advocate John's knowledge of one of Mark's sources). The arguments which are adduced against the supposition of a literary connection between John and the Synoptics are chiefly two: a) The number of the texts for which a dependence of John upon the Synoptics can be defended with any reason is astonishingly small, and by closer inspection even for these texts the number of divergencies is far greater than that of the agreements. b) The total plan of John diverges from that of the Synoptics and proves that John in no case could have learned from the Synoptics the tradition which was used by the Synoptics, and perhaps did not even know the same tradition. In addition to a) and b) arguments are brought forth stating that a Gospel originating from an eyewitness cannot be dependent upon "Vorlagen" which do not stem from eyewitnesses, and that the superiority of the Johannine account in historical particulars is explicable only if John reproduces a tradition which is independent of the Synoptics and is in part superior to them (e.g., Michaelis). We need not consider such argumentation, because its premises must first be secured, in order to permit any inferences to be drawn.

Since even the first two mentioned arguments are hardly sufficient to exclude the supposition of a knowledge or use of the Synoptics by John, some scholars summarily affirm a knowledge of the Synoptics by John (Höpfl-Gut, McNeile-Williams, Lightfoot, Maurer, Goodwin, Hirsch). Others maintain that John was dependent upon Mark and Luke (Sparks, Howard, Barrett, Streeter, *Four Gospels* [see above, p. 33], Teeple), or only upon Mark (Meinertz, R. M. Grant, HarvThR 1942, Lee) (only Sparks has expressly advocated a knowledge of Matthew). In favor of John's knowledge of Mark is the fact that several scenes and shorter historical notices in John are encountered in the same sequence as in Mark, and that in numerous of these places clear linguistic reminiscences are also found (see the lists in Barrett, Commentary, 34 ff.). Especially striking is the agreement of Jn. 6:7 with Mk. 6:37 διακοσίων δηναρίων ἄρτοι, of Jn. 5:8 with Mk. 2:11 ἆρον τὸν κράβατόν σου, of Jn. 12:3 with Mk. 14:3 (λίτραν) μύρου νάρδου πιστικῆς πολυτελοῦς or πολυτίμου (in all three cases only Mark, in addition to John, offers this wording). In a series of additional instances the contact of John with Mark is likewise unmistakable (Jn. 4:44 par. Mk. 6:4; Jn. 6:20 par. Mk. 6:50; Jn. 12:7 f. par. Mk. 14:7 f.; Jn. 19:17 par. Mk. 15:22; Jn. 19:29 par. Mk. 15:36), but in these cases Matthew is parallel with Mark, so that only a parallel with Mark *or* Matthew can be maintained (additional examples in Lee).

The literary connection of John with Luke is also indisputable. This statement is supported by the presence of the same names (Mary and Martha, Lazarus, Annas) and individual features (Jn. 13:2, 27 par. Lk. 22:3; Jn. 13:38 par. Lk. 22:34; Jn. 18:10 par. Lk. 22:30), but chiefly by the account of the anointing (Jn. 12:3 ff. par. Lk. 7:36 ff.). The Johannine account of the foolish action of Mary in anointing Jesus' feet and then drying them with her hair is explained in either of two ways: 1) John combined the narrative of the anointing of Jesus' head by a woman (Mk. 14:3 ff. par. Mt. 26:6 ff.) with the narrative of Lk. 7:36 ff., in which, according to the text of the great majority of the manuscripts, a sinful woman wets Jesus' feet with her tears, dries them with her hair, and anoints them. 2) According to the illuminating argument of K. Weiss, John had not yet read in Lk. 7:46 τοὺς πόδας μου (these last words are missing in the "Western" witnesses DW 079 b q), so that Luke originally spoke only of the wetting, drying, and kissing of Jesus' feet, and of the anointing of Jesus, i.e., his head (cf. also Jn. 11:2!), but John then misunderstood this account to the effect that the woman anointed Jesus' feet and then dried them (Jn. 12:3). In both cases, however, a knowledge of Luke by John is certainly to be supposed.

We cannot decide so clearly whether John also knew the Gospel of Matthew. The features which are factually parallel (Jn. 18:11 par. Mt. 26:52; Jn. 20:23 par. Mt. 18:18) strongly diverge from each other linguistically. The saying about slave and master (Jn. 15:20; cf. 13:16) not only has a clear parallel in Mt. 10:24 f. but also to the wider context (see Sparks), but this parallel is not close enough to be considered as evidence for a literary dependence (cf. Gardner-Smith, JThSt 1953; Dodd, NTSt 1955-56, 76 f.). The supposition that there is a literary relation between John and Matthew can appeal only to those texts cited above where we can just as well suppose John's dependence upon Mark as upon Matthew.

If, therefore, the question must remain undecided whether John knew Matthew, John's knowledge of Mark and Luke can be maintained with great probability. But as we have seen in connection with the question of the literary relationship of the Synoptics (see above, p. 60), we certainly must not picture this dependence as a direct revision of a written "Vorlage." Apparently the author had the Gospels of Mark and Luke in mind and used them from memory, so far as they appeared suitable to him (cf. Lee). But he used his sources in a manner entirely different from the way the Synoptics used theirs. On the one hand, he took up only a small part of the material known to him from the Synoptics and also used none of these earlier Gospels as the basis of his Gospel, but occasionally inserted some of the material known to him from the Synoptics into his presentation. On the other hand, John acted completely freely with the sources he took over, as Goodwin has shown by the manner in which John newly formed and combined from memory his quotations from the OT (also according to Noack, 84, the OT quotations are cited from memory). Consequently, the texts taken over from the Synoptics are thoroughly incorporated into John's account both linguistically and formally, and compose only *one* woof in the fabric of the entire Gospel. The hypothesis of John's literary connection with Mark and Luke thus explains the reminiscences of the Synoptics in John, but in no way makes understandable the origin and the literary character of John.

Our comparison of John with the Synoptics has shown not only a difference in material but also in chronological framework. If we examine this framework more closely, immediately a series of striking contradictions appears (cf. Wellhausen, Komm., 5 f.; Schweizer, 84 f.). In Jn. 6:1 it is presupposed that Jesus is in Galilee, though according to 5:1 he is in Jerusalem. 7:3 f., in spite of 2:23 and 5:1, seems to presuppose that Jesus has not yet worked in Jerusalem. 7:19-23 refers back to the attempt on Jesus' life, reported in 5:18, and lying at least half a year in the past. In 10:19-29 there arises a controversy over the event of 9:1 ff., which occurred at least a quarter of a year earlier. 10:33 alludes to a remark about Jesus made half a year previously. At the end of the farewell discourse is this concluding sentence: "Rise, let us go hence" (14:31). Yet the discourse in chaps. 15, 16 continues with the same themes.

To such contradictions in the course of the narrative may be added breaks in the train of thought of the discourses: 3:31 ff. is poorly suited to the mouth of the Baptist, but fits well in the mouth of Jesus in connection with 3:21. Following the conclusion of 12:36b-43, 12:44 ff. is a completely situationless discourse. Jesus' designation of himself as "the door" (10:7, 9) is ill-adapted to the shepherd's discourse (10:1-6, 11 ff.). Since the time of Tatian, who arranged ch. 6 before ch. 5, and since the time of the *Syrus Sinaiticus* (see below, p. 371), which rearranged the scene before Annas and Caiaphas (18:13-24; see the apparatus in Nestle to 18:13), these and similar difficulties have pointed to a hypothesis which has been very widespread since the beginning of the twentieth century (see above, pp. 141 f.): The text of John has not been transmitted to us in the sequence intended by the author, either because the author died before concluding his work or because the text subsequently fell into disorder through dislocation of sheets, or the like. Attempts have been made to show that the original, meaningful sequence can be restored by placing ch. 5 after ch. 6, or 10:19-29 before 10:1, etc. Recently, transpositions have been assumed to a lesser extent by Howard, Menoud, Schweizer, Jeremias, Grundmann, Guilding, and to a greater extent by Bacon, Bernard, Wikenhauser, Macgregor, Hirsch, Bultmann, Käsemann, Mendner, Merlier, Wilkens, Eckhardt. But there are weighty considerations against this supposition (see Michaelis, Goodspeed, Klijn, Dodd, Barrett, Lightfoot, W. G. Wilson, Parker, JBL 1956, Teeple, JBL 1962). Above all, it is very improbable paleographically. If it were simply a matter of displacement of sheets, then the contents of the displaced sheets must always have about the same extent. But the attempts to prove that (see Schweizer, 110 f.) founder on the fact that in no case do the intervals between the alleged dislocated sheets have the same extent or a multiple thereof (see W. G. Wilson and Parker). There are, to be sure, isolated examples from antiquity showing that such displacement of sheets took place (Schweizer, 109, note 161), but none of these examples involves a series of sections in the same work. The advocates of this view not only are forced to suppose that sections of varying length were dislocated, but they must also face the fact that there is no proof that drafts were generally written on separate sheets. But if we suppose that the sheets of the original manuscripts were promiscuously arranged, then it is strange that the sheets which allegedly have gotten into the wrong place still should always begin and end with complete sentences. It also strikes us as peculiar that the pupils, who themselves had these sheets in hand, were not able to restore these sheets to their proper order, whereas we are supposed to succeed in doing that, even though we do not possess the sheets. But if we suppose not only the dislocation of larger sections but of smaller textual units (according to Bultmann, e.g., the order of the section 6:27-59 was originally 6:27, 34 f., 30-33, 47-51a, 41-46), then, first of all, it is completely inexplicable in what form these small pieces of text were supposed to have lain before the redactor. Moreover, the supposition of secondary transpositions in many instances presupposes what must first of all be established as the correct presupposition, namely, that the author thought in terms of presenting a framework free of topographical and chronological contradictions and in terms of the logical progression of the discourses of Christ. Surely, we cannot always recognize a meaningful composition by the evangelist, and in these cases the exegete who rejects the supposition of secondary transpositions should "stop with the establishment of the aporiai [unsolved difficulties]" (Bultmann, NTSt 1954-55, 86). But on the whole it still holds true that "no one yet has demonstrated convincingly that the gospel has been disarranged" (Teeple, JBL 1962, 286), and therefore the hypothesis of a secondary transposition cannot solve the literary problem of John.

Now, to be sure, a few scholars have traced the secondary transposition of John back to the evangelist himself. In this case, the paleographical difficulty does not exist. According to Wilkens, the basic Gospel of the author was a "Gospel of Signs," which contained only narratives, and according to which Jesus, as in the Synoptics, made only one journey from Galilee to Jerusalem. The evangelist expanded this basic Gospel through discourses of Jesus, which he had formed before he inserted them into the Gospel, without thereby changing the draft of the basic Gospel. And, finally, through rearrangement of the entire Gospel and the incorporation of additional material, he transformed the Gospel into a Passion Gospel, without being able to finish it entirely. But if this history of the origin of John is conceivable, it is still neither provable nor even probable (cf. Barrett's criticism). Why should the author later have systematically disrupted his beautifully constructed basic Gospel and thus have created the difficulties whose origin the theory seeks to explain? The same objection also applies to Parker's theory (JBL 1956). Parker renounces transpositions, and supposes that the author later not only added ch. 21 to his own Gospel, but also 2:1-12 and chaps. 4 and 6, without checking to see whether these additions were suitable to their context.

Other scholars seek to solve the literary problem of John by supposing the later revision of the Gospel by a redactor, in part in connection with the conjecture of systematic transpositions. As a rule, the starting point for these hypotheses is the observation that additions are doubtless found in 7:53-8:11 and ch. 21. That the pericope of the adulteress (7:53-8:11) does not at all belong to the original traditon of John, is shown by its manuscript witnesses (it is lacking already in $\mathfrak{P}^{66}$ and $\mathfrak{P}^{75}$), its linguistic form, and its disturbing and fluctuating position. It was probably inserted here as an illustration to 8:15 (cf. the excurses by Zahn, Bauer, and Barrett, *ad loc.*, and on the great age of the account, J. Blinzler, NTSt 4, 1957-58, 32 ff., and E. Stauffer, "Neue Wege der Jesusforschung," *Gottes ist der Orient*, Festschr. O. Eissfeldt, 1959, 178 f.).

That ch. 21 represents a supplement is indisputable, for 20:30 f. is clearly the conclusion of the original Gospel. The only question is whether this supplement stems from the evangelist or from a strange hand. According to the manuscript tradition accessible to us, John never circulated without ch. 21. Yet Jn. 21 exhibits several striking contrasts to chaps. 1–20: in 21:2 the sons of Zebedee, who otherwise are missing, suddenly appear; the Christophany of 21:3 ff. takes place in Galilee, whereas ch. 20 is localized in Jerusalem; in 21:23 the death of the Beloved Disciple is probably presupposed, but in 21:24 he is attested as the author of John. Whereas the author could have said concerning himself, "This is the disciple who is bearing witness to these things, and who has written these things" (21:24a), 21:24b could not have originated with him, "and we know that his testimony is true." Likewise it would have been difficult for the indication of his death in 21:23 to have stemmed from him. Also 21:25, with its hyperbolic and aretalogical style, does not at all fit the Johannine style. Hence some scholars have attempted to join the supposition of the composition of 21:1-23 by the evangelist with the supposition of the unauthenticity of 21:24, 25 (or at least 21:25), so that 20:30 f. can be interpreted as the original conclusion of John, which at first stood after 21:23. This original conclusion was then shifted to its present position when pupils of the evangelist wished to add their testimony (21:24, 25) (Lagrange, Vaganay [regards also 21:24 as authentic], Menoud). But this solution of the difficulty is impossible. It cannot explain how 20:30 f. could have been inserted secondarily before 21:1. And if 20:30 f. had always stood where it now is, then 21:23 or 21:24a would not be a suitable conclusion of the document, and 21:24b would in no case be possible in the mouth of the author. Most writers who want to maintain that Jn. 21 is a supplement from the author of Jn. 1–20 do not suppose any transposition but simply interpret 21:24 f. as an addition by pupils of the author (Meinertz, Schäfer, Höpfl-Gut, Tenney, Howard, Jeremias, Ruckstuhl, Wilkens, Grundmann; Tasker regards only v. 25 as an addition). But the hypothesis that Jn. 21 stems from the author still confronts weighty difficulties. That vs. 24 f. must be separated in order to be able to maintain the same authorship for 1–20 and 21:1-23 is questionable, since on other grounds there exists no cause for that. In addition, there are the already mentioned factual difficulties and the improbability that the same author would have attached a supplement of such a nature without transferring or removing 20:30 f. But chiefly there exist linguistic difficulties. To be sure, Schweizer (108, note 158) and Boismard (RB 1947, 474 ff.) have pointed to linguistic agreements between ch. 21 and the remainder of John (e.g., ἀνθρακιά, ὀψάριον, μέντοι, 21:24 cf. with 5:32), but these parallels can be thoroughly understood as conscious or unconscious literary adaptations. Over against that there are numerous and important linguistic differences (see Boismard, *ibid.*, 484 ff.; Merlier, 151 ff.), not only words not otherwise found in John (e.g., ἰσχύειν), but also divergent linguistic usages (e.g., ἀπό in partitive sense; ἐπιστραφείς instead of στραφείς), which are hardly conceivable in the same author (the objections by Ruckstuhl, 143 ff., against these statements are simply evasions). It follows from all of these observations that Jn. 21, with the greatest probability, must be regarded as an appendix from a strange hand (e.g., Michaelis, Wikenhauser, Albertz, McNeile-Williams, Feine-Behm, Goodspeed, Bultmann, Barrett, Goguel, Dibelius, Lightfoot, Dodd, Hirsch, Strathmann, Käsemann, H. Braun, Eckhardt, Teeple; Schnackenburg and Grundmann conjecture use of the author's material; Jülicher, Schweizer, Feuillet in Robert-Feuillet regard a decision as impossible; the entire chapter stems from the author of 1–20 according to Bauer and Kragerud, on the one hand, and Schlatter and Cassian, on the other). We cannot make a conjecture about the purpose of this supplement before we consider the question of authorship.

If ch. 21 was attached by a strange hand, then it is natural to ask whether the hand of this redactor can be traced elsewhere. Since 19:35 speaks about the trustworthiness of the witness for the events connected with the death of Jesus in a manner similar to that in which 21:24 speaks about the author of the Gospel, and since 19:35 interrupts the connection, 19:35 has often been regarded as an insertion by the author of the supplement (Wikenhauser, Bacon, Goguel, Hirsch, Bultmann; Jeremias only for 21:24; 19:35). If a redactor interfered with the Gospel at all, then the question arises as to whether other verses may not also be the work of a redactor: remarks which disrupt the connection, or which assimilate to the Synoptics (e.g., 1:22-24, 27, 32; 3:24; 4:2; 11:2; 16:5b; 18:9, 13b, 14, 24, 32), or also texts which in respect to content are in tension with Johannine teaching (the futuristic eschatological sayings [5: 28 f.; 6:39 f., 44b, 54; 12:48]; or the references to baptism and Lord's Supper [3:5; ὕδατος καὶ]; 6:51b-58; 19:34b). In favor of this possibility linguistic arguments can partly also be adduced (thus in various ways, Bacon, Jeremias, Bultmann, Käsemann, Temple, JBL 1961, Teeple, JBL 1962). Others go further and seek to reconstruct a "Grundschrift," which a redactor extensively expanded by means of synoptic material and other additions (Wellhausen, Schwartz, Hirsch, Merlier, Mendner, Temple, JBL 1961). Preisker reconstructs an original eschatological Gospel. According to Eckhardt, Ignatius revised a Johannine draft, and then this writing was expanded twice. Boismard (RB 1962) concludes from the contradictions in Jn. 4:46 ff. and 20:24 ff., and from the reminiscences of Luke, that Luke combined the Johannine material into one account and used particular scenes.

It is thoroughly possible that interpolations were inserted into the text of the Gospel before the manuscript was written to which our entire manuscript tradition goes back (similarly as 5:4 was later inserted and made its way into the manuscript tradition). And that the text reads smoothly after the removal of the pieces of text which are felt to be disruptive, is self-evident. If, therefore, there are no fundamental considerations against the hypothesis of isolated redactional additions, then it is still very questionable whether awkwardnesses in the presentation cannot just as well go back to the evangelist as to a redactor. That the futuristic, eschatological texts mentioned above were interpolated, is very improbable, in view of the eschatological teaching of the Gospel as a whole, for the futuristic eschatology is also found in 3:5; 10:9; 12:32; 14:3; 17:24; and is theologically indispensable (cf. W. G. Kümmel, *Die Eschatologie der Evv.*, 1936, 22 ff.; Ruckstuhl, 159 ff.; Schulz, *Menschensohn*, 109 ff., 159 ff.; L. van Hartingsveld, *Die Eschatologie des Joh.*, 1962, 194 , 200 ff. On Boismard's supposition of two layers of Johannine eschatology [RB 1961], see below, pp. 153 f.). As for the section referring to the Lord's Supper (6:51*b*-58), which is frequently characterized as a sacramental insertion (see those cited in Schultz, *Menschensohn*, 115 f.; also G. Bornkamm, "Die eucharistische Rede im Joh.," ZNW 47, 1956, 161 ff.; E. Lohse, "Wort und Sakrament im Joh.," NTSt 7, 1960-61, 117 ff.), it is, linguistically speaking, thoroughly Johannine (cf. Ruckstuhl, 169 ff., 220 ff.). This section is contestable on the basis of content only if one is already convinced, upon the basis of a spiritualizing or existential exegesis of John, that John can have no sacramental interests. Such an exegesis, however, has no solid foundation. If there are, therefore, good reasons for regarding 6:51*b*-58 as an original part of John (see lately P. Borgen, "The Unity of Discourse in John 6," ZNW 50, 1959, 277 f.; H. Schürmann, "Joh. 6:51*c*, ein Schlüssel zur grossen joh. Brotrede," BZ, N.F. 2, 1958, 245 ff.), then there exists no reason at all to explain the words ὕδατος καί (3:5) and 19:34*b* as interpolations because they are thought to refer to baptism and the Lord's Supper. Thus the hypothesis that a redactor first gave to John its present order also cannot be made more probable by an appeal to a series of redactional additions, and vice versa.

The more far-reaching hypotheses of Wellhausen, Schwarz, and Hirsch, according to which John arose through extensive expansion of a "Grundschrift," can only be designated as arbitrary and undemonstrable. The "aporiai," which Mendner and Merlier have recently attempted to point out, are aporiai only if a completely unsuitable standard of logic and consistency of narration is applied to the text. And even if the Nicodemus discourse, which is now in Jn. 3, really did stand originally between 7:45-52*a* and 8:13 f., and included only 3:2, 3*a*, 7*b*, 9 f., 12*b*, 13*a*, 31*a*, 32*a*, 33, 34*a*, 35 (Mendner, JBL 1958), then Streeter's objection to older source theories will serve as a warning to the literary critic against the construction of such theories: "If the sources have undergone anything like the amount of amplification, excision, rearrangement, and adaptation which the theory postulates, then the critic's pretence that he can unravel the process is grotesque. As well hope to start with a string of sausages and reconstruct the pig" (*Gospels* [see above, p. 33], 377). According to Eckhardt's redaction hypothesis, Ignatius, before the destruction of Jerusalem, delivered the unfinished exemplar of the Gospel from Jerusalem to Antioch and revised it, etc. This many-staged hypothesis allows itself considerably more unverifiable conjectures than can be permitted in the context of serious historical investigation. Finally, Boismard's conjecture of a Lukan revision of John does rest upon observations which are to be taken seriously. But, in the first place, Boismard applies an altogether too strict standard of consistency to the Johannine account and can, e.g., not make it evident that an account in 4:46*b*, 47, 50 ever existed independently; and, in the second place, he overlooks the fact that the author very probably knew the Gospel of Luke, so that linguistic and factual parallels can better be made understandable upon that basis.

Thus without needing to speak yet of the "unity" of John, we can say that "neither displacement theories nor redaction theories are needed to explain the present state of the gospel" (Barrett, Comm., 20). Rather, if we are not able to explain the difficulties on the basis of a later alteration of Jn. 1–20, then at once the question arises all the more urgently about the sources and the aim of the Gospel. For the view that the author as eyewitness simply drew upon his memory and, therefore, could not have used any sources (Michaelis; Edwards thinks of the author's own notes!), is, in view of the difficulties of his account, little convincing. Indeed, it is to be denied because John, as we have seen, knew, and occasionally used, at least Mark and Luke. A knowledge of the collection of Pauline epistles (as Hirsch, Goodspeed, R. M. Grant, JBL 1950, maintain), is, on the other hand, unprovable (Feine-Behm). The OT is quoted directly relatively seldom, and then from memory in a very free way (Goodwin) (that an Exodus typology lies at the basis of John [H. Sahlin, *Zur Typologie des Joh.*, Uppsala Universitets Aarsskrift 1950, 4], is completely unproved). Yet the greatest part of the material of John is taken over neither from the OT nor from the Synoptics. These observations raise the question whether John used sources for this material. Even though Broome claims to have discovered seven sources, his proof is hardly convincing (cf. Ruckstuhl, 17 ff.). Macgregor and Morton have attempted to establish a second source by means of statistical calculations based upon Morton's conception of average sentence length and standard-sized codices. The author joined this second source to his Gospel in alternating blocks. This view runs aground not only on paleographic errors and impossibilities, but also on the fact that the character of this second source and the meaning of the combination of both sources cannot be made clear (see Haenchen, ThLZ 1962, 487 ff.). On the other hand, Bultmann's source theory has rightly been much discussed (see RGG [3] III, 842 f.). He proceeds from the observation that the enumeration of the σημεῖα in 2:11 and 4:54 cannot have originated with the evangelist, since the evangelist ascribes to Jesus a larger number of σημεῖα (2:23; 4:45). Although 20:30 ("Now Jesus did many other signs in the presence of the disciples") is hardly suitable as a conclusion of John, it is probably fitting as the ending of a "σημεῖα-source" (cf. also 12:37). From stylistic observations, which he had first made in I John (see below, p. 308), Bultmann then inferred an originally Gnostic source of "revelation discourses," which the evangelist modified, glossed, and placed at the basis of his Jesus discourses. As the third source Bultmann conjectured a collection of passion and resurrection narratives, whose existence can be recognized by redactional additions of the evangelist (e.g., 18:13*b*, 14, 24) (cf. the summary of the Bultmannian sources in Ruckstuhl, 25, 31 f.). The supposition of a miracle source found agreement with Käsemann (VuF 1946-47, 186) and

Haenchen (ThRdsch 1955, 303), who would like to think of the Gospel of the evangelist's home church. Becker, critically following Bultmann, has sought to reconstruct the source of "revelation discourses" against the background of Gnostic parallels, whereas Käsemann (*ibid.*, 187 f.) and Haenchen (*ibid.*, 306 f.) critically stand over against the supposition of such a source. A special written source for the Johannine passion narrative had already been conjectured by others (M. Dibelius, *Die atl. Motive in der Leidensgeschichte des Petrus- und des Johannes-Evangeliums*, Beih. ZAW 33, Festschr. W. Baudissin, 1918, 125 ff. = *Botschaft und Geschichte* I, 1953, 221 ff.; Goguel, *Intr.* II, 436 ff.; V. Taylor, *The Formation of the Gospel Tradition*, 1933, 53 f.; P. Winter, "On the Trial of Jesus," *Studia Judaica* I, 1961, 33 ff., leaves undecided whether the evangelist used and expanded a written passion narrative, or whether his presentation was expanded by an interpolator).

Attempts have been made to test and to refute the possibility and the correctness of this and earlier source theories by seeking to establish the linguistic and stylistic peculiarities of John and then by showing that they can be observed to transverse all supposed sources. From these studies the conclusion has been drawn with more or less certainty that the supposition of written sources in John contradicts these linguistic and stylistic findings (Schweizer, 87 ff.; Jeremias, 35 ff.; Menoud, *L'évangile*, 15 f.; Ruckstuhl, 190 ff.; a list of these "Johannine characteristics" in F.-M. Braun, *Jean*, 401 ff.). Others, however, have objected to this method because the particular linguistic characteristics are of very different value and very probably could have been inserted by the evangelist as he took up the pieces of sources. Thus by means of these linguistic observations nothing decisive against this or that source hypothesis is established (Hirsch, ZNW, 1950-51, 134 ff.; Haenchen, ThRdsch 1955, 307 ff.; cf. the discussion of principles by Schulz, *Menschensohn*, 51 ff., and Teeple, JBL 1962). These investigations have doubtless shown that the linguistic peculiarities of John are distributed over the entire Gospel, and that, therefore, the identification of connected sources upon the basis of linguistic and stylistic arguments is hardly possible. On the other hand, these studies have also shown that in individual pericopes the characteristics designated as Johannine are so obviously lacking that we must suppose that here traditions have been taken up (Schweizer, 100; Schulz, *loc. cit.*, 56 f.; above all, 2:1-10, 13-19; 4:46-53; 12:1-8, 12-15). But that in no wise leads to a written "signs source" lying before the evangelist. And also with respect to the passion narratives the hints of a special tradition are hardly sufficient to establish a connected written "Vorlage" in addition to the knowledge of Mark and Luke (see Barrett, Comm., 18).

But the most difficult question concerns the origin of the Johannine discourses. Two decisive objections speak against the hypothesis of a "revelation source." a) Käsemann (VuF 1946-47, 187) has pointed out that behind the prologue of John a strictly constructed hymn can be recognized, to which nothing corresponding can be found in all the remainder of John, with the result that stylistic analysis can have no certain foothold in the rest of John. b) The stylistic features employed by Bultmann are not plain enough to distinguish between source and revision (Noack, 18 ff.), especially since Bultmann repeatedly finds it necessary to ascribe to the evangelist an influence on the source. Against Becker's reconstruction of the source we must object that the arguments adduced from time to time in favor of this reconstruction often point to a contradictory conclusion, and that "*if* John used a source, and *if* he reshaped it as radically as Becker thinks he did, that source is now irrecoverable" (Barrett, ThLZ 1957, 912). Hence the view that the Johannine discourses are taken from a written source is not only unproved but is also improbable because precisely in this extensive part of the Gospel the author himself seems to speak. He uses his own language in shaping the discourses in the form of dialogues and in the interpretation of the narratives. But if, according to every appearance, neither the narratives nor the discourse material stems from a written source, then the other contention often advanced is most questionable, namely, that there lie at the basis of John two different layers of tradition, narratives and discourses (Käsemann, VuF 1946-47, 185; Grundmann, 14 f.; Wilkens; other advocates of this view in Schweizer, 85, note 22), since often in John narratives form the starting point for discourse compositions (cf. against this theory Barrett, Comm., 17; Teeple, JBL 1962, 280 f.).

If thus it is improbable that the evangelist used any connected written sources (apart from the Synoptics), that does not at all mean that he was dependent upon no kind of tradition. Already the difficulties within the course of the narrative and of the structure of the discourses force us, if they are not the consequence of later interference with the original Gospel, to suppose that the author used strange traditions or those of his own. We have already seen that linguistic studies prove that separate pieces of narrative were taken over. That doubtless also holds true for the prologue of the Gospel. The extensive recent discussion about the origin and the original form of Jn. 1:1-18 is largely unanimous about the view that a "λόγος-hymn" composed in strophes was expanded by the evangelist and shaped into the prologue of the Gospel. In favor of this theory are not only the numerous words not found elsewhere in the Gospel for themes which are major in the Gospel (χάρις, πλήρωμα, κόλπος, ἐξηγέομαι; see Teeple, JBL 1962, 284), but also the prose interpolations which express characteristic thoughts of the evangelist (e.g., 1:6-8, 13, 15, 17). In other respects opinions vary widely. Is the revised hymn of Christian origin (the view which will probably yet prove to be right; see especially E. Käsemann, "Aufbau und Anliegen des joh. Prologs," *Libertas Christiana*, Festschr. F. Delekat, 1957, 75 ff.; R. Schnackenburg, "Logoshymnus und joh. Prolog," BZ, N.F. 1, 1957, 69 ff.) or a Baptist hymn (so Bultmann, Komm.; Schulz, *Reden*, 7 ff., here also the history of criticism)? Which verses are original and which are additions? Here it becomes evident in an exemplary fashion that we are able to recognize with great probability large pieces of narrative and discourse material of John as taken over from the oral tradition (e.g., Noack, 108, 124, 136), but that we can hardly determine the exact extent and the exact form of the tradition which has been taken up.

The solution advocated by Boismard (RB 1961) that the author of John combined various drafts of his own, which, e.g., can be distinguished through a development from a traditional futuristic eschatology to a present eschatology, is noteworthy, even if the difficulty is not thereby solved as to why the author did not harmonize the differing texts. The fact that the insight into the dependence of John upon oral tradition certainly does not mean that "the beginnings of the Johannine tradition are just as old as those of the Synoptic" (Gyllenberg, 146), will come to light when we ask about the comparative-religion background of this tradition.

But before that we must once more take up the question of how we can explain the presence in John of numerous contradictions and abrupt shifts in thought. We shall mention here two theses which seek to solve this problem without the supposition of later tampering with the Gospel. According to the one view, the inconcinnities are explained on the grounds that in John we have to do with the work of an old man (Hoffmann, Michaelis, Albertz, Strathmann, Grundmann). It is, however, very questionable whether anyone would have hit upon this view upon the basis of the Gospel itself, if the tradition of the early church did not exist that the apostle John wrote this Gospel at a great age. But this tradition is late (see below, pp. 168 ff.), and the psychology of old age can hardly explain topographical and chronological inconsistencies. To be taken more seriously is the other view that the author left his work uncompleted when he died (Feine-Behm, Strathmann, Schnackenburg, LThK V, 1101, F.-M. Braun, *Jean*, 24 f., Wilkens; questioningly, Käsemann, NGG 1957, 147). Methodologically, there is no objection against this proposal, though we cannot quite understand why the editor did not remove the all too obvious difficulties (6:1!). If this conjecture remains as a possibility, then we may ask whether the intention of the author does not offer another possibility of explanation.

4. The Relation of the Gospel of John to Contemporary Religious Thought

The most striking difference between the discourses of the Johannine Jesus and the Jesus of the Synoptics is the completely different language which Jesus speaks in John. We mean language, not so much in a grammatical and stylistic sense, as the world of concepts. To be sure, the language of John in the narrower sense presents a problem. For in view of the strongly Semitic character of the language of John a translation of John out of the Aramaic has often been conjectured (Burney, Torrey, de Zwaan, Eckhardt; Boismard, RechB III, 41 ff., gives fanciful examples of Aramaisms which are supposed to be found in manuscript variants), or occasionally a translation has been proposed only in respect to a source used in the Gospel (Manson, Bultmann, RGG III, 844, Hunter; cf. also Feuillet in Robert-Feuillet, 659). But Bonsirven has pointed out numerous features in John's Greek which cannot be explained by a translation from the Aramaic. Colwell has shown the relationship of the language of John to that of Epictetus, and Kilpatrick the close proximity to the language of the LXX. Barrett has demonstrated that we do not need to suppose any faulty translations. The supposition of a translation of John out of the Aramaic is, therefore, to be rejected. Yet we must grant that the author either thinks in Aramaic, but writes in Greek (Dodd, Bultmann, Barrett), or at least lives in a bilingual environment.

The actual historical problem, however, is the origin of the conceptual world in which, in John, the evangelist himself, as well as Jesus, the Baptist, and the Jews speak. This language is characterized by the opposites of light and darkness, falsehood and truth, above and below, ὁ πατήρ as related to ὁ υἱός, the numerous ἐγώ εἰμι-sayings of Jesus, salvation concepts like water of life, bread of life, and light of the world. This Johannine language describes Jesus as "him whom the Father has sent," who has ascended into heaven, etc., and in all these ways is differentiated from the Palestinian-Jewish conceptual world of the synoptic Jesus. In spite of that, attempts have repeatedly been made to understand John exclusively against the background of the OT and of rabbinic Judaism (Schlatter, Büchsel [see WGK, NT, 500 ff.], Hoskyns, F.-M. Braun, RB 1955). But these attempts fail to see that the Johannine Christology, with its myth of the Son who returns to the Father, can as little have its roots in Pharisaic Judaism as can the dualistic language. Moreover, any kind of familiarity with the views of the rabbis nowhere is evident in John (against Dodd, Interpretation, 75 ff.; correct: Haenchen, ThRdsch 1955, 322 f., Schulz, Reden, 151 f.). Just as little can the language of John be explained against the background of the Greeks or of philosophical Hellenism. The earlier favorite view that the λόγος-concept of the prologue and the Johannine "God mysticism" have their nearest parallels in Philo (earlier views in Schmid, 14 ff.) is today chiefly advocated by Dodd (John "certainly presupposes a range of ideas having a remarkable resemblance to those of Hellenistic Judaism, as represented by Philo." Interpretation, 73; cf. also Goodspeed, 308 (see p. 28): "In fact, the gospel [of John] may be said to be intensely Greek from Prologue to Epilogue in every fiber of both thought and language"; Heard, Klijn). It is noteworthy that Dodd also would like to suppose a decided relationship of John to the Hermetic writings (see H. Schwabl, LTHK V, 1960, 257 f.; Dörrie, RGG [3] III, 1959, 265). For the indubitable similarity of John to many conceptions of this late Hellenistic, philosophical, mystical religiousness (cf. the parallels in Dodd, Interpretation, 34 f., 50 f., and F.-M. Braun, Revue Thomiste 1955, 259 ff., 263 ff., 275 ff.), precisely like his parallels with Philo, is not based upon John's connection with the Hellenistic interpretation of the world and his attempt to make the Christian message acceptable to the educated Greek ("John sets forth a synthesis of Jewish and Greek thought," Barrett, Comm., 32). On the contrary, fundamental concepts of the Hermetica are missing in John (see Kilpatrick, 40), and the glittering and finally impersonal λόγος-concept of Philo cannot explain the personal λόγος of John. That John indeed shows a striking relationship to Philo and the Hermetica rests rather upon the fact that the Hellenistic Jew, as well as the Gentile mystic, took up concepts from that form of religion in late antiquity which also influenced John, namely, Gnosticism (see Bultmann, NTSt 1954-55, 78 f.).

Since the conceptual world of John can be explained neither from orthodox Palestinian Judaism nor from Hellenistic philosophy and mysticism, scholarship in recent decades has more and more drawn upon two other phenomena in order to make intelligible the origin of the Johannine conceptual world, Gentile Gnosticism, especially that of the Mandaeans, and heterodox Judaism, chiefly that in the writings of the Qumran community. Already J. D. Michaelis noted in John a polemic "against disciples of John, Mandaeans," i.e., he observed a polemic connection with non-Christian Gnosticism (see above, p. 27; II, [4]1788, 1140). In 1903 W. Wrede (see WGK, NT, 384 f.) sketched hastily the conjecture "that views conditioned by Gnosticism lie at the basis of the Gospel." But the question of a Gnostic background of John first became of pressing importance in 1925 when R. Bultmann drew upon the writings of the Mandaeans (which in the meantime had been made accessible through translation by Lidzbarski) and further upon the half-Jewish, half-Christian, Gnostic "Odes of Solomon" and Manichean texts, in order to reconstruct the Gnostic myth used by John. Also W. Bauer in his commentary (Hdb., [2]1925) made extensive use of Mandaean texts for the clarification of John. But against this usage of the Mandaean texts there arose a strong opposition. Especially H. Lietzmann (*Beitrag zur Mandäerfrage*, 1930) made an impact through his contention that the Mandaeans were a religious community which first arose in the Byzantine-Arabic period in the region of the Euphrates, so that primitive Christianity could not have had any contact with it (see on this entire discussion, WGK, NT, 449 ff.). Whereas most scholars rejected this supposition of the connection of John with an Oriental Gnosticism, especially as understood by the Mandaeans, Odeberg (1929), Bauer (Hdb., [3]1933), and Bultmann (Meyer II [10], 1941) made the thesis of a Gnostic background for John the basis of their commentaries. Schweizer and Becker pointed out in detail the nearness of the Johannine conceptual world to Oriental Gnosticism. At that time the question was already raised upon the basis of later Jewish mystical texts whether already at the time of primitive Christianity there was not a Jewish Gnosticism which was especially related to Mandaean conceptual forms, and which we are to suppose was the spiritual foundation for the Johannine conceptual world (Odeberg, Komm., 215 f.; H. Schlier, "Zur Mandäerfrage," ThRdsch, N.F. 5, 1933, 32; Fischel).

The publication since 1948 of the writings of the community at Qumran created a new situation. Already upon the basis of the first publications of fragments K. G. Kuhn maintained: "In these new texts we get to lay hold upon the native soil of John, and this native soil is . . . a Palestinian-Jewish sectarian piety of Gnostic structure" ("Die in Palästina gefundenen hebr. Texte und das NT," ZThK 47, 1950, 210). Since then the comparison of the extensive published texts with John has convinced many scholars that in some way the author of John was influenced by the concepts of the Qumran community (see K. G. Kuhn [lately in 1962], F.-M. Braun, RB 1955, Mowry, Albright, Boismard, BdJ, Schnackenburg, LThK V, J. A. T. Robinson, StEv, Hunter, Schulz, *Reden*, 161, Stauffer, Smith, Grundmann, O. Cullmann, "The Significance of the Qumran Texts for Research Into the Beginnings of Christianity," in *The Scrolls and the NT*, edited by K. Stendahl, 1957, 25 ff., etc. Brown and Higgins think of an indirect connection). Some have also thought it possible to clarify this connection more precisely: The evangelist was a pupil of John the Baptist, and the Baptist grew up in the Qumran community, or in any case belonged to it for a while (F.-M. Braun, Brown, Stauffer, J. A. T. Robinson). As an alternative, the possibility has been discussed that the evangelist, who wrote in Ephesus, could have come into contact with the thought-world of Qumran through the Baptist's disciples in Ephesus (Acts 19:1 ff.) or through Qumran people who after the year 70 came to Ephesus with their writings (Brown, F.-M. Braun). Cullmann seeks to show that the "Hellenists" in Acts 6:1; 9:29 are identical with the ἄλλοι, who, according to Jn. 4:38, began the Samaritan mission, and that the opposition to the temple which characterizes both groups also characterizes John. He would like to conclude from these observations that the author of John, like the "Hellenists," stemmed from a syncretistic Judaism standing near to Qumran.

These attempts to make understandable a supposed influence upon John by the thought-world of Qumran are, to be sure, hardly tenable. That the evangelist was a pupil of John the Baptist proves true only under the supposition that the evangelist is identical with the "Beloved Disciple," and that the Beloved Disciple in turn is identical with one of the two brothers whom we find presupposed in 1:40, all of which is extremely questionable (see below, pp. 165 ff.). Moreover, no one has made it probable that John the Baptist was ever a follower or a disciple at Qumran (cf. H. Braun, ThRdsch 1962, 202 f., 209 f.). Especially the alleged influence of Qumran upon the evangelist in Ephesus is completely a fabrication. Cullmann's suggestion that the ἄλλοι mentioned in Jn. 4:38 were missionaries to Samaria and were identical with the "Hellenists" is an unprovable conjecture, particularly since the opposition against the temple in Jerusalem in Jn. 4 and in Qumran has a completely different character (see H. Braun, *ibid.*, 212, 214).

But even if the attempts to trace back historically the connection of John with the thought-world of Qumran are not tenable, the question remains whether this connection is not forced upon us by virtue of the similar conceptions of John and the Scrolls. We are referred to the ethical dualism, joined with the conception of creation, to the predestinarian distinction between "the sons of light'" and those who "remain in darkness," between men who "are of the truth" and those who "are of your father the devil," and to concepts like "to bear witness to truth," "light of life," etc. We cannot deny that these are striking parallels, and that occasionally a Johannine expression is attested elsewhere only in Qumran (μαρτυρεῖν τῇ ἀληθείᾳ Jn. 5:33, compared with "witnesses of the truth" 1 QS 8, 6; cf. H. Braun, *ibid.*, 214 f.). But in answer to that, we observe, on the one hand, that the parallels of the Qumran texts to John are found in the majority of cases also in other late Jewish writings, above all in the apocalypses (see the evidence in Teeple, NovT 1960, 18 ff., and H. Braun), and, on the other hand, that the context of thought of the dualism in Qumran is completely different from that in John: In Qumran it describes the relation to the radically interpreted cultic law and to the organized group of the "unity" (jáchad); in John, the decision according to faith for the "Sent One" and the "being at one," "as Christ and the Father are one" (Jn. 17:22). The conception of the "new covenant," which is characteristic of Qumran, is missing from John. Conversely, the figure of a divine redeemer plays no role at all in Qumran (the messianic expectation is purely futuristic). But above all, the following have no point of contact at all in Qumran: the mythological Christology of John and, connected with that, the Gnosticized discourses of John about, e.g., the "coming from the Father," the "being born again from above," and the ἐγώ εἰμι-predicates. We must conclude, therefore, that John and the community at Qumran presuppose a common background, but that the thought-world of Qumran cannot be the native soil of the Johannine thought-forms (so Bultmann, Baumbach, Teeple, NovT 1960, H. Braun).

Because in the writings of the Mandaeans we find not only numerous parallels to the dualistic language of John, but also because the Mandaean myth of the heavenly Revealer shows clear parallels to the Johannine conception of the One sent from heaven, Bultmann, Bauer, and others have drawn extensively upon Mandaean mythological Gnosticism as a help in reconstructing the spiritual background of John. They presuppose that the Mandaean religion, which we first learn to know in its writings from the seventh and eighth centuries in the region of the Euphrates, goes back in its early stages to the time of late Hellenism and the Syrian Occident. In support of this presupposition they adduce, in addition to linguistic and historical reasons, the relationship of the "Odes of Solomon" (preserved in Syriac manuscripts) with the Johannine and Mandaean conceptual world. On the other hand, H. Lietzmann and many others have denied the correctness of this argumentation (on the state of the discussion at that time see, on the one hand, H. Schlier, "Zur Mandäerfrage," ThRdsch, N.F. 5, 1933, 1 ff., 69 ff., and Schweizer, 46 ff.; and, on the other hand, against a western origin of the Mandaean religion, F. Rosenthal, *Aramaistische Forschung* [see above, p. 45], 224 ff.). But the investigation since about 1940, based upon texts newly published by Lady Drower and upon work undertaken in separating the layers within the Mandaean texts, in increasing degree has agreed upon the fact that the Mandaean religion, in any case in its roots, belongs to the chronological and spatial proximity of primitive Christianity, and either originated directly from a Gnosticized Judaism, or at least appeared very early in a polemical exchange with a syncretistic Judaism: "In its fundamental features the Mandaean religion stands in the circle of Judaized (western) Gnosticism, which made itself known in the eastern regions bordering the Syrian-Palestinian cultural sphere in the form of baptismal sects" (K. Rudolph, *Die Mandäer. I. Prolegomena: Das Mandäerproblem*, FRLANT 74, 1960, 175. Besides this comprehensive work (bibl.!), there are the following surveys: W. Baumgartner, "Der heutige Stand der Mandäerfrage," ThZ 6, 1950, 401 ff.; *idem*, "Zur Mandäerfrage," *Hebrew Union College Annual* 23, 1950-51, 41 ff.; Haenchen, ThRdsch 1955, 314 ff.; R. Macuch, "Alter und Heimat des Mandäismus nach neuerschlossenen Quellen," ThLZ 82, 1957, 401 ff.; Schulz, *Reden*, 170 ff.; *idem*, "Die Bedeutung neuer Gnosisfunde für die ntl. Wissenschaft," ThRdsch, N.F. 26, 1960, 301 ff.; C. Colpe, art. "Mandäer," RGG [3] IV, 1960, 709 ff.; J. Schmid, art. "Mandäismus," LThK VI, 1961, 1343 ff.; G. Widengren, "Die Mandäer," *Handbuch der Orientalistik* I, 8, 1961, 83 ff.). With these insights it is confirmed that John could not have been influenced by the Mandaean texts which have been preserved, indeed, that a direct connection of John with Mandaean or primitive Mandaean circles is out of the question. Yet the similarity of the Johannine and the Mandaean conceptions, repeatedly observed (Rudolph, Widengren), points to the conclusion that the Mandaean texts are late and deformed witnesses for a Jewish Gnosticism which took form on the edge of Judaism, and which is to be accepted as the spiritual background of John.

This problem of a pre-Christian Gnosticism and of a Gnosticizing Judaism is still completely in flux. Yet two facts can hardly be denied: a) The "Odes of Solomon" (translation by W. Bauer, "Die Oden Salomos," Kleine Texte 64, 1933 in Hennecke-Schneemelcher, NT Apocrypha, II), which originated in the second century, are doubtless documents of a Christian Gnosticism, but a Gnosticism whose dualism was softened through Jewish influence (conception of creation, eschatology). The original language of these poems, which have been transmitted in Syriac (in part, also Coptic; one ode in Greek), has not been established, yet there is something to be said for Syriac as the original language (see A. Adam, "Die ursprüngliche Sprache der Salomo-Oden," ZNW 52, 1961, 141 ff.; cf. in general S. Schulz, art. "Salomo-Oden," RGG [3] V, 1961, 1339 ff.; J. Schmid, art. "Oden Salomos," LThK VII, 1962, 1094 f.). In any case, there exist strong similarities between the "Odes of Solomon," John, and Ignatius. A dependence of the "Odes of Solomon" upon John (Schmid, *op. cit.*) is extremely improbable. For the "Odes of Solomon," whose Gnostic Christianity doubtless results from a touching up of the original, presuppose a Gnosticism influenced by Judaism, which is related as well with John as with the writings of the Mandaeans (see R. M. Grant, JBL 1944). b) There doubtless was a Jewish Gnosticism late in the second century which speculated over divine figures of revelation, the throne of Yahweh, journeys to heaven, etc. Evidence of this Jewish Gnosticism is found in certain Talmudic traditions, the Apocalypse of Abraham, and particular components of the earlier apocalyptic (e.g., Apocalypse of Enoch, 14). But we are not able to know about these currents with detailed precision (cf. Fischel; P. Winter, ThLZ 1955, 144 ff.; Wikenhauser, *Introd.*, 310 ff.; G. Scholem, *Major Trends in Jewish Mysticism*, 1941, pp. 73 ff.; Quispel would prefer to speak of a "Jewish pre-Gnosticism," and similarly Higgins, 17).

These two observations permit us to suppose with certainty that Gnosticism as a dualistic-mythological religion of redemption through revelation and knowledge was pre-Christian. And observations based upon the opponents of Paul in Corinth and Colossae, upon the false teachers of Jude and I John, and likewise upon the earliest witnesses of Christian Gnosticism and the prehistory of the Mandaean religion also point in the same direction (see below, §§17:3; 21:3, 4; 29:2; 31:3; cf. W. Foerster, "Das Wesen der Gnosis," *Die Welt als Geschichte*

14, 1954, 100 ff.; R. Schnackenburg, in "Kerygma und Mythos" V, 1955, 89; E. Haenchen, art. "Gnosis und NT," RGG ³ II, 1958, 1652 ff.; S. Schulz, "Die Bedeutung neuer Gnosisfunde für die ntl. Wissenschaft," ThRdsch, N.F. 26, 1960, 209 ff., 301 ff., especially 329 ff.; Barrett, Piper-Festschr.—The existence of a pre-Christian Gnosticism has recently been denied by C. Colpe, art. "Gnosis, Religionsgeschichtlich," RGG ³ II, 1958, 1648 ff.; J. Munck, "The NT and Gnosticism," *Current Issues in NT Interpretation*, Festschr. O. Piper, 1962, 224 ff.; K. G. Kuhn, 121 f.).

From all of these considerations, there follows undoubtedly the probability that the background of the Johannine thought-world was a form of Jewish Gnosticism, which bore a stronger mythological character than the thought-world of the Qumran community, and which, above all, knew the myth characteristic of John, that of the descending and ascending envoy (thus besides Bultmann: Käsemann, VuF 1946-47; R. M. Grant, JBL 1950, 321 f.; F. C. Grant, *The Gospels*, 1957, 159, 58 f.; Haenchen, ThRdsch 1955, 324 ff.; Schulz, *Reden*, 123, 186; J. A. T. Robinson, NTSt 1959-60, 130; H. Braun, ThRdsch 1962, 219; with reservations, Schnackenburg, LThK V, 1102). As confirmation of this contention is the observation that the Johannine Christological self-predications with ἐγώ εἰμι nowhere have such close parallels as in Mandaean texts (Schweizer, Schulz, *Reden*, 119 ff.). There is also the proof of the stylistic closeness of the Johannine to the Gnostic revelation discourses (see above all Becker, 14 ff.). In addition, two other statements serve to confirm this view. a) F.-M. Braun (Cullmann-Festschr.) has again pointed out that the prologue of John and the Johannine conception of Jesus' revelation of the divine mysteries to his own is reminiscent in many respects of conceptions and formulations of the Jewish wisdom literature. Already Bultmann had called special attention to this relationship and indicated that these sayings about wisdom belong within the conceptual range of the descending Revealer which comes to expression with special clarity in Gnostic contexts ("Der religionsgeschichtliche Hintergrund des Prologs zum Joh.," *Eucharisterion* II, Festschr. H. Gunkel, FRLANT, N.F., 19, 2, 1923, 3 ff.). The parallels of John with wisdom literature in these conceptions, therefore, prove that John could find a part of the conceptions presupposed for Jewish Gnosticism already in the wisdom literature influenced by Hellenism, whereas neither the ethical dualism nor the combining of preexistence Christology with the myth of the descending Revealer can be explained from wisdom literature alone. b) Barrett (Piper-Festschr.) has compared John with one of the Gnostic writings which belongs to the find of Gnostic manuscripts in the Coptic language from Nag Hamadi, the "Gospel of Truth" (on this manuscript discovery, to which belongs also the Gospel of Thomas mentioned above, pp. 57 f., cf. the report by S. Schultz, ThRdsch, N.F. 26, 1960, 237 ff., and especially on the Gospel of Truth, pp. 258 ff.; English translation by K. Grobel, *The Gospel of Truth*, 1960). This sermon, stemming from the middle of the second century, has incorrectly received the designation of "gospel." Whether this writing belongs to the "Valentinian" form of Christian Gnosticism is disputed. Barrett shows that John and this original Gnostic writing, in spite of their many linguistic parallels, diverge completely in their use of central theological concepts, and infers correctly that John consciously took up pre-Christian Gnostic language in an anti-Gnostic sense, because "Gnosticism raised questions which the theologian could not overlook."

Thus we can see clearly that John is considerably indebted for his conceptual world, especially as it appears in the Johannine Jesus discourses, to a heterodox Jewish-Gnostic milieu, which must be supposed on the edge of Palestinian Judaism, and which was strongly influenced by a Syrian mythological Gnosticism. Although a direct connection of John with the form of heterodox Judaism as it has become known to us from the writings of the Qumran community has turned out to be improbable, the literature from Qumran can teach us two things about the position of John in respect to other religions. 1) In addition to Pharisaic orthodoxy there were quite diverse forms of Jewish thought and life, to which belonged not only the Qumran community and Jewish syncretistic baptismal groups but also Jewish-Gnostic groups (see J. Thomas, "Le mouvement baptiste en Palestine et Syrie," Dissertationes theologicae Lovanienses II, 28, 1935). 2) The fact that we previously had no idea of the form of Jewish thought which the accidental discovery of the caves at Qumran made accessible to us, must make us consider the possibility that still other forms of Jewish thought not directly available to us could have existed. Although we can only approximately delimit the spiritual background of John, we have, nevertheless, obtained an important indication of the circumstances of the origin of John.

5. The Purpose and Theological Character of the Gospel of John

In his conclusion (20:30 f.), the author of John himself expresses the aim which he follows: "Now Jesus did many other signs in the presence of the disciples, which are not written in this book; but these are written that you may believe that Jesus is the Christ, the Son of God, and that believing you may have life in his name." It cannot be decided with certainty whether in 20:31 πιστεύητε (B ℵ* Θ) or πιστεύσητε (the majority of manuscripts) is to be read (probably the present tense). But even if πιστεύητε is original, in view of the irregular use of tenses in John we cannot decide upon this basis whether the readers presupposed are Christians who are to be strengthened in the faith, or men who are to be won to the faith (see Barrett, ZsystTh 1953, 258). Accordingly, the following proposals have been advanced: 1) The author is thinking primarily of non-Christians, to whom the Christian faith is supposed to be made intelligible (Dodd; similarly C. F. D. Moule, "The Intention of the Evangelists," NT Essays in Memory of T. W. Manson, 1959, 168). 2) John is a "Programmschrift" to Baptist communities (Stauffer, ThLZ 1956, 146). 3) John writes for Jews and for Gentiles influenced by Hermetic religiousness (F.-M. Braun, Revue Thomiste 1955, 294). 4) John is written to win Jews of the Diaspora to faith in Jesus the Messiah (a view which Smith, van Unnik, and J. A. T. Robinson [NTSt 1959-60] have attempted to demonstrate in detail). Now just as it is correct to say, on the one hand, that John strives to show that Jesus of Nazareth is the one "of whom Moses in the law and also the prophets wrote" (1:45), so it is also correct to say, on the other hand, that the Jesus of John designates himself as the "good shepherd" and the "true vine" (10:11, 14; 15:1), and thereby separates himself polemically from thieves and hirelings (10:8, 10, 12), i.e., from salvation figures who erroneously claim this title (see Schulz, *Reden*, 122 f.). Although John thus plainly seeks to establish that faith in Jesus is the fulfillment of Judaism, as well as the true Gentile religion, the missionary character is missing throughout the Gospel. That becomes clear, not only in that the evangelist repeatedly alludes to states of affairs which are reported in the Synoptic Gospels, but above all in those statements of the Gospel which summon Christians to "continue in my word" (cf. 6:67 f.; 15:4 ff.). John is, therefore, primarily written in order to establish and secure the faith of Christians (e.g., Feine-Behm, Barrett, ZsystTh 1953, 272, Higgins, 13 f., 21, Schnackenburg, LThK V, 1102).

In the light of this intention we can understand the polemical features which John exhibits. 1) Irenaeus (*Haer*. III, 11, 7) supposes that John polemizes against the Gnostic, Cerinthus, and this view has found supporters to this day (Wikenhauser, Meinertz, Höpfl-Gut, Grundmann). But what we know about Cerinthus (the separation of an upper and lower God, separation of the Spirit from Jesus before the passion—see R. M. Grant, JBL 1950, H. Rahner, LThK VI, 1961, 120), is no object of John's polemic (as also of I John; see below, §31:3), and thus the statement of Irenaeus hardly proves true (so R. M. Grant, *loc. cit.*, Michaelis, Michel, CBL). We are not denying that John contains a polemic against Gnostic thoughts, which follows not only from the formulations which exclude all Docetism (like 1:14; 6:53 f.; 19:34), but also from the exclusive claim to salvation-predicates for Jesus which were ascribed to Gnostic figures of revelation (shepherd, vine, the envoy, etc., Jn. 10:11; 15:1; 5:36, etc.; cf. Schulz, *Reden*, 121). John lays claim to the language of Gnosticism in order to show to Christians that Jesus is the true Revealer.

2) As Bretschneider already noted, some texts of John (1:7 f., 15, 20-27; 3:26-30; 5:33-36; 10:41) show a front against John the Baptist and his disciples. Since Baldensperger, many have accepted this interpretation (e.g., Michaelis, Wikenhauser, Feine-Behm, Henshaw, Howard, Michel, Schnackenburg, *Johannesjünger;* to the contrary, Smith, 50 f., J. A. T. Robinson, NTSt 1959-60, 130). The Baptist himself in John stresses repeatedly that he is not the prophet, not the Messiah, and points to Jesus, who alone must increase. Such statements are clearly directed against the overestimation of the Baptist which appears to have prevailed in the circles of the Baptist's disciples (on the disciples of John cf. Acts 19:1 ff., and Schnackenburg, *loc. cit.*). If John does polemize against such veneration of the Baptist, then it must have been a certain danger for the reader. Yet this polemic is only a relatively slightly emphasized motif.

3) Weizsäcker first called attention to a polemical opposition to Judaism in John. Wrede, Jülicher-Fascher, and R. M. Grant (JBL 1950) have seen the actual purpose of John in the refutation of Jewish charges against Christianity.

But for Wikenhauser, Meinertz, Feine-Behm, Henshaw, Riddle-Hutson, and Schnackenburg (LThK V) such a refutation is only a secondary purpose. Miss Guilding has sought to prove that John was written for Jewish Christians who recently had been excluded from the synagogue. As proof of the fulfillment of the Jewish system of worship in Jesus, John reproduces, in their original liturgical context, the sermons of Jesus, which originally were delivered in the context of the Jewish ecclesiastical year (pp. 54, 231). Now there can be no doubt that John polemizes especially sharply against "the Jews," who from the beginning wanted to destroy Jesus (cf. 5:16, 18, 37 f., 45; 7:1, 19; 8:22-24, 37-59; 10:31-39; 19:7). And this opposition is so sharp that Jesus can speak to the Jews of "your law" (8:17; 10:34; see also "the word that is written in their law" [15:25] in the mouth of Jesus! Cf. Bultmann, Komm., Meyer II [10], 59, and supplement [2], 16). That this picture of the opposition between Jesus and the Jews who deny him (there is also reference to believing Jews in 8:31; 11:45; 12:11) gets its sharpness from the violent enmity between Jews and Christians at the time of the composition of John is proved by 16:2 f.: "They will put you out of the synagogues." At the same time the enmity of the κόσμος against Jesus and his own (see the connection of 15:18 f. with 16:1 f.) is concretized in the enmity of the Jews against the Christians. Thus the polemic against Judaism certainly is an actual motif of John. But at the same time this polemic is taken up into the fundamentally dualistic representation of the opposition between the ἄρχων τοῦ κόσμου τούτου and the Christ, who has overcome the κόσμος (12:31; 16:33). Miss Guilding's conception of John's apologetic purpose surely originated out of pure fantasy, for her proof is not successful in showing that the discourses of Jesus in John are arranged in connection with the OT readings of the synagogical year (see Haenchen's criticism).

If, therefore, John was written to encourage the faith of specific Christians and to strengthen it through polemic defense, then another problem forces itself upon us: How does the author of John want us to understand his representation of Jesus, which is so different from that of the Synoptics? Clement of Alexandria (according to Eus., EH VI, 14, 17), beginning with the presupposition that the author of John knew the Synoptics, was the first to advocate the thesis that John, by complementing them, wished to excel them: "John, as the last, because he perceived that the corporeal things (τὰ σωματικά) are presented in the Gospels, at the exhortation of his friends and impelled by the divine Spirit, wrote a spiritual Gospel (πνευματικὸν ποιῆσαι εὐαγγέλιον)." This "complement hypothesis," which often has been advocated until the present (cf., e.g., Goguel, Schäfer, Sigge, Boismard, BdJ, Höpfl-Gut; in a limited way, Meinertz; for the history of the problem, Windisch, Johannes, 1 ff.), and the related view, that John, upon the basis of better knowldege, wanted to correct the Synoptics (Stauffer, Historische Elemente, 33), have against them the fact that John nowhere clearly says that he is adding something new to that which is already known, and just as little says that he is correcting that which is already known. Hence Windisch has attempted to establish the thesis (already occasionally advocated before him) that John did not use the Synoptics and did not presuppose that they were known by his readers. Rather, John wished to put the absolute gospel in the place of the Synoptics (then also Riddle-Hutson, Bauer, ThRdsch 1929, 139, R. M. Grant, HarvThR 1942, 95). But Windisch's thesis is contrary to our conclusion that John obviously knew at least Mark and Luke and occasionally took them over (see above, pp. 143 f.). Furthermore, John more than once alludes to the account of the Synoptics and thereby clearly presupposes that the readers can expand the allusions upon the basis of their knowledge of the Synoptics, or at least of the synoptic tradition (1:25, baptismal activity of the Baptist; 1:32 f., baptism of Jesus; 3:24, imprisonment of the Baptist; 6:67, 70; 20:24, existence of the circle of the twelve; 12:16, participation of the disciples in the journey of Jesus to Jerusalem; 18:40, alternative of releasing Jesus or Barabbas). But if John intends to be neither a complement nor an improvement nor a replacement of the Synoptics, which it knows and presupposes as somehow known by the readers, then there remains only one possibility: Under the tacit persupposition of acquaintanceship with Gospels already in existence, John, for its part, wants to give a representation of Jesus which will make known in a consummate manner that "Jesus is the Christ, the Son of God" (20:31). John thus "attempts to express adequately what already was contained in the earlier tradition" (Barrett, ZsystTh 1953, 269; similarly, Lightfoot, Bultmann).

This independent representation of Jesus seeks, therefore, to give perfect expression to the Christian faith in Jesus, the Messiah and Son of God, and thus consistently proceeds from the image of faith of the Christian community: John "presents in a more systematic, more independent, and in a more grandiose manner than the Synoptics, not what Jesus was, but what the Christians have in Jesus" (Dibelius, RGG[2] III, 350; similarly, E. Gaugler, "Das Christuszeugnis des Joh.," in *Jesus Christus im Zeugnis der Heiligen Schrift und der Kirche*, Beih. 2 to EvTh, 1936, 41 f., Strathmann, NTD [6], 22 f., and others). We are not saying that John wished to narrate no historical events and had at his disposal no historical traditions. The opposite is doubtless the case, as is shown by the repeated topographical and geographical data of John. But the contention repeated again and again that the author of John claims to write as an eyewitness (e.g., Michaelis, Meinertz, Boismard, BdJ, Feine-Behm, Feuillet in Robert-Feuillet, Nunn, Stauffer, Eckhardt), simply does not prove true for chaps. 1–20: The first person plural in 1:14 (ἐσκήνωσεν ἐν ἡμῖν, ἐθεασάμεθα τὴν δόξαν αὐτοῦ) is doubtless the same as in 1:16 (ἐκ τοῦ πληρώματος αὐτοῦ ἡμεῖς πάντες ἐλάβομεν) and designates, therefore, the Christian experience of faith (see Bultmann and Barrett, *ad loc.*), and 19:35 appeals to the witness of a ἑωρακώς but in no wise indicates that the author is identical with this witness. And the thesis, which is defended in ever new form, that the author shows himself by his exact knowledge of geography and chronology and of particulars in the history of Jesus to be a Jerusalemite and an eyewitness (thus in varying form Michaelis, Feine-Behm, Albright, Potter, Hunter, Smith, Higgins, Gyllenberg, Manson, Sanders, Stauffer; for the authenticity of the discourses of Jesus, Albright, Guilding, Eckhardt), not only rests upon a fallacy, but is objectively false. Although we do not deny that John contains historical reports (that perhaps holds true for the date of Jesus' death or for the going over of the Baptist's disciples to Jesus), that can be proved only from case to case, and permits no inference as to whether or not the author was an eyewitness. And Eckhardt's contention that Johannine discourse "is in truth Jesus' manner of discourse" (Eckhardt, 52), is false, because the Gnosticized language of the Johannine Jesus obviously is that of the evangelist, and in any case cannot be that of Jesus of Nazareth, whom we learn to know in the Synoptic traditions. If, therefore, John wants to report history but consistently shapes it according to his faith in the Risen One, then the theological question about John which corresponds to the content of the Gospel is not the question, justified in itself, about John's contribution to the history of Jesus, but the question whether John's portrayal of Jesus, based upon faith, as the Son of God come from heaven is an interpretation in conformity with the essence of God's historical act of salvation in Jesus. For the answer to this question it is immaterial that the author cannot have been an eyewitness (as is proved in any case by his reproduction of the discourses of Jesus).

6. The Author

Since the days of the Alogoi, and especially since the beginning of the nineteenth century, the problem of the authorship of John has been encumbered in a twofold way. On the one hand, composition by John, the son of Zebedee, who is named in the tradition, has been passionately defended by those who thought that the apostolic authority or the historical trustworthiness of John was dependent upon it. On the other hand, this tradition has been attacked just as violently because with the incorrectness of this tradition the historical or theological doubtfulness of this Gospel appeared to be established. Since both conclusions are false, we should, in our own discussion of the question of authorship, seek to state dispassionately what we really can and cannot know.

John does not name its author in chaps. 1–20, and where the author includes himself with others in a "we," he does not indicate that he writes as an eyewitness, as we have already seen. In the second half of the Gospel we meet the disciple ὃν ἠγάπα or ἐφίλει ὁ Ἰησοῦς (13:23-25; 19:26 f.; 20:2-8), but the Gospel itself offers no help in the identification of this person. It is only clear that this "Beloved Disciple" stands with Peter in some kind of competitive relationship. We can also ask whether the ἄλλος μαθητής (18:15 f.), who, as an acquaintance of the high priest, leads Peter into the court of the high priestly palace, is identical with the Beloved Disciple, for the latter is also designated as ὁ ἄλλος μαθητής in 20:3, 8. But since this characterization in 20:3 refers back to τὸν ἄλλον μαθητὴν ὃν ἐφίλει ὁ Ἰησοῦς in 20:2, the question about the identity of the ἄλλος μαθητής (18:15 f.) cannot be clearly answered. Should the Beloved Disciple also be meant here, there results here, too, a superiority of the Beloved Disciple over Peter; that he was then designated as an acquaintance of the high priest helps no further. If the reference in 19:35 were certain, this passage would be more significant than 18:15 f. In 19:26, outside of the women standing by the cross, only the Beloved Disciple is mentioned, to whom Jesus entrusts his mother (19:26 f.). Then the death of Jesus and the confirmation of his death by the soldiers are reported, in connection with which water and blood flow out of Jesus' spear-pierced side (19:28-34). Then in 19:35 follows the sentence: "He who saw it has borne witness—his testimony is true, and he knows that he tells the truth—that you also may believe." Since only the Beloved Disciple was mentioned as present at the cross (in addition to the women), it is natural to find him mentioned in the ἑωρακώς and witness of 19:35, though, to be sure, that is not clearly said. Yet it remains unclear whether ἐκεῖνος in v. 35b also means the ἑωρακώς or another person (e.g., Jesus, according to Bultmann, Hoskyns, Strathmann, ad loc., and others). But the equating of ἐκεῖνος and ὁ ἑωρακώς is by far the most natural hypothesis (see Barrett, ad loc.). If both suppositions prove true, that in 19:35 the Beloved Disciple is meant and that knowledge concerning the truth of his witness is ascribed to him, then it follows that the evangelist, at least for what took place at Jesus' death, can cite an eyewitness as authority. If that all does turn out to be correct, then the question still remains fully open of how far beyond the scenes at which he is mentioned this Beloved Disciple is presupposed as a witness, and his identity then also remains unknown. But according to 19:35, he can hardly be identical with the author. In view of Jn. 1–20 we can come no further. The Gospel of John is, therefore, anonymous.

The Gospel of John, of course, has been handed down only together with the supplement, ch. 21. We have seen that factual and linguistic reasons make it very probable that this supplement was attached to the Gospel by a strange hand, yet the linguistic relationship indicates that the enlarger(s) was strongly dependent upon the author. Here we meet again the juxtaposition of Peter and the Beloved Disciple (21:7). Peter, to whom Jesus gave the commission to lead the disciples but also prophesied his martyrdom (21:15-19), then sees the Beloved Disciple, asks Jesus about him, and receives the puzzling answer, "If it is my will that he remain until I come, what is that to you?" (21:22). If 21:23 stresses that Jesus did not intend to say that the Beloved Disciple would not die before the parousia, then this correction would have meaning only if the Beloved Disciple had died in the meantime. 21:24a follows with the statement that this Beloved Disciple "is the disciple who is bearing witness to these things, and who has written these things." In all probability περὶ τούτων as well as ταῦτα refers to the entire Gospel. It is, therefore, maintained that the Beloved Disciple, who has died in the meantime, is an eyewitness (at least according to 19:35) and the author of John. 21:24b adds, "and we know that his testimony is true," which can only mean that the Christians or the Christian churches, quite generally, which are speaking here can certify to the trustworthiness of the author of the Gospel (cf. 3:11). From 21:23 on, the author himself cannot be speaking, and since there is no sufficient reason for detaching these verses from the remainder of ch. 21, the insight is confirmed that the entire ch. 21 cannot stem from the author of Jn. 1–20. The author of ch. 21, in attaching the supplement, follows in any case the intention of designating the Beloved Disciple as the author of the Gospel, something which the author of chaps. 1–20 did not do, and which does not correspond to the manner in which the Beloved Disciple is spoken of in chaps. 13–20.

Ch. 21 certainly also does not help us any further in the identification of the Beloved Disciple. To be sure, we must conclude from 21:7 that the Beloved Disciple named there must belong to those named in 21:2 and to those who went fishing together, according to 21:3. Besides the three disciples who are named, there are enumerated there "the (sons) of Zebedee, and two others of his disciples." The ever-repeated contention, on the basis of the Synoptics, that the Beloved Disciple must be one of the two sons of Zebedee (e.g., Michaelis, Feine-Behm, Wikenhauser), is, in view of this text, completely unfounded. With the same right, the Beloved Disciple can be sought in one of the two unnamed disciples mentioned. Thus the secret about the figure of the Beloved Disciple is also not disclosed in ch. 21. For that reason, the author of John, upon the basis of his own statements, remains unknown, even if the equating of the author with the Beloved Disciple, which is in discord with chaps. 1–20, could prove correct.

Naturally, many have not rested content with the statement that the identity of the Beloved Disciple remains unknown to us. The traditional argumentation seeks to clarify his identity through a comparison with the Synoptics. Reference is made to the inference that the "disciple, whom Jesus loved" must be one of the three who, according to Mk. 5:37 par.; 9:2 par.; 14:33 par., were with Jesus when he took only the most intimate ones with him, Peter and the sons of Zebedee, James and John. Since Peter is named in addition to the Beloved Disciple, and James had already died in 44, it is only a matter of John, the son of Zebedee, as the Beloved Disciple and author of John. Some find a confirmation to this conclusion in 1:40 f. They contend that if we emphasize πρῶτον and read that *first of all* Andrew brought his brother Simon Peter to Jesus, then it follows that the remaining, unnamed second one of the disciples of the Baptist who came over to Jesus, likewise brought his brother to Jesus, so that John, like the Synoptics (Mk. 1:16 ff.), presupposes the call of the sons of Zebedee at the beginning of Jesus' activity (e.g., Michaelis, Feine-Behm, Wikenhauser in the supposition that the Beloved Disciple is the author; McNeile-Williams, Hunter, Tasker while denying this supposition). But this entire chain of reasoning is full of flaws. In the first place, it is very questionable whether we may generally so supplement John from the Synoptics, and, on this basis, presuppose that the author of John, with the designation, "the disciple, whom Jesus loved," could only mean one of Jesus' three most intimate disciples mentioned in the Synoptics, and hence, in connection with the second pair of brothers in 1:40 f., must have had in mind the sons of Zebedee, even if he does not name them. In the second place, if the Beloved Disciple belonged to the disciples from the beginning, it is hardly comprehensible why he plays no role until Jn. 13. Finally, neither does this chain of reasoning explain why John, the son of Zebedee, is designated with this pseudonym, nor does it make understandable why the reference to the turning of the second pair of brothers to Jesus (a reference made only by means of the πρῶτον [1:41], which has to be strongly emphasized) should be so unclear. Thus this kind of attempt to equate the Beloved Disciple with John, the son of Zebedee, does not succeed.

Others have sought for another identification. According to F. V. Filson ("Who Was the Beloved Disciple?" JBL 68, 1949, 83 ff.), Sanders (NTSt 1954-55), and Eckhardt, the Beloved Disciple is Lazarus, who was raised by Jesus, of whom it is said: "Lord, he whom you love is ill" (11:3). Eckhardt then succeeds also in equating the Beloved Disciple with the son of Zebedee, in that he explains the name Lazarus in chaps. 11, 12 as an interpolation upon the basis of Lk. 16:19 ff.! E. L. Titus ("The Identity of the Beloved Disciple," JBL 69, 1950, 323 ff.) conjectures Matthias (Acts 1:15 ff.), and still other names have also been defended (see the enumeration in Kragerud, 42 ff.). Since all of these attempts are unverifiable fancies, and John seems strictly to preserve the anonymity of the Beloved Disciple, some scholars want to see in the Beloved Disciple an ideal figure (Jülicher-Fascher, Dibelius, Botschaft I, 214, Bacon, E. Kraft, "Die Personen des Joh.," EvTh 16, 1956, 18 ff.: type of the disciples; H. Lietzmann, *The Beginnings of the Christian Church*, I. Tr. Bertram Lee Woolf, 1937, 1953, 233, R. M. Grant, HarvThR 1942, 116, E. Käsemann, *Exegetische Versuche und Besinnungen* I, 1960, 180: the ideal bearer of the apostolic witness; Bultmann: Gentile Christianity as the true Christianity; Kragerud: the Johannine prophethood in opposition to ecclesiastical office; all references to the Beloved Disciple are explained as interpolated by those named in Kragerud [11 f.], also by Goguel [*Intr.* II, 362 ff.], and A. Harnack, *Studien zur Geschichte des NT* I, AKG 19, 1931, 126, note 2). The contention that all references to the Beloved Disciple are interpolated is wholly arbitrary. The interpretation of the Beloved Disciple as an ideal figure is especially improbable, because his rivalry with Peter must then unavoidably lead to the conclusion that Peter also is an ideal figure. And it would be inexplicable that the author would then have ascribed to this ideal figure such a slight role. If 18:15 f. is also supposed to refer to the Beloved Disciple, then this notice expressed about an ideal figure would be totally senseless. And the author of the supplement in 21:23 indeed knew of the death of the Beloved Disciple and the reflections connected with it.

Thus the problem remains. There is no possibility of establishing the identity of the disciple whom the Gospel of John cites as its authority for its report about the passion of Jesus. The supposition which continues to be the most probable is that the author of John was associated with a disciple who lived very long, and upon whom had been bestowed the title of honor, "he, whom Jesus loved" (cf. W. Bauer, Komm, Hdb.[3], excursus to 13:23). But so far as the clarification of the problem of authorship is concerned, this statement helps us no further.

We have yet to ask the question whether the ecclesiastical tradition can help us identify the author of John. The tradition that John, the son of Zebedee, wrote the Gospel of John at Ephesus when very old is first found with certainty in Irenaeus (*Haer.* III, 1, 2, = Eus., EH V, 8, 4,): "Afterwards [after the three Synoptic Gospels] John, the disciple of the Lord, who also had leaned upon his breast, himself published his Gospel, while he was living at Ephesus in Asia." In this statement from his chief work, *Adversus haereses*, written about 180, Irenaeus obviously relates especially the tradition of his home in Asia Minor, but also the Roman tradition. For Bishop Polycrates of Ephesus, around 190 in a letter to the Roman Bishop Victor (preserved in Eusebius, EH V, 24, 2 ff), refers to the witnesses of the tradition of Asia Minor, and mentions in that connection (V, 24, 3): "Furthermore, also John, who lay upon the breast of the Lord. . . . He is buried in Ephesus." Bishop Melito of Sardis (c. 175) refers to the Gospel of John in a similar manner as to the Synoptics (cf. Barrett, Comm., 94). In the *Epistula apostolorum*, which supposedly was written about the same time in Asia Minor, the Gospel of John is not only repeatedly used and cited, but also John is named as the first in the list of apostles. Upon the basis of this data, R. M. Grant would like to conclude that the Fourth Gospel was regarded as the Gospel of John (HarvThR 1942, 104), an inference which is not at all certain. Just as the report of Irenaeus proves to be the tradition of Asia Minor in the last quarter of the second century, the statement of the Muratorian canon (lines 9 ff.) establishes the same for Rome:

The fourth of the Gospels, that of John, (one) of the disciples. When his fellow-disciples and bishops urged him, he said: Fast with me from today for three days, and what will be revealed to each one let us relate to one another. In the same night it was revealed to Andrew, one of the apostles, that, whilst all were to go over (it), John in his own name should write everything down. . . . For so he confesses (himself) [in I John 1:1] not merely an eye and ear witness, but also a writer of all the marvels of the Lord in order (Hennecke-Schneemelcher [see above, p. 60], I, 43).

That the Gospel of John was written by the apostle John, who was identical with the Beloved Disciple, is thus the tradition of Asia Minor and of Rome in the last quarter of the second century. There can be no doubt that Irenaeus meant by this disciple of the Lord John the son of Zebedee since he quotes Jn. 1:14 with the formula, ὁ ἀπόστολος εἴρηκεν (*Haer.* I, 1, 19), and says of the church at Ephesus: "The church at Ephesus, which was founded by Paul, where John continued to abide with them until the time of Trajan, is a true witness of the tradition of the Apostles" (*Haer.* III, 3, 4 = Eus., EH III, 23, 4). It is all the more striking that Irenaeus almost always calls this John "the disciple of the Lord," and uses this phrase in the singular number for no other person (see Burney, 138 f., and Bernard, I, XLVII f.), and that the author of John in the Muratorian canon is also called "John, one of the disciples" [Johannes ex discipulis] (line 9, corrected text). This designation, "the disciple of the Lord," in the tradition which we meet at the end of the second century, therefore plainly belongs to the John who was regarded as the author of John. Yet from the end of the second century the composition of the Gospel of John by John, the son of Zebedee, is undisputed.

Of course, this view was not yet generally recognized in the second half of the second century, as the derivation of John from the Gnostic Cerinthus by various anti-Montanists in this time shows (see above, pp. 139 f.). We must, therefore, ask from where Irenaeus obtained his information that John stems from the apostle John, the disciple of the Lord. Irenaeus refers to two sources of tradition: a) In a letter to the Gnostic Florinus (in Eus., EH V, 20, 4) he says:

The presbyters who were before us, who had dealings with the apostles, did not hand down these teachings to you. For I saw you when I was still a child, in lower Asia Minor with Polycarp. . . . [I can remember exactly] how [the blessed Polycarp] told about his familiar intercourse with John and with the others who had seen the Lord, and how he remembered their discourses, and what it was that he had heard from each about the Lord, about his miracles and his teaching.

From this statement of Irenaeus there follows no more than that Polycarp knew a John who had seen the Lord. Irenaeus no more says here that John was the apostle than that Polycarp had met John in Asia Minor. Now Irenaeus, according to his own statement, was a παῖς when he met Polycarp. A. Harnack has calculated that Irenaeus could not have been more than fifteen years old at the death of Polycarp (*Geschichte der altchristlichen Literatur bis Eusebius* II, 1, 1897, 342 ff.). But Polycarp himself, in his letter to the Philippians, does not refer to his relation with an apostle. In view of this fact it is very questionable whether Irenaeus was not deceived when he regarded the John (of whom he as a child had heard Polycarp speak) as the apostle and removed to Asia Minor.

b) Irenaeus also appeals for his knowledge of the apostle John to "all the presbyters, who had met in Asia with John, the disciple of the Lord. . . . But some of them not only saw John but also other apostles" (*Haer.* II, 33, 3, partly also in Eus., EH III, 23, 3). Who these presbyters were is not ascertainable with certainty. According to Harnack (*loc. cit.*, 334 ff.), they are identical with Papias. But against that is the fact that Irenaeus (*Haer.* V, 33, 3, 4; partly also in Eus., EH III, 39, 1) names "the presbyters who have seen John, the disciple of the Lord," side by side with "Papias, the hearer of John and companion of Polycarp." But whoever these presbyters were, it is, again, said of them only that they knew John, the disciple of the Lord. It remains unclear whether the statement that this meeting took place in Asia belongs to the tradition of the presbyters or was appended by Irenaeus. From this statement, then, there is nothing more to gather than that Irenaeus knew of a disciple of the Lord, John, whom the presbyters of Asia Minor had heard. In the tradition of the presbyters there is no talk of an apostle John. And, according to that which Irenaeus reports, this disciple of the Lord, John, is designated as author of a Gospel neither by Polycarp nor by the presbyters. That is, the tradition which is recognizable as Irenaeus' source knows only of a disciple of the Lord, John, and whether this John was in Asia Minor and known as the author of a Gospel is uncertain.

What can we recognize about the view of Papias, who, in any case, was contemporary with the "presbyters" of Irenaeus? Eusebius reports nothing of a statement by Papias about the Gospel of John. The completely corrupt Latin prologue to John, according to which Papias somehow had traced back the Gospel of John to John (text in K. Bihlmeyer, *Die apostolischen Väter I*, 1924, 139 f.), is completely uncertain in respect to its age and is useless (the attempt of F.-M. Braun, *Jean*, 345 ff., to reconstruct a genuine kernel, is hardly tenable. Cf. to the alleged "anti-Marcionite" prologues, below, pp. 342 f.). Thus we do not have a sure witness that Papias knew the Gospel of John. And what is called an indication of Papias' acquaintanceship with the Gospel of John (Iren., *Haer.* II, 33, 4 and V, 36, 1; Eus., EH III, 39, 3 f.; cf. R. Heard, NTSt 1, 1954-55 [see below, p. 337], 131), points only to a probability (see R. M. Grant, HarvThR 1942, 100, Bultmann, RGG [3] III, 849). On the other hand, Irenaeus clearly maintains that Papias was a hearer of John ('Ιωάννου ἀκουστής) (Iren., *Haer.* V, 33, 4 = Eus., EH III, 39, 1). But this statement of Irenaeus does not agree with Papias' own words in the proemium of his "Exposition of the Lord's Sayings." This much-disputed text reads (Eus., EH III, 39, 3 f.):

I shall spare no pains to present all that I once learned well from the presbyters (παρὰ τῶν πρεσβυτέρων) and remembered well, together with my expositions [of the Lord's sayings], in that I can vouch for their truth (αὐτῶν ἀλήθειαν). For, unlike the masses, I took delight, not in those who have much to say, but in those who teach the truth, also not in those who talk about strange precepts, but in those who relate precepts given by the Lord to the faith, and which are derived from the truth itself. But if anyone came who had followed the presbyters, I was accustomed to inquire about the sayings of the presbyters, what Andrew or what Peter had said (εἶπεν), or Philip or Thomas or Jacob or John or Matthew or any other of the Lord's disciples; and what Aristion and the presbyter John, the disciples of the Lord, say (ἅτε 'Αριστίων καὶ ὁ πρεσβύτερος 'Ιωάννης οἱ τοῦ κυρίου μαθηταὶ λέγουσιν). For I do not regard that which comes from books as so valuable for myself as that which comes from a living and abiding voice.

In view of this text, the discussion centers about the twofold appearance of the name "John" and about the meaning of οἱ πρεσβύτεροι and τοῦ κυρίου μαθηταί. It is hardly understandable that the first question is at all disputed and the contention always repeated that Papias spoke of only one John (Michaelis, Meinertz, Feine-Behm, Nunn, Edwards). An unbiased exegesis of the text permits no doubt that Papias says that whenever he had opportunity he inquired of followers of the πρεσβύτεροι about the sayings of the πρεσβύτεροι, and thus he learned 1) what the seven named and any other of the Lord's disciples had said, and 2) what the Lord's disciples Aristion and the πρεσβύτερος John were saying (so already Eus., EH III, 39, 5; recently, Barrett, Comm., 88 ff.; F.-M. Braun, *Jean*, 357 ff.; Merlier, 224 ff.; J. Munck, "Presbyters and Disciples of the Lord in Papias," HarvThR 52, 1959, 223 ff.). Papias, therefore, mentions two persons with the name John, concerning whose teaching he had inquired. The one stands together with names of the circle of the twelve, and is plainly, like the others of this group, no longer living; here can be meant only John, the son of Zebedee. The other is obviously known by the designation, "the presbyter John," and is like Aristion still living. But Papias has heard of both groups only through their followers (παρηκολουθηκώς τις τοῖς πρεσβυτέροις). Hence it follows that the statement of Irenaeus that Papias was a "hearer of John" does not prove true. The supposition that Papias first of all heard the presbyters directly on journeys and later their followers in Hierapolis is forced into the text by Munck (*loc. cit.*, 229). Barrett's suggestion (Comm., 89 f.) that Papias was separated from the apostles by the two links of the presbyters and their hearers does not follow from the text either.

Although we have been able to interpret Papias' text thus far with some degree of certainty, we cannot answer the second question with complete confidence. The concept, πρεσβύτεροι, which is met here as a collective characterization of the men regarded by Papias as bearers of the tradition and also as the characterizing designation of the second John in our section, in the sense of Papias can in both cases designate only the generation of the bearers of tradition. "The presbyter John" is thus the man who, to be sure, does not belong to the circle of the twelve, but yet also, like Aristion, can pass on "precepts given by the Lord to the faith." Why he in particular is called ὁ πρεσβύτερος is indiscernible to us. It is also not clear what is meant by τοῦ κυρίου μαθηταί. That it is synonymous with οἱ πρεσβύτεροι, is improbable according to the context. Munck (*loc. cit.*, 32) is probably right with his conjecture that in this context it is supposed to designate "personal disciples of Jesus." If that turns out to be correct, then "the presbyter John," of course, was no member of the narrower circle of disciples, but still somehow a personal disciple of Jesus. But Papias heard from the apostle John as well as from the presbyter John only through their followers. In regard to the question whether Papias knew the Gospel of John, this statement does not help us further.

Some have thought they could establish Papias' knowledge of the Gospel of John in another manner. Parker (JBL 1960) seeks to show that all that we know about John Mark (see above, pp. 69 f.) is excellently suited to the author of John, and that the remarks of Papias concerning the Gospel of Mark and its author, Mark (Eus., EH III, 39, 15; see above, p. 43), are equally suitable to the Gospel of John. He conjectures that Papias in these remarks in reality wanted to speak about the Gospel of John and, therefore, the Gospel of John stems from John Mark. But even if it proves true that the reports about John Mark and the remarks of Papias concerning the Gospel of Mark are suitable to the Gospel of John and its author (most of the agreements adduced by Parker are by no means obvious), it still remains inexplicable how Eusebius could be so deceived about which Gospel Papias intended to speak, since he indeed had Papias' book itself before him and could even refer his readers to the books of Papias (Eus., EH III, 39, 14). That Papias knew the Gospel of John cannot be made certain in this way.

The tradition, which is first palpable for us toward the end of the second century, that the Gospel of John was written in Ephesus by John, the son of Zebedee, can therefore hardly be traced back further. For in connection with

Polycarp and the presbyters, who are alleged by Irenaeus to be tradition transmitters, we find only the report that they had dealings with a disciple of the Lord, John. Although Irenaeus himself regards the author of John as the apostle, he almost always calls him "the disciple of the Lord." From the tradition handed down by Irenaeus, we can infer only that a disciple of the Lord, John, was author of the Gospel of John. But this inference is weakened by the statement that Polycarp in his epistle reveals no knowledge of the Gospel of John (probably, however, I John; see R. M. Grant, HarvThR 1942, 100). Whether this disciple of the Lord, John, is identical with the Lord's disciple whom Papias calls the presbyter John, is no more ascertainable.

But for that reason it is also very questionable whether we may further infer the following: The only tradition to be taken seriously about the author of John in the early church traces back the Gospel of John to a disciple of the Lord, John. If the equating of this John with the son of Zebedee is not attested before Irenaeus and on other grounds is impossible (see below), then there is every probability that the author of John is to be sought in the presbyter John, with whom Papias was connected. And this probability becomes a certainty if the Johannine epistles stem from the same author, since the author of II and III John calls himself ὁ πρεσβύτερος (see also §32,3). The supposition proved by this or similar reasoning that the Gospel of John stems from the presbyter John of Papias (Bernard, Bauer, Dibelius, Sparks, Henshaw, McNeile-Williams, Grundmann, Merlier), is, to be sure, opposed by the fact that we can *conclude* only that the tradition to which Irenaeus refers traces the Gospel of John back to John the Lord's disciple, and that the equating of John the Lord's disciple with the presbyter John in Papias must also remain uncertain. Although the composition of the Gospel of John and of the Epistles of John by the presbyter John is not unthinkable, this supposition has no secure evidence in its favor and can at the most be characterized as a possibility (Barrett).

If, then, the great age of the tradition which is first recognizable to us at the end of the second century that John, the son of Zebedee, was the author of John cannot be demonstrated, we still must ask whether this tradition is not correct after all, as a large number of scholars maintain (cf., e.g., recently in addition to the Catholic scholars, Michaelis, Feine-Behm, Klijn, Tenney, Lightfoot, Strathmann, Menoud, Edwards, Stauffer, Albright). The question would surely be answered in the negative if it could be proved with certainty that John, the son of Zebedee, died early as a martyr. As testimony for this fact the following support is adduced: a) the prophecy of Jesus (Mk. 10:39 par.); b) according to late accounts, Papias handed down the tradition that "John the theologian and his brother James were killed by the Jews"; c) some old lists of martyrs also mention the martyrdom of John (thus since E. Schwartz many; recently, e.g., Bauer, Jülicher-Fascher, Dibelius, Bultmann, R. M. Grant, HarvThR 1942). The proofs for this thesis are certainly of unequal value. Whereas we can hardly explain the reproduction of the prophecy in Mk. 10:39 par. if it had been contradicted by the facts, the report from Papias has been transmitted very undependably, and the historical value of the lists of martyrs is disputed (see above all Barrett, Comm., 86 f., and F.-M. Braun, *Jean*, 375 ff.). And even if there is some probability that John died as a martyr, it remains completely uncertain when and where that happened. Hence this argument cannot speak decisively against the composition of John by John, the son of Zebedee.

On the other hand, several other facts weigh conclusively against the correctness of this tradition of Johannine authorship. We have already seen that the Gnostic language of the Johannine Jesus discourses makes impossible the composition of John by an eyewitness. Moreover, if from the beginning the composition of John by an apostle had been recognized, it is completely incomprehensible why John was able to make its way only so slowly and against opposition (Barrett, Käsemann). Further, the dependence upon Mark by a member of the circle of the twelve is hardly conceivable, and the schematization of Jesus' altercation with "the Jews" reveals no knowledge of the actual altercation with the Pharisees, Sadducees, and scribes. To these arguments, which make the composition of John by a member of the circle of the twelve, in general, seem impossible, we may add the facts which exclude John, the son of Zebedee, in particular, as author (see the evidence by Merlier, 200 ff., and Parker, JBL 1962): All the events in which John, the son of Zebedee, decisively participated are missing in John: call of the sons of Zebedee (Mk. 1:19 f. par.); healing of Peter's mother-in-law (Mk. 1:29); choice of the twelve (Mk. 3:13 ff. par.); raising of Jairus' daughter (Mk. 5:37 par.); transfiguration (Mk. 9:2 ff. par.); petition of the sons of Zebedee, with prophecy of their martyrdom (Mk. 10:35 ff. par.); and Gethsemane (Mk. 14:22 ff. par.). James, the brother of John, is never mentioned; although the sons of Zebedee were Galileans, all interest in Galilee is lacking; according to Acts 4:13, Peter and John were ἄνθρωποι ἀγράμματοι, but John is written in good, even if Semitized, Greek. The composition of John by the son of Zebedee is, therefore, excluded.

That is to say, the author of John is unknown to us. It has often been maintained that he must have been a born Jew (lately, e.g., Smith, Schnackenburg, Grundmann). But this supposition is not convincing at all, since the citation of a series of geographical data which are lacking in the Synoptics can readily be explained by the taking up of topographical traditions of the Christian congregations. If he were a former Jew, we might conjecture that he had belonged to a Gnosticizing group before he became a Christian; yet that is pure speculation. It is certain only that he had come into contact with a Palestinian Christian who somehow had participated in the passion history of Jesus, and whom he named "the disciple whom Jesus loved," without our knowing whether this designation was handed down or not. We do not know more about the author of John, and all additional conjectures about the origin of the later tradition about John, the son of Zebedee, as the author of John, contribute nothing to its understanding.

7. Time and Place of Composition

The dating of John is possible today with tolerable certainty within relatively narrow limits. The question about which writers at the beginning of the second century knew John is disputed now as before: I Clement hardly knows John (in spite of Boismard, F.-M. Braun), and equally as little Barnabas and Hermas (against F.-M. Braun; correctly Boismard, RB 1960, 593 ff.). On the other hand, some contend that Ignatius knew John (cf. Maurer, F.-M. Braun, Nunn, and others; opposed, e.g., Barrett). But for the establishment of the *terminus ad quem* for the composition of John the deciding of this question is no longer very important. For Papyrus 52 from the early second century is a fragment of a manuscript of John (see below, p. 363), and the fragment of the "Unknown Gospel," which was written about the same time, likewise knows John (see G. Mayeda, *Das Leben-Jesu-Fragment Papyrus Egerton 2 und seine Stellung in der urchristlichen Literaturgeschichte*, 1946; see above, p. 60). If, therefore, John was known in Egypt in the first quarter of the second century, then the beginning of the second century is a certain *terminus ad quem*. On the other hand, if John most probably knows Luke, then it cannot have been written before about 80-90 (Gardner-Smith, Hunter, Mendner would like to date it earlier). Thus today it is almost common opinion that John was written in the last decade of the first century.

More difficult is the determination of the place of composition. Composition in Ephesus is advocated by the supporters of the ecclesiastical tradition of authorship, but also by Barrett, because in this way the tradition in Irenaeus can best be explained, and by Aland, because the Montanists appeal to John, and the ecclesiastical tradition concerning locations is to be trusted. Since, apart from the very late tradition, nothing in John makes us think of an origin in Asia Minor, attempts have been made to connect the tradition with the other references to the origin of John: The tradition about the Gospel of John came from Alexandria to Ephesus (Stauffer, Snape), or stems out of Jerusalem and was brought via Antioch to Ephesus (Manson, R. M. Grant, JBL 1944, Feuillet in Robert-Feuillet, Eckhardt). Such constructions, though, are without possibility of proof, and the home of the Johannine conceptual world is doubtless not Alexandrian. There are, however, marked parallels in subject matter with the "Odes of Solomon," which supposedly belong to Syria, and with Ignatius of Antioch, who apparently is the oldest user of John. The linguistic form of John also causes us to think of a Greek-speaking author in a Semitic environment. Furthermore, the conceptual world shows relationship with the Gnosticizing circles on the edge of Judaism. Thus the supposition that John originated somewhere in Syria is probably the best conjecture (so Jülicher-Fascher, Burney, Bauer, Schweizer, Haenchen, ZThK 1959). That Ephraem's commentary on the Diatessaron already held this view, as, e.g., W. Bauer maintains upon the basis of an ancient Latin translation of the Armenian translation of this commentary, is surely false, as W. Leloir has demonstrated ("L'original syriaque du commentaire de S. Ephrem sur le Diatessaron," Bb 40, 1959, 965 f.).

B. THE EPISTLES

§11. The Epistle as a Literary Form in the New Testament

A. Deissmann, *Bibelstudien* 1895, 187 ff.; *Bible Studies*. Tr. Alexander Grieve with author's additions, 1901; *idem, Licht vom Osten,* ⁴1923, 116 ff.; *Light from the Ancient East.* Tr. Lionel R. M. Strachan, 1910, 143 ff.; P. Wendland, *Die urchristlichen Literaturformen,* ²/³1912 = Hdb. I, 3, 342 ff.; M. Dibelius, *Geschichte der urchristlichen Literatur* II, 1926, 5 ff.; E. Lohmeyer, "Probleme paulinischer Theologie I: Die brieflichen Grussüberschriften," ZNW 26, 1927, 158 ff.; O. Roller, *Das Formular der paulinischen Briefe,* BWANT, 4. Folge, 6, 1933; L. G. Champion, "Benedictions and Doxologies in the Epistles of Paul," Diss. Heidelberg, 1934; P. Schubert, *Form and Function of the Pauline Thanksgivings,* Beih. zur ZNW 20, 1939; J. T. Sanders, "The Transition from Opening Epistolary Thanksgiving to Body in the Letters of the Pauline Corpus," JBL 81, 1962, 348 ff.; J. Schneider, RAC II, 564 ff.; E. Fascher, RGG³ I, 1412 ff.; B. Rigaux, see lit. to §12, 163 ff.—Good comparative materials from the papyrus letters are found in S. Witowski, *Ep. privatae Graecae,* 1906; A. Deissmann, *loc. cit.;* B. Olsson, *Papyrusbriefe aus der frühesten Römerzeit,* 1925.

Twenty-one writings in the NT have the form of the epistle. But not all of them are actually letters, i.e., writings directed on specific occasions to specific persons or circles of persons, written for the purpose of private communication, without a thought of wider circulation. In James, e.g., everything actually letterlike is missing. The Apocalypse, to be sure, is cast in an epistolary framework, but literarily speaking belongs to the category of the apocalypses. In connection with Hebrews, views vary widely as to whether it is to be regarded as a genuine letter or an artistically constructed essay directed to a broader public, and which uses the form of a letter only as a veil. Among the Catholic epistles, only II and III John are actual letters to exact, specific addressees.

The scheme according to which the epistles are laid out is as follows: At the beginning a formula of salutation, with the names of the sender and the recipient; then thanksgiving to God; and at the conclusion messages of greeting and good wishes in one's own hand, which replace our customary signature. This pattern is, on the whole, the usual one of the Hellenistic epistles of the time, of which the papyrus finds of recent decades have supplied illustrative material in full. Yet Paul in his address formula follows more closely the Oriental-Jewish practice, whereas James and the epistles of Acts 15:23 and 23:26 follow the Hellenistic usage in this respect. But the Pauline epistles assume a superiority over the artless, folk letter through free, deliberate transformation of these pieces, especially of the address which, according to the occasion of the letter, varies the formula which at its beginning and ending is formally structured (Schubert, Sanders). Standing nearest to the ancient private letters are Philemon, II and III John. But even such brief, intimate lines from Paul or the "elder," which in their intimations and allusions are fully understandable only to those most closely involved, are, like Paul's longer epistles, no private correspondence, but the fruits of early Christian missionary work. The epistles of Paul which have been preserved are epistles of the apostle in his official character; they serve to advance his missionary activity from afar. Under the hand of the apostle, the form of the epistle assumes all stylistic forms of oral missionary discourse, generally speaking, of the preaching of the Word in worship: sermon, paraenesis, doctrinal exposition, prophetic witness, and hymn, and consequently in the earliest church becomes the form for writing down edifying or theological trains of thought. Occasionally Paul took up units which had previously been formed, either in his own usage or in the primitive Christian tradition (e.g., I Cor. 15:3-5; Rom. 1:3, 4; Phil. 2:6-11; Col. 1:15-20; yet the wording and origin of such pieces can be ascertained only conjecturally).

In view of the special manner of using the epistolary form in the primitive Christian mission, the lines between actual letters and epistles in the NT cannot always be sharply drawn. An epistle written for a special occasion, which expressly is to be read to all Christians at a place (I Thess. 5:27), an epistle to a particular church, which in exchange the neighboring church is to receive also (Col. 4:16), or epistles to several congregations (Gal. 1:2; cf. II Cor. 1:1), are on the way to becoming literary texts with an official character. On the other hand, in epistles of such general bearing as I Peter or Hebrews there is not lacking a glance at special congregations and states of affairs. The driving force for the independent formation of the epistolary form into a means of literary self-communication of Christianity was the actual need of the mission for edification and instruction, admonition and pastoral work, defense against erroneous ideas, and the securing of ecclesiastical order. The form of the more general epistles contained in the NT is not directly connected with the Hellenistic epistle (cf. Epicurus, Seneca) or the Jewish-Hellenistic epistle (e.g., the Letter of Aristeas).

I. The Pauline Epistles

§12. GENERAL

W. G. KÜMMEL, "Paulusbriefe," RGG³ V, 1961, 195 ff. (lit.); B. RIGAUX, *Saint Paul et ses lettres, Studia Neotestamentica*, Subsidia II, 1962.

The NT canon contains thirteen epistles which cite Paul as the author in the address. Hebrews, which was first regarded as Pauline in the Alexandrian Church, then generally in the East, and since the fourth century in the West, certainly does not stem from Paul. Among the Pauline epistles, the so-called Pastoral epistles (I, II Timothy, Titus) form a special group. We may also classify the epistles which Paul wrote in prison (Philippians, Colossians, Philemon, Ephesians) as "Prison epistles." Outside of the Pastoral epistles and the Epistle to Philemon, all of the Pauline epistles are directed to congregations.

At the beginning of the nineteenth century the Pauline origin of a number of the epistles was called into question—first of all, the Pastorals, then also Thessalonians, Ephesians, Philippians, and Colossians. Then F. C. Baur and the

Tübingen school regarded only the so-called "pillar epistles" (Galatians, I, II Corinthians, Romans) as authentic documents of the apostle, because only these epistles could be understood as witnesses of the struggle between Paul and the Judaizers. But it soon became apparent that the Tübingen School had stretched the historical picture of primitive Christianity on a framework which was too narrow. The advocates of "radical criticism" (Br. Bauer, Pierson, Naber, Loman, van Manen, van den Bergh van Eysinga, Steck) denied even Paul's authorship of the four "Pillar epistles," and explained them as the sediment of antinomian streams around 140. They proceeded from untenable presuppositions and from a forced construction of history, as did later constructions by J. G. Rylands, A. Loisy, H. Delafosse, and others. Together with the four "Pillar epistles," I Thessalonians, Philippians, and Philemon are definitely to be regarded as authentic, whereas the Pauline authorship of the Pastorals is certainly to be denied, and the genuineness of the remaining three epistles (II Thessalonians, Colossians, Ephesians) is debatable. It is also disputed whether the authentic epistles contain unauthentic components, and are partly to be explained as compilations of several epistles or pieces of epistles.

Paul doubtless dictated his epistles (Rom. 16:22), but, according to the usage of the time, characterized them as authentic by a concluding greeting in his own hand. This practice doubtless holds true for all of the Pauline epistles but is expressly noted down in some, for, when the epistles were read aloud, it was only in this way that the congregations could know that this addition was from Paul's own hand (I Cor. 16:21; Gal. 6:11; Col. 4:18; II Thess. 3:17; Phlm. 19). The supposition that Paul entrusted the formulation of his epistles to secretaries (Roller, see to §11) is, in view of the numerous indications that Paul's dictated words were interrupted, and in view of the unity of the specifically Pauline language, impossible.

All of the Pauline epistles which have been preserved stem from the time of the peak and termination of the apostle's missionary activity. From the first decade and a half of his work evidence from his hand is missing. But already in the next to oldest of his epistles Paul speaks of his epistolary habit (II Thess. 3:17). His earlier epistles have, therefore, been lost.

The apostle himself mentions two epistles to the Corinthians which have not been preserved (I Cor. 5:9; II Cor. 2:4), and likewise an epistle to Laodicea (Col. 4:16). This latter reference has occasioned the fabrication of an "Epistle of Paul to the Laodiceans" (a thoughtless compilation of Pauline phrases, especially from Philippians; German reproduction in E. Hennecke, *NTl. Apokryphen*, [2]1924, 150 f.; English tr. in M. R. James, *The Apocryphal NT*, 1924, pp. 478-79; cf. W. Foerster, RGG [3] IV, 1960, 231). The author of the apocryphal Acts of Paul (c. 180), in connection with I Cor. 7:1; 5:9, invented or took up an epistle of the Corinthians to Paul and an answer of Paul (III Corinthians) (see W. G. Kümmel, RGG [3] V, 1961, 194; German in E. Hennecke, *loc. cit.*, 207 ff., II [3], 259 f. The Latin epistolary exchange between Paul (six epistles) and the philosopher Seneca (eight epistles) is an artificial production, probably of the fourth century (edition by C. W. Barlow, 1938, Papers and

Monographs of the American Academy in Rome X; cf. K. Pink, "Die pseudo-paulinischen Briefe," Bb 6, 1925, 68 ff., 179 ff.).

§13. THE CHRONOLOGY OF THE LIFE OF PAUL

Earlier literature in A. JÜLICHER-E. FASCHER, Einl. in das NT, [7]1931, 40, more recent in H. BRAUN, RGG[3] I, 1694 f. On the Gallio-inscription: A. DEISSMANN, Paulus, [2]1925, 203 ff.; Paul, a Study in Social and Religious History. Tr. William E. Wilson from 2nd ed. (1925), 1926; DBS II, 355 ff. (lit.).—D. W. RIDDLE, Paul, Man of Conflict, 1940, 201 ff.; J. KNOX, Chapters in a Life of Paul, 1950, 47 ff.; J. DUPONT, "Chronologie Paulinienne," RB 62, 1955, 55 ff.; TH. H. CAMPBELL, "Paul's 'Missionary Journeys' as Reflected in His Letters," JBL 74, 1955, 80 ff.; E. HAENCHEN, Die Apg., Meyer III[13] 1961, 53 ff.; M. J. SUGGS, "Concerning the Date of Paul's Macedonian Ministry," NovT 4, 1960-61, 60 ff.

Until the beginning of the twentieth century, there was no fixed date for an absolute chronology of Paul, i.e., the numerical arrangement of the events of his life in the context of the general chronology.

And even today the references of Acts and of the Pauline epistles to historical events and persons (Acts 12:1 ff., Herod Agrippa I; 13:7 ff., the proconsul Sergius Paulus; 18:2, Jewish edict of Claudius; 18:12, Gallio the proconsul; chaps. 23 ff., procurators Felix and Festus; II Cor. 11:32, the ethnarch of the Nabatean king, Aretas) cannot, with one exception, be clearly established chronologically. At first, we might think that the transfer of the procuratorship in Palestine from Antonius Felix to Porcius Festus could offer the handle for a definite beginning. But the statements of the sources (Jos., Ant. 20, 118 ff.; Tacitus, Annals 12, 54) are contradictory, and it is difficult to decide with certainty whether the διετία (Acts 24:27) refers to Felix' years in office or to Paul's imprisonment. If, upon the basis of Josephus' statements and the referral of the διετία to Felix' years in office, we calculate that Festus assumed office in 55 (Haenchen), then Paul must have come to Rome about 56. But that would be acceptable only if we completely disregarded the statements of Acts about the journeys of Paul as historically useless. That is done by Riddle, Knox, and Suggs, according to whom either the activity of Paul in Greece began already very soon after his conversion (Suggs, cf. Phil. 4:15 ἐν ἀρχῇ τοῦ εὐαγγελίου ὅτε ἐξῆλθον ἀπὸ Μακεδονίας), or almost the entire activity of Paul took place in the fourteen years before the apostolic council (Riddle, Knox, cf. Gal. 2:1; II Cor. 12:2). Thereby we would arrive at an interval of twenty years at the most from Paul's conversion to his journey to Rome and to a still earlier date for this journey. But Campbell has convincingly demonstrated that the sequence of Paul's missionary activity to be inferred from his epistles so excellently agrees with the statements of Acts that we have every reason to infer the relative chronology of Paul's activity from the combination of both sources.

Since the date of Festus' assumption of office is not useful in establishing an absolute chronology, we have only one possibility of arriving at an absolute chronology, namely, the mention of Gallio the governor, before whom Paul was accused toward the end of his activity in Corinth (Acts 18:12-18). An inscription, which was found in Delphi and published for the first time in 1905, reproduces an epistle of Emperor Claudius to the city of Delphi. It was written when Claudius, after a military success, had been proclaimed "imperator" for the twenty-sixth time. It names Lucius Junius Gallio as proconsul of the province of Achaia at that time. According to Claudius' rule (Dio Cassius 60, 17), the proconsuls, in order to assume office, had to leave Rome by the middle of April. In the senatorial provinces, to which Achaia belonged, the proconsuls were in office one year. Since the twenty-sixth acclamation of Claudius must have taken place between 25 January 52 and 1 August 52, and since the time from Gallio's possible assumption of office in May 52 until the twenty-sixth acclamation of Claudius mentioned in the epistle of the emperor is hardly sufficient for the events presupposed in the epistle, Gallio's term of office is probably to be placed in the year 51-52 (52-53, however, is not excluded). Paul's encounter with Gallio perhaps took place in May or June of 51. At the time Paul had already been in Corinth one and a half years (Acts 18:11), thus since the end of 49. Acts 18:2 reports that Paul, when he came from Athens to Corinth, dwelt with the couple Aquila and Priscilla, who, because of the Jewish edict of Claudius, had recently (προσφάτως) come from Italy to Corinth. This expulsion of the Jews from Rome (Suetonius, *Claudius* 25: "He [Claudius] expelled the Jews from Rome, since they were continually making disturbances with Chrestus as the instigator" [Judaeos impulsore Chresto assidue tumultuantes Roma expulit]) may also have occurred in the year 49. Although we cannot ascribe events with precision to any one year, we can, on the basis of this one, absolute, fixed point, and upon the basis of the relative chronology to be inferred from the Pauline epistles and Acts, establish the following chronology: According to the most probable calculations, there were about sixteen years between the call of Paul and the apostolic council (Gal. 1:18; 2:1). Three years are hardly too much for the time from the apostolic council to the end of Paul's more than eighteen months of activity in Corinth (Gal. 2:1, 11; I Thess. 2:2; Phil. 4:15 f.; I Thess. 3:1; II Cor. 11:7-9; Acts 15:30–18:18*a*). And the time for the return from Corinth to Asia Minor via Palestine, the more than two-year sojourn in Ephesus, the journey to Corinth via Macedonia with the three-month stay in Achaia, and the time for delivering the collection to Jerusalem (I Cor. 16:8; II Cor. 2:12 f.; 9:4; Rom. 15:25-27; Acts 18:18*b*–21:15), include undoubtedly more than three years. Reckoned from the Corinthian stay (49-51), the following dates result:

Conversion	31/32
First visit to Jerusalem	34/35
Abode in Syria and Cilicia	34/35-48
Apostolic council	48
First journey to Asia Minor and Greece	48-51/52
Second journey to Asia Minor and Greece	51/52-55/56
Arrival in Jerusalem	c. 55/56

From there on reasonably certain statements about chronology cannot be made, since we do not know how long the trial of Paul in Caesarea lasted. Like the view that Paul was martyred under Nero (I Clem. 5:7; 6:1), the view that Paul was freed after his two-year imprisonment (Acts 28:30) and traveled to Spain (cf. Rom. 15:24; I Clem. 5:7) remains only a probable supposition.

§14. THE FIRST EPISTLE TO THE THESSALONIANS

Commentaries, see p. 390. Studies: W. LÜTGERT, *Die Vollkommenen in Philippi und die Enthusiasten in Thessalonich*, BFTh 13, 6, 1909, 55 ff.; W. HADORN, *Die Abfassung der Thessalonicherbriefe in der Zeit der dritten Missionsreise des Paulus*, BFTh 24, 3-4, 1919-20, 67 ff.; W. MICHAELIS, *Die Gefangenschaft des Paulus in Ephesus und das Itinerar des Timotheus*, NTF I, 3, 1925, 65 ff.; T. W. MANSON, "St. Paul in Greece: The Letters to the Thessalonians," BJRL 35, 1952-53, 428 ff. (= Manson, St., 259 ff.); C. E. FAW, "On the Writing of First Thessalonians," JBL 71, 1952, 217 ff.; K.-G. ECKART, "Der zweite echte Brief des Apostels Paulus an die Thessalonicher," ZThK 58, 1961, 30 ff.; W. G. KÜMMEL, "Das literarische und geschichtliche Problem des ersten Thessalonicherbriefes," *Neotestamentica et Patristica, Freundesgabe O. Cullmann*, NovT Suppl. 6, 1962, 213 ff.

1. Contents

After the introductory greetings (1:1) follows thanksgiving for the exemplary manner in which the congregation has received the Christian faith (1:2-10). Then Paul retrospectively defends his missionary work in Thessalonica (2:1-12), and enters anew into the attitude of the readers (2:13-16). He concludes the first part of the Epistle (which remains within the framework of the epistolary introduction) with a thankful portrayal of his relations with the church (2:17–3:10), and intercession (3:11-13). In chaps. 4–5 follow warnings and instructions: a reminder of the moral duties of the Thessalonians as Christians with a pagan past (4:1-12), an eschatological instruction concerning the fate of those church members who have fallen asleep before the parousia, with a call for watchfulness to the living (4:13–5:11), and a series of particular directions for the life of the congregation (5:12-22). Closing prayer and benediction (5:23-28).

2. The Founding of the Church

Thessalonica, until 1937, Salonica, the capital of the Roman province Macedonia, lay on the great military road, the "via Egnatia" (Dyrrhachium-Byzantium), which connected Rome with the East. At that time it was already a populous city, which also had a synagogue (Acts 17:1), with numerous non-Jewish "God-fearers" (Acts 17:4).

On the so-called second missionary journey, perhaps in the year 49, Paul, supported by Silvanus (or, as Acts calls him, Silas) and Timothy, came from Philippi to Thessalonica and founded the Christian church there. I Thess. 1:1,

5-8; 2:1-14; 3:1-6; Phil. 4:16, and Acts 17:1-10; 18:5, give sketches of the history of the founding. The congregation was almost entirely Gentile-Christian (1:9; 2:14; Acts 17:4). According to Col. 4:10 f., Aristarchus, who hailed from Thessalonica, was a Jewish Christian (Acts 20:4).

Acts 17:2 does not prove that Paul worked there only three to four weeks. An intimate and loving relationship between Paul and the church, as is shown in 2:9-12, 17, 19 f.; 3:6, could not have originated in so short a time, just as little as the exemplary faith of the Thessalonians (1:8 ff.). If, according to Phil. 4:16, the Christians from Philippi more than once sent support to Paul in Thessalonica, then his sojourn here must have been of a longer duration. Paul did not create a fixed church organization in Thessalonica. In 5:12 there is no talk of administrators in the official sense (cf. I Tim. 5:17) but of congregational members, who voluntarily assist the brethren. The imperatives in 5:14 are not intended for any kind of officeholders but summon the congregation itself to pastoral care of its members.

The congregation must soon have enjoyed a gratifying development (1:3 f.; 2:13); indeed, Paul characterizes them as exemplary for the believers in Macedonia and Achaia (1:7 f.). But the Jews stirred up the rabble of the city against Paul and Silas, so that they had to flee by night to Berea (Acts 17:5 ff.). There also successful preaching was violently obstructed by the Jews from Thessalonica (Acts 17:13 f.). Then Paul went to Athens and hence to Corinth. According to Acts 17:14 f., Silas and Timothy remained behind in Berea but received a command from Paul in Athens to come to him as soon as possible, and, coming from Macedonia, they met again with Paul in Corinth (Acts 18:5). But these statements do not agree entirely with I Thess. 3:1-6. Here Paul says that in his heated desire for a report from the young congregation, which he had had to leave so suddenly, "we were willing to be left behind at Athens alone, and we sent Timothy" (3:1 f.), namely, to Thessalonica. Once more he says the same thing in v. 5: "I sent . . . ," so that v. 5 resumes the thought of v. 2 (editorial "we" = I of 3:6 ff., and often in Paul). The expression, "we were willing to be left behind at Athens alone," presupposes the presence of Timothy in Athens. The various attempts to solve this contradiction are unprovable and probably unnecessary, because Acts was not precisely informed about the travels of Paul's companions (cf. v. Dobschütz, Komm., 13 ff.).

3. Time and Occasion of the Epistle

The statements in I Thessalonians itself presuppose a situation according to which Paul had sent Timothy from Athens to Thessalonica (3:1 f.) in order to learn something about the continuing existence of the church. Since, according to 1:1 and 3:6, Timothy and Silvanus are with Paul, and Timothy has brought reports from Thessalonica; since, moreover, Athens is so mentioned in 3:1 as if Paul were no more there, it is the predominant view that I Thessalonians was written in Corinth, where also, according to Acts 18:5, Timothy and Silvanus had again met Paul. Since for the journey of Timothy from Athens to Thessalonica and back to Corinth and for the publication abroad in Macedonia and Achaia of the Thessalonians' condition of faith (I Thess. 1:8 f.) some time must have passed, I Thessalonians may have been written about the year 50. I Thessalonians is, therefore, the oldest preserved Pauline epistle. Against this dating, Lütgert, Hadorn, Michaelis, and Schmithals (ZNW 51, 1960, 230, 232 f.) have raised several objections: a) The opponents of Paul who are combated in I Thessalonians advocate the same views as those attacked in Galatians and II Corinthians (according to Schmithals, Jewish-Christian-Gnostic views), and Paul must defend himself against the same charges. That compels us to suppose that I Thessalonians was written during the same period of Paul's activity as Galatians and II Corinthians (according to Schmithals also I Corinthians, Philippians, and Rom. 16). b) The reports concerning the spread of the information about the Thessalonians' faith in Macedonia and Achaia, indeed, everywhere (1:8 f.); the reports about the persecution of the church (2:14), and the organization already existing in it (5:12), refer to an interval from the time of the founding of the church which must be greater than a few months. c) The occurrence of several cases of death in the congregation is not conceivable within so short a time. d) Since according to Acts 17:14 and 18:5 Timothy was not with Paul in Athens, but I Thess. 3:1 f. presupposes that he was, the stay in Athens mentioned in I Thessalonians cannot be identical with that mentioned in Acts. Consequently, I Thessalonians must have been written either during the third missionary journey when Paul made his "intermediate visit" to Corinth (II Cor. 2:1) (and then we must conjecture that on this journey Paul, accompanied by Timothy, stayed in Athens), or Paul during his stop in Corinth from 50-52 must have been once more in Athens and sent Timothy from there to Thessalonica (so Michaelis as a possibility).

But these arguments are not convincing. a) It is correct that in I Thess. 2:1 ff. Paul defends himself against similar charges as in Galatians and II Corinthians: false leadership (I 2:3 = II Cor. 6:8); deceit (I 2:3 = II Cor. 4:2); greed (I 2:5 = II Cor. 12:16-18); seeking of personal glory (I 2:6 = II Cor. 10:17 f.; 4:5; 3:1); not allowing himself to be supported by the congregation (I 2:7 = II Cor. 11:9); flattery and pleasing of men (I 2:4 f. = Gal. 1:10) (cf. the exaggerated compilation by Schmithals, ZNW 51, 1960, 228). But this argument is no reason to date I Thessalonians from the time of the Apostle's struggle against the Judaizers and the Gnostics. Jews, Judaizers, and Gnostics often used the same weapons against Paul. In Thessalonica it was the Jews there who appeared against him with great bitterness, drove him away, and pursued him to Berea. They obviously were the ones who persuaded the young Christian congregation that Paul was a false leader, a sorcerer with a mean disposition, who worked with all the tricks of selfish, ambitious propaganda. It is against such charges that Paul defends himself in 2:1 ff., 18 f.; 3:9 f., and not against false teachings which have infiltrated the congregation. He feared that the Jewish calumnies of his person could make an impression upon the Christians, since he had left so quickly and did not return. If this is the historical background, then it also accounts for the sudden attack against the Judaism which was hostile to Christians (2:14-16). b) The references to the spreading reputation of the Thessalonians' belief and persecution befalling them demand no longer interval, and there is no talk of a fixed organization (see above, p. 182). c) A few cases of death could occur in a shorter period. d) Acts was hardly so precisely oriented about the journeys of Paul's companions. But more important than these negative statements as arguments against the composition of I Thessalonians several years after the departure of Paul from Thessalonica, is what the Epistle itself tells us about the previous relations of Paul to the congregation. Already 1:5–2:12 is saturated with allusions to the period of Paul's first missionary activity in Thessalonica (1:5, 9; 2:2, 8 f., 12). It tells us of his arrival among them (1:9; 2:1); it speaks of how unobjectionable his appearance in Thessalonica was, and how the Thessalonians through their conversion became imitators of Paul and Christ (1:6), and thereby examples for others (1:7). In ever new phrases the Apostle reminds them of these facts: "you know" (1:5; 2:1 ff., 5), "you remember" (2:9), "you are witnesses" (2:10). These all seem to be entirely fresh recollections. Further, 2:17 f.: Paul after his departure πρὸς καιρὸν ὥρας was bereft because of his separation from the readers; therefore he was away from Thessalonica a very short time. Then the desire for his church so overcame him that he once, indeed twice, decided to travel to Thessalonica, in order to see whether the church in its times of tribulation and persecution was standing firm (3:2 f.), but "Satan hindered" him. Then, when he could bear it no longer to remain without a report from Thessalonica, he sent Timothy there from Athens (3:1 f., 5), received with great thankfulness and joy the good news which Timothy brought back to him, and immediately wrote this Epistle (3:6 ff.). Accordingly, the Epistle can have been written only a few months after the founding of the church, as the first epistle of the Apostle to them since their separation.

According to 3:6, I Thessalonians was written directly after Timothy's return to Paul. Paul had traveled again from Athens to Corinth and had begun to preach in the synagogue there, until finally Silas and Timothy should meet him again (Acts 18:1-5). According to that, several months, but not more, could very well lie between the separation of Paul from the Thessalonians and the composition of the Epistle. Paul, therefore, received the inducement to write I Thessalonians through the fresh reports which Timothy brought him from Thessalonica, whereby the *possibility* exists that Paul in chaps. 4 and 5 is answering a letter from the church (Faw, with reference to περί in 4:9, 13; 5:1, 12). The reports freed Paul from heavy solicitude: The church stands fast in faith and love (3:6). His deep joy over this report compels him to the discussion which serves at the same time to strengthen the congregation's faith and to defend Paul against the accusations brought against him. In this connection we see not only the difficulty into which the Christians who were formerly Gentiles fell through the preaching of the imminent eschatological glory (cf. 4:11 f., 13 ff.; 5:1 ff., 14), but also the necessity of bringing into living harmony the certainty of imminent justification before God with sober moral duty in the present (5:6 ff.; 4:3 ff.; 5:12 f., 19 f.). On the other hand, in I Thessalonians there is no systematic instruction, for this writing, which arose out of a particular, unique situation, is an actual epistle, a through and through personal and original witness to Pauline missionary work.

4. Authenticity

Baur and a part of his school (Volkmar, Holsten) denied the authenticity of this Epistle because it is lacking in originality and significant doctrinal ideas; it is dependent upon other NT writings; it contains nothing about justification by faith, no polemic against Judaizing teaching about the Law, and no OT quotations; finally, the apocalypticism in chaps. 4 and 5 is non-Pauline. The alleged literary parallels, however, do not exist, and in Thessalonica the battle against the Judaizers about justification by faith played no role. In vocabulary, style, and direction of thought the Epistle is genuinely Pauline. No later writer would have attributed to Paul the unfulfilled expectation of living to see the parousia (4:15, 17). There is no reason for denying to Paul the apocalyptic thoughts of the Epistle—they are also found in I Cor. 15:23 ff., 51 ff. The recent attempt to show that I Thessalonians is a piecing together of two genuine epistles to the Thessalonians (E. Fuchs, Thv 7, 1960, 46 ff.; Eckart) is insufficiently grounded. The additional supposition that the sections 2:13-16; 4:1-8, 10b-12, 18; 5:12-22, 27 are un-Pauline additions of the redactor (Eckart) runs aground on the incontestably Pauline language of these sections, and also on the fact that nothing convincing can be adduced against these texts. There can be no justifiable doubt that all of I Thessalonians is of Pauline origin.

§15. THE SECOND EPISTLE TO THE THESSALONIANS

Besides the lit. to §14: W. WREDE, *Die Echtheit des II Thess.*, TU, N. F. 9, 2, 1903; A. HARNACK, *Das Problem des II Thess.*, SBA 1910, 560 ff.; J. WRZOL, "Die Echtheit des II Thess. untersucht," BSt 19, 4, 1916; J. GRAAFEN, *Die Echtheit des 2. Briefes an die Thessalonicher*, NTA 14, 5, 1930; E. SCHWEIZER, "Der II Thess. ein Phil.?," ThZ 1, 1945, 90 ff., 286 ff.; 2, 1946, 74 f., contrariwise W. MICHAELIS, *ibid.* 1, 282 ff.; J. KLAUSNER, *Von Jesus zu Paulus*, 1950, 229 ff.; *From Jesus to Paul.* Tr. from Hebrew by William F. Stinespring, 1943; H. BRAUN, "Zur nichtpaulinischen Herkunft des zweiten Thessalonicherbriefes," ZNW 44, 1952-53, 152 ff. (= Gesammelte Studien zum NT und seiner Umwelt, 1962, 205 ff.).

1. Contents

After introduction and greeting (1:1-2), Paul gives thanks for the preservation of the church in faith and love, especially for their endurance in suffering, refers to parousia and last judgment, and concludes his epistolary introduction with intercession for the congregation (1:3-12). The actual letter begins, in view of reports from the church, with an attempt to keep the Thessalonians from an exaggerated expectation of the parousia: The day of the Lord is not yet there; before that the antichrist must come; he is working already in secret but is restrained by a power known to the congregation; after his revelation he will immediately be destroyed by the Lord's parousia (2:1-12). There follow thanks for the election of the Christians, admonition to firmness, and renewed intercession, with reference to the steadfastness of Christ and God (2:13–3:5), then special instructions in respect to the disorderly, who, because of the nearness of the parousia, lead a life of laziness (3:6-16). Epistolary conclusion in Paul's own hand (3:17-18).

2. Chronological Sequence of I and II Thessalonians

Since Hugo Grotius (1640) several scholars have placed II before I (recently, e.g., J. Weiss, *Earliest Christianity*. Translation edited F. C. Grant, 1959, I, 289 ff.; Hadorn [see §14], 116 ff.; de Zwaan, Appel [II was only *sent* before I!], T. W. Manson [see §14], Albertz). The reasons for this predating of II are: 1) In the canon, I was placed first because it is longer than II. 2) When Timothy was sent to Thessalonica he would have taken an epistle with him. 3) The troubles are present in II, past in I. 4) The disorders are something new in II 3:11; on the other hand, in I 5:14 the unorderly are mentioned as already dealt with; I 4:10, 12 is so short that this admonition can be understood only from II 3. 5) The reference to the personal subscription (II 3:17) would have meaning only in the first epistle. 6) The remark that the congregation has no need of instruction about times and seasons (I 5:1) is more suitable if the congregation had already read II 2. 7) The references with περί (I 4:9, 13; 5:1) to questions which are problematic in the congregation are best explained if these questions were raised in the congregation through the statements in II. But these reasons are by no means convincing: 1) For a disarrangement in connection with the collection of the Pauline epistles there is no criterion. 2) Timothy is the cosender and thus not the bearer. 3) The difficulties continue after I 3:3 f. and, considering the state of affairs in Thessalonica, could be renewed any day, and, as II 1:4 ff. shows, that actually happened. 4) According to I 4:11, Paul, in connection with the founding of the church, already had to ward off a tendency toward sloth on the part of enthusiastic eschatologists. He confronts this inclination in I 4:10 f.; 5:14. But in II, in the meantime, energetic measures have become necessary, in connection with which Paul naturally appeals to fundamental oral instructions, not to I 4:10 f.; 5:14. 5) Paul refers to earlier epistolary communications not only in I Cor. 5:9; II Cor. 2:3 ff.; 7:8, 12, but also in II Thess. 2:15; and in II 2:2 he perhaps presupposes that a forged letter supposedly from him is in circulation in Thessalonica. This conjecture abundantly justifies his remark in II 3:17 about his mode of letter writing. 6) I 5:1 f. alludes to oral instruction just as does I 4:9. 7) Nothing points to the idea that the questions which arose in the congregation were raised by a letter from Paul. But the fact that I 2:17–3:10 could stand only in the first letter to the congregation speaks decisively against the hypothesis that I Thessalonians is the second letter to the congregation. The canonical sequence must, therefore, be the original one.

3. Occasion

The letter cannot have been composed long after I, that is, 50-51 in Corinth, for the inscription to II also names, in addition to Paul, Silvanus and Timothy. But, according to Acts, Silvanus accompanied the Apostle only during the so-called second missionary journey. The situation of the congregation presupposed in II is the same as in I, but Paul has received new reports from Thessalonica: "we hear" (3:11; cf. 2:2). The congregation had not wavered in persecutions and afflictions (1:4), but there had developed within it fantastic conceptions of the parousia. False teachers had spoken of alleged revelations (διὰ πνεύματος 2:2), and appeals seem to have been made to oral and epistolary statements of Paul to the effect that the day of the Lord had already come (2:2). The apocalyptic fanaticism exercised such a bad influence upon the moral behavior of some church members that Paul commanded that the means of church discipline be used against this fanaticism (3:6 ff., 11 ff.). The things mentioned were the chief occasion of II. Paul guards against epistolary forgery (2:2), gives the characteristic of his genuine letters, i.e., the conclusion in his own hand (3:17), and teaches about the parousia (2:1-12).

4. Authenticity

For history of criticism cf. B. Rigaux, Comm, 124 ff. The first to deny the authenticity, fundamentally only the authenticity of 2:1-12, was J. E. Christian Schmidt, *Vermutungen über die beiden Briefe an die Thessalonicher*, 1801. According to Schmidt, Paul would have had to call to mind I Thessalonians if he wanted to warn the congregation to have confidence in a letter written in his name, in which the imminent parousia of Christ was maintained. In II 2:1-12 those warnings as well as the fancies about the antichrist connected with them are un-Pauline. In the first edition of his *Einl.* De Wette took up Schmidt's doubt but later decided in favor of authenticity (4th ed.). In an exhaustive investigation F. H. Kern (TZTh 1839, 145 ff.) opposed the Pauline origin of II. He placed the chief emphasis of his investigation upon 2:1-12. This apocalyptic portrayal is comparable to Rev. 13:3 ff.; 17:8 ff., and hence is to be dated during the period 68-70. A Paulinist put this apocalyptic picture into a frame which he took from the materials of I. Thus the impression of literary dependence of II upon I formed for Kern a secondary argument against authenticity. Kern also referred to other questionable instances, such as II 3:17, the statement of the characteristic of all genuine Pauline epistles, a notice which Kern regarded as an attempt to secure recognition for the unauthentic letter. He also found un-Pauline phrases in II. For decades Kern's investigation was decisive. Many accepted it (Baur, Hilgenfeld, Pfleiderer, Hausrath, and others; some placed II in the time of Trajan).

Weizsäcker (*The Apostolical Age of the Christian Church*. Tr. James Millar, from 2nd ed. [1892], 1897, i, 295 ff.) was the first who based the critical considerations principally upon II's literary dependence upon I. According to Holtzmann, the chief question about the unauthenticity of II hinges upon the relation of II 2:1-12 to I 4:13–5:11 (the pictures of the future in these two passages are irreconcilable) ; added to that, II consists almost entirely of extracts, paraphrases, and variations of I. Wrede in his proof of the unauthenticity of II emphasized the literary relation of II to I: II is almost completely dependent upon I, and was composed around 100, with I as a basis. In addition, Wrede also urged that if Paul had believed, as must be concluded from II 2:2; 3:17, that his name was misused in a forgery, then he must have pursued this matter, but he does not do that. Today where the authenticity of II is doubted, Wrede's criticism continues to exercise influence. Critics also point to the incompatibility of II 2:1-12 with the eschatological sections in I 4:13 ff. and I Cor. 15:20 ff. (Masson), or to the moralizing in II 1:5 ff.; 2:12, in comparison with Paul (Braun). There are to be named as advocates of unauthenticity besides those already mentioned Jülicher, R. Bultmann, *Theology of the NT*, II, 142, H. J. Schoeps, *Paul*, Tr. Harold Knight, 1961, 51, E. Fuchs, Thv 7, 1960, 46, G. Bornkamm, RGG [3] V, 1961, 167, K.-G. Eckart (see to §14), J. C. Beker, JR 38, 1958, 132, by connecting ὁ κατέχων II 2:7 to Paul.

Yet weighty considerations oppose the supposition of a non-Pauline origin of II Thessalonians. The reasons against authenticity based upon the difference between the expectation of the end in I and II cannot be considered as valid. The illustrative material in II 2:3 ff. does not originate from the history of the time but is traditional apocalyptic material. Both "the man of lawlessness" (II 2:3) and the κατέχων (II 2:7) are traditional apocalyptic figures (see Dibelius, *ad loc.*,), and the events, which II 2:3 ff. presuppose, are to be joined together with I Cor. 15:23 ff. in a coherent eschatological picture no better and no worse than I 4:13 ff. with I Cor. 15:51 ff. The contradiction between I and II, that the parousia according to I 5:2 comes suddenly like a thief in the night, whereas according to II 2:3 ff. not until after the appearance of various signs (rebellion, revelation of the man of lawlesnes, who takes his seat in the temple in a blasphemous arrogance and proclaims himself to be God, removal of the restraining power), does not appear strange, so long as we keep in mind that both conceptions—the end comes suddenly, and it is historically prepared for —go together and are viewed together in the apocalypticism of Judaism and primitive Christianity. J. Klausner has rightly drawn our attention to the fact that in other times in history great spirits have expressed themselves differently in style and content in writings chronologically close to one another. Moreover, in spite of the reference to the delayed events, II 2:7 also says: "The mystery of lawlessness is already at work"; the eschatological drama, whose goal is the parousia of Christ, has already begun. Occasioned by reports from Thessalonica, Paul supposes that a forged epistle, supposedly from him, is circulating in Thessalonica (2:2; 3:11), and once for all states the characteristic of his genuine epistles (3:17), without finding it necessary to go further into the question of an unauthentic epistle. And in view of the overheated eschatological expectation on the part of some Christians in Thessalonica, Paul had occasion to point out

that the parousia would be delayed, in spite of the fact that he still held fast
to the expectation of the parousia.

The language and style of II Thessalonians are, apart from particular words,
thoroughly Pauline: ἐπιφάνεια is found only in II 2:8 and in the Pastorals for
the parousia, but in II Thessalonians it is not used as an isolated *terminus technicus*. And if occasionally in II Thessalonians (2:13; 3:16) κύριος appears for
θεός in I Thessalonians (1:4; 5:23), such changes are also found otherwise (I
Thess. 2:12, cf. with Col. 1:10). The literary connection of II Thessalonians
with I Thessalonians is doubtless very close (cf. the lists in Rigaux, Comm.,
133 f.). But against Wrede's contention, the parallels are not in the same
sequence and extend to only about a third of the Epistle, so that nothing compels
us to suppose a literary dependence of II upon I. And the change of tone (cf.
II 1:3; 2:13 εὐχαριστεῖν ὀφείλομεν with I 1:2; 2:13 εὐχαριστοῦμεν) is understandable in view of the censure which Paul has to express in II Thessalonians and,
besides that, corresponds to liturgical style (I Clem. 38:4; Barn. 5:3). And if
Braun wants to find in II Thessalonians a moralizing development of the theology of I Thessalonians because of II's presupposition of divine judgment upon
those who afflict the congregation (II 1:5 ff.), in I 2:16 there is also found
an analogous judgment upon the Jews who are hostile to the mission. And II
1:11 shows that Paul by no means relies upon a general acceptance of Christians *as* Christians in the judgment.

The hypothesis of unauthenticity is subject to criticism, not only on the
grounds of eschatology and language, but in and of itself. Since II Thessalonians
from the early second century on (Polycarp, Phil. 11:4; Marcion) belonged
indisputably to the Pauline writings, it must have been written at the latest by
the beginning of the second century. But the eschatological teaching, which
forms the center of the Epistle, cannot be understood from post-Pauline tendencies of the first century. II 2:4 was obviously written while the temple was
still standing. The fact that the addition of μεθ' ἡμῶν (II 1:7) is good Pauline
style (cf. I 3:12 and v. Dobschütz, *ad loc.*) and would be very improbable for
an imitator, also speaks in favor of the Pauline origin of II Thessalonians. And
likewise the premature conclusion of II 3:1-5 is more suitable to Paul who is
dictating his correspondence in a vivid way than to an author who is consciously imitating him.

With the supposition of the authenticity of II Thessalonians, there naturally
remains the striking fact that Paul must have written to the same congregation
after a relatively short time an epistle so similar in many respects to the first one.
Attempts have been made to elude this difficulty by supposing that II Thessalonians was originally directed to a Jewish-Christian minority in Thessalonica
(Harnack, Albertz), or to a special group within the congregation (Dibelius),
or even to the church at Berea (Goguel) or Philippi (Schweizer). But weighing
against all these hypotheses are the facts that then the original address of the
Epistle must have been altered (why?), and that according to II 2:15 Paul
already had written an epistle to the same congregation.

II Thessalonians remains best understood if Paul himself wrote II a few weeks after I, when I was still fresh in his memory. Thus, on the one hand, the apocalyptic teaching becomes understandable, which now, as an elaboration of Paul's original oral missionary preaching, shows the other side of the question, and, on the other hand, the peculiar mixture of components of the new letter with material from I, whereby I 2:1–3:10 remains basically unused. The somewhat changed situation also makes understandable the amplification of those points of view which already were treated in I, such as the duty of suffering, the threat of judgment against the persecutors of the church, and the reproof of the slothful and fanatics. If there remain some details in II (and even in I) which are not as clear to us as we would like for them to be, we still have no cause to doubt the authenticity of II, for this lack of clarity is the consequence of II's being a real letter.

§16. The Epistle to the Galatians

Commentaries, see p. 389. Studies: W. M. RAMSAY, *The Church in the Roman Empire*, [3]1894, 74 ff.; W. LÜTGERT, *Gesetz und Geist. Eine Untersuchung zur Vorgeschichte des Gal.*, BFTh 22, 6, 1919; J. H. ROPES, *The Singular Problem of the Epistle to the Galatians*, HarvThSt 14, 1929; T. W. MANSON, "St. Paul in Ephesus: (2) The Problem of the Epistle to the Galatians," BJRL 24, 1940, 59 ff. (= MANSON, St., 168 ff.); B. ORCHARD, "A New Solution of the Galatians Problem," BJRL 28, 1944, 154 ff.; F. C. CROWNFIELD, "The Singular Problem of the Dual Galatians," JBL 64, 1945, 491 ff.; C. H. BUCK, "The Date of Galatians," JBL 70, 1951, 113 ff.; J. MUNCK, *Paulus und die Heilsgeschichte*, Acta Jutlandica 26, 1, 1954, 79 ff.; *Paul and the Salvation of Mankind.* Tr. Frank Clarke, 1959, 87 ff.; W. SCHMITHALS, "Die Häretiker in Galatien," ZNW 47, 1956, 25 ff.; G. STÄHLIN, RGG[3] II, 1958, 1187 ff.; H. SCHLIER, LThK IV, 487 f.; C. E. FAW, "The Anomaly of Galatians," BR 4, 1960, 25 ff.; G. KLEIN, "Gal.2,6-9 und die Geschichte der Jerusalemer Urgemeinde," ZThK 57, 1960, 275 ff.; A. VIARD, DBS VII, 1961, 211 ff. (bibl.); K. WEGENAST, *Das Verständnis der Tradition bei Paulus und in den Deuteropaulinen*, WMANT 8, 1962, 36 ff.

1. Contents

After the address, which has been expanded by apology (1:1-5), there follows, contrary to epistolary custom, no thanksgiving for the addressees, but Paul begins immediately with reference to the situation in the churches, in that he censures the readers because of their desertion of the gospel, and his judgment falls upon their seducers (1:6-10). Then follows, first of all, in the First Part (1:11–2:21) Paul's personal defense against attacks on his apostolic office: His gospel does not stem from men; he has received it directly from God in the revelation of Christ before Damascus—hence his independence in his missionary calling from the first days on (1:11-24). His gospel in its peculiarity was expressly approved and recognized by the primitive church in Jerusalem and the primitive apostles at the apostolic council (2:1-10). In connection with a visit of Peter to Antioch, Paul showed his independence of men, even in respect to the leading primitive apostle, and defended the truth of his law-free gospel (2:11-21).

The Second Part (3:1–4:31) demonstrates in an exegetical way, and with reference to the experience of the readers, the necessity of freedom from the Law: Faith, not works, obtains salvation; justification is not connected with the fulfillment of the Law but with the promise. The readers know that from their own experience (3:1-5); the example of Abraham attests that to them (3:6-9); rightly understood, the entire OT already says that to them (3:10-14), for in the OT Law and faith oppose each other as two exclusive opposites. Through Christ the Law is now abrogated (3:15-24), and the time of the free adoption of God has broken in (3:25-4:7). Therewith slavery to the elements of the world is abolished, and therefore the Galatians must not subject themselves to them again for any price (4:8-11). After a personal appeal to the Galatians to consider the love which existed between them and their apostle (4:12-20), there follows, somewhat unexpectedly, a scriptural proof for the freedom of Christians through an allegorical interpretation of the OT narrative of Hagar and Sarah (4:21-31).

The Third Part (5:1–6:10), which is attached with a paraenetic οὖν (see W. Nauck, ZNW 49, 1958, 134 f.), exhorts them to preserve the gift of freedom through obedience to the Spirit in freedom from the Law, and closes with concrete instructions. The epistolary conclusion in Paul's own hand warns anew about self-seeking false teachers but contains no personal greeting, only Paul's good wishes.

2. The Territory of Galatia

The Galatians, in the narrower sense, who alone were thought to be the addressees until the eighteenth century, were Celts, who had settled in central Asia Minor in the first half of the third century before Christ. Around 240 B.C. King Attalos of Pergamum limited their territory to the river regions of the Halys and the Sangarios, with the cities Ancyra, Pessinus, and Tavium. In 25 B.C. the last king of the Galatians, Amyntas, left behind his kingdom to the Romans, who made a province out of it, with Ancyra as the capital. This province included, in addition to the actual land of Galatia, several other territories, including Pisidia, Isauria, parts of Lycaonia, Phrygia, Paphlagonia, and Pontus. The extent of the territories and cities assimilated into the province of Galatia was changed more than once. Officially, it bore no uniform name. The abbreviated designation of the province with the name Galatia appears occasionally in writers of the age of the emperors, but not in inscriptions. The name "Galatian" is found only for the inhabitants of the territory of Galatia (see PW 7, 1 = 13, 556 f.).

3. The Recipients of the Epistle

In Galatia at the time of Galatians there existed several churches in unnamed places (1:2). Concerning the time of their founding, the Epistle says nothing.

Acts mentions the land of Galatia twice: 16:6 says only that the Apostle and his companions passed through the region of Phrygia and Galatia; according to 18:23, there were disciples at the beginning of the so-called third missionary journey in the region of Galatia and Phrygia, i.e., congregations existed there. Did Paul write to these congregations in "the region of Galatia"?

Two answers stand opposed to each other, the falsely so-called "south Galatian" and "north Galatian" theories. The south Galatian hypothesis, or better, "province hypothesis" ["Provinzhypothese"], refers to the congregations at Antioch, Lystra, Derbe, Iconium, and others, in Pisidia and Lycaonia, founded on the first missionary journey (Acts 13, 14), which Paul again visited on the so-called second missionary journey (Acts 16:1 ff.). The north Galatian hypothesis, or better, "territory hypothesis" ["Landschaftshypothese"], seeks the addressees of the Epistle in the actual land of Galatia, in the territory of Galatia. Since, according to Acts 18:23, congregations are presupposed there, one must, according to this hypothesis, in spite of the silence of Acts, suppose that Paul, on his passage through the Galatian territory (Acts 16:6), gave the impetus to the founding of these congregations.

The "province hypothesis" appeared for the first time in Joh. Joach. Schmidt (1748) and J. P. Mynster (1825). W. M. Ramsay and Zahn advocated it most effectively. Today it has numerous supporters (e.g., Goodspeed, T. W. Manson, Orchard, Heard, Henshaw, Albertz, Ridderbos, R. T. Stamm, McNeile-Williams, Michaelis, Guthrie, Klijn). The chief arguments for this hypothesis are the following: 1) Paul was accustomed to use as designations of the lands through which he passed the Roman provincial names, not the names of the territories. Lycaonia and Pisidia, however, belonged to the province Galatia. 2) In the churches of Galatia there were born Jews, which proves true only of the province Galatia, since we know practically nothing of Jews in the territory of Galatia. 3) According to Acts 20:4, Paul has Christians from the province Galatia (Gaius of Derbe, Timothy of Lystra) among the bearers of the collection, but no delegates from the territory of Galatia, whereas according to I Cor. 16:1 the collection was also gathered in Galatia. 4) The activity of the envoys from Jerusalem in Galatia in the south of the Taurus mountains is more probable than in the hardly accessible inner Asia Minor. But none of these arguments is really effective: 1) The contention that Paul used only the official names of the provinces cannot be maintained. In Gal. 1:21 Paul mentions his journey from Jerusalem and names Syria as the territory for which he first sets out. Here, however, he speaks of Syria, not in the broader, official sense of the Roman province, to which Jerusalem also belonged, but in the narrower sense of Seleucidian Syria, in which Antioch lay. When he refers to the Christian congregations in Judea (I Thess. 2:14), he is thinking of the territory of Judea (likewise in II Cor. 1:16). And Arabia, to which Paul went after his Damascus experience (Gal. 1:17), was no official name for the kingdom of the Nabateans. 2) The places which could point to Jewish Christians in the congregations (3:2 f., 13 f., 23 f.; 4:2, 5; 5:1), speak generally of the Christians there; but, according to 4:8; 5:2 f.; 6:12 f., it is certain that the Galatians were Gentile Christians. As a matter of fact, the passages cited testify only to the opinion natural to Paul as a former Jew that the OT Law has validity for all mankind, and, therefore, through Christ's redemptive death the Gentiles also were freed from the Law. 3) In Acts 20:4 there are also no bearers from Achaia in the collection deputation, who would be expected according to I Cor. 16:1 ff. Moreover, it is questionable whether Gaius was not a Macedonian (cf. Acts 19:29 and 20:4 $\Delta o v \beta[\eta] \rho \iota o s$ according to D gig). 4) If, in connection with the opponents in Galatia, it is actually supposed to be a matter of envoys from Jerusalem (see below, pp. 193 ff.), then we know in any case nothing at all about their journeys, and even the supposition would be *conceivable* that they also were active in the churches founded by Paul on the so-called first missionary journey, before they went into the territory of Galatia, without our learning anything of this activity. This argument is, therefore, completely useless.

On the other hand, at least two arguments speak for the supposition that Galatians was directed to Christian congregations in the *territory* of Galatia: 1) If Galatians were sent to the congregations founded on the so-called first missionary journey, then Paul would not have said: "Then I went into the regions of Syria and Cilicia" (1:21), but something like this: Then I went to Syria, Cilicia, and to you. 2) Paul could not possibly have addressed Lycaonians or Pisidians "O foolish Galatians" (3:1), particularly since this linguistic usage is generally not attested. The same linguistic usage as in Acts and contemporary writers, who clearly distinguish the Galatians from their neighboring tribes, must also be presupposed in Paul, a native of Asia Minor. Thus the supposition that the addressees are the Galatians living in inner Asia Minor, whom Paul visited on his second and third missionary journeys, is most nearly suited to the indications of the Epistle. This judgment, to be sure, can first be considered to some degree certain if it can be shown that the historical situation presupposed in Galatians corresponds to this supposition.

4. The Historical Situation

The determination of the historical occasion of the Epistle presupposes the answer to two questions, both of which are very controversial: a) Who are the opponents whom Paul battles in Galatians? b) Which events in the life of Paul does Galatians presuppose as already having occurred?

a) It is clear that the Epistle is directed against an agitation in the Galatian churches, which was brought into the churches from the outside. Persons who "pervert the gospel" (1:7) and "unsettle the congregations" (1:7; 5:10, 12) have appeared suddenly since Paul's last visit in Galatia. They are doubtless Christians (1:6 f.) who want to cause the congregations to accept circumcision (5:2; 6:12 f.), and evidently also demand the following of the Law (3:2; 5:4). Possibly the Galatians already observe certain festivals (4:10); but in general they appear not yet to have succumbed to the propaganda of the intruders (4:9; 6:13, 16). Paul turns sharply against these intruders; he curses them, if they preach another gospel, which is no gospel (1:6 ff.); he reproaches them for following impure motives (4:17; 6:13), for not keeping the Law themselves (6:13), and sarcastically summons them to castrate themselves (5:12). It is not clear whether a specific leading person is behind these intruders (5:7, 10). (Contrary to H. Lietzmann [*Kleine Schriften* II, TU 68, 288], Paul here in no case alludes to Peter, for such an allusion would be inconsistent with the tone with which Paul speaks of Peter in 1:18 and 2:8 ff. Moreover, we lack any report that Peter was in Asia Minor.) Since the second century (Marcionite prologue to Galatians: "The Galatians . . . were tempted by false apostles to turn to the Law and circumcision" [Galatae . . . temptati sunt a falsis apostolis, ut in legem et circumcisionem verterentur]) scholars generally have concluded from these statements that radical, Jewish-Christian opponents of Paul, the so-called "Judaizers" from Jerusalem, had infiltrated the churches, and had sought to convince the uncircumcised Gentile Christians living free of the Law to accept circumcision and thereby to take upon themselves the Jewish Law. Recently this supposition has been questioned from various sides. On the one hand, it has been maintained that the opponents in Galatia could only be Gentile Christians, who wanted to win other Gentile Christians to circumcision which they had accepted; only thus can be explained the sarcastic exaggeration of the demand for circumcision (5:12), the present tense οἱ περιτεμνόμενοι (6:13), and the contention that the opponents themselves do not keep the Law (E. Hirsch, ZNW 29, 1930, 192 ff.; Lietzmann, Beyer, Munck). On the other hand, it has been observed that Paul must defend himself against charges that his apostolic office was a commission received only from men (1:1, 11), and at the same time repulse libertine views which cannot be directed against the Judaizers (5:13, 16; 6:1, 8). In the light of these observations some have concluded that Paul struggled on two fronts, against both Judaizers and libertine "pneumatikoi," who battled each other within the congregations (5:15; Lütgert, Ropes). Others, however, have correctly objected against this thesis that in Galatians there is no trace of a polemic alternating between two fronts. Therefore, attempts have been made to do justice not only to the observations of Lütgert and Ropes but also to the reasons for the traditional interpretation that the opponents were Judaizers, by describing the Galatian opponents as syncretistic Jews, who strove through casuistic legalism for higher enlightenment (Crownfield), or as Gnostic Jewish Christians (Schmithals, Wegenast). Schmithals based his thesis upon the following argumentation: a) Judaizers did not reproach Paul for dependence upon the primitive apostles. b) As opponents of the Gentile mission, Judaizers could not promote the Gentile mission. c) Paul was the first to draw to the attention of the Galatians that if circumcised they had to keep the entire Law (5:3; Gnostic circumcision never obliged one to keep the Mosaic Law). d) The observance of particular times in connection with the worship of angels (4:9 f.) is, like the above, understandable only from Gnostic presuppositions. Contrary to Schmithals, we hold that no one can deny that the Galatian intruders demanded the acceptance of the Law (2:16; 3:21*b*; 4:21; 5:4). In 5:3 Paul did not make known to the Galatians a new fact, but only wanted to remind them anew of a known fact which they had not sufficiently taken into consideration. In any case, the Galatian opponents were advocates of a Jewish legalism. Certainly the interpretation of their demand for circumcision as a means of releasing oneself symbolically from the lordship of the flesh has no basis at all in Galatians. And since Paul interprets the subjection to the Jewish Law in 4:3 ff., 8 ff., as well as service to the elemental spirits, as the veneration of the φύσει μὴ ὄντες θεοί, the *basis* for the observance of particular times in 4:10 is not recognizable with certainty but is better understood in connection with renewed obedience to the Law. Hence, if the reasons for regarding the opponents as Gnostics fall to the ground, then it is also clear at the same time that their Gentile origin can hardly be established (περιτεμνόμενοι 6:13 compared with 5:3 is no proof for a circumcision not practiced until now; whether 5:12 would be intolerable if directed against Jews is a subjective judgment; and if 3:7 strongly emphasizes that only men of faith are Abraham's sons, then such a proof in respect to newly circumcised Gentile Christians is not probable, since the proselytes were not called "sons of Abraham"). The opponents were, therefore, doubtless Jewish Christians who preached circumcision and fulfillment of the Law. That they were connected with Jerusalem is not clearly said. Nevertheless, it seems that Paul not only was reproached in general because his apostolic dignity was merely dependent upon men, but also in particular because he was dependent upon the apostles of Jerusalem and was, therefore, no true apostle, charges which he seeks to prove are not historically correct (1:15 ff.). Thus there exists some probability that the Galatian opponents were somehow connected with the primitive church in Jerusalem, certainly not with the "pillars," as 2:6 ff. shows, but with the "false brethren" mentioned in 2:4, who in no case were still Jews (so Schmithals). Precisely on the basis of Gal. 2:1 ff., we cannot deny, as do Schmithals and Munck, that the Jerusalem church, in addition to the "pillars," also had a radical wing which opposed the law-free Gentile mission (not any Gentile mission). 5:13 ff., however, is not fighting against an antinomian libertinism. Rather, it combats the conclusion which was either actually drawn by the Galatian Christians, or which was falsely maintained by the opponents as the consequence of Pauline teaching, that freedom from the Law leads to licentiousness. Here Paul opposes their conclusion by linking Christians to the leadership of the divine Spirit. At any rate, the opponents of Paul in Galatia were Jewish Christians true to the Law, and whether Gnostic features must also be ascribed to them (Schlier, Stählin, H. Köster, RGG [3] III, 1959, 18; Beyer-Althaus think of "Hellenistic Judaizers"), is not certain. This statement helps to make comprehensible the concrete occasion of Galatians, but permits no more precise historical definition of the Epistle.

b) The dating of the Epistle depends above all upon the answer to the question, How is the account of the meeting of Paul and Barnabas with the "pillars" in Jerusalem (Gal. 2:1 ff.) related to Paul's journeys to Jerusalem reported in Acts and to the report of the apostolic council in Jerusalem (Acts 15:1 ff.)? Since Paul tells of two journeys to Jerusalem up to and including this meeting (Gal. 1:18; 2:1), but Acts mentions three (9:26; 11:30; 12:25; 15:4), the

decisive question is whether both accounts (Gal. 2:1 ff.; Acts 15:1 ff.) refer
to the same event. If that is the case, how can the difference in the number of
journeys to Jerusalem in both sources be reconciled?

1) We can obtain this harmonization most simply by denying that the two
accounts in Gal. 2:1 ff. and Acts 15:1 ff. are speaking of the same event. In
favor of this supposition one can especially point out that thus the lack of the
apostolic decree (Acts 15:22 f.) in the account in Gal. 2:1 ff. becomes understandable, and that then there is no necessity of ascribing to the author of Acts
an error in the number or arrangement of Paul's journeys to Jerusalem. For in
this case the journey of Paul and Barnabas to Jerusalem reported in Gal. 2:1 can
readily be identified with the journey mentioned in Acts 11:30; 12:25. Then the
apostolic council of Acts 15:1 ff. takes place after the composition of Galatians.
But in order to place the composition of Galatians before the apostolic council
of Acts 15:1 ff., it must be supposed that εὐηγγελισάμην ὑμῖν τὸ πρότερον (4:13)
refers to only one visit of Paul in the churches in the province of Galatia (or
at the most to the stay when the churches were founded [Acts 13:13–14:20]
in comparison with the return journey of Acts 14:21 ff.; so recently Heard,
Henshaw, Orchard, Guthrie, Klijn). In this case Galatians would be the oldest
preserved Pauline epistle, composed between the missionary journey of Acts
13, 14 and the apostolic council of Acts 15. But this attempted solution comprises too many improbabilities. That the two accounts in Gal. 2:1 ff. and Acts
15:1 ff. do not intend to report the same event is most unlikely, since both
accounts have to do with the same question of circumcision and of responsibility
toward the Law, involving Paul and Barnabas and the apostles of Jerusalem.
Furthermore, if we adopt this position, then we must accept the "province
hypothesis," in spite of its problematical nature. And, finally, it is to be said
against this solution that τὸ πρότερον (4:13) in Hellenistic Greek *can* mean "the
previous" in the sense of "the only earlier," but then the addition of this expression in Gal. 4:13 would be entirely superfluous. Rather, 4:13, according
to the most natural interpretation, presupposes two visits of Paul in Galatia.

2) If, therefore, the equating of the events reported in Gal. 2:1 ff. and
Acts 15:1 ff. is the most probable supposition, then there remain two possibilities of exposition in respect to the Jerusalem journeys: Either the event reported in Acts 15:1 ff. (= Gal. 2:1 ff.) has been placed erroneously after the
journey narrated in Acts 13, 14 and actually took place at the time of Acts
11:30 and 12:25, with the result that the Jerusalem journey mentioned in Acts
15:1 ff. is a mistaken doubling; or Acts 15:1 ff. stands in the right place, so
that the reference to Paul's journey to Jerusalem in Acts 11:30 and 12:25
between the two journeys (Gal. 1:18 = Acts 9:26 and Gal. 2:1 = Acts 15:4)
rests upon an error. In both instances there is an error in the account of Acts.
According to the first supposition, which has found numerous advocates (see
W. G. Kümmel, ThRdsch N.F. 17, 1948-49, 29 f.; 18, 1950, 26 f.; Bonnard),
we must not only transfer the account of the so-called first missionary journey
(Acts 13, 14) to a position after the apostolic council (so also G. Bornkamm,
RGG ³ V, 1961, 172), for which there is no reason, but also utilize the doubt-

less fragmentary notice (Acts 11:27 ff.; 12:25) as a useful account, which likewise is thoroughly improbable. The second supposition is, therefore, much more reasonable. If, as has already been said, Gal. 4:13 presupposes, according to the most probable interpretation, two visits of Paul to Galatia, then it follows that the composition of Galatians after the apostolic conference reported in Acts 15 thoroughly admits of the adoption of the "territory hypothesis."

It would now be a substantial support for this conclusion if we could make probable in another way the composition of Galatians after Acts 18:23, i.e., after Paul's second visit to the territory of Galatia, and thus at the earliest during his stay in Ephesus (Acts 19:1 ff.). And that is indeed the case. Scholars have correctly indicated that the terminology and language of Galatians are strikingly parallel with that of Romans, chiefly in the terminology of justification, which is extensively displayed only in these two epistles, but also otherwise (cf. Gal. 5:13-25 with Rom. 8:2-25). Moreover, some have concluded that Paul in Galatians and II Corinthians is defending himself against the same charges (cf. Gal. 1:6, 10; 2:4 with II Cor. 11:4; 5:11; 11:26, and Buck, J. N. Sanders, NTSt 2, 1955-56, 140 f.; J. Dupont, RB 64, 1957, 46). Beyond that, others have wanted to show that Romans combines conceptions from Galatians and II Corinthians (Buck), or that Galatians in its development of the teaching about the Spirit and the valuation of the cross and resurrection of Jesus stands between II Corinthians and Romans (Faw, who also points out that only in Romans and Galatians there is to be found an omission of associates and an emphasis upon the apostolic office in the address). It is questionable whether such developments can be convincingly grounded on the slight source material for such comparison, but we may regard it as certain that these observations show that the composition of Galatians cannot be chronologically far from that of II Corinthians and Romans. Hence also from this point of view the "territory hypothesis" alone is demonstrated to be probable.

5. Time and Place of Composition

The time and therewith the place of compositon of Galatians can hardly be determined precisely within the limits given above. In any case, if the Epistle was written after the arrival of Paul in Ephesus on the so-called third missionary journey (therefore after Acts 19:1), we may then allege in favor of an early date in Ephesus that Paul in Gal. 1:6 speaks of such a quick desertion by the Galatians and probably would not be so astonished over this desertion if he had already experienced the Corinthian confusion. But these arguments for a composition of Galatians in Ephesus before I Corinthians (Feine-Behm; cf. already the Marcionite prologue: "writing to them from Ephesus" [scribens eis ab Epheso]) are not really convincing. A date in a later period of the Ephesian sojourn, or after that in Macedonia in about the same time as II Corinthians, may be advocated just as well, and even more convincingly (Goguel, Jülicher, Sanders, Dupont, Viard). It is less probable that Galatians was composed in Corinth only shortly before Romans (at the time of Acts 20:2, so Bonnard), for then the differences which exist between Galatians and Romans are not explainable. Thus it is possible to date the composition of Galatians in Ephesus or Macedonia about 53-55.

6. Authenticity

Doubt about the authenticity of Galatians, which was probably known already by Polycarp (3:3; 5:1), was expressed by Br. Bauer, *Kritik der paulinischen Briefe*, 1850-52, and the radical Dutch critics (see above, §12), supported by the Swiss scholar, R. Steck, *Der Gal. nach seiner Echtheit untersucht*, 1888. On this untenable criticism, see J. Gloël, *Die jüngste Kritik des Gal. auf ihre Berechtigung geprüft*, 1890. Interpolation or compilation hypotheses for Galatians (cf. C. Clemen, *Die Einheitlichkeit der paulinischen Briefe*, 1894, 100 ff.) have not been advocated recently, doubtless correctly so. That Galatians is a genuine, authentic Epistle is indisputable. Its significance lies not only in what it teaches us about the history of Paul and his dispute with the radical, Jewish-Christian contraction of the gospel, but especially in the fact that, occasioned by this dispute, it became the first classical formulation of the freedom of the Christian from the regulation of the Law and his capacity for responsible obedience in the Spirit of God.

§17. The First Epistle to the Corinthians

Commentaries, see pp. 388 f. Studies: K. Lake, *The Earlier Epistles of Paul*, 1911; W. Lütgert, *Freiheitspredigt und Schwarmgeister in Korinth*, BFTh 12, 3, 1908; A. Schlatter, *Die kor. Theologie*, BFTh 18, 2, 1914; H. v. Soden, *Sakrament und Ethik bei Paulus*, Marburger Theologische Studien I, 1931, 1 ff. (= Urchristentum und Geschichte I, 1951, 239 ff.); T. W. Manson, "St. Paul in Ephesus: (3) The Corinthian Correspondence," BJRL 26, 1941-42, 101 ff. (= Manson, St., 190 ff., 210 ff.); J. T. Dean, *Saint Paul and Corinth*, 1947; P. Cleary, "The Epistles to the Corinthians," CBQ 12, 1950, 10 ff.; J. Munck, see §16, 127 ff.; Eng., 135 ff.; W. Schmithals, *Die Gnosis in Korinth. Eine Untersuchung zu den Korintherbriefen*, FRLANT, N.F. 48, 1956; U. Wilckens, *Weisheit und Torheit. Eine exegetisch-religionsgeschichtliche Untersuchung zu 1 Kor. 1 und 2*. BhTh 26, 1959; E. Dinkler, RGG³ IV, 1960, 17 ff.; D. Georgi, review of Schmithals, Gnosis (see above), VuF 1958-59, 1960, 90 ff.

1. Contents

After the address and thanksgiving for God's action in the congregation, Paul immediately mentions, on the basis of reports (1:11), quarrels in the congregation (1:10–4:21): Over against the false overestimation of baptizers, Paul sets forth the insignificance of the individual preachers of the gospel, since the gospel is no human wisdom (1:13–3:17) (by way of excursus in 2:6-16 he points out that there certainly is a wisdom for the mature), attacks human glory by calling attention to the smallness of the apostles (3:18–4:13), and refers to his plans concerning the congregation (the resultant sending of Timothy, plan of his own coming). Upon the basis of a further report (5:1), a discussion of sexual problems follows: a case of incest (5:1-13); intercourse with prostitutes (6:12-20); in between these two sections is inserted catchwordwise a section treating the problem of lawsuits between Christians (6:1-11). 7:1-40 discusses, upon the basis of a written inquiry from the Corinthians, problems of marriage, and 8:1–11:1 the eating of meats offered to idols (by way of excursus, 9:1-27 takes up the right of the Apostle to support, his renunciation and his adaptation for the sake of the mission). 11:2–14:40 turns to questions about worship: One after another, the problems of covering of women's heads in worship (11:3-16), the correct celebration of the Lord's Supper (11:17-34), and the role of spiritual gifts in the assembly of the church (12:1–14:40) are discussed. Again by way of excursus, 13:1-13 is inserted as a hymnic description of ἀγάπη. 15:1-58 deals with the resurrection of Christians. In 16:1-18 follow epistolary notes: collection (16:1-4), travel plans (16:5-12), concluding exhortations (16:13 f.), and notes (16:15-18). 16:19-24: greetings and benediction.

The Epistle clearly has no connected train of thought, and there are no connecting links between the separate sections. Rather, upon the basis of reports from the congregation and in answer to a congregational letter, Paul handles various questions about the life of the community. We may suppose that not only 7:1 ff. but also the sections introduced with περὶ δέ (8:1 ff.; 12:1 ff.; 16:1 ff.) answer questions in the letter from the Corinthians (7:1). And in respect to 11:18 ff. and 15:12 ff., it is clear that Paul takes reports from the congregation as starting points. It is striking that more than once (6:1 ff.; 9:1 ff.; 13:1 ff.) a connected theme is interrupted by an excursus.

2. Founding of the Congregation

On Corinth, see Th. Lenschau, PW, Suppl. 4, 1924, 991 ff.; 6, 1935, 182 ff.; *Ancient Corinth. A Guide to the Excavations,* [6]1960.—Wealthy, magnificent, ancient Corinth was destroyed in 146 B.C. Caesar first refounded the city as a Roman colony. Since 29 B.C. Corinth was the residence of a proconsul, the capital city of the senatorial province of Achaia. Situated on two seas, with harbors on the east (Cenchreae) and on the west (Lechaeum), it was destined to be a world city, the natural trading center between the East and the West. Religious syncretism flourished in the heterogeneous population. The famed temple of Aphrodite (who had assumed features of the Phoenician Astarte) on the rocks of the Acrocorinth, possessed, according to Strabo (8, 6, 20), more than one thousand prostitutes, who devoted themselves to the glory of the goddess. The wickedness of the city was proverbial. I Cor. 5, 6 vividly shows the perilous milieu of the young Corinthian congregation. On the so-called second missionary journey, perhaps in the year 49, Paul, coming from Macedonia to Athens, appeared in Corinth, preaching the gospel. His assistants were Silvanus and Timothy (II 1:19; Acts 18:5). Acts 18:1-17 gives what is surely a very fragmentary report of his work there, but this report is expanded manifoldly through I and II Corinthians. Paul taught first of all in the synagogue, then, after the conflict with the Jews, in the house of the proselyte, Titus Justus (Acts 18:4 ff.). Whereas in Thessalonica he allowed himself to be supported partly by the Philippians, in Corinth he supported himself entirely through his own trade (Acts 18:2 f.; I 4:12; 9:1 ff.; II 11:7 ff.). After Paul's activity of a year and a half in Corinth (Acts 18:11), there existed a flourishing congregation. It consisted of Gentile Christians (I 12:2), predominantly from the lower classes (I 1:26 ff.), but there was also a Jewish-Christian element (Acts 18:4; I 7:18), and an admixture of those of higher social and economic status (I 11:21 ff.; Acts 18:8; Rom. 16:23). After Paul, Apollos, an eloquent, theologically trained Jewish Christian from Alexandria, whom Aquila and Priscilla had won to Christianity (Acts 18:24 ff.; I 3:5 ff.), worked there for a while in a similar manner.

Before I Paul had already written an epistle to the Corinthians (I 5:9 ff.). In it he had forbidden the congregation any association with immoral men. In Corinth that command was so interpreted as if the Apostle meant immoral men outside of the congregation. The question, whether this "Vorbrief" is lost or can be restored wholly or in part from the preserved Corinthian Epistles, can be answered only in connection with the question about the unity of both Epistles.

3. Occasion of the Epistle

The immediate occasion was an epistolary inquiry from the Corinthian congregation (7:1: "about which you wrote") to the Apostle about a series of questions (see above, p. 199). Perhaps the Corinthians Stephanas, Fortunatus, and Achaicus had delivered the letter to Paul (I 16:17 f.). He had also received reports about the congregation through "Chloe's people" (I 1:11), persons known to Paul and to the congregation, but about whom we know nothing further. The picture of the congregation which Paul derived from all of these reports was little gratifying. In the sexual sphere the congregation tolerated lapses which were condemned even by the pagans: A Christian was living with the wife of his father, his own stepmother, without any interference from the congregation (I 5:1 ff.). With great earnestness the Apostle must insist that intercourse with prostitutes is immoral (I 6:12 ff.). On the other hand, there was among the Christians from Corinth an ascetic view, which regarded marital intercourse as something sinful (I 7). In everyday quarrels the Christians had sought justice before pagan judges (I 6:1 ff.), whereas cultic groups insisted on settling these matters in their own circles. Some accepted invitations to dinner at which meat offered as a sacrifice was served (I 10:27 f.) and participated in meals in pagan temples (I 8:10). At the Christian love feasts it happened that the rich ate heartily of the food and drink which they had brought with them, whereas the poor remained hungry (I 11:17 ff.). There was disorder in the worship services, since the glossolalia, glorified as the Christian charisma, threatened to supplant all other works of the Spirit (I 14). The general Christian faith in the resurrection of the dead was denied by a part of the congregation (I 15:12).

But Paul is most strongly upset by the report of quarrels and divisions within the congregation. At the beginning of his discussion of this situation (I 1-4) Paul speaks of people in the church who characterize themselves as belonging to Paul, Apollos, Cephas, or Christ. Noting this passage, scholars since F. C. Baur ("Die Christuspartei in der korinthischen Gemeinde," etc., TZTh 4, 1831, 61 ff.; excerpts in WGK, NT, 158 ff.) have spoken of the *parties* in Corinth. They have attempted to determine the character of the individual "parties," and to allocate the polemic of the Epistle among the individual "parties." On the basis of the report in Gal. 2:11 ff. the view can easily be formed that the followers of Peter are advocates of a Jewish Christianity which appeals to the primitive apostles of Jerusalem, though we hear nothing of a demand for fulfilling the Law in I Corinthians and know nothing of a stay of Peter in Corinth (against H. Lietzmann, *Kleine Schriften* II, TU 68, 1958, 288 f.; Appel, Lake, Craig, and others). On the basis of Acts 18:24 and I 1:18 ff., the Apollos-people can be regarded as advocates of a cultured Christianity of eloquent wisdom. Then we may think of the followers of Paul as such Christians who agreed with Paul and who must have defended Paul's conception of Christianity. But there is no convincing proof that Paul in particular sections is turning against each of these "parties" one at a time. Especially we cannot establish satisfactorily what kind of view the Christ party is supposed to have advocated. Some have sought to define their view in terms of radical Jewish Christianity (Baur, Feine-Behm), libertine Gnosticism (Lütgert, Schmithals), connection with James the Lord's brother (E. Bammel, ThZ 11, 1955, 412), or the preaching of God, freedom, and immortality (Manson). Others have ascribed to them the view of which Paul alone approved (R. Reitzenstein, *Hellen. Mysterienreligionen*, [3]1927, 334), or rejected (Schmithals). Still others, noting that all of the above contentions are unprovable and that in I 3:22 and I Clem. 47:3, in enumerations similar to I 1:12, the name of Christ is omitted, have supposed that ἐγὼ δὲ Χριστοῦ is a gloss in I 1:12 (Heinrici, J. Weiss, Goguel, Michaelis, Héring, Wilckens). But quite apart from the unanswerable question of why this phrase should have been interpolated, we object to this hypothesis on the grounds that I 1:13 (μεμέρισται ὁ Χριστός;) is best understood if the contested phrase ἐγὼ δὲ Χριστοῦ had stood before it. But in reality the supposition is completely erroneous that Paul reckons with the existence of closed groups in the congregation. In I 1-4 he always polemizes against, or speaks to, the entire congregation (cf. Munck). The division is not caused by the presence of different doctrines or tendencies in the congregation, but by the Corinthians' overestimation of human teachers and baptizers as the result of an understanding of baptism like that of the mystery religions (I 1:12 ff.; 4:15). How the supposed particularistic claim to belong to Christ is related to this union of definite circles of the Corinthian congregation around one of the baptizers (Paul, Apollos, Cephas) we can in no wise determine, but just as little can we ascertain that Paul judged such a claim differently from the previously named group slogans.

Hence the supposition that Paul in I Corinthians polemizes against two (or more) fronts cannot be grounded upon the discussion in I 1–4. And otherwise this supposition is also very improbable. For there is nothing in I Corinthians of a polemic against "Judaizing" (radical Jewish-Christian) views (against Manson, H. J. Schoeps, *Paul*, 1961, 78). Rather, the entire epistle shows a front against a new Gnostic interpretation of the Christian message (Dinkler, Schmithals), an interpretation which ascribed complete salvation and unconditional moral freedom to the "pneumatikos," as one who had been freed from the σάρξ. But it is very questionable whether we can, starting from the presupposition that Paul was inadequately instructed concerning the views of the Gnostics, establish also a genuine Gnostic Christology on the part of the opponents in Corinth (Schmithals). Although it is clear that Paul discusses also questions and views in the congregation which only *forcibly* can be traced back to Gnostic presuppositions (I 7: restraint in respect to marriage; I 11:3 ff.: the aversion of the women toward covering their heads), this consideration does not change anything in respect to the fact that Paul in I Corinthians basically sees only one front over against him, even the Gnostic, and that Paul regards the abandonment of Gnostic views as a presupposition for holding fast to the proclamation of Jesus Christ, the Crucified and Risen One.

4. Authenticity and Integrity

The authenticity of I Corinthians is not disputed. The Epistle was already clearly known by I Clem. 37:5; 47:1-3; 49:5; Ign., Eph. 16:1; 18:1; Rom. 5:1; Philad. 3:3. I 1:2*b* (J. Weiss, Dinkler, W. Schmithals, ZNW 51, 1960, 240 [lit.]) and I 14:33*b*-35 (J. Weiss, G. Zuntz [see below, p. 359], 17, and others) have often been regarded as un-Pauline interpolations. The addition, "with all those who in every place call on the name of our Lord Jesus Christ, both their Lord and ours" (I 1:2*b*), to the usual address in the dative case, "to the church . . . at Corinth," is said to be impossible, because the very concrete epistle directed to the Corinthians could not also be intended for the whole of Christendom. Others explain this "ecumenical" addition on the basis of their contention that I Corinthians was placed at the beginning of the oldest collection of Pauline epistles. But if it proves true that we know nothing certain about the oldest sequence in the collection of the Pauline epistles (see below, pp. 338 f.), then this explanation of the addition lacks probative force. On the other hand, we cannot avoid the difficulty by limiting the ἐπικαλούμενοι to the "official liturgists" (P. Gaechter, *Petrus und seine Zeit*, 1958, 311 ff.), or in the addition, "with all who call on . . . ," see the sender and the addressees united (U. Wickert, ZNW 50, 1959, 73 ff.). Rather we must maintain that Paul in I 1:2*b* expands the address through a liturgically qualified characterization of the totality of Christendom (see Lietzmann-Kümmel, *ad loc.*). If the liturgical origin explains the formality of the formulation, it cannot yet be clearly explained why here this reference to all Christendom is added. But this lack of insight is no adequate reason for the supposition of an interpolation, which cannot be convincingly grounded.

The command "Let a woman be silent in church" ([mulier taceat in ecclesia] I 14:33*b*-35) does stand in a certain tension with I 11:3 ff. But the contradiction is explained by the almost universally shared view that in I 14:33*b*-35 only "disputation" is forbidden. Hence the supposition of an interpolation here is also unnecessary.

Although the Pauline origin of I Corinthians is not in dispute, its integrity, together with that of II Corinthians, is a moot point (see the survey in Rigaux, see lit. to §12, 153 ff.). Proceeding from the fact that Paul in I 5:9 and II 2:4 mentions an epistle which must be lost, and from the supposition that it is improbable that "only a part of the epistles of the Apostle were preserved or published" (Schmithals), scholars have called our attention to contradictions in I Corinthians and from them drawn the conclusion that I Corinthians was worked up out of two Pauline epistles. This thesis, which was advocated earlier in the most divergent ways (cf. Goguel, *Intr.* IV 2, 86 ff.), recently has been proposed again in various forms, especially by Schmithals, Dinkler, and Héring. Whereas Héring, Manson, Craig, Guthrie, Dean, Henshaw, and Klijn find a fragment of the "Vorbrief" only in II 6:14–7:1, Schmithals (and similarly Dinkler) reconstructs the "Vorbrief" from II 6:14–7:1; I 9:24–10:22; 6:12-20; 11:2-34; 15:1-58; 16:13-24, and sees in the second epistle (I 1:1–6:11; 7:1–9:23; 10:23–11:1; 12:1–14:40; 16:1-12) the answer to the letter from the Corinthians and the basis of our I Corinthians, in which the material of the "Vorbrief" was incorporated (still more complicated by Cleary). Héring, however, dissects I Corinthians into two epistles: A (1–8; 10:23–11:1; 16:1-4, 10-14) and B (9:1–10:22; 11:2-15:58; 16:5-9, 15-24). Schmithals and Héring regard I Cor. 13 as Paul's hymn inserted at the wrong place. As the basis for the supposition that I Corinthians was compiled from two epistles the following contentions are especially cited: In I 4:19 Paul promises a quick coming to Corinth; in I 16:3 ff. he presupposes a longer interval until the journey to Macedonia; in I 10:1-22, he rejects any participation in cultic meals; in I 8 and 10:23–11:1 he forbids the eating of meat offered as a sacrifice, but only out of consideration for the weak; in I 9 Paul defends his apostleship against charges, whereas 1–4 does not presuppose that the apostolic dignity of Paul is impugned. In I 11:18 ff. Paul appears to hear of disputes for the first time, whereas in I 1–4 he is more precisely informed. As grounds for the later weaving together of the originally independent epistles, it is adduced that in connection with the collecting of the Pauline epistles into a seven-letter corpus, a process which took place at Corinth at the end of the first century, smaller epistles had to be pieced together into larger ones, especially if one wanted the epistles to Corinth to stand at the beginning of the corpus (Schmithals, ZNW 51, 1960, 240 ff.; likewise Müller-Bardorff [see to §20], 601 f.), and that perhaps a piece of an epistle had been broken off or the beginning of an epistle had become illegible (Héring). Now certainly I 5:9 cannot be used to prove II 6:14–7:1 or perhaps the epistle reconstructed by Schmithals out of I Corinthians as the "Vorbrief" or a part of the "Vorbrief," for the warning against association with the πόρνοι is not found in this hypothetical epistle. The "Vorbrief," then, in any case is not preserved. But also the reasons for the dissection of I Corinthians into two epistles are not convincing (cf. also Michaelis, Einl.[3], supplement, 25 f.) : The allusions to Paul's intention to come to Corinth are in no wise mutually exclusive since ταχέως (I 4:19) is thoroughly compatible with the plans in I 16:3 ff. Moreover, Paul in the course of the composition of the Epistle, which indeed was not necessarily dictated all at once, could have worked out his plans in more detail. The explanations concerning right and wrong in the question about eating meat offered to idols (I 8:1–11:1) are only formally contradictory. Factually they are completely homogeneous, since Paul maintains the danger of demons (whose existence is not denied) even for the "strong" Christians, if these think that with their "strength" they can exult before God (cf. H. v. Soden, Urchristentum und Geschichte I, 1951, 254 ff.; G. Bornkamm, Studien zu Antike und Urchristentum, BeTh 28, 1959, 173 ff.). And if Paul in I 1–4 does not explicitly defend his apostleship against charges, but certainly does so in I 9, we must recognize that in I 4:9 he does allude to the scorning of his apostolic dignity, and I 3:5 ff. and 4:1 ff. do presuppose a criticism of his activity in founding the congregation. On the other hand, the reference to his rights as apostle in I 9:1 ff. may be explained as the taking up by way of excursus the theme of his readiness for renunciation. The arguments adduced for the hypothesis of the secondary compilation of I Corinthians out of two epistles are thus in no instance conclusive. Moreover, the occasionally somewhat disconnected transition from one theme to another in I Corinthians is explained by the special nature of this Epistle, which handles questions and reports one after another, and thereby uses the literary method of the excursus several times (2:6-16; 9:1-27; 13:1-13; also 10:1-22). In addition, we must consider the fact that it "is equally possible that St. Paul was great enough to be inconsistent at some points and that he did not have the thoroughness of the German or the lucidity of the French mind" (McNeile-Williams, Intr., 136).

But the weightiest consideration against this hypothesis of a secondary composition of I Corinthians is the fact that the historical probability for such a secondary composition cannot be made evident. The supposition that on the occasion of the first collection of the Pauline epistles in Corinth the complete correspondence of Paul with Corinth was combined into two epistles, is just as much pulled out of the air as the supposition that the epistles originally were carelessly preserved, mutilated, or that the beginning of one of the epistles was illegible. Also the contention that each epistle of Paul must have been preserved and later published is a mere postulate. But above all, no one has yet adduced really convincing motives for weaving together several documents from the same author by a strange hand (cf. W. Michaelis, "Teilungshypothesen bei Paulusbriefen," ThZ 14, 1958, 321 ff.). And if we here disregard for the moment the hypothetical partition of other Pauline epistles (II Corinthians, Romans,

Philippians), then the only alleged parallel is the one adduced by G. Bornkamm (see lit. to §18, 34, note 131), Polycarp's Epistle to the Philippians. Bornkamm's suggestion, however, proves nothing, for even if it is probable that this epistle was secondarily joined out of chaps. 1–12 and 13, 14 (cf. lately H. v. Campenhausen, RGG[3] V, 1961, 449), then we have in this case two epistles joined to each other and not thrown together in confusion. Moreover, the hypothesis of a secondary piecing together of I Corinthians presupposes that an epistolary introduction and a conclusion were cut off, for which no plausible motive can be alleged. The supposition of a secondary composition of I Corinthians is, therefore, to be rejected as extremely improbable.

5. Time and Place of Composition

Some time before the composition of I Corinthians Paul sent Timothy via Macedonia to Corinth (I 4:17; 16:10; Acts 19:22). Paul expects that Timothy will arrive there later than the Epistle sent by the direct route. In the meantime the envoys of the Corinthians have come to him. To them he probably gives I Corinthians, which answers the questions of the church as well as sets forth the things about which he has heard otherwise. The Epistle is written in Ephesus (16:8). The Sosthenes mentioned in the address is possibly the former Jewish ruler of the synagogue (Acts 18:17). Since Paul sends greetings from the churches of Asia (16:19), he has, therefore, already worked a while in the province. He has not been in Corinth for a long time (4:18), but is now thinking of a visit there, if possible, for an entire winter (16:6). At the time at which he writes it is spring (16:8; but the Epistle is no "avowed Easter Epistle," so K. H. Rengstorf, *Die Auferstehung Jesu*, [4]1960, 64), and surely according to all probability the spring before the end of Paul's stay in Ephesus. Hence I Corinthians is to be dated in the spring of 54 or 55.

§18. THE SECOND EPISTLE TO THE CORINTHIANS

Commentaries, see p. 389. Studies: besides the works cited before §17 by T. W. Manson, J. T. Dean, P. Cleary, W. Schmithals, E. Dinkler, D. Georgi: A. Hausrath, *Der Vier-Capitel-Brief des Paulus an die Korinther*, 1870; J. H. Kennedy, *The Second and Third Epistles of St. Paul to the Corinthians*, 1900; H. Preisker, "Zur Komposition des zweiten Korinther-Briefes," ThBl 5, 1926, 154 ff.; E. Käsemann, "Die Legitimität des Apostels," ZNW 41, 1942, 33 ff.; R. Bultmann, *Exegetische Probleme des zweiten Korintherbriefes*, SBU 9, 1947; L. P. Pherigo, "Paul and the Corinthian Church," JBL 68, 1949, 341 ff.; C. H. Dodd, NT Studies, 1952, 80 ff.; J. Munck, see §16, 162 ff.; Eng., 168 ff.; W. Schmithals, "Zwei gnostische Glossen im Zweiten Korintherbrief," EvTh 18, 1958, 552 ff.; G. Bornkamm, *Die Vorgeschichte des sog. Zweiten Korintherbriefes*, SHA 1961, 2; J. A. Fitzmyer, "Qumran and the Interpolated Paragraph in 2 Cor. 6:14–7:1," CBQ 23, 1961, 271 ff.

1. Contents

The Epistle falls into three parts which are not clearly connected: 1–7; 8–9; 10–13. The First Part opens with introduction (1:1, 2) and thanksgiving (1:3-11) for the deliverance of Paul from danger of death in Asia. Then Paul immediately proceeds to defend himself, first of all against charges of inconstancy in view of the change in his travel plans. Paul characterizes this change as having originated out of his solicitude for the congregation, even as did his "stern" Epistle to Corinth (1:12–2:4). An appeal for milder discipline of a member who led a revolt against Paul follows in 2:5-11, and then Paul begins with the description of the events which directly preceded the composition of the present Epistle (2:12, 13). This description is interrupted by a thanksgiving (2:14), which passes on to an apology for Paul's apostleship, which reaches to 7:4, whereas the description of the prehistory of the Epistle is not resumed until 7:5 ff. The apology for his apostleship, which runs from 2:14–7:4, portrays, first of all, the Apostle's self-confidence upon the basis of his divine commission (2:14–4:6), then his necessary sufferings (4:7–5:10), and the commission of the Apostle (5:11–6:10), whereas 5:14–6:2, excursuswise, describes the contents of this commission. 6:11-13 points back to the address to the congregation; yet this address is interrupted by means of a general warning against relations with unbelievers (6:14–7:1), and not completed until 7:2-4. In 7:5-16 Paul brings to an end the report about the prehistory of the Epistle.

Second Part. Without transition there follows in 8:1-24 the recommendation of the collection for Jerusalem and the colaborers of Paul sent to gather it. 9:1-15 renews the discussion of the collection question, mentions anew the sending of Paul's associates, and closes with an exclamation of thanksgiving.

Third Part. 10:1 signifies a completely new beginning with a sharp warning and defense against charges (10:1-18), which (11:1–12:13) continues further with "foolish" self-praise for the purpose of defense. 12:14–13:10 wards off the charge of robbing the church and discusses travel plans. 13:11-13 contains concluding wishes and a triadic benediction.

2. Prehistory and Occasion

The Epistle doubtless makes a very contradictory impression. Not only is there no clear connection between the three parts, 1–7; 8, 9; and 10–13; not only is the collection theme in chaps. 8 and 9 dealt with twice without a clear reference to each other; and not only does 10–13 speak in a completely different tone to the church from 1–9, but also the first larger section, 1–7, is not homogeneous: The narrative concerning the prehistory of the Epistle is interrupted in 2:13 and in 7:5 taken up again; the transition from 6:2 to 6:3 is very rough, and 6:3 would be better connected to 5:13, so that 5:14–6:2 has the effect of an excursus. The general warning (6:14–7:1) interrupts the personal address (6:11-13; 7:2-4) very clumsily. It is understandable that the original unity of this Epistle as a whole has been widely doubted.

The difficulty we encounter in determining clearly the prehistory and occasion of the Epistle lends support to the supposition that II Corinthians is not intact. Since Acts (20:1-3) mentions only one visit of Paul to Greece after the close of his Ephesian sojourn (out of which I Corinthians stems), we know concerning Paul's relations with the Corinthian church after the composition of I Corinthians only that which we can infer from II Corinthians. And these statements are partly very dark. Possibly the following can be concluded: 1. II Corinthians is later than I. Not long before the composition of II Paul was rescued from the gravest danger to life in Asia (Paul here cannot be alluding only to the effect upon him of the bad reports from Corinth which Titus had delivered, as Dean thinks). He then traveled from Ephesus via Troas to Macedonia, where he stayed at the time of II (II 1:8 ff.; 2:12 f.; 7:5; 9:2). The situation plainly corresponds to Acts 20:1 f., according to which Paul, because of the uproar of the silversmith, concluded his three-year stay in Ephesus, possibly in the early spring of 54 or 55 (see p. 180), and went to Macedonia. In that case II shows the matter of the collection for Jerusalem at a more advanced stage than I. The collection mentioned only briefly in I 16:1 ff., even if already presupposed as known, is treated in II 8, 9 in detail and urgently, because it is supposed to be concluded and delivered (II 8:6, 11, 14). The remark that it has been going on already "since last year" (II 8:1; 9:2), reaches back to the first beginnings, which lay yet before the instructions of I 16:1 ff., and is chronologically not useful.

2. Among other things, II follows the purpose of settling finally the serious conflict of the Apostle with the congregation. According to II 12:14; 13:1, Paul intends shortly to come to Corinth for the third time. On his second visit Paul warned them that if he returned he would not spare them (II 13:2; cf. 12:20 f.). Therefore, his second visit took place in the midst of signs of tension between him and the church. II 2:1 ff. continues further. According to it, Paul was once troubled in Corinth. And we may be sure that he caused the Corinthians trouble as well as they him.

This second visit cannot have taken place before I Corinthians. In I nothing points to tension of such a nature. There Paul speaks throughout to the church in the expectation that they will unconditionally obey him. Nothing hinders him, by virtue of his authority as apostle, to whom the congregation is subordinate, and for whose directions they have asked, from reprimanding them and from taking them to task.

Therefore, the second visit lies between I and II ("intermediate visit").

To be sure, the statements about Paul's travel plans are not entirely uniform. Whereas he obviously plans a third visit to Corinth soon according to II 12:14; 13:1, 10, he apologizes in II 1:15 f. for having to give up his plan to come to Corinth a second time, then to travel to Macedonia, and from there to return to Corinth and bases the default of a further visit to Corinth (II 2:1) upon his purposeful solicitude for the Corinthians. It is disputed whether Paul here speaks of a plan which he has not at all begun to carry out or of a plan only half carried out. And we cannot ascertain with certainty whether Paul informed

the Corinthians in writing (cf. II 1:13) or orally about this plan which he
had abandoned. But even if, according to the most probable exposition, Paul had
begun to carry out this plan (δευτέρα χάρις = intermediate visit, II 1:15), he
here in any case maintains that he has given up the original plan of going, after
this visit in Corinth, to Macedonia and then to Corinth again; and this change
of plans (II 2) is explained on the basis of his solicitude for the Corinthians.
Since that does not sound like his intention to come to Corinth soon, it is,
therefore, adduced as an argument against the original unity of II 1–9 and
II 10–13 (see below, pp. 211 f.).

3. The reason for the turbidity of the relations between Paul and the congregation is difficult to determine exactly. According to II 12:21 and 13:2,
Paul on his second visit must have experienced sorrow for members of the
congregation, who still had not repented of their immoral lives. But since 13:2
also speaks of "all the others" (sinners), we must also consider other lapses. We
find additional light on the situation in 7:12, where there is reference to a member of the congregation who had personally wronged Paul (ὁ ἀδικήσας). And
in 2:5 ff. we learn of someone who had not "caused pain" to Paul, but to the
majority, indeed, in principle, to the entire congregation. The occurrence, to
which both passages allude, happened at a time when Paul himself was present
(2:1) and can have occurred only on his second stay in Corinth (1:15), not
on the first one, when he founded the church. The evildoer (II 2:5; 7:12)
is not identical with the incestuous man (I 5:1 ff.). Weighty reasons speak
against this equating, already denied by Tertullian (de pudit. 13). Paul's command to deliver the sinner to Satan (I 5:3 f.; i.e., to exclude him from the
congregation) in no wise harmonizes with the mildness of II 2:6 ff.: "For
such a one this punishment by the majority is enough." It is inconceivable that
the Paul who wrote I 6:12 ff.; I Thess. 4:3 ff.; Rom. 13:12 ff., etc., sometime
later should have accepted so lightly that gross case of sexual lapse. The wrong
toward Paul, however, cannot have consisted of the charge that he used the
collection money for himself (II 12:16 ff.), for this accusation is not ascribed
to a specific evildoer, and could not be designated as distress in respect to the
entire congregation (II 2:5). What the nature of the wrong done to Paul was
remains in the dark. To connect this wrong against Paul to the agitation against
Paul which arose in Corinth in the meantime is no more than a conjecture.
Obviously the evildoer was a member of the church, for the congregation had
passed judgment upon him.

4. Since the sending of I Corinthians, the polemic against Paul in the Corinthian congregation seems to have been intensified. On the one hand, through
the entire Epistle Paul must counter charges against his person: The change of
his travel plans reveals his inconstancy (1:15 ff.); his epistles do not say clearly
what he means (1:13 f.); he has no letter of recommendation (3:1; 4:2); his
gospel is not clear (4:3); his conduct is unintelligible and offensive (5:11 ff.;
6:3; 10:2); he injures the congregation and enriches himself (7:2; 12:16); he
is bold only at a distance (10:1, 10); he cannot claim to belong to Christ
(10:7); his speech is unskilled (10:11; 11:6); he came to Corinth without

commission (10:13 f.); he is inferior to the persons he calls "superlative apostles" (11:5; 12:11); he does not dare have himself supported by the congregation (11:7 ff.; 12:13); he is, in general, no apostle (12:12); indeed, Christ does not speak through him (13:3). It is entirely clear that Paul in II Corinthians, contrary to I Corinthians, polemizes not only against a new Gnostic interpretation of the Christian message, but against persons in Corinth who disparage his person as an apostle of Jesus Christ and dispute his apostleship. But beyond that, we can recognize that Paul in II Corinthians polemizes against specific persons, who have attacked him in the congregation. A minority (2:6; 10:2), which seeks personal profit (2:17; 11:20), and which found entrance into the congregation through letters of recommendation and through self-recommendation (3:1; 10:12, 18), boasts of definite advantages (5:12; 11:12, 18): they have ecstasies (5:13; 12:1, 7); they know Christ and belong to him (5:16; 10:7; 11:23); they claim the apostleship, which they deny Paul (11:5, 13; 12:11); they know themselves superior to Moses (3:4 ff.) but are proud of their undeniable Jewish origin (11:22). Paul reproaches them for proclaiming another Christ and another God (11:4); they operate in strange mission territory (10:15 f.); they live riotously but do not repent (12:21; 13:2); they compare themselves only with themselves and for that reason boast without limit (10:12 f.); they are servants of Satan (11:13-15). That a definite person leads them is probably not to be inferred from 11:4 (cf. 10:2). It is clear that the presence and agitation of these people represent a different state of affairs in the life of the congregation from that discernible in I Corinthians. Thus the supposition that Paul struggles here only against the same Gnostic opponents as in I Corinthians (Bultmann, Schmithals, Dinkler) does not explain the facts of the case. On the other hand, since there is no trace of a polemic against any demand from the opponents that the Corinthians fulfill the Law, it is, therefore, unjustified to equate them with the Judaizers in Galatia (H. J. Schoeps, *Paul*, 1961, 78 ff.; J. Jervell, *Imago Dei*, FRLANT, N.F. 58, 1960, 177, note 20) or to ascribe to them support from the primitive apostles in Jerusalem (Manson, Käsemann). But neither is it enough to describe the opponents simply as Jewish-Christian wandering preachers after the type of Hellenistic wandering preachers (Georgi, Bornkamm), or to declare their origin as unknown (Munck). Rather, it is clear that Jewish Christians have come into the Corinthian church who boast of their indubitable apostolic dignity, their Palestinian origin ('Εβραῖοι II 11:22; cf. ThWB III, 393), their contact with the earthly Jesus, their irreproachable Jewish descent, and also their spiritual gifts; they have letters of recommendation and deny all of these advantages to Paul. The intruders, who originated from Palestine, are, therefore, not "Judaizers," but Palestinian opponents of the Pauline mission and apostolic dignity. They joined themselves with the Gnostic opposition against Paul recognizable in I Corinthians, or already before his coming to Corinth assumed Gnostic-pneumatic features. Thus Paul in II Corinthians, polemizes, to be sure, not against a "double front" (Lietzmann-Kümmel, Wikenhauser), but against a definite Gnostic, Palestinian, Jewish-Christian opposition created by new additional opponents, who forced

Paul to defend the "legitimacy" (Käsemann) of his apostleship throughout the entire Epistle.

5. Between I and II Paul wrote to the church an epistle, "out of much affliction and anguish of heart and with many tears" (2:3 f.), the so-called "intermediate epistle" or "Epistle of Tears." This epistle had caused the Corinthians sadness (7:8 ff.; 2:9). In it Paul had demanded the punishment of the ἀδικήσας (7:12). Thus the "stern" epistle is related to the conflict between Paul and the congregation; it belongs in the period of the greatest tension. The bearer of the intermediate epistle was, according to all appearances, Titus. Paul credited Titus with the tenacity, the caution, and the tact to subject the church again to his authority. The difficult task of persuading Titus even to undertake this mission cost Paul considerable effort (7:13 f.). Paul and Titus agreed precisely upon the way and time of the return journey. Paul expected to join Titus in Troas (2:12 f.). The nonarrival of Titus so upset Paul that in spite of great missionary success he went to Macedonia to meet Titus (2:13; 7:5). Here at last the arrival of Titus relieved him of all cares: Titus brought the good report that the Corinthian congregation was seized by repentance and by the wish for reconciliation with Paul (7:6 f.). Titus also was able to carry out the additional task of working in Corinth for the collection (8:6; 12:17 f.).

6. Thus there results from the events between I and II Corinthians something of the following picture. The sending of Timothy to Corinth (I 4:17; 16:10) seems to have had no complete success; rather, Timothy probably brought with him bad reports out of Corinth. Even I Corinthians had not lastingly established Paul's authority. Then Paul, perhaps soon after I Corinthians, crossed over from Ephesus to Corinth, in order to create order. But he experienced a great disappointment. The visit to the church, which was close to open revolt against him, caused him deep sorrow, especially an injustice which a Corinthian inflicted upon him, and which the church permitted to happen. He did not succeed in becoming master of the situation. In displeasure and sadness he broke off the visit and returned to Ephesus, but promised to come again to Corinth soon. Whereas he abstained from this new visit out of consideration for the Corinthians, he won Titus to the task of restoring order to the church, and gave to him a stern epistle, the "Epistle of Tears." Under the eyes of Titus a sudden change took place in Corinth. The majority of the congregation submitted and repented of their insubordinate behavior. Paul, full of unrest, traveled to meet Titus and joined him in Macedonia. The good success of the mission filled him with joy and contentment. Immediately he sent Titus once again to Corinth, in order energetically to bring the business of the collection to its end before his own arrival in Corinth. Titus was accompanied by two brothers (II 8:16 ff.). Strange to say, Paul does not call them by name. Among them was probably the brother who, according to 12:18, had been his helper the previous time in connection with the solicitation of the collection. Paul gave to Titus II Corinthians as a harbinger of his own coming (II 12:20; 13:2). To be sure, this picture of the events between I and II Corinthians is

tenable only if II Corinthians in its transmitted form represents an original unity, a contention which is much disputed.

3. Authenticity and Unity

The authenticity of II Corinthians as a whole is undisputed. On the other hand, the Pauline origin of II 6:14–7:1 has long been denied (recently, e.g., by Jülicher, Bultmann, Dinkler, Bornkamm, Georgi, Fitzmyer). With respect to this supposition the indisputable fact that this section fits very poorly in its context is not so very decisive, for, indeed, the text could be Pauline, but wrongly inserted here (so Goguel, Schmithals). What is decisive is the relative large number of words not found in Paul or otherwise in the entire NT, the combinations unusual for Paul μολυσμὸς σαρκὸς καὶ πνεύματος (7:1) and κοινωνία πρός (6:14), and the strikingly strong relationship with conceptions of the Qumran community (cf. thereto also H. W. Huppenbauer, *Der Mensch zwischen zwei Welten*, AThANT 34, 1959, 59, note 222). Hence K. G. Kuhn supposes that Paul himself Christianized an "Essene" text (RB 61, 1954, 203, note 2), whereas Fitzmyer prefers to think of a non-Pauline interpolation. But as correct as it is that the dualism of God and Belial is characteristic of Qumran, and that Paul speaks of it otherwise as little as of μολυσμὸς σαρκὸς καὶ πνεύματος, still we must note that Paul does not have a fixed linguistic usage for the devil and that also I 7:34 presupposes the possibility of the defilement of σῶμα καὶ πνεῦμα. That the section must be Pauline cannot be proved (but cf. for all that the parallelism between κοινωνία and μετέχειν in I 10:16 with II 6:14!). But just as little can it be proved that it could not stem from Paul and must stem from Qumran circles. Only its poor connection in the context demands an explanation. Furthermore, Schmithals has sought to show that II Cor. 3:17, 18*b* and 5:16 are Gnostic glosses, which could not have been formulated by Paul, and probably were written by Gnostic opponents of Paul in Corinth in the margin of the Pauline epistle, and while being copied "slipped into the text." But the consistent Gnostic interpretation of these verses is only then convincing if a consistent Gnostic Christology may be ascribed to the Corinthian Gnostics, which is very questionable (see above, p. 202). And that glosses of Paul's opponents could have succeeded in getting unnoticed into the text of the archetype lying at the basis of our manuscripts is extremely improbable.

Although there are therefore no adequate reasons for considering smaller pieces of text of II Corinthians as non-Pauline insertions, the difficulty of looking upon the transmitted text of II Corinthians as a whole as an original unity remains so great that this unity has been questioned in the most diverse ways. This question applies above all to the relationship of II 10–13 to II 1–9: Whereas in II 1–7 Paul expresses his joy because he and the congregation have made up their quarrel and he can even warn about a too strict punishment of the ἀδικήσας (II 2:7 f.), 10:1 begins anew with "I, Paul, myself"; he attacks "some" (10:2), "such people" (10:11), "those who would like to claim" (11:

12), "false apostles" (11:13), servants of Satan, who "disguise themselves as servants of righteousness" (11:15), etc. He fears that he may come and not find the Corinthians as he would wish (12:20); he warns he "will not spare them" (13:2) and hopes that when he does come he will "not have to be severe" (13:10). Inasmuch as there thus comes to light in II 10–13 a completely different position of Paul in respect to the church from that in II 1–9, since the time of J. S. Semler (*Paraphrasis II. Epistulae ad Corinthos,* 1776), II 10–13 has been viewed as an independent epistle or as a fragment of an epistle, that was written either later than II 1–9 (so Semler, and recently Windisch, and Pherigo, who removes this epistle to the end of Paul's first stay in Rome, and hesitatingly Jülicher), or between I and II Corinthians ("intermediate epistle," first by A. Hausrath [1870], recently, e.g., Goguel, de Zwaan, Héring, Filson, Cleary, T. W. Manson, Dodd, Dean, Sparks, Bultmann, Dinkler, Schmithals, Klijn, and others). Many scholars go yet a step farther and point out that in 2:13 the discussion of the settlement of the untoward incident is interrupted by a long defense of Paul's apostolic office and not resumed until 7:5, where once again we find clear linguistic harmony with 2:13. And as already noted, the general exhortation in 6:14–7:1 produces the effect of an extraneous insertion into the personal address to the congregation (6:11-13; 7:2-4). And both appeals in behalf of the collection (chaps. 8, 9) seem not to have belonged together originally. Consequently some declare as unavoidable the supposition that not only II 10–13, but also II 2:14–7:4; II 6:14–7:1, and II 9, stem from one or more other epistles of Paul, whereby either 2:14–6:13; 7:2-4, together with chaps. 10–13, are regarded as fragments of the intermediate epistle (Bultmann, Dean, Dinkler), or 2:14–6:13 and 7:2-4 were drawn from an epistle preceding the intermediate epistle (Mitton [see p. 337], Bornkamm, Schmithals), whereas ch. 9 represents an isolated epistolary fragment (additional hypotheses in Goguel, *Intr.,* IV 2, 86 ff., and Guthrie, see pp. 62 ff.). Naturally, we may not object to these reconstructions of several original epistles of Paul to the Corinthians on the grounds that the differences among the various hypotheses demonstrate their untenability, because hypothetical reconstructions, even if they are well grounded, always leave open several possibilities corresponding to their hypothetical character.

Rather, in view of these literary-critical hypotheses, the answer to two questions is decisive: a) Does the transmitted text compel us to the supposition of a secondary combination? b) Can we recognize a convincing motive for this "combination"?

a) The decisive problem is the question whether II 1–9 and II 10–13 could have stood in the same epistle, for in connection with the relation of these two sections to each other it is not only a matter of a smooth continuity of thought but also of varying attitudes of Paul to the situation in the congregation. As little as this difference (see above, pp. 211 f.) can be denied, so little may we overlook the fact that also in II 1–7 Paul by no means presupposes that in Corinth everything is now in order. Rather, this part of the Epistle is also permeated with defenses against a misinterpretation of his conduct (1:13 ff., 23 ff.; 4:2 f.;

5:11 ff.; 7:2) and a polemic against other missionaries (2:17 f.). Only a minority of the congregation complied with Paul's wishes (2:6). And just as little as Paul in II 10–13 can suddenly address a minority in the congregation, so clearly does he also presuppose here that only *specific* persons are attacking him (10:2, 7, 11 f.; 11:5, 12 f., 18, 20; 12:11, 21; 13:2), and the remainder of the congregation is endangered by these people (11:1*b*, 4, 16; 12:11, 19; 13:2). Other considerations also preclude the identification of II 10–13 with the intermediate epistle: II 12:18 clearly looks *back* upon the sending of Titus and of a "brother" mentioned in II 8:6, 16-18; the event, which, according to II 2:3-5, 9, was dealt with in the intermediate epistle, is not treated in II 10–13; and, conversely, II 2:3 ff. and 7:8 ff. do not speak of how the congregation reacted to the polemic against the "superlative apostles" in II 10–13, which could hardly have been omitted if II 10–13 belonged to the intermediate epistle. The supposition that II 10–13 belongs to an epistle which was composed later than II 1–9 is confronted with the difficulty that II 10–13 contains no hint of the fact that Paul had received information that the situation in Corinth had deteriorated since the composition of II 1–9, which also could hardly have been left unmentioned. Moreover, both the hypotheses of the intermediate epistle and that of a later epistle demand the supposition that the ending of the epistle II 1–9 and the beginning of the epistle II 10–13 (or of the more comprehensive epistle containing this piece) were broken off, for which no plausible reason can be assigned. Although it is hardly possible that II 1–9 and II 10–13 were dictated one right after the other, it cannot be declared as inconceivable that Paul, after a certain interval of time, added to the epistle a conclusion in which he expressed more sharply his continuing concern for the congregation, and in which he also discussed his travel plans for the near future, which he had not treated in II 1–9. But we should forego proposing more specific hypotheses for the clarification of this joining, for they are nothing more than unprovable conjectures (Paul himself takes the pen in 10:1, Feine-Behm, Dibelius; he received new reports, Munck; between II 1–9 and II 10–13 lies a sleepless night, Lietzmann; Paul suddenly had doubts about the genuineness of the turning in Corinth, Guthrie, etc.).

Can we, however, maintain the original unity of II 1–9? Although II 2:14–7:4 no doubt interrupts the account of the congregation's reaction to Paul's intermediate epistle, it is still understandable that Paul, when mentioning his meeting with Titus (2:13), would feel motivated to give a doxology (cf. II 8:16; Rom. 9:5), and then allow himself to be led to an apology for his apostleship, from which in 6:11-7:4 he would slowly return to the original theme. The formulation in 7:5 as the resumption of the theme thus becomes understandable, whereas directly after 2:13 it would represent a very striking linguistic repetition. Having seen that there is no real necessity to regard 2:14–7:4 as a secondary insertion, we still find it surprising that Paul in II 9 takes up anew the discussion of the business of the collection after he had finally summarized the exhortations of 8:1-23 in 8:24. But 9:1 is no completely new effort (cf. γάρ). The necessity of help for Jerusalem is generally discussed no more, but only the necessity of giving generously. Hence II 9 could not by itself have formed an epistle or a part of an epistle. But it is conceivable that Paul, after an interruption of his theme, takes it up once more and gives to it a new, forceful expression.

Only II 6:14–7:1 forms a difficulty probably not to be solved, for this section is without thematic connection to its context and interrupts the good connection between 6:13 and 7:2. If, as we have already seen (above, pp. 211 f.), there is no adequate reason for designating the text as un-Pauline, then the most that we can say to explain the presence of this section in this place is that Paul, very hesitatingly and intermittently, from 6:3 on returns to his actual correspondence, and the exhortation to reconciliation begun in 6:1 continues factually in 6:14–7:1, whereas 6:3-13, as the beginning of this return to the correspondence, interrupts this exhortation (6:3 also doubtless connects very badly with 6:2!). Since this attempted explanation is not very convincing, the supposition of a secondary insertion of a Pauline fragment here naturally suggests itself. But what could be the reason for such an insertion?

b) For now the decisive question is whether we can find a convincing motive for combining Pauline texts so as to form a complete epistle. We have already spoken of the general grounds against such combination hypotheses (see pp. 204 f.). But the arguments which are especially cited to clarify the combination of II Corinthians are also not convincing. For why should Paul himself have agreed that in Corinth 2:14–7:4 should be inserted into the "Epistle of Reconciliation" (II 1–8) in order not so to emphasize the controversy treated here (so Dean)? Bornkamm, however, would like to explain the attachment of II 10–13 to the ending of the epistle on the basis of the literary convention of placing at the conclusion of a text a warning against false teachers at the close of the age. He grounds the insertion of 2:14–7:4 in the tendency of the redactor to interpret Paul's activity as a divine, triumphal procession (2:14 ff.), even in its failures (cf. 2:12 f.). But the second motive follows in no wise from the text, and the first would be convincing only if it were previously explained what caused someone to remove the introductions and conclusions of various Pauline epistles, and to piece the epistles together so as to make a conglomeration. Bornkamm also can bring up no real reason for the insertion of II 9.

Viewed as a whole, the best supposition remains that II Corinthians as transmitted forms an original unity. Since Paul dictated the Epistle in the midst of interruptions the possibility of unevennesses existed from the beginning. Precisely when we understand II Corinthians as an actual epistle out of the uniqueness of a developing historical situation does it become comprehensible as a historical entity. And there are not lacking in it connecting threads between the various parts. In the first chapters Paul treats that which freed him from his great solicitude for the Corinthian congregation, the settlement of the conflict. But through all the joy there repeatedly sounds here the note that there remains much to be desired for the church: "you have understood in part"

(1:14); "punishment by the majority" (2:6), etc. The fact that chaps. 8, 9 have their own tone in respect to the discussions before and after results from the subject matter. The fact that Paul solicits for the collection with a certain timidity in tortuous trains of thought is explicable in the light of his situation in respect to a congregation which has only recently been won again. With 10:1 the Apostle once more prepares to add a concluding word. But as he begins, he again is overcome by bitterness over all that he had experienced in recent months at the hands of the congregation and by his solicitude for the future of the congregation still constantly threatened by opponents. Gal. 6:12 ff., I Cor. 16:22, and Rom. 16:17 ff. present shorter parallels to that kind of sharp conclusion. But a more irenic wish and greeting conclude the Epistle.

4. Place and Time of Composition

If the reconstruction of the events between I and II Corinthians proposed above (pp. 207 ff.) is correct, then the following events are to be placed between the composition of I Corinthians in the spring of 54 or 55 and the composition of II Corinthians: the return of Timothy from Corinth, the journey of Paul to Corinth, his return to Ephesus, the sending of Titus to Corinth, the beginning and the breaking off of Paul's missionary activity in Troas, his journey to Macedonia, and his meeting there with Titus. This journey from Ephesus to Macedonia must correspond to that mentioned in Acts 20:1 f., and Paul must, if Acts 20:2-16 is correct, have traveled again to Corinth soon after the composition of II Corinthians, spent three months there, and at the time of the Passover was again in Philippi. Since it is completely possible to accommodate in half a year the events supposed to have taken place between I and II Corinthians, and since the journey from Macedonia to Greece, the three-month stay there, and the return to Macedonia must be placed after the composition of II Corinthians, it follows that the time of composition of II Corinthians was the late fall of the year 55 or 56. The indication in II 8:10 and 9:2 that the collection in Corinth was being pushed forward ἀπὸ πέρυσι also points to the same conclusion, since, according to this dating, between the beginning of the collection directed in I 16:1 f. and the composition of II Corinthians could lie the beginning of a new year which commenced in autumn (Michaelis). There is no reason for the supposition that there was a year and a half between the composition of I and II Corinthians. II Corinthians was doubtless written in Macedonia.

That II Corinthians effected the final settlement of the conflict with the Corinthian congregation is probable, because the Epistle to the Romans, presumably written in Corinth, reveals none of the difficulties with the congregation in which Paul finds himself. In addition to its elucidation of the difficulties of the Pauline mission, the significance of II Corinthians lies in the insight into Paul's apostolic consciousness of mission which the Epistle imparts to us.

§19. THE EPISTLE TO THE ROMANS

Commentaries, see p. 388. Studies: W. LÜTGERT, *Der Röm. als historisches Problem*, BFTh 17, 2, 1913; R. SCHUMACHER, *Die beiden letzten Kapitel des Röm.*, NTA 14, 4, 1929; R. M. HAWKINS, "Romans: A Reinterpretation," JBL 60, 1941, 129 ff.; R. BULTMANN, "Glossen im Röm.," ThLZ 72, 1947, 197 ff.; J. DUPONT, "Pour l'histoire de la doxologie finale de l'Épître aux Romains," RBd 58, 1948, 1 ff. (lit.); T. M. TAYLOR, "The Place of Origin of Romans," JBL 67, 1948, 281 ff.; T. W. MANSON, "St. Paul's Letter to the Romans—and Others," BJRL 31, 1948, 224 ff. (= Manson, St., 225 ff.); A. FEUILLET, "Le plan salvifique de Dieu d'après l'Épître aux Romains," RB 57, 1950, 336 ff.; 489 ff.; E. J. GOODSPEED, "Phoebe's Letter of Introduction," HarvThR 44, 1951, 55 ff.; S. LYONNET, "Note sur le plan de l'Épître aux Romains," RScR 39-40, 1951-52, 301 ff.; N. A. DAHL, "Two Notes on Romans 5," StTh 5, 1951, 37 ff.; H. PREISKER, "Das historische Problem des Röm.," *Wissenschaftl. Zeitschr. der Friedrich Schiller-Univers.* Jena 1952-53, 25 ff.; G. SCHRENK, *Der Röm. als Missionsdokument*, "Studien zu Paulus," AThANT 26, 1954, 81 ff.; J. MUNCK, see §16, 190 ff.; Eng., 196 ff.; J. DUPONT, "Le problème de la structure littéraire de l'Épître aux Romains," RB 62, 1955, 365 ff.; J. KNOX, "A Note on the Text of Romans," NTSt 2, 1955-56, 191 ff.; W. SCHMITHALS, "Die Irrlehrer von Rm. 16:17-20," StTh 12, 1958, 51 ff.; N. KRIEGER, "Zum Röm.," NovT 3, 1959, 146 ff.; G. HARDER, "Der konkrete Anlass des Röm.," Thv 6, 1959, 13 ff.; T. FAHY, "St. Paul's Romans were Jewish Converts," *The Irish Theological Quarterly* 26, 1959, 182 ff.; E. TROCMÉ, "L'Épître aux Romains et la méthode missionaire de l'apôtre Paul," NTSt 7, 1960-61, 148 ff.; G. FRIEDRICH, RGG [3] V, 1961, 1137 ff.

1. Contents

After the address (1:1-7), expanded by a definition of the contents of the "gospel," and the introductory thanksgiving (1:8-15), which explains how Paul came to write this Epistle, follows the theme of the Epistle (1:16-17): "The gospel ... is the power of God for salvation to every one who has faith, ... for in it the righteousness of God is revealed through faith." This theme is carried out by means of the negative and the positive proof of God's saving act in Christ, which makes possible justification through faith alone (1:18-4:25). Negatively it is shown that apart from the gospel all men stand under the wrath of God (1:18-3:20). Then there follows the positive proof (3:21-4:25): the new righteousness of God by grace through faith in Christ (3:21-26); through God's new revelation of faith all boasting is excluded (3:27-30); the objection that the Law has been abrogated is refuted with the reference to Abraham, who was justified by faith.

After this demonstration that salvation is founded in God's act, there follows the description of the actuality of the new being of the Christian (5:1-8:39; that the new train of thought commences, not after 5:21, so lately Gaugler and Goguel, and not after 5:11, so Feuillet, Leenhardt, but after 4:25, has been established by Dahl, Lyonnet, Dupont, cf. also Dodd, Nygren, Michel). First of all, Paul shows that with justification certainty of salvation is given (5:1-

11); Christ as the second Adam is the bringer of life (5:12-21). Against the charge that the proclamation of justification by grace alone creates indifference toward sin, Paul retorts: On the basis of baptism, the new life is in principle freed from sin (6:1-14); it is obedience and service (6:15-23); it is freedom from the Law (7:1-6), which in men under the Law only reveals sin and works death, but which, thanks to the saving act of Christ, has no more power (7:7-25); he who is controlled by the Spirit is free from sin and death (8:1-11); the possession of the Spirit guarantees the certainty of salvation (8:12-17); in any case, the hope in final salvation is certainly secured (8:18-30), for which Paul gives thanks with rejoicing (8:31-39). Then in 9–11 Paul raises the question about the unbelief of the Jews in the dawning time of salvation. The shocking fact of their present rejection is manifest (9:1-5), but God with their rejection has not violated his promise to Israel, for he has the freedom to reject (9:6-29). Human guilt is the cause of the rejection (9:30–10:21), but the rejection of the Jews is a temporary expedient of grace (11:1-32). A hymn concludes this chain of thought (11:33-36).

With 12:1, 2, Paul introduces a series of paraeneses. There follow general exhortations for the relations of Christians to one another: principles for the attitude of Christians toward non-Christians (12:14-21); duties of Christians toward the state (13:1-7); the love of neighbor as the highest duty (13:8-10); the imminent end as an impulse to moral earnestness (13:11-14). In 14:1–15:6 is discussed the concrete question of the strong and the weak in the Roman congregation (14:1-12, Paul's judgment; 14:13-15, six exhortations for the strengthening of faith); generalization of the exhortation with reference to the example of Christ (15:7-13). In the personal conclusion Paul justifies his writing (15:14-21), speaks about his travel plans, and gives notice of his visit to Rome (15:22-33). Recommendation of Phoebe (16:1-2); greetings (16:3-16); sudden warning against false teachers (16:17-20); greetings from the associates of Paul (16:21-24); doxology (16:25-27).

2. The Beginnings of the Roman Church

The oldest certain witness to the existence of the Roman Church is the Epistle to the Romans itself. Then follows Acts 28:15, the account of the meeting of Paul in Rome by the Christians there. In Rom. 15:22 ff. (cf. 1:13), Paul writes that for many years he has had the intention to come to the brethren in Rome. According to that, at least at the beginning of the fifties, there were already Christians in the capital city of the "Imperium Romanum." The remark of the Roman writer, Suetonius, in his *Vita Claudii* 25 (c. 120), must point still further back: "He [Claudius] expelled the Jews from Rome, since they were continually making disturbances with Chrestus as the instigator" [Judaeos impulsore Chresto assidue tumultuantes Roma expulit]. Since "Chrestus" is simply another form of "Christus," Suetonius undoubtedly refers, not to a Jewish agitator in Rome named "Chrestus," but to Jesus Christ, whose gospel brought great unrest to Roman Jewry and became the occasion for

Emperor Claudius to expel the Jews, or a part of them. The report, which is not entirely clear, probably is based upon the heathen writer's inexact information. We do not need to conclude from this notice that Christianity first penetrated to Rome shortly before the Jewish edict of Claudius, which was issued in the year 49 (see p. 180). But it must have actually spread at that time among the Roman Jews, so that severe struggles arose between the old believers and the Christian believers.

In any case, Peter was not the founder of the Roman Church, nor did he work in Rome before Paul wrote the Epistle to the Romans. The following verses speak against the supposition that Peter promoted the mission in Rome before Paul (so H. Lietzmann [see above, p. 194] 290 f.; E. Hirsch, ZNW 29, 1930, 63 ff.): Gal. 2:7; Rom. 15:20; II Cor. 10:15 f. (Paul does not interfere in strange mission territory), and I Cor. 9:5, which mentions Peter's missionary, itinerant preaching, but says nothing about his settling in a community founded by him.

Nowhere does the Epistle to the Romans allude to persons to whom the congregation is indebted for the gospel, not even where it would be natural (e.g., 1:8 ff.; 15:14 ff.). It is probable that Christianity came to the capital city of the empire, not through a particular apostle or missionary, but early over the routes of world commerce through the agency of the great Jewish diaspora of Rome. A sign of the religious ties between Roman Jews of the diaspora and Jerusalem is perhaps the fact, attested by Acts 6:9, that in Jerusalem the Libertines had a synagogue of their own, among whom some scholars conceive chiefly the offspring of Jews who were shipped to Rome by Pompey in 61 B.C. as prisoners of war, but later were released and formed a strong element in Roman Jewry (see E. Haenchen, Apg., Meyer III [13], 1961, 223, note 3; otherwise, H. J. Leon, The Jews of Ancient Rome, 1960, 156). Christianity in Rome already had a bit of history behind it when Paul wrote his Epistle to the Romans.

3. The Composition of the Congregation at the Time of the Epistle

The Epistle to the Romans bears a double character: It is basically a dialogue of the Pauline gospel with Judaism, so that the conclusion, the readers are Jewish Christians, seems obvious. And yet the Epistle contains expressions which definitely characterize the congregation as Gentile Christian. The suppositions that the Roman congregation consists of a majority of Jewish Christians (W. Manson, The Epistle to the Hebrews, 1953, 172 ff.; according to T. Fahy [see p. 216] 182 ff., the Roman congregation is supposed to consist basically of converted diaspora Jews), or that Paul seeks to win the Jewish Christians in Rome for the Gentile mission (Krieger), or that Paul battles against Jewish Christians who had returned to Rome, who wanted to gain ground again (Michel), can appeal only to Paul's lively discussion with Jewish arguments (cf. 2:17; 3:1; 4:1; 7:1, 4), but not to any text which characterizes the majority of Roman Christians as former Jews. Also nothing points to the related supposition that the Gentile Christians in Rome had had themselves circumcised before their baptism (Michaelis), or that there were in the Roman congregation, in addition to Jewish Christians, circumcised and uncircumcised Gentile Christians (Harder), for in Romans (contrary to Galatians) there is lacking any argument against the acceptance of circumcision by Gentile Christians. Rather, everything favors the conclusion that the Roman congregation at the time of Paul consisted in its majority of former pagans.

The Epistle unambiguously designates its readers as Gentile Christians. In 1:5 f., Paul introduces himself to them as the bearer of the apostleship "among all the [Gentiles], including yourselves," the Christians in Rome. In 1:13 he expresses the wish that he "may reap some harvest among you as well as among the rest of the Gentiles" (similarly in 15:15 ff.). In 11:13 he writes: "I am speaking to you Gentiles," thus addressing his readers as Gentile Christians, in contradistinction to the unbelieving Jews. And in 9:3 ff.; 10:1 f.; and 11:23, 28, 31, Paul speaks to non-Jews about his own people.

Any attempt to obtain a picture of the readers of Romans must proceed from this fixed point. To that even 4:1 and 7:1 ff. offer no hindrance. For in 4:1 Paul imagines himself in discussion with a Jewish opponent and includes himself as a Jew with him. But the imaginary opponent is just as little to be sought among the readers of Romans as the rhetorical, apostrophic Jew of 2:17. In 7:1 he calls the readers "those who know the law." If Paul here actually means the Law of Moses, then he can presuppose this knowledge on the part of the Gentile Christians without more ado, for the OT was their Bible as well as that of the Jewish Christians. Gentile Christians were completely familiar with the OT through constant use in worship and instruction. Gentile Christians as well as Jewish Christians were set free from the Law through death (7:4; cf. Gal. 4:1 ff., 8 ff.; 5:1, 13: all of pre-Christian mankind stood under the Law and became free from it through Christ).

Nevertheless, the Roman congregation was certainly not pure Gentile Christian (against Munck). That the contrast between "strong" and "weak" in the question of eating meat (14:1 ff.) goes back to the contrast between Jewish Christians and Gentile Christians, as is often supposed, is very questionable, since in Judaism we know no vegetarianism based on principle. But the history of the origin of the Christian community in Rome makes a Jewish-Christian admixture in it probable. Nevertheless, after the Jewish edict of Claudius its composition may have changed radically. But above all the admonition to mutual acceptance, with an allusion to the effect of the incarnation of Christ upon Jews and Gentiles, would be pointless if both groups were not presupposed in the congregation (15:7 ff.). Moreover, the repeated reference to the equal responsibility of Jews and Greeks before God (1:16; 2:9 ff., 25 ff.; 3:29; 10:12), and the broad discussion of the reasons for the unbelief of the majority of the Jewish people, with its proclamation of God's still continuing goal of salvation for Israel (9–11), would be incomprehensible if no Jewish Christians belonged to the Roman congregation. And if ch. 16 should belong to Romans (see below, pp. 224 ff.), 16:7, 11 shows the presence of former Jews in the Roman congregation.

4. Time, Place, Occasion, and Purpose of Romans

The Epistle was most probably written in Corinth during Paul's last, three-month-long stay there, perhaps the spring of 55 or 56 (according to Acts 20:6 Paul at Passover time was again in Philippi; but nothing in Romans points to Rengstorf's claim that Paul wanted Romans to be known at Easter in Rome; see K. H. Rengstorf, pp. 64 f. [see above, p. 205]; cf. Acts 20:2 f.). Not long after II Corinthians, the Apostle himself came from Macedonia to Corinth, where he rested before commencing the collection journey to Jerusalem (15:25). From the years of Paul's mission in Asia Minor and Greece, we know of no time which is better suited for the composition of such an extensive, well-considered, and detailed writing as Romans is. Even the recommendation of Phoebe from Cenchreae, the harbor city of Corinth (16:1 f.), would point to Corinth as the place of composition. Paul regards his task in the East as fulfilled. Now his glance is turning toward the West, the other half of the Roman Empire: He wants to make Rome the base of his mission in the West, and via Rome push on to Spain (15:24, 28). But before that, in order to wind up the business of the collection, it is a question of undertaking a journey to Jerusalem, dangerous because of the hate of the Jews in Judea against the apostate. For this situation the three-month stay in Corinth presents the most evident hypothesis, whereas there is no reason to take seriously Athens (Pherigo, see §18), or Philippi (Taylor, hesitatingly Michaelis). Duncan's suggestion that Romans (or its chief part) was composed during Paul's Asia Minor period (G. S. Duncan, ExpT 68, 1955-56, 164 f.) is not even worthy of advocacy for the chief part of Romans, in view of the priority of Galatians in subject matter (see above, pp. 197 f.).

From the situation and the plans of the Apostle follow the occasion and purpose of Romans. Previously, Paul had not known the Christians of Rome personally. Through the Epistle he sought to gain rapport with them. According to that which he has in view, it is plainly an imperative of missionary strategy for him to establish relations with the church of the capital city of the empire. He needs it as a basis of operations for his further work (cf. Schrenk). Although Paul does not come to the strange congregation in Rome as its missionary, he is prepared as a guest traveling through to serve them with the gospel. Above all, however, he wants to enlist their brotherly help in the execution of his plans. But the announcement of his visit, the explanation of his intentions, and the wooing of understanding and help from the Christians in Rome in respect to the goal of his mission, which he is pursuing, explain only the external occasion and the immediate purpose of the Epistle. The broad, theological discussion and the controversy with the Jews which permeates the book must have other, more deeply lying foundations.

The old view that Romans is a systematic, doctrinal presentation of Christian belief (church fathers, reformers, etc.; cf. Melanchthon: "a compendium of Christian doctrine" ["doctrinae Christianae compendium"]), is untenable, for important elements of Pauline teaching, such as Christology and eschatology, do not receive full attention, and some, such as the Lord's Supper and church polity, are not touched upon at all. On the other hand, the entire Epistle is conditioned by the fact that Paul, in seeking an association with the Roman Christians in the interests of his further missionary work, introduces himself to them and says to them what to him is the essence of Christianity and the content of the gospel, which he as apostle of the Gentiles proclaims. His desire to introduce himself to the Christians in Rome, to tell them who he is and what he preaches, gives Paul the opportunity to express himself at length concerning the basic truths of Christianity as he sees and teaches them. Romans is the theological self-confession of Paul, which arose out of a concrete necessity of his missionary work.

But this self-confession in no wise creates "the impression of a monologue" (Feine-Behm; to the contrary, Michel). Rather, we repeatedly get the impression that Paul is polemizing against false views being advocated in the Roman congregation: the criticism of the "weak" by the "strong" and the disregard of the "strong" for the "weak" (14:1–15:7); the creation of "dissensions and difficulties, in opposition to the doctrine which you have been taught" (Rom. 16:17 f.); Jewish errors and criticism of the gospel (2:17; 3:1-31; 4:1; 7:13; 9:31 f.; 11:11); libertine-antinomian deductions from the message of the freedom of the Christians from the Law (3:8, 31; 6:1, 15; 7:7 ff.), and Gentile-Christian arrogance (11:13 ff.). We can hardly explain this double polemic with the supposition that Paul in the well-defined structure of 1:16–15:13 sent to the Romans in an epistolary frame a document already written for a situation that he frequently encountered in his missionary activity, i.e., a document which was formulated for the instruction of Christian congregations which were separating from the synagogue, so that in the chief part of Romans we hear an echo of Paul's controversies with Judaizers and antinomians (Trocmé; similarly W. Manson, Munck). For that does not explain the polemic as dialogue and it especially does not fit 14:1–15:13. On the other hand, it is characteristic of many suppositions that they seek to have too precise knowledge and reach out beyond that which can be recognized with certainty. Such suppositions include the following: Paul in Romans intervenes in the discussion between Jewish Christians and antinomian Gentile Christians in Rome (Preisker); he struggles only against antinomianism in the congregation (Lütgert); he attacks only the Jewish Christians who do not want to allow the Gentile Christians to be regarded as full Christians (Harder); he defends his view against that of the circumcised Gentile Christians in Rome (Michaelis); he seeks to make the most amiable possible approach to the Roman congregation, whom he fears will reject him (J. Knox). In truth, we can say with certainty only that Paul set forth his views against the Jewish teaching of salvation and against antinomian charges against his message of the gospel (carried by him to the Romans from a concrete, missionary impetus, as the saving power for everyone who believes) because he expected such objections from the Roman congregation. Moreover, it is also certain that he interfered in the controversy between vegetarians and their opponents in Rome, of whom he must have heard, but that he did not need to have in mind a threat to the community through Judaizing propaganda. And in spite of this actual ramification of the Epistle, we need not doubt that Paul himself with this extensive, argumentative, and transcending representation gives an account of his gospel which he previously preached and which he is now bringing to the far West.

5. Authenticity and Integrity of the Epistle

The authenticity and unity of Rom. 1–15 admit of no serious doubt (Hawkins' supposition of extensive interpolations is completely arbitrary, and for the thesis that ch. 16 was attached to the authentic Romans in the Roman Church J. Knox can adduce no convincing argument). Bultmann's supposition of the interpolation of particular verses (2:16; 6:17; 7:25b; 8:1; 10:17) has found only isolated agreement, especially for 7:25b, but is in no instance conclusive. On the other hand, the ending of Romans presents weighty text-critical difficulties.

In Marcion's *Apostolikon* there is a shorter text of Romans. Origen, *Commentaria in epistolam ad Romanos* (VII, 453 Lommatzsch), says about it:

Marcion, by whom the evangelical and apostolic writings were falsified, completely removed this section (16:25 ff.) from this Epistle; and not this alone, but also from that place where it is written: "For all which is not based upon faith is sin" (14:23), he cut it all off right up to the end. (Caput hoc [16:25 ff.] Marcion, a quo scripturae evangelicae et apostolicae interpolatae sunt, de hac epistula penitus abstulit; et non solum hoc, sed et ab eo loco, ubi scriptum est: "omne autem, quod non est ex fide, peccatum est" [14:23] usque ad finem cuncta dissecuit.)

That is, Marcion cut off chaps. 15 and 16 (dissecuit = desecuit); his Romans concluded with 14:23. Marcion's text of Romans without chaps. 15 and 16 later affected some manuscripts of the Western Church, which, after 14:23, have only the doxology of 16:25 ff. (cf. J. Dupont, RBd 58, 1948, 6 f.). 15:1–16:23 is undeniably Pauline, but the doxology of 16:25 ff. is found in the text tradition not only after 14:23 but in strikingly varying positions:

a) 1:1–14:23;	15:1–16:23; 16:25-27	$\mathfrak{P}^{61}$ ℵ B C bo sa D d e f vg sy^p
b) 1:1–14:23; 16:25-27;	15:1–16:23; 16:25-27	A P min
c) 1:1–14:23; 16:25-27;	15:1–16:24	$\mathfrak{K}$ sy^h Chrys
d) 1:1–14:23;	15:1–16:24	F G g Archetype of D
e) 1:1–14:23; 16:24-27;		vg^{2089} Old Latin according to chaps. lists Cypr
f) 1:1–15:33; 16:25-27;	16:1-23	$\mathfrak{P}^{46}$

The doxology cannot originally have stood after 14:23 *and* 16:23, especially since after 14:23 it destroys the connection. But if it originally stood after 16:23, how did it get after 14:23? The conjecture that Marcion's text (i.e., without chaps. 15 and 16) played a role here urges itself upon us, especially since the text form (e) also existed in ecclesiastical circles. Upon the basis of these observations, P. Corssen (ZNW 10, 1909, 1 ff., 97 ff.), and D. de Bruyne (RBd 25, 1908, 423 ff.), independently of each other, first advocated the evident hypothesis that Marcion's shortened text represents the starting point of the textual tradition which is discernible to us, since the doxology was attached to this shortened text (text e). The Great Church accepted this textual form, and from the confrontation of this textual form (e) with the primitive Pauline text, which had been preserved elsewhere, arose the various textual forms, in that the doxology remained in its original place (text c), was omitted (text d), was shifted after 15:33 or 16:23 (texts f and a), or remained and was appended (text b). There results, then, the following family tree of the textual forms:

primitive text (1:1–16:23)
|
Marcion's text (1:1–14:23)
|
Marcion's text expanded by means of the doxology (e)
|
combination of primitive text and text e: a,b,c,d,f.

The presupposition of this hypothesis, which is approved by the great majority of scholars (16:25-27 after 16:23 is still defended as original by Höpfl-Gut, Meinertz, Nygren, Cambier in Robert-Feuillet, Guthrie; after 15:33 by Feuillet), is certainly that 16:25-27 is either a fragment of another Pauline epistle (Schumacher, Michaelis, Feine-Behm, Wikenhauser), or a non-Pauline addition (Dupont, T. W. Manson, G. Zuntz [see pp. 359] 227, E. Kamlah, ThLZ 81, 1956, 492, K. G. Kuhn, NTSt 7, 1960-61, 336). In and of itself the preservation of such a small Pauline fragment is not probable, but the composition of a liturgical conclusion to the shortened text in ecclesiastical circles is likely (Kamlah refers to relationship with the Pastorals; Klijn supposes attachment in connection with the collection of the Pauline epistles), or in Marcionite circles after Marcion (A. Harnack, *Studien zur Geschichte des NT und der Alten Kirche* I, 1931, 184 ff., Goguel, Lietzmann, Zuntz, T. W. Manson). In fact, the unusualness of the style as a whole plus the expressions αἰώνιος θεός, μόνος σοφὸς θεός, γνωρίζειν τὸ μυστήριον, weigh against the Pauline authorship of this section, but especially the thoughts that the gospel "was kept secret for long ages" and "is now disclosed and through the prophetic writings is made known." These conceptions would be well explained in connection with Marcionite origin, but whereas this question must remain open, it may be certain that the doxology does not stem from Paul and originally was created as a conclusion following 14:23. We do not know the origin of the mutilated textual form 1:1–14:23, which for us is attested only for Marcion. It is just as possible that Marcion found the text mutilated as that he himself shortened it. But in any case it follows that the archetype, to which our textual tradition goes back, included only 1:1–16:23.

By reference to two facts, some scholars have denied that a text of this extent represents Paul's original Romans. 1) They have noted that before the writing of the oldest preserved copy of Romans, Papyrus 46 from the end of the second century (see below, p. 363), Romans could have included only chaps. 1–15, since only in this way can the position of the doxology after 15:33 in $\mathfrak{P}^{46}$ be explained (Friedrich). Hence T. W. Manson (followed by Munck) concluded that Paul wrote 1:1–15:33 for Rome and sent it to Rome, and then sent to Ephesus a copy of this text, expanded through ch. 16. Albertz would like to see in ch. 16 a second Romans which Paul in Puteoli (cf. Acts 28:13) attached to first Romans. No convincing argument can be adduced in favor of Albertz' hypothesis. Moreover, the presence of the doxology after 15:33 in $\mathfrak{P}^{46}$ in no wise proves that there ever was a manuscript which ended with 15:33, not to mention that this form of the text was sent by Paul to Rome, especially since $\mathfrak{P}^{46}$ itself contains ch. 16.

2) T. W. Manson's hypothesis, however, coincides with earlier observations on ch. 16. C. A. Heumann (1755) raised the question for the first time whether chaps. 12–15 and 16 were Pauline supplements to Romans. J. S. Semler (1769, see WGK, NT, 79) designated chaps. 15 and 16 as appended Pauline essays. But D. Schulz (ThStKr 2, 1829, 609 ff.) was the first to regard ch. 16 as a fragment of a Pauline epistle to the Ephesians. This hypothesis, with slight differences (e.g., 16:1, 2 still belong to Romans, according to Feine-Behm, Michaelis), is advocated today by numerous scholars (e.g., Henshaw, Heard, McNeile-Williams, Goodspeed, T. W. Manson, Munck, Leenhardt, Feuillet, Schmithals, T. M. Taylor, Friedrich, Bultmann, *In memoriam E. Lohmeyer*, 1951, 190), and rests upon the following arguments:

1. The list of personal greetings (16:3-16) presupposes that Paul has a strikingly large number of personal acquaintances in a congregation yet unknown to him. But even if we take into consideration the freedom of movement in that age, it is difficult to conceive that all of these persons in the meantime had emigrated from the Orient to Rome. And it would hardly have served the purposes which Paul was pursuing in Rome with the Epistle if he had greeted so emphatically his old friends instead of the leading personalities of the congregation. That we encounter only a few Latin names in the list of greetings does not need to speak against Rome, for Greek was the language of Christians in Rome throughout the first century. Yet all attempts to prove the names found in ch. 16 by means of the inscriptions and literary documents of the time as from the city of Rome are not successful. The names are attested throughout the most diverse parts of the "Imperium Romanum" and cannot be fixed locally.

2. We would seek "the first convert in Asia" (16:5) in Ephesus, not in Rome. Likewise, Prisca and Aquila with their household church, who were

banished from Rome (Acts 18:2), first settled in Corinth, and then in Ephesus (Acts 18:18 f., 26; I Cor. 16:19).

3. The sharp warning against those who create dissensions (16:17-20) is neither suitable in the framework of Romans nor to the situation of the readers. The paragraph also has an authoritative tone which is incompatible with the guarded contacts in 1:10 ff.; 15:14 ff.; 12:3 ff. This argument especially has value if we see Judaizers opposed here as in Galatians.

4. 15:33 has the character of the solemn epistolary conclusion, likewise 16:20. This duplication is quite unusual in Paul.

5. It is extraordinary for Paul to greet so many individual Christians at the end of an epistle.

The most probable reasons for the hypothesis that basic parts of Rom. 16 were originally directed *to Ephesus* are given in arguments 1–3. But this hypothesis is not at all convincing: 1. Paul by no means knows all of the persons greeted; we *must* suppose only that nine out of the twenty-six emigrated from the East to Rome (Prisca and Aquila, Epaenetus, Andronicus and Junias, Ampliatus, Stachys, Rufus and his mother). And even if considerably more of those greeted had come from the East to Rome, still it would be a matter of only a small number of Christians, who had traveled to the capital city during the course of several years, which is not inconceivable (Lietzmann referred to the analogy of a Bacchian Thiasos, who, according to an inscription published in the *American Journal of Archaeology* 37, 1933, 115 ff., came from the East to Rome).

2. The first convert of Asia, Epaenetus, can without further ado be thought of as now in Rome; the reference to his special role in Asia is even basically more natural in an epistle to Rome than in one to Ephesus, where his role was known. And the conjecture that Prisca and Aquila, in the meantime, returned home after the lifting of Claudius' Jewish edict following his death in 54, is not to be rejected out of hand.

3. It is not clearly ascertainable against whom the sharp warning of 16:17-20 is directed; nothing points to "Judaizers" true to the law; some also think of Gnostics (Michel, Preisker, Schmithals), though that is not exactly demonstrable. But a warning of a threat to the congregation which has not yet become a reality, would be as conceivable in respect to Rome as in respect to Ephesus.

4. The concluding benediction of 15:33 within a Pauline epistle is not at all impossible (cf. I Thess. 3:11-13; Phil. 4:9).

5. But two reasons speak decisively against the Ephesian hypothesis: a) The Epistle 16:1-23 or 16:3-23 would have an impossible literary character. No one yet has established the existence in antiquity of a letter consisting mainly of greetings (not even in a letter of recommendation for a woman, in which that would be necessary, according to Goodspeed), and particularly to the congregation to which Paul had attended for years could he hardly have written so trivially. b) Neither the supposition that someone "piously added" to Romans as the conclusion of the collection of Pauline epistles "what was still found in the archive of Pauline materials" (Feine-Behm; but did Romans stand at the

end of the earliest Pauline collection?), nor the conjecture that Paul, by means of this appendix, made Romans also suitable for Ephesus, can explain why someone cut off from the Romans which ended with 15:33 the greetings which are indispensable there and cut off the address from the alleged epistle to the Ephesians. And the supposition that ch. 16 is only a fragment of an epistle to the Ephesians especially makes the preservation of such a fragment still more incomprehensible. On the other hand, Col. 4:10 ff., which likewise was written to a congregation unknown to Paul, shows that Paul had good reasons in such cases to use all personal contacts. Karl Holl (*Gesammelte Aufsätze* II, 1928, 47, note 2) also has stressed correctly that the greeting from "all the churches of Christ" (16:16) was basically more suitable in an epistle to Rome in this situation than in respect to Ephesus. The supposition that the original text of Romans contained 1:1–16:23, therefore, explains the textual tradition the most convincingly (so, e.g., Lietzmann, Jülicher, Goguel, Michel, Huby-Lyonnet, Gaugler, Barrett, Wikenhauser, Guthrie, Preisker, Harder).

§20. THE EPISTLE TO THE PHILIPPIANS

Commentaries, see p. 389. Studies: W. LÜTGERT, *Die Vollkommenen in Philippi und die Enthusiasten in Thessalonich*, BFTh 13, 6, 1909, 1 ff.; P. FEINE, *Die Abfassung des Phil. in Ephesus*, BFTh 20, 4, 1916; W. MICHAELIS, *Die Gefangenschaft des Paulus in Ephesus und das Itinerar des Timotheus*, NTF, I, 3, 1925; idem, *Die Datierung des Phil.*, NTF I, 8, 1933; G. S. DUNCAN, *St. Paul's Ephesian Ministry. A Reconstruction with Special Reference to the Ephesian Origin of the Imprisonment Epistles*, 1929; J. SCHMID, *Zeit und Ort der paulinischen Gefangenschaftsbriefe. Mit einem Anhang über die Datierung der Past.*, 1931; T. W. MANSON, "St. Paul in Ephesus. The Date of the Epistle to the Philippians," BJRL 23, 1939, 182 ff. (= Manson, St., 149 ff.); C. H. DODD, *NT Studies*, 1953, 85 ff.; G. S. DUNCAN, "Were Paul's Imprisonment Epistles written from Ephesus?," ExpT 67, 1955-56, 163 ff.; idem, "Paul's Ministry in Asia—the Last Phase," NTSt 3, 1956-57, 211 ff.; idem, "Chronological Table to Illustrate Paul's Ministry in Asia," NTSt 5, 1958-59, 43 ff.; P. N. HARRISON, "The Pastoral Epistles and Duncan's Ephesian Theory," NTSt 2, 1955-56, 250 ff.; L. JOHNSON, "The Pauline Letters from Caesarea," ExpT 68, 1956-57, 24 ff.; W. SCHMITHALS, "Die Irrlehrer des Phil.," ZThK 54, 1957, 297 ff.; J. MÜLLER-BARDORFF, "Zur Frage der literarischen Einheit des Phil.," *Wissenschaftl. Zeitschrift der Friedrich Schiller-Universität* Jena 7, 1957-58, Gesellschafts- und sprachwissenschaftl. Reihe 4, 591 ff.; B. D. RAHTJEN, "The Three Letters of Paul to the Philippians," NTSt 6, 1959-60, 167 ff.; B. S. MACKAY, "Further Thoughts on Philippians," NTSt 7, 1960-61, 161 ff.; G. DELLING, RGG [3] V, 1961, 333 ff.; G. BORNKAMM, "Der Phil. als paulinische Briefsammlung," *Neotestamentica et Patristica, Freundesgabe O. Cullmann*, NovT Suppl. 6, 1962, 192 ff.; H. KÖSTER, "The Purpose of the Polemic of a Pauline Fragment (Phil. III)," NTSt 8, 1961-62, 317 ff.

1. Contents

After the address (1:1 f.) and epistolary introduction (1:3-11), in which Paul gives thanks for the condition of the church and prayerfully mentions their further advancement, follow reports about the Apostle's situation (1:12-26). Although he is imprisoned, the cause of the gospel is not hindered, but advanced; his associates have thereby received a stimulus to the joyful confession and proclamation of the gospel (1:12-18a); even his personal prospects are auspicious: Filled with a desire for death, he, nevertheless, sees a favorable outcome to his trial, his acquittal; he knows that he will remain in the flesh, that he will remain to support his churches, and that he will see the Philippians again (1:18b-26). To that are connected exhortations to the congregation (1:27–2:18): First, an exhortation to brave perseverance in the struggle for the faith (1:27-30); then the admonition to cultivation of a right disposition, which above all things is humility and unselfishness as a member of the body of Christ (2:1-5). This admonition becomes the occasion for the incorporation of the Christ psalm (2:6-11), in which Paul praises Jesus Christ as the foundation of a disposition which is prepared for self-forgetting renunciation, even unto the uttermost. The paraenesis rings out with a repeated admonition to struggle for salvation, from which joy originates for Paul and the readers themselves (2:12-18). In 2:19-30 follow notes about Timothy and Epaphroditus: Timothy, whose faithfulness Paul praises, is supposed to come to Philippi soon; the Philippian, Epaphroditus, who in connection with his visit to Paul became sorely sick, has recovered and is now setting out upon his journey home. 3:1a seems to prepare for the epistolary conclusion. But then once more the Apostle commences longer expositions, whose changed tone is striking: 3:1b-21 forcibly warns of persons who have false confidence in the flesh, which Paul has given up, in order, on the basis of faith, to strive after the goal of the upward call, and sets up Paul as a pattern for those people who live as enemies of the cross of Christ. Short, specific admonitions and renewed general exhortations are attached to this general warning (4:1-9). Finally, Paul thanks the Philippians for a gift, over which he rejoices as evidence of their inner unity with him (4:10-20). General greetings (4:21 f.) and the benediction (4:23) form the conclusion.

2. Paul and the Church at Philippi

The founding of the church was the first act of Paul on European soil when, in the year 48/49 on his so-called second missionary journey, he came from Asia Minor to Macedonia. Philippi, built by Philip of Macedon, the father of Alexander the Great, and named after him, since 42 B.C. was a Roman military colony, "Colonia Augusta Iulia Philippensis," whose inhabitants enjoyed the privileges of the "ius Italicum" (cf. P. Lemerle, *Philippes et la Macédoine orientale à l'époque chrétienne et byzantine*, 1945, 7 ff.). The history of Paul's first mission in Philippi is known from Acts 16:12-40. It follows from I Thess. 2:2 and Phil. 1:30 that the Apostle on this occasion was beset by conflicts and abuse. His first stay does not seem to have been of long duration, nor to have led to the founding of a large congregation. Acts mentions only the proselyte Lydia, a dealer in purple from Thyatira, with her household (16:14 f., 40), and the jailer (16:33 f.). Otherwise, we know only the members of the congregation mentioned in Philippians, who perhaps were not converted until later: Epaphroditus (2:25 ff.; 4:18), Euodia, Clement, and the unnamed "fellow workers" (4:2 f.; a proper name, Σύζυγος, is not attested). Already these names cause us to conclude that this congregation was basically Gentile Christian, and 3:3 also presupposes that the readers were not circumcised Jews. In the salutation Paul greets especially "overseers" and "assistants" (ἐπίσκοποι καὶ διάκονοι; 1:1): The congregation has persons for definite, practical tasks whose services are characterized with designations traditional in the surrounding associations and cultic fellowships. Through the years Paul had not again visited Philippi. But the ties with the Christians there were firmly knit together, as is shown already by the gifts of money with which they helped him immediately in Thessalonica and also later in Corinth (4:15 f.; II Cor. 11:8 f.). And possibly 3:1 (τὰ αὐτὰ γράφειν ἐμοὶ οὐκ ὀκνηρόν), and perhaps also 3:18, refer to earlier epistles of Paul to Philippi. The sending of Timothy to Macedonia (Acts 19:22) was certainly also intended for the Philippians. Paul himself, probably first in the late spring of 54 or 55, came again to Macedonia (Acts 20:1 f.). During the stay there he doubtless also stopped at Philippi, and perhaps here met Titus who came from Corinth, and here wrote II Corinthians (see p. 215). Finally, he visited the congregation in the spring of 55 or 56 when he traveled from Corinth via Macedonia to Jerusalem to deliver the collection, and probably celebrated Passover in their midst (Acts 20:3 ff.).

3. The Occasion of the Epistle

a) Paul had recently received another gift of money from Philippi. Epaphroditus delivered it under commission of the congregation (4:14, 18; 2:25). The Epistle expresses thanks for the evidence of love which has been received. Paul dispatches the Epistle by means of Epaphroditus, who had been very sick when with Paul, but has now recovered (2:28). b) Between the arrival of Epaphroditus with Paul and the Epistle to the Philippians a report concerning the illness of Epaphroditus must also have reached Philippi (2:26), and it is usually concluded from the formulation, he "has been distressed because you heard that he was ill," that a report about the distress of the Philippians likewise must already have arrived back at the place where Paul and Epaphroditus were, but that by no means follows with certainty from this formulation (cf. Mackay). In any case, the Epistle to the Philippians also wishes to inform the Philippians that since the illness of Epaphroditus, which he contracted in the service of Christ, brought him near to death, he should be received with even greater esteem by the Philippians (2:27-30). c) Paul also desires to furnish the congregation in Philippi with a report about his condition (1:12 ff.), especially since he cannot come at the moment because of his imprisonment. In addition, he wants to inform them that he hopes to send Timothy to Philippi soon, because he is waiting upon reports from the congregation (2:19 ff.). d) Paul also longs to help the congregation, since he himself, for the present, cannot come. To be sure, the

condition of the congregation hardly gives Paul occasion for exhortatory intervention. 1:3 ff.; 2:12; 4:1 show the picture of a congregation which deserves
the full confidence of its Apostle. Only the vigorous reminder of the duty of
concord (1:27–2:18) points to a definite lack in the moral conduct of the
congregational members, which in the single case of 4:2 has mounted to the
crass form of a quarrel between two women. Yet Paul wants to warn the congregation of persons whom he characterizes as "evil workers" (3:2) and
"enemies of the cross of Christ" (3:18), and who could make an impression
upon the Philippians (3:2, 15, 17), even though he does not observe that the
congregation is already threatened.

The reasons for the composition of this very personal writing are, therefore,
so numerous that its origin becomes readily comprehensible. All the more unclear
are the immediate historical circumstances of its composition.

4. Place and Time of the Composition of the Epistle

Paul writes as a prisoner (1:7, 13, 17; which Manson disputes for insufficient
reasons), but the Epistle manifests nothing of apprehension about the outcome.
Rather, Paul sees his situation developing for the advancement of the gospel:
It has become known throughout the entire praetorian guard and to all the rest
that his imprisonment is as a Christian missionary, not as a common criminal
(1:12 f.). His trial can end with a judgment of death (1:20; 2:17). But most
probably he will be acquitted. Hence he is in good spirits, and hopes soon to
be working in freedom again, and to be able to come to Philippi (1:25; 2:24).
Around him there prevails a lively, joyful activity of evangelization (1:14 ff.).
Timothy is found among Paul's associates (1:1; 2:19, 23).

When was Paul in a situation to which these data of Philippians are suited?

From Acts 23:33–26:32 and 28:14–31 we know of two imprisonments of
Paul, that in Caesarea and that in Rome. How long Paul sat under investigation
during the proceedings in Caesarea, which followed the arrest of the Apostle
in Jerusalem around Pentecost in 57 or 58, we do not know. Although Acts
24:27 gives two years, it is questionable whether this statement also in the
source referred to the time of Paul's confinement (cf. E. Haenchen, *Die Apg.*,
Meyer III[13], 1961, 60 ff.). In Rome Paul sat two years in "custodia libera,"
according to Acts 28:30. Does Philippians originate from one of these two
imprisonments or from a hypothetical imprisonment in Ephesus?

1. The traditional view has Philippians composed in Rome (since the Marcionite prologue of the second century until the eighteenth century this view
was undisputed; recently, e.g., Jülicher, Heard, Henshaw, Sparks, J. J. Müller,
Beare, Guthrie, Dodd, J. Schmid, Harrison, Mackay, Rahtjen, etc.). Above all,
the following arguments are cited in favor of this position:

a) 1:13, πραιτώριον = praetorian guard, which stood in Rome. According
to Acts 28:16, Paul, in the "custodia libera" in his own quarters, had a soldier
with him as guard. He was, therefore, placed under the surveillance of praetorian
guards, who relieved one another.

b) The expression "οἱ ἐκ τῆς Καίσαρος οἰκίας" (4:22), which, according to the linguistic usage of the time of the emperors (cf. Latin, "domus" or "familia Caesaris"), designates "members of the imperial household," "the attendants of the emperor," "slaves and free men." Nowhere was there a better opportunity to meet slaves of the emperor and to win them to Christianity than in Rome.

c) The situation of the imprisoned Paul. That in his place of residence preachers of the gospel were active in numbers (1:14 ff.) is readily understood in Rome with its distinguished Christian church. But even the Apostle's personal situation corresponds to a Roman imprisonment: His trial before the imperial judge is coming to a close. Philippians stems from the time close before the end of the proceedings. Paul is mindful of the judicial decision as an alternative between judgment of death or acquittal (1:19 ff.). A hearing has already taken place (1:7; ἀπολογία, βεβαίωσις); thereby it was shown that he was arrested and brought to trial only as a missionary of Christianity for the sake of Christ (1:12 f.). His freedom to send letters and to associate with his missionary companions also fits Paul's situation as portrayed in Acts 28:16, 30 f.

But against the Roman origin of Philippians we may bring forth strong considerations. a) From Rome Paul wanted to go on to Spain (Rom. 15:24, 28). But how do these plans agree with the announcement of a visit to Philippi, which Paul promises after a favorable outcome of the trial (2:24; 1:26)?

b) In view of the great distance between Rome and Philippi, how is the quick communication and exchange of reports through letters and messengers between Paul and the church conceivable, as presupposed in Philippians? It has been calculated that before the composition of the Epistle the distance between the place of Paul's imprisonment and Philippi must have been traversed four times (the Philippians heard of Paul's arrest and sent Epaphroditus to him; the latter's illness was reported to Philippi, and the concern of the Philippians reported back), and that between the composition of Philippians and the projected journey of Paul to Philippi the same distance would have to be traversed yet three more times (Epaphroditus returns to Philippi with the Epistle to the Philippians; Timothy is supposed to follow soon, and bring back reports from Philippi; cf. Michaelis). In whatever way we reckon the duration of a journey from Rome to Philippi, these numerous journeys demand in any case several months. Could Paul have waited for months to thank the Philippians for the gift (4:10 ff.)? Could he have characterized a projected journey which was to take place only after months as "coming soon" (2:24)?

c) "According to 1:30; 4:15 f. (cf. also 2:12; 1:26 and 2:22), Paul obviously had not been to Philippi since the founding of the church" (Michaelis) —a statement which does not apply to the time of the Roman imprisonment (cf. Acts 20:1 ff.).

d) In 3:2 ff. Paul polemizes against Judaizers in a manner similar to that in Galatians and II Corinthians. Romans shows, however, that at that time there was no Judaizing danger either in Corinth or in Rome. This polemic is thus incomprehensible at the time of Paul's Roman imprisonment (so Feine).

These reasons for and these objections against the composition of Philippians in Rome are largely without real probative force.

a) The reference to the publication of Paul's imprisonment as a Christian ἐν ὅλῳ τῷ πραιτωρίῳ (1:13), and the greetings from the emperor's slaves (4:22), agree, to be sure, especially well with Rome. But these allusions would likewise have been possible in Caesarea or Ephesus, because πραιτώριον can also characterize the residence of Roman governors and other Roman official houses, and there were slaves of the emperor in many places.

b) From 1:14 f. we can no more infer anything certain about the size of the local Christian church than about the number of the missionaries active there. Paul's personal situation, with the alternative of death sentence or acquittal, certainly does fit best his trial before the emperor in Rome, against whom there was no further appeal. But it is completely unknown to us, e.g., whether Paul, perhaps in Caesarea, had had the intention from the beginning of his imprisonment to appeal to Caesar (Acts 25:11; 26:32; 28:19).

c) We know nothing as to whether Paul during his two-year Roman imprisonment gave up or postponed his plan of a journey to Spain, in order to travel after his release first to the East and hence also to Philippi. Nevertheless, here is a real difficulty for the supposition that Philippians was composed in Rome.

d) The journeys presupposed and projected in Philippians between Paul's residence and Philippi can doubtless be better explained if Paul were closer to Philippi than in Rome or Caesarea. Yet it is by no means correct that before the composition of the Epistle this distance must have been traversed four times (cf. Mackay). It is nowhere said that the Philippians sent their gift through Epaphroditus after they had heard of Paul's imprisonment, and from 2:26 it by no means follows that Epaphroditus learned how the Philippians reacted to the report of his illness. From Philippians we can suppose with certainty nothing more than that Paul, after Epaphroditus had overcome his disease, thanks the Philippians for their gift delivered by Epaphroditus. Hence the interval of time between the receipt of the gift and the composition of the epistle of thanks is independent of the duration of a journey between the residence of Paul and Philippi. On the other hand, 2:19, 24 presupposes that Timothy is supposed to travel to Philippi and back, before Paul himself departs "soon" for there, a situation more difficult to conceive in connection with the great distances from Rome or Caesarea than from Ephesus.

e) From no place in Philippians does it follow that Paul was no more in Philippi after the founding of the church there; hence this argument does not speak against Rome or Caesarea.

f) It is debatable against whom the polemic in 3:2 ff., 17 ff. is directed, but the claim that Paul here polemizes against Judaizers (Appel, Feine-Behm, McNeile-Williams, Cerfaux in Robert-Feuillet, Beare, Martin, J. J. Müller, Delling, Bonnard, T. W. Manson, O. Cullmann, *Peter* . . . Tr. F. V. Filson, 1962, 105, B. Reicke, *Diakonie, Festfreude und Zelos*, 1951, 298 ff.), is extremely improbable, because any polemic against the adoption of circumcision and of the observance of the Law by Christians and any defense of Paul's apostleship is lacking. Thus on the basis of this point no convincing objection can be raised to the composition of Philippians in Rome. But it cannot generally be determined with complete certainty against whom this polemic is directed. Those who have denied the interpretation which identifies the opponents as Judaizers, have largely thought in terms of Jewish propagandists (Dibelius, Goguel, Meinertz, Jülicher, Lohmeyer, Duncan, Albertz, J. Munck, see bibl. to §16, p. 274). To their propaganda for circumcision ἐν σαρκί the statement, "We are the true circumcision" (3:3), was placed in contrast. To be sure, some advocates of this view hesitate to interpret 3:17 ff. as directed against the same Jews, and refer 3:17 ff. to base Christians (Dibelius, Michel, CBL), or, in connection with an interpretation which refers 3:2 ff. to Judaizers, refer 3:17 ff. to libertines (Lütgert, Appel, Beare, Martin, Delling), because the charges in 3:19, "their god is the belly, and they glory in their shame," fits neither Jews nor Judaizers. Others want to regard the entire polemic in 3:2 ff. and 3:17 ff. as directed against the same Jewish-Gnostic opponents of the Pauline mission who also had to be fought in Corinth (Schmithals; somewhat differently, Köster, Bornkamm). Unequivocal Gnostic features certainly are not found in 3:2 ff., 17 ff. (the contention that the opponents maintain the Resurrection as already past is dragged in), and that abusive term, κύνες (3:2), just like the contrast between ἡμεῖς and those attacked (3:2 f., 19 f.), refers to Jews rather than to Christians. The supposition that the opponents whom Paul attacks in ch. 3, opponents who only threaten the congregation without already belonging to it, are the same Jewish propagandists in 3:2 ff. as in 3:17 ff. calls forth fewest doubts, but remains uncertain. Hence we cannot use the character of the opponents in Phil. 3 to determine the place where the Epistle was composed. If it is a matter of the Christian congregation over against hostile Jews, then this polemic agrees with every place at which a Christian congregation was found.

2. If there are no clear-cut arguments for the composition of Philippians in Rome, and if a few arguments speak against it, then it is understandable that since H. E. G. Paulus (1799) numerous scholars have expressed themselves in favor of the composition of the Epistle in the other imprisonment known from Acts, that in Caesarea (see J. Schmid, 2, note 1; lately, Lohmeyer and L. Johnson). To be sure, the difficulty which has already been shown to arise from the journeys to and from Philippi speaks as well against Caesarea as against Rome, even if the voyage from Caesarea to Philippi is calculated to be somewhat shorter than the journey from Rome to Philippi. In favor of Caesarea would be the consideration that the congregation at the place of confinement does not seem to have been founded by Paul (cf. 1:13-17). Likewise, the plan mentioned in Philippians of a renewed journey to Philippi would blend smoothly with the plan mentioned in Romans of missionary activity in Spain, if we would suppose that Paul at a point of time before Acts 25:11 could have reckoned with the possibility of his acquittal. Since that is not provable, this localization of Philippians is today almost generally, but yet probably all too quickly, denied.

3. The problem of establishing the place where Philippians was written is

not necessarily bound to the alternative of Caesarea or Rome. Already before the years of investigation, of which Acts 23 ff. reports, Paul, according to his own testimony, was imprisoned more than once (II Cor. 11:23; 6:5; I Clem. 5:6 knows that Paul "wore chains seven times"). Accordingly, there always exists the possibility that Philippians stems from an imprisonment of Paul of which the NT gives no direct information but for whose historicity there are indications in the sources. In the opinion of many scholars it is a question of an imprisonment in Ephesus.

The Ephesian hypothesis first appears in a quite eccentric form in H. Lisco (1900), but was then thoroughly grounded by Deissmann, Feine, Michaelis, and Duncan (who thinks of the first of several Ephesian imprisonments), and today has numerous supporters (e.g., Goguel, Appel, Albertz, McNeile-Williams, de Zwaan, Feine-Behm, Klijn, Bonnard, Benoit, BdJ 499, Delling, Riddle-Hutson, W. Manson, Lemerle [see p. 227] 49 ff., Schmithals, Müller-Bardorff, G. Bornkamm, Friedrich).

The most important arguments are the following:

a) According to language, literary manner, and thought-content, Philippians fits better closer to the earlier epistles than to the other prison epistles, which are to be located in Caesarea or Rome. Feine (43 ff.) has cited observations concerning the linguistic relationship of Philippians with I and II Corinthians and Romans. But Schmid's opposing studies (122 ff.) of the linguistic relationship of Philippians with Colossians (and Ephesians) show that neither with the one nor with the other group of Pauline epistles is there a one-sided relationship in language. And the lists of "Parallels between Philippians and the other Pauline Epistles" (compiled by C. L. Mitton, *The Epistle to the Ephesians*, 1951, 322 ff.) clearly show that there are parallels with almost all the Pauline epistles.

b) Phil. 3 fits only into the time of Paul's struggles with the Judaizers or Gnostics, whose literary monuments are Galatians and II Corinthians. This argument is untenable, if in Phil. 3 it is a matter of warning against Jewish propaganda. But even if Paul is supposed to be warning against the same Judaizing or Gnostic danger as in Galatians or II Corinthians, it is by no means certain that a similar danger could not have been in Paul's mind in a later time on the basis of new experiences.

c) The process of Paul in Phil. 1, 2 cannot be the same as that introduced in Acts 23 ff. Phil. 1:7, 12 f., 16; 2:17 show that Paul's proclamation of the gospel has somehow become the occasion for his judicial prosecution, but according to Acts 21:28; 25:7 ff.; 28:17 ff. it is a matter of alleged offenses of Paul against the Jewish Law together with profanation of the temple. If Paul in Philippians were standing before the last stages of his process which was begun in Jerusalem and Caesarea and then referred to the imperial tribunal in Rome, then the allusions to the process would have to sound different. "Defense and confirmation of the gospel" (1:7; cf. 1:16) lie upon a different level from the defense against Jewish accusations in Acts. This argument, however, has probative power only if we regard the charges mentioned in Philippians, based upon the proclamation of the gospel, as somewhat different from the accusations in Acts, based upon teaching which is hostile to the Law. Especially since the statements in Acts about the process of Paul are by no means clear, this distinction is hardly valid.

d) There can be no doubt that the "praetorian guard" (1:13), as well as the "slaves of the emperor" (4:22), were at Ephesus, for Ephesus was also a praetorian garrison, and there were imperial slaves or freed men in the empire generally, where imperial property was to be managed. But since this argument also applies to Caesarea, it is not convincing (see p. 231).

e) The journeys between Paul's place of residence and Philippi, which the Epistle presupposes (see p. 230), are more easily conceivable from Ephesus than from Caesarea or Rome. Paul's plans to come to Philippi after his acquittal, and before that to send Timothy there and to await his return, are suitable to Acts 19:22; 20:1; I Cor. 4:17; 16:5, 10. Yet we certainly must note that this argument encounters the difficulty that Paul himself in I Cor. 4:17 and 16:10 does not suggest that he is sending Timothy via Macedonia to Corinth, and that Acts 19:22 does not indicate that Paul expects Timothy back before his departure. Concerning Timothy's fate according to Acts 20:6, following the departure from Philippi after Paul's last stay there, we know nothing, so that the supposition is thoroughly possible that Paul wanted to send him from Caesarea or Rome to Philippi. Therefore, this argument also is not compelling.

f) In 1:30 Paul compares his conflict with the authorities in Philippi (Acts 16:19 ff.) with a similar experience about which the Philippians are *now* hearing. That points to an event of the most recent past, not to the imprisonment in Caesarea and Rome lasting several years. But 1:30 presupposes that the Philippians are hearing now for the first time in more detail about Paul's present ἀγών, and it shows nothing at all in respect to the duration of his imprisonment up to this time.

In addition, there is the indubitable difficulty that the fact of an imprisonment in Ephesus cannot be proved directly from the sources. The only thing settled is that Paul experienced severe suffering there. He writes from Ephesus: "Why am I in peril every hour? I protest, brethren, by my pride in you which I have in Christ Jesus our Lord, I die every day! What do I gain if, humanly speaking, I fought with beasts at Ephesus?" (I Cor. 15:30 ff.). Paul's reference to fighting with beasts is probably to be understood figuratively (cf. Schmid, 39 ff.), and cannot be used as evidence for a longer imprisonment. And in II Cor. 1:8 ff. Paul says retrospectively about the period lying behind him in Ephesus:

For we do not want you to be ignorant, brethren, of the affliction we experienced in Asia; for we were so utterly, unbearably crushed that we despaired of life itself. Why, we felt that we had received the sentence of death; but that was to make us rely not on ourselves but on God who raises the dead; he delivered us from so deadly a peril, and he will deliver us; on him we have set our hope that he will deliver us again (cf. also 4:8 ff.; 6:9 f.).

But the text does not show that this danger of death was connected with an imprisonment. And even though there are still today in Ephesus ruins called the

"Prison of Paul," the origin of this local tradition, authenticated only since the seventeenth century, has not yet been discovered.

Thus we are wanting any convincing evidence for an imprisonment of long duration of Paul in Ephesus (cf. the journeys to and from Philippi!). And there remains the difficulty that Acts is silent about Paul's painful experiences in Ephesus, which, in spite of the silence of Acts, probably include an imprisonment. But this difficulty exists even without the fusion of the question about the home of the Epistle to the Philippians with the fate of Paul in Ephesus, and we cannot simply put it out of the way with the unfounded hypothesis that the author of Acts "intentionally said nothing about an imprisonment in Ephesus" (Michaelis).

The question of where Philippians was written cannot, then, be answered with certainty without new sources (Dibelius, Martin, Wikenhauser). But we can say that the probability of the Ephesian hypothesis is the slightest. Thus the time of composition is most likely a matter of the years 56/58 (Caesarea) or 58/60 (Rome).

5. Authenticity and Unity

The doubts of Baur's school about the authenticity of this Epistle (attested already by Polycarp, Phil. 3:2) have disappeared since Holsten. Attempts to separate unauthentic pieces from Philippians have miscarried (lately, Riddle-Hutson, *NT Life and Literature*, 1946, 123, maintained the secondary insertion of 1:1b, since Paul does not speak of ἐπίσκοποι). On the other hand, the view repeatedly advocated since the seventeenth century has recently been established again in the most varied forms (cf. Goguel, *Intr.* IV, 1, 404 f.): The transmitted Philippians has secondarily been joined together out of two or three originally independent epistles or fragments of epistles. Advocates of this view point out that Paul in Philippians "until 3:1 offers the paragon of a clear and precise Epistle" (Schmithals), but that in 3:1 an epistolary conclusion begins, which is interrupted in 3:2 by a warning about opponents which is completely different in tone and contents from the preceding chapters, whereas 4:4 connects very well with 3:1. On the basis of these considerations some critics suppose an interpolation of 3:2–4:3 (or 3:2–4:1, McNeile-Williams, J. Weiss, *Earliest Christianity*, 1959, I, 387; or 3:2–4:20, Goodspeed; or 3:1b–4:9, Friedrich). Others find that the thanks for the gift of the Philippians (4:10-20) is also out of place at the end of the Epistle, especially in view of the long time required by 2:25 ff., and separate out this section as a previously existing thanksgiving epistle. Moreover, 3:2–4:3 presupposes no imprisonment of Paul (Bornkamm). As a result, we have the supposition, in slightly varying forms, that Philippians is composed of three Pauline epistles to Philippi, each following chronologically after the other: 4:10-20 / 1:1–3:1; 4:2-9, 21-23 / 3:2–4:1 (Beare); 4:10-23/1:1–3:1; 4:4-7/3:2–4:3, 8 f. (Schmithals); 1:1–3:1; 4:4-7, 21-23 / 3:2–4:3 / 4:10-20 (Bornkamm); 4:10-20 / 1:1–2:30; 4:21-23 / 3:1–

4:9 (Rahtjen). Of these epistles, the first was written soon after the arrival of Epaphroditus, the second after his recovery, and the third later after the receipt of new reports (so also Köster, without exact demarcations). Müller-Bardorff, however, regards the connection within the first two chapters also as intolerable, and constructs the three epistles in the following manner: 4:10-20 / 1:1-26; 2:17 f.; 1:27–2:16; 4:1-3; 2:19-30; 3:1*a*; 4:4-7; 4:21-23 / 3:2-21; 4:8 f. Others quite generally regard the composition of Philippians out of several epistles as certain or probable (Riddle-Hutson, Wikenhauser, Benoit, in BdJ). As confirmation of this supposition, some refer to Polycarp's remark about Paul: ὅς καὶ ἀπὼν ὑμῖν ἔγραψεν ἐπιστολὰς, εἰς ἃς ἐὰν ἐγκύπτητε . . . , (Phil. 3:2). Hence Polycarp must still have known of several epistles of Paul to Philippi. As a motive for the combination of two or three epistles into one Epistle to the Philippians, the same motive is adduced as for the combination of the two Epistles to the Corinthians (see p. 204): The "most exceedingly prudent man," in the interest of disseminating the Pauline epistles throughout the entire church, so joined together the writings to one congregation that they would become obligatory for the entire church (Schmithals, Müller-Bardorff). Bornkamm would like to suppose another redactor than the one connected with Corinthians, who wanted to make the epistles to Philippi accessible to other churches. This entire argumentation, however, is not convincing (cf. on the other hand Guthrie, Mackay, Delling, Michaelis, *Einl.*, supplement). The new beginning in 3:2 is, of course, surprising, and we are not prepared for the sharpness of the warning in 3:2 ff., 18 f. But, on the one hand, 1:28 already contains a warning against ἀντικείμενοι, and, on the other hand, Paul elsewhere also shows abrupt shifts in style (Rom. 16:17 ff.; I Thess. 2:15 f.; I Cor. 15:58). Further, the invective in 3:2 ff. is useful to Paul in connection with the resumption of the ethical admonition of 2:12 ff. in 3:15 f., and the resumption of the reference to his example in 1:30 in 3:17. The conjecture that 3:2–4:3 presupposes no imprisonment of Paul can be maintained only after the removal of the text from its context. And I confess that I cannot perceive why Paul could not wait to join his gratitude in 4:10 ff. to the loosely connected personal epistolary conclusion in 4:2 ff., especially since 1:7 and 2:25 clearly allude already to help from the Philippians. But surely the discovery of strange features within the context of thought in chaps. 1 and 2 proves no secondary transpositions, and the question, Who was supposed to have undertaken such changes in a text which, according to Müller-Bardorff, already was regarded as "Holy Scripture"? points to the decisive objection against all of these combination theories: They presuppose not only arbitrary combinations but at the least the excision of introductions and conclusions, and possibly even the composition of a connective sentence (3:1*b*) by the redactor (Beare, Müller-Bardorff). How anyone could believe a "most exceedingly prudent man" capable of such arbitrariness is beyond comprehension, and "an also otherwise usual method" (Bornkamm) is by no means present (see p. 205). The remark of Polycarp is certainly striking. If here there is not simply an error, it is most likely to be made understandable as a false deduction from 3:1*b*. But in any case it does not prove that in our

Philippians several epistles are combined. Moreover, Mackay has correctly called our attention to the fact that definite motifs permeate all of the alleged separate pieces of the epistle, above all, the motif of joy (1:4, 18; 2:2, 17; 3:1; 4:1, 4, 10) but also, e.g., the motifs of Paul's contentment in any situation (1:21 ff.; 4:12 f.) and his confidence in the church (1:9; 4:1, 18 f.). There is, therefore, no sufficient reason to doubt the original unity of the transmitted Philippians. And even if the very widespread, but by no means certain, supposition is correct that Paul in 2:6-11 took up an early Christian hymn (cf. R. Martin, *An Early Christian Confession. Phil. 2:5-11 in Recent Interpretation,* 1960; lit.), or a hymn of a companion (Beare), then Paul, through this adopted text, doubtless only gave expression to his own proclamation of Christ (cf., e.g., J. M. Furness, ExpT 70, 1958-59, 240 ff.).

§21. The Epistle to the Colossians

Commentaries, see pp. 389 f. Studies: Duncan, Schmid, Dodd, Johnson see on Phil.; H. J. Holtzmann, *Kritik der Epheser- und Kolosserbriefe,* 1872; M. Dibelius, *Die Geisterwelt im Glauben des Paulus,* 1909, 125 ff.; J. Knox, "Philemon and the Authenticity of Colossians," JR 18, 1938, 144 ff.; E. Percy, *Die Probleme der Kolosser- und Epheserbriefe,* Skrifter utgivna av Kungl. Humanistiska Vetensskapssamfundet i Lund XXXIX, 1946 (thereto E. Käsemann, Gn 21, 1949, 342 ff.); G. Bornkmamm, "Die Häresie des Kol.," ThLZ 73, 1948, 11 ff. (= Das Ende des Gesetzes, BeTh 16, ²1958, 139 ff.); P. N. Harrison, "Onesimus and Philemon," AThR 32, 1950, 268 ff.; W. Bieder, *Die kolossische Irrlehre und die Kirche von heute,* ThSt 33, 1952; J. Coutts, "The Relationship of Ephesians and Colossians," NTSt 4, 1957-58, 201 ff.; E. Käsemann, RGG³ III, 1959, 1727 f.; P. Benoit, DBS VII, 1961, 156 ff. (bibl.); G. Bornkamm, "Die Hoffnung im Kol.—Zugleich ein Beitrag zur Frage der Echtheit des Briefes," *Studien zum NT und zur Patristik, Festschr. E. Klostermann,* TU 77, 1962, 56 ff.

1. Contents

After the address (1:1 f.) follow thanks to God for the good condition of faith in the congregation founded by Epaphras (1:3-8) and intercession for the further growth of their knowledge (1:9-12). To that is attached, by means of a relative pronoun (ὅς), a hymnic description of the significance of Christ: He is mediator of creation, reconciler of the world, head of the church (1:13-20). The Colossians also have experienced salvation in Christ (1:21-23). The imprisoned Apostle, as servant of the church, has the task of proclaiming the divine mystery, even to the Colossians, who are personally strange to him (1:24–2:5). Then he turns to them in their situation in which they are especially threatened by false doctrine (2:6-23): They should not allow themselves to be blinded by a philosophy which would subject them to angelic powers, above whom Christ is highly exalted; in Christ dwells the fullness of the Godhead bodily; he is the head of all angelic and spiritual powers; dependence upon Christ sets one free from ties to the world elements, and tolerates no ascetic, ritualistic piety. After this polemic follows the ethical paraenesis (3:1–4:6), first of all, in principle (3:1-4), then in individual admonitions placed in relation to Christ (3:5-17), and finally in an address to the particular classes within the congregation: wives, husbands, children, fathers, slaves, and masters ("Haustafel," or table of household duties; 3:18–4:1), ending in exhortation to prayer, also for the Apostle (4:2-4), and to wise conduct toward non-Christians (4:5 f.). Then follows the actual correspondence: recommendation of Tychicus, the bearer of the letter, who is accompanied by Onesimus, a Christian from Colossae (4:7-9); greetings and instructions (4:10-17); greeting and benediction with Paul's own hand (4:18).

2. The Origin of the Church

The Phrygian city of Colossae, on the upper Lycus, a tributary of the Meander, situated on the great highway from Ephesus to the East, was at the time of Paul an insignificant market town, in contrast to the larger and more lively neighboring cities of Hierapolis and Laodicea. In these three places lying close together there existed, according to Colossians, Christian congregations with close connections to one another (4:13, 15 f.). Paul did not found the church at Colossae, nor had he visited it before writing Colossians (2:1; cf. 1:4, 7 ff.). On his journeys through Phrygia (Acts 16:6; 18:23), the Apostle probably did not touch the southwestern part of the territory in which Colossae lay. The church, like those at Laodicea and Hierapolis (4:13), was founded by the Colossian, Epaphras (1:7; 4:12). That Epaphras worked in Colossae under commission of Paul probably follows from 1:7 (reading ὑπὲρ ἡμῶν), and in any case Paul regarded the churches as belonging to his missionary territory in the province of Asia, and recognized Epaphras as a "faithful minister of Christ on our behalf," who rightly preached "the word of the truth, the gospel" (1:5 ff.; 2:6).

The size of the congregation, of which two household churches are mentioned (Col. 4:15, 17; cf. Phlm. 2), cannot be discerned from the Epistle. It probably consisted predominantly of Gentile Christians (2:13; 1:21, 27). A Jewish-Christian admixture in the church, which was thoroughly possible in regions with numerous Jews, nowhere stands out. Paul writes the Epistle as a prisoner (4:3, 10, 18; 1:24). Scattered remarks about Epaphras inform us that he was a fellow prisoner of Paul (Phlm. 23); he told the Apostle of the congregation's love (Col. 1:8); and greets the congregation (Col. 4:12). On the basis of these statements it is well to infer that he had sought Paul because of the situation in Colossae and had willingly shared his imprisonment. Under the impression of his report, Paul wrote Colossians. Tychicus delivered the Epistle, while Epaphras remained with Paul (4:7 f., 12 f.). Ἐπαφρᾶς is the shortened form of the very widespread name Ἐπαφρόδιτος. The identity of the Epaphras of Colossians and Philemon with the Epaphroditus of Philippians is not even to be considered.

3. Occasion of the Epistle

The Christians at Colossae were threatened with danger from false teachers who had appeared among them. Yet they had no success (2:4, 8, 20; on δογματίζεσθε 2:20 = you are burdened with regulations; cf. Masson, *ad loc.*); Paul is full of gratitude for the Christian condition of the Colossians, full of joy over the order in their ranks and over the firmness of their faith in Christ (1:3 ff.; 2:5). However, he regards as necessary the perfecting and establishing of the congregation's Christian knowledge (1:9 ff.; 2:6 f.). The false teachers demand observance of festivals, new moon, and sabbath (2:16), and they prescribe regulations for food (2:16, 21), whose observance in strict asceticism (2:20 ff.) is supposed to serve to mortify the flesh (2:23). That the characterization of baptism as a "circumcision made without hands" (2:11) refers to the heretics' demand for circumcision is improbable. If already the ascetic bent in these ethical precepts, which is expounded in spiritual pride (2:18), seems to be Gnostic, so especially does the religious, cultic doctrine of angels, which the false teachers advocate. They demand a "worship of angels" (θρησκεία τῶν ἀγγέλων 2:18), of "the elemental spirits of the universe" (τὰ στοιχεῖα τοῦ κόσμου 2:8; cf. Gal. 4:9), of spiritual beings, who fill the world and have power over men, and perhaps also of powers of the stars (2:16; Bornkamm). Asceticism and the cult "in humility" (2:18, 23) plainly are supposed to make one ripe for direct encounter with the angelic powers, which takes place in visions (2:18). Paul condemns the ritualistic commands of the false teachers, because they make things into chief things, which are only "a shadow of what is to come" (2:17 f.) and therefore are of no consequence religiously. The Gnostic secret wisdom, with the Gnostic concept of "philosophy" characterized as a doctrine of revelation, is, in Paul's eyes, only apparent wisdom, in truth, "empty deceit, according to human tradition" (2:8, 22 f.). The "cult devised according to the fancy of the devotees," "humility," and "mortification of the flesh" (2:23) derive from a sensuous mind and a foolish imagination (2:18, 22 f.). Perhaps this worship of angels had the form of the mysteries (cf. ἐμβατεύων 2:18; ἐθελοθρησκία 2:23; and the characterization of Christ as μυστήριον 2:2), but was, in any case, connected with the Christian faith. With the false doctrine of the false teachers, Paul contrasts the true: Christ is the origin and the head of all things, of all living creatures, even of all angelic beings, the bringer of reconciliation for them as well as for men; his cross is the victory over spiritual powers; in him dwells all the fullness of the Godhead bodily; in him the entire world has all fullness of being, of salvation, of wisdom, and of knowledge.

Concerning the nature of the Colossian heresy, views formerly varied widely (cf. H. J. Holtzmann, *Einl.*[3], 250). Today there are hardly any differences in basic opinion. Paul, with obvious correctness, sees in the heretical teaching Gnosticism, secret wisdom of a syncretistic sort (2:8, 18), which combines ascetic, ritualistic worship of the elements with Jewish ritualism and Jewish speculation about angels. Influences of specific Gentile, Oriental cults cannot with certainty be demonstrated. Also, a connection with the dualistic Torah piety of the sect of Qumran is hardly provable (against W. D. Davies, in: *The Scrolls and the NT*, ed. K. Stendahl, 1957, 166 ff.). It is nothing unusual for that period that Judaism or Jewish Christianity and Gnosticism should meet one another, especially since Phrygia was a soil well-suited for such an encounter (for details, cf. Bornkamm, Dibelius-Greeven on 2:8, 23, Guthrie, 162 ff.).

Thus, according to all probability, the Colossian heresy represented a form of Jewish Gnosticism combined with Christianity. The preference for the term "Prägnosis" (Meinertz, Cerfaux in Robert-Feuillet) is only a terminological difference. On the other hand, the denial of an angelic cult by Percy, Bieder, Masson, and Klijn is untenable. Because the Colossian false teachers doubted the conquest of the spiritual world by Christ and therefore sought to win the good favor of these powers, Paul accents Christ's cosmic role and his victory over the spiritual powers (1:15-17, 19; 2:9 f., 15).

4. Authenticity and Integrity

For the history of the problem see Percy, 5 ff. The Pauline origin of Colossians was first denied by Mayerhoff (1838), who found in the Epistle dependence upon Ephesians, un-Pauline thoughts, and opposition to Cerinthus. Its authenticity was then refuted by F. C. Baur and his pupils, who traced the Epistle back to Gnostic circles of the second century. Holtzmann supposed a shorter authentic Colossians, which the author of Ephesians revised according to an anti-Gnostic purpose, in order to have the canonical Colossians thus produced issued as a counterpart to Ephesians. Interpolations in a genuine Pauline epistle without thorough rewriting was conjectured also by J. Weiss, *Earliest Christianity*, I, 150 f., Harrison, J. Knox, *Jesus, Lord and Christ*, 1958, 158, note 20. And Masson, independently of Holtzmann, arrived at a similar hypothesis: An authentic Pauline epistle (1:1-4, 7 f.; 2:6, 8 f., 12a, 16, 20 f.; 3:3 f., 12, 13a, 18-22a, 25; 4:1-3a, b, 5-8a, 9-12a, 14 [15], 17 f.) was interpolated by the author of Ephesians. After the recognition of the Pauline origin of Colossians had widely prevailed in recent decades because of the works of Dibelius, Lohmeyer, and Percy, lately doubt has been established again more than once (Bultmann, *Theology of the NT*, II, 175 ff., Käsemann, Bornkamm, E. Schweizer, ThLZ 86, 1961, 246 ff., E. Fuchs, *Die Freiheit des Glaubens*, BeTh 14, 1949, 30, H. J. Schoeps, *Paul*, 1961, 51, K.-G. Eckart, "Exegetische Beobachtungen zu Kol. 1:9-20," Thv 7, 1960, 95 ff.; the question remains open for Beare).

1) Language and style, 2) theology (especially the Christology of the Epistle), and 3) its relation to Ephesians give reason for painstaking examination of the authenticity of Colossians.

1. Certainly in vocabulary and sentence structure Colossians has much that is peculiar. Besides thirty-three actual hapax legomena, Holtzmann also found fifteen words which appear elsewhere in the NT but not in Paul. Moreover, there occurs the heaping of synonyms (as, "praying and asking, in all spiritual wisdom and understanding" [1:9], "holy and blameless and irreproachable" [1:

22]) and genitival connectives (as, πᾶν πλοῦτος τῆς πληροφορίας τῆς συνέσεως [2:2], τῆς πίστεως τῆς ἐνεργείας τοῦ θεοῦ [2:12]; cf. Percy, 20 f., 26 f.). The style is cumbersome, verbose, and surfeited to opacity with subordinate clauses, participial and infinitive constructions or substantives with ἐν (e.g., 1:9-20 [one sentence!]; 2:9-15). Several noted Pauline concepts are missing, as righteousness, justification, law, salvation, revelation. But in part the different linguistic manner is explained by a more considerable use of liturgical, hymnic style, in which prayers and thanksgivings are also couched in epistles recognized as Pauline (Percy, 38); in part by the polemical purpose of the Epistle: The peculiarities of language and manner of expression are found most extensively in the sections of Colossians in which Paul polemizes against the new heresy or, with a glance at it, develops his own thought in hymnic form (1:10-20; 2:16-23). And the absence of well-known Pauline concepts proves nothing, because analogous observations can also be made about other Pauline epistles (cf. Lohmeyer, 12 f.). Also the lack in Colossians of the address otherwise met in all Pauline epistles, ἀδελφοί or ἀδελφέ (see E. Schweizer, ZNW 47, 1956, 287) hardly proves anything, because Paul does not always use this address throughout long texts (Rom. 1:14-6:23; II Cor. 1:1-7:16).

On the other hand, Colossians shows clear stylistic peculiarities of Paul: Pleonastic καί after διὰ τοῦτο (1:9) is found in the NT only in Paul (I Thess. 2:13; 3:5; Rom. 13:6; cf. also Rom. 9:24 [and Eph. 1:15 borrowing from Col. 1:9]); οἱ ἅγιοι αὐτοῦ in NT only in Col. 1:26; I Thess. 3:13; II Thess. 1:10; χαρίζεσθαι = forgive, 2:13; 3:13; otherwise in NT only in II Cor. 2:7, 10; 12:13 (and Eph. 4:32 = Col. 3:13); ἐν μέρει, 2:16 = "with regard to" in NT otherwise only in II Cor. 3:10; 9:3; Col. 1:10, πᾶν ἔργον ἀγαθόν, is found only in Paul in II Cor. 9:8; II Thess. 2:17 (likewise the singular ἔργον ἀγαθόν alone in Rom. 2:7; 13:3; Phil. 1:6); on the other hand, the plural ἔργα ἀγαθά is found only in Eph. 2:10; I Tim. 2:10; Acts 9:36 in the NT.

The language and style of Colossians, therefore, give no cause to doubt the Pauline origin of the Epistle.

2. That Colossians presents a front against Gnostics could make us suspicious of its authenticity so long as we knew Gnosticism only as a phenomenon of church history embodied in the Gnostic systems of the second century. Today we know that there were Gnostic, syncretistic groups and propaganda already at the time of Paul (see §17, 3), and that Gnosticism was a pre-Christian movement (cf. the surveys in S. Schulz, ThRdsch, N.F. 26, 1960, 330 ff.; E. Haenchen, RGG [3] II, 1958, 1652 ff.), so that the Jewish-Christian Gnosticism attacked in Colossians was altogether possible at the time of Paul. But does not the manner in which Colossians resists this heresy, this "anti-Gnostic Gnosticism" (Albertz), point to an author other than Paul? In particular, critics have referred to the cosmic character of the Christology (1:16-19; 2:9 f., 19), and to the conception of Christ as "the head of the body, the church" (1:18; cf. 2:19), but also in general to the doctrinarianism and moralism, the relaxation of theological argumentation, and the conception of salvation as something realized here and now. And some students have also sought to show that in 1:

15-20 a pre-Christian or Hellenistic-Christian hymn was taken up, which the
author of the Epistle Paulinized, whereby he stretched the Pauline Christology
cosmically, and at the same time reshaped the cosmic statements of the hymn
in an ecclesiastical direction. In so far as these critical objections are concrete
and tangible, their probative power is dependent upon agreement in respect to
the stylistic analysis and derivation of the hymn in 1:15-20, upon the history-
of-religions judgment concerning the relation of the κεφαλή-conception to the
concept of the church in the undisputed Pauline epistles, and upon the understanding of ἐλπίς in Colossians.

Now it is certainly not to be denied that 1:15-20 bears a hymnic character,
but the numerous reconstructions proposed since Lohmeyer's analysis (to the
literature cited by J. M. Robinson, JBL 76, 1957, 270 f., notes 5-7, should be
added, in addition to Robinson, above all E. Schweizer, ThLZ 86, 1961, 241 ff.;
E. Bammel, ZNW 52, 1961, 88 ff., H. Hegermann, *Die Vorstellung vom
Schöpfungsmittler im hellenistischen Judentum und Urchristentum*, TU 82,
1961, 88 ff.) have hardly led to a fully convincing result, since the presupposition is thoroughly unproved that a hymn constructed according to a strict
scheme was used, and that, therefore, every sentence fragment exceeding that
scheme must derive from the author of Colossians. The pre-Christian origin of
the inferred hymn (so Käsemann, *Essays on New Testament Themes*, 1964,
149 ff., Bultmann, U. Wilckens, *Weisheit und Torheit*, BhTh 26, 1959, 200 f.,
Eckart) is, in view of πρωτότοκος ἐκ τῶν νεκρῶν (1:18), as good as excluded.
Moreover, since the supposition of an insertion of the interpretation τῆς ἐκκλησίας
(1:18) or of 1:18c is demonstrable only from the certainly doubtful presupposition of a strict scheme, the widespread supposition that a pre-Pauline hymn
was taken up (lately, Schweizer, Bammel, Hegermann, J. Jervell, *Imago Dei*,
FRLANT, N.F. 58, 1960, 198 ff.) is by no means proved. Rather, it is completely possible that the author of Colossians himself formed this hymn on the
basis of traditional material (thus C. Maurer, *Wort und Dienst*, N.F. 4, 1955,
79 ff., Moule). If this supposition proves correct, then the contention that in
the manner of the postapostolic age the apostolic office in Col. 1:21 ff. is placed
side by side with the church confession in 1:12-20 (Käsemann) proves to be
just as unfounded as the assertion that the author of Colossians, like the author
of Ephesians, transformed the cosmic statement of the hymn into an ecclesiastical
statement (Schweizer). Rather, the author places in antithesis to the teaching
of the false teachers the mediator of creation, whose role comprehends the
cosmos, as well as the Christ, who through death and resurrection conquered the
cosmic powers (1:15-17, 20a; 2:10, 15), and who comprises within himself
the church as his body (1:18, 19, 20b, 24; 2:19). But the cosmic Christology
appearing therein had its beginnings in the recognized Pauline epistles (I Cor.
2:8; 8:6; II Cor. 4:4; Gal. 4:3, 9; Phil. 2:10), a fact to which Dibelius already
called attention.

The idea of Christ as the "head of the body, the church" (1:18; 2:19), which
is new in respect to the recognized Pauline epistles, is not striking within the
framework of the Pauline ecclesiology, if we observe that Paul even in the

recognized epistles (in addition to the comparison of the church with a σῶμα Rom. 12:4 f.; I Cor. 12:12, 14 ff.; cf. also Col. 3:15) knows the conception of the identity of the ἐκκλησία as the "body of Christ" with Christ himself (I Cor. 1:13; 12:12c, 13; Gal. 3:28), and that thereby the conception of Christ as the "makroanthropos" is given, wherever we might derive this conception. Viewed in this light, κεφαλή, as the controlling reality in the "body" (2:19), is a natural, precise statement which is not out of line with the idea of the body in the recognized epistles (cf. E. Best, *One Body in Christ*, 1955, 115 ff.).

Bornkamm contends that in Col. 1:5, 23, 27 "hope" is no longer understood in the sense of "historical" eschatology, and also that ἐλπίς (1:5), in the sense of "the possession of hope," is unusual in Paul. Indeed, in Col. 1:26 f., he detects a "Gnostic, spherical thought." But against Bornkamm we must say that ἐλπίς in Rom. 8:24 is found in the sense of "possession of hope," that the thought of the mystery concealed since eternity and now revealed corresponds to I Cor. 2:7 and Rom. 3:21 (νῦν δέ 1:26 is by no means a "stereotype"!), and that neither 1:26 nor 3:4 is a spherical conception, but rather a genuine eschatological tension as in Paul.

If the differences in content between Colossians and the recognized Pauline epistles can accordingly be thoroughly understood in relation to the anti-Gnostic polemic of the Epistle (so also H. Chadwick, NTSt 1, 1954-55, 270 ff.), then several facts which are also in the realm of content give positive support to the supposition of the Pauline origin of the Epistle. a) The relation of the writer to the readers presupposed in Colossians corresponds in several points to that of Philemon: In both Epistles Epaphras, Aristarchus, Mark, Luke, and Demas send greetings (Col. 4:10 ff.; Phlm. 23 f.); in both Epistles there is talk of sending Onesimus (Col. 4:9; Phlm. 12), and Archippus is addressed (Col. 4:17; Phlm. 2). Since these agreements are not found in the same contexts and formulations, the thesis that the non-Pauline author of Ephesians imitated the indubitably Pauline Philemon only in respect to these personal remarks is not convincing. b) The "Haustafel" (Col. 3:18–4:1) reveals a strikingly slight Christianization, especially as compared with Eph. 5:22–6:9. That is basically less easy to understand on the part of a post-Pauline author of Colossians than on the part of Paul himself (cf. Dibelius-Greeven on Col. 3:18–4:1). c) The use of the formulas ἐν Χριστῷ and ἐν κυρίῳ in Colossians corresponds completely with Pauline usage, in contrast with Ephesians (see F. Neugebauer, *In Christus*, 1961, 175 ff.). d) J. Knox has suggested that this Epistle, which is also designated for Laodicea (4:16a), was probably sent to the smaller city of Colossae because Onesimus' home was in Colossae and Paul sought contact with the church in which the master of Onesimus lived, to whom the Epistle to Philemon carries such a great petition. A pseudo-writer would hardly have thought of addressing it to Colossae instead of to Laodicea. And besides that the disproportionate attention to master-slave relations (3:22-25) is best explained if the matter of the slave Onesimus was to be settled at about the same time. Even if not all of these arguments are forceful in the same way, together they strengthen the supposition of the Pauline origin of Colossians.

3. The supposition of a revision of Colossians by the author of Ephesians (see p. 240) is based upon the doubtless close relationship of Colossians with Ephesians. But the arguments lately brought forth by Masson for the dependence of the greater part of Colossians upon Ephesians are in no wise convincing, for, on the one hand, the Pauline origin of the very short epistle which is separated out as original can be established only negatively by means of the lack of parallels with Ephesians, entirely apart from the improbability of such a revision, and because, on the other hand, the gradient of the development of thought clearly proceeds from Colossians to Ephesians and not vice versa (see §23, 3). Jülicher correctly stated that "the suspicion of such interpolations and revisions would never have been raised against Colossians, which pursues its course like a quiet stream without inconcinnities and without lacunae, if we had not also had Ephesians" (cf. on Masson also W. Bieder, ThZ 8, 1952, 139 ff.). Coutts's supposition that Colossians as a whole is dependent upon Ephesians rests upon the unprovable presuppositions that the smoother wording of Ephesians in contrast to the difficulties of Colossians is primary and that every parallel in wording with disconnected passages of the other Epistle must be explained as literary dependence.

Colossians, which probably was used already by Justin (*Dial.* 85, 2; 138, 2), and which stood also in Marcion's canon, is accordingly to be regarded as doubtless Pauline.

5. Place and Time of Composition

Paul is in prison (4:3, 10, 18). In Ephesus, Caesarea, or Rome (see §20)?

Ephesus, to which also the Marcionite prologue to Colossians (but not to Philemon!) points: "Therefore the Apostle already in bonds writes to them from Ephesus" [ergo apostolus iam ligatus scribit eis ab Epheso] (cf. Preuschen, *Analecta,* 87), has recently been advocated by Appel, Michaelis, Duncan, Masson, Harrison, Riddle-Hutson, etc. It is natural to think the Epistle was written in the capital city of the province Asia, to which also the cities in the Lycus valley belonged, where Epaphras had the shortest route to Paul, and where the Apostle might be surrounded by a large number of helpers in the missionary work, as 4:10 ff. presupposes. Paul's request to prepare a guest room (Phlm. 22), which was written in the same place and at about the same time, is also well-suited to Ephesus, which is not far from Colossae. Several factors, however, stand in the way of the Ephesian hypothesis. In the list of names we find Luke and Mark. Luke, in any case, was not then with Paul in Ephesus, if the "we" of Acts is supposed to indicate his participation in the events reported (see §9, 4), and we know that Mark did not take part in Paul's so-called second missionary journey (Acts 15:37-39). And even if we cannot demonstrate a development of the Pauline style and thought, the peculiarities of style and of thought of Colossians do not speak directly for a chronological nearness to Galatians, I II Corinthians, entirely apart from the assumption of a Pauline imprisonment in Ephesus (see §20, 4). Therefore, some place the Epistle in

Caesarea (Goguel, Lohmeyer, de Zwaan, Dibelius, Johnson). That Aristarchus shares Paul's imprisonment (4:10) is consistent with Acts 20:4 and 24:3, and Luke is suited as well to Caesarea as to Rome. To which place the escaped slave Onesimus could most easily have turned is an unanswerable question. Paul's plea for quarters (Phlm. 22) is then possible in Caesarea, if Paul does not yet have to reckon with the necessity of appealing to the emperor. The only consideration weighing against Caesarea is that such a small city was hardly the place for the missionary work of the many companions of Paul, among whom were only a few Jewish Christians (4:11). Thus to this day the early view (John Chrysostom) that Colossians stems from Rome has prevailed overwhelmingly.

The imprisonment in Rome, with its "custodia libera" (Acts 28:16, 30 f.), made it possible for the Apostle to do his own preaching and to have active association with an imposing staff of coworkers corresponding to the great city. His joy over the victorious march of the gospel through the entire world (1:6, 23) also suits Rome well. Epaphras' visit with Paul is certainly more difficult to conceive in Rome than in Caesarea, and Paul's plea for quarters (Phlm. 22) presupposes the abandonment of Paul's Spanish plans (cf. the corresponding difficulty in connection with the supposition of the Roman composition of Philippians, pp. 230 f.). Thus various factors support the composition of Colossians in Caesarea, but composition in Rome is also not excluded. The time of composition would then be either 56/58 or 58/60.

§22. THE EPISTLE TO PHILEMON

Commentaries, see p. 390. Studies: see J. KNOX and P. N. HARRISON on Col.; further J. KNOX, *Philemon among the Letters of Paul* (1935) [2]1959; TH. PREISS, "Vie en Christ et éthique sociale dans l'Épître à Philémon," in *La vie en Christ*, 1951, 65 ff.; "Life in Christ and Social Ethics in the Epistle to Philemon" (tr. Harold Knight), *Life in Christ*, 1954, 32-42; H. GREEVEN, "Prüfung der Thesen von J. Knox zum Phlm.," ThLZ 79, 1954, 373 ff.; U. WICKERT, "Der Philemonbrief—Privatbrief oder Apostolisches Schreiben?" ZNW 52, 1961, 230 ff.

1. Contents

Address (1-3). Gratitude to Philemon for his love and his faith (4-7). Plea to Philemon to pardon his slave Onesimus, who ran away from him and in the meantime was converted to Christianity, and to receive him as a Christian brother and helper of Paul, who himself hopes to come to Philemon as guest (8-22). Greetings (23 f.) and benediction (25).

2. Occasion, Time, and Place

Philemon is an epistle to a particular person, to Philemon, a wealthy Christian, presumably personally unknown to Paul (5; cf. Col. 1:4). His slave, Onesimus, escaped (15 f.), it seems, after a theft (18). Philemon lives with

his sister Apphia and with Archippus (who often are designated without adequate reason as wife and son of Philemon), and his household church (2), evidently in Colossae, for Onesimus originates from there (Col. 4:9—"who is one
of yourselves"). Archippus, mentioned in addition to Philemon (Phlm. 2),
is also to be sought in Colossae, according to Col. 4:17. The runaway Onesimus
met with the imprisoned Paul, for unknown reasons (Had he become acquainted
with Paul in connection with Philemon, or was he accidentally brought to the
same prison?). Onesimus was converted by Paul (10), and entered into close
personal relations with him (12 f., 16 f.). The Apostle would have preferred
most of all to keep Onesimus with him in the service of the gospel, but, recog-
nizing the legal claim which Philemon had upon his slave, he sent him back to
his master. The Epistle pleads for the fugitive, who otherwise would have had
to look forward to severe punishment. Paul does not command, though he could
have on the basis of his apostolic authority (8 f., 14, 21; cf. Wickert, who correctly with Lohmeyer, Moule, and Preiss also takes πρεσβύτης [9] in the sense of
"ambassador"). That Paul in his hope that Philemon "will do even more than
I say" (21) expects the release of Onesimus (Knox) is improbable (cf. Preiss).
It is clear only that Paul requests the restoration of Onesimus to the household
of his master Philemon (17). The thesis advocated by Knox (with partial
agreement from Greeven and W. Schmauch, EKL III, 183) that the master of
Onesimus was Archippus, who was admonished to free Onesimus (Col. 4:17),
and that the epistle "from Laodicea" (Col. 4:16) was the Epistle to Philemon,
shatters on the natural exegesis of Phlm. 1, 2 and Col. 4:17, as well as upon the
fact that Marcion knew both an epistle to Philemon and an epistle to Laodicea
(against Knox, Guthrie, and Moule). The conjecture advanced by Goodspeed,
Knox, Harrison, and Moule that Onesimus was identical with the bishop of
Ephesus mentioned by Ignatius (Eph. 1:3; 2:1; 6:1), is a mere possibility.

Since Onesimus returned to Colossae with Tychicus, the bearer of Colossians
(Col. 4:7 ff.), and since among the associates of Paul according to Philemon
and Colossians the same persons are named (see above, p. 243), Philemon is
to be dated like Colossians (see above, p. 245).

3. Authenticity

Only "tendency criticism" could doubt the authenticity of this Epistle, which
already stood in Marcion's canon (e.g., F. C. Baur and still C. Weizsäcker, *The
Apostolical Age*, 1897, ii, 383). This Epistle, which of all the Pauline epistles
stands the closest to the ancient private letter, has in its personal character the
marks of uninventable lifelikeness. In Philemon we have a practical illustration
of Paul's views on slavery as expressed in I Cor. 7:20 ff. and Col. 3:22 ff. Paul
did not shake the social and legal orders. In Philemon there is no word about
freeing Onesimus. But Paul knew that the Christian faith binds men together
as brothers across the barriers of class. Just as he expected the runaway slave to
return to his master, so also he expected the master to extend a forgiving reception to the "beloved brother" (16).

§23. THE EPISTLE TO THE EPHESIANS

Commentaries, see p. 389. Studies: HOLTZMANN, PERCY, COUTTS see to Col.; further A. HARNACK, *Die Adresse des Eph. des Paulus*, SBA 1910, 696 ff.; J. SCHMID, *Der Eph. des Apostels Paulus*, BSt 22, 3-4, 1928 (lit.); E. J. GOODSPEED, *The Meaning of Ephesians*, 1933; W. OCHEL, *Die Annahme einer Bearbeitung des Kol. im Eph. in einer Analyse des Eph. untersucht*, Diss. phil. Marburg, 1934; M. GOGUEL, "Esquisse d'une solution nouvelle du problème de l'épître aux Ephésiens," RHR 111, 1935, 254 ff.; 112, 1936, 73 ff.; P. BENOIT, "L'horizon Paulinien de l'Épître aux Éphésiens," RB 46, 1937, 342 ff. 506 ff. (= Exégèse et théologie II, 1961, 53 ff.); N. A. DAHL, "Adresse und Prooemium des Eph.," ThZ 7, 1951, 24 ff.; C. L. MITTON, *The Epistle to the Ephesians*, 1951; C. MAURER, "Der Hymnus von Eph. 1 als Schlüssel zum ganzen Brief," EvTh 11, 1951-52, 151 ff.; W. NAUCK, "Eph. 2:19-22 ein Tauflied?" EvTh 13, 1953, 362 ff.; G. SCHILLE, "Liturgisches Gut im Eph.," ThLZ 80, 183 (Diss. Göttingen); F. CORNELIUS, "Die geschichtliche Stellung des Eph.," ZRGG 7, 1955, 74 ff.; *Studies in Ephesians*, edited by F. L. CROSS, 1956; J. COUTTS, "Ephesians 1:3-14 and I Peter 1:3-12," NTSt 3, 1956-57, 115 ff.; E. J. GOODSPEED, *The Key to Ephesians*, 1956; J. A. ALLAN, "The 'In Christ' Formula in Ephesians," NTSt 5, 1958-59, 54 ff.; E. KÄSEMANN, RGG [3] II, 1958, 517 ff.; H. J. CADBURY, "The Dilemma of Ephesians," NTSt 5, 1958-59, 91 ff.; H. SCHLIER, LThK III, 1959, 916 ff.; L. CERFAUX, "En faveur de l'authenticité des Épîtres de la Captivité," Littérature et théologie Pauliniennes, RechB V, 1960, 60 ff.; H. CHADWICK, "Die Absicht des Eph.," ZNW 51, 1960, 145 ff.; K. G. KUHN, "Der Eph. im Lichte der Qumrantexte," NTSt 7, 1960-61, 334 ff.; P. BENOIT, DBS VII, 1961, 195 ff. (bibl.); P. POKORNÝ, "Eph. und gnostische Mysterien," ZNW 53, 1962, 160 ff.

1. Contents

Apart from the address and conclusion, the Epistle falls into two parts: 1:3–3:21 treats the mystery of the call of the Gentiles within the framework of the introductory intercession, and 4:1–6:20 at once attaches admonitions to it (thus the usual core of a Pauline epistle is omitted; I Thessalonians is of similar form). After the address (1:1 f.), follows a hymnic praise of God (1:3-14), who has drawn "us" and "you" (probably author and readers) into his cosmic plan of salvation. Joined to that is the gratitude which is characteristic of the epistolary introduction, with intercession for the readers that they may have right knowledge of the world-wide salvation given us in Christ (1:15-23). As former heathen, the readers were once lost as were "we" (probably the Jewish Christians), but all have been saved through Christ (2:1-10). Hence the readers are to meditate upon the removal of the separation of Israel and the Gentiles through the reconciling act of Christ (2:11-22). The apparent resumption of the petition in 3:1 leads to the description of the office with which Paul has been commissioned, the office of the calling of the Gentiles (3:2-13). 3:14-19 brings the petition for the complete insight of the readers into the breadth of the mystery of Christ to an end, so that a doxology (3:20 f.) can conclude the epistolary introduction.

The paraenesis begins with a summons to unity in faith and love in connection with all the wealth of gifts of grace effective in the church (4:1-16), and then urgently warns the readers to renounce the heathen manner of living (4:17-24), and to test the Christian manner of living in all areas (4:25–5:21) and in all ranks (5:22–6:9) ("Haustafel," treated extensively, especially 5:22 ff.: marriage as the image of the relation between Christ and the church). In conclusion the readers are exhorted to put on the armor of God, to fight against the devil and the spiritual powers of darkness, and to pray for all the saints and the imprisoned Apostle (6:10-20). With a recommendation of Tychicus, the bearer of the Epistle (6:21 f.), and with benedictions (6:23 f.), the Epistle closes.

2. The Literary Problem

This Epistle, according to the superscription Πρὸς Ἐφεσίους (so all manuscripts since the end of the second century), and according to the text in 1:1 in the great majority of the manuscripts since the end of the fourth century (Schmid, 66 f.), was sent by the apostle Paul to the congregation in Ephesus. Compared with the other Pauline epistles, this Epistle is striking because of the almost complete lack of concrete details. To be sure, the imprisonment of Paul is mentioned (3:1; 4:1; 6:20; cf. 3:13), but the author seems to have no kind of contacts with the readers: He has heard of the faith and the love of the readers (1:15), and addresses them as Gentile Christians (2:1 ff., 11 ff.; 3:1 f.; 4:17) who are in danger of losing their ties to Jewish Christianity (2:11 ff.; Käsemann), but he does not enter into the concrete problems of the congregation. All personal greetings are also omitted, a feature which has a parallel only in the polemical Epistle to the Galatians. Conversely, the author must first introduce himself as the missionary to the Gentiles commissioned by God (3:2 ff.) and can allude to the preaching which the congregation has heard as something strange to him (4:21).

Since Paul worked more than two years in Ephesus, and the Epistle, by reason of its contents, could in no case have been written before this time, it is inconceivable that Paul wrote it to the Christian community in Ephesus. But the earlier text of Ephesians by no means presupposes that. For to whom the Epistle is directed can be determined with certainty neither from the superscription (Πρὸς Ἐφεσίους) nor from the address (1:1). The superscription first originated at the time of the collection of the Pauline epistles, and therefore repeats only an early Christian opinion about the addressees, which was taken over by the earliest codices since 𝔓⁴⁶. And in the text of 1:1 the words ἐν Ἐφέσῳ are not original.

B, ℵ, Codex 1739 (which goes back to a very early "Vorlage"; see p. 368), and the corrector of minuscle 424, who used a very good text, do not offer these two words. Origen did not find them in his text (J. A. F. Gregg, JThSt 3, 1902, 235). 𝔓⁴⁶, the earliest manuscript of the Pauline epistles (beginning of the third century), reads τοῖς ἁγίοις οὖσιν καὶ πιστοῖς. Already Marcion (c. 140) did not read "in Ephesus" in the text of Eph. 1:1, as is shown by Tertullian's polemic against Marcion (*Adv. Marc.* 5:11, 17), for it seems that Tertullian and Marcion read the same text. According to Tertullian, Marcion undertook an interpolation in the "titulus" of the Epistle. By the "titulus" Tertullian means not the address (1:1 f.) but the superscription, for he speaks of the Epistle, "which we have with the superscription to Ephesus" ["ad Ephesios praescriptam habemus"], the heretics (i.e., Marcion) as Epistle to the Laodiceans ["ad Laodicenos"]. If "in Ephesus" had already at that time stood in 1:1, Tertullian would certainly have discovered the contradiction in which Marcion was entangled. Thus he presupposes that Marcion's text did not have the two words in 1:1. We do not know how Marcion came to give the Epistle the superscription "to the Laodiceans." Marcion could just as well have found the conjecture already derived from Col. 4:16 as have advanced it himself. Two factors militate against the possibility that Tertullian used a text of 1:1 with ἐν Λαοδικείᾳ instead of ἐν Ἐφέσῳ: Tertullian's testimony, to which we have just referred, and the lack of any trace of such a text in the tradition. Marcion probably knew as little about the original destination of the Epistle as did the creator of the superscription "to the Ephesians," whose view about the address the ecclesiastical tradition adopted as its own since the end of the second century (Muratorian canon, Irenaeus, Clement of Alexandria, Tertullian, etc.). Upon the basis of this tradition, ἐν Ἐφέσῳ crowded its way into the text of the address before the end of the fourth century.

If, then, ἐν Ἐφέσῳ was doubtless lacking in the archetype lying at the basis of our textual tradition, then the question arises as to whether in lieu of this place-name another originally stood. It would be a question only of Laodicea, upon the basis of Marcion's superscription and with reference to Col. 4:16. This hypothesis, advocated by Harnack, Roller (see in bibl. §11, pp. 199 ff., 520 ff.), Meinertz, Schäfer, and Masson, has against it not only the want of any other testimony to such an address of the Epistle, but in the Epistle itself there is nothing which especially points to Laodicea. It would have been absurd that Paul, when he sent Colossians and Ephesians (= Epistle to the Laodiceans) at the same time (see Col. 4:16), did not draw up orders for the Laodiceans in the epistle to them but took the roundabout way via Colossae (Col. 4:15 f.). Moreover, it is not clear why then the name Laodicea would have been stricken from the address. To be sure, Harnack wanted to explain the suppression of the original epistolary address by his suggestion that the church at Laodicea through inner degeneration had temporarily as good as dissolved (Rev. 3:14 ff.), and, therefore, no one would wish to read a Pauline epistle to them. But where in primitive Christianity was there the inclination to literary proscription and at what time would they have been able to accomplish it? And Masson's supposition (similarly Wikenhauser, Dahl; cf. also Klijn) that in Ephesus, from where the Epistle to the Ephesians was placed in circulation, "in Laodicea" (or another name) was expunged, because the Epistle was not at all directed to a particular congregation, is based upon modern points of view. But Ochel's thesis, that "in Colossae" stood in the address of Ephesians, which was intended as a substitute for the Pauline Colossians, but was replaced by "in Ephesus" during canonization, is not only arbitrary, but also does not explain the lack of any place-name in the earliest textual tradition. Therefore, it is very improbable that any kind of name originally stood in the address of Ephesians.

Consequently, the hypothesis expressed by Beza and Grotius and established by James Ussher (1654), has found numerous supporters. According to this hypothesis, Ephesians was not composed as an epistle to a particular congregation, but as a circular letter to several congregations, which either contained a blank in its address, to be filled in from time to time with the name of the church addressed (most recently, Henshaw, Cerfaux in Robert-Feuillet, Albertz, Percy, Schlier; similarly, Klijn), or whose address without names preserved in the earliest manuscripts served as a general address (Michaelis, Guthrie, Feine-Behm, Cadbury, Sanders in Cross; Goguel and Schmid regard τοῖς οὖσιν as a later addition; Benoit deems the reading of 𝔓⁴⁶ as possibly the primitive text). We cannot, however, explain why an epistle destined for several congregations should not contain a general address like Galatians, II Corinthians, and I Peter. Albertz attempted to solve the problem with his conjecture that Paul granted authority to Tychicus (6:21) to supply the name of each church as the letter was read. But an epistle with a blank in the address for the later insertion of the addressee is without any parallel in antiquity (even Zuntz [see p. 359] 278, note, helps no further), entirely apart from the fact that then our manuscripts must have descended from the Pauline original, which was not at all intended for circulation in *this* form. Moreover, the position of the inserted place-name in the address of Ephesians before καὶ πιστοῖς, compared with Col. 1:2, would be completely inexplicable. But if we regard the text of the archetype of our manuscripts τοῖς ἁγίοις οὖσιν καὶ πιστοῖς as the primitive Pauline text, then it is incomprehensible what τοῖς οὖσιν καὶ πιστοῖς as a closer definition of τοῖς ἁγίοις would have meant to Paul, for to Paul there would be no "saints" who were not "also faithful in Christ Jesus" (see the evidence in Schmid, 110 ff., Percy, 450 f.; the lack of the article before οὖσιν in 𝔓⁴⁶ and D changes nothing thereby, and the deletion of τοῖς οὖσιν does not explain how these words came into the textual tradition without place-names). Although the earliest text of the address attainable by means of textual criticism is impossible for Paul, it offers no difficulty once we abandon the attempt to ascribe the letter to Paul and think in terms of an unknown author who, according to 2:19, could have understood οἱ ἅγιοι in the sense of the ancient people of God, whereby πιστοί as characterization of the "believers" (in Christ) is not an equivalent, but a necessary qualification to "the saints" (Beare). From that it follows that the question about the original text of the address cannot be answered by the supposition of authenticity; on the other hand, by the supposition of pseudepigraphical composition the text of the earliest manuscripts can be regarded as possibly the primitive text.

Although the address of Ephesians can give no certain information about the literary character of the writing, the facts set forth above on pp. 248 f. show that in Ephesians it is not a matter of an epistle to a specific congregation, and just as little a matter of a circular letter for several specific congregations. For only 1:15 speaks of the faith and love of the readers (and even here, quite generally), whereas in all other places, where a "you" is distinguished from the totality of Christians or of Jewish Christians (3:18; 6:18; 1:13; 2:1, 11 f., 13; 3:1; cf. Schlier, 17), no local, limited readership becomes evident. The only exception to this fact is the note about the sending of Tychicus to the readers (6:21 f.), which corresponds almost verbatim to Col. 4:7. Some scholars, on the basis of this concluding sentence, have suggested that Ephesians is directed to Christian churches which lie upon the route of Tychicus who is traveling to Colossae (Dahl, Schlier, Michaelis). But then it is completely incomprehensible why Paul, otherwise than in Romans and Colossians, establishes no personal bonds of connection with these readers, and the totally nonepistolary character of the remainder of this piece of writing stands clearly in tension with 6:21 f. Hence nothing points to an actual circular letter. On the other hand, some contend that Ephesians is a "post-baptismal mystery discourse" addressed to recently baptized Christians to remind them of their baptism. Thus in 1:3-14; 2:19-22, and elsewhere, parts of the baptismal liturgy are said to be taken up (Dahl, Nauck, Schille, Coutts, Schlier, S. Lyonnet, "La bénédiction de Éph. I, 3-14 et son arrière-plan judaïque," *Mémorial A. Gelin*, 1961, 341 ff.). But this thesis is not sufficient to demonstrate that the Epistle was sent to concrete addressees. For even if baptismal songs are originally supposed to have lain at the basis of 1:3 ff. and 2:19 ff. and in 5:14 an eschatological hymn is interpreted as a baptismal song (so B. Noack, StTh 5, 1951, 52 ff.), we still find only very isolated direct references to baptism (1:13; 4:5; 4:30; 5:26). And because of "the entire high level of the Epistle" (Michaelis), the addressees could not have been newly founded churches. Rather, there is every reason to believe that in Ephesians, apart from the epistolary framework and 6:21 f., we do not have to do with a writing which has definite readers in mind. In this respect Ephesians is differentiated from all previously discussed Pauline epistles. Having recognized this unepistolary nature of Ephesians, Sanders characterized it as "the spiritual testament of Paul to the Church" (in Cross), Guthrie as "a meditation about great Christian themes," and H. Rendtorff as Paul's "Epistle directed to no specific address" (NTD, 1933, 44). Indeed, that would be the only possible characterization of the Epistle, if there were no weighty considerations against the composition of Ephesians by Paul.

3. Authenticity

Without question Ephesians was extraordinarily well attested in the early church (cf. Schmid, 16 ff., Mitton, 160 ff.): Ignatius, Pol. 5:1, and Polycarp, Phil. 1:13; 12:1, remind us clearly of Ephesians. Since Marcion, Ephesians was an uncontested part of the canon of Pauline epistles, and since Irenaeus and Clement of Alexandria, the Epistle was undisputed as the Epistle of Paul to the Ephesians. Erasmus was the first to state that the style of Ephesians diverges so markedly from Paul, "that it can seem [to be the writing] of another" [ut alterius videri possit], without drawing consequences from this observation (for the history of criticism, see Schmid, 1 ff., Percy, 1 ff.). After Edward Evanson in 1792, on the basis of the contradiction between address and contents, had designated Ephesians as a forgery, de Wette in 1826 was the first to deny Ephesians to Paul because of the address, style, its relationship to Colossians, and individual statements. F. C. Baur and his pupils removed the Epistle to the second century as typically primitive Catholic, whereas Holtzmann sought to prove it to be a revision of Colossians, which had not yet been interpolated (see p. 240) with the use of other Pauline epistles. In addition to Catholic scholarship Ephesians today is defended as Pauline by numerous scholars (cf., e.g., Appel, Albertz, Henshaw, Lo Bue, Michaelis, Rendtorff, Simpson, J. N. Sanders in Cross, Cornelius, Schille, Dahl, also Klijn, especially Percy and Guthrie), whereas the number of those who deny the authenticity likewise is quite impressive (cf., e.g., Sparks, Heard, Beare, Masson, Dibelius-Greeven, Maurer, Allan, D. E. Nineham in Cross, Käsemann, Pokorný, F. Lang, CBL, 266 ff., C. K. Barrett, *Studia Paulina*, 1953, 13, Harrison and Bornkamm, see to §21, Conzelmann, especially Mitton and Goodspeed with their followers Riddle-Hutson, Lake, W. L. Knox, *St. Paul and the Church of the Gentiles*, 1939, 182 ff., S. G. F. Brandon, *The Fall of Jerusalem and the Christian Church*, 1951, 215 f., J. Knox, see to §22). How difficult a decision in this question is, is shown by the fact that Goguel believed himself able to defend the Pauline origin of Ephesians only through the certainly unprovable supposition of extensive interpolations, and that several scholars leave the question undecided (Jülicher, McNeile-Williams, Cadbury), or combine the supposition of authenticity with the limitation that Paul entrusted a pupil with the finishing touches of the writing (Appel, Albertz, Benoit, Rigaux, see lit. to §12). This "amanuensis hypothesis," which is based on nothing, can, at the most, explain the style and language of the Epistle, but not the more decisive questions about the relation to Colossians and about the theology of Ephesians.

1. Language and style (cf. Schmid, 131 ff., Percy, 179 ff., Mitton, 8 ff., 29 ff.). The appearance of numerous words not encountered in Paul, but in the later writings of the NT and in the apostolic fathers (e.g., ἀσωτία, εὔσπλαγχνος, ὁσιότης, πολιτεία), is striking only in connection with the fact that Ephesians also uses other vocables than Paul uses for important concepts (ἐν τοῖς ἐπουρανίοις 1:3, 20; 2:6; 3:10; 6:12 is found in addition to οἱ οὐρανοί, which alone is met in Paul; ὁ ἠγαπημένος 1:6 as predicate for Christ; the sequence αἷμα καὶ σάρκα 6:12; χαριτόω 1:6 instead of the Pauline χάριν δίδωμι). More important is the fact that the heaping up of synonyms and genitival connectives, already observed in Colossians, is found in Ephesians to a still more considerable extent (see Percy, 186 ff., e.g., ἐνέργεια τοῦ κράτους τῆς ἰσχύος 1:19; κατὰ τὸν αἰῶνα τοῦ κόσμου τούτου 2:2; διὰ πάσης προσευχῆς καὶ δεήσεως . . . ἐν πάσῃ προσκαρτερήσει καὶ δεήσει 6:18, etc.), and proceeds with the predilection for overly long conglomerations of sentences which can hardly be classified (1:15-23; 4:11-16, etc.). And this language, which is reminiscent of the language in the Qumran texts, shows "such Semitic, syntactical phenomena four times as often as all other epistles of the Pauline corpus" (K. G. Kuhn, 334 f.; that also applies to

the relation of Semitic and Greek influence on the syntax of the conditional sentences, cf. K. Beyer, *Semitische Syntax in Nt* I, 1, 1962, 298). As little as such and related linguistic and stylistic differences taken alone prove the Pauline composition of Ephesians as impossible, they nevertheless make more difficult the supposition that Paul wrote Ephesians in its transmitted form.

2. More fundamental to deciding the problem of authorship is the relationship of Ephesians to Colossians (cf. Percy, 360 ff., Mitton, 55 ff., 279 ff.), which is doubtless considerably greater than the relationship of any other Pauline epistle to the remainder of the Pauline epistles: About one third of the words in Colossians are found again in Ephesians (Mitton), and this verbal parallel runs throughout the entire Epistle to the Ephesians, and only short, connected pieces of Ephesians (e.g., 2:6-9; 4:5-13; 5:29-33) have no verbal parallels in Colossians (of 155 verses of Ephesians, 73 have verbal parallels with Colossians, Goguel). In spite of these extensive agreements, however, only the notice about Tychicus (Eph. 6:21 f.) agrees so exactly with Col. 4:7 f. that a written "Vorlage" must have been used directly, in case the same author at almost the same time did not dictate the same thing two times. But this supposition is already much questioned because Ephesians also exhibits in basically greater extent than all other Pauline epistles verbal parallels with all the other Pauline epistles (except II Thessalonians) (Mitton, 98 ff., has convincingly shown that, using Philippians as an example). And these parallels are found repeatedly in related sections of the other epistles (cf., e.g., Rom. 3:20-27; 11:32–12:5 with Eph. 1:19; 2:5, 8; 1:7; 3:8, 21; 4:1; 5:10, 17; 3:7; 4:7, 4, 25 and the lists in Mitton, 120 ff., 333 ff.), both of which in the same author would be very striking.

But speaking decisively against the supposition that the same author very quickly wrote Colossians and Ephesians one after the other are the instances where Ephesians clearly exhibits a) a literary dependence or b) a basic, factual difference in respect to Colossians. a) Thus Col. 3:7 says quite naturally after a catalog of vices ἐν οἷς (sc. the vices) καὶ ὑμεῖς περιεπατήσατέ ποτε, whereas Eph. 2:2 f. first naturally affixes to ἁμαρτίαι the relative clause ἐν αἷς ποτε περιεπατήσατε . . . , in order then to attach awkwardly to the reference to the activity of the adversary ἐν τοῖς υἱοῖς τῆς ἀπειθείας the relative clause ἐν οἷς καὶ ἡμεῖς πάντες ἀνεστράφημέν ποτε, in clear reminiscence of Col. 3:7. And the "Haustafel" of Eph. 5:22 ff. is not only a strong Christianizing of the "Haustafel" of Col. 3:18 ff., which manifests the same sequence and largely the same wording, but the command to wives to obey their husbands ὡς ἀνῆκεν ἐν κυρίῳ (Col. 3:18), in Eph. 5:22 is intensified to subordination ὡς τῷ κυρίῳ. b) In Col. 1:26 f. Paul designates with μυστήριον God's eschatological act of salvation in Christ (likewise 2:2; 4:3) in agreement with I Cor. 2:1, 7; but in Eph. 3:3 ff. μυστήριον indicates in clear linguistic reminiscence of Col. 1:26 the share of the Gentiles in salvation with the Jews, and besides that μυστήριον (Eph. 1:9) serves to describe the uniting of the all in Christ, and 5:32 to denote the hidden analogy between marriage, on the one hand, and Christ's relation to the church, on the other. These three meanings of μυστήριον are completely strange to Paul. It is similar with the use of οἰκονομία. In Col. 1:25 Paul signifies with this word, as in I Cor. 4:1; 9:17, the commission to preach about the mystery of Christ. In Eph. 3:2, on the contrary, and in spite of clear reminiscence of Col. 1:25, the word means God's plan of salvation, and has the same sense in Eph. 1:10; 3:9, according to which this plan of salvation has mystery in its content, of which there was talk even in reference to Eph. 1:9; 3:3 ff. We may regard the possibility as excluded that Paul in a writing of almost the same time as Colossians should have given such completely new meanings to the words μυστήριον and οἰκονομία.

3. If both of these complexes speak in the highest degree against a Pauline origin of Ephesians, then the theology of Ephesians makes the Pauline composition of the Epistle completely impossible, as also becomes evident first of all in comparison with Colossians. If Col. 2:7 says that the Christians are "rooted and built up in him," in Eph. 2:20 f. that becomes, "built upon the foundation of the apostles and prophets, Christ Jesus himself being the chief cornerstone," which represents a clear displacement in respect to the exclusive statement of I Cor. 3:11. But when the related passage, Eph. 3:5, describes the revelation of the mystery to "his holy apostles and prophets," whereas Col. 1:26 speaks of the revelation to "his saints," then this evaluation of the apostles as the foundation of the church is just as impossible for Paul as the designation of the apostles as "holy" in a special sense. A related fact is that in Ephesians ἐκκλησία is used exclusively of the universal church (1:22; 3:10, 21; 5:23-25, 27, 29, 32), whereas in all the Pauline epistles, even in Colossians, ἐκκλησία indicates the individual congregations as well as the total church. Furthermore, the μυστήριον τοῦ Χριστοῦ (Eph. 3:4 f.), which is now revealed, is not Christ, as in Col. 2:2, but the unity of Gentiles and Jews in the body of Christ, so that "now the Christology also is interpreted almost exclusively by the ecclesiology" (Käsemann, ThLZ 86, 1961, 3). And therein the Christology of Ephesians also shows a development beyond Paul in respect to the agent of reconciliation. In spite of the fact that the same verb is used in Eph. 2:16 and Col. 1:20 (ἀποκαταλλάσσειν—a verb common only to Eph. 2:16 and Col. 1:20), the subject of this verb in Eph. 2:16 is Christ, contrary to Paul's only use of this verb in Col. 1:20, where God is the subject. Similarly, in Eph. 4:11 Christ (not God, as in I Cor. 12:28) appointed the apostles and prophets.

If these developments *beyond* Paul are inconceivable in an epistle which is to be placed at almost the same time as Colossians, other conceptions and formulations of Ephesians stand in any case in an irreconcilable *contrast to* Paul. Characteristically, we find that "every good work" in Col. 1:10 becomes ἔργα ἀγαθά in Eph. 2:10, a plural which was avoided by Paul, even in Colossians (see p. 241). It is likewise characteristic that Ephesians (in contrast to Colossians) knows several ἐν-formulas, which Paul does not have (ἐν τῷ Χριστῷ Ἰησοῦ 3:11; ἐν τῷ Ἰησοῦ 4:21; ἐν τῷ κυρίῳ Ἰησοῦ 1:15), and in 1:15 joins πίστις with κύριος, whereas in Paul we find only the connection with Χριστός (F. Neugebauer [see p. 243] 176, 179 ff., Allan). And it also may be no accident that only in Eph. 1:17 and 3:14, in contrast to all other Pauline epistles, is the address of God as Father in supplication found (G. Harder, *Paulus und das Gebet*, NTF I, 10, 1936, 186). Still more basic than these divergences, however, are three other facts which are not compatible with Pauline origin. For one, in contrast to all Pauline epistles, and even to Col. 3:4, any mention of the parousia is lacking. Eph. 3:21, in the formula εἰς πάσας τὰς γενεὰς τοῦ αἰῶνος τῶν αἰώνων, is hardly counting upon an imminent eschaton. Second, the evaluation of marriage as the image of the heavenly union of Christ and church (5:25 ff.) is scarcely possible to the Paul who wrote I Cor. 7. And finally, the statement that the office to which Paul was commissioned was the proclamation of the unity of Jews and Gentiles in the promise of Christ (3:2 ff.) contradicts Paul's own statements, even Col. 1:25 ff.; and Paul's designation of himself as ἐλαχιστότερος πάντων ἁγίων (3:8) is hardly a comprehensible exaggeration of ἐλάχιστος τῶν ἀποστόλων (I Cor. 15:9).

In view of these linguistic, literary, and theological facts of the case, we cannot seriously doubt that Ephesians does not derive from Paul and is, therefore, a pseudonymous writing. And, in view of the theology of Ephesians, which is not only further developed than Paul's theology, but in part stands clearly in contradiction to Paul, we cannot simply explain the difference by saying that we should designate this Epistle, not as " 'Kerygma' in the strict sense," but as "Sophia, Sophia of the mystery, . . . meditation of the wisdom of the mystery of Christ himself" (Schlier). Nor can we extricate ourselves from this difficulty by referring to Cerfaux's contention that "the symphony of the Pauline doctrine is transposed as a whole from a lower manual to a higher one: The Gospel becomes the Mystery." By means of such formulations the clear historical results are simply covered with a smoke screen. It remains only to ask what purpose this pseudonymous writing serves and in which historical context it is to be placed.

Against the supposition that in Ephesians we are dealing with a pseudonymous writing, the objection has been raised (which is also of importance for the NT epistles yet to be discussed) that the practice of pseudonymous epistles in the environment of Christianity hardly existed, and that such a deception in religious writings, which especially accent their responsibility to truth (cf. 4:15, 25; 6:14), is hardly conceivable (Guthrie, 282 ff., Michaelis, *Einl.*, 2 f.). No one, however, can deny that not only in general in antiquity there were numerous pseudonymous writings, but that the literary genus of pseudonymous writings precisely in the period of Hellenism was very widespread, and that out of late Judaism as well as out of early Christianity there is reliable evidence for it (Epistle of Jeremiah, Epistle of Aristeas, Acts 23:26 ff., epistolary exchange of Paul with Corinth = III Corinthians; cf. also the possibility presupposed by Paul [II Thess. 2:2; 3:17] of a forged Pauline epistle). The admittedly still fully inadequate discussion of the problem of pseudonymity in antiquity has, nevertheless, clearly shown that there were very different kinds, degrees, and motives of pseudonymous writing, and that in primitive Christianity the preaching moved by the Holy Ghost was uncritically regarded as apostolic, so that the intention of *deception* may not be attributed to the pseudonymous writer without special reasons (cf. F. Torm, *Die Psychologie*

der Pseudonymität im Hinblick auf die Literatur des Urchristentums, 1932;
A. Meyer, "Religiöse Pseudepigraphie als ethisch-psychologisches Problem,"
ZNW 35, 1936, 262 ff.; E. J. Goodspeed, "Pseudonymity and Pseudepigraphy
in Early Christian Literature," in *New Chapters in New Testament Study*,
1937, 169 ff.; J. C. Fenton, "Pseudonymity in the NT," *Theology* 58, 1955,
51 ff.; J. A. Sint, "Pseudonymität im Altertum," *Commentationes Aenipontanae*
15, 1960 [critique of M. Forderer, Gn 33, 1961, 440 ff.]; K. Aland, "The
Problem of Anonymity and Pseudonymity in Christian Literature of the First
Centuries," JThSt, N.S. 12, 1961, 39 ff.; D. Guthrie, "The Development of
the Idea of Canonical Pseudepigrapha in NT Criticism," VE, 43 ff.). In any
case, there exists no adequate reason for declaring pseudepigraphy as impossible
in respect to primitive Christian epistolary literature and as contradictory to
truthfulness. And even if no pseudonymous epistolary literature could be proved
in late Judaism and early Christianity (as Guthrie, certainly wrongly, maintains; see above), this statement, in view of the undoubted appearance of other
pseudonymous writing in late Judaism and late primitive Christianity (cf.
only Wisdom of Solomon and Didache), can indicate nothing in the case where
the supposition of pseudonymous writing in respect to a primitive Christian
epistle unavoidably forces itself upon us. But indeed, if the supposition of pseudepigraphical composition turns out to be necessary, the question must be clarified as to which kind of pseudonymous writing is present and what purpose the
piece of writing in question served.

4. Purpose, Historical Position, and Time of the Epistle

In clear agreement with the situation and language revealed in Colossians,
Ephesians attributes itself to Paul (1:1; 3:1; 4:1; 6:19-22), without characterizing this historical situation any more precisely. Just as little is the situation
of the readers indicated, except that they are Gentile Christians (2:1 ff., 11 ff.;
3:1, 13; 4:17). There is also lacking any concrete discussion of heresy or abuses
of the readers. The Epistle lays stress on only one thing, and, to be sure, in
connection with the commission of the writing "Paul" even as in connection
with the readers: The Gentiles now have a share in Christ in the people of God,
and through the death of Christ the wall between both has been broken down,
and "through him we both have access in one Spirit to the Father" (2:11 ff.;
3:1 ff.; 4:3). And in order to expound this comprehensive interpretation of
Christ, the Epistle speaks of the all embracing working of God's activity in
Christ (1:10, 20 ff.; 3:10, 18; 4:10), and, therefore, it stresses the eternal
connection between Christ, the head, and his body, the church (1:4 f., 22 f.;
2:15 f., 21 f.; 4:13, 15 f.; 5:23 f., 29, 32), and the necessity for the readers to
consider the significance of their membership in this body and to prove themselves worthy of it (1:18 f.; 2:11; 4:1 ff., 20 ff., 25; 5:22 ff.). We cannot,
however, recognize what concrete occasion there was for the transformation of
the Pauline preaching through the emphasis upon the unity of the church made

up of Gentiles and Jews (strained relations between Gentile Christians of the churches in Asia Minor and Jewish Christians who had immigrated from Palestine after the Jewish war is out of the question, against W. Grundmann, NTSt 5, 1958-59, 194, note). We also cannot be satisfied to see in Ephesians only "a comprehensive summary of Paul's message" (Mitton), or a "commendation of Paul's theology to the church of another generation" (Beare). Rather, Chadwick has seen correctly that Ephesians speaks in reaction to a general spiritual crisis of post-Pauline Gentile Christianity, in connection with which it must be emphasized that the church of the Gentiles includes the Jewish past of the church, because it is the universal church in every sense, which will yet succeed in attaining "to the measure of the stature of the fullness of Christ" (4:13). But that Paul, moreover, as Chadwick thinks, is supposed to be recommended to the Gentile-Christian churches not founded by him as "their unique representative," is hardly demonstrable.

The author of this "Epistle," which speaks to a concrete post-Pauline situation of Gentile Christendom, appears especially well acquainted with Colossians and also with the remaining Pauline epistles, but he must have had the wording of Colossians before him only for 6:21 f. Beyond that, the author is clearly dependent upon a double history-of-religions situation. On the one hand, there comes to light in the religious terminology as well as in the paraenesis a striking parallel with the literature of the sect from Qumran (Käsemann, D. Flusser, *Scripta Hierosolymitana* 4, 1958, 263, note 163 f., especially Kuhn). On the other hand, not only the "Haustafel" (probably taken over from Colossians) stems from Hellenistic-Jewish tradition, but the shaping of the Christology and ecclesiology, especially the conceptions of Christ as the primitive man [Urmensch], of the syzygy between Christ and the church, and of the church as the body of Christ the head, can be made understandable only against the background of Christianized, mythological Gnosticism (Käsemann, Schlier, P. Pokorný, "Σῶμα Χριστοῦ im Eph.," EvTh 20, 1960, 456 ff., and *idem*, lit. to §23). In view of this state of affairs and the strongly Semitized language of Ephesians, the supposition is natural that the author was a Jewish Christian, as he himself seems to indicate (2:3, 11, 17; Beare). The only certain thing is that he stands in connection with a Gentile Christianity which has been considerably influenced by Gnostic mythology and perhaps also by a strongly Hellenized Judaism (so C. Colpe, "Zur Leib-Christi-Vorstellung im Eph.," *Festschr. J. Jeremias*, Beih. ZNW 26, 1960, 172 ff.). He recognizes that this Gentile Christianity is threatened by possible separation from its connection through salvation history to the ancient people of God. Thus, in spite of considerable dependence upon Pauline conceptions and formulations, there arises a recognizable further development of the Pauline theology, through the disappearance of the eschatological emphasis, stronger mythologizing of the Christology and ecclesiology, and moralization (3:10!), which exhibits, at least to some extent, features of that phenomenon which is so difficult to delimit in detail, "primitive Catholicism" (see F. Mussner, LThK VI, 89 f.).

All of which is to say that Goodspeed's thesis, which is very widespread in

English-speaking regions, that Ephesians was composed as a covering letter on the occasion of the first collection of the Pauline epistles, cannot be regarded as probable. Against this theory weighs not only the fact that according to our knowledge Ephesians never stood at the beginning of a collection of Pauline epistles (see p. 338), but above all the fact that the special purpose of Ephesians cannot be explained upon the basis of this supposition (for criticism of this thesis, cf. Schlier, 26 f., Guthrie, 132 f.).

If the composition of Ephesians be established in the post-Pauline period, then it follows from Ignatius' acquaintanceship with Ephesians (see p. 338 f.) that the first decade of the second century is the *terminus ad quem*. A possibility of more precise dating would open if a literary dependence of I Peter upon Ephesians could be demonstrated, as, e.g., Mitton (who dates Ephesians 87-92) and Cornelius (who has Ephesians composed at the time of Peter in Rome!) assume. But because of the common paraenetic tradition, that supposition is not convincing. Since Ephesians, however, was acquainted with the totality of the Pauline epistles, no early dating is probable. Its composition cannot be determined more closely than about 80-100. In view of the special acquaintanceship with Colossians, we would like most to look for the place of composition in Asia Minor, but that is no more than a conjecture.

§24. The Pastoral Epistles: I and II Timothy, Titus

Commentaries, see p. 390. Studies: H. J. HOLTZMANN, *Die Past., kritisch und exegetisch bearbeitet*, 1880; W. LÜTGERT, *Die Irrlehrer der Past.*, BFTh 13, 3, 1909; P. N. HARRISON, *The Problem of the Pastoral Epistles*, 1921; idem, "The Authorship of the Pastoral Epistles," ExpT 67, 1955-56, 77 ff.; idem, "The Pastoral Epistles and Duncan's Ephesian Theory," NTSt 2, 1955-56, 250 ff.; W. MICHAELIS, "Past. und Wortstatistik," ZNW 28, 1929, 69 ff.; idem, *Past. und Gefangenschaftsbriefe*, NTF I, 6, 1930; W. BAUER, *Rechtgläubigkeit und Ketzerei im ältesten Christentum*, BhTh 10, 1934, 225 ff.; R. FALCONER, *The Pastoral Epistles*, 1937; C. MAURER, "Eine Textvariante klärt die Entstehung der Past. auf," ThZ 3, 1947, 321 ff.; H. SCHLIER, "Die Ordnung der Kirche nach den Past.," Festschr. F. Gogarten, 1948, 38 ff. (= *Die Zeit der Kirche*, 1956, 129 ff.); O. MICHEL, "Grundfragen der Past.," Festgabe für Th. Wurm, 1948, 83 ff.; idem, CBL, 1959, 992 ff.; H. VON CAMPENHAUSEN, *Pol. und die Past.*, SHA 1951, 2; idem, *Kirchliches Amt und geistliche Vollmacht in den ersten drei Jahrhunderten*, BhTh 14, 1953, 116 ff.; W. NAUCK, "Die Theologie der Past. I," ThLZ 79, 1954, 124 f. (Diss. Göttingen); R. BULTMANN, *Theologie des NT*, [3]1958, 468, 533 ff.; *Theology of the NT*. Tr. Kendrick Grobel, 1951-55, II, 183 ff.; B. M. METZGER, "A Reconsideration of Certain Arguments Against the Pauline Authorship of the Pastoral Epistles," ExpT 70, 1958-59, 91 ff.; E. SCHWEIZER, *Gemeinde und Gemeindeordnung im NT*, AThANT 35, 1959, 67 ff.; *Church Order in the NT*. Tr. Frank Clarke, 1961; W. KASCH, EKL III, 1959, 78 f.; J. MÜLLER-BARDORFF, "Zur Exegese von I Tim. 5:3-16," Festgabe für E. Fascher, 1959, 113 ff.; K. GRAYSTON and G. HERDAN, "The Authorship of the Pastorals in the Light of Statistical Linguistics," NTSt 6, 1959-60, 1 ff.; E. E. ELLIS, *Paul and His Recent Interpreters*, 1961, 49 ff.; J. JEREMIAS, "Zur Datierung der Past.," ZNW 52, 1961, 101 ff.; W. SCHMITHALS, RGG [3] V, 1961, 144 ff.; C. SPICQ, DBS VII, 1961, 1 ff.; (bibl.); K. WEGENAST,

Das Verständnis der Tradition bei Paulus und in den Deuteropaulinen, WMANT 8, 1962, 132 ff.

The name "Pastoral Epistles" for these epistles appeared in the eighteenth century (first attested for Titus in D. N. Bardot, 1703; for all three epistles by P. Anton, *Exegetische Abhandlungen der Past. Pauli*, 1753-55): They contain instructions and admonitions for the conduct of the pastoral office in the Christian congregations. These instructions are directed to two of Paul's closest colaborers in the form of epistles, which, however, do not carry the features of private letters, but of writings for the ministry, "for the regulation of ecclesiastical discipline" (Muratorian canon). But also in respect to content the three epistles, of which I Timothy and Titus stand especially close to each other, form a group in themselves among the traditional Pauline epistles: They presuppose the same false teachers, the same organization, and quite similar conditions in the churches, move in the same theological conceptual world, and have the same peculiarities of language and style.

1. Contents

I Timothy. After the address (1:1 f.) follows a summons to Timothy to battle against false teachers, who have lost themselves in mythical speculations concerning genealogies, desiring thereby to be teachers of the Law, without understanding the true meaning of the Law (1:3-11). Paul, the former persecutor, through God's mercy has been entrusted with the gospel which saves sinners (1:12-17). Accordingly, Timothy is supposed to keep the Christian tradition in faithfulness (1:18-20). There follow directions concerning congregational prayer (2:1-7) and the conduct of men and women in worship (2:8-15), concerning the requirements which the holders of the office of bishop (3:1-7) and the office of male and female deacons (3:8-13) should meet, and in conclusion a word to Timothy concerning the importance of such instructions: They have to do with the house of God, the church, the guardian of the great mystery of God (3:14-16). Ch. 4 prophesies the appearance of false teachers and gives instructions for their control (4:1-10) and reminds Timothy of the duties which the charisma, bestowed upon him through laying on of hands, enjoins upon him (4:11-16). The next section (5:1-6:2) gives directions for conduct in respect to the various stages of life and to the different sexes (5:1-3), regulations for the classes of widows (5:4-16) and elders (5:17-22) (partly addressed to Timothy), personal advice to Timothy (5:23), a reference to the fact that sooner or later sins and good works will be manifested (5:24 f.), and finally rules of conduct for Christian slaves (6:1 f.). A group of general admonitions fills out the last section (6:3-21a): warning against false teachers and love of money (6:3-10), exhortation to Timothy to adhere to the faith (6:11-16), advice for pastoral care of the rich (6:17-19), final warning against false knowledge (6:20-21a). Benediction (6:21b).

II Timothy. To the address (1:1 f.) is joined the intercession for Timothy

(1:3-5), exhortation to him to adhere to the charisma imparted through the laying on of hands (1:6-14), and reference to experiences of Paul with his closest associates (1:15-18). Ch. 2 admonishes Timothy to unflinching endurance in suffering like Paul in connection with faithful protection of the tradition (2:1-13), and to correct handling of the truth while avoiding foolish disputes with those who have gotten onto wrong ways (2:14-26). There follows a prophecy of the appearance of false teachers in the last days, who especially lead astray weak women (3:1-9); all the more Timothy should continue in that which he has learned from Paul and the Holy Scriptures (3:10-17), and proclaim "sound teaching" (4:1-5). Finally, Paul describes his situation: He looks forward to death as a martyr (4:6-8), gives information about his co-laborers (4:9-12), orders to Timothy (4:13-15), last reports concerning the seriousness of his situation (4:16-18), delivers greetings (4:19-21). Benediction (4:22).

Titus. The verbose address also describes the contents of Paul's message (1:1-4). In 1:5-16 Titus receives rules concerning the installation and the character of elders or bishops in Crete (1:5-9), with a view to the false teachers who have appeared there, who, out of avarice, spread abroad Jewish myths and ascetic commands (1:10-16). Ch. 2 directs the teaching of all classes in the congregation ("Haustafel"; 2:1-10), corresponding to the grace of God which was revealed in Christ and which brings salvation (2:11-15). In 3:1 f. follow admonitions to obedience to authorities and to courteous conduct toward all men, again grounded through a reference to the goodness and loving-kindness of God which appeared in Christ (3:3-7), which leads to good works (3:8 f.). Repeated warning against false teachers (3:10 f.), orders and greetings (3:12-15a). Benediction (3:15b).

2. The Addressees

The Pastorals indicate as addressees Timothy in Ephesus (I 1:3; II 1:15), and Titus in Crete (Tit. 1:5). Both men are well-known coworkers of Paul from the years of his great mission. Timothy, from Lystra in Lycaonia, was the son of a Gentile father and of a Jewish-Christian mother (Acts 16:1; according to II 1:5, his mother's name was Eunice). Perhaps already won through the first mission of Paul in his hometown (Acts 14:6 ff.), he was chosen by the Apostle on his second visit in Lystra as a missionary companion and was circumcised (Acts 16:3). Henceforth, he was a constant companion of Paul (Acts 17:14 f.; 18:5; 19:22; 20:4; I Thess. 1:1; II Thess. 1:1; II Cor. 1:1, 19; Phil. 1:1) and at intervals was sent by Paul to particular churches with special tasks (I Thess. 3:2, 6; I Cor. 4:17; 16:10; Phil. 2:19, 23). On the collection journey to Jerusalem he was in the company of Paul (Acts 20:4) and, according to Col. 1:1 and Phlm. 1, with him at the place of his imprisonment (see pp. 229 ff.). Phil. 2:20 ff. shows the Apostle's great appreciation of the personality and the service of Timothy. What is historical in Hb. 13:23, the last place in the NT which mentions Timothy, lies in darkness.

Titus, a Gentile Christian, concerning whom Acts, strange to say, is silent, is first named by Paul in Gal. 2:1, 3 as one of his companions on the journey to the apostolic council, where the Apostle successfully withstood the demand to circumcise Titus. According to II Corinthians, he delivered the "intermediate epistle" to the Corinthian congregation. He settled the discord which existed between Paul and Corinth, and actively promoted the business of the collection (2:13; 7:6 f., 13 ff.), and after the fulfillment of this mission he once more came from Macedonia with II Corinthians as forerunner of Paul to Corinth (8:6, 16 ff.; 12:18). II Tim. 4:10 speaks yet of a journey of Titus from Rome, where he was with Paul, to Dalmatia.

3. The Historical Problem

The historical and theological problem of the Pastorals is inextricably intertwined with the question of whether or not these epistles stem from Paul.

Their external attestation in the primitive church is unfavorable. In Marcion's canon the Pastorals are wanting. But in spite of Tertullian's statement (*Adv. Marc.* V, 21: "he [Marcion] rejected" [recusaverit]), the view that Marcion knew but rejected these epistles (Spicq, Michaelis) is just as little demonstrable as the opinion that the epistles could not yet have existed at the time of the formation of Marcion's canon (Bauer, v. Campenhausen). Tatian, according to the report of Hieronymus (foreword to Titus), denied the authenticity of I Timothy for ascetic reasons, but recognized Titus. But from the end of the second century on, the Pastorals were regarded without controversy as epistles of Paul (Muratorian canon, Irenaeus, Tertullian). Hence we cannot interpret the fact that in $\mathfrak{P}^{46}$ (see p. 363) the Pastorals had no place at the (not preserved) end of the papyrus quire only by saying that the writer did not *want* to include the Pastorals. In the first half of the second century the points of contact between Ignatius and the Pastorals concern only isolated expressions, for which no dependence is obvious. And the linguistic agreements between the Pastorals and Polycarp (cf. Spicq, XCVII) prove no more than that they both stood in the same ecclesiastical and cultural tradition (see v. Campenhausen, *Polycarp*, 28 f.). Thus we have no certain evidence for an acquaintanceship with the Pastorals before the third quarter of the second century, which, however, permits no clear judgment about their age.

The Pauline origin of the Pastorals was not challenged from the time of their recognition as canonical writings toward the end of the second century till the beginning of the nineteenth century. But after J. E. C. Schmidt (1804) had expressed doubt about the authenticity of I Timothy, F. Schleiermacher, in his "Sendschreiben an J. C. Gess" (1807), disputed the Pauline composition of I Timothy on the basis of the language and the biographical statements. Several years later J. G. Eichhorn (1812), with reference to the divergent religious language, extended this judgment to all three Pastorals. Then F. C. Baur (1835) closed the circle through his proof that the polemic of the Pastorals was connected with the Gnosticism of the second century (cf. WGK, NT,

100 f., 161 f.). Since H. J. Holtzmann collected all the objections, the insight
into the impossibility of the Pauline composition of the Pastorals has widely
prevailed (thus, e.g., Jülicher, Goodspeed, Dibelius-Conzelmann, Bultmann,
W. Bauer, Gealy, Maurer, v. Campenhausen, Müller-Bardorff, Schweizer, Kasch,
Wegenast), whereas numerous scholars more or less confidently suppose at the
same time the incorporation of genuine Pauline fragments (see Appel, Goguel,
Harrison, Falconer, McNeile-Williams, Henshaw, Heard, Sparks, Easton, Scott,
Michel, Schmithals). Likewise the conviction that the Pastorals, directly or
indirectly, go back to Paul still has numerous advocates (in addition to the
Catholic theologians, cf. Roller [see p. 176], Albertz, de Zwaan, Schlatter, Jeremias, Feine-Behm, Michaelis, Guthrie, Klijn, L. Goppelt, *Die apostolische und
nachapostolische Zeit*, Die Kirche in ihre Geschichte I, A, 1962, 71). The objections against the Pauline composition of the Pastorals are based chiefly upon
1. language and style; 2. the presupposed historical situation; 3. the opposition
to the false teachers; 4. the congregational situation; 5. the theology of the
Pastorals.

1. Language and style. The first doubts as to the authenticity of the Pastorals proceeded from their language. H. J. Holtzmann already demonstrated
in detail the great difference between the language of the Pastorals and that
of the other Pauline epistles. Then Harrison (1921) sought to establish by
means of statistics that the Pastorals, through lesser use of particles, through
the number of words otherwise not encountered in Paul, and through their
relationship to the language of the second century, clearly diverge from the
language of the Pauline epistles. Harrison's method was called into question by
Michaelis, because Harrison compared the vocabulary of individual pages with
one another instead of entire epistles. Metzger has objected that in view of the
shortness of the texts of the Pastorals word statistics generally cannot be employed (additional literature in Guthrie [see p. 28] 221). Certainly with word
statistics we cannot prove more than that the language of certain pieces of
writing diverges in a striking manner from other comparable writings. But
that is, to an indisputable degree, the case when we compare the Pastorals
with the other Pauline epistles. In his statistics Morgenthaler has pointed out
([see pp. 22] 28, 38) that the Pastorals, with 335 vocables in their special material, exhibit two and one half times the number of such words as over against
the cross section of the Pauline epistles. The mathematically improved statistical
method of Grayston and Herdan has confirmed these results, and in addition
has shown that the ratio of the logarithms of vocabulary and text length in
the Pastorals diverges considerably from the same ratio in the Pauline epistles
as a whole (including Colossians, Ephesians, and II Thessalonians). Statistics
about the ratio of Greek and Semitic conditional sentences in the NT writings
indicate that the Pastorals exhibit ten to twenty times as many "Grecisms"
as the Pauline epistles (see K. Beyer, *Semitische Syntax im NT* I, 1, 1962, 232,
295, 298). Moreover, Harrison (ExpT 1955-56) could refer to a larger number
of words and phrases in the Pastorals which are not attested before the second
Christian century. The result of these observations is that the language and

style of the Pastorals do not allow the possibility that Paul wrote them. We cannot avoid this conclusion by contending that between the earlier Pauline epistles (supposing the composition of the "prison epistles" in Ephesus) and the Pastorals there was an interval of from five to seven years, which permitted a considerable change in Paul's style (Michaelis), or by making responsible for this change the influence of Latin upon Paul who was imprisoned the second time in Rome (Spicq). For even if these thoroughly questionable influences could have changed the vocabulary, it would still be completely incomprehensible that thereby the ratio of the logarithms of vocabulary and text length would change so decisively.

Along with these statistical observations about the language and style of the Pastorals, there appear additional linguistic facts which clearly carry even greater weight. For one, there are lacking in the Pastorals numerous shorter words of all kinds otherwise used often by Paul (e.g., ἄν, ἄρα, διό, εἴτε, ἔκαστος, ἔτι, νυνί, οὐκέτι, πάλιν, σύν, ὥσπερ, ὥστε; cf. the lists in Harrison, 1921, 37), and, as a rule, the use of precisely such words takes place instinctively. Still more significant is the use of different words for the same things: κύριοι for the owners of slaves (Col. 3:22; 4:1), δεσπόται (Pastorals); ἀρχαί in Paul for spiritual powers, but in Tit. 3:1 for earthly rulers; in Paul, εὐχαριστεῖν in epistolary introductions in respect to God, but χάριν ἔχειν in I Tim. 1:12 and II Tim. 1:3, whereas this word combination in II Cor. 1:15 means "to receive grace." Finally, if we exclude here for the moment the problem of the theological conceptual world, there occurs the repeated appearance of phrases which otherwise are not found in Paul: e.g., διαβεβαιοῦσθαι περί τινος (I Tim. 1:7; Tit. 3:8); διαμαρτύρεσθαι ἐνώπιον τοῦ θεοῦ (I Tim. 5:21; II Tim. 2:14; 4:1); πιστὸς ὁ λόγος, five times; δι᾽ ἣν αἰτίαν, three times. If we consider all of these facts together, then we cannot deny that already the language and the style speak decisively against the Pauline origin of the Pastorals.

To be sure, that which H. A. Schott (1830) already expressed as a conjecture, O. Roller ([see p. 176] 20 ff.) has sought to establish, namely: Paul himself did not dictate the Pastorals, but had them written from his statements by an amanuensis, and then only corrected the text and subscribed it in his own hand, as corresponds not only to the circumstances presupposed in almost all other Pauline epistles, but follows with necessity from the situation recognizable in II Tim. 1:8, 16; 2:9 of Paul as a chained prisoner. This thesis appears to numerous scholars as an adequate explanation of the juxtaposed Pauline and un-Pauline features in the language of the Pastorals. Conjectures have centered around Luke or Tychicus as the secretary (Albertz, Jeremias, Feine-Behm, Benoit, BdJ; as a possibility, Spicq, Guthrie). However, Roller's denial of the fact that Paul dictated his epistles is untenable (see p. 178). Nor is there any trace of a hint in favor of the supposition that a secretary was involved in the composition of the Pastorals (and, to account for the unity of the language, always the same one!). Moreover, even if the work of an amanuensis could explain the linguistic and stylistic variations from the other Pauline epistles, it would not remove the additional difficulties to be discussed below (see also Michaelis, 242 ff.). And if Jeremias, following Roller, mentions as a formal sign of authenticity that the epistolary form of the Pastorals corresponds exactly to the development of this form in the last of the Pauline epistles, in Colossians, then that is not entirely correct in so far as the introductory greeting (χάρις, etc.) of all three Pastorals diverges from that of all other Pauline epistles (see table 3 in Roller). Besides that, an imitator could connect just as well to one of the last as to one of the earlier Pauline epistles. Thus, in the face of the linguistic data, the amanuensis hypothesis cannot secure even the indirect composition of the Pastorals by Paul.

2. The presupposed historical situation. I Timothy presupposes that until recently Paul and Timothy had worked together in Ephesus. Then Paul traveled to Macedonia and left Timothy behind to resist the false teachers in Ephesus (1:3). The Epistle is a directive to Timothy as to how he should conduct his office during the temporary absence of Paul (3:14; 4:13). But this directive is not primarily intended for Timothy—for that purpose the detailed, written repetition of the oral instructions which the Apostle had already given his tested helper (1:3 ff.) would not have been necessary, especially since Paul himself wanted to return to him soon—it is aimed first of all at the congregations in which Timothy is supposed to work in the highest official capacity.

According to Titus, Paul was at Crete and left Titus there to complete the organization already begun of the congregations in the cities of the island (1:5 ff.). The purpose of the Epistle is to give instructions for this matter, and formally to certify to the congregations that Titus, like Timothy in I Timothy, is Paul's deputy. Perhaps the lawyer Zenas and Apollos are the bearers of the Epistle (3:13). Paul wants to have Titus relieved soon by Artemas or Tychicus. Then Titus is to come as quickly as possible to Paul at Nicopolis, where he has decided to spend the winter (3:12). Of the many cities with this name, we need consider seriously only Nicopolis in Epirus.

According to II Timothy, in which official and personal matters are more entwined than in I Timothy and Titus, Paul is in prison in Rome (1:8, 16 f.; 2:9). Once already he has had to defend himself before the court, forsaken by all his friends, but he has been rescued from the lion's mouth (4:16 f.). Onesiphorus visited him (1:17). Now only Luke is with him (4:16 f.). Crescens has gone to Gaul (or Galatia?), Titus to Dalmatia; Tychicus has been sent by Paul to Ephesus, and Demas has forsaken him (4:10 ff.), likewise the brethren from Asia, among them Phygelus and Hermogenes (1:15). Alexander the coppersmith proved himself a bitter enemy of Paul, and Paul warns Timothy against him (4:14 f.). Paul feels that he is close to death (4:6 ff., 18). Timothy is to hasten to come to him (1:4; 4:9) before winter sets in (4:21), and to bring Mark with him (4:11). Paul was recently at Troas, where he left his cloak and books with Carpus, which Timothy is to bring to him (4:13), and at Miletus, where he had to leave behind the ill Trophimus (4:20). Obviously Timothy does not yet know all of this news. Where Timothy is staying is not directly said. 4:13 points to Asia, and the greeting to Prisca and Aquila (4:19) to Ephesus, where, according to I Timothy, is Timothy's working place.

None of the situations indicated here fits into the life of Paul from Damascus to Rome, as we know it from the other Pauline epistles and Acts.

I Timothy. After three years of activity in Ephesus Paul traveled from Ephesus to Macedonia (Acts 20:1 f.; cf. 19:21). But at that time he had not left Timothy behind in Ephesus but had sent him ahead to Macedonia (Acts 19:22). His additional travel goals were Corinth and Jerusalem (Acts 20:2 ff.). He did not touch Ephesus again (Acts 20:16 ff.). And Timothy, who already must have met again with Paul in Macedonia (II Cor. 1:1), belonged to his companions on the journey to Jerusalem (Acts 20:4 ff.).

Titus. According to our knowledge, Paul was never on Crete and in Nicopolis during his great mission. The voyage of the imprisoned Paul led alongside Crete (Acts 27:7 ff.), but there was no missionary opportunity even while anchoring at Fair Havens. We do not know whether Titus at that time was with Paul. The next winter brought Paul to Malta (Acts 28:1 ff.), not to Nicopolis.

II Timothy. Paul visited Corinth, Troas, and Miletus on the journey depicted in Acts 20:2 f., 5 f., 15 ff. But II Timothy, especially 4:9 ff., cannot refer to this journey, in which Timothy took part as a companion of Paul, and concerning which he would therefore not need to be informed by letter. If Timothy went at that time with Paul to Jerusalem (Acts 20:4 ff.), then he could not be ordered to bring with him to Rome the things which Paul had left in Troas, and that not until after several years (4:13). And Trophimus came at that time with Paul to Jerusalem (Acts 21:29), whereas here he remains behind in Miletus because of illness (4:20). And Paul must not have reported this illness to Timothy until after several years. In the imprisonment from which Colossians stems, Paul had Timothy with him (1:1). In case that was in Rome (see p. 245), that would contradict the summoning of Timothy from Ephesus to Rome (4:9, 21).

The situations presupposed in the Pastorals must, therefore, in so far as they are historical, belong to the time after the Roman imprisonment of Acts 28.

But is there historical information about Paul's life after the end of Acts? a) The report that Paul, like Peter, was a martyr in the Neronian persecution of the year 64, first appears with complete certainty in the so-called "Decretum Gelasianum" III, 2, which stems from the beginning of the sixth century. The end of Acts (28:30 f.) gives no indication of what happened to Paul after his two years of confinement and unhindered preaching in Rome. Some contend that Paul *must* have been released because Acts 25:20 and 26:32 presuppose the innocence of Paul as the view of Festus and Agrippa (Guthrie), and that Paul's death could not have followed immediately after Acts 28:30 f., because then the author of Acts must have mentioned it (Michaelis). These contentions overlook the facts that we know absolutely nothing about whether any appellate process would be properly decided in Rome, that the apologetic goal of Acts has obviously been reached in 28:30 f., and we are not able to postulate what its author must have written or omitted. On the other hand, Acts 20:25, 38 clearly proves that Paul, according to the opinion of the author of Acts, was not able to return anymore to his churches in the East. The ending of Acts, therefore, leaves the possibilities open that Paul was released or executed after his two-year Roman imprisonment, but excludes a new journey to the East.

b) Should Paul have been set free, then the two early reports that Paul worked as a missionary in Spain as he had planned in Rom. 15:24, 28 could prove true. I Clem. 5:7 (end of the first century) concludes its praise of Paul, the champion of the faith, with the words: "He taught righteousness to the whole world and reached to the bounds of the West (ἐπὶ τὸ τέρμα τῆς δύσεως ἐλθών), and he bore witness before rulers; then he was taken out of the world." That was written in Rome; from the standpoint of the Romans, τὸ τέρμα τῆς δύσεως can only be Spain. The Muratorian canon (see §35, 3) says of Acts that Luke, as an eyewitness of the several events, wrote Acts, "and he makes this plain by omitting the passion of Peter and Paul's journey from Rome to Spain." Here the journey of Paul to Spain is presupposed as a fact as well known as the martyrdom of Peter. Paul's journey to Spain could have been deduced by the author of the Muratorian canon from his knowledge of the Epistle to the Romans, but not the passion of Peter. Thus at the basis of this account of Paul's trip to Spain there probably lies a tradition which at the end of the second century could very well have been legendary. On the other hand, it is less probable that the Roman author of I Clement at the end of the first century no longer had an independent tradition about the end of Paul's life, and since he obviously wants to speak in chaps. 5 and 6 about Roman martyrs, there is a considerable probability that he reliably knew that Paul yet labored as a missionary in Spain and then died as a martyr in Rome (see E. Dinkler, ThRdsch 25, 1959, 209 f.). Thus there exists the possibility, or probability, that Paul in Rome once again was released and later became a martyr in Rome. But the situations presupposed by the Pastorals for a journey in the East are not given by these witnesses, and just as little for a second Roman imprisonment, in which Paul expected to be imprisoned long enough after his first defense that he can yet ask Timothy to hasten to come to him before "the time of his departure has come" (II Tim. 4:6 ff., 16, 18, 21).

The report of Paul's second Roman imprisonment (first cited by Eus., EH II, 22, 2), from which II Timothy stems, and the related supposition of Paul's journey in the East, which is defended by all modern advocates of the Pauline composition of the Pastorals, has, therefore, no kind of testimony for it outside the Pastorals, and must be characterized as an unfounded construction.

3. The opposition against the false teachers. If we may regard the false teachers against whom the Pastorals are directed as a unified entity (in spite of Michaelis, *Past. und Gefangenschaftsbriefe*, 102 ff.), then within this entity there are two prominent characteristics inextricably connected: Judaism or Jewish Christianity and Gnosticism.

The opponents belong mostly to the περιτομή (Tit. 1:10), want to be teachers of the Law (I Tim. 1:7), instigate quarrels over the (Mosaic) Law (Tit. 3:9), and take money for their doctrinal discourses (Tit. 1:11; I Tim. 6:5). They give "heed to Jewish myths" and "commands of men" (Tit. 1:14). They lead "dissensions, and quarrels over the [Mosaic] law" (Tit. 3:9). Adherence to ritualistic regulations about clean and unclean (Tit. 1:14 f.) also shows a Jewish root of the heresy. However, it is not only Jewish Christians who are the spreaders of improper teaching (Tit. 1:10 ff.). Although this statement expressly refers to Crete, it also applies to I and II Timothy. The false teachers boast of their higher knowledge (I Tim. 6:20), speculate about series of eons (I Tim. 1:4; 4:7; Tit. 3:9), and practice asceticism through forbidding marriage and foods (I Tim. 4:3; Tit. 1:14 f.), and accordingly hold the Gnostic view that redemption comes through searching into the secrets of the upper world and through practice of asceticism. On that basis we can also understand the decidedly Gnostic concept, "the resurrection is past already." Two of the church members, Hymenaeus and Philetus, by holding to this false teaching, have "swerved from the truth" (II Tim. 2:18). The false teachers make an impression upon credulous souls, chiefly upon unstable women (II Tim. 3:6 f.; Tit. 1:11). Their preaching, which falsifies the truth and undermines morality, is the precursor of frightful eschatological errors in all areas of life (I Tim. 4:1 ff.; II Tim. 3:1 ff.; 4:3 f.).

If the Pastorals are concerned with a Gnosticism more or less modified by Jewish Christianity, then that corresponds exactly with that which we have observed as the danger to the congregation in Colossae (see pp. 239 f.). Although the false teachers who are opposed are Gnostics, there is, therefore, not the slightest reason for relating them to the great Gnostic systems of the second century. The supposition has been repeatedly advocated that the antiheretical polemic of the Pastorals is directed against Marcion, and that in connection with the ἀντιθέσεις τῆς ψευδωνύμου γνώσεως (I Tim. 6:20) we are to think of the 'Αντιθέσεις of Marcion, that great work in which the words and deeds of the creator of the world and of the good God were contrasted with one another (Goodspeed, Riddle-Hutson, J. Knox [see to §35, 2], 74, Gealy, v. Campenhausen; W. Bauer uncertain). This supposition, however, is prohibited not only by Marcion's harsh opposition to the OT and Judaism, but also by the lack of any polemic in the Pastorals against specific Marcionite views.

The Jewish-Christian, Gnostic heresy which the Pastorals combat is thus quite conceivable in the lifetime of Paul. But it is striking that in addition to prophecies about appearance of false teachers "in the last days" (I Tim. 4:1 ff.; II Tim. 3:1 ff., 13; 4:3 f.), we also find hints of the present activity of false teachers and instructions for their opposition (I Tim. 1:3 ff., 19 f.; 6:20 f.; II Tim. 2:16 ff.; 3:8; Tit. 1:10 ff.; 3:9 ff.). Moreover, we are unable to distinguish between the teaching of those who are active in the present and those who are to come "in the last days." Since in the Pastorals we nowhere find an allusion to the consciousness of living "in the last days," the prophecy of the end-time, which obviously describes present phenomena, can only be a traditional literary device ("vaticinium ex eventu"), which "Paul" now uses. It is still more striking *how* the struggle against the false teachers takes place. In marked contrast to other Pauline epistles, even one so late as Colossians, the views of the false teachers are not refuted by confrontation with the preaching of Christ, but they are simply contrasted with the traditional teaching, from which the false teachers have fallen away, and to which one ought to adhere (I Tim. 4:1; 6:20; II Tim. 1:14; 2:2; Tit. 3:10 f.). We cannot base this lack of factual controversy on the claim that Paul regards the babble of the false teachers as not worthy of refutation and presupposes that Timothy and Titus themselves know what is to be advanced against the false teachers (Guthrie), for then there would be no necessity to call the attention of the addressees to the danger of the heresy in detail. Rather, this lack points clearly to the supposition that Paul is not writing here.

4. The congregational situation. In the instructions which Timothy and Titus receive for the establishment of the churches, the officials stand in the foreground: presbyters, bishops (I Tim. 3:1 ff.; 5:17 ff.; Tit. 1:5 ff.) as leaders of the congregation, ordained through laying on of hands (I Tim. 5:22), and supported by the congregation (5:17 ff.); in addition, deacons (3:8 ff.) and widows (5:9 ff.). The chosen officeholders are the guardians of order in the individual congregations; therefore, every importance is placed upon the requirements which they must satisfy. Bearers of the Spirit, prophets, are mentioned only in passing (I Tim. 1:18; 4:14). To be sure, the presbyters or bishops are not all preachers and teachers (I Tim. 5:17), but in the epistles extraordinarily much depends upon administrators who are well prepared to proclaim the Word, since they have to lead the battle against the false teachers (I Tim. 3:2; II Tim. 2:2; Tit. 1:9).

We can hardly determine precisely whether in the Pastorals, in addition to the ἐπίσκοπος (I Tim. 3:2; Tit. 1:7), as a monarchical office, there is a majority of πρεσβύτεροι (I Tim. 5:17, 19; Tit. 1:5), and, therefore, a monarchical episcopal office is presupposed (v. Campenhausen), or the bishop is at least the chief of the presbyters, though of the same status as the presbyters (Spicq), or whether ἐπίσκοπος represents only another designation for the πρεσβύτεροι (Schweizer). There would be no problem at all if πρεσβύτεροι in the Pastorals were always only a designation of age, as in I Tim. 5:1, and if ἐπίθεσις τῶν χειρῶν τοῦ πρεσβυτερίου (I Tim. 4:14) were to be translated, "laying on of hands, which makes a man an elder" (Jeremias). This translation, however, is untenable, for it is constructed upon a technical rabbinic term, which would not have been understandable to a Greek reader, and it contradicts the usual NT use of πρεσβυτέριον. Furthermore, in Tit. 1:5 πρεσβύτεροι clearly designates an office. Since in Tit. 1:5, 7 πρεσβυτέρους is taken up by τὸν ἐπίσκοπον, and the "management" referred to in I Tim. 3:4 f. and 5:17 is applied similarly to a bishop and to a presbyter, the Pastorals probably designate with ἐπίσκοπος and πρεσβύτερος the same office, which is not yet monarchical. The change to the singular τὸν ἐπίσκοπον in Tit. 1:7 is explained by the adoption of a bishop's rule (Dibelius-Conzelmann). If, therefore, the Pastorals know only presbyter-bishops and, in addition, deacons (I Tim. 3:8, 12), then the office of presbyter-bishop is a civil office which has claim to payment (I Tim. 3:1; 5:17). As Timothy himself was ordained by the presbytery when the elders laid their hands upon him (I Tim. 4:14), Timothy ordains others to the office of presbyter-bishop by laying his hands upon them (I Tim. 5:22). Correspondingly, Tit. 1:5

directs Titus to ordain presbyters. Some scholars regard the office of Timothy or Titus, which is superior to the local church, as the actual bishop's or metropolitan's office (Easton, Gealy), or interpret these pupils of the Apostle as apostolic delegates (Guthrie). But v. Campenhausen has rightly emphasized that "the presupposed situations yet remain much too indefinite" to identify the position of Timothy and Titus with a later ecclesiastical office. But we can recognize without further ado that the actual task of Timothy and Titus consists in preserving and handing down to their pupils the orthodox teaching which they have received from Paul (I Tim. 1:11; 6:20; II Tim. 1:14; 2:2). As little as the chain of *succession* from Paul through his pupils to officials in the congregations is established (against Schlier, Schmithals), so much is the chain of *tradition* emphasized, which begins with the Apostle (II Tim. 2:2, 8). The presupposition behind this central role of the tradition is a church, which, in contrast to Paul's imminent expectation, is already making provision for the time after the death of the tradition-bearers installed by the Apostle's pupils (II Tim. 2:1 f.). If Paul doubtless did not know the task of the preservation of the tradition by ordained presbyters (πρεσβύτερος is not found in Paul as a designation of an office!), then the ecclesiastical office of the widows (I Tim. 5:3 ff.), whose basic task is continual prayer in connection with complete sexual abstinence (Müller-Bardorff), is especially strange to Paul. Although it is questionable whether the Pastorals presuppose the distinction between clergy and laity (Schlier, Spicq), there is nowhere anymore any consideration of an active cooperation and responsibility on the part of the congregation. In view of these factors we see that the Pastorals are the document "of an already rather highly developed canon law" (v. Campenhausen) in a church which is establishing itself in the world, a church such as Paul did not know.

5. The theology of the Pastorals. The Pastorals' theological world of conceptions corresponds fully with the above findings. To be sure, the Pastorals contain a series of sayings which are in line with the central thoughts of Paul: the salvation of the sinner through Christ (I Tim. 1:15 f.), the revelation of the grace of God now through the appearance of Christ (II Tim. 1:9 f.), justification not by works (Tit. 3:5), faith as the way to eternal life (I Tim. 1:16). On the other hand, we encounter Hellenistic terms for the event of salvation which would be strange to Paul: ἐπεφάνη ἡ χάρις . . . σωτήριος . . . παιδεύουσα ἡμᾶς (Tit. 2:10 f.), ὅτε . . . ἡ φιλανθρωπία ἐπεφάνη τοῦ σωτῆρος ἡμῶν θεοῦ (Tit. 3:4); and for the gift of salvation: προσδεχόμενοι τὴν μακαρίαν ἐλπίδα καὶ ἐπιφάνειαν τῆς δόξης τοῦ μεγάλου θεοῦ καὶ σωτῆρος ἡμῶν Ἰησοῦ Χριστοῦ (Tit. 2:13); for God: ὁ μόνος ἔχων ἀθανασίαν, φῶς οἰκῶν ἀπρόσιτον (I Tim. 6:16), ὁ μακάριος καὶ μόνος δυνάστης (I Tim. 6:15); and Christ: ἐπιφάνεια and σωτήρ for the earthly appearance of Christ (II Tim. 1:10; Tit. 3:6), εἷς μεσίτης θεοῦ καὶ ἀνθρώπων (I Tim. 2:5). The supposition that Paul since the beginning of his first Roman imprisonment expanded his mental range "in an entirely new environment," which led "him to incorporate into his vocabulary words previously foreign to him," especially words from the terminology of the emperor cult (Michaelis), makes Paul into a syncretist.

The description of the Christian life found in the Pastorals is even more striking than the divergent formulation of soteriological statements. Frequently the correct attitude of the Christian is called εὐσέβεια (I Tim. 2:2; 4:7 f; 6:3, 5 f., 11; II Tim. 3:5; Tit. 1:1); πίστις, to be sure, still often designates the attitude of faith (e.g., I Tim. 1:5), but also the rule of faith (I Tim. 3:9; 6:10; II Tim. 4:7, etc.), so that more than once the formula ἐν πίστει is encountered (I Tim. 1:2; 2:7, etc.); parallel with πίστις in this sense stands then καλὴ διδασκαλία (I Tim. 4:6), ἡ κατ᾽ εὐσέβειαν διδασκαλία (I Tim. 6:3), and above all ὑγιαίνουσα διδασκαλία (I Tim. 1:10; II Tim. 4:3; Tit. 1:9; 2:1), or ὑγιαίνοντες λόγοι (I Tim. 6:3; II Tim. 1:13). From Christians is, therefore, demanded ὑγιαίνειν ἐν τῇ πίστει (Tit. 1:13; 2:2); σωφρόνως καὶ δικαίως καὶ εὐσεβῶς ζῆν (Tit. 2:12); ἤρεμον καὶ ἡσύχιον βίον διάγειν ἐν πάσῃ εὐσεβείᾳ καὶ σεμνότητι (I Tim. 2:2). To this rational, ethicized description of the Christian life and the Christian demand corresponds the fact that, as in Eph. 2:10, the plural ἔργα ἀγαθά likewise is found emphasized in I Tim. 2:10 and Tit. 2:14, like ἀγαθὴ or καθαρὰ συνείδησις in I Tim. 1:5; 3:9, etc.; that ἐν Χριστῷ Ἰησοῦ appears connected only with concepts of salvation, not with persons (e.g., II Tim. 1:1; I Tim. 3:13); that πνεῦμα is found only twice as designation of the Spirit of God given to the Christian (II Tim. 1:14; Tit. 3:5; in the second passage limited to the salvation in the λουτρὸν παλιγγενεσίας); and σῶμα does not appear at all. If we add the facts that, in spite of adherence to a coming final consummation (I Tim. 6:14; Tit. 2:13, etc.), there exists no living expectation of the end, as the provision for coming generations shows (see Schweizer, 67 f., Bultmann, 468, 535), and that in I Tim. 1:15 we find the same coarsened version of the Pauline self-judgment (I Cor. 15:9 f.) as in Eph. 3:8, then there can be no doubt that in these epistles it is not Paul who speaks but a Christian of later primitive Christianity. M. Dibelius called this Christianity which is settling down in the world and which speaks a strongly Hellenistic language a "bourgeois" Christianity (see excursus to I Tim. 1:10; 2:2), and thereby doubtless hit upon an essential characteristic of this "piety." But at the same time it is "a somewhat faded Paulinism" (Bultmann), for the grace which has appeared qualifies the Christian first of all for a pious life in this aeon (Tit. 2:11 f.). Therefore, it certainly induces a falsification into the Pauline theology if we include the Pastorals in our representation of Pauline thought (Cerfaux in Robert-Feuillet, 529 [with agreement by B. Rigaux, see lit. to §12, 152], in spite of his adherence to the Pauline composition of the Pastorals, demands that we should not "use the Pastorals in pure scientific work for the determination of the theology of the Apostle or for the reconstruction of primitive Christian history without plain caution"!). To say that the Pastorals do not reproduce the theology of Paul, is not at all to say that their "bourgeois Christianity" does not in many respects represent a necessary new interpretation of the primitive message under the presupposition of the abandoned imminent expectation. The question as to whether the Pastorals represent a relevant and necessary development of the Pauline proclamation, or its full or partial falsification, cannot be answered by a literary judgment in respect to their author but only by a critical, theological examination of them.

4. Purpose, Time, and Place of Composition

As literary entities, the Pastorals are not homogeneous. On the one hand, in I Timothy and Titus the directions for organization of the churches, teaching of the classes, and opposition to the false teachers form the actual contents, so that in essence these two Epistles treat ecclesiastical order. On the other hand, II Timothy consists of an admonition of Paul, who is going to his death, to his pupil to stand firm and to fight heresy, i.e., the Epistle has the form of a literary testament. And whereas in all three Epistles Paul plainly appears as the author, it is only in II Timothy that we find personal correspondence to a considerable extent. If the Pastorals, on the basis of the numerous facts already discussed, cannot be Pauline epistles, then they are pseudonymous writings. Hence we must ask what character this pseudonymity has, or, how we are to judge concerning the personalia of the Epistles. Because some of these notices sound as if they are personal reports without any tendency (especially II Tim. 4:9-21; Tit. 3:12 f.), scholars since 1836 have advocated the thesis in the most varied ways that the Pastorals contain a series of fragments of authentic Pauline epistles, which the author of the Pastorals has inserted into his compositions (see the enumeration in Goguel, *Intr.*, IV, 2, 500 note). Especially Harrison has taken pains to piece together from separate verses, first, five, later three, genuine notes, which originally belonged together. He then placed these notes within the history of Paul up to his imprisonment in Rome (see further Appel, Goguel, Falconer, McNeile-Williams, Henshaw, Heard, Sparks, Scott, Schmithals; Easton and Michel, uncertain). Two decisive reasons, however, weigh against this supposition (cf. also Guthrie, 224 ff.): a) It is not clear how such small epistles or epistolary fragments of Paul could have been preserved nor why the author of the Pastorals should have inserted them so splintered into his epistles. b) The arrangement of these fragments, which only hint at their situation, into the life of Paul that is known to us is only possible hypothetically. Thus we can obtain no certainty as to whether a section really is a genuine fragment simply because it fits into a situation known to us; and there is no other criterion of authenticity in this case. But in any event, we must consider that this theory, if it possesses probability, presupposes the oddity that the author of the Pastorals writes in the name of Paul and thinks that he is able to give these pseudonymous writings the appearance of authenticity through insertion of genuine fragments.

Rather, we must recognize the fact that the three Pastorals, which presumably stem from the same author, purport to be Pauline epistles not only through their addresses but also through personal remarks, the mention of additional persons, and greetings. According to Harrison, the writer only intended to express in the well-known form of the Pauline epistles what, in his opinion and the opinion of his readers, "the Apostle would have said had he been still alive";

the reader was not at all to suppose that it was a question of genuine Pauline epistles (ExpT 1955-56, 77). Since nothing in the Pastorals indicates that they were intended to be Pauline only in appearance, Harrison's view is extremely improbable. But precisely if we must suppose that the author really writes in the role of Paul, and that the pseudonymity, in contrast to Ephesians, is carried out with emphasis (v. Campenhausen, *Kirchliches Amt*, 121 f. rightly compares II Peter), then it is questionable whether the biographical situation of each individual epistle is so thought through that the writer was clear in which period of the Pauline activity (known to us or imagined by him) the individual epistle was to be placed (Maurer's attempt to reconstruct the situation presupposed by the author from the supposition that the doubtless secondary reading προσελθόντες [Acts 20:5] lay before the author, is not feasible; see Michaelis, *Einl.*, 250 ff.). We probably cannot determine either the presupposed situation of the individual epistles or the sequence of their composition. Rather, the author wants to support the churches near to him (in Asia Minor?) in the danger which is indicated by the false teaching. Writing as a pupil of Paul in the name of Paul, he shows the churches how to repulse the false teachers through correct order in the churches, through sound doctrine, and through a pious life according to the teaching of Paul, to the end that Christians may "become heirs in hope of eternal life" (Tit. 3:7).

We know nothing concrete concerning the author. According to v. Campenhausen the author was Polycarp of Smyrna. But this hypothesis is incompatible with the striking literary difference between the Pastorals and Polycarp's Epistle to the Philippians, as well as with the already mentioned improbability of placing the Pastorals after Marcion (see also E. Käsemann, VuF 1949-50, 1951-52, 215). And the suggestion that the author possessed rabbinic schooling (Michel, Nauck) is as little demonstrable as the proposal that he himself was an office-holder (v. Campenhausen). The factual and linguistic relationship of the Pastorals with Polycarp prompts the supposition that the Pastorals arose in Asia Minor, though no actual proof is possible. A too late dating is opposed not only by the strong Pauline heritage which obviously stems "from living church tradition" (Käsemann), but also by the rudimentary character of the Gnosticism which is resisted (see pp. 266 ff.). Thus the time best suited for composition is just after the turn of the second century.

APPENDIX

§25. The Epistle to the Hebrews

Commentaries, see p. 390. Studies: W. Wrede, *Das literarische Rätsel des Hb.*, 1906; R. Perdelwitz, "Das literarische Problem des Hb.," ZNW 11, 1910, 59 ff. 105 ff.; Th. Haering, "Gedankengang und Grundgedanken des Hb.," ZNW 18, 1917, 145 ff.; A. C. Purdy, "The Purpose of the Epistle to the Hebrews," in: *Amicitiae Corolla*, 1933, 253 ff.; E. Käsemann, *Das wandernde Gottesvolk*, FRLANT, N. F. 37, 1938 (= ⁴1961); T. W. Manson, "The Problem of the Epistle to the Hebrews," BJRL 32, 1949-50, 1 ff. (= Manson, St., 242 ff.); A. Oepke, *Das neue Gottesvolk*, 1950, 17 ff., 57 ff.; W. F. Howard, "The Epistle to the Hebrews," Int 5, 1951, 80 ff.; W. Manson, *The Epistle to the Hebrews*, 1953; G. Schille, "Erwägungen zur Hohepriesterlehre des Hb.," ZNW 46, 1955, 81 ff.; idem, "Erwägungen zu Hb. 11," ZNW 51, 1960, 112 ff.; F. Lo Bue, "The Historical Background of the Epistle to the Hebrews," JBL 75, 1956, 52 ff.; C. P. M. Jones, "The Epistle to the Hebrews and the Lucan Writings," StG, 1957, 113 ff.; H. Thyen, *Der Stil der Jüdisch-Hellenistischen Homilie*, FRLANT, N. F. 47, 1956, 16 ff.; Y. Yadin, "The Dead Sea Scrolls and the Epistle to the Hebrews," *Scripta Hierosolymitana* IV, 1958, 36 ff.; J. Daniélou, *Qumran und der Ursprung des Christentums*, 1958, 148 ff.; *The Dead Sea Scrolls and Primitive Christianity*. Tr. Salvator Attanasio, 1958; C. Spicq, "L'Épître aux Hébreux, Apollos, Jean-Baptiste, les Hellénistes et Qumran," RdQ 1, 1958-59, 365 ff.; idem, DBS VII, 1961, 226 ff.; H. Kosmala, "Hebräer—Essener—Christen," *Studia Post-Biblica* I, 1959, 1 ff.; J. Schneider, RGG³ III, 1959, 106 ff.; F. C. Synge, *Hebrews and the Scriptures*, 1959; W. Nauck, "Zum Aufbau des Hb.," *Judentum, Urchristentum, Kirche, Festschr. J. Jeremias*, Beih. ZNW 26, 1960, 199 ff.; F. J. Schierse, LThK V, 1960, 45 ff.; R. Schnackenburg, *Die Kirche im NT*, 1961, 81 ff.; J. Betz, *Die Eucharistie in der Zeit der griech. Väter* II, 1, 1961, 144 ff.; W. L. Dulière, "Antioche et la lettre aux Hébreux," ZRGG 13, 1961, 216 ff.; J. Coppens, "Les affinités qumrâniennes de l'Épître aux Hébreux," NRTh 94, 1962, 128 ff., 257 ff.; B. Rigaux, see lit. to § 12, 201 ff.

1. Contents

The plan of Hebrews is characterized by two peculiarities: 1) the expositions begin at once, without an epistolary introduction; 2) contrary to most Pauline epistles, the exhortatory section does not come only at the conclusion of the "Epistle," but the expositions are more than once interrupted by paraeneses (2:1-4; 3:7–4:11; 4:14-16; 5:11–6:12; 10:19-39; 12:1–13:17), which evidently are the actual goal of all the expositions (Michel, Kuss, Nauck). The very diverse attempts to distinguish between a dogmatic and a paraenetic part (lately Coppens), or to discover an arrangement on the basis of the Christological concepts of the Epistle (cf. the survey in Spicq, *Ét. bibl.* I, 27 ff., and Rigaux, 212 ff.) are as little convincing as the supposition that Hebrews is divided according to the scheme of Greek exhortatory discourses into prologue

(1:1–4:13), two expositions about Jesus the High Priest (4:14–6:20; 7:1–10: 18), and epilogue (10:19–13:25) (Haering, Windisch). Rather, Nauck has shown that Hebrews is organized by means of paraeneses, which from time to time stand in parallel form at the beginning and ending of a larger section (similarly Schierse). Upon the basis of this insight there results the following train of thought in three chief parts:

I. Hear the word of God in the Son Jesus Christ, who is higher than the angels and Moses (1:1–4:13). In 1:1-4a the eschatological superiority of the Son of God over the prophets and angels as the bearer of the word of God and destroyer of sins is stressed thematically. Then Jesus' superiority over the angels is shown through a scriptural proof: He has the higher name of the Son (1:4b-14). Therefore, we must give heed to his word (2:1-4). He was made lower than the angels, in that he became man and suffered death, in order that according to God's will he might thus become the perfect pioneer of salvation for his brethren (2:5-18). Jesus is also exalted above Moses, for Moses was only a servant in God's house, whereas Jesus as the Son is Lord over God's house (3: 1-6). Hence Christians must beware of losing the promised rest of God through unbelief and disobedience, as did the contemporaries of Moses (3:7-19). They must do their utmost to win their share in the promise which applies to them as the people of God (4:1-11), for God's word impels to decision (4:12 f.).

II. Let us draw near to the High Priest of the heavenly sanctuary and hold fast to our confession (4:14–10:31). We ought to hold fast to Jesus, the heavenly High Priest (4:14-16). He proves his high priesthood by the fact that he shares in human weakness, is appointed by God, and has perfected his calling through the obedience of suffering (5:1-10). There follows a paraenetical interlude which is to arouse the readers to attention to the fundamental truths of the Christian faith, which are developed here (5:11–6:20): They must overcome their obtuseness, which actually makes necessary a repetition of elementary Christian instruction (5:11–6:18), and lay hold upon the certainty of hope, for God has authenticated the goal of their salvation by an oath (6:9-20). Then the portrayal of Jesus' high priesthood is resumed; he is the perfect, eternal High Priest after the order of Melchizedek—holy, sinless, guarantor of a better order of God, whose everlasting priesthood guarantees full salvation (ch. 7). He is the heavenly High Priest upon the basis of his definitive, once-and-for-all self-sacrifice (8:1–10:18); as priest in the heavenly sanctuary he serves the new order of God, which is better than that of the OT (ch. 8). In place of the insufficient sacrifices in the earthly sanctuary he has offered himself, and through his own blood has effected an eternally valid redemption (9:1-15). But this once-and-for-all self-sacrifice of Christ was necessary (9:16-28) and provides the perfect forgiveness of sins, which the sacrifice of animals in the OT cultus was unable to accomplish (10:1-18). Let us, therefore, hold fast to this High Priest in confession and not fall back into sin (10:19-31).

III. Hold fast to Jesus Christ, the pioneer and perfecter of our faith (10:32–13:17). Since the readers earlier had stood firm in suffering, now they ought also to wait on the coming of the Lord in steadfast patience (10:32-39). For the power of such faith, which hopes in future things and is certain of invisible things, there is a cloud of witnesses, from Abel unto Jesus, the pioneer and perfecter of faith (11:1–12:3). In the sufferings, which are a divine means of discipline, let us look to Jesus and faithfully persevere (12:4-17). We dare not reject God's unique revelation in Christ, else God's frightful judgment threatens us (12:18-29). Thence there follows the duty of brotherly love, of a chaste and frugal life, of patient endurance, and of following the leaders (13:1-17). Then comes the epistolary conclusion (13:18-25): personalia, greetings, and benediction.

2. The Tradition About the Epistle

Hebrews was already known and esteemed by I Clem. 17:1; 36:2-5, without being cited by title and author's name. The superscription, "To the Hebrews" (Πρὸς Ἑβραίους), is first attested by Pantaenus (in Eus., EH VI, 14, 4), then by Clement of Alexandria and Tertullian; also the earliest manuscripts ($\mathfrak{P}^{46}$) have it already. It obviously stems from the time of the collection of primitive Christian epistles, and gives expression to the opinion that Hebrews was written to Jewish Christians (the contention that Πρὸς Ἑβραίους means "*Against* the Jews" is not tenable, even with reference to the polemical parts of the Epistle, against Synge). Marcion does not have the Epistle in his *Apostolikon*. According-ing to early Alexandrian tradition, Hebrews was regarded as a Pauline epistle, as is shown by Pantaenus' reflections about the missing address, Clement of Alexandria's conjectures about Luke as the translator of the Hebraic Pauline epistle (Eus., EH VI, 14, 2f.), and the alignment of Hebrews in the Pauline corpus after Romans ($\mathfrak{P}^{46}$). Origen regarded it as Pauline, to be sure, only indirectly. A pupil wrote down the thoughts of the Apostle but set them forth in his own style: τίς ὁ γράψας τὴν ἐπιστολήν, τὸ μὲν ἀληθὲς θεὸς οἶδεν (in Eus., EH VI, 25, 11 ff.; see WGK, NT, 5).

In the entire Greek and also Syrian Church Hebrews, since the third century, was classed, without exception, among the canonical Pauline epistles. In most manuscripts it stands after the congregational epistles (after II Thessalonians) and before the private epistles (I Timothy, etc.), but in the western tradition at the close of the Pauline epistles, after Philemon. In the earlier tradition, the place of Hebrews is unique in $\mathfrak{P}^{46}$—between Romans and Corinthians; yet this arrangement is also occasionally found later (see W. H. P. Hatch, "The Position of Hebrews in the Canon of the NT," HarvThR 29, 1936, 133 ff.).

In the West Hebrews was not regarded as a Pauline epistle until the fourth century. Just as it is missing in the Muratorian canon, so also in the African canon of c. 350 (see Preuschen, *Analecta*, 37). The anti-Montanist, Gaius (c. 200), does not classify it among the Pauline epistles, and still at the time of Eusebius the Roman Church is of the same opinion (see Eus., EH VI, 20, 3; VI, 13, 6). Cyprian, Ambrosiaster, and others do not mention it. Irenaeus and Hippolytus know it but deny its composition by Paul (Th. Zahn, *Geschichte des Ntl. Kanons* I, 1888, 296, note 2). We first find a tradition about Barnabas as author of the Epistle in Tertullian (*de pud.*, 20). Tertullian cites Hebrews as noncanonical, but as a widely recognized ecclesiastical writing: "For there exists [an Epistle] to the Hebrews [with the] superscription of Barnabas, a man with sufficient authorization from God" [extat enim et Barnabae titulus ad Hebraeos, a deo satis auctorati viri]. We do not know the origin of this tradition. Only from the second half of the fourth century on, under the influence of inter-communication among Western and Eastern theologians, was the Western canon assimilated to the Eastern, and Hebrews recognized as the fourteenth Pauline epistle (see §36, 2).

In the Reformation period doubts again emerged, first by Erasmus and Cajetan, in connection with Hieronymus' reports about criticism in the early church (see WGK, NT, 10). Luther separated Hebrews from the Pauline epistles, and placed it with James, Jude, and Revelation after the "really certain principal books of the NT," chiefly because the Epistle declares as impossible a second repentance after apostasy from faith (see "Preface to the Epistle to the Hebrews," 1522). Melanchthon, Calvin, and Beza regarded it as non-Pauline. The Council of Trent decreed the existence of fourteen Pauline epistles in the NT, and thereby the composition of Hebrews by Paul. From the end of the six-teenth century on, almost all Protestants returned to the supposition of Pauline origin. But with the Enlightenment doubt was again awakened (J. D. Michaelis; see WGK, NT, 85), and Bleek in 1828 brought forth the conclusive proof of its non-Pauline origin.

In 1914 the papal biblical commission decided that Hebrews is to be classified among the authentic Pauline epistles; on the other hand, Paul need not have published Hebrews "in that form in which it stands [now]" [ea forma qua prostat] (*Enchiridion Biblicum*, [3]1956, 129 f.). Since then, however, an ever greater number of Catholic scholars have accepted the view that Hebrews does not derive even indirectly from Paul, but is the work of an independent Pauline pupil (Wikenhauser, Schäfer, Benoit in the BdJ, Cambier in Robert-Feuillet, Kuss, Schierse, Spicq, Rigaux). It is expressly declared that since the scholar is free in respect to the decisions of the biblical commission in so far as they do not touch the "truth of faith and morals" [veritas fidei et morum], he is also free to question the authorship (cf. E. Vogt, Bb 36, 1955, 564 f.; J. Dupont, RB 62, 1955, 414 ff.).

3. Literary Character

The plan of Hebrews is not the same as that of the Pauline epistles. As a rule, Paul has an exhortatory concluding section follow the doctrinal or controversial questions. In Hebrews, on the other hand, the doctrinal discussions are frequently interrupted by shorter or longer exhortations (see p. 273 f.). Also style, language, and manner of expression are different from those of Paul. Only the epistolary conclusion (13:18 ff.) has frequent points of contact with Paul and can point to connections with Paul. But Hebrews has its own vocabulary and refined stylistic taste, which reveal a writer who, in quite a different degree from

Paul, relies upon the means of expression of Greek rhetoric (cf. Spicq, *Ét. bibl.* I, 351 ff.). The Epistle is one of the books written in the best Greek in the NT.

The theology of Hebrews also is not Pauline. To be sure, much is reminiscent of Paul: e.g., Christ the Son, the pre-existent agent in creation; Christ's death for sins as the central expression of salvation; the conception of "God's new order" (καινὴ διαθήκη; cf. I Cor. 11:25; II Cor. 3:6, 14; Gal. 4:24); the decisive significance of faith; use of similar passages in scriptural proof (10:38; cf. Rom. 1:17; Gal. 3:11: Hab. 2:4 or 2:6 ff.; cf. I Cor. 15:27: Ps. 8); reminiscences of Paul's statements (cf. 5:12 ff. with I Cor. 3:1 ff.). Somehow, the conceptual world of Hebrews must have been touched by the spirit of Paul. But Hebrews, in its erudite form, is definitely differentiated from that of the Apostle. None of the features mentioned is carried out in Paul's manner. Where Paul speaks of Christ's resurrection, Hebrews speaks of his exaltation in heaven. The result of Christ's saving work, which Paul summarizes as reconciliation with God, Hebrews preferably calls purification, sanctification, perfection (καθαρίζειν, ἁγιάζειν, τελειοῦν). The chief, prevailing conception of Hebrews' Christology, Christ's high priesthood, is missing in Paul. The concept of God's new order is independently developed by Hebrews and placed in the center of things. Hebrews has as little to say about justification by faith, not by works of the Law, as about the dichotomy between flesh and spirit, or about σὺν Χριστῷ. The concept of Gentiles and Jews plays no role in Hebrews' theology of history. Quite differently from Paul, Hebrews views the Law essentially from the aspect of cult, as an institution of atonement, which is supposed to remove sins of weakness; it does not stand in opposition to the NT revelation of salvation, but is its incomplete preparation. Paul nowhere maintains the impossibility of second repentance (6:4 ff.; 10:26; 12:17; cf. Spicq, *Ét. bibl.* I, 145 ff.).

Even Hebrews' relation to other religions is different from that of Paul. Points of contact between Hebrews and the spirit of Alexandrian Judaism, especially Philo, are clear. Unimpeded by the historical meaning of the scriptural words, Hebrews uses and interprets the OT in the manner of the Alexandrians, thinking entirely of ascertaining the deeper, truer sense. That is accomplished by artistic introduction of the author's own thoughts (4:3), by interpretation of proper names (7:2), by relating as many scriptural passages as possible to Christ (1:5 ff.; 2:6 ff., 12 f.; 10:5 ff.), by means of allegorical exposition, which extracts from the scriptural word a mysterious meaning with reference to the present (11:13 ff.; 13:11 ff.), and above all by comparison of OT persons and institutions with the ideal NT ones, to which they correspond, i.e., by typological exegesis. Melchizedek is the type of the true NT High Priest (ch. 7); the earthly tabernacle is the shadowy copy of the heavenly sanctuary (8:2, 5); the Law contains only a silhouette of the good things to come, not the form of these realities themselves (10:1). With ever new variations Hebrews alludes to the contrast between shadow and reality, earthly and heavenly (9:23 f.; 8:1 ff.), created and uncreated (9:11), past and future (9:1 ff.; 13:14; 2:5), transient and permanent (7:3, 24; 10:34; 12:27; 13:14). It intends to convince the readers of the sole reality of the invisible, heavenly realities to come (11:1;

6:4 f.; 11:16; 12:22; 10:1). Although Hebrews' direct acquaintanceship with Philo is improbable (against Spicq, Purdy), it is clear that it was strongly influenced by the spirit and forms of expression of the Hellenistic synagogue (Michel, Thyen, Coppens). According to form and content, Hebrews stands closer to the Hellenistic literature and intellectual world than do the Pauline epistles.

Moreover, Hebrews in its Christology, as well as in its prevailing conception of the "wandering people of God," shows a clear connection with Gnostic ideas (Käsemann, Michaelis, Albertz), which likewise goes far beyond that which can be observed in connection with Paul. Further, certain scholars recently, and in various ways, have attempted to establish that the intellectual world of Qumran influenced Hebrews (Schnackenburg, Betz), or at least that Hebrews is an appeal to former members of the Qumran sect of Essenes whose theological proclivities were similar to those of the author (Kosmala, Yadin). Coppens, on the other hand, has convincingly demonstrated that no specific parallels between Hebrews and the intellectual world of Qumran appear; rather, distinctive Qumran language has no analogy in Hebrews. Hebrews belongs entirely in the sphere of influence of Hellenistic Judaism and of the original Gnosticism which came into contact with part of this Judaism.

If, in spite of some parallels, Hebrews varies decisively from Paul literarily and theologically, as well as in respect to its relations with other religions, then the question about its literary character becomes all the more urgent. Since Hebrews has no epistolary introduction, but does have an epistolary conclusion reminiscent of Paul's epistolary style, some scholars have sought to trace back this lack of epistolary introduction to accidental or intentional excisement (Jülicher, Feine, *Einl.*[6]), or to the literary intention of the writer of the Epistle (Goguel, Windisch, T. W. Manson, Spicq, Feine-Behm), and on the basis of this supposition to regard Hebrews as an actual epistle. Since both suppositions are hardly evident, and the "Epistle" otherwise shows no epistolary character, others have conjectured that the author, through the addition of the epistolary ending, wanted to create the impression of a Pauline epistle (Wrede, Dibelius, Goodspeed), or the epistolary ending was attached by a strange hand, in order to send the unepistolary document to another congregation (Perdelwitz, Thyen). But at most the mention of Timothy (13:23) could merely have suggested to the original readers that Paul was the writer of the Epistle, and nothing points to an addition by a strange hand.

It is, therefore, most improbable that the entire piece of writing was composed or prepared as a real or alleged epistle. Rather, there is every reason to believe that here we have to do with a discourse. The expression ὁ λόγος τῆς παρακλήσεως (13:22), which, after all, stands next to ἐπέστειλα ὑμῖν, does not point so much in the direction of a discourse as do the frequent references to the author's speaking (2:5; 5:11; 6:9; 8:1; 9:5), and especially to the lack of time for the discourse (11:32). On the other hand, this discourse obviously presupposes definite Christians as listeners, into whose special situation the writer enters (5:11 ff.; 6:9 f.; 10:25, 32 ff.; 12:4 f.). The promise to come soon (13:19, 23), like the greeting in 13:24, has meaning only in respect to certain readers. The supposition, which was first advocated by J. Berger (1797), that Hebrews is a sermon sent to another congregation has rightly gained wide recognition in a modified form: A sermon which was written down for a particular community, was sent, with an epistolary conclusion, by the author to that community (cf., e.g., Albertz, McNeile-Williams, Wikenhauser, Klijn, Schierse, Windisch, Strathmann, Kuss, Spicq, Oepke, Nauck). The suggestion that this sermon is a homily on a specific passage of Scripture, such as Jer. 31:31-34, cannot be proved. Likewise, the conjecture that the sermon is based upon earlier separate treatises of the author (Spicq, Michel, Schneider) is unnecessary. Especially the suppositions of a secondary joining together of exegetical and paraenetic pieces by a redactor (Synge) and of interpolations of 5:11b-14 and 6:5, 6b (Kosmala) are completely arbitrary. It is altogether probable that the author used previously fixed traditions (e.g., in 1:3; 11:1-38; 13:14; cf. Michel, *ad loc.*, and Käsemann, ThLZ 75, 1950, 428), even if the reconstruction of such pieces of tradition by Schille is not convincing. But what intention the author followed in composing and sending this unusually long sermon to a congregation known to him, we can recognize only when we have asked about the readers addressed.

4. Readers

For a long time Hebrews, even independently of its superscription, was generally regarded as an epistle for Jewish Christians. In support of this view scholars appealed to the manner of argumentation, which moves entirely within OT conceptions and presupposes the most precise knowledge of Jewish views and concepts, especially of the nature of OT sacrifices. They also cited the abundance of OT quotations and the extent of scriptural proof. They called attention to the theological discussions directed toward Jews about the superiority of God's new order over the old, about the high priesthood of Jesus and his service of sacrifice, and especially about Jesus' preeminence over Moses (3:1 ff.). Hence these scholars readily sought the readers in the original home of Jewish Christianity, Palestine or Jerusalem. Recently, scholars in various ways have advocated the thesis that the addressees were Essene priests (Daniélou, Spicq, RdQ, DBS), or former members of Qumran (Yadin, Betz), who perhaps had not yet accepted Jesus as Messiah (Kosmala).

But neither the priestly nor the Qumran origin of the readers can be made probable in any way, and it follows clearly from 3:1 f., 4; 6:4-6, 9; 10:23, 26; and 12:22-24 that the readers were Christians. Moreover, the Epistle certainly is not addressed to Jerusalem. The primitive church was poor and needed the support of foreign congregations (cf. the collections for them in Antioch and in Paul's missionary territory). But the receivers of Hebrews themselves repeatedly supported others (6:10). 2:3 f. and 13:7 also are not suitable to the members of the primitive community. And the one persecution, to which the readers were exposed soon after their conversion (10:32 ff.), does not coincide with the periods of suffering of the Christians in Jerusalem known to us from Acts.

But also the hypothesis of Jewish-Christian readers outside of Palestine, which is advocated either generally (Appel, Strathmann, Meinertz, Schäfer, Cambier in Robert-Feuillet, Benoit in the BdJ, Coppens), or with limitation to a Jewish-Christian minority (Howard, W. Manson, Lo Bue, Spicq, *Ét. bibl.*, Guthrie), is extremely improbable, in view of the reference to the necessity of faith in God (6:1; 11:6). And contrary to Appel and W. Manson, we nowhere note that the readers manifest an inclination toward Judaism.

A supposition with greater probability was first advocated by E. M. Roeth (1836): The readers were predominantly Gentile Christians or simply Christians (thus, e.g., Jülicher, Wrede, Windisch, Michaelis, Albertz, Henshaw, Schierse, Michel, Oepke, Feine-Behm, Käsemann, Kuss). At an early date the Gentile Christians were also regarded as heirs of the blessings and promises of the OT people of God. As Christians, they are the true Israel, the chosen people (Gal. 6:16; I Cor. 10:1, "our fathers"; I Pet. 2:9), for whom the OT was written (Rom. 15:4; I Cor. 10:11; I Pet. 1:12). The mission of primitive Christianity generally made the OT into the Bible of the new congregations, in which they were thoroughly steeped; thus for them it was an incontestable authority and a conclusive source of proof. Already in Galatians Paul expects ordinary Gentile Christians to understand difficult OT scriptural proofs. How much more can that happen in respect to readers for whom such a highly finished epistle as Hebrews is intended, readers who thus must stand upon a certain cultural level. If the author had wanted to inculcate Jewish Christians anew with the fundamental teachings of Christianity (5:12 ff.), then he would not have cited "repentance from dead works and . . . faith toward God, . . . instruction about ablutions, the laying on of hands, the resurrection of the dead, and eternal judgment" (6:1 f.), but the person and work of Christ and the presence of God in the Spirit. What he enumerates are fundamental articles of Gentile mission preaching (Windisch). 13:9 refers to Jewish teachings and food regulations as something strange and unfamiliar, and those who occupy themselves with such matters are held before the readers as a warning. That is not possibly intended for Jewish Christians. The warning against "falling away from the living God" (3:12) points rather to Gentile-Christian than to Jewish-Christian readers. Hebrews does not know the contrast between Jews and Gentiles at all, and does not even have the words Ἰουδαῖος and ἔθνη. The author writes to Christians as Christians.

These Christians, however, are not endangered by a definite heresy. What is meant by the "foods" which do not strengthen the heart (13:9) is not at all plain, but the readers are not decisively characterized by the evaluation of foods which is rejected here. In spite of their admirable Christian past (6:10; 10:32 ff.), the readers are marked by lassitude of faith, fear of suffering, and lack of faithfulness toward the congregation (5:11 f.; 10:25, 35; 12:3 f., 12 f.;

13:17). Against such "general weaknesses" (Kuss), Hebrews intends to warn its readers by portraying the greatness of the salvation which is at stake and by referring to the eschatological urgency of renewed earnestness in respect to the enlightenment once received (6:4). Here we obviously find ourselves in a later period of Christian development.

Where to seek for the readers is a question which, in view of the lack of concrete data in Hebrews, is answered in the most varied ways. Scholars have conjectured Corinth (Lo Bue), Ephesus (Howard), the Lycus Valley (T. W. Manson), Antioch (Spicq), and Cyprus (Riggenbach).

Recently it has often been supposed that the Epistle was directed to Rome (Michaelis, McNeile-Williams, Strathmann, W. Manson, Feine-Behm, Goodspeed; Michel and Albertz think of an Italian church outside Rome). In favor of Rome we can cite these points: 1) Hebrews was first attested in Rome by I Clement. 2) The characterization of the administrators of the congregation as οἱ ἡγούμενοι (13:7, 17, 24) is the same as in I Clem. 1:3; cf. 21:6; Herm., v. II 2, 6; III 9, 7 (προηγούμενοι). 3) "Those who come from Italy send you greetings" (13:24), can most naturally be understood by assuming that the writer is outside of Italy and that the Italians who are among his associates send greetings to their fellow countrymen. But since this reference can also be understood as a greeting from Italy (see Spicq, Ét. bibl. I, 261 ff.), Rome or another Italian congregation remains only one possibility as the address of Hebrews.

5. Author

Since the author of Hebrews keeps himself entirely in the background—only his close connection with Timothy (13:23) points to the Pauline circle, if here the well-known companion of Paul is meant—the most diverse possibilities have been discussed, of which we mention the following:

1. Paul. This supposition today is advocated only seldom, even on the Catholic side; we have already shown that it is untenable (see pp. 276 f.).

2. Luke. Clement of Alexandria (see p. 275), because of Hebrews' stylistic relationship with Acts, regarded Luke as the translator of the epistle written by Paul in Hebrew. But Hebrews is no translation and diverges so strikingly from Acts in style and theological peculiarity that the author of Acts is not to be considered as the author of Hebrews.

3. Clement of Rome. This early hypothesis, known already by Origen (see p. 275), runs aground on the impossibility of considering Hebrews and I Clement as the work of the same man, and upon the literary dependence of I Clement upon Hebrews.

4. Apollos. First discussed by Luther and emphatically advocated by Bleek, this hypothesis has found many supporters (lately, Zahn, Appel, Howard, T. W. Manson, Lo Bue, Spicq). Apollos was an Alexandrian Jewish Christian and authority on the Scriptures, who at the same time had a Greek rhetorical

education at his disposal (Acts 18:24 ff.). Independently of Paul, he promoted a mission (I Cor. 1:12; 3:4 ff.; 16:12). Although Apollos may very well be recognized as the "auctor ad Hebraeos," we do not know whether he was active literarily, nor whether he was the only one among the Christian διδάσκαλοι of the apostolic age who could have written an epistle like Hebrews.

5. Barnabas. In line with the tradition attested by Tertullian, many until today have ascribed Hebrews to Barnabas (such as Riggenbach and Strathmann). Barnabas was a Levite from Cyprus (Acts 4:36), who then became a resident in Jerusalem and a distinguished member of the primitive community (Acts 9:27; 11:22). Is it conceivable that a man like Barnabas could have abandoned so completely the attitude of the primitive church to the OT Law and cultus, and could have been so rhetorically trained and so definitely Alexandrian as the author of Hebrews?

In reality, the person of the author is no longer ascertainable (thus Origen, and since Eichhorn and de Wette most recent scholars). W. Manson would like to see the author "in direct succession to the teaching of Stephen," but not once is there more than an occasional point of contact with Stephen's speech in Acts 7, and the character of Hebrews, which was doubtless influenced by Hellenistic Judaism and Gnosticism, speaks against a Palestinian origin of the author of Hebrews. On the other hand, Jones has demonstrated that Hebrews linguistically and conceptually is most closely related to Luke-Acts within the NT, so that the author of Hebrews, though certainly a Hellenistic Jewish Christian, may have been at home in a Gentile-Christian congregation, with whose tradition the author of Luke-Acts also stands related. Concerning the place of authorship, nothing more precise can be determined, though critics have advanced the most diverse conjectures (Rome, Egypt, Ephesus, Antioch).

6. Time of Composition

To the obvious question whether Jerusalem is yet standing (13:13 f.) and the cult of the temple is still functioning (9:9 f.), Hebrews gives no answer. In its timeless, scribelike movement of thought, only the OT sanctuary plays a role, not the Herodian temple. Neither from the silence about the catastrophe of the year 70, nor from the phrase in 8:13 that the old order of God "is ready to vanish away," can an origin before 70 be inferred (against Guthrie, who wants to date it before 70 or before the Neronian persecution). And the intellectual relationship with Luke-Acts points doubtless to the post-Pauline period. Hebrews was written before 96 (I Clement) (Dulières' dating of 115-17 is arbitrary). Timothy, who as a young man was a missionary helper of Paul, is still alive (13:23). Author and readers belong to the second Christian generation (2:3). The recent sufferings which threaten the readers cause us to think of the time of Domitian (81-96). Accordingly, the Epistle was probably composed between 80 and 90.

II. The Catholic Epistles

§26. GENERAL

E. Fascher, *Kath. Br.*, RGG³ III, 1959, 1198 f.

In addition to the collection of Pauline epistles, the NT contains a second group of epistles, the seven so-called Catholic epistles, which in the manuscripts from time immemorial (cf. already $\mathfrak{P}^{72}$, see p. 364) carried as a superscription the names of the authors, not the addressees (as in the case of the Pauline epistles): James, I II Peter, Jude, I II III John. Even though there are seven so-called open letters in the Apocalypse, and there are two times seven Pauline epistles, the Catholic epistles did not come to be seven in number as the result of an intentional process, but rather because of a slow, fluctuating historical development (see §36). Eusebius (EH II, 23, 24 f.) was the first to speak of the Epistles of James, Peter, John, and Jude as the "seven Catholic epistles." Earlier, individual epistles already were designated as "Catholic": thus by Dionysius Alexandrinus, I John (Eus., EH VII, 25, 7); by Origen, I John, I Peter, Jude, and also Barnabas. At the close of the second century the anti-Montanist, Apollonius, reproached the Montanist, Themison, for drawing up a certain Catholic epistle in imitation of the Apostle (probably John) (cf. Eus., EH V, 18, 5). Apparently I John was the first to receive the designation, "Catholic epistle," which was supposed to characterize the indefiniteness and broadness of its address, in contrast to the strictly defined addresses of II and III John, and then this designation flowed over to the entire group of epistles, among which I John was classified. In any case, the term "catholic" in reference to the extra-Pauline epistles of the NT meant to the earliest Greek ecclesiastical writers not "recognized in the catholic church," but rather the term "catholic" meant to them "intended for the catholic church." But the designation preferred in the West, "Canonical epistles," shows that the original sense of the name was not preserved in its purity.

Of the Catholic epistles, II and III John are clearly not destined for the catholic church. Of the remaining five Catholic epistles, only I Peter has a geographically limited address, whereas the addressees of James are not limited geographically, Jude and II Peter address all Christians, and I John has no address at all. Only the investigation of each epistle can determine whether it is actually intended for a general circle of readers.

In the canon of the Greek Church, the Catholic epistles stand after Acts and before the Pauline epistles. Acts, which began with the history of the primitive church, was followed at once by the epistles of the primitive apostles and members of the primitive church. In the canon of the Latin Church the Pauline epistles, as the earliest apostolic witnesses, precede the Catholic epistles.

§27. The Epistle of James

Commentaries, see pp. 390 f. Studies: A. Meyer, *Das Rätsel des Jk.*, Beih. ZNW 10, 1930 (thereto M. Dibelius, ThRdsch, N.F. 3, 1931, 216 ff. and G. Kittel, DLZ, 3. Folge 3, 1932, 50 ff.); H. Schammberger, *Die Einheitlichkeit des Jk. im antignostischen Kampf*, 1936; G. Kittel, "Der geschichtliche Ort des Jk.," ZNW 41, 1942, 71 ff. (thereto K. Aland, ThLZ, 69, 1944, 97 ff.); *idem*, "Der Jk. und die Apostolischen Väter," ZNW 43, 1950-51, 54 ff.; W. L. Knox, "The Epistle of St. James," JThSt 46, 1945, 10 ff.; J. Bonsirven, DBS 4, 1949, 783 ff. (bibl.); H. J. Schoeps, *Theologie und Geschichte des Judenchristentums*, 1949, 343 ff.; W. Bieder, "Christliche Existenz nach dem Zeugnis des Jk.," ThZ 5, 1949, 93 ff.; M. Lackmann, *Sola fide*, BFTh II, 50, 1949; D. Y. Hadidian, "Palestinian Pictures in the Epistle of James," ExpT 63, 1951-52, 227 f.; G. Eichholz, *Jakobus und Paulus. Ein Beitrag zum Problem des Kanons*, ThEh, N.F. 39, 1953; *idem*, EKL II, 1958, 234 f.; *idem*, *Glaube und Werke bei Paulus und Jakobus*, ThEh, N.F. 88, 1961; J. Jeremias, "Paul and James," ExpT 66, 1954-55, 368 ff;. H. Thyen, *Der Stil der Jüdisch-Hellenistischen Homilie*, FRLANT, N.F. 47, 1956, 14 ff.; L. E. Elliott-Binns, *Galilean Christianity*, StBTh 16, 1956, 45 ff.; M. H. Shepherd, "The Epistle of James and the Gospel of Matthew," JBL 75, 1956, 40 ff.; E. Lohse, "Glaube und Werke—zur Theologie des Jk.," ZNW 48, 1957, 1 ff.; J. B. Souček, "Zu den Problemen des Jk.," EvTh 18, 1958, 460 ff.; W. Marxsen, *Der "Frühkatholizismus" im NT*, 1958, 22 ff.; O. Michel, CBL, 1959, 586 f.; K. Aland, RGG ³ III, 1959, 526 ff.; J. Blinzler, LThK V, 1960, 861 f.; G. Braumann, "Der theologische Hintergrund des Jk.," ThZ 18, 1962, 401 ff.

1. Contents

James begins with the address (1:1): "James, a servant of God and of the Lord Jesus Christ, to the twelve tribes in the dispersion: Greeting." We cannot recognize any methodical train of thought in the content of the Epistle (1:2–5:20). It consists of a chain of separate admonitions of greater and lesser extent, of groups of sayings and shorter sayings, which are arranged more or less at random one after another. The catchwords of the admonition are: Rejoice over trials, which are a school of testing before God, from whom come only good gifts (1:2-18). Hear God's word but also be doers of it (1:19-27). Beware of partiality for the rich against the poor; rather, fulfill the royal law of love (2:1-12). To that is attached, catchwordwise, a reference to the necessity of mercy (2:13). Mere faith is worthless. Right action is what counts, as the examples of Abraham and Rahab show (2:14-26). Watch your tongues (3:1-12). Abandon earthly wisdom and seek the heavenly wisdom (3:13-18). Do not quarrel but have peace, which comes from bowing before God (4:1-10). Do not slander (4:11-12). You merchants, when formulating your plans, do not forget that you stand under God (4:13-16). Again, catchwordwise, the statement is appended, we must do right (4:17). You rich, recognize your guilt and your deserved punishment (5:1-6). Brethren, wait patiently in view of the imminent judgment of God (5:7-11). Swear not (5:12). Reference to the effects of prayer (5:13-18). Save the erring brother (5:19-20). With that, the writing stops short, without an epistolary ending.

2. The Epistle's Lot

From early times until today opinions about the origin and character, time and value of James have varied widely (cf. the detailed presentation in A. Meyer, 8 ff.). Already in I Clement and the Shepherd of Hermas are found echoes of James, but they are not so clear that they would not be understandable from common dependence upon paraenetic tradition (see Dibelius, 30 ff.). The Epistle is missing from the Muratorian canon and the chief witnesses of the "Vetus Latina." It is never quoted by Tertullian, Cyprian, Irenaeus, and Hippolytus. Not until after 200 do definite traces of James appear in Palestine and Egypt, in the epistles "De virginitate," falsely ascribed to Clement of Rome, in the papyrus fragment $\mathfrak{P}^{20}$, and in Origen, who often cites it as "Scripture," but once as ἡ φερομένη Ἰακώβου ἐπιστολή (Commentary on John, 8, 24; edited by Preuschen, 325), and thereby hints that it is disputed. Eusebius (EH II, 23, 25; III 25, 3) still enumerates James among the "Antilegomena," but mentions for the first time that many recognize the Lord's brother as the author. In the Syrian Church scruples against James did not cease, even after James was taken up into the Peshitta. Theodore of Mopsuestia rejected it. In the Greek Church, however, James was generally recognized since the Synod of Laodicea (360) and Athanasius. In the West the earliest witness is the Codex Corbeiensis (ff), which reproduces an old Latin translation from the fourth century. Under the influence of Hilary, Hieronymus, and Augustine, James was defined as canonical at the Synods of Rome (382) and Carthage (397). Yet Hieronymus' *de viris illustribus* 2 carried doubts about the authenticity of James into the Middle Ages, to which were joined the cautious doubt of Erasmus and the sharp polemic of Luther.

Luther's critical judgment about the Epistle is well known ("Preface to the NT" [1545 (1522)] [tr. C. M. Jacobs], in *Works of Martin Luther*. "The Philadelphia Edition," Vol. VI [1932], pp. 439-44; "Preface to the Epistles of Saint James and Saint Jude" [1545 (1522)], *ibid.*, pp. 477-79. See A. Meyer, 4 ff., and WGK, NT, 17 ff.): Because it teaches justification by works, in contradiction to Paul, does not preach Christ, but the Law and a general faith in God, James does not belong in the Bible among the legitimate, principal books of the NT ("a right strawy Epistle in comparison with them, for it has no evangelical manner about it"). Even though there may be many good sayings in it, it is unorganized and Jewish, and therefore not an apostolic writing. Luther would have liked most of all to eliminate James from his Bible, and still in 1543 he rejected the Epistle for use in dogmatic proof.

The opposition to James on dogmatic grounds in the early church (not apostolic, not canonical) and by Luther (irreconcilable with the Pauline gospel), was succeeded in the nineteenth century by doubt of its authenticity on historical-critical grounds. De Wette pronounced the Epistle as unauthentic chiefly because of its language: We cannot believe James the Lord's brother capable of using such fluent Greek. The tendency criticism of the Tübingen school contended that although James combats Paul's doctrine of justification it no longer does so from the standpoint of the earliest, legalistic Jewish Christianity. Hence the Tübingen critics removed the Epistle to the second century and saw in it the pseudepigraphical work of a Jewish Christianity which was drawing near to catholicism. But even after Baur's scheme of primitive Christian history had collapsed, the opinion was still widely held that James belongs to the postapostolic age (see recently, e.g., Jülicher-Fascher, Dibelius, Windisch-Preisker, Ropes, Goodspeed, Aland, Henshaw, Shepherd, Thyen, Souček, Lohse, Easton, Eichholz, Marxsen). The thesis of Spitta and Massebieau (1895-96) gave a new direction to the criticism of James: James is a Jewish writing, which was transformed into a Christian writing simply by the interpolation of the name "Christ" in two places (1:1: καὶ κυρίου Ἰησοῦ Χριστοῦ; 2:1: τοῦ κυρίου ἡμῶν Ἰησοῦ Χριστοῦ). A. Meyer goes farther in this direction in that he interprets James as a Christian revision of a Jewish "Grundschrift," which launched forth into a continuous allegory about Jacob and his twelve sons. The Jewish writing lying at the basis of James, which is to be thought of as related to the Testaments of the Twelve Patriarchs, works systematically with an artistic, allegorical interpretation of the names of Jacob's family. A number of scholars incline toward A. Meyer's hypothesis, which has been worked out with acumen (Jülicher-Fascher, Windisch, A. Farrer, *A Study in Mark,* 1951, 320, Thyen, Easton). Most scholars, however, reject this hypothesis as being too artificial, especially since there is no example of an allegory upon names standing only in the background of a text without any reference to its presence. Dibelius evaluated James from the viewpoint of primitive Christian paraenesis and examined it as a writing without tangible historical points of contact, detached from the author's name, which means no more than a label pasted on; James offers a collection of material from impersonal paraenetic tradition, an arranging together of admonitions of general ethical content, according to the manner characteristic of Greek and Jewish proverbial wisdom. Nonetheless, up to now there has been no lack of scientific theologians whom James reminds primarily of the discourses of Jesus, especially the Sermon on the Mount, and who, therefore, understand the Epistle as the word of a man of the first generation (among others, Feine-Behm, Zahn, Schlatter, Michaelis, Sparks, Heard, Ross, Tasker, Stauffer, Kittel, Lackmann, Michel, Elliott-Binns, Klijn, Guthrie, and the Catholic scholars, among whom Blinzer, however, would not like to reject out of hand composition by a later Jewish Christian). But even in this circle, critics are not agreed as to whether James knew Paul and his theology. Did James write before Paul as the earliest primitive Christian writer known to us (especially Kittel and Michaelis)? Or, does the Epistle advance a polemic against Paul or a misunderstood Paul and belong in the later apostolic age (e.g., Feine-Behm; Guthrie even supposes that Paul polemizes against a misunderstood James!)? In order to elude objections against composition by James, the Lord's brother, an unknown Christian with the widespread name of James is also taken into consideration as the author (cf. Appel, Hauck, Marty, Henshaw, de Zwaan).

3. The Literary Peculiarity of James

According to 1:1, the writing is an epistle of a Christian, James, "to the twelve tribes in the dispersion." This description of the recipients is ambiguous. It can designate Jews outside of Palestine (cf. Schlatter). But the contents of the Epistle nowhere indicate that a Christian is speaking to Jews, and in it there is lacking any characteristic of a missionary writing. If Christians are meant, then we can think of the Jewish Christians of the diaspora (Michaelis, Wikenhauser, Michel, Guthrie, etc.), but that is improbable, because the writer could hardly have designated only the Jewish Christians as "the twelve tribes." Thus there remains only the possibility that James is addressed to Christians as the true Israel, which lives on the earth as sojourners, and has its home in heaven (in the sense of Gal. 6:16; Phil. 3:3; I Pet. 1:1, 17; 2:11; Rev. 7:4; 14:1; Shepherd of Hermas, IX, 17, 1). Yet that is not clearly said. The vagueness of the destination, the impersonal attitude of the contents, and the lack of an epistolary conclusion make doubtful the epistolary nature of James. Certainly the supposition that the epistolary address of James was not attached until later (Goodspeed, Albertz, Elliott-Binns) is improbable, in view of the play on words (χαίρειν 1:1; χαράν 1:2). But the entire writing creates the impression of an essay in epistolary form, which is directed to a wide circle of readers, not to be sharply defined. And the supposition that 2:2 f.; 3:1 f.; 4:13 ff.; 5:1 ff. are allusions to concrete events in a particular congregation (Michaelis, Kittel, Feine-Behm) overlooks the typical character of these warnings which criticize so severely these phenomena of that period. From the point of view of form criticism James, on the whole, gives the undivided impression of being a paraenetic didactic writing which joins together a series of aphorisms and brief discussions. By this literary character its lack of connection is caused: Besides the three longer expositions (2:1 ff., 14 ff.; 3:1 ff.) are found only small groups of aphorisms or even separate aphorisms, which occasionally are connected by means of catchwords, but also often show no kind of recognizable connection. This fact, which was already recognized by Luther ("he makes a jumble of things," "Preface to the Epistles of Saint James and Saint Jude," 1522), corresponds to the character of paraenesis, and should restrain us from establishing artificial connections. Literary critics have correctly pointed to James's relationship with the paraenetic parts of the Pauline epistles and other primitive Christian writings like Hebrews, I Clement, Barnabas, Didache, and Shepherd of Hermas. And Dibelius stretched the framework of observation still further and placed James in the history not only of the Jewish, but also of the Greek and Hellenistic, paraenetic tradition.

In addition to this lack of connection, a second striking fact is the Jewish character of James. This peculiarity was also noted by Luther, who contended that James is the work of a Jew who had only a woolly notion of Christianity (*Luthers Werke*, Weimar edition, *Tischreden*, Vol. V, No. 5443: "Ich halt, dass sie irgend ein Jude gemacht hat, welcher wohl hat hören von den Christen läuten, aber nicht gar zusammenschlagen"). The name of Christ is encountered only in 1:1 and 2:1, and in both places can be omitted without difficulty, though there certainly is no necessity for that (on 2:1 cf. J. Brinktrine, Bb 35, 1954, 40 ff.). The life, death, and resurrection of Christ are not mentioned. The paraenesis does not point to Jesus as an example, but rather to the OT prophets, Job, and Elijah (5:10 f., 17). The thesis of the original Jewish origin of James (see p. 286) is, therefore, thoroughly understandable. But against that thesis certainly is the consideration that in addition to the mention of the name of Christ in 1:1 and 2:1 there is an entire series of features which are understandable only in connection with Christian origin: "Of his own will he brought us forth by the word of truth that we should be a kind of first fruits of his creatures" (1:18), is impossible as a Jewish affirmation about God, but on the other hand is quite understandable as a description of the effect of baptism (cf. W. Nauck, see to §31, 90 ff.; Braumann). "The implanted word, which is able to save your souls" (1:21) cannot be a designation of the Law. "The perfect law . . . of liberty" (1:25) is without parallel as a Jewish expression, even in Qumran (see W. Nauck, ZNW 46, 1955, 138 ff.). "That honorable name by which you are called" (2:7) would be a very unusual designation of the name Yahweh. "The coming of the Lord is at hand" (5:8) in this formulatation is not attested in Jewish sources. The prohibition of swearing (5:12) can be comprehended only as a primitive form of Jesus' saying in Mt. 5:37. And ἐκκλησία as a designation of a particular congregation is not Jewish. Moreover, we find in James numerous parallels with Jesus' sayings, e.g., ask for good gifts (1:5, 17 = Mt. 7:7 ff.); hearers and doers of the word (1:22 = Mt. 7:24 ff.); judge not (4:12 = Mt. 7:1); prayer without doubt (1:6 = Mk. 11:23 f.) (see the list in Kittel, ZNW 41, 84 ff.). These parallels do not rest, however, upon literary dependence on Matthew (Shepherd), but upon the paraenetic tradition of Jesus' sayings which precisely in the postapostolic period was especially widespread (Lohse).

All of these facts show clearly already that James was conceived as a Christian writing. But we can establish this conclusion beyond the shadow of a doubt by examining the relation of 2:14-26 to Paul. Admittedly, this relation is especially debated. For although James's denial of the proposition that man is justified by faith alone (2:24) sounds like a polemic against Rom. 3:28, the contention is often advanced that James by no means presupposes the specific theology of Paul. Rather, "James and Paul come from the same Jewish school" (Thyen, A. Meyer; similarly, Schlatter, Bieder, Michel). To be sure, this contention that James is polemizing against Rom. 3:28 has also been opposed by those scholars who regard James as a writing of the Lord's brother from the beginning of the sixties and suppose as a presupposition of the polemic "a misinterpretation and distortion of the Pauline thesis" (Feine-Behm, Tasker). Indeed, there can be no doubt that Jas. 2:14 ff. is inconceivable without the preceding activity of Paul. For in this section there is not only a polemic against the lack of works, but at the same time it makes two points: 1) Gen. 15:6 proves that in the case of Abraham "faith was active along with his works," which is not obvious in the Genesis text in and of itself; 2) the supposition is untenable that "faith alone" can justify, a supposition not found before Paul. Hence it is unquestionable that James is controverting a view which finally goes back to Paul (cf. Eichholz, Souček, Lohse, etc.). A knowledge of the Pauline epistles, however, is very improbable, in view of the complete misunderstanding of the Pauline formulations (James speaks no more of ἔργα νόμου in contrast to πίστις). James opposes a "Paul who had become formalized" (Eichholz) and presents an inner-Christian controversy, which no longer has Paul for a direct opponent.

Neither is there a clearly recognizable literary connection with other primitive Christian writings. The parallels are strongest with I Peter (cf. Jas. 1:2 f. with I Pet. 1:6 f.; Jas. 4:1 f. with I Pet. 2:11; cf. A. Meyer, 75 ff.). But in none of these instances do the parallels go beyond common dependence upon paraenetic tradition, which in James is less Christianized and actualized than in I Peter (see Lohse, 13 ff.). This paraenesis, which was much alive in Jewish tradition, exhibits a very pure Greek. In the vocabulary of James are found linguistic materials from high style koine, as κατήφεια (4:9), ἀποκνέω (1:15, 18), δελεάζομαι (1:14), τὰ ἐπιτήδεια τοῦ σώματος (2:16). He likes to use rhetorical devices—plays upon words: φαινομένη-ἀφανιζομένη (4:14); διεκρίθητε-κριταί (2:4); ἀδιάκριτος-ἀνυπόκριτος (3:17); χαίρειν-χαράν (1:1 f.); ἔργων-ἀργή (2:20); alliteration: πειρασμοῖς περιπέσητε ποικίλοις (1:2); μικρὸν μέλος-μεγάλα (3:5). The presentation of thoughts in discourse and counter-discourse, question and answer (2:18 f.; 5:13 f., etc.), reminds us of the Hellenistic diatribe. The hexameter in 1:17 is also an indication of the author's literary skill. On the other hand, non-Greek features in language and sentence structure are striking, e.g., τῶν ἵππων τοὺς χαλινοὺς εἰς τὰ στόματα βάλλομεν (3:3); οὔτε ἁλυκὸν γλυκὺ ποιῆσαι ὕδωρ (3:12); 4:13 ff. The translation Greek of the LXX occasionally makes itself noticeable, e.g., 2:1, 9, 13, 16; 5:17. On the whole, however, the Greek is that of an educated Hellenist, of whom the pure Greek address (1:1; otherwise in the NT only in Acts 15:23) is characteristic.

With these statements about the literary character of James, the position of James in respect to other religions, and the language of James, the problems of its authorship and time of composition are raised.

4. Author and Time

Who is the James who introduces himself with the straightforward self-designation, "a servant of God and of the Lord Jesus Christ" (1:1)? In the NT five men are called by this name:

1. James, the son of Zebedee (Mk. 1:19; 3:17 par., etc., Acts 12:2);
2. James, the son of Alphaeus (Mk. 3:18 par.);
3. James, the brother of Jesus, son of Joseph and Mary (Mk. 6:3 par.; I Cor. 15:7; Gal. 1:19; 2:9, 12; Acts 12:17; 15:13; 21:18; Jude 1);
4. James, the younger (Mk. 15:40 par.), son of a Mary (cf. Mk. 16:1);
5. James, the father of the apostle Judas (= Thaddaeus or Lebbaeus?) (Lk. 6:16; Acts 1:13).

The author of James, who without further ado claims authority for his word, cannot be an unknown man without a history. Hence we need not consider the Jameses in the NT of whom we know nothing except the name (#2, #4, #5). #1 is also eliminated, since he became a martyr already in A.D. 44, which doubtless preceded the composition of James. There remains only #3. Indeed, in primitive Christianity there was only one James who was so well known and who assumed such a transcending position that his mere name would identify him sufficiently, James the brother of the Lord. Without doubt, James purports to be written by him. Even if the Epistle is not authentic, it claims the famous James, with all the importance of highly esteemed personality, as the authority for its contents.

This James, having remained in the background during Jesus' lifetime, seems to have been converted soon after Easter by an appearance of the Risen One (I Cor. 15:7; Gospel of the Hebrews, according to Hieronymus, *de viris illustribus* 2; cf. E. Hennecke-W. Schneemelcher, *NT Apocrypha*, I, 165). As the Lord's brother, he became the head of the primitive church (Acts 12:17; Gal. 1:19; Acts 21:18). In his report of the apostolic council Paul names him before Peter among the authorities in highest position (Gal. 2:9). Also according to Acts 15:13 ff. James spoke the decisive word at that time. On the basis of I Cor. 9:5 we may conjecture that James also promoted a mission outside of Jerusalem. The attitude of James toward the primitive Christian conflict over the question of the Law is debated. According to Gal. 2:12, he seems to have belonged to the legalistic wing of the primitive church but hardly to that party which was hostile to Paul (cf. Gal. 2:9). And the picture of the Jewish saint sketched by Hegesippus (in Jos., *Ant.* XX, 200) is doubtless legendary. He died as a martyr in the year 62.

Only two reasons favor the Lord's brother as author of the Epistle:

1. The simplicity of the majestic self-designation (1:1), in which an eminent man cites nothing except his name and his commission as a special instrument in the service of God and of the Lord Jesus Christ;

2. Close, but not literary, parallels with major pieces of gospel tradition.

These arguments, however, not only do not prove much, but are opposed by very weighty difficulties:

1. The cultured language of James is not that of a Palestinian. Hence most advocates of the composition of James by the Lord's brother attribute the linguistic form of James to a Hellenistic Jew who assisted in the writing of the Epistle. Against that, we can say in the first place that the text itself nowhere suggests that a secretary created the linguistic form of the Epistle. In the second place, the question remains completely unanswerable as to what extent the actual author and the secretary shared in the production of the Epistle.

2. It is hardly comprehensible that the Lord's brother, who was so true to the Law, could speak of "the perfect law of liberty" (1:25) and could concretize the Law by means of ethical commands (2:11 f.) and yet not even by way of suggestion call attention to any of the cultic, ritualistic commands.

3. Would the Lord's brother really omit every allusion to Jesus and his relation to him, though he emphatically introduces himself in his authoritative role?

4. The controversy in 2:14 ff. with a misunderstood aftereffect of Pauline theology presupposes such a temporal distance from Paul that it could not have been written by James who was killed in the year 62. Furthermore, this passage reveals such a complete ignorance of the polemic meaning of the Pauline theology that we may hardly attribute it to James, who as late as c. 55/56 met with Paul in Jerusalem (Acts 21:18 ff.).

5. As the history of the canon shows (see p. 285), James was only very slowly, and against opposition, recognized as the work of the Lord's brother, and hence as apostolic and canonical. Accordingly, there seems to have been no early tradition concerning its origin from the Lord's brother.

Thus if there can be no doubt that an unknown Christian placed his exhortatory writing under the authority of the former leader of the church in Jerusalem, then it is very difficult to determine exactly the circumstances of its origin. In view of the author's life in the Jewish tradition, it is very probable that he was a Jewish Christian, but he did not belong to the "Ebionite" circles which were separating from Gentile Christianity (Schoeps). His familiarity with the LXX, his literary language, and his designation of the Christians as people of the diaspora (1:1) speak against the supposition that the author was a Palestinian (Michaelis, Hadidian; contrary, Eichholz, Easton). Nothing favors composition in Galilee (Elliott-Binns), whereas in behalf of composition in Syria Shepherd can at least adduce the fact that the earliest attestation of James in the third century is found in works which originated in Syria. Any other place of eastern Jewish Christianity is just as conceivable, but Rome (Henshaw) is quite improbable.

The time of composition of James can hardly be determined more precisely than at the end of the first century. A much later dating is unfounded, for the contention that James shows signs of the anti-Gnostic struggle (Schammberger, Schoeps), rests upon an exaggerated interpretation of certain Hellenistic formulations. But James cannot be dated earlier in view of its doctrinal separation from Paul.

5. The Theological Problem

A theological problem in connection with James has existed ever since Luther (1522) established an irreconcilable antithesis between James and Paul. Our insight into the origin of James at the end of the first century, as well as the exact exegesis of Jas. 2:14 ff., have shown that a pre-Pauline composition of James can be as little supposed as a direct opposition to Paul by James. If it proves true that there is "no actual encounter between James and Paul in Jas. 2" (Eichholz, 1953, 41), then it also turns out to be correct that "as propositions the statements of James cannot be brought into harmony with those of the real Paul, and that there exists not only tension, but opposition, in respect to content" (Souček). This statement points to a genuine theological problem, for Paul and James stand in the canon of the NT and are, therefore, bearers of revelation, however we may determine the character of the norm of the canon (see §37). In view of these facts, it is natural to brush off the contrast and to interpret the discourse about "justification by works" (Jas. 2:24) as referring to the believer, "who claims for himself the guilt- and sin-offering of Christ, which sanctifies him unto the obedience of faith" (Lackmann, 65), or to see the man of faith in James's sense caught up "into that movement which the Lord, in view of his parousia, will enkindle in the poor chosen by him" (Bieder, 100; cf. James 2:5). But even if we refrain from such an introduction of Pauline theology into James, the contentions hardly prove true that James in his struggle with a Paul who has been formalized says the same thing in his time as Paul did in his (Eichholz), or that James, like Paul, repeats what Jesus said, only the former corresponds to the beginning and the latter to the ending of the Sermon on the Mount (Jeremias). On the one hand, we must properly take into consideration the terminology and the divergent polemic direction of Paul and James, and thus be able to establish a considerably greater mutuality between both forms of theological address than Luther saw. On the other hand, some have incorrectly denied that in James in contrast to Paul there is a "synergistic understanding of faith and works," and have likewise wrongly maintained that also in James "the imperative is not without the indicative, which establishes it" (Eichholz, 1961, 38).

If we want to solve properly the problem caused by the juxtaposition of Paul and James in the canon, then we must carefully distinguish between two questions: 1) Schlatter is doubtless correct in saying that the churches "have seriously harmed themselves by granting to James only a completely superficial hearing." Thus we can regard James as thoroughly indispensable to Christianity (Eichholz), because he seeks "to maintain the solidarity of the life of the community" (Souček), over against the danger of a mere internalization of faith. In other words, we must answer the question in the affirmative whether James, when he is interpreted according to his concrete purpose, does not have something decisive to say to a Christianity which in some respects exhibits the same degenerate "faith" which he attacked. 2) On the other hand, we must say at once that in view of the lack of the actual Christian message in James and in view of his contradiction of the central Pauline proclamation, we "are called to an evangelical criticism of James, not of his practical sayings, but of his form of theology" (P. Althaus, in "Das Menschenbild im Lichte des Evangeliums," *Festschrift für E. Brunner*, 1950, 48). Where James "is no more understood as a correction but as the basis" (Marxsen), there is a theological misuse of this writing. James can perform his indispensable task in the canon only where Christians have previously heard the message of Jesus or of Paul, and then let their eyes be sharpened for the exhortation to the work of faith which is already contained in this message, but not so exclusively formulated.

§28. The First Epistle of Peter

Commentaries, see p. 391. Studies: R. PERDELWITZ, *Die Mysterienreligionen und das Problem des I Pt.*, RVV 11, 3, 1911; W. BORNEMANN, "Der I Pet.—eine Taufrede des

Silvanus?," ZNW 19, 1919-20, 143 ff.; L. RADERMACHER, "Der I Pet. und Silvanus," ZNW 27, 1926, 287 ff.; B. H. STREETER, *The Primitive Church*, 1929, 115 ff.; W. C. VAN UNNIK, *De verlossing I Petrus 1:18-19 en het probleem van den eersten Petrusbrief*, Mededeelingen der Nederlandsche Akademie van Wetenschappen, Afdeeling Letterkunde, Nieuwe Reeks, Deel 5, Nr. 1, 1942; *idem*, "Christianity According to I Peter," ExpT 68, 1956-57, 79 ff.; R. BULTMANN, "Bekenntnis- und Liedfragmente im I Pet.," *Conjectanea Neotestamentica XI in honorem A. Fridrichsen*, 1947, 1 ff.; E. G. SELWYN, "The Persecutions in I Peter," SNTSB 1950, 39 ff.; J. DANIÉLOU, *Sacramentum Futuri*, 1950, 140 f.; C. L. MITTON, "The Relationship Between I Peter and Ephesians," JThSt, N.S. 1, 1950, 67 ff.; PH. CARRINGTON, "Saint Peter's Epistle," *The Joy of Studies*, Festschr. F. C. Grant, 1951, 57 ff.; J. KNOX, "Pliny and I Peter," JBL 72, 1953, 187 ff.; F. C. CROSS, *I Peter. A Paschal Liturgy*, 1954; E. LOHSE, "Paränese und Kerygma im I Pet.," ZNW 45, 1954, 68 ff.; W. NAUCK, "Freude im Leiden," ZNW 46, 1955, 68 ff.; C. F. D. MOULE, "The Nature and Purpose of I Peter," NTSt 3, 1956-57, 1 ff.; M.-E. BOISMARD, "Une liturgie baptismale dans la Prima Petri," RB 63, 1956, 182 ff.; 64, 1957, 161 ff.; S. J. BUSE, in "Christian Baptism," ed. by A. Gilmore, 1960, 170 ff.; S. E. JOHNSON, "The Preaching to the Dead," JBL 79, 1960, 48 ff.; T. C. G. THORNTON, "I Peter, a Paschal Liturgy?," JThSt, N.S. 12, 1961, 14 ff.; E. FASCHER, RGG [3] V, 1961, 257 ff.; R. P. MARTIN, *The Composition of I Peter in Recent Study*, VE 29 ff.

1. Contents

A simple organization of I Peter cannot be given because of its paraenetic character. Each delineation is no more than a possibility. After the address (1:1), follows praise of God, by whose mercy the readers have been born anew to hope in future salvation, which is certain in spite of present suffering, especially since the prophecies of the prophets are now fulfilled (1:3-12). Thereupon follow admonitions to adhere to this hope with confidence in the blood of Christ, to live as those who have been born again, and to be built into the spiritual temple of Christ (1:13–2:10). A second group of exhortations deals with the relation to the world (2:11–4:6): maintain good conduct among outsiders (2:11 f.); be subject to rulers (2:13-17); "Haustafel" (2:18–3:12); readiness for suffering, responsibility toward non-Christians, renunciation of sins (3:13–4:6), after which general admonitions and a doxology form a conclusion (4:7-11). Then the exhortation to proper endurance of suffering begins anew (4:12-19), and there follow admonitions to elders and those who are younger (5:1-5), which again are concluded by general exhortations (5:6-11). Concluding epistolary ending and greetings (5:12-14).

2. Readers

According to the address, the apostle Peter writes "to the exiles of the dispersion (ἐκλεκτοῖς παρεπιδήμοις διασπορᾶς) in Pontus, Galatia, Cappadocia, Asia, and Bithynia." If these names are supposed to designate the Roman provinces (Schelkle), then the Epistle is directed to the Christians in Asia Minor in general; yet Lycia, Pamphylia, and Cilicia in the south are omitted. However, these names can also refer to the old territories. In favor of this alternative, Wikenhauser and Michaelis point out that the readers, according to 1:14, 18; 2:9 f.; 4:3 f., are clearly Gentile Christians. But in the south of the province Galatia (Iconium, Lystra, Derbe) there was no lack of Jewish Christians (Acts 13, 14). Moreover, I Peter, when the names are interpreted as referring to the territories, is not directed to Paul's mission region. Nevertheless, these arguments are hardly sufficient for a decision one way or the other, and therefore the author's selection of these geographical names remains inexplicable. And the idea that the southern territories are omitted because no "ecclesiastically" colored Christianity existed there (W. Bauer, *Rechtgläubigkeit*, see to §24, 85 f.) is completely unprovable. Since the Epistle is intended for Gentile Christians, the "exiles of the dispersion" in the territories named are to be understood figuratively. The Christians are thought of as members of the true people of God, who live scattered as exiles upon the earth, since their true home is in heaven (cf. Gal. 6:16; Phil. 3:20; Hb. 13:14; also I Pet. 1:17; 2:11). The supposition that these Gentile Christians had previously adhered to synagogues as "Godfearers" (van Unnik, Klijn) is arbitrary.

3. Purpose and Literary Character

The Epistle presents itself as a writing of comfort and exhortation (5:12). In the face of persecution, hate, suffering, and humiliating defamation, the readers should remain steadfast in their Christianity, in the "true grace of God," in view of the heavenly goal, which beckons to all who hold fast to the Christian faith and in good conduct do not go astray. What is the nature of the persecution to which the addressees see themselves exposed? It has often been suggested that obviously calumnies from the side of Gentile fellow countrymen (2:12, 15; 3:14 ff.; 4:3 f., 14 f.) have led to false accusations against the Christians in court, which the Christians experience as surprising (1:6; 4:12); a civil persecution is by no means present, and in view of the positive attitude toward the state (2:13 ff.) is inconceivable (e.g., Wikenhauser, Albertz, Meinertz, Feine-Behm, Höpfl-Gut, Selwyn, Moule, Schelkle, Fascher, van Unnik, Guthrie). Just as it is plain that the personal animosity of Gentile countrymen caused the action against these Christians, it is also clear that they were arraigned ὡς Χριστιανός (4:16) and not on the basis of charges as moral wrongdoers (2:20; 4:15). Further, these accusations are not locally limited, but befall all of Christendom (5:9), and therefore should be interpreted as the beginning of the final judgment (4:7, 17). In view of the inherent danger of apostasy (5:8 ff.), the author wants to convince the readers that such suffering must be regarded as God's means of testing before the imminent appearance of Christ (1:6 f.; 4:12 f., 19), and the traditional admonition to obedience in no wise stands in tension therewith (2:20!).

Students of I Peter have called our attention to the fact that the situation of the addressees does not seem to be the same throughout the Epistle. Whereas in 4:12, 14, 19; 5:6, 8 the suffering is described as a present condition, 1:6;

2:20; and 3:14, 17 reckon only with the possibility of suffering. Moreover, since 1:3–4:11 bears no kind of epistolary character, and closes in 4:11 with a doxology, while on the contrary 4:12 ff. addresses Christians in a concrete situation of suffering, as well as πρεσβύτεροι and νεώτεροι, some critics see here a further indication of the divergent origin of 1:3–4:11 and 4:12 ff. Finally, it has also been pointed out that in 1:3, 12, 23; 2:2, 10, 25; 3:21, and thus only in the section 1:3–4:11, we find clear allusions to the fact that the Christians addressed were recently baptized. From all of these observations, scholars have drawn a series of very diverse conclusions. Some regard the differences between 1:3–4:11 and 4:12 ff. as inconsequential and interpret 1:3–5:11 as a baptismal sermon which secondarily was given an epistolary framework (Bornemann, Albertz; with questions, Fascher; A. Adam, *Wort und Dienst, Jbch. der Theologischen Schule Bethel* 1952, 20, and J. Daniélou, *Sacramentum Futuri*, 1950, 141, think of a baptismal sermon during Passover week). Others suppose that a baptismal sermon (1:3–4:11) and an exhortatory writing by the same author (Perdelwitz, Streeter, Windisch, Beare[1], Schneider, W. Nauck, see to §31, 48, note 9), or a baptismal discourse before and one after baptism (Buse, Martin), or two epistles, one to those not yet persecuted, and the other to those being persecuted (Moule), were joined together into one writing. Preisker wants to see in I Peter the compilation of liturgical pieces of a baptismal service, in which we are to think of the baptism as taking place between 1:21 and 1:22, which is not mentioned because of secret discipline (similarly, in connection with another arrangement, Boismard). Cross concludes from the repeated emphasis upon πάσχειν and πάθος, and from parallels with Hippolytus' *Apostolic Tradition*, that at the basis of I Peter lie instructions for the bishop's baptism during the Passover season. And A. Strobel speaks of a "passover festival circular letter" and of a "passover baptismal ritual" (NovT 2, 1958, 210, 212, 219). Thornton has correctly objected against the last mentioned thesis that the connection between πάσχα and πάσχειν is first attested in the late second century, and is still unknown in the first century, and that otherwise nothing in I Peter refers to the Passover festival. And apart from all other difficulties, the following consideration speaks decisively against the supposition of a "liturgy": we cannot conceive how "a liturgy-homily, shorn of its 'rubrics,' . . . but with its changing tenses and broken sequences all retained, could have been hastily dressed up as a letter and sent off (without a word of explanation) to Christians who had not witnessed its original setting" (Moule, 4). Likewise, the presupposition that 1:3–4:11 and 4:12 ff. presuppose a different situation of the readers in respect to suffering hardly proves correct. In the first place, the first section already presupposes the readers' experiences of suffering (1:6, λυπηθέντες 2:12; 3:16; 4:4). In the second place, Nauck has shown that I Peter's conceptions of "joy in suffering" originated in a "Jewish, primitive Christian persecution tradition," in which the suffering experienced was interpreted as the eschatologically necessary and expected suffering (ZNW 46, 1955, 79 f.). The supposition of a compilation of I Peter from two parts is, therefore, unnecessary and improbable (so also Michaelis, Selwyn, Lohse, Nauck, Beare[2], Martin, Thornton, van Unnik,

Guthrie). And the supposition that the epistolary framework (1:1 f.; 5:12-14) was later placed around 1:3–5:11 is opposed by the clear contacts this framework exhibits with the body of the Epistle (cf. παρεπίδημοι 1:1 with 1:17; 2:11 and 5:12 with 4:12). The eulogy in the epistolary introduction (1:3 ff.) and the "Haustafel" (2:18 ff.) also favor our view that I Peter was conceived as an "Epistle."

Certainly, then, the undeniable references in I Peter to baptism must be explained. A complete baptismal sermon sent out as an epistle hardly need be considered, because the "Haustafel" (2:18 ff.) and the paraenesis (3:8 ff.; 4:7 ff.) are not suited to a baptismal sermon. Lohse has correctly emphasized that the actual theme of the Epistle is the strengthening of Christians for suffering, and that the references to baptism are found almost entirely in 1:3–2:10. In addition, it appears that possibly several hymns were assimilated (2:6-8, Selwyn; 2:21-25, Lohse; 3:18-22, Lohse, Johnson; Bultmann seeks to combine 1:20; 3:18 f., 22 into a confession; for criticism, cf. Martin, 31 ff.). Even if the reconstruction of these hymns remains uncertain, their absorption also speaks against a complete baptismal sermon. And finally we must note that the readers' situation of suffering doubtless presupposes that the Christians addressed had not been newly baptized (Michaelis). If we take together all of these facts, we shall regard I Peter as an exhortatory writing formed from traditional paraenetic and possibly liturgical material, addressed to young Christian communities, whereby the reminder of the gift of baptism and the eschatologically grounded universality of this suffering serves to place before the eyes of these Christians in a convincing manner the necessity and the power to persevere in suffering.

4. Author

In the address the author calls himself "Peter, an apostle of Jesus Christ," and designates himself as συμπρεσβύτερος καὶ μάρτυς τῶν τοῦ Χριστοῦ παθημάτων (5:1). He writes διὰ Σιλουανοῦ (5:12), and from "Babylon" (5:13). Although the address clearly points to Peter as the author, "witness of the sufferings of Christ" hardly designates an eyewitness of Christ's own sufferings (Feine-Behm), but a Christian, who, like the Christians addressed, has experienced "the sufferings of Christ" and can witness to them (H. v. Campenhausen, *Die Idee des Martyriums in der alten Kirche*, 1936, 64 f.; H. Strathmann, ThWB IV, 498 f.; W. Michaelis, ThWB V, 934), or, who, like them, is a "witness for the sufferings of Christ" (J. Schneider; Bauer-Arndt-Gingrich, *Lexicon*, 495). To this understanding of 5:1 points the apposition, "a partaker in the glory that is to be revealed," since the state of being a witness is parallel to future participation in glory. Hence the self-designation of the author in 5:1 does not point especially to an apostle or eyewitness of Jesus. The Silvanus mentioned in 5:12, according to all probability, is identical with Paul's pupil Silvanus (I Thess. 1:1; II Thess. 1:1; II Cor. 1:19), and with Paul's companion, Silas (Acts 15:22-32; 15:40–18:5). Otherwise, we hear nothing of a connection between Silvanus-Silas and

Peter. And also Μᾶρκος ὁ υἱός μου (5:13) was, to be sure, a Jerusalemite (Acts 12:12) but is met otherwise only as a colaborer with Paul or Barnabas (Acts 13:5, 13; 15:37, 39; Col. 4:10; Phlm. 24), not in connection with Peter. Thus all of these data cannot serve to support the statement of 1:1 that Peter was the author of I Peter. Neither does 1:3 ff. point to a witness of the resurrection (Feine-Behm), nor the reference to the example of the suffering Christ (2:21-24) to a personal disciple of Jesus (Wikenhauser). At the most, the naming of "Babylon" (5:13) as the place of composition of I Peter, could or should support the statement of 1:1. For it is very improbable that this reference is to the Mesopotamian Babylon (Schlatter, J. Munck, see to §16, 141n, 275), or even to an Egyptian military post of this name (de Zwaan; with hesitation, Klijn), because no tradition is known that Peter was ever in these places. On the other hand, in the Jewish apocalyptic of the first century after Christ, and correspondingly also in Rev. 14:8; 16:19; 17:5; 18:2, 10, 21, "Babylon" is a pseudonym for Rome (see Windisch and Schelkle on I Pet. 5:13), and "Babylon" may also have this meaning in I Pet. 5:13. Then this statement of place pre-supposes the composition of I Peter in Rome, since the conception of a Roman stay by Peter is doubtless attested at the end of the first century (cf. O. Cullmann, *Peter*, 1962, 82 ff.; E. Dinkler, ThRdsch, N.F. 25, 1959, 206 ff.; 27, 1961, 37 f.).

There are, however, several decisive arguments against the derivation of I Peter from Peter, a derivation which is advocated in the epistolary framework of I Peter but in other respects not amplified at all:

a) The language of I Peter is in impeccable Greek, which uses numerous rhetorical devices: word order (1:23; 3:16); parallel clauses (4:11); series of similar compounds (1:4), etc. (cf. Selwyn, 26; Schelkle, 13; Radermacher, 287 f.). And the numerous OT quotations and allusions stem without exception from the LXX. Both are inconceivable for the Galilean Peter.

b) I Peter presupposes Pauline theology, not only in the general sense that for Gentile-Christian readers, the "people of God" (2:10), the problem of the fulfillment of the Law generally seems to exist no more, but also in the special sense that as in Paul the death of Jesus atones for the sins of Christians and effects righteousness (1:18 f.; 2:24); Christians should suffer with Christ (4:13; 5:1); obedience toward civil rulers is demanded (2:14 f.); and the Pauline formula ἐν Χριστῷ (3:16; 5:10, 14) is encountered. The repeatedly advocated supposition of a literary dependence of I Peter upon Romans (and Ephesians) (McNeile-Williams, Beare, Feine-Behm, Mitton) is, of course, improbable, because the linguistic parallels can be explained out of the common catechetical tradition (see the proof by Selwyn, 365 ff.). Yet we cannot doubt that the author of I Peter stands in the succession of Pauline theology (otherwise Guthrie, who thinks that Peter heard Paul preach in Rome!). Is that conceivable of the Peter who still at the time of Gal. 2:11 ff. was able to follow only with uncertainty the Pauline principle of Gentile-Christian freedom from the Law?

To be sure, numerous scholars would like to refute both of these arguments

by supposing, upon the basis of 5:12 (διὰ Σιλουανοῦ ὑμῖν . . . ἔγραψα) that
Silvanus was the actual author, to whom Peter simply gave the order to write
(besides the Catholics, e.g., Michaelis, Feine-Behm, Lo Bue, de Zwaan, Klijn, van
Unnik, McNeile-Williams, Henshaw, Heard, Schneider, Hunter, Selwyn, Stibbs-
Walls, Carrington, L. Goppelt, *Die apostolische und nachapostolische Zeit*, 1962,
75, 153; Guthrie, as a possible alternative to direct composition by Peter).
Selwyn even thinks that he can show clear similarities in the language of I II
Thessalonians, I Peter, and Acts 15:29, which point to the common authorship
of Silvanus. But these linguistic parallels are far too insignificant to carry much
weight, and elsewhere the distinction in style between I II Thessalonians and
I Peter is significant. Nor has anyone yet demonstrated that γράφω διά τινος can
mean to have a piece of writing composed by another. Moreover, Peter then in
no wise would be the actual author of I Peter (cf. against this "secretary hypothesis" Beare[2], 188 ff.).

If, however, attempts can be made to counter arguments a) and b) by referring the composition of I Peter to Silvanus on order of Peter, then there are
two additional and irrefutable arguments against tracing back the Epistle to
Peter:

c) I Peter contains no kind of hint of an acquaintance with the earthly
Jesus, his life, teaching, and death, but refers only generally to the "suffering"
of Christ. That Peter should neither have strengthened his authority through
reference to his personal relationship to Jesus nor have alluded in any way to
the example of Jesus is hardly conceivable.

d) The situation of persecution of the addressees can be understood only as
the beginning of civil persecution (see pp. 294 f.). According to the unanimous
early ecclesiastical tradition, the first persecution of Christians which was not
merely local (cf. 5:9) took place under Domitian (Melito in Eus. EH IV,
26, 9), which doubtless takes us far beyond the lifetime of Peter.

I Peter is, therefore, doubtless a pseudonymous writing (so, first, H. H.
Cludius, 1808; recently, Albertz, Goodspeed, Jülicher-Fascher, Riddle-Hutson,
Beare, Windisch, F. Hauck, NTD 10, 1933, 36; the question of authorship is
left open by Cross, Moule, Schelkle). Certainly the pseudonymity is carried
out only in the epistolary framework, and even there extremely cautiously. It
is also clear that the uncertain conduct of the churches in Asia Minor at the
beginning of the persecution occasioned the author to write. He claims Peter
as his authority for his exhortation, into which he has incorporated much traditional paraenetic material. Yet we cannot recognize why this Gentile Christian
drew upon the authority precisely of Peter, unless the place of composition provided the opportunity for that. Our inability to determine the motive for
pseudonymity does not tell against its existence (against Guthrie).

5. Place and Time of Composition

If by "Babylon" (5:13) Rome is meant (see p. 297), then I Peter by all means
could have been written in Rome, where Peter supposedly died, and where

early appeals were made to his authority (I Clem. 5:3 f.). That I Peter was known in the East already by Polycarp (Phil. 1:3; 8:1; 10:2) and Papias (according to Eus., EH III, 39, 17), whereas in the West it is missing from the Muratorian canon (according to Guthrie because of a lacuna!), and certainly is cited by Irenaeus and Tertullian, proves only that I Peter was known in the church in the East, but nothing about the place of composition. As the time of composition we have to suppose the period of Domitian's reign, since there is no reason at all to go down into the beginning of the second century because of the persecution "as Christians" (4:16) (Beare), or to the time of Trajan's persecution (Riddle-Hutson, Knox, Lake). 90-95 is, therefore, the most probable time of composition.

§29. THE EPISTLE OF JUDE

Commentaries, see p. 391. Studies: B. H. STREETER, *The Primitive Church*, 1929, 178 ff.; A. MEYER, *Das Rätsel des Jk.*, Beih. ZNW 10, 1930, 82 ff.; R. LECONTE, DBS IV, 1949, 1285 ff.; E. FASCHER, RGG [3] III, 1959, 966 f.; J. BLINZLER, LThK V, 1960, 1155 f.

1. Contents

After the address (1 f.), the author gives the occasion of his writing—the appearance of false teachers, who deny God and Christ. In the face of such sacrilege, there is an urgent need to contend for the faith which has been delivered (3 f.). Similar judgment threatens them as met Israel in the wilderness, the fallen angels, and Sodom and Gomorrah (5-7). The picture of the false teachers (8-16) shows libertinism: They resemble Cain, Balaam, Korah; they destroy the life of the congregation (love feasts) with their debaucheries; but they themselves face a frightful judgment, as Enoch prophesied. The readers should remember the preaching of the apostles, who predicted the appearance of such scoffers in the last time (17-19). Hold fast to faith, prayer, love, and hope in final salvation (20 f.). In respect to the erring ones, combine abhorrence for their sins with saving love (22 f.). Conclusion: Doxology (24 f.).

2. Purpose and Literary Character

The Epistle fights against libertine, Gnostic, false teachers. They have gained admission into the congregation; they set up divisions (19), and they defile the love feasts (12). Their mouths speak excessively (16), probably in consciousness of their pneumatic superiority. They want to be *pneumatikoi*, but this predicate is denied to them: They are worldly people (19) and dreamers (8), i.e., probably visionaries. They turn away from the grace of God and deny the only Master and Lord, Jesus Christ (4). They place themselves above all God-ordained spiritual authorities (8). Scorn of God and Christ and of the good heavenly angelic powers is their religious sacrilege, like that of Korah, who rebelled against God's order (11). With the pride of fanatical *pneumatikoi* they combine the offense of exciting, voluptuous living. They pervert the grace of God into licentiousness (4), and defile their flesh. Like dumb animals, they follow their physical desires (7 f., 10, 18), and, like wild waves of the sea, they foam out their own shame (13). They are, therefore, advocates of a Gnostic trend, which contended that the real pneumatic being is not touched by what the flesh does. This characteristic does not fit any specific Gnostic system of the second century.

Libertine Gnosticism of a similar sort, however, is resisted in Rev. 2:6, 14 f., 20 ff., in the Pastorals, and to some extent in I Corinthians. But it is not possible to draw lines of connection between the related phenomena here and there. In the age of syncretism, during which primitive Christianity spread, similar phenomena could appear spontaneously at any time and any place.

It is, nevertheless, significant that the views of the Gnostics are not actually refuted in particular. Rather, the false teachers are reviled and threatened with God's judgment (5-7, 12 f., 15), whereas the addressees are admonished to hold fast to "the faith which was once for all delivered to the saints" (3, 20). Although such a brand of polemic against heretics is contradictory to the usual NT struggle against false teachers, it does correspond with the fact that the Epistle contains no real proclamation of Christ at all. Jude, with its "primitive catholic" concept of faith, stands in irreconcilable discord with the understanding of faith in the principal NT witnesses.

The form of Jude is hardly epistolary: address, "to those who are called, beloved in God the Father and kept for Jesus Christ" (1), and liturgical conclusion (24 f.). Although 4, 12 allude to the appearance of Gnostics in the congregations, it is not at all obvious that the "Epistle" is directed to specific congregations (so Michaelis, Wikenhauser, Lo Bue, Schneider, Schelkle). We cannot discern clearly whether the Christians addressed were former Jews or Gentiles, yet the intemperance criticized makes us think rather of Gentile Christians.

3. Author and Time of Composition

The author calls himself "Jude, a servant of Jesus Christ and brother of James" (1). There can be no doubt which of the various bearers of the name Jude known in the NT is meant. As "brother of James" he is characterized clearly enough. There was only one eminent, well-known James, the brother of the Lord (Jas. 1:1; Gal. 1:19; 2:9; I Cor. 15:7). Then Jude is one of the brothers of Jesus, the third named in Mk. 6:3, the fourth in Mt. 13:55. Otherwise, we know nothing about this Jude. Of course, we have Hegesippus' report (in Eus., EH III, 20, 1 ff.). According to Hegesippus, at the end of Domitian's reign (c. 95), two grandsons of Jude, the brother of the Lord, were accused of belonging to the family of David, whom Domitian had ordered slain. The emperor, having personally examined the two grandsons, dismissed them as harmless.

They were then rulers of the churches (ἡγήσασθαι τῶν ἐκκλησιῶν) and lived until the time of Trajan (98-117). But from that account we learn only that the name of this brother of Jesus was still known toward the end of the first century.

Obviously, the Epistle of Jude pretends to be written by this brother of Jesus. For the supposition that the author was an otherwise unknown Jude who had a brother James (Appel, Henshaw) is extremely improbable in view of the linguistic accord between Jude 1 and Jas. 1:1. And the equating of the author of Jude with Bishop Jude named in the old Jerusalem list of bishops (H. Grotius, Streeter; similarly A. Adam, ZKG, 4, Folge 6, 1957, 46, and G. Klein, *Die Zwölf Apostel*, FRLANT, N.F. 59, 1961, 100) runs aground on the fact that we know nothing as to whether this bishop had a brother named James. Can Jude be written by Jude, the brother of Jesus?

The author was likely a Jewish Christian, for he knows Jewish apocalyptic writings, the *Assumption of Moses* (9), the *Apocalypse of Enoch* (14), and the Jewish Legend (9, 11). The author, however, "speaks of the Apostles as a disciple long afterwards" (17; Luther, "Preface to Jude," 1522), and presupposes not only the conception of "the faith which was once for all delivered to the saints" (3), but he also quotes in a similar manner late Jewish and primitive Christian prophecy concerning false teachers at the end of time (14 f., 17). Such factors point to the late period of primitive Christianity. Furthermore, Jude's pure Greek language, like his quotation of the Greek translation of the *Apocalypse of Enoch* (see J. Cantinat in Robert-Feuillet, 603), fits poorly a Galilean. The repeatedly advocated supposition that Jude actually derives from the brother of the Lord (thus most of the Catholic scholars, plus, e.g., Heard, Sparks, Feine-Behm, Schneider, Guthrie) is therefore extremely unlikely, and Jude is probably a pseudonymous writing (Knopf, Windisch-Preisker, Barnett, Jülicher-Fascher, Dibelius, Michaelis, Henshaw, Goodspeed, A. Meyer; with questions, Schelkle), especially if Jude 1 refers back to a pseudonymous James (see pp. 290 f.).

The early ecclesiastical attestation is at first good but then becomes uncertain. II Peter used Jude (see §30), and the Muratorian canon, Tertullian, and Clement of Alexandria regarded it as canonical. On the other hand, Origen quoted it, but did not regard it as a part of the canon (Eus., EH VI, 25). Eusebius (EH II, 23, 25; III, 25, 3), like Hieronymus, considered Jude as among the "disputed" writings. Nevertheless, this doubt of the canonicity of Jude obviously does not rest upon an independent tradition, but upon the offense caused by Jude's use of the Apocrypha. In the canonical lists of the Western Church, Jude has stood uncontested since the fourth century. Luther, regarding Jude as dependent upon II Peter and as postapostolic, did not enumerate it among "the true, undoubted principal books of the NT." Luther found only a few followers until J. D. Michaelis.

Jude doubtless belongs in the late period of primitive Christianity, but we lack all ways and means of determining more precisely the time of its origin. The reference to James points to the end of the first century as *terminus a quo*, but there is no adequate reason for placing it as late as c. 125 (Goodspeed, Barnett). The most probable dating is around the turn of the century. We know nothing about the place of composition.

§30. THE SECOND EPISTLE OF PETER

Commentaries, see p. 391. Studies: U. HOLZMEISTER, "Vocabularium secundae epistolae S. Petri erroresque quidam de eo divulgati," Bb 30, 1949, 339 ff.; E. KÄSEMANN, "Eine Apologie der urchristlichen Eschatologie," ZThK 49, 1952, 272 ff. (= Exegetische Versuche und Besinnungen I, 1960, 135 ff.); W. MARXSEN, Der "Frühkatholizismus" im NT, 1958, 7 ff.; G. H. BOOBYER, "The Indebtedness of 2 Peter to 1 Peter," NT Essays in Memory of T. W. Manson, 1959, 34 ff.; E. FASCHER, RGG [3] V, 1961, 259 f.

1. Contents

After the address (1:1 f.), there follow as epistolary introduction a reminder to the readers of all the great things which the divine Power has granted to them, and an admonition to be most zealous in escaping from worldly corruption and in obtaining knowledge, in order thus to gain entrance into the eternal kingdom of Christ (1:3-11). Peter, with his death in view, wants to refer the readers once more to the transfiguration of the Lord, of which he was a witness, as a preview of the coming parousia, and to the trustworthy prophetic word of the OT (1:12-21). An important concern of the Epistle is the urgent warning against false prophets (ch. 2), who will seek to bring in destructive heresies, who do not recognize Christ as Lord, who give themselves over to licentiousness, voluptuous living, and base greed, and with their wiles constitute a danger to those just converted. These false teachers are prophesied (2:1-3), and described as present (2:9-12). 3:1-13 refers to ch. 1 and warns of scoffers who will say that the parousia will not occur at all. As there has already been one world catastrophe, the deluge, so also the imminent day of the Lord will destroy the world through fire, and it will be a day of judgment. Concluding exhortation (3:14-18): Therefore, let us prepare ourselves for the parousia, as also Paul demanded, and grow in the grace and knowledge of Christ.

2. Author and Authenticity

The Epistle clearly raises the claim to be written by the apostle Peter. It begins (1:1) with the author's self-designation: "Simon Peter, a servant and apostle of Jesus Christ." The author speaks as an eyewitness of Jesus' transfiguration (1:16 ff.). 1:14 refers to a saying of Jesus about Peter's martyrdom. In 3:15 f. the author places himself on the same level of apostolic authority as his "beloved brother Paul." 3:1 obviously alludes to I Peter: "This is now the second letter that I have written to you." Thus II Peter is written in the form of a testament of Peter, who sees his death approaching (1:13 ff.).

But Peter cannot have written this Epistle.

1. Petrine authorship is forbidden by the literary relation to Jude. II Pet. 1 and 3 have several parallels with Jude (cf. II Pet. 1:5 with Jude 3; II Pet. 1:12 with Jude 5; II Pet. 3:2 f. with Jude 17 f.; II Pet. 3:14 with Jude 24; II Pet. 3:18 with Jude 25). Especially the portrayal of the false teachers in II Pet. 2 shows the most striking agreements with Jude, even in the illustrations from the OT, pictures from nature, and extensive agreements in wording and sequence. The false teachers deny the Lord Christ and lead a licentious life (II Pet. 2:1 f. = Jude 4); they despise and blaspheme the good angelic powers (II Pet. 2:10 f. = Jude 8 f.); they speak loud boasts (ὑπέρογκα; II Pet. 2:18 = Jude 16); they are moral blemishes at their feasts (σπίλοι συνευωχούμενοι; II Pet. 2:13 = Jude 12); they are clouds driven by the wind, waterless, for whom the gloom of darkness has been reserved (II Pet. 2:17 = Jude 12 f.); they are reproached for fleshly defilement and licentious living (II Pet. 2:10, 12 ff., 18 = Jude 7 f., 10, 12, 16). The sequence of the three OT examples of punishment (Israel in the wilderness, the fallen angels, Sodom and Gomorrah) in Jude 5 ff. is arranged historically and modified in II Pet. 2:4 ff. (fallen angels, deluge, Sodom and Gomorrah), because this Epistle uses the example of the deluge against the deniers of the parousia. The general saying in II Pet. 2:11 first becomes understandable when we have before our eyes the concrete example cited in Jude 9. The picture in Jude 12 f. is more authentic and more plastic than its parallel in II Pet. 2:17.

This material shows already that II Peter is the dependent work. Furthermore, we may observe that the quotation from a non-canonical writing (Jude 14 f. = Apocalypse of Enoch 1:9; 60:8) is lacking in II Peter, and that additional allusions to apocryphal writings (Jude 6, fall of the angels; 9, struggle of the archangel Michael with the devil) are obscured by omission of essential features. Thus we see that although Jude takes a naïve attitude toward this literature, II Peter hesitates to use it. In contrast to Jude, who characterizes the false teachers as present, II Peter betrays literary reflection in that it seeks to portray the false teachers of its time as future: Peter's prediction (2:1 ff.; future tense), 3:3, 17 (προγινώσκοντες), but in spite of that also the present tense (2:10, 12 ff., 20), and even the preterit (2:15, 22) is used. Hence the judgment that II Peter is dependent upon Jude, and not vice versa, is today generally recognized (otherwise yet Guthrie). If in II Pet. 3:3 ff. the libertines also are pictured as deniers of the parousia, then here too II Peter offers the more developed, Jude the simpler, state of affairs, for Jude does not know that the false teachers, against whom he directs his polemic, would have doubted the parousia. Since Jude belongs in the postapostolic period, Peter cannot have written II Peter.

2. The conceptual world and rhetorical language of II Peter are too strongly influenced by Hellenism to be attributed to Peter, or to a helper or pupil who wrote the Epistle under his command, even some time after the apostle's death (as de Zwaan still regards as possible).

To this Hellenistic influence we owe concepts like ἀρετή of God (1:3); "virtue" in addition to "faith" (1:5); "knowledge" (1:2, 3, 6, 8; 2:20; 3:18); "you may escape from the corruption that is in the world because of passion, and become partakers of the divine nature" (θείας κοινωνοὶ φύσεως 1:4); the term ἐπόπται from the language of the mysteries (1:16); the juxtaposition of a quotation from the canonical book of Proverbs (26:11) and a familiar quotation from Hellenistic tradition (2:22), etc.

3. One lively interest of the Epistle is to oppose the denial of the Christian expectation of the parousia. Already 1:12 ff. treats the hope in the parousia of Christ, which is authenticated through the fact of Jesus' transfiguration and by OT prophecy. 3:3 ff. is a direct polemic against deniers of the parousia. These scoffingly ask, "Where is the promise of his coming?" and appeal to the observation that "ever since the fathers fell asleep, all things have continued as they were from the beginning of creation" (3:4). Also in I Clem. 23:3 f. and II Clem. 11:2 ff. is cited a writing obviously read in Christian circles, which raises the charge: "We heard that already in the days of our fathers, and, behold, we have become old, and nothing of it has happened to us." I Clement was written about 95, II Clement hardly much earlier than 150. Thus from the end of the first century on the sneering skepticism, to which II Pet. 3:3 ff. refers, can be historically attested. The Gnostics of the second century, however, opposed the doctrine of the parousia and gave it a new meaning by spiritualizing it. They are also probably meant as the preachers of "cleverly devised myths" (1:16) and of "knowledge" (see 2). In addition, libertinism and impudent disrespect of spiritual powers are their hallmarks (see 1). Accordingly, II Peter presents a front against a movement which bears the essential characteristics of second-century Gnosticism. A closer definition is, however, impossible.

4. The second century is again indicated by appeals not only to a collection of Pauline epistles, whose statements are "hard to understand" and are misinterpreted by the false teachers, but also to other normative writings, probably both the OT and the NT, which was in the process of development (3: 16). In view of this difficulty in understanding the "scriptures" and of the ambiguity of the "scriptures," II Peter advocates the thesis that "no prophecy of scripture is a matter of one's own interpretation," because men moved by the Holy Spirit have spoken (1:20 f.). Since not every Christian has the Spirit, exposition of the Scriptures is reserved to the ecclesiastical teaching office (Käsemann, 152 f.; Marxsen, 16 f.; Schelkle, ad loc.). With this attitude we find ourselves doubtless far beyond the time of Peter and in "primitive catholicism" ["Frühkatholizismus"].

It is certain, therefore, that II Peter cannot have originated from Peter. Today, this result is accepted by most Catholic scholars (Schäfer, Chaine, Benoit, BdJ, Cantinat in Robert-Feuillet, Michl, Schelkle; otherwise still Meinertz, Holzmeister, Höpfl-Gut; Wikenhauser undecided), in addition to almost all Protestants (otherwise Guthrie). Two additional facts confirm this conclusion:

5. Pseudonymity in II Peter (similarly as in the Pastorals) is consistently carried out by means of strong emphasis upon Petrine composition (see above, p. 302). The author, however, derives his authority not only from the fiction of a "testament of Peter," but also from the reference to I Peter in 3:1 f., whereby II Peter wants to "remind" (1:12, 15; 3:1 f.) its readers only of that

which has been said in I Peter which corresponds to the interpretation which the author of II Peter gives to I Peter (cf. Boobyer). This appeal to the apostolic authority of Peter and his Epistle is, however, clearly occasioned by the sharpening of the Gnostic heresy opposed in Jude through consistent denial of the parousia by the false teachers. Hence the apostle becomes "the guarantor of the tradition" (1:12 f.), and the parousia, in connection with abandonment of the imminent expectation (3:8), is stripped of its Christological character and aligned with an anthropologically oriented doctrine of rewards (Käsemann). The consistent character of this pseudonymity betrays the late origin of II Peter.

6. In spite of this strong emphasis upon Petrine composition, II Peter is nowhere mentioned in the second century. The apologists, Irenaeus, Tertullian, Cyprian, Clement of Alexandria, and the Muratorian canon are silent about it. The first certain witness is Origen, but, according to him, the Epistle is disputed (ἀμφιβάλλεται). Eusebius classifies it among the "Antilegomena." Hippolytus knows II Peter, and likewise Firmilian, Bishop of Caesarea in Cappadocia († 268) (according to Cyprian, Ep. 75, 6). Still in the fourth century it is widely unknown or not recognized (cf. Hieronymus: "It is rejected by the majority" [a plerisque negatur]). Then gradually it achieves recognition. The canonical lists of Athanasius, Cyril of Jerusalem, Gregory of Nazianzus, and others, have it. Under the influence of Hilary, Ambrose, and Augustine, it found final acceptance in the Western canon. *The Peshitta* does not have II Peter; it has never obtained full canonical authority among the Syrians.

3. Time and Place of Composition

Every clue to a precise dating of II Peter eludes us. The time of composition of Jude is the *terminus a quo*. The development of Gnosticism traceable in II Peter makes it natural to think of the second quarter of the second century, whereas the lack of Christological heresy advises against coming down as late as 150, as do Fascher, Barnett, and Käsemann. We know nothing about the place of composition. Rome (Goodspeed, Barnett, Michl) can only be conjectured.

The "primitive catholic" features already mentioned, the Hellenistic anthropology, the Hellenistic understanding of salvation (1:3 f.), and the abandonment of the primitive Christian eschatology and its replacement by "that apocalyptic which Jews and Gentiles also esteem and preach" (Käsemann), make it plain that, in connection with II Peter as probably the latest writing in the NT canon, the problem of the "inner limits of the canon" stands out in special sharpness, and forces us to consider the normative character of this theology (see §37).

§31. THE FIRST EPISTLE OF JOHN

Commentaries, see p. 391. Studies: E. v. DOBSCHÜTZ, "Johanneische Studien," ZNW 8, 1907, 1 ff.; R. BULTMANN, "Analyse des I Joh.," *Festgabe für A. Jülicher*, 1927,

138 ff.; *idem,* "Die kirchliche Redaktion des I Joh.," *In memoriam E. Lohmeyer,* 1951, 181 ff.; *idem,* RGG³ III, 1959, 836 ff.; E. LOHMEYER, "Über Gliederung und Aufbau des I Joh.," ZNW 27, 1928, 225 ff.; F. BÜCHSEL, "Zu den Johbr.," ZNW 28, 1929, 235 ff.; C. H. DODD, "The First Epistle of John and the Fourth Gospel," BJRL 21, 1937, 129 ff.; O. A. PIPER, "1 John and the Didache of the Primitive Church," JBL 66, 1947, 437 ff.; W. F. HOWARD, "The Common Authorship of the Johannine Gospel and Epistles," JThSt 48, 1947, 12 ff.; W. G. WILSON, "An Examination of the Linguistic Evidence Adduced Against the Unity of Authorship of the First Epistle of John and the Fourth Gospel," JThSt 49, 1948, 147 ff.; R. LECONTE, DBS IV, 1949, 797 ff.; E. KÄSEMANN, "Ketzer und Zeuge," ZThK 48, 1951, 292 ff. (= Exegetische Versuche und Besinnungen I, 1960, 168 ff.); H. BRAUN, "Literar-Analyse und theologische Schichtung im I Joh.," ZThK 48, 1951, 262 ff. (= Gesammelte Studien zum NT und seiner Umwelt, 1962, 210 ff.); H. CONZELMANN, "Was von Anfang war," *Ntl. Studien für R. Bultmann,* Beih. ZNW 21, 1954, 194 ff.; A. P. SALOM, "Some Aspects of the Grammatical Style of I John," JBL 74, 1955, 96 ff.; J. HÉRING, "Y a-t-il des aramaïsmes dans la Première Épître Johannique?," RHPR 36, 1956, 113 ff.; W. NAUCK, *Die Tradition und der Charaker des I Joh.,* WUNT 3, 1957; H. STRATHMANN, EKL II, 1958, 363 f.; O. MICHEL, CBL, 1959, 655 ff.; E. HAENCHEN, "Neuere Literatur zu den Johbr.: A," ThRdsch, N. F. 26, 1960, 1 ff.; J. A. T. ROBINSON, "The Destination and Purpose of the Johannine Epistles," NTSt 7, 1960-61, 56 ff.

1. Contents

The Epistle has no clearly recognizable plan, but presents frequent variations on two themes: right faith in Christ and the necessary connection between faith and proper conduct. Consequently, attempts to point out an ingenious plan of seven groups (Lohmeyer, Albertz) are not convincing. Neither have other endeavors to outline a symmetrical organization (see the summary by A. Feuillet in Robert-Feuillet, 687 f.) proved successful. As in the case of I Peter (see above, p. 293), each attempt at a division can be nothing more than that.

In the "address" (1:1-4), the author attests the reality of the life revealed through the incarnated Logos, which also gives to the readers fellowship with God. In the First course of thought (1:5-2:27), there are two theses, an ethical thesis (walking in the light), and a Christological thesis (confession of Jesus as the Christ). First, the ethical thesis is discussed in detail: walking in the light includes no absolute sinlessness (1:5-10); warning and comfort in view of the reality of sin in the Christian life (2:1 f.); keeping of the commandments as indication of knowledge of God and Christ (2:3-6); brotherly love as proof of walking in the light (2:7-11); reminder to the readers of their possession of salvation and urgent warning against love of the world (2:12-17). Then briefly, and with sharp remarks against the false teachers, the Christological thesis is developed (2:18-27).

The theme is repeated with another variation in the Second course of thought (2:28-4:6): doing righteousness and confessing Jesus as the Christ as marks of God's sovereignty. Here also the carrying out of the ethical thesis, doing righteousness, i.e., especially active brotherly love (2:28-3:24), receives greater attention: doing righteousness and self-purification characterize the children of God and enable them to pass safely through the judgment before him (2:28–3:6); committing sin characterizes the children of the devil, not committing sin (exercising love), the children of God (3:7-17); energetic brotherly love and faith in Christ and love of the brethren among themselves are the guarantee of fellowship with God (3:18-24). And then the Christological thesis: The confession, "Jesus Christ come in the flesh is the sign of origin from God" (4:1-6), is again expounded in a sharp, antiheretical formulation.

In the Third course of thought (4:7–5:13), love and faith connect the lines of the meditation, in that in 4:7-21 love based upon faith and in 5:1-13 faith based upon love prove to be the marks of being engendered by God. Concluding thoughts (5:14-21): the certainty of having life gives joyousness to prayer (14 f.) and intercession (except in connection with mortal sin; 16 f.); the basic truths stand fast: not sinning as a result of being born of God, and adherence to the confession of God in Jesus Christ (18-20); finally, the warning, "keep yourselves from idols" (21).

2. Literary Character

I John lacks the characteristics of an epistle: address and conclusion with greetings and benediction. It contains no names (except "Cain," 3:12), and no concrete personal references. Hence it makes a nonepistolary impression. It appears to be a tractate intended for all of Christendom, an encyclical directed to all fellow believers, a "manifesto" (Knopf, Windisch, Jülicher-Fascher, Riddle-Hutson, Klijn, Lohmeyer, Bultmann, Boismard, BdJ, and others). Other scholars object to this supposition on the grounds that I John presupposes a specific historical situation, that it (especially clearly in 2:18 ff.; 4:1 ff.) contends against the acute danger of a heretical belief, toward which the readers themselves have already taken a position (2:21; 4:4). The author has in mind a circle of readers somehow limited. The addressees, "children" (2:1, 12, 14, 18, 28; 3:7, 18; 4:4; 5:21), and "beloved" (2:7; 3:2, 21; 4:1, 7, 11), also cause some to conclude that here we have to do with the intimate relationship between a spiritual leader coming forward with fatherly authority and those committed to his care. Thus in spite of the lack of an epistolary framework I John is said to be an actual epistle. However, the polemic against heretics in no wise alludes to concrete relations, and the discourses do not indicate a personal relation to the readers. That the readers were former Jews of the diaspora (Robinson) cannot be concluded from their acquaintance with Cain (3:12), from the moral standards presupposed for them, and not at all from the "Judaizing" character of the opposed heresy. The Gentile origin of the readers also is not stressed, because upon the basis of a special situation the entirety of Christendom is addressed. And Bultmann's supposition that 1:1-4 imitates an epistolary address, whereas 5:13 is an epistolary conclusion, so that 5:14-21 turns out to be a secondary appendix, is not at all convincing, for apart from the question whether

5:14 ff. is to be regarded as an addition (see below, p. 309), 1:4 and 5:13 cannot by any means be shown to be transformed introductory and concluding greetings. I John is in no way to be understood as a writing for specific readers.

Scholars have attempted to explain the special literary nature of I John by various theories of secondary compilation (see the summary in Nauck, 1 ff.). First of all, v. Dobschütz separated out of 2:28–3:17 four antithetical sentences (e.g., 3:9aa and 3:10ba), which the author of the Epistle elaborated and commented upon. Then Bultmann, using criteria based upon style and content, separated from the entire Epistle a "Vorlage" consisting of twenty-six antithetical couplets. He distinguished the poetical material of this "Vorlage" from the homiletical reworking which it received from the writer of the Epistle. Moreover, Bultmann designated this "Vorlage" as part of the Gnostic source of "revelation discourses," which he also finds in the Gospel of John (see above, pp. 151 ff.). Bultmann later expanded this analysis with the hypothesis that an ecclasiastical redactor not only added an appendix (5:14-21), which, through its conceptions, proves to be a "foreign body," but he also undertook interpolations in 2:28; 3:2; 4:17 and 1:7; 2:2; 4:10, which introduce the ecclesiastical eschatology and the conception of expiation through the blood of Christ. Bultmann found agreement with his source analysis from Windisch, Wilder, and Preisker. Preisker, in the new edition of Windisch's commentary, instead of revision, wanted to assume a second "Vorlage," which seeks to establish the traditional eschatology. Braun, who agreed in principle with Bultmann's method, sought to expand somewhat the extent of the source lying at the basis of I John, denied the pre-Christian origin of this source, and distinguished the standpoint of the source from that of the revision as "genuine Christian" and "primitive catholic." Finally, Nauck held fast to the distinction between "Vorlage" and revision, but traced both back to the same author: Originally, the author, with the antithetically formulated "Vorlage," had intervened in the situation of the church endangered by heresy and now with his commentary intends to lead the church finally to a sure attitude.

The observation of the stylistic distinction between short, sententious sentences (e.g., 2:9) and broad, homiletical discussions (e.g., 2:1 f.) is absolutely correct. But the bounds between these two stylistic forms can be so little sharply drawn that during analysis the necessity repeatedly arises of supposing an interweaving of the "Vorlage" with the revision and vice versa, or of admitting the uncertainty of the separation (Braun, 215; Nauck, 74 ff., 123), thus showing that the separation cannot be undertaken convincingly upon the basis of stylistic peculiarities. On the other hand, if it can be established that also the "Vorlage" must be of Christian origin (Braun), but that between "Vorlage" and revision no clear theological difference exists (Käsemann, 182 f., note 47; Haenchen, 32 ff.), then even this criterion for the separation of sources collapses. And Nauck's supposition of the same authorship of "Vorlage" and revision is untenable, for we cannot understand why a writer should subsequently have so disrupted his own artistic work that we can observe nothing at all of the original. The supposition of a "Vorlage" and its revision is, therefore, unproved and improbable. As for the differences in style, we may trace them back to the use of traditional material (cf. Piper).

But is Bultmann's supposition of an ecclesiastical redaction of I John tenable (cf. thereto Schnackenburg, 12 f.; Nauck, 128 ff.)? Since the offenses in the context are of no great significance, Bultmann's excision of the references to futuristic eschatology and the expiating work of Jesus' blood can be convincingly established only by maintaining a contrast to Johannine theology. But even in connection with the Gospel of John, this contention can be maintained only through the supposition of interpolations (see above, pp. 149 f.) and is thus not justified. More noteworthy are some reasons which can be adduced for the secondary addition of 5:14 ff. (cf. the cautious agreement by Feuillet in Robert-Feuillet, 693 f., and Schnackenburg, 12 f.): the distinction between two classes of sins is lacking otherwise in I John, and stands in tension with 1:5 ff.; ἥκει (5:20) for the coming of the Son of God is peculiar, and 5:21 is linguistically un-Johannine. Since, however, these divergences or singularities are not actual contradictions to the remainder of I John, 5:14 ff. can be thoroughly understood as forming an integral part of the Epistle, even if that naturally cannot be proved. That I John in the form in which it lies before us is the work of one author must, therefore, be considered as probable.

Obviously, the Trinitarian addition in 5:7 f., the so-called *Comma Johanneum* (see H. Greeven, RGG³ I, 1854; W. Thiele, "Beobachtungen zum Comma Johanneum," ZNW 50, 1959, 61 ff.), is to be excluded from this judgment. This section is missing in all Greek manuscripts outside of three minuscules of the fourteenth to sixteenth centuries, in the original Vulgate and the Oriental translations. It was first taken up in the third edition of Erasmus, and from there came into the Textus Receptus (see below, p. 380). Today, without exception, 5:7 f. is recognized as a later addition. The earliest sure witness is Priscillian (end of the fourth century). Whether the addition is somewhat older is debatable, but its interpolation already into the Greek text (Thiele) is very improbable.

3. Purpose

I John wants to warn against heretical teachers who have arisen in the Christian churches (2:18 f., 26; 3:7). Many false prophets have gone out into the world (4:1). I John calls them "antichrists" (2:18; cf. 4:3). Since many have appeared, the readers know the parousia of Christ is close at hand (2:18; cf. Mk. 13:22 par.). The seriousness of the dawning age demands that Christians distinguish between the spirit of error and the spirit of truth (4:6). The Christians to whom the Epistle is directed already have resisted mightily the seducers (4:4). The false spirits went out of the congregation (2:19), but their dangerous influence has not yet been broken (4:1 ff.). What they want and promote is revealed by their features to which I John calls special attention: They boast about their knowledge of God (2:4; 4:8), love of God (4:20), and fellowship with God (1:6; 2:6, 9). They claim for themselves unique pneumatic experiences (4:1 ff.) and think that they are exalted above sin (1:8, 10). They deny that Jesus is the Christ (2:22 f.), the Son of God in the sense of primitive Christian belief (4:15; 5:5, 10 ff.). They reject the confession of the full historical humanity of Jesus, who came in the flesh (4:2), whose earthly work began with his baptism, and concluded with his death (5:6). It was, therefore, a Gnostic, enthusiastic movement, which advocated a Docetic Christology, in contrast to which the identity of the man Jesus with the Son of God and Christ (4:15; 5:1, 5) and the redemptive power of his death (5:6; 1:7; 2:1 f.; 3:16; 4:10) must be regarded as essential parts of the certainty of Christian faith. With their opposition to the Christian confession of faith was joined a basic moral outlook which scorned the firm bond between Christian faith and life. The keeping of Jesus' commandments did not appear to them as a basic demand (2:4), and they placed no importance upon the doing of righteousness (3:7, 10), active brotherly love (2:9, 11; 3:10 ff.; 4:20), and help for the poor (3:17). They made concessions to the world, instead of separating themselves from it (4:5; 2:15 ff.), and in so doing claimed moral perfection (1:8, 10). By way of contrast, I John stresses most emphatically that knowledge of God and walking in the light are inseparable, and only Jesus Christ who became flesh brought sin-destroying love.

The variety of primitive Christian Gnosticism which I John combats cannot with certainty be identified with names from the history of heresy. To be sure, scholars have often supposed that I John strikes out at the heresy of Cerinthus, which appeared at the end of the first century in Asia Minor (e.g., Wikenhauser, de Zwaan, Feuillet in Robert-Feuillet, Feine-Behm, Chaine, Ross, Robinson, Bultmann; to the contrary, especially Schnackenburg, 15 ff.). But I John shows no trace of Cerinthus' characteristic view that the Christ was joined only temporarily with the man Jesus, nor does I John polemize against the separation of an upper from a lower God. And the ethical danger, against which I John warns, is also not demonstrable in connection with Cerinthus. Thus if the Gnostic heresy cannot be fixed precisely historically, it is nevertheless significant that here, in contrast to Colossians, the Pastorals, Jude, and II Peter, the enthusiastic Gnosticism also has Christological effects. Hence we have to do here with a developed form of Gnosticism. The attack upon this Gnostic heresy takes place, however, in a language influenced by Gnosticism, a language closely parallel with the conceptual world of John (see above, p. 157). The proof that I John stands in history-of-tradition connection with Qumran and Christian baptismal ritual (Nauck, with agreement from M.-E. Boismard, RB 66, 1959, 146) is thus hardly successful, since reminiscences of single motifs prove no history-of-tradition dependence (see Haenchen, 21 ff., 41 f.).

4. Author and Relation to the Fourth Gospel

As Dionysius of Alexandria already saw (in Eus., EH VII, 25, 18 ff.), the relationship of I John with the Gospel of John is the most striking fact in connection with the historical criticism of I John. Dionysius concluded from the agreement in language and conceptual world that both writings have the same author. This view remained uncontested until the beginning of the nineteenth century and today is shared by the majority of scholars, independent of the question about the person of the author. But especially since the Tübingen school directed attention to the differences from which different authors can be inferred, this opinion has repeatedly come into the foreground (cf. lately, e.g., Moffatt, Dibelius, Goguel, Windisch, Wilder, Dodd, McNeile-Williams, Klijn, Bultmann, Conzelmann, Haenchen). Reasons based upon language and upon content are adduced for both views.

a) That I John and John are extraordinarily closely related in vocabulary and style is undisputed (cf. Brooke, 1 ff.; Chaine, 104 ff.), which seems to indicate the same author. In contrast to that, Dodd has pointed out that I John uses significantly fewer prepositions, particles, and verbal compounds than John, and that numerous expressions and words of John are missing in I John. Especially striking is the lack of οὖν (194 times in John); δόξα (18); κρίνειν (19); and γάρ is found sixty-three times in John, but only three times in I John. Howard and Wilson have questioned the probative force of these statements by pointing out that the frequency of use of particles, etc., and the presence of favorite particles corresponding to the length of the pieces of writing and the subject treated vary even in the same author, so that no conclusions can be drawn therefrom. Moreover, Salom has shown that both writings coincide remarkably in frequence of sequence of sentence parts and in individual stylistc peculiarities (e.g., ἐν τούτῳ . . . ὅτι or ἐάν). On the other hand, Haenchen, taking up again Dodd's observations, stresses that a difference in use of prepositions (John has, e.g., παρά with the genitive 25 times; I John has for it ἀπό) allows us to presume another author. Indeed, an observation like the latter one is notable (e.g., in connection with the verbs αἰτεῖν and ἀκούειν), but against it stands the contrary observation that I Jn. 4:13 and Jn. 6:11 go together in the strange connection διδόναι or διαδιδόναι ἔκ τινος. Even if a certain linguistic difference between John and I John cannot be denied, it hardly goes further than is conceivable in the same writer at two different times sufficiently far apart.

b) Decisive, however, is the question whether I John differs basically from John in content. Also here no one denies that both writings largely advocate the same ideas (cf. Windisch's summary at I Jn. 1:3). Yet clear differences doubtless exist: In I John all OT citations are lacking; futuristic eschatology is emphasized (2:28, παρουσία; 3:2; 4:17); the false teachers are characterized as present ἀντίχριστοι (2:18, 22; 4:3); παράκλητος designates Jesus Christ (2:1), not the Spirit, as in John; only in I John is the atoning character of Jesus' death presented (1:7, 9; 2:2; 4:10); John does not speak of rebirth through Christ (2:29). From these and other differences, Dodd has concluded that I John stands closer to common Christianity than John, Haenchen that I John is more strongly connected to primitive catholicism than the Pastorals, and Conzelmann that I John already refers back to John as tradition. On the other hand, we must say, in the first place, that some of these conceptions are certainly found also in John: futuristic eschatology (5:29; 12:48; 14:3); Christ indirectly as παράκλητος (14:16); and Jesus' atoning death (1:29; 3:14 ff.; 6:51b; 12:24). Secondly, we note that some differences are explained by the polemic against heretics in I John: false teachers as ἀντίχριστοι; emphasis upon the connection between love of God and love of brother; or by the presumed chronological distance between the composition of both writings—rebirth through Christ. But above all it is not only unproved that I John refers back to John as tradition, but it is thoroughly questionable whether the comparison between John and I John justifies the conclusion that "the great sayings of the past . . . are worn from constant handling like long used coins" (Haenchen, 39), because the practical, paraenetic nature of I John, in contrast to the more strongly kerygmatically aligned Gospel, inevitably leads to formulations which are better suited to the concrete difficulties of the Christian life.

Thus there hardly exists adequate reason to suppose another author for I John than for John. And since the earliest tradition (in Irenaeus, Haer. II, 17, 5, 8, and in the Muratorian canon, 26 ff.) simply refers to the evangelist as the author of I John, and thus offers no independent tradition about his person, we can hold only to that which we know about the author of John (see above, pp. 165 ff.) That the author was a man with a Semitic mother language or Semitic thought patterns (Schnackenburg, Héring) can hardly be demonstrated.

5. Time of Composition

If I John and the Gospel of John stem from the same author, then I John was not written long before or after John. The attempts to prove I John earlier (lately, Strathmann, Klijn) or later (lately, Ross, Robinson, Haenchen, Guthrie) than John are not convincing. Since I John was already known in the second quarter of the second century (Polycarp, Phil. 7:1: "everyone who does not confess that Jesus Christ has come in the flesh is an antichrist," presupposes I Jn. 4:2 f., and Papias, according to Eus., EH III, 39, 17 "used testimonies from the first Epistle of John"), it could not have been written later than toward the end of the first quarter of the second century. Most probably we can date the origin of I John between 90-110. Concerning the place of origin, we know nothing. If John belongs to Syria (see above, p. 175), we may also conjecture that for I John (so also Nauck).

§32. The Second and Third Epistles of John

Commentaries, see p. 391. Studies: see to §31, besides A. HARNACK, Über den III Joh., TU 15, 3, 1897; H. v. CAMPENHAUSEN, Kirchliches Amt und geistliche Vollmacht in den ersten drei Jahrhunderten, BhTh 14, 1953, 132 ff.; R. SCHNACKENBURG, "Der Streit zwischen dem Verf. von 3 Joh. und Diotrephes . . . ," MThZ 4, 1953, 18 ff.; G. BORNKAMM, art. πρέσβυς, ThWB VI, 1959, 670 ff.; A. KRAGERUD, Der Lieblingsjünger im Joh., 1959, 100 ff.; E. HAENCHEN, "Neuere Literatur zu den Johbr.n: B," ThRdsch, N.F. 26, 1960, 267 ff.

1. Contents

II John. "The elder" writes the Epistle to "the elect lady and her children," without mentioning any names. In the address (1-3) the author emphasizes the bond of love which unites him and all who have recognized the truth with the addressees. An admonition to walk in truth and love, and a warning against deceivers who do not confess Jesus Christ who has come in the flesh and who preach progressivism, form the actual contents of the Epistle (4-11). The Epistle closes with the expressed hope of soon meeting personally (12), and with greetings from the "children of the elect sister" of the addressees (13).

III John. Here "the elder" writes to a particular person, Gaius. After the short address (1) there follows in the epistolary introductory intercession (2-4) an expression of joy over the good testimony which traveling brethren give concerning Gaius. The theme of the Epistle is hospitality toward traveling brethren (5-12): Gaius is encouraged further to establish his tried and tested hospitality (5-8). 9 f. is a polemic against Diotrephes, because he provides opposition to the writer. Demetrius is praised (11 f.). Conclusion (13-15): the Epistle is so brief because "the elder" hopes soon to meet Gaius in person (13 f.). Wish for peace, and greetings (15).

2. Form, Destination, and Purpose

No other NT epistle, not even Philemon, has so much the form of the Hellenistic private letter as II and III John. Both are actual letters. But they do not treat private concerns, but matters of the faith and life of Christian congregations, and, as remarks of an ecclesiastical person of authority, they bear a certain official character.

II John is directed to a congregation. κυρία (1, 5) can be, of course, a personal name or official address of a woman (thus falsely Albertz: "head of a household church"; Ross, Guthrie: "elect lady"), but according to the entire attitude of the Epistle we must suppose that the word κυρία here has a metaphorical meaning. The one so designated is connected by the bond of mutually binding love with "all who know the truth" (1, 5). Her "children," many in number (4), are, like the "children" of the "elder" (III 4), not physical but spiritual children. The Epistle treats problems of Christian congregational life (5 f., 7 ff., 10 f.). "Lady" is thus a pictorial designation of a congregation, a carry-over of a political expression to an ecclesiastical community (see W. Foerster, ThWB III, 1938, 1095, and F. J. Dölger, "Domina Mater Ecclesia und die 'Herrin' im II Joh.," Antike und Christentum, 5, 1936, 211 ff.). As an ecclesiastical community it is called "elect," like its "elect sister" (13; cf. I Pet. 5:13), the congregation at the place from which the "elder" writes. II John is intended for a concrete, particular church (4, 12 f.).

Of Gaius, to whom III John is sent, nothing otherwise is known. We know just as little about Diotrephes (9) and Demetrius (12). Gaius was probably converted through the "elder" (4) and obviously lives in a community in which he and his "friends" (15) stand apart from Diotrephes (9), who domi-nates the congregation, and his circle. It is not clear whether Demetrius also belongs to the congregation and to the friends of Gaius, or is the bearer of the Epistle, or is one of the "strange brethren" (5). The congregation is certainly a different one from that of II John, for the figure of Diotrephes would not fit into the harmonious picture of II John. That III 9 refers to II John, which was written earlier (thus, e.g., Dibelius, Jülicher-Fascher, McNeile-Williams, Strathmann), is very questionable, in view of the difference in the situation (cf. Schnackenburg, Haenchen, Guthrie)—the similarity of form points to the origin of both Epistles at about the same time. Particulars about the place of destination can no more be determined for III John than for II John.

The purpose of both Epistles is different. In II John "the elder" warns the addressed congregation against false teachers who deny the incarnation of Jesus Christ and preach progressivism, and thus against Gnostics similar to those com-bated in I John. Here they are also equated with the antichrist, and "the elder" commands the congregation to enter into no kind of relationship with such people. Upon the basis of what authority "the elder" gives this instruction to the addressed congregation cannot be determined.

In III John "the elder" praises Gaius, because he has extended hospitality to missionary brethren. He commands him to continue to do so, not allowing himself to be hindered by Diotrephes, who rejects "the elder" and "prates against him with evil words" (9 f.). Diotrephes does not welcome to the congregation the brethren sent by "the elder," prevents the members of the congregation from welcoming them, and puts them out of the church when they resist him. What kind of situation is presupposed in III John is disputed (cf. the report by Haenchen). Harnack wanted to see expressed here the struggle of the old pro-vincial missionary organizations against the individual churches which had been consolidated under monarchical leadership (similarly, Kragerud, Schneider, Schnackenburg). But there is not even a clue to a provincial missionary organiza-tion or something similar. Also the attempts to show that Diotrephes is a Gnostic (W. Bauer, see to §24, 97), or to see in the "elder" one of the false teachers excommunicated by Diotrephes, the orthodox congregational leader (Käse-mann), are untenable, because there is no mention of the "elder's" false teaching or of his excommunication. Preferably we can think of a conflict between a fixed ecclesiastical organization and an earlier, freer charismatic situation (Jülicher-Fascher, Bultmann, Michel, v. Campenhausen, Bornkamm). Yet it is not clear that "the elder" represents the freer charismatic situation. It is clear only that, according to the opinion of "the elder," Diotrephes has usurped an ex-clusive role, to which he has no right, in spite of his de facto role of leadership. Thereby Diotrephes hinders the missionary activity supported by "the elder" and some members of Diotrephes' congregation. Obviously, "the elder as speaker of one congregation turns to another congregation" (Haenchen). Like Diotre-phes, he is probably a congregational leader, but as "the elder" he enjoys a more than local authority, which Diotrephes obviously denies to him. Thus we can clarify the historical difficulty only by determining who this elder was.

3. Author

II and III John have the same author. They speak the same language. They nearly agree in length and in epistolary form (address, introduction, conclusion). They carry at their head the same characteristic self-designation of the author, ὁ πρεσβύτερος. This title, which is used instead of a name, at this time hardly indicates "the presbyter" (of whom there were many), but "the elderly man." The riddle of this designation is to be solved as little from the Epistle alone as the problem of the person of the author in general. Now both Epistles are closely related to the Gospel of John and I John in language, style, and world view (summary of the material in R. H. Charles, *The Revelation of St. John*, ICC, I, XXXIV ff., XLI ff.). The emphasis upon the truth of the author's testimony in III 12 is similar to that in Jn. 19:35 and 21:24. III 11 expresses the characteristic Johannine view that one's fundamental being is to be inferred from the way one acts. II 4 ff. is full of parallels to conceptions from I John. The front of heretical Gnosticism, against which II 7, 9 is directed, is the same as in I John. II and III John are either artificial creations prepared in conscious imitation of Johannine writing (so Dibelius, Jülicher-Fascher)— but their unpretentiousness militates against that—or they stem from the same author as I John and John. These two Epistles, written for particular occasions, probably owe their preservation solely to the respect that their author enjoyed as the author of two more significant larger writings.

Certain scholars, of course, have sought to ascribe II and III John to a different author from that of I John, because of particular differences in thought and language (e.g., Jülicher-Fascher, J. Jeremias, "Joh. Literarkritik," ThBl 20, 1941, 43, note 39, Bultmann). The following are not supposed to agree with Johannine thought: designation of a single false teacher as "the antichrist" (II 7); no "progressivist" (II 9) is to be received by the congregation (10 f.); Jesus Christ who "is come in the flesh" (I 4, 2) is called Jesus Christ who "comes in the flesh" (II 7); in contradiction to Jn. 1:18 and I 4:12a, III 11 says, "he who does evil has not seen God." These differences, however, are too trivial to be taken seriously.

But who is the author who simply calls himself ὁ πρεσβύτερος? It is as improbable that the name has been omitted as that it designates an office. In so far as the early ecclesiastical tradition traced John and I II III John back to the same author (see above, p. 310), it supposed that John the son of Zebedee was also the author of II III John (concerning the slight age of this tradition, see above, pp. 168 ff.). If II III John stem from the same author as I John, then the arguments already presented against authorship by the son of Zebedee also apply to these small writings. But on the other hand, it also follows that the author of these four writings could call himself ὁ πρεσβύτερος and thereby be understood. Then two possibilities remain: Either a man unknown to us, who perhaps belonged to a πρεσβυτέριον (cf. I Tim. 4:14), bore this title in a special sense, though we can know no details about it, or ὁ πρεσβύτερος is an allusion to the membership of this man in that circle of "those 'presbyters'" whom Papias and Irenaeus and Clement represented as custodians and transmitters of the apostolic tradition" (Haenchen, 291). If this second supposition is more probable, because only it makes understandable the authoritative use of the title by the author of II III John, then we may further ask whether perhaps the one whom Papias calls ὁ πρεσβύτερος Ἰωάννης (in Eus., EH III, 39, 4; see above, pp. 171 f.) designated himself in this manner. But to this question there is no certain answer.

4. Time of Origin

We first find an acquaintance with II III John in Clement of Alexandria, who, according to Eus., EH VI, 14, 1, commented upon all the Catholic epistles. But Irenaeus quoted only II John, and the Muratorian canon speaks only of two Johannine epistles which were accepted in the Catholic Church. Since, according to the proof by T. W. Manson (JThSt 48, 1947, 32 f.), III John was independently translated into Latin, III John obviously came into the canon in the West later than II John. And yet Origen (in Eus., EH VI, 25, 10) and Eusebius (EH III, 25, 3) know that the authenticity of the small Johannine epistles is not generally recognized, and Hieronymus (vir. ill., 9) reports that II III John are ascribed to the presbyter John. If, therefore, II III John were only hesitatingly taken up into the canon and possibly were not known until late (in any case III John), there is hardly any special tradition about the author. Rather, for both Epistles, in addition to their brevity, the title ὁ πρεσβύτερος was a hindrance, as it does not point to an apostle. Since we can recognize nothing about the time of origin either from the tradition or the Epistle itself, and we also know nothing at all about the sequence of the Epistles, we must think of the same time as for I John, therefore approximately 90-110.

C. THE APOCALYPTIC BOOK

§33. APOCALYPTICISM AND APOCALYPSES

Literature: A. HILGENFELD, Die jüdische Apokalyptik, 1857; W. BOUSSET-H. GRESSMANN, Die Religion des Judentums im späthellenistischen Zeitalter, Hdb. 21, ³1926, 11 ff., 242 ff.; J.-B. FREY, DBS I, 1928, 326 ff. (lit.); E. STAUFFER, "Das theologische Weltbild der Apokalyptik," ZsystTh 8, 1931, 203 ff.; P. VOLZ, Die Eschatologie der jüdischen Gemeinde im ntl. Zeitalter, 1934; J. SICKENBERGER, RAC I, 1950, 504 ff.; H. H. ROWLEY, The Relevance of Apocalyptic, ²1947 (lit.); J. BLOCH, On the Apocalyptic in Judaism, Jewish Quarterly Review, Monograph Series 2, 1952; W. FOERSTER, Ntl. Zeitgeschichte, UB 26, 1, ³1955, 78 ff.; H. RINGGREN-R. SCHÜTZ, Apokalyptik I—III, RGG³ I, 1957, 463 ff.; H. GROSS-J. MICHL-F. J. SCHIERSE, Apokalypsen, Apokalyptik, LThK I, 1959, 696 ff.; B. REICKE, "Official and Pietistic Elements of Jewish Apocalypticism," JBL 79, 1960, 137 ff.—The Jewish apocalypses in the original text are available only in separate editions, but in translation in the following collections: E. KAUTZSCH, *Die Apokryphen und Pseudepigraphen des AT* II, 1900; R. H. CHARLES, *The Apocrypha and Pseudepigrapha of the Old Testament in English* II, 1913; P. RIESSLER, *Altjüdisches Schrifttum ausserhalb der Bibel*, 1928; J. MAIER, *Die Texte vom Toten Meer* I, 1960.

The concept "apocalypticism" designates, on the one hand, a phenomenon in the history of religion, a religious attitude which is characterized by a peculiar eschatological world of thought, and, on the other hand, a literary category, in which such eschatological thoughts are expressed. Generally, where religions are occupied with the problem of the end of the world and the close of history, we meet apocalyptic thoughts and their literary deposits, especially in the Orient, and particularly in Iranian religion, but also in Hellenistic syncretism and among the ancient Germans. Apocalypticism developed most profusely on the soil of Judaism and primitive Christianity. The name is based upon Rev. 1:1: "The revelation (ἀποκάλυψις) of Jesus Christ, which God gave him." Here for the first time such a book which unveils the divine secrets of the end-time carries the title "Apocalypse," "Book of Revelation." Nevertheless, the Apocalypse of John had predecessors, for the origin of this literary category lies in Judaism. Jewish apocalypticism, for its part, arose out of, and continued, Israelite prophecy, and by adopting various kinds of materials strange in form and thought succeeded prophecy.

Since the time of Ezekiel and Deutero-Isaiah the expectation of the imminent end of the world as cosmic catastrophe more and more comes to the fore. The future kingdom of God assumes the features of a kingdom not of this world, whose arena is the new heaven and the new earth. Isa. 24–27, Zech. 9–14, Joel, and other works are prophecies of an apocalyptic nature. The true Jewish apocalypses present complete books of prophecy in pseudonymous form. The first and most significant among the preserved apocalypses is the book of Daniel, written 165/164 B.C., in the time of the Maccabean revolt. The period from the Maccabean wars until the turn of the second century A.D. is the golden age of Jewish apocalypticism: Books of Enoch, the Testaments of the Twelve Patriarchs, the Jewish Sibyllines, the Assumption of Moses, II (IV) Ezra, the Syrian Apocalypse of Baruch, the "War Scroll" found at Qumran, etc. The Jewish apocalyptists do not dare to step forth personally, but conceal themselves behind the authority of some ancient worthy, such as Enoch, Noah, Abraham, the twelve patriarchs, Moses, Elijah, Daniel, Baruch, and Ezra. They write history in prophetic form from the time of the alleged author until the end of the world. About the time of the actual author, which is treated with special accuracy, there often occurs a break between representation of past history and construction of future history, which gives a clue to the time of composition. The apocalyptists receive their revelations in ecstatic visions or dreams, but the vision also becomes simply the stylistic form of apocalypticism. Their most essential means of expression are parable (allegory) and symbol: Persons are represented in the form of animals and historical events in the form of natural phenomena. Colors and numbers have secret meanings. The meaning of the numbers is connected with the ancient Oriental world picture [Welt-bild]. The images often have a history behind them; they stem from the mythological, cosmological, and astrological tradition of the Orient as of the West, a tradition which more or less determines their meaning.

Apocalypticism is controlled by a historical, ethical dualism. The present aeon is evil, standing under the lordship of demons; God has turned away from the earth; his will was formerly manifested in the history of the fathers; in the time of the end he will again reveal himself mightily and will finally prevail. The world lies in wickedness, but God will help. This aeon of the godless, earthly kingdom is coming to an end; the new aeon of God's transcendental kingdom stands at the door. Apocalypticism spreads out before us like a vast panorama a religious view of history, which sees the course of world history predestined to the smallest detail, according to a fixed, meaningful plan of God. Apocalyp-ticism, certain of the goal of history, infers from past history the laws accord-ing to which the course of the world will terminate. It calculates the inbreaking of the end, which is prepared for by a chain of catastrophes on the earth and in the cosmos, and finally resolves the conflict between God's will and present reality, between his holiness and man's sin. "Their [the apocalyptists'] despair of the world that was living without God was coupled with the lively hope that all things work together for good to them that love God" (Rowley, 163). The seriousness of the threat of judgment and the glow of hope in imminent salvation through God's wonderful rule exercised strong influence upon Jewish piety in the centuries around the turn of our era.

Primitive Christianity was most strongly influenced by apocalyptic concep-tions, which above all refer to the inbreaking of God's kingdom and the parousia of Christ. In Jesus' eschatological words, and in the expectation of the end held by Paul and I II John, resound thoughts of the book of Daniel and of later Jewish apocalypticism. Mk. 13 par.; I Thess. 4:15-17; II Thess. 2:1-12; I Cor. 15:20-28; II Cor. 5:1 ff.; 12:4; Hb. 12:22 ff. are signs that Christianity soon independently used and developed apocalyptic conceptions. Later the Christians went even further and created a Christian apocalyptic literature, either by revising Jewish apocalypses in a Christian direction (e.g., II [IV] Ezra, Testa-ments of the Twelve Patriarchs, Ascension of Isaiah, Christian Sibyllines), or by composing new apocalypses (before the middle of the second century, Apocalypse of Peter, Shepherd of Hermas; see the survey LThK I, 698 ff., and the translations in E. Hennecke-W. Schneemelcher, NT Apocrypha, II). The earliest and most significant apocalyptic work from Christian hands is the Apocalypse of John.

§34. The Apocalypse of John

Commentaries, see p. 391. Studies (in addition to those cited in §33): E. Vischer, *Die Offenbarung Johannis, eine jüdische Apk. in christlicher Bearbeitung*, TU II, 3, ²1895; L. Brun, "Die römischen Kaiser in der Apk.," ZNW 26, 1927, 128 ff.; H. Windisch,

RGG² III, 330 ff.; R. Schütz, *Die Offenbarung des Johannes und Kaiser Domitian,* FRLANT, N.F. 32, 1933; H. Strathmann, *Was soll die "Offenbarung" des Johannes im NT?,* (1934) ²1947; E. Lohmeyer, "Die Offenbarung des Johannes, 1920-34," ThRdsch, N.F. 6, 1934, 269 ff.; *ibid.* 7, 1935, 28 ff.; G. Bornkamm, "Die Komposition der apokalyptischen Visionen in der Offenbarung Johannis," ZNW 36, 1937, 132 ff. (= Studien zu Antike und Urchristentum, BeTh 28, 1959, 204 ff.); H.-D. Wendland, *Geschichtsanschauung und Geschichtsbewusstsein im NT,* 1938, 49 ff.; M.-E. Boismard, " 'L'apocalypse' ou 'les apocalypses' de S. Jean," RB 56, 1949, 507 ff.; A. Farrer, *A Rebirth of Images,* 1949; M. Rissi, *Zeit und Geschichte in der Offenbarung des Johannes,* AThANT 22, 1952; E. Stauffer, *Christus und die Cäsaren,* ³1952, 160 ff.; *Christ and the Caesars: Historical Sketches.* Tr. K. & R. Gregory Smith from 3rd ed. (1952), 1955; J. W. Bowman, "The Revelation to John: Its Dramatic Structure and Message," Int 9, 1955, 436 ff.; S. Giet, *L'Apocalypse et l'histoire,* 1957 (cf. thereto J. Schmid, ThLZ 84, 1959, 428 ff.); J. Michl, LThK I, 690 ff.; A. Feuillet, "Essai d'interprétation du chapître XI de l'Apocalypse," NTSt 4, 1957-58, 183 ff.; L. Goppelt, EKL II, 365 ff.; G. Delling, "Zum gottesdienstlichen Stil der Johannes-Apk.," NovT 3, 1959, 107 ff.; C. C. Torrey, *The Apocalypse of John,* 1958; O. A. Piper, RGG³ III, 822 ff. (bibl.); O. Michel, CBL, 1959, 957 ff.; S. Läuchli, "Eine Gottesdienststruktur in der Johannesoffenbarung," ThZ 16, 1960, 359 ff.; E. Lohse, "Die atl. Sprache des Sehers Johannes," ZNW 52, 1961, 122 ff.; T. Holtz, *Die Christologie der Apk. des Johannes,* TU 85, 1962.

1. Contents

After the introduction the Apocalypse is clearly organized into two principal parts: chaps. 2, 3 are words of admonition to the church of the author's time (the seven so-called open letters); chaps. 4–22 disclose the future. Only the second principal part, which comprises almost three fourths of the entire book, is apocalyptic in the strict sense. But the introductory account of the Christ-vision of John the seer on Patmos (1:9-20), which is preceded by a preface (1:1-3) designating the contents of the book as divine revelation to John and by an epistolary introduction (1:4-8), also places the open letters under the apocalyptic keynote of the entire book, and 22:21 terminates it like an epistle. The book, according to 1:4, 11 is intended for the seven churches in the cities of Ephesus, Smyrna, Pergamum, Thyatira, Sardis, Philadelphia, and Laodicea.

The open letters (chaps. 2, 3) are symmetrically constructed epistles, of exhortatory, comforting, and censorious contents, which the heavenly Christ writes to the churches through John. Each church receives, according to its condition, praise and blame; the brightest light falls upon the church of Philadelphia, the darkest shadow upon that of Laodicea.

In a long series of visions, which appear predominantly in groups of seven, the actual apocalypse (chaps. 4–22) reveals and points out the things to come. Preceding the vision of seven seals (6:1–8:1) is a prelude in heaven (4:1–5:14): John, carried away into heaven, beholds God upon his throne, surrounded by the twenty-four elders and the four living creatures (ch. 4), the sealed scroll which no one is able to open (5:1-5), and the Lamb, who is to break the seals

(5:6-14). The opening of the first six seals permits the Seer to view the four horsemen of the apocalypse (6:1-8), the souls of the martyrs under the altar (6:9-11), and the shaking of the structure of the world (6:12-17). Then an interlude is inserted: the sealing of the 144,000 from the tribes of Israel (7:1-8), and the great multitude of martyrs before God's throne (7:9-17). With the opening of the seventh seal, silence commences in heaven (8:1). Forthwith, however, a second group of seven begins—the vision of the seven trumpets (8:2–11:19). After an introduction (8:2-6; prayers of the saints upon the heavenly altar; fire cast upon the earth) the first four trumpets (8:7-12) bring frightful catastrophes upon the earth, sea, inland waters, sun, moon, and stars. The continuation is prepared for by the eagle's threefold cry of woe (8:13). After the fifth (9:1-12) and sixth (9:13-21) trumpets there follow demonic locusts and a wild host of cavalrymen. An interlude brings to the Apocalyptist, who again finds himself upon the earth, two visions (10:1–11:14): an angel comes down from heaven, promises that in the days of the seventh trumpet the mystery of God will be fulfilled, and gives the small open scroll lying in his hand to the Seer to eat, which first tastes sweet and then bitter (ch. 10). Then the Seer must measure the temple. He hears the prophecy from the two witnesses, who appear as preachers of repentance, and are killed by the beast out of the abyss, but rise again and ascend into heaven (11:1-14). The seventh trumpet (11:15-19) calls forth heavenly hymns and the appearance of the ark of the covenant in the heavenly temple, but also cosmic woes. Then follows a long interruption of the series of seven (chaps. 12–14): the dragon and the Lamb—war and victory. The heavenly woman with the child is threatened by the dragon, and the child carried up to God (12:1-6). Michael triumphs over the dragon (12:7-12), which vainly pursues the woman on the earth (12:13-17). Two beasts emerge (13:1-18): the first out of the sea, with the mortally wounded and healed head, which persecutes the Christians (13:1-10); the second from the land, the importunate, wooing companion of the first (13:11-17); the number of the first beast, the number of a man, is 666 (13:18). By way of contrast, there appears the vision of the Lamb and of 144,000 sealed (14:1-5), and the announcement and execution of judgment (14:6-20). Next appears the third group of seven, the vision of the seven bowls (chaps. 15, 16), with the dreadful plagues, which are poured out from the bowls of God's wrath upon the earth one after another, but do not yet bring the end. Not until the fall of Babylon (17:1–19:10) does the judgment of God begin, which leads to the final triumph of the eternal Lord of history: judgment upon the harlot Babylon and the beast (ch. 17), with the lament over Babylon's fall (ch. 18), and joy in heaven (19:1-10). The final section, the coming of Christ and the consummation (19:11–22:5), portrays the victory of the Christ (who appears on a white horse and whose names are ὁ λόγος τοῦ θεοῦ, "King of Kings," and "Lord of Lords") over the antichrist and his followers (19:11-21), the thousand-year kingdom, in which the pious who have been certified through death participate, judgment upon Satan, who once more has become free (20:1-10), the last judgment (20:11-15), and the heavenly Jerusalem (21:1–22:5).

The conclusion (22:6-21) contains the verification of the Apocalypse as a prophetic witness of divine truth, a renewed promise of Christ's parousia, and a benediction.

2. The Apocalypse of John as an Apocalyptic and Prophetic Book

The Apocalypse is most closely connected with the apocalyptic literature of Judaism (see §33). Mythical material, mysterious numbers, visions and apparitions out of heaven as the chief means of revealing transworldly things, reproduction of that which has been seen in richly embellished, fanciful images, but also frequent dependence upon the OT, characterize the Apocalypse as a work which belongs to the same literary category as the Jewish apocalypses. A chain of visionary images represents "what must soon take place" (1:1; 22:6), "what is and what is to take place hereafter" (1:19): the last phase of the history of God with mankind and the universe.

The Seer of the Johannine Apocalypse, however, in more than one way makes himself free in a characteristic manner from the scheme of apocalyptic literature and draws up a picture of history of quite a different sort from that of Jewish apocalypticism.

The Johannine Apocalypse is no pseudonymous book: John writes under his own name (1:1, 4, 9; 22:8) and does not conceal himself behind the mask of an ancient worthy, as was the custom of the Jewish apocalyptists. John is presumably a real visionary, but when he depicts that which he has experienced, he does not get lost in cosmological or astronomical secret wisdom. He does not write secret wisdom, allegedly out of primordial times; rather, he gives unsealed, open, clear, eschatological prophecy and exhortation related to the present (22:10). The book is directed to a large circle of readers, the seven churches as the church in John's field of vision, and is intended to be read aloud (1:3, 4; 22:16, 18). The epistolary framework, on which the Apocalypse appears to be stretched between the address (1:4 ff.) and the conclusion (22:21), is not traditional and is reminiscent of the literary form which primitive Christian literature at first mostly took (see §11). The elevated liturgical tone, which characterizes the Apocalypse far beyond its hymns, doxologies, and prayers, causes us to recognize that it was written with the thought of being read aloud in worship. Here too the practice of primitive Christian life had a voice in the shaping of the literary form.

The apocalyptic book of the NT is contrasted still more strongly with the Jewish type in its view of history.

In the history of his time John sees a mighty drama taking place. The stage is the earth, more precisely, the world controlled by the Roman Empire, and, in particular, the sector of it in which John lives, the province of Asia. The Christian church and the pagan political power are pitted against each other in the severest struggle. The Roman state gives color to the "beast," the bitter enemy of the church (13:1 ff.), heathen Rome to the "harlot," who sits upon the beast (17:1 ff.). Rome prepares itself for the assault upon Christianity: The churches of Asia Minor have to suffer under its vexation (2:3, 10; 3:8); in Pergamum the blood of martyrs has already flowed (2:13). Even in the vision of the seals a multitude of Christian martyrs under the altar in heaven appears in the eyes of the Seer (6:9). But these events of the past and present are only the gentle prelude to the coming great decisive struggle, which the nearest future will bring, "the hour of trial which is coming on the whole world" (3:10), in which the number of martyrs predestined by God should be complete (6:11), and in which the Christians who are faithful until death are to obtain the crown of victory (3:11; 2:10; 13:10, etc.). The Seer already sees the endless multitude of martyrs, who come out of the great tribulation, in the adornment of the victors, clothed in white robes, with palm branches in their hands, standing before the throne of God, beside the "sea of glass" (7:9 ff.; 15:2). He hears their praise in the hymn of the angel (12:10 ff.). He views them as participants in the reign and joy of the thousand-year kingdom (20:4, 6). Enthusiastically he summons the faithful to battle and victory in this unparalleled time of martyrdom: " 'Blessed are the dead who die in the Lord henceforth.' 'Blessed indeed,' says the Spirit, 'that they may rest from their labors, for their deeds follow them!' " (14:13).

This drama, however, plays only upon the proscenium, so to speak. Along with and behind this drama a yet much vaster plot unfolds, in which heaven and hell are in action—the war of God with Satan (see especially chaps. 12 ff.). The beast with the seven heads and ten horns, which rises up out of the sea, this apocalyptic symbol of "Imperium Romanum," has his power from the dragon, that old serpent, the deceiver of the whole world; it is the servant of the devil, the executor of his will upon the earth (13:2). The Roman Empire is the Satanic world power, because it fosters and demands emperor worship (13:4 ff.). The subordinate figure of the second beast shows still more crassly the empire's anti-God activity. It rises out of the earth and entices the inhabitants of the earth to worship the image of the first beast (13:12 ff.)—for good reason we see in the second beast, in the "false prophet" (16:13; 19:20; 20:10), the imperial priesthood of the province (or an individual out of its midst) with its fanatic promotion of the emperor cult (see, e.g., Bousset and Lohse, *ad loc.*). The dragon, which lay in wait for the messianic child and sought to storm heaven (12:4, 7), is also the driving power in connection with the persecution of the Christians (12:17), who refuse to worship the beast. But the struggling Christian church has yet a stronger patron: Christ, the Son of man (1:13; 14:14), the Lamb with the healed mortal wound (5:6), who, as the firstborn of the dead, was raised up to heaven, and as God's partner on the throne has become ruler over the kings of the earth (1:5), is victor (5:5; 3:21), the Lord of the new aeon. God Almighty had previously frustrated the assault of Satan, saved the messianic child from him (12:5), and cast Satan himself with his angelic host out of heaven (12:9). God's victory in heaven guarantees his coming victory on earth. God has predestined the course of things; the δεῖ γενέσθαι of the sovereign divine will stands above the events of the nearest future. He will direct the course of history so that the combatants who have "not worshiped the beast or its image" and have "not received its mark on their foreheads or their hands" (20:4) will receive the prize of victory.

God's immutable will over the last act in the world drama is written down in the secret scroll with the seven seals, which the Apocalyptist sees in the right hand of the Majesty upon the heavenly throne (5:1). Before the eyes of the Seer Christ receives this scroll, the testament of God, in order to execute it immediately and uninterruptedly (5:7, 9; chaps. 6 ff.). Its contents, in spite of dreadful terrors, are gospel, consummation of salvation (14:6; 10:7). The might of the empire is broken by Christ—he conquers and destroys the two opponents of the faithful, the beast and the false prophet (19:11 ff.). Then follows the triumph of the martyrs, the thousand-year reign, during which the resurrected, tried, and tested warriors reign with Christ, while Satan lies chained in the abyss (20:1 ff.). Then, after a brief release of Satan for the final, frightful madness upon the earth, comes the final destruction of God's archenemy (20:7 ff.). Following the last judgment (20:11 ff.) there is revealed a luminous view of a new, glorious world, with the new Jerusalem, the blessed inheritance of the victors in eternal fellowship with God (21:1–22:5).

The new in the Apocalypse of John here is, first of all, the total transformation of the Jewish into a Christian apocalypticism of history [Geschichtsapokalyptik]. From John, and through the historical appearance of Jesus, the apocalyptic view of history received a new foundation, upon which now the entire weight of the structure rests. Whereas Daniel and his successors had to turn their glance far toward the past to the God of their fathers, in order to find clear clues of his helping might in the great times of the past of the people of Israel and to rejoice with full pride over these events (cf. Dan. 2:23; Jub. 45:3; Test. Jud. 19; Assumption of Moses 3:9; II [IV] Ezra 3:15), for John the starting point of his eschatological hope is faith in the saving act of God in Jesus and in his saving work which portends victory. This event, which the first Christians themselves experienced at first hand, is for John the pivot of his confidence in the historically powerful God. As little as the Apocalypse dwells on the earthly life of Jesus, the appearance of Jesus, symbolized by the birth of the messianic child (12:5), by Jesus' redemptive death (1:5; 7:14; 12:11), and his victorious exaltation (3:21; 5:5; 17:14; cf. 1:7), is the eschatological turning point of history, the pledge of its divine consummation. The conception of salvation history, in whose center Jesus stands, lies at the basis of the Apocalypse's philosophy of history, gives to it the tone which comes from the certainty of salvation: the battle in heaven has been fought; Satan has fallen (12:7 ff.); "now the salvation and the power and the kingdom of our God . . . have come" (12:10) (cf. on the Apocalypse's view of history the works cited above of Wendland, Rissi, 66 ff., Holtz, 95 ff., 212 ff.).

The prophetic Seer, who speaks in the Apocalypse, writes a book of comfort for the church, which is on the point of becoming a martyr church. To that end he interprets the events of the present and the recent past and prophesies the development of things in the short span of time until the end of the world and the establishment of God's sovereignty. A definite situation of the primitive Christian churches, which in the shortest time must lead to the bloody persecution of all of Christendom, and the confident, victorious outlook beyond the coming time of suffering to the imminent parousia of Christ and the destruction of all antidivine powers, provide us with a secure basis for interpreting the Apocalypse, an interpretation which the Apocalypse itself demands. The Apocalypse is a book of its time, written out of its time and for its time, not for the distant generations of the future or even of the end-time. It is an occasional writing [Gelegenheitsschrift], as much so as are the epistles of the NT, and which, therefore, as a matter of principle should be understood in relation to the history of its time. With this insight into the nature of the Apocalypse we must combine our understanding of it as a work determined by the apocalyptic tradition and yet written according to a new Christian-prophetic point of view.

3. Sources, Literary Form, and Plan of the Apocalypse

This message, however, is presented in a form which gives rise to many questions. On the one hand, the Apocalypse creates the impression of a systematic and careful plan. The order to the Seer to write "what you see, and what is and what is to take place hereafter" (1:19) is carried out in succession in 1:10-18; 2-3; 4:1-22:5. By means of the Epistles, seals, trumpets, and bowls, the number seven is stressed by explicit enumeration, and since elsewhere in the Apocalypse the number seven plays an accentuated role (seven spirits, 3:1; seven lampstands, 1:12; seven stars, 1:16; seven heads, 5:6; 12:3; 17:3; seven angels, 8:2, etc.), scholars have tried to explain the plan of the entire Apocalypse even in detail according to the principle of the number seven (cf. recently, e.g., Lohmeyer [likewise Rist], Charles, de Zwaan, Goppelt, Albertz, Lohse, Bowman). In the section (12–14) standing between the seven trumpets and the seven seals, e.g., we can easily differentiate seven scenes: 12:1-18; 13:1-10; 13:11-18; 14:1-5; 14:6-13; 14:14-20; 15:2-4 (so Bowman). But here there is no recognizable indication that precisely this sevenfold division was intended. A comparison of the proposed arrangements (cf. only the table in Bowman, 444) shows that the various proposals by no means agree and give the impression of artificiality. On the other hand, if we view the whole of the Apocalypse, then we can much rather say that "the book shows no clearly recognizable arrangement" (Piper). But beyond that we must note that the Apocalypse offers numerous doublets (the seven trumpets and the seven bowls; the last judgment, 14:14 ff. and 20:11 ff.; description of the heavenly Jerusalem, 21:1 ff. and 21:9 ff.); that the visions in 7:1-17 and 10:1–11:14 interrupt the series of the seven seals and the seven trumpets; that the seventh trumpet (11: 15-19) combines heavenly songs of praise, a vision of salvation, and cosmic catastrophes; that a chronological sequence of the things seen is difficult to carry out (11:1 ff. seems to point to the time shortly before the destruction of the temple in Jerusalem; 12:1 ff. reports the birth of Jesus, and 17:5 ff. belongs at the earliest in the time of Vespasian). Since the time of H. Grotius (1641), these numerous contradictions have caused many scholars to explain the origin of the Apocalypse with literary-critical conjectures. Some thought of the weaving together of various Jewish or Christian written sources by the author. Others suggested a manifold changing of a "Grundschrift" by redactors (see the reports in Bousset, 108 ff., and Lohmeyer, ThRdsch 7, 1935, 35 ff.). Since all of these hypotheses have been unconvincing, scholars in recent decades have only occasionally sought to explain the difficulties by the supposition of sources or interpolations (McNeile-Williams, Charles, Windisch; Giet, 182 ff., regards 19:9–22:21 as a later addition). But it has especially been supposed that the Apocalypse in its transmitted form was put together out of two writings composed at different times by the same author (de Zwaan: visions of the years 70 and 79-96; E. Hirsch, *Studien zum 4. Ev.*, BhTh 11, 1936, 156 ff.: 1:1-3, 7; 4:2–22:10, 18 f. stem from the year 68/69, and 1:4-6; 1:8–3:22; 22:11-17, 20 f. from the end of Domitian's reign; M. Goguel, *The Birth of Christianity*. Tr. H. C. Snape, 1954, 525 f.: 1:4–3:22 from the years 80-85; 4:1 ff. from the end of Domitian's reign; Boismard: two parallel texts were woven together, the one beginning with 10:2 was written under Nero, the one beginning with 4:1 at the beginning of Domitian's rule, and chaps. 1–3 somewhat later). But none of these hypotheses has been able to make it plain why the author fitted his own earlier and unimproved writing to or into a later writing. Hence this approach to a solution of the literary problem of the Apocalypse is not successful (cf. also Michaelis, 307 f.). We are faced, then, with two facts: The Apocalypse does not owe its literary form alone to intentional shaping by the author, and neither connected sources nor secondary interpolations can be convincingly demonstrated. Only the supposition that the author used various traditional materials in an independent manner takes into account these two facts (so lately Piper). In view of these heterogeneous materials, the unavoidable question arises: Is this *particular* complex of tradition, or this *particular* conception, of pagan, Jewish, or Christian origin? Although this question cannot always be answered with certainty, its answer is indispensable to the exposition of individual texts. For the understanding of the Apocalypse as a whole, however, this problem in comparative religion is largely without significance, because John in any case found his material in Jewish, if not already in Christian, form and dealt with it freely.

The linguistic and stylistic form, in which the author expressed the traditional material on the basis of personal visionary experience and of the situation of the church of his time, is certainly very remarkable. The language of the Apocalpse is saturated with countless verbal reminiscences of the OT, yet we find not a single verbatim quotation. These reminiscences, to be sure, are parallel more than once with the LXX and later versions of the OT, but manifest in the majority of cases an exact knowledge of the Hebraic and Aramaic primitive texts of the OT (proof in Charles I, LXV ff.). But the author consequently writes not only in a strongly Semitized, hieratic style, with the result that his OT form of expression can be used as an aid in textual criticism (Lohse), but also "throughout the entire book we find peculiar (and in such abundance only in the Apocalypse) demonstrable grammatical and stylistic crudities, especially neglect of congruity, which lend to the linguistic character of the Apocalypse its special stamp" (Bousset; see on the language of the Apocalypse, Bousset, 159 ff.; Charles I, CXVII ff.: "A Short Grammar of the Apocalypse"; J. Schmid, *Studien zur Geschichte des griech. Apk.-Textes* II, MThSt, 1. Erg. Bd., 1955, 173 ff.). This form of the Greek language, which is characteristic of the Apocalypse, is hardly an indication of faulty command of the language (Feine-Behm), but an intentional peculiarity of the Apocalyptist, and therefore not the secondary result of a "careful" translation out of Aramaic (Torrey).

In addition to this peculiarity of language in the narrower sense, the Apocalypse shows in its hymns and songs of praise an abundance of material in poetic form (1:5 f.; 4:8, 11; 5:9 f., 12 f.; 7:10, 12; 11:15, 17 f.; 12:10-12; 15:3 f.; 19:1 f., 5-8; 22:13). It has often been supposed that John cites liturgical pieces from the Christian worship of his time (e.g., O. Cullmann, *Early Christian Worship*. Tr. A. S. Todd and J. B. Torrance from 2nd ed., 1953; Lohse, excursus to 7:17), or even in his hymnic texts follows the liturgy of Asia Minor (Läuchli). But this supposition is undemonstrable and arbitrary, since John according to his own statement participates in heavenly worship (see E. Stauffer, *NT Theology*. Tr. John Marsh from 5th ed. [1948], 1956, 202). Delling has shown that the liturgical pieces, which are formed extensively out of OT materials, assist the author in his interpretation of the visions and therefore probably to a great extent were formulated by the author himself for this purpose. It is not the course of an earthly or of a supposed heavenly worship service which conditions the structure of the Apocalypse, but it is the sequence of the expected eschatological events and presumably also the visionary experience of the author which is decisive for the structure of the entire writing. Yet it is precisely this course of expected eschatological events which seems to be interrupted by chronological retrospections and repetitions (see above, pp. 324 f.). A unilinear, logical, consistent succession of eschatological events cannot be known, and we can hardly speak of a "homogeneous composition" (Goppelt). Rather we can readily understand that since Victorinus of Pettau (†304) there have been those who have sought to explain the repetitions with the supposition that the same future, eschatological events are described several times in succession (recapitulation theory; similarly, lately Rissi). But we may note that contrary to this supposition the text contains no kind of indication which points to an intentional repetition. Instead, the visions of the bowls clearly represent an advance beyond the visions of the trumpets. Hence Bornkamm's supposition is correct: The sections 6:1–8:1; 8:2–14:12, and 15:1–22:6 follow one after another in the relationship of overture, preparation, and final events. But even this explanation does not solve all the riddles of the course of the prophecies, such as the retrospection in 12:1 ff. and the prospection of the last judgment in 14:14 ff. The result of the discussion about the correct exposition of the Apocalypse, a discussion carried on since antiquity and marked by many changes (see the survey in Bousset, 49 ff.; lately, especially Piper), is that John wants to describe the imminent end-time beginning in his present with materials containing traditional conceptions. If we may adhere to this conclusion, then we must also say that the actual goal of the prophetic-apocalyptic portrayal is not the course of the eschatological events, but their significance for the church of his time ("kerygmatic picture of reality," Goppelt). Therefore to understand the message of the Apocalypse a knowledge of the external circumstances of its origin is especially indispensable.

4. Time of Composition of the Apocalypse

According to the earliest tradition, Irenaeus (Haer. V, 30, 3 = Eus., EH III, 18) reports that John "saw the revelation . . . at the close of Domitian's reign" (81-96). The testimony of the book itself favors an origin in the province of Asia when the Christians were severely oppressed, a time best conceivable under Domitian. In the open letters of the Apocalypse, persecutions are expected at the hands of the authorities (2:10); the blood of martyrs has already flowed (2:13; 6:9); frightful danger threatens all of Christendom (3:10): the outbreak of a general persecution of Christians by the Roman state is imminent. In 17:6 John sees the harlot, Babylon-Rome, drunk from the blood of the saints and from the blood of the witnesses of Jesus (cf. 18:24; 19:2; 16:6; 6:10). In 20:4 participation in the thousand-year kingdom is promised to the martyrs, who for the sake of the testimony to Jesus and for the word of God fell to the ax, and who did not worship the beast and its image and did not receive its mark upon their foreheads and their hands, i.e., to those who refused divine worship to the emperor (13:4, 12 ff.; 14:9, 11; 16:2; 19:20). Christianity has collided with the state and the state's religion, the Christ cult with the emperor cult. For the sake of the faith the Apocalypse raises vehement opposition against Rome and the emperor cult. That corresponds to the situation under Domitian.

The state religion had not turned against Christians before Domitian. Nero's raging in Rome against the Christians had nothing to do with the cult of the emperor. Under Domitian, who according to Oriental pattern claimed divine worship for himself as emperor during his lifetime (title, "our Lord and our God" [dominus ac deus noster], see Suetonius, *Domitian* 13, and L. Cerfaux and J. Tondriau, *Le culte des souverains dans la civilisation gréco-romaine*, 1957, 355 ff.), persecution of Christians by the state on religious grounds took place for the first time. In 96, members of the emperor's house in Rome were called to account because of ἀθεότης, an offense against the state religion. And in the Christian tradition Domitian is unanimously regarded as the first persecutor of the Christians after Nero (Melito, in Eus., EH IV, 26, 9, etc.). In the province of Asia the cult of the emperor was promoted with special zeal. Under Domitian Ephesus received a new temple to the emperor (Schütz, 18 ff.). But Giet's contention that Vespasian placed special emphasis upon the emperor cult contradicts all that we know (see Cerfaux-Tondriau, *loc. cit.*, 354 f.).

Precisely in the province of Asia, the classical land of the emperor cult, at the time of Domitian all prerequisites are given for the severe conflict between Christianity and the state religion which the Apocalypse has in mind (cf. also I Peter!). To be sure, the Seer nowhere alludes to Domitian as the very emperor reigning then. The "beast" (13:1 ff.) does not bear the features of a definite historical ruler, but rather the features of the demonic figure of *Nero redivivus,* this figure being very much alive in the popular expectation of that time. But the picture of the time which the Apocalypse sketches coincides with no epoch of the primitive history of Christianity so well as with the period of Domitian's persecution.

It is unfortunate that we cannot calculate even from chaps. 13 and 17 which Roman emperor was reigning when the Apocalypse was written. The seven heads of the beast (13:1), according to 17:9 f., represent seven emperors: "They are also seven kings, five of whom have fallen, one is, the other has not yet come, and when he comes he must remain only a little while" (17:10). In both chapters the interest is not at all fixed on the last in the series: 13:3 points in particular to one of the heads of the beast, which "seemed to have a mortal wound, but its mortal wound was healed." 17:11 transcends the number seven and poses the riddle: "as for the beast that was and is not, it is an eighth but it belongs to the seven, and it goes to perdition." Here as there the thought is of the demonic figure of Nero returned from the dead (see on the myth of Nero, Bousset, Charles, Lohmeyer, *ad loc.*) : The antichrist embodies himself in the demonic form of a ruler, Nero, who returns from the kingdom of the dead in a future emperor, who should not be counted because he breaks the rule of the cosmic number seven, and he already was one in the series of seven. Although the author's interest is focused, not on the last of the series, but on the yet expected (seventh and) eighth emperor, in 17:9*a* he thinks it important for the reader to note who is reckoned as the sixth emperor. For us, however, there is still the difficulty that we do not know with which emperor the enumeration is supposed to begin. Usually we calculate from Augustus on and regard Vespasian as the sixth emperor (Augustus, Tiberius, Caligula, Claudius, Nero, Vespasian; the soldier-emperors, Galba, Otho, Vitellius 68/69, are not taken into consideration). Giet would like to count from Caesar on, and thus regards Vespasian as the seventh or the tenth emperor. But Giet overlooks the fact that the "ten kings," according to 17:12, are yet completely future. In connection with the usual enumeration we must either suppose that the Apocalypse was written under Vespasian (but Vespasian was no promoter of the emperor cult and no persecutor of the Christians), or that the author took up a fragment which originated under Vespasian, without adapting the enumeration to the present (but 17:7 ff. doubtless is the author's own interpretation). Feuillet's supposition that the author who wrote under Domitian fictitiously backdated his writing to the time of Vespasian is especially arbitrary. Thus there remain only two possibilities: First, the author generally was not concerned about agreement between the enumeration which, for him, was dogmatically fixed, and historical reality (thus, e.g., Bousset, Lohse). But then he could hardly have written

17:9*a*. Or second, we must suppose with Brun that John begins the series of the Roman emperors regarded as enemies of God with Caligula. John, then, would resemble the author of the Apocalypse of II(IV) Ezra, who likewise wrote under Domitian, and who counted the three Flavians separately because of their hostility toward the Jews. If this supposition proves true, then Domitian would be the sixth emperor starting with Caligula, and the enumeration of the Roman emperors by the author would agree with the origin of the Apocalypse under Domitian. But as probable as this supposition is, it remains a hypothesis, and it is unable to secure the dating of the Apocalypse during Domitian's reign. And especially the mysterious number 666 (13:18) can contribute nothing to the dating, since its solution remains completely uncertain, and several emperors' names can be proposed with good reason.

In favor of an origin of the Apocalypse toward the end of the first century we may also note that according to 2:8-11 the congregation at Smyrna had been tried for a long time, whereas according to Polycarp, Phil. 11, it did not yet exist at all in the time of Paul. And 3:17 describes the church at Laodicea as rich, though this city was almost completely destroyed by an earthquake in A.D. 60/61.

All probability thus favors the view that the Apocalypse was written in Asia Minor toward the end of Domitian's reign, thus about 90-95. Its purpose was to encourage the Christian churches which were threatened by destructive persecution to resistance and to perseverance, and to assure them of Christ's early victory over the powers of the antichrist.

5. Author

The Seer of the Apocalypse and the author of the book mention his name "John" in four places (1:1, 4, 9; 22:8). Since he receives the first vision on the Isle of Patmos, which lies off the coast of Asia Minor by Miletus (1:9), and directs his book in the form of a circular letter to the seven churches in Asia (1:4; cf. 1:11), whose situation he knows quite exactly, as chaps. 2, 3 show, he himself without question belongs in this province. He bears no title which indicates his position to the readers. He asks a hearing as "servant" of God (or Jesus Christ) (1:1), as "brother" of the addressed Christians who shares with them "in Jesus the tribulation and the kingdom and the patient endurance" (1:9). The plain name "John" points to a personality known to all, and the matter-of-fact way in which he demands to be heard, to a man of high authority. He has been a prophet only since the vision of his call (1:9 ff.). The only datum out of his life which he supplies is that he "was on the island called Patmos on account of the word of God and the testimony of Jesus" (1:9), i.e., he was a preacher of the gospel, and as such he was obviously prominent, if the early interpretation of his stay on Patmos as banishment is correct (Tertullian, *Praescr. Haer.* 36; Clement of Alexandria, *Quis Div. Salv.* 42).

Already in the second century the apostle John, the son of Zebedee, was named as author, first, before 160, by Justin, *Dial.* 81, 4 (with reference to Rev.

20:4): ἀνήρ τις, ᾧ ὄνομα Ἰωάννης, εἷς τῶν ἀποστόλων τοῦ Χριστοῦ ἐν ἀποκαλύψει γενομένῃ αὐτῷ . . . προεφήτευσε, and soon thereafter by Clement of Alexandria, *Quis Div. Salv.* 42: Ἰωάννου τοῦ ἀποστόλου. Papias designated the Apocalypse as trustworthy (according to the commentary of Andreas of Caesarea, in J. Schmid, *Studien* [see above, p. 326], I Text, 10), and Melito of Sardis (in Eus., EH IV, 26, 2) wrote about it. Thus the Apocalypse from the end of the second century on in the West was regarded as apostolic and canonical without exception, and generally in the East until the middle of the third century.

This opinion certainly was not uncontested. Marcion's rejection of the Apocalypse as Jewish (according to Tertullian, *adv. Marc.* 4, 5) means nothing. The fact, however, that the anti-Montanist opponents of the Gospel of John in Asia Minor, the so-called Alogoi (see above, p. 140), and the Roman anti-Montanist, Gaius (c. 210), could trace the Apocalypse, which was prized by the Montanists, back to the Gnostic Cerinthus, proves that at the beginning of the third century the apostle John's authorship of the Apocalypse was by no means generally recognized. This relative uncertainty explains the fact that about the middle of the third century Bishop Dionysius of Alexandria, in connection with a polemic against the apocalyptic false teaching of chiliasm, could deny the Apocalypse to the apostle John and trace it back to another inspired man by the name of John. Dionysius pointed out the great linguistic and stylistic differences between the Apocalypse, on the one hand, and John and the Johannine epistles, on the other hand (in Eus., EH VII, 25, 1 ff.; *Ante-Nicene Fathers*, Vol. VI, pp. 81-84; German in WGK, NT, 6 ff.). From then on the apostolic origin of the Apocalypse was long disputed in the East. Eusebius vacillated between "recognized" and "forged" (see below, p. 349). Thus the Apocalypse is missing from several canonical lists of Asia Minor and Palestine and from most of the Greek manuscripts of the NT until the ninth and tenth centuries (cf. J. Schmid [above, p. 326] II, 31 ff.), and it first came into the Syriac NT through the revision of Philoxenos (see below, p. 354). But after Athanasius in his thirty-ninth Easter epistle, and the Latin Church under the influence of Augustine toward the end of the fourth century, had accepted the Apocalypse in their canonical lists, it was no more officially contested as a part of the NT. And since Hieronymus in his catalog of writers did not mention that the canonical status of the Apocalypse was disputed, the Middle Ages knew nothing about it. Erasmus was the first to refer again to the considerations which weigh against the composition of the Apocalypse by John the evangelist. Luther, to whom the Apocalypse was offensive by reason of its contents, declared in his "Preface to the Revelation of Saint John," 1522, that he regarded the book as "neither apostolic nor prophetic" (see *Works of Martin Luther*, "The Philadelphia Edition," Vol. 6 [1932], pp. 488 f.), and he also held fast to this judgment about the author in his more positive preface of 1530. Although Zwingli and Calvin also opposed the Apocalypse with reserve, J. S. Semler first again denied the Apocalypse to the apostle John by reason of its theology and its position in the context of the history of religions (see WGK, NT, 74 f., 79), and since then the view that the Apocalypse and John cannot derive from the same author has made much headway (recently, e.g., Bousset, Heard, Lohse, McNeile-Williams, Jülicher-Fascher, Rist, Henshaw). Yet the supposition that the apostle John is the author of John and the Johannine epistles as well as of the Apocalypse now as then has numerous supporters (so, e.g., outside of most of the Catholic scholars, Michaelis, Albertz, Hadorn, de Zwaan, Klijn, Feine-Behm, Guthrie, E. Stauffer, *NT Theology*, 1956, 40 f., etc.; Lohmeyer and Farrer assume the same author, but not the apostle; for Piper, Michl, Boismard, and Wikenhauser, the question of authorship remains undecided).

In favor of equating the author of the Apocalypse with the author of John and the apostle John, one points, in addition to the great age of this tradition, especially to the agreements in language and conceptual world. But in all these respects it becomes evident that the apocalyptist John cannot be identical with the author of John and of the Johannine epistles. The language is completely different, as especially Charles has shown (I, XXIX ff.; Rev.: ἀρνίον, Ἰερουσαλήμ, ἔθνος, ἔθνη = heathen; John: ἀμνός, Ἰεροσόλυμα, ἔθνος = the Jews). More important, the eschatology of the Apocalypse is most strongly determined by futuristic apocalyptic conceptions, of which John generally manifests nothing. Similarly, John is strongly interested in the earthly life of Jesus, whereas the Apocalypse mentions Jesus' birth only once and his death repeatedly. The Apocalypse and the Gospel of John speak and think so fundamentally differently that the early tradition (which in no way is undisputed) of the identity of the author of John and the Apocalypse cannot be based upon dependable knowledge, but must owe its origin to an earlier judgment in connection with the canonization of both writings.

Then we know nothing more about the author of the Apocalypse than that he was a Jewish-Christian prophet by the name of John. For he cannot be identical with John the son of Zebedee, if the son of Zebedee died as a martyr long before the end of the first century (see above, pp. 173 f.). And the "presbyter" John mentioned by Papias belongs by no means certainly to Asia Minor; rather the possibility exists of his identity with the presbyter of II III John (and then probably also John and I John). John, the author of the Apocalypse, does not have his authority through his relation to the Palestinian primitive church, but as a former witness for Jesus in the churches of Asia Minor (1:9) and as a present witness for Jesus in respect to all that he saw and that which God gave him to show to his servants (1:1 f.).

6. The Theological Problem

Whereas in the discussion about the historical criticism and canonical status of James the theological problem of its message was never included until Luther, this discussion in connection with the Apocalypse flared up from the beginning on in respect to the contents of this writing. Dionysius of Alexandria raised questions about the author of the Apocalypse because the advocates of an earthly eschatological hope (the "Chiliasts"), whom he opposed, appealed to Rev. 20. In order to dispute the right of the false teachers to claim that their doctrine was in conformity with Scripture, he denied, with historical arguments, the apostolic origin of the Apocalypse, and added that the book exceeded his capacity (Eus. EH VII, 25). Quite corresponding to that, Luther declared at the beginning of the Reformation that "his spirit" could not "accommodate itself to the book," because the Apocalypse has altogether too much to do with visions and symbols, and Christ is neither taught nor recognized therein. Appealing to the discussion in the early church, Luther stated that he regarded the book as neither apostolic nor prophetic. Once more, at the beginning of conscious historical criticism of the NT Semler said "the tone of the Apocalypse" was "displeasing and offensive" to him, and therefore he could not regard the book as inspired and must deny it to the author of John (see above, p. 330). Thus because of its visionary and symbolic contents, which are unusual in the NT framework, and its abstruseness, the Apocalypse has been theologically controversial in all periods of church history. So it remains until today: Whereas some will find in the Apocalypse a "genuine apostolic representation of the history of the end" (Goppelt), for others it is only "a valuable monument from a historical crisis in the history of our faith" (Rist, p. 359), its Christianity "a weakly Christianized Judaism" (R. Bultmann, *Theology of the NT*, II, 175). To be sure, today we are one in principle in respect to the correct method of exposition of the Apocalypse, at least where such exposition proceeds from scientific presuppositions: The Apocalypse can only be understood in accordance with the intentions of the author and with our historical distance from his time, if we first of all ask about the traditional meaning of the images and conceptions [traditionsgeschichtliche Methode], then seek to determine which expectations the author proclaims in respect to the imminent end [endgeschichtliche Methode], and finally observe to what extent, by means of reference to the history of the immediate past or present, the time of the end is regarded as already realized in the present [zeitgeschichtliche Methode]. But even if through conscious combination of these methods we reach a somewhat certain view of the intended meaning of the numerous symbols and concepts, the theological problem still remains as to what extent the eschatological view of history proclaimed in the Apocalypse harmonizes with the remainder of the NT message, and what existential meaning for us today this apocalyptic portrayal of the future, which is so strange to us, still has. In view of the repetitions and contradictions in the Apocalypse, and in view of the fact that the past of Christ's appearance and the present of the church's experience are included in the history of the end, there can be no doubt that the Apocalypse intends to offer no "chronology of eschatological dates" (Michaelis), as realistically as the author understood his prophecies, but a "picture of the essence of the totality of events," which is accessible only to the faithful (Goppelt). This picture of the essence is by no means only a superficially Christianized Judaism, as the central significance of the present and future Christ for the total view of the divine history and the present situation of the Christian church shows (see Holtz, 212 ff.). Yet the conceptions and symbols which form this picture of the essence presuppose to an unusually large extent not only the ancient world picture [Weltbild], but also conceptions of

Judaism and Hellenism which are in tension or even in contradiction with the central NT proclamation (e.g., the cry for vengeance in 6:10, or the expectation of an earthly millennium, 20:2 ff.). In so far as such conceptions and symbols stand in irreconcilable contradiction to this proclamation, the theological task of exposition of the Apocalypse can be properly fulfilled only if the impropriety of these conceptions and symbols is expounded and maintained. Just as there is no reason to exclude the Apocalypse as a whole from the NT, so there is every reason to regard detailed theological criticism of this writing as indispensable. For if some difficulties, such as Luther's, may disappear by reason of a more adequate knowledge of the contemporary conceptual world, there still remains no doubt that the Apocalyptist is in danger of falsifying the message of God's goal with world history. Therefore, internal criticism of the canon in respect to the Apocalypse is especially necessary, and always indispensable in ascertaining its actual message. Like James, the Apocalypse can declare its message with validity only within the framework and limits of the NT.

PART II

The Origin of the Canon of the New Testament

TH. ZAHN, *Geschichte des NTl. Kanons* I, 1888-89, II, 1890-92 (uncompleted); *idem, Forschungen zur Geschichte des NTl. Kanons und der altkirchlichen Literatur* 1-10, 1881-1929 (also contains works of other scholars); *idem, Grundriss der Geschichte des NTl. Kanons,* ²1904; A. HARNACK, *Das NT um das Jahr 200,* 1889; *idem, Die Entstehung des NT und die wichtigsten Folgen der neuen Schöpfung,* 1914; *The Origin of the NT and the Most Important Consequences of the New Creation.* Tr. J. R. Wilkinson, 1925; *idem, Die Briefsammlung des Apostels Paulus,* 1926; *idem, Die ältesten Evv.-Prologe und die Bildung des NT,* SBA 1928, 337 ff.; J. LEIPOLDT, *Geschichte des NTl. Kanons* I. II., 1907-8; E. J. GOODSPEED, *The Formation of the NT,* 1926; M.-J. LAGRANGE, *Introduction à l'étude du NT I: Histoire ancienne du canon du NT,* 1933; A. SOUTER, *The Text and Canon of the NT,* Revised by C. S. C. WILLIAMS, 1954, 137 ff.; H. HÖPFL-L. LELOIR, *Introductionis in Sacros utriusque Testamenti libros compendium,* vol. I: *Introductio generalis,* ⁶1958; E. HENNECKE-W. SCHNEEMELCHER, *NTl. Apokryphen* I, ³1959, 1 ff.; *NT Apocrypha* I. Tr. R. McL. Wilson et al., from 3rd ed. (1959), 1963, 21 ff.; also the relevant sections in the NT introductions. The most important texts, see E. PREUSCHEN, *Analecta* 2, ²1910; ZAHN, *Grundriss;* SOUTER-WILLIAMS, *Text and Canon,* 188 ff.; W. W. GROSHEIDE, *Some Early Lists of the Books of the NT,* Textus minores 1, 1948; HENNECKE-SCHNEEMELCHER, *loc. cit.,* 19 ff.; in part also in *Enchiridion Biblicum,* ³1956.

§35. THE DEVELOPMENT OF THE NEW TESTAMENT CANON UNTIL THE END OF THE SECOND CENTURY

1) The Authorities of Primitive Christianity

G. SCHRENK, art. γράφω etc., ThWB I, 1933, 742 ff.; *Theological Dictionary of the NT.* Tr. and edited Geoffrey W. Bromiley, 1964, 742 ff.; R. MEYER-A. OEPKE, *Kanonisch und apokryph,* ThWB III, 1938, 979 ff.; A. JEPSEN, "Kanon und Text des AT," ThLZ 74, 1949, 65 ff.; *idem,* RGG ³ I, 1957, 1123 ff.; G. DELLING, *Der Gottesdienst im NT,* 1952, 89 ff.; *Worship in the NT.* Tr. Percy Scott, 1962, 92 ff.; O. EISSFELDT, *Einleitung in das AT,* ²1956, 691 ff.; *Introduction to the OT.* Tr. P. R. Ackroyed from 3rd ed. (1964), 1964; P. KATZ, "The Old Testament Canon in Palestine and Alexandria," ZNW 47, 1956, 191 ff.; A. C. SUNDBERG, "The Old Testament of the Early Church," HarvThR 51, 1958, 205 ff.

The twenty-seven writings whose origin we have discussed in Part I are for us preserved almost exclusively in the context of ecclesiastical collections, and hence not in direct copies of the individual originals. We cannot decide whether some of the few fragments of papyrus from the second or third centuries (see below, pp. 363 ff., and K. Aland, FuF 31, 1957, 50) are an exception to this statement. How these collections, and finally the collection of the NT, arose, the history of the canon seeks to clarify.

Although the NT writings have been handed down to us only as part of an ecclesiastical collection, they all presumably were not written for absorption into such a collection. Even if there was a collection of Pauline epistles perhaps already at the end of the first century, they were not regarded as "Holy Scripture." Yet Jesus and primitive Christianity were not without Holy Scriptures. They took over the OT as "the scriptures" (Mk. 12:24) from Judaism and quoted from all three parts of the later OT canon. Thus from the beginning it was self-evident to the primitive church that God's revelation was set down in written form. On the other hand, it is very questionable whether before the end of the first century there already existed a closed canon of the OT and whether primitive Christianity recognized the OT as an entity with precise limits. The Pentateuch, of course, was completed in the third century before Christ, and the grandson of Jesus Sirach (preface to Sir., c. 117 B.C.) seems to know ὁ νόμος and οἱ προφῆται as closed collections, whereas the ἄλλα πάτρια βιβλία were not yet delimited. So certainly as there were "Holy Scriptures" in the Judaism of the first century before Christ, so little was there already a definitely fixed "canon." This state of affairs must have existed until the end of the first century A.D. for the Judaism of Palestine as well as of the diaspora. For texts were used as "Scripture" by the Jewish community at Qumran as well as within the Christian churches which had come forth out of Palestinian Judaism, texts which did not stand in the later canon of the rabbis (cf. I Cor. 2:9; Jas. 4:5; Jn. 7:38; Jude 14 f.). The NT writers designated the Scriptures as a whole as "law and prophets," a designation also known to contemporary Judaism (Mt. 5:17; additional evidence in W. G. Kümmel, ZNW 33, 1934, 111, note 23), but in the NT we do not find the division of the "Scriptures" into "the Law, the Prophets, and the Writings," which was used since the end of the first century A.D. in rabbinic Judaism (Talmud Babli, Sanhedrin 90b in the mouth of Gamaliel II.; Lk. 24:44 is no counterproof, since ψαλμοί cannot designate the entire collection of the "Writings"). The limitation of the Holy Scriptures to the Masoretic canon of thirty-nine writings, accomplished by the rabbis at the end of the first century A.D. (first witnesses are II [IV] Ezra 14:45; the transcribed list in ZNW 44, 1952-53, 222, and an inference from the decision concerning the Song of Solomon and Ecclesiastes at Jamnia, Mishna Jadajim 3, 5), was for centuries not accepted by the Christian church. Rather, the church itself delimited its extensive "Old Testament" from the second Christian century on in varying ways (cf. A. Jepsen and A. C. Sundberg). Thus primitive Christianity possessed "Holy Scriptures," yet did not know the concept of a clearly limited "canon" and an exclusive norm. These "Holy Scriptures," however, did not have their authority in and of themselves, for already Jesus and the primitive church submitted them, for their worth and understanding, to the critical authority of Jesus or of the Spirit of God bestowed by the Risen One (cf. Mt. 5:21 ff.; II Cor. 3:12 ff.; Jn. 5:39 ff.; 10:35 f.; II Tim. 3:15; Heb. 8:13).

Since the regular reading of OT texts in Christian worship services of the apostolic period cannot be proved, we cannot on that basis recognize an exclusive, normative character of rigidly delimited Holy Scriptures in primitive Christianity.

Hence it is not surprising that within the church—especially recognizable in Paul—there appears by the side of, or superior to, the norm of the OT, the new norm of the earthly and risen κύριος. For Paul, a saying of the Lord answers a debatable question of doctrine, faith, or life, just as categorically as a scriptural saying. In I Thess. 4:15 he gives eschatological instruction on the basis of a saying of Jesus. In I Cor. 9:9, 13, 14 he places the authoritative instruction of the Lord alongside of the scriptural proof. In I Cor. 11:23 ff. he designates word and deed of Jesus in connection with the institution of the Lord's Supper as the norm for its celebration in the churches, and in I Cor. 15:1 ff., "the gospel I preached to you," as the foundation of primitive Christian belief. In I Cor. 7:10, 12, 25 he notes the wide distance between the command of the Lord, which is unconditionally binding, and the personal instructions of the apostle commissioned by the Lord. And at the end of the apostolic age we find the same unconditional authority of the Lord's sayings which have been handed down in the church or spoken by the Risen Lord himself (Acts 20:35; Rev. 2:1, 8, etc.).

At the same time, however, another development is under way. Not only is the authority of the κύριος unconditional, but Paul, where he himself has to decide a matter, appeals to his claim that he is one "commissioned by the Lord," and has the Spirit of God (I Cor. 7:25, 40); his instructions, therefore, κυρίου ἐστίν, i.e., the Lord himself speaks through him. And as ἀπόστολος διὰ Ἰησοῦ Χριστοῦ καὶ θεοῦ πατρός he claims that he may put under the curse any other gospel as not derived from God (Gal. 1:1, 7 ff.; cf. II Thess. 3:17). Likewise, the later teachers of the apostolic age claim authority in their own names (Heb. 10:26 f.; 13:18 f.; III Jn. 5 ff.; Rev. 1:1-3), or under the authority of one of the earliest apostles (Eph. 4:1; I Tim. 5:14; 6:13 ff.). But this derived authority of the apostles of Jesus Christ is, like that of the κύριος, a living authority which becomes actual in preaching, not the authority of Scriptures on a level with the "Scriptures" of the OT (even the Apocalypse, which was intended for reading aloud in worship services, claims only inspiration and hence inviolability for the writing of the Seer, but not "canonical status"—22:18 f.). Paul presumably presupposes that his epistles will be read in the assemblies of the congregations to which he writes, and occasionally also exchanged among the churches (cf. I Thess. 5:26 f.; the liturgical conclusion of I Cor. 16:20-23; Rom. 16:16; II Cor. 13:12; 1:1; Col. 4:16). Hb. (11:32) and I Pet. (5:14) obviously are also intended for reading aloud. Yet this liturgical usage is no indication that the primitive Christian writings were placed on a par with the "Scriptures" of the OT. From all of these facts we may conclude with probability that a new, living norm was developing in the church, a norm which included the Lord *and* the apostles, who from the first witnessed to the message from the Lord.

2) Preliminary Stages in the Formation of the Canon in the Postapostolic Age

The NT in the Apostolic Fathers, by a Committee of the Oxford Society of Historical Theology, 1905; A. v. HARNACK, "Über das Alter der Bezeichnung 'Die Bücher' ('Die Bibel') für die heiligen Schriften in der Kirche," *Zentralblatt für Bibliothekswesen* 45, 1928, 337 ff.; C. MAURER, *Ignatius von Antiochien und das Joh.*, AThANT 18, 1949; É. MASSAUX, *Influence de l'Évangile de saint Matthieu sur la littérature chrétienne avant saint Irénée* (Universitas Catholica Lovaniensis, Dissertationes . . . II, 42), 1950; R. HEARD, "Papias' Quotations from the NT," NTSt 1, 1954-55, 130 ff.; H. KÖSTER, *Synoptische Überlieferung bei den Apostolischen Vätern*, TU 65, 1957; R. GLOVER, "The Didache's Quotations and the Synoptic Gospels," NTSt 5, 1958-59, 12 ff.—A. HARNACK, *Die Briefsammlung* (see above, p. 334); E. J. GOODSPEED, *An Introduction* (see above, p. 28), 222 ff.; A. E. BARNETT, *Paul Becomes a Literary Influence*, 1941; J. KNOX, *Marcion and the NT*, 1942, 39 ff.; 172 ff.; L. MOWRY, "The Early Circulation of Paul's Letters," JBL 63, 1944, 73 ff.; C. H. BUCK, "The Early Order of the Pauline Corpus," JBL 68, 1949, 351 ff.; K. L. CARROLL, "The Expansion of the Pauline Corpus," JBL 72, 1953, 230 ff.; C. L. MITTON, *The Formation of the Pauline Corpus*, 1955; J. FINEGAN, "The Original Form of the Pauline Collection," HarvThR 49, 1956, 85 ff.; J. KNOX, *Philemon Among the Letters of Paul*, ²1959; W. SCHMITHALS, "Zur Abfassung und ältesten Sammlung der paulinischen Hauptbriefe," ZNW 51, 1960, 225 ff.—O. CULLMANN, "Die Pluralität der Evv. als theologisches Problem im Altertum," ThZ 1, 1945, 23 ff.; K. L. CARROLL, "The Creation of the Fourfold Gospel," BJRL 37, 1954-55, 68 ff.; J. H. CREHAN, "The Fourfold Character of the Gospel," StEv, 1959, 3 ff.

The attitude of the Christians toward the norms of Christian teaching and Christian life to be observed at the end of the apostolic age (i.e., toward the end of the first century), can also still be observed at the beginning of the postapostolic age, especially in the earliest of the "apostolic fathers." The "Scriptures" and the λόγοι τοῦ κυρίου Ἰησοῦ, or the "words of the holy prophets" and "the ἐντολή τοῦ κυρίου handed down by the apostles" are placed side by side as having equal worth (I Clem. 13:1f.; 46:2 f., 7 f.; II Pet. 3:2). Correspondingly, Ignatius of Antioch names as authorities "the prophets, but especially the gospel" (Smyrn. 7:2), and superior to that which "stands written" in the "records," i.e., in the OT, he places "Jesus Christ," whose cross, death, resurrection, and the faith awakened by him are "the holy records" (Philad. 8). Concerning the "Lord," however, Ignatius says that he did nothing without the Father, with whom he was one, "neither he personally nor through the apostles" (Magn. 7:1; cf. 13:1), and thus shows that the revelation of Christ is mediated through his own word or that of the apostles. Hence alongside the OT as "Scripture," there also appeared the authority of the "Lord," which from the first was available in the sayings of the Lord himself in exactly the same way as in the testimony of the apostles. But it is significant that in connection with the quotation of the Lord's sayings there is no reference to their being written down, and even to this day no unanimity can be reached as to whether I Clement and Ignatius knew (Massaux) or did not know (Köster) a gospel writing. Since "the Lord" and "the apostles" in this period were "a purely ideal canon, intangible, unverifiable" (A. Jülicher), sooner or later, with the dying out of the generation of the apostles and their direct hearers, the necessity must inevitably arise of seeking the authoritative voice of the Lord *and* of the apostles in writings, where they alone could still be heard. And then sooner or later the question must be raised as to the authority of these *writings*.

The collection of primitive Christian writings which was beginning in this period abetted this development. According to all probability the collection of Pauline epistles arose already at the end of the first century. Granted, a collection of ten Pauline epistles (without the Pastorals) is not clearly attested until Marcion around 140, but it is very improbable that Marcion was the first to collect these epistles. Already I Clement, which originated in Rome, uses not only Romans (35:5 f.), but also refers the Corinthians to whom it is addressed to τὴν ἐπιστολὴν τοῦ μακαρίου Παύλου. In that connection Clement cites from I Corinthians (47:1-3; cf. also 37:5; 49:5), of which he must know a copy. Ignatius writes to the Ephesians that Paul mentions them in every epistle (Ignatius, Eph. 12:2), thus revealing his knowledge of a collection of Pauline epistles, which includes Ephesians. Other passages in Ignatius also show clear contacts with several of Paul's epistles (Romans, I Corinthians, Colossians; cf. Ignatius, Eph. 18:1, 2; Rom. 5:1; 9:2; Smyrn. 1:1; Magn. 1:1). II Pet. 3:15 f. speaks of "all the epistles" of our beloved brother Paul, and presupposes that they are in the hands of the readers. At least by the beginning of the second century, then, a collection of Pauline epistles was known in Asia Minor, and it is thoroughly probable that this canon already contained all of the ten epistles in Marcion's canon.

Some scholars have wanted to explain the origin of the Pauline collection still more precisely with the hypothesis, advocated in various forms, that this collection was created after the end of the first century as a result of the appearance of Acts, which newly awakened interest in the completely forgotten Pauline epistles. This collection of seven epistles (I-II Corinthians were combined into one epistle, as were I-II Thessalonians, and Colossians-Philemon) was arranged according to length, and Ephesians was written as an introduction to the collection. The publication of this collection in Ephesus occasioned the composition of numerous Christian epistles and the origin of additional collections of epistles (Rev. 2, 3; Ignatius) (Goodspeed, Barnett, Knox, Mitton, Carroll). Several reasons, however, militate against this hypothesis. We have no kind of testimony that Ephesians ever stood at the head of the collection (Buck, Finegan). In view of the many difficulties connected with the suggestion that I-II Corinthians, like I-II Thessalonians, and Colossians-Philemon, were originally joined into one epistle, this suggestion cannot be grounded alone on the lack of prologues to II Corinthians, II Thessalonians, and Philemon among the "anti-Marcionite Pauline prologues" (see p. 342). And the supposition that the Pauline epistles were completely forgotten until the beginning of the second century lacks probative force (cf. rather I Peter and Hebrews). Thus there remains of this hypothesis only the probable conjecture that in the first collection the

Pauline epistles were arranged basically according to length (Finegan) and that this collection arose in Asia Minor (not in Corinth, so Harnack). Schmithals' supposition that the earliest collection of seven Pauline epistles (without Colossians, Ephesians, Philemon) arose in Corinth around 80 through a redaction of fourteen original Pauline epistles, collapses with the questionableness of the supposition of such a redaction and of the arbitrary exclusion of Colossians, Ephesians, and Philemon. But even if the details remain uncertain, we may be sure that since the beginning of the second century a collection of Pauline epistles was circulated. Although this collection enjoyed high authority, it in no way was regarded as on the same level as the "Holy Scriptures" of the OT.

We must answer with still less certainty the question when a collection of the Gospels had its inception, especially since we cannot determine clearly whether I Clement and Ignatius knew gospel writings at all (see above, pp. 337 f.). Even if Ignatius knew the Gospel of Matthew and probably also the Gospel of John (so Massaux, C. Maurer, with good reasons), he refers to no written source, and thus reveals no knowledge of a collection of gospels. The contention that the collection of four Gospels existed already at the beginning of the second century (Harnack, Goodspeed, Crehan) is not provable. Toward the middle of the second century, however, the situation appears to have changed. II Clement knows Matthew and Luke, as probably does the principal part of the Epistle of Polycarp (chaps. 1–12), which originated in the thirties of the second century. The "Unknown Gospel," from the second quarter of the second century (H. I. Bell and T. C. Skeat, *Fragments of an Unknown Gospel,* 1935), reveals knowledge of all four Gospels (see J. Jeremias, ThBl 15, 1936, 34 ff.). Papias not only expressed himself about the circumstances of the composition of Matthew and Mark, but also compared Mark with another Gospel (probably Matthew) (see above, p. 43), and probably also knew John (cf. Heard). If the supposition that Tatian created his Diatessaron (see below, pp. 369 f.) before his break with the Great Church (cf. C. Peters, Diatessaron [see below, p. 370], 211 f.) could be established, a four-Gospel canon would be clearly attested for this period. But even if the existence of a collection of the four Gospels were plainly attested already for the end of the first half of the second century, Tatian's uniting of the texts of the four Gospels into one connected account, like Papias' preference for the living tradition of the κύριος (τὰ παρὰ ζώσης φωνῆς καὶ μενούσης) over against "the contents of books" (Eus., EH III, 39, 3 f.), would show that the later canonical Gospels were beginning to achieve growing significance and recognition as sources of the tradition but were not yet regarded as an exclusive and inviolable norm and were still not equally esteemed with the OT "Scriptures." Moreover, far into the second century "apocryphal" gospel writings and oral Jesus tradition from ecclesiastical writers were still used along with the canonical Gospels (cf. E. Hennecke-W. Schneemelcher, see above, p. 334). For the liturgical reading of the Gospels during this period, we still have no witness.

Parallel to this collection of writings of the apostolic age, there appeared another development which was to lay the foundation for the origin of a second body of "Holy Scriptures." The chief part of the Epistle of Polycarp, which, in addition to two gospel writings (see above, p. 339), also uses the Pauline epistles and I Peter, makes allusion with certainty only to the κύριος (Polycarp, Phil. 2:3; 7:2), and to the commands of the Lord, of the apostles, and of the prophets (καθὼς αὐτὸς ἐνετείλατο καὶ οἱ εὐαγγελισάμενοι ἡμᾶς ἀπόστολοι καὶ οἱ προφῆται οἱ προκηρύξαντες τὴν ἔλευσιν τοῦ κυρίου ἡμῶν 6:3), and therefore places alongside the OT only the proclamation of the Lord and of the apostles (cf. Phil. 11:2: "as Paul teaches" [sicut Paulus docet]), but not new Holy Scriptures (also Phil. 12:1 hardly offers an exception; cf. J. Leipoldt [see above, p. 334], I, 191). And yet a little later the so-called II Clement (14:2) names as authorities for the teaching that the church stems from above, τὰ βιβλία καὶ οἱ ἀπόστολοι and thereby places, according to the most probable meaning of the text, the apostles as living authorities side by side with the OT Scriptures (Harnack). But the same II Clement, which repeatedly introduces OT quotations with λέγει ἡ γραφή, λέγει ὁ κύριος (14:2; 13:2) and similar, in 2:4, after OT quotations, introduces the Jesus-saying (Mt. 9:13b) with the formula: καὶ ἑτέρα δὲ γραφὴ λέγει. And if it doubtless proves correct that here a gospel writing is placed on a par with the OT, because it contains testimony to the sayings of the Lord (Massaux), then it cannot be denied that therewith a gospel writing appears beside the OT as authority, though it is not recognizable whether the fathers were already clear about the existence of a new written norm. About the same time, the Epistle of Barnabas (4:14) introduces the Jesus-saying (Mt. 22:14) with the quotation formula which it repeatedly uses for OT texts: ὡς γέγραπται. Since the writer, however, does not positively indicate that he is quoting a saying of the Lord, the possibility cannot be precluded that the author of the epistle was deluded about the origin of the quotation. Yet there exists no necessity for this supposition, and we may thus point also to Barn. 4:14 as evidence that a gospel writing was beginning to be valued equally with an OT writing. In this way the first tendency to new "Scriptures" is given. But at first only "the Gospel" is accorded this place of honor, whereas for such an evaluation of apostolic writings we have no testimony until the middle of the second century (II Pet. 3:16 is still no witness that the Pauline epistles were classified as γραφή). Since, however, from the beginning of the postapostolic period sayings of the Lord and the living testimony of the apostles were cited in the same manner as divine norms (see above, p. 336), a twofold corpus of sacred Scripture must of inner necessity emerge, especially with the growing distance from the apostolic age.

3) The Beginnings of the Formation of the Canon in the Second Half of the Second Century

K. L. CARROLL, "The Earliest NT," BJRL 38, 1955-56, 45 ff.—G. KLEIN, Die zwölf Apostel, FRLANT 77, 1961, 192 ff. (on Justin); O. PIPER, "The Nature of the Gospel According to Justin Martyr," JR 41, 1961, 155 ff.—A. v. HARNACK, Marcion. Das Evangelium vom fremden Gott, TU III 15, ²1924; J. KNOX, Marcion

(see above, p. 337); E. C. BLACKMAN, *Marcion and His Influence*, 1948, 23 ff.—
R. M. GRANT, *Tatian and the Bible*, Studia Patristica I (= TU V 8), 1957, 297 ff.;
idem, "The Bible of Theophilus of Antioch," JBL 66, 1947, 173 ff.—W. C. VAN
UNNIK, "De la règle Μήτε προσθεῖναι μήτε ἀφελεῖν dans l'histoire du canon," VC 3,
1949, 1 ff.—G. BONNER, "The Scillitan Saints and the Pauline Epistles," *Journal of
Ecclesiastical History* 7, 1956, 141 ff.—D. DE BRUYNE, "Prologues bibliques d'origine
Marcionite," RBd 24, 1907, 1 ff.; P. CORSSEN, "Zur Überlieferungsgeschichte des
Römerbriefes," ZNW 10, 1909, 37 ff.; W. MUNDLE, "Die Herkunft der 'marcionitischen' Prologe zu den paulinischen Briefen," ZNW 24, 1925, 56 ff.; A. v. HARNACK,
"Der marcionitische Ursprung der ältesten Vulgata-Prologe zu den Plsbr.n," ZNW 24,
1925, 205 ff.; *idem*, "Die Marcionitischen Prologe zu den Plsbr.n, eine Quelle des Mura-
torischen Fragments," ZNW 25, 1926, 160 ff.; M.-J. LAGRANGE, "Les prologues pré-
tendus marcionites," RB 35, 1926, 161 ff.—D. DE BRUYNE, "Les plus anciens prologues
latins des évangiles," RBd 40, 1928, 193 ff.; A. v. HARNACK, *Die ältesten Evangelien-
Prologe und die Bildung des NT*, SBA 1928, 322 ff.; M.-J. LAGRANGE, review of
De Bruyne, RB 38, 1929, 115 ff.; B. W. BACON, "The Anti-Marcionite Prologue to
John," JBL 49, 1930, 43 ff.; R. G. HEARD, "The Old Gospel Prologues," JThSt, N.S. 5,
1954, 1 ff.; A. STROBEL, "Lukas der Antiochener," ZNW 49, 1958, 131 ff.; E. HAEN-
CHEN, *Die Apg.* (Meyer III [13]), 1961, 8 ff.—M.-J. LAGRANGE, "Le canon d'Hippolyte
et le fragment de Muratori," RB 42, 1933, 161 ff.; A. T. EHRHARDT, "The Gospels in
the Muratorian Fragment," *Ostkirchliche Studien* 2, 1953, 121 ff.; G. BARDY, art.
"Muratori (Canon de)," DBS V, 1954, 1399 ff.; P. KATZ, "The Johannine Epistles in
the Muratorian Canon," JThSt, N.S. 8, 1957, 273 f.; N. A. DAHL, "Welche Ordnung
der Plsbr. wird vom muratorischen Kanon vorausgesetzt?" ZNW 52, 1961, 39 ff.;
idem, "The Apocalypse of John and the Epistles of Paul in the Muratorian Fragment,"
Current Issues in NT Interpretation, Essays in honor of O. A. Piper, 1962, 239 ff.—
W. L. DULIÈRE, "Le canon néotestamentaire et les écrits chrétiens approuvés par
Irénée," *Nouvelle Clio* 6, 1954, 199 ff.—J. RUWET, "Clément d'Alexandrie, canon des
Écritures et apocryphes," Bb 29, 1948, 94 ff., 391 ff.

Shortly after the middle of the second century Justin Marytr (*Apol.* 67, 3)
reports that in Sunday worship τὰ ἀπομνημονεύματα τῶν ἀποστόλων ἢ τὰ συγγράμματα τῶν προφητῶν are read liturgically, and he means by these "Memoirs of the
Apostles," according to his own statement (*Apol.* 66, 3), the Gospels. Correspondingly, Justin repeatedly cites Synoptic texts as γέγραπται ἐν τοῖς ἀπομνη-
μονεύμασι τῶν ἀποστόλων or similarly (e.g., *Dial.* 101, 3; 104, 1), and expressly
emphasizes that these memoirs were composed "by the apostles or those who
followed them" (*Dial.* 103, 8), and includes in this manner in the "Memoirs
of the Apostles" also the Gospels of Mark and Luke, composed according to the
tradition by pupils of the apostles. Justin does not clearly include the Gospel
of John in the "Memoirs of the Apostles," but quotes from it with the formulas
ὁ Χριστὸς εἶπεν and ἐν τῷ εὐαγγελίῳ γέγραπται (*Apol.* 61, 4; *Dial.* 100, 1), so
that Justin presumably knows the four-Gospel canon. But in any case, Justin
places a collection of gospel writings for use in worship as normative "Scriptures" on a par with the OT. Thus, so far as the reading of Scripture in worship is concerned, a new canon, having only one part, appears along with the
OT canon (incorrectly denied by Piper). But when Justin goes further and

classifies the Revelation of John among the ἡμέτερα συγγράμματα (*Apol.* 28, 1), and to the testimony of the apostle John ἐν ἀποκαλύψει γενομένῃ αὐτῷ adds ὅπερ καὶ ὁ κύριος εἶπεν (*Dial.* 81, 4), he is preparing the way for the according of normative status to an "apostolic writing," though he does not grant it equal rank with the Gospels. Although Justin probably knew the Pauline epistles, he neither quotes them nor appeals to Paul, but does not intentionally ignore him (against Klein). A two-part canon, in addition to the OT, was thus developing.

Shortly before 150, however, Marcion of Asia Minor, who already was stoutly opposed at home because he rejected the OT, came to Rome and there was excluded from the church (c. A.D. 144). He then organized his own church, and, since he completely repudiated the OT, he gave to his church new Holy Scriptures, consisting of Luke and ten Pauline epistles (without the Pastorals). Intending to restore the original text, Marcion considerably shortened the "Western" text he had found of these eleven writings, and in numerous places altered them in an anti-Jewish direction. Marcion's text is not preserved as a whole, but can be partly reconstructed from the polemic of the church fathers (see Harnack, *Markion*, 40*ff.). Perhaps Marcion also expanded the text of the "Apostolos" by placing prologues before the individual Pauline epistles, which, in addition to the circumstances of origin, emphasize Paul's polemic against the legalistic "false apostles." It has been established by de Bruyne, Corssen, and Harnack (and not disproved by Mundle and Lagrange) that the prologues to Galatians, Corinthians, Romans, Thessalonians, Colossians, Philippians, and Philemon, which stand in numerous manuscripts of the Vulgate, originated in the second century, were of Marcionite origin, and originally also contained a prologue to Ephesians designated as Epistle to the Laodiceans, whereas the prologues which have been preserved to Ephesians and the Pastorals were of later origin in the Great Church (text in Preuschen, *Analecta*, 85 ff.). This two-part canon of Marcion's doubtless was precisely delimited Holy Scripture. Since the days of the church fathers, scholars have thought that Marcion chose his canon from the more extensive ecclesiastical canon (thus still Feine-Behm). But in opposition to this view, Harnack advanced the thesis that Marcion was the first to advocate the conception of new Holy Scriptures, as well as its twofold division, and the church followed him in both. And J. Knox went still further and maintained that the church saw itself *compelled* by Marcion's canon to put the four-Gospel canon in the place of his one mangled gospel and the collection of the thirteen Pauline epistles and additional apostolic writings in the place of his collection of ten Pauline epistles (similarly Carroll: The NT was consciously created in Rome between 170 and 180 to ward off the flood of apocryphal writings). But all of these theses are very questionable. On the one hand, as we cannot determine whether Marcion knew the four-Gospel canon and the Pastorals at all, we cannot say that he consciously excluded from his canon writings already regarded as canonical. On the other hand, when Marcion gave his church his two-part canon, the four-Gospel canon was already in development, and the authority of the apostolic writings had already begun to appear, in addition to that of the gospel writings. Hence Marcion's formation of his canon hardly occasioned the ecclesiastical formation of the canon. But the fact that Marcion had precisely established the canonical authority of Paul doubtless strengthened the tendency already existing in the church toward a normative evaluation of apostolic writings along with the gospel writings and toward explicit delimitation of these new "Holy Scriptures." This development was probably still further accelerated by the necessity for emphasizing the consummation of the new covenant in Christ and the apostles over against Montanism (Blackman). Thus Marcion's canon did not occasion the ecclesiastical formation of the canon, but it did encourage it. Furthermore, the church took over not only Marcionite text-forms (doxology of Romans, see above, pp. 222 ff.), and the Marcionite Pauline prologues, but also the "Epistle to the Laodiceans." This epistle originated in the Marcionite church, and is found in many Latin Bibles from the sixth century on, but already in the Muratorian fragment from the end of the second century was rejected as a Marcionite forgery (see Harnack, *Markion*, 134* ff.). As for the prologues to Mark, Luke, and John (text in Huck-Lietzmann, *Synopse*, VIII), which since de Bruyne and Harnack have been almost universally regarded as anti-Marcionite introductions to the church's four-Gospel canon from the second half of the second century which was placed against the "gospel" of Marcion's church (so also Feine-Behm, Michaelis, Wikenhauser, Strobel), they very probably do not belong together at all, but arose later and separately, though we cannot determine with certainty the circumstances of their origin (cf. Lagrange, Bacon, Heard, Haenchen). But in no case do these prologues prove that the church in the second half of the second century consciously advanced a NT canon overlapping Marcion's canon.

To be sure, we are inadequately informed about the development of the NT canon from Justin till the end of the second century.

The apologist Tatian, a native Syrian, pupil of Justin, and later head of an Encratic sect, introduced Jn. 1:5 with the formula, τὸ εἰρημένον (*Oratio ad Graecos* 13, 1, c. 176), that is, with the solemn manner of a scriptural citation. In spite of that, Tatian produced a gospel harmony, the Diatessaron, almost exclusively out of our four Gospels, by omitting the parallels and harmonizing the discrepancies (see pp. 369 f.). His harmony was used for centuries in the Syrian Church. The composition of the Diatessaron confirms the existence of the four Gospels whose text was not yet inviolable. He also used the Pauline epistles, including Hebrews (supposedly altering them linguistically; Eus., EH IV, 29, 6), and thus knew the beginning of a two-part NT.

The Valentinians knew and used the ecclesiastical four Gospels. From the Valentinian Heracleon stems the earliest commentary on the Fourth Gospel. The Valentinians also used Pauline epistles, likewise following the ecclesiastical usage.

The apologist Athenagoras (c. 180) quotes texts from the OT and the Gospels with φησί (*Apology* 10:3; 32:1; 33:2), and also refers to Paul (*de resurrectione* 18) with the formula κατὰ τὸν ἀπόστολον. If already here Paul is always valued almost equally with the Gospels, then Theophilus of Antioch (end of the second century) quotes Isaiah, τὸ εὐαγγέλιον and ὁ θεῖος λόγος = Paul, side by side, and calls John "Holy Scripture" (*ad Autolycum* III, 14; II, 22). And about the same time Ptolemy the Gnostic in his Epistle to Flora (in Epiphanius, *Panarion haer.* 33, 5, 10.15 Holl) quotes the σωτήρ in association with Παῦλος ὁ ἀπόστολος. As in the East the Pauline epistles were placed as norm alongside the Gospels, without being directly designated as "Scripture," so in the West one of the martyrs from Scilla answered the question of the proconsul (in the year 188): "What are those things in your satchel?": "Books and Epistles of Paul, a just man" ["Quae sunt res in capsa uestra?": "Libri et epistulae Pauli uiri iusti"] (R. Knopf-G. Krüger, *Ausgewählte Märtyrerakten,* Sammlung ausgewählter kirchen- und dogmengeschichtlicher Quellenschriften, N.F. 3, ³1929, 29), thus showing clearly that the Gospels, together with the OT, were valued as "The Books," but that the Pauline epistles, in spite of their practically equal position, had not quite received the same rank.

That a two-part new canon was in development at the end of the second century is also shown by the epistle of the churches in Vienna and Lyons from the year 177, which quotes Revelation as γραφή (in Eus., EH V, 1, 58). About 180 Melito of Sardis advanced a catalog of books τῆς παλαιᾶς διαθήκης (in Eus., EH IV, 26, 14), from which we may conclude, *e contrario*, the developing conception of a "NT." And it is indubitable that the anti-Montanist writing around 192 (in Eus., EH V, 16, 3; Polycrates of Ephesus?), with the designation ὁ τῆς τοῦ εὐαγγελίου καινῆς διαθήκης λόγος means a collection of writings which are called the καινὴ διαθήκη, to which one may "add nothing and take away nothing" (van Unnik). Although the church was thus gradually becoming aware of a new scriptural norm, this collection was by no means yet generally delimited in the same way. Indeed, the consciousness was largely lacking that a delimitation was necessary. Thus around 170 the anti-Montanists known as "Alogoi" could reject the Gospel of John and the Apocalypse of John as alleged works of the Gnostic Cerinthus, without thereby falling out of the framework of the church. Conversely, Bishop Serapion of Antioch (c. 200) could permit the reading of the Gospel of Peter (not having perused it himself, he had to withdraw this permission when he became acquainted with its heretical contents; Eus., EH VI, 12, 2 ff.). The circle of the accepted writings of the "new covenant" was, therefore, not yet closed.

We also find this state of things in the great church fathers of the outgoing second century and in the earliest preserved list of the canon.

Irenaeus (*Haer.* III, 11, 11), who knows the churches of Asia Minor, Rome, and Gaul, stresses the authority of the εὐαγγέλιον τετράμορφον: According to God's eternal decree, four Gospels are entrusted to the church, not more, not less. As there are four world regions, four chief winds, four divine διαθῆκαι, so four Gospels as the chief pillars of the church. For Irenaeus the second part of the NT canon consists of the thirteen Pauline epistles—for this number of the Pauline epistles he is the first witness—further, Acts, Apocalypse, I Peter, I II John. He is still undecided about Hebrews and III John, II Peter, James, and Jude. He quotes Hermas (IV, 34, 2) in connection with Genesis, Malachi, Ephesians, and Matthew as γραφή. He also prizes highly I Clement, yet probably not as "Holy Scripture" (III, 3, 2 f.).

Tertullian as witness for the church of Africa knows "the complete instrument of each testament" [totum instrumentum utriusque testamenti]; side by side with the "Law and the prophets" [lex et prophetae] stand "evangelical and apostolic writings" [evangelicae et apostolicae litterae]. Hence there is an OT and a NT. The canon of the Gospels is closed, but not yet the canon of the apostolic writings. In *Adv. Marc.* IV, 2, 5, Tertullian clearly attests the four Gospels and calls them "scripturae" (*De carne Christi,* 3). To "the Apostolos" belong, for him, thirteen Pauline epistles, Acts, Apocalypse, I John, I Peter, Jude. Not mentioned are II III John, James, and II Peter among the Catholic epistles. On the other hand, he cites Hebrews as the Epistle of Barnabas (*de pud.,* 20) and calls it "better received among the churches" [receptior apud ecclesias]. In his pre-Montanist period he treated the Shepherd of Hermas as *scriptura,* but in *de pud.* 10 rejected it as *apocryphus.*

Clement of Alexandria knows "the four Gospels delivered up to us" (*Strom.,* III 13, 93), and in the second part of the canon fourteen Pauline epistles (inclusive of Hebrews), plus Acts and the Apocalypse. According to Eusebius (EH VI, 14, 1), Clement in his *Hypotyposeis* also expounded all the Catholic epistles, including Jude, as well as Barnabas and the Apocalypse of Peter. His NT, however, included still more works. Of the gospels he used the Gospels of the Hebrews and of the Egyptians, but not as equally authoritative. As apostolic writings, he also regarded as inspired the Apocalypse of Peter, the Preaching of Peter, the Epistle of Barnabas, I Clement, Didache, and the Shepherd of Hermas.

Thus the three great theologians at the end of the second century knew a NT that contained the four-Gospel canon and an apostolic part, to which belonged incontestably thirteen Pauline epistles, Acts, I Peter, I John, and the Apocalypse. However, the status of the other Catholic epistles and of Hebrews was not yet established, and also additional writings were used as canonical. The so-called Muratorian fragment, or the Muratorian canon, attests that this state of affairs also held true for the Roman congregation. This fragment was discovered in 1740 by L. A. Muratori, librarian in the "Bibliotheca Ambrosiana" in Milan, in a manuscript of the eighth century, in a not always understandable Latin (text in the collections named on p. 334; also in H. Lietzmann, *Kleine Texte* I ²1933; English in Hennecke-Schneemelcher, *NT Apocrypha,* I, 42 ff.). This fragment reproduces a text most probably translated from the Greek into barbarous Latin, which is mutilated at the beginning and perhaps also at the end. The unknown author wrote toward the end of the second century in Rome. That he was the Roman "counter-bishop," Hippolytus (Zahn, Lagrange), is not demonstrable (on the other hand, Harnack, ZNW 24, 1925, 1 ff., Bardy). Likewise, A. Ehrhardt's view that it was an official Roman document originally written in Latin cannot be established. The fragment offers an authoritative list of the Scriptures "received" in the Catholic Church and to be read publicly, together with explicit rejection of writings to which other ecclesiastical Christians or heretics want to attribute equal worth. The text begins with the last words concerning Mark. Since it then designates Luke as the third and John as the fourth Gospel, the mention of Matthew as the first Gospel has been broken off. The statements about Mark and Luke show that eyewitnessship is highly valued. For Mark "was present at some events and thus set them down." Luke "had not seen the Lord in the flesh," but he related the events as far as he could ascertain them. The Fourth Gospel, composed by the disciple John, was written down under explicit request and approval of his fellow disciples and bishops; also the Johannine epistles guarantee that John had seen and heard the Lord and thus presents in his Gospel all the wonderful deeds of the Lord in the right order. The fragmentist knows the differences among the Gospels, but finds that they make no difference to the faith of believers, since the chief facts of the evangelical history "are declared by the one guiding Spirit" [uno ac principali spiritu declarata sint]. In connection with Acts, the most important fact is that "the several events took place in his [Luke's] presence" [sub praesentia eius (Luke) singula gerebantur]. Therefore the contents of the book are well authenticated. Luke does not report the *Passio Petri* and the journey of Paul from Rome to Spain because he was not present at these events (cf. p. 266). The seven churches to whom Paul wrote epistles symbolize to the author, just as the seven churches in the Apocalypse, the totality of the Christian church and hence the nature of the Pauline epistles as intended for the entire church. In Romans the struggle of Paul against heresy and his understanding of the OT are especially emphasized as significant. The four epistles to individual persons who were close to the Apostle (Philemon, I II Timothy, Titus) have achieved canonical recognition because they contain regulations for church discipline. Spurious Pauline epistles, which stem from heretical circles, like the epistles to the Laodiceans or to the Alexandrians, are rejected ("cannot be received into the Catholic Church" [in catholicam ecclesiam recipi non potest]), for "it is not fitting for gall to be mixed with honey." Nothing is said about the reasons for receiving three Catholic epistles (Jude, I II John). Strange to say, the Wisdom of Solomon is classified with them as a canonical book. There follow two apocalypses, the Apocalypse of John and the Apocalypse of Peter, the latter with the qualification, "which some of us do not wish to be read in church" [quam quidam ex nostris legi in ecclesia nolunt]. On the other hand, it is explained in connection with the Shepherd of Hermas: It ought also to be read, but not "publicly in church to the people" [se publicare in ecclesia populo], for it belongs neither in the completed OT canon of the prophets nor among the apostles, to the end of time. Indeed, it was written very recently in Rome by the brother of Bishop Pius. The list finally names the writings of Arsinous, Valentinus, Miltiades, and a book of psalms attributed to Marcion, but of these it says: "we accept nothing at all" [nihil in totum recipimus].

This enumeration of the writings which are received agrees essentially with that which had been established by the contemporary fathers of the West. The omission of I Peter is surprising, but not of Hebrews, James, and III John (Katz's conjecture that the reference was originally to three Johannine epistles is not convincing). Although the forged Pauline epistles and the Shepherd of

Hermas are excluded, the Apocalypse of Peter is recognized (the mention of the Wisdom of Solomon in this connection is certainly to be understood only as a mistake). It is important that here we learn something of the motives for the exclusion and inclusion of individual writings. The consciousness that in addition to the completed number of the prophetic writings "the apostle" must also be exactly limited, and hence that the new canon must also be closed, is clear. Decisive for the admission of a writing is, however, not its contents, but its composition by an apostle. Therefore the authors of Luke and probably also of Mark are authorized through the relationship of pupil to an apostle, and Acts is designated as "the acts of all the apostles" [acta omnium apostolorum], whereas the Shepherd of Hermas is excluded because its late origin precludes an apostle as author. In addition, a second motive for ecclesiastical recognition of a writing comes to light: It must be intended for the entire "ecclesia catholica." This principle creates some difficulty for the author in connection with the Pauline epistles. He overcomes this problem, however, by comparing them to the seven epistles of the Apocalypse (see Dahl). If yet in addition direct eyewitnessship is emphasized for John and Acts, and indirect eyewitnessship for Luke (something similar about Mark must have stood in the original), the polemical sense may have been: Over against the apocryphal gospels and acts is placed the certain connection of the canonical writings with the apostolic tradition. The delimitation of the canon through the exclusion of nonapostolic writings is thus completed in the case of "the gospel" by the end of the second century, but "the apostle" is still in flux. The practical consequence of such inclusion or exclusion was, first, the permission or prohibition of reading in worship and, second, as a consequence of that, in course of time the acceptance or rejection of a writing for inclusion in the manuscripts intended for use in worship.

§36. The Closing of the New Testament Canon in the Early Church

J. Ruwet, "Les 'Antilegomena' dans les œuvres d'Origène," Bb 23, 1942, 18 ff.; idem, "Le canon Alexandrin des Écritures. Saint Athanase," Bb 33, 1952, 1 ff.; C. F. F. Andry, "Barnabae Epist. ver. DCCCL," JBL 70, 1951, 233 ff.; W. Bauer, Der Apostolos der Syrer, 1903; M. Jugie, Theologia dogmatica Christianorum orientalium ab ecclesia catholica dissidentium 5, 1935, 25, 369.

1) The New Testament in the Greek Church from Origen Until the End of Antiquity

Within the history of the NT canon the great Alexandrian, Origen († 253/54), is of special import. His significance does not consist in active intervention in the course of the development which determined the extent of the NT essentially different from what it was when he found it. Rather, his service is that he ascertained the existing use of the NT writings in the particular ecclesiastical provinces of his time, and upon the basis of this investigation drew certain

results with a cautious hand. His scholarly studies, as well as his visits in various
cities and countries (Rome, Athens, Antioch, Arabia, Cappadocia, Palestine),
had given him a comprehensive knowledge of the usage in the various churches.
Upon this knowledge he based his judgment about the canonical recognition
of NT writings. Because of the great esteem which Origen enjoyed, his views
became influential in the following period.

The most important feature of Origen's work on the canon is that he determined for the first time which writings had general ecclesiastical recognition,
and that in this way he was led to distinguish various classes of ecclesiastical
writings (cf. Eus., EH VI, 25, 3 ff.). 1) His first class is the ἀναντίρρητα or
ὁμολογούμενα ("which are undisputed in the Church of God throughout the
whole world"). To this class belong the four Gospels, thirteen Pauline epistles,
I Peter, I John, Acts, and the Apocalypse. 2) The ἀμφιβαλλόμενα = disputed
writings, i.e., II Peter, II III John, Hebrews, James (*Tomoi in Jn.* 20, 10, 66),
and Jude (*Tomoi in Mt.* 17, 30). Although he cites the Shepherd of Hermas,
Barnabas, and Didache as γραφή, he seems not to have classified them as canonical. 3) The ψευδῆ, the Gospels of the Egyptians, Thomas, Basilides, and Matthias, which are rejected as heretical forgeries. On the whole, it becomes evident
in connection with Origen as well as with his predecessor Clement, that the
church in Alexandria was more broad-minded in its use of Scriptures than the
churches elsewhere. The criterion of separation between ὁμολογούμενα and ἀμφιβαλλόμενα was the recognition or rejection of a writing as "authentic," i.e.,
apostolic, by the majority of the churches. The limits of the canon were thus
not yet finally fixed. Through the use of the majority decision in respect to a
question which is ultimately historical, the judgment in particular cases remained
yet in abeyance (especially in respect to Hebrews and the Apocalypse), and
writings which were later excluded were still regarded here and there as canonical.

That becomes clear in the other witnesses of the third century. A catalog in
Latin which stands in Codex Claromontanus (D) of the Pauline epistles (see
below, p. 366), between Philemon and Hebrews (text in Preuschen, *Analecta*
2, 41 f.), is most probably translated out of the Greek and stems from the third
century (so Zahn, Leipoldt, Lagrange, Wikenhauser); it gives the number of
lines of the biblical writings. In this list are enumerated the four Gospels, thirteen
Pauline epistles (Philippians and I II Thessalonians can only inadvertently be
missing), the seven Catholic epistles, the Apocalypse, and Acts. Thus Hebrews
is omitted, which Origen traced back to Paul only indirectly. Instead of it
the following are cited as components of the NT: Epistle of Barnabas (not =
Hebrews! cf. the proof by Andry), Shepherd of Hermas, Acts of Paul, and
Apocalypse of Peter. But the partiality toward apocalypses which can be traced
here was shaken when Dionysius of Alexandria, in his writing, "On the Promises"
(c. 260; in Eus., EH VII, 25; *Ante-Nicene Fathers*, Vol. VI, pp. 81-84; German
in WGK, NT, 6 ff.), using evidence based upon language, style, and contents,
declared that the Apocalypse of John cannot stem from the author of John
and I John. Although Dionysius himself did not venture to reject the Apocalypse
because "many brethren prize it highly," as a result of his criticism the canonical

recognition of the Apocalypse in the East was violently shaken. Inasmuch as in these witnesses of the third century there still comes to light an uncertainty about the canonical recognition of Hebrews, the Apocalypse, several Catholic epistles, and some writings which finally were not received into the canon, the development continued yet further which led to the delimitation of the NT in the sense at last defined. Methodius of Olympus, Origen's opponent in Asia Minor, cites all the writings of the NT as canonical, and also the Apocalypse of Peter and perhaps the Epistle of Barnabas and the Didache. Papyrus 72 (see below, p. 364) from the third century contains Jude and both Epistles of Peter, designating the second one explicitly as the second Epistle, and therefore presumably knows these three writings as a part of the NT canon.

This uncertainty concerning the delimitation of "the apostle" still appears clearly also in the detailed discussion which Eusebius of Caesarea gives to the NT in his Ecclesiastical History (c. 303). He distinguishes three classes of writings (EH III, 25): 1. "Homologoumena," 2. "Antilegomena," 3. "altogether absurd and impious writings" (ἄτοπα πάντη καὶ δυσσεβῆ), fictions of heretical men deviating from sound orthodoxy. For Eusebius the Homologoumena are the four Gospels, Acts, (fourteen) Pauline epistles (including Hebrews), I Peter, I John, and, "if it seem correct" (εἴ γε φανείη), the Apocalypse of John. Among the Antilegomena he distinguishes two groups, writings with better and inferior reputation. The first he calls "Antilegomena which are approved by many": James, Jude, II Peter, II III John. The second group are the νόθα, the spurious Acts of Paul, the Apocalypse of Peter, Shepherd of Hermas, Barnabas, Didache, and, εἰ φανείη, the Apocalypse of John. Moreover, there are some, he says, who number among the writings in this group the Gospel of Hebrews, a gospel used by the Jewish Christians. The curious fact that he first enumerates the Apocalypse among the Homologoumena and then among the spurious Antilegomena is explained by the widespread opposition, since Dionysius of Alexandria, against the apostolic origin of the Apocalypse, whereas the earlier ecclesiastical tradition and Origen recognized it as canonical.

This scholarly classification gives, however, no complete picture of the state of affairs at the time of Eusebius. The Greek Church of his time generally knew seven Catholic epistles, as Eusebius himself certifies (EH II, 23, 24 f.), so that according to his presentation if one would join the Homologoumena and the first group of the Antilegomena he would have the NT in the modern sense. Yet at his time the seven Catholic epistles were not yet generally recognized, though according to Eusebius the name "Catholic epistles" was customary. Perhaps even a definite sequence of these epistles existed (cf. EH II, 23, 24): Ἰάκωβον, οὗ ἡ πρώτη τῶν ὀνομαζομένων καθολικῶν ἐπιστολῶν εἶναι λέγεται. But the recognition of the four small epistles was not generally fixed in his day. Above all, the Apocalypse was still disputed. From the fourth century we have enumerations of twenty-six books (i.e., without the Apocalypse) in Cyril of Jerusalem (c. 350), in the fifty-ninth (or sixtieth) canon of the synod of Laodicea (after 360), and in Gregory of Nazianzus († 390). Also Amphilochius of Iconium († c. 394) indicates that most declare the Apocalypse to be spurious.

Epiphanius, bishop on Cyprus († 403), though, cites the Apocalypse as the last NT book.

On the one hand, then, the canonical status of some of the Catholic Epistles and the Apocalypse was still disputed. On the other hand, other writings which finally were not recognized as canonical were even yet treated as components of the NT: the *Codex Sinaiticus* (see p. 365) still contains after the Apocalypse the Epistle of Barnabas and the Shepherd of Hermas; the *Codex Alexandrinus* (see p. 366), I II Clement; and the Didache is cited as γραφή by the writing which probably arose in Egypt in the fourth century and was falsely attributed to Athanasius, "Concerning Virginity."

The thirty-ninth Festal Letter of Athanasius, written in 367, put an end to this uncertainty about the delimitation of the NT canon. This Festal Letter is almost entirely preserved in Greek, Syriac, and Coptic (text in the collections listed on p. 334; English in E. Hennecke-W. Schneemelcher, *NT Apocrypha*, I, 59 f.). In this pastoral epistle he was the first to establish a fixed, circumscribed canon of the OT and NT, within which also the separate classes of writings and their sequence are defined. He designates the twenty-seven books of our NT as alone canonical. They are the four Gospels, after which follow Acts and the seven Catholic epistles (James, I II Peter, I II III John, Jude), then the fourteen Pauline epistles (Hebrews after II Thessalonians and before the Pastorals and Philemon), and the Apocalypse. No one should add anything to these nor take anything away from them. In addition to the canonical books (κανονιζόμενα) and the books which the church has rejected (ἀπόκρυφα), he cites yet a third class, the books for reading aloud (ἀναγινωσκόμενα), which the church may use in baptismal instruction: besides the Wisdom of Solomon, Sirach, Esther, Judith, and Tobit, Didache (because of the "two ways," chaps. 1–6), and the Shepherd of Hermas (because of the "Mandata"). Athanasius was also the first to call this ecclesiastically fixed collection of Holy Scriptures κανών (he says Hermas "is not of the canon" [μὴ ὄν ἐκ κανόνος]: "De decretis Nicaenae synodi" 18, 3; = Athanasius' *Werke* II, 1, 1935 ff., 15; = *A Select Library of Nicene and Post-Nicene Fathers of the Christian Church*, IV, p. 162).

Because of Athanasius' authority, the canonicity of the seven Catholic epistles quickly prevailed within the Greek Church. But the attitude toward the Apocalypse continued to be ambiguous. Chrysostom and Theodoret, the great doctors of the Antiochian school, were against it, as were also the three great Cappadocians. The Quinisextine Council (692) advanced one NT canonical list with the Apocalypse and one without it. A scriptural catalog of the ninth century, the so-called Stichometry of Nicephorus, expressly does not count the Apocalypse among the books of the NT. Until in the late Byzantine period, only a very few of the preserved Greek manuscripts of the NT text contain the Apocalypse, and most of the Greek manuscripts of the Apocalypse offer the text of it either as part of a commentary or together with nonbiblical writings. Not until the tenth-eleventh century on did the situation slowly change (cf. J. Schmid, *Studien* [see p. 326], 31 ff.). Thus we can say that the number of twenty-seven canonical writings of the NT did not finally prevail in the Greek Church until about the tenth century.

2) The New Testament in the Latin Church from Cyprian to the Fifth Century

In the Latin Church, in contrast to the Greek Church, the final determination of the canon came about earlier. Here the Apocalypse, because its recognition as canonical was already attested in the Muratorian canon, was almost never attacked, and other apocalypses after the third century were only rarely cited as canonical. Yet in the West, Hebrews and five Catholic epistles were long unrecognized or disputed.

In addition to the Gospels, Acts, and thirteen Pauline epistles, the Roman Novatian (c. 250) cites only I John and the Apocalypse as "Scripture." In the works of Cyprian (†258) we can see the contents of the NT in Africa around the middle of the third century, since he quotes numerous biblical passages, especially in his *Testimonia*. Only I John and I Peter are cited among the Catholic epistles; Hebrews does not appear; yet the Apocalypse is Holy Scripture.

The Latin church has no scholar to point to who, like Eusebius, intervened in the history of the canon with an organizing hand. On the whole, however, the formation of the canon here was accomplished more simply, corresponding to the strongly impressed sense of law and order in the Latin Church. As is shown by Hieronymus in particular, Greek theological literature generally acquired a strong influence in the West. Hieronymus made a basic contribution to the elimination of the differences between the canons of the East and of the West. Pope Damasus listened to him in connection with the determination of the Roman canon. Also Athanasius worked in the same direction during his various stays in Rome and other places of the West.

Especially in the evaluation of Hebrews, the influence of the Greek Church is clearly recognizable in the West. Originally in the Latin Church the Epistle was not regarded as Pauline. Tertullian ascribed it to Barnabas. The Roman Christian who expounded the Pauline epistles around 370, the so-called Ambrosiaster, limited himself to the thirteen Pauline epistles, without Hebrews, as did Pelagius in his commentary written around 400 in Rome. Both, however, knew Hebrews, and also cited it as Scripture, but not as Pauline. The first certain Latin canonical catalog after the Muratorian canon, an African canon from the period around 360, called Canon Mommsen after its editor (text in Preuschen, *Analecta* 2, 37 f.), names the four Gospels (Matthew, Mark, John, Luke), thirteen Pauline epistles, Acts, Apocalypse, then "epistulae Johannis" III ("una sola"), "epistulae Petri" II ("una sola"). Only one of the two manuscripts from which we know the canon, that from Cheltenham, has "una sola" in parentheses in both places. These words, whose originator wanted to recognize only one Johannine epistle and only one Petrine epistle, seem to be a later correction. Hebrews, James, and Jude, however, are missing altogether.

In the second half of the fourth century the influence of the East made itself noticeable. Hilary of Poitiers (†367), who was banished for several years to Asia Minor, cited Hebrews, James, and II Peter as apostolic. Lucifer of Calaris (†370/71), who also was in the East in exile, judged likewise about Hebrews, Jude, and II Peter. Hieronymus, who already during his Roman sojourn (382-85) placed the Athanasian extent of the NT at the basis of his revision of the Latin NT (see below, pp. 374 f.), after his emigration to the East (394) expressly described this extent in an epistle (*Ep. ad Paulinum* 53, 9) but by no means suppressed his doubts about the Pauline origin of Hebrews. In his catalog of writers (*de viris illustribus*, 392) he placed together the reports known to him about the doubts of the apostolic origin of II Peter, James, Jude, Hebrews, and the Apocalypse, and thus they were handed down to the Middle Ages. Under the influence of Hieronymus, Augustine (*De doctrina christiana II,* 13; c. 396) advocated the canon of Athanasius, in which Hebrews was cited as the last of the fourteen Pauline epistles. Already shortly before, an African synod of Hippo Regius (393; we possess only the repetition of its resolution on the canon from a synod of Carthage, 397) established the same extent of the canon, indeed formulated: "Of the apostle Paul, thirteen epistles" [Pauli apostoli epistulae tredecim]."Of the same, to the Hebrews, one" [Eiusdem ad Hebraeos una] (not until a new Catholic synod in 419 was it said: "Of the apostle Paul, fourteen epistles" [Pauli apostoli epistulae quatuordecim]!). When Pope Innocent I was asked by a Gallic bishop about the canon, he cited the Athanasian canon with fourteen Pauline epistles and seven Catholic epistles (*Epist.* 6, from the year 405).

With these African and Roman decisions the question of the canon was finally decided for the West. To be sure, practice did not immediately keep pace with this decision: Hebrews for a long time was occasionally omitted in biblical manuscripts (in the pseudo-Augustinian *Speculum,* stemming from the fifth century, and in *Codex Boernerianus* of the ninth century; see below, p. 367). Cassiodorus around the middle of the sixth century still knew no Latin commentary on Hebrews. On the other hand, until the end of the Middle Ages the apocryphal Pauline epistle to the Laodiceans is found in manuscripts of the Vulgate. But such variations do not call into question the fact that the extent of the NT of the Latin Church was irrevocably defined at the beginning of the fifth century.

3) The New Testament in the Oriental National Churches

The history of the canon in the Syrian national Church, whose center was in the lands of the Euphrates, underwent a peculiar development, in part diverging from the course of things in the Greek and Latin Churches. In Edessa, the capital of the principality of Osroëne, Christianity obtained a foothold in the last third of the second century. The *Doctrina Addai,* a Syrian legend probably from the beginning of the fifth century (see G. Philipps, *The Doctrine of Addai*, 1876), reports that the founder of the Church of Edessa, in his farewell speech to his follower Aggai, ordered that besides the OT no other writings than the Gospel, the Epistles of Paul, and Acts, in which the divine truth is enclosed, should be read in the churches (cf. Zahn, *Geschichte des Ntl. Kanons* I, 373). The early canon of the Syrians was accordingly much more limited than that of the Greeks and Latins: Instead of the four Gospels, the Diatessaron was used, and the Catholic epistles and the Apocalypse were omitted. Under Greek influence Hebrews was regarded as Pauline, whereas Philemon was either ignored as un-Pauline or rejected (see J. Leipoldt [see above, p. 334], 208 ff.). In its place the Syrian fathers of the fourth century cited III Corinthians as canonical, together with an Epistle of the Corinthians and a narrative connecting piece. This apocryphal exchange of epistles either arose independently (now known from Papyrus Bodmer X of the third century) or was taken out of the apocryphal Acts of Paul.

From the period around 400 a Syrian canonical catalog is preserved (German in Preuschen, *Analecta* 2, 67 f.). It also names from the NT only Gospels, Acts, and Pauline epistles, and after Philemon, the last Pauline epistle, remarks: "The entire 'Apostolos,' 5076 stichoi," i.e., the Pauline epistles, including Philemon, but without III Corinthians, form with Acts the entire "Apostolos." On the other hand, this canonical catalog specifies the *four* Gospels. Yet the Doctrina Addai, Aphraates, and Ephraem (both in the fourth century) still attest the ecclesiastical use of the Diatessaron, as does Eusebius (EH IV, 29, 6). Theodoret (†c. 466), bishop of Cyrrhos on the Euphrates, collected and destroyed more than 200 copies of the Diatessaron in his diocese and introduced in its place the four Gospels (*Haereticarum fabularum compendium* 1, 20). Similarly Bishop Rabbula of Edessa (†436) instructed his priests to take heed that in all churches the four "separated" Gospels be present and read. Yet such intervention of the bishops could not entirely displace the Diatessaron. It was still highly prized for a long time, especially by the Nestorians, even though they also had the Peshitta as their church Bible and therein the four Gospels.

At the beginning of the fifth century, under direction of the episcopacy, the Syrian ecclesiastical Bible, the so-called "Peshitta," was created (see p. 371 f.). It represents an assimilation of the canon of the Syrians to that of the Greeks. At its head stood the "separated" Gospels; III Corinthians was removed; there remained, with Hebrews, fourteen Pauline epistles. In addition, there were three Catholic epistles, James, I Peter, and I John. Like the Apocalypse, the other Catholic epistles remained excluded. Thus the canon contained twenty-two writings. With that, the formation of the canon was completed for a large part of the Syrian Church. Further assimilation to the Greek canon did not ensue here. Toward that direction there was even less occasion when, after the Synod of Ephesus (431), the East Syrians as Nestorians separated themselves from the Great Church. The Ethiopian Church, however, added to the twenty-seven part canon of the Greek Church the Shepherd of Hermas, I II Clement, and the eight books of the Apostolic Constitutions. On the other hand, in West

Syria, which remained in closer contact with neighboring churches, the canon was completed. The revision or new translation of the NT, the so-called *Philoxeniana*, prepared in 508 at the order of Bishop Philoxenus of Mabbug, and its revision by Thomas of Harkel in the year 616 (see p. 372), also contained II III John, II Peter, and Jude, as well as the Apocalypse. Still in the fifth and sixth centuries James and the four smaller Catholic epistles did not yet have canonical authority everywhere, and also the Apocalypse only slowly won ecclesiastical esteem.

§37. The Canon in the Western Church Since the Reformation and the Theological Problem of the Canon

H. J. Holtzmann, *Lehrbuch* (see p. 28), 154 ff.; J. Leipoldt, *Geschichte* (see p. 334) II; H. Strathmann, "Die Krisis des Kanons der Kirche," ThBl 20, 1941, 295 ff.; W. G. Kümmel, "Notwendigkeit und Grenze des NTl. Kanons," ZThK 47, 1950, 277 ff.; E. Käsemann, "Begründet der ntl. Kanon die Einheit der Kirche?," EvTh 11, 1951-52, 13 ff. (= Exegetische Versuche I, 214 ff.); H. Diem, "Das Problem des Schriftkanons," ThSt 32, 1952; O. Weber, *Grundlagen der Dogmatik* I, 1955, 274 ff.; O. Cullmann, *Die Tradition als exegetisches, historisches und theologisches Problem*, 1954; "The Tradition. The Exegetical, Historical and Theological Problem" (tr. A. J. B. Higgins), in *The Early Church. Historical and Theological Studies* (ed. A. J. B. Higgins), 1956, 57-99; F. V. Filson, *Which Books Belong in the Bible?*, 1957; H. Bacht, "Die Rolle der Tradition in der Kanonbildung," *Catholica* 12, 1958, 16 ff.; H. Braun, W. Andersen, W. Maurer, *Die Verbindlichkeit des Kanons*, Fuldaer Hefte 12, 1960; W. Marxsen, "Das Problem des ntl. Kanons aus der Sicht des Exegeten," NZSTh 2, 1960, 137 ff.; C. H. Ratschow, "Zur Frage der Begründung des ntl. Kanons aus der Sicht des systematischen Theologen," NZSTh 2, 1960, 150 ff.; W. Marxsen, "Kontingenz der Offenbarung oder (und?) Kontingenz des Kanons?," NZSTh 2, 1960, 355 ff.; P. Lengsfeld, *Überlieferung. Tradition und Schrift in der evangelischen und katholischen Theologie der Gegenwart*, 1960, 71 ff.; K. Aland, "Das Problem des ntl. Kanons," NZSTh 4, 1962, 220 ff.

For the Catholic Church of the Middle Ages there was no problem of the extent of the NT. The NT canon which was received from the early church was indisputable authority. If Thomas Aquinas and especially Nicholas of Lyra (†1340) discussed doubts about Hebrews as rightly belonging to the canon, it was done precisely in order to demonstrate that it is a canonical epistle. Following the reports of Hieronymus, historical criticism of Hebrews, some Catholic epistles, and the Apocalypse, made itself felt in Humanism (Erasmus, Cajetan), yet no one dared dispute seriously their canonicity. The Council of Trent (Sessio IV, 8 April 1546: "Decretum de canonicis scripturis," text in *Enchiridion Biblicum*, 23 f.) declared the entire Bible of the OT and NT, of the same extent as the Vulgate, as canonical. The individual books were enumerated (among them Hebrews as the fourteenth Pauline epistle and James as the epistle of the apostle James). The Council placed an equal valuation upon all the component parts of the canon, but at the same time demanded that "the oral traditions" should be received "with equal affection and reverence of piety" [sine scripto traditiones pari pietatis affectu ac reverentia].

In spite of the objections which the reformers raised against individual books, the Protestant churches also confirmed the canon of the NT of the same extent which the early church had given it. For Luther (see especially "Prefaces to the NT," 1522) that is canonical which is apostolic. However, he understands the expression "apostolic" in a twofold sense: Apostolic is now what the apostles have written, then, what has apostolic nature in it, even if not written by apostles. "The correct touchstone by which to criticize all books is to see whether they promote Christ or not. What does not teach Christ is not apostolic, even if Peter or Paul should teach it; on the other hand, what preaches Christ is apostolic, even if Judas, Annas, Pilate, and Herod should teach it" ("Preface to James"). From this point of view, Luther removed four of the seven writings which had been disputed in antiquity and by the humanists to the end of the NT, and did not enumerate them with the rest. In this way he made it plain that he did not reckon these four books, which "formerly had another reputation," among "the truly certain principal books of the NT," because only these "present me Christ bright and clear." Luther's juxtaposition of theological criticism of contents with the historical question of authorship inevitably caused him in time to modify his opinions somewhat, and from the outset he expressly emphasized that he wanted to force his views upon no one. As little as anything was changed in respect to the extent of the canon by this theological criticism of the contents, fundamentally the question about the theological justification of the early ecclesiastical delimitation of the canon was raised but certainly was not taken up for some time. Just as little did the historically understood distinctions between "canonical" and "apocryphal," or "protocanonical" and "deuterocanonical" writings of the NT have any practical significance for Lutheran theologians from Joh. Brenz to Leonh. Hutter. They were expressly opposed from Joh. Gerhard on and then abandoned, whereas in the Reformed Church such distinctions never arose. From the Reformation period the removal of Hebrews, James, Jude, and the Apocalypse to the end of the Lutheran edition of the Bible (and in no other translations of the reformers!) alone was continued. In confessions of the Reformed churches there are differences in the classification of Hebrews: The "Confessio Belgica" (1561) enumerates it as the fourteenth Pauline epistle, whereas the "Confessio Gallicana" (1559) and the "Westminster Confession" (1647) place it among the Catholic epistles. But nowhere was anything else changed in the contents of the NT.

Although the external history of the NT canon was at an end, since the theology of the Enlightenment the correctness of this ecclesiastical delimitation of the canon and the binding force of the canon for Protestant theology have become problems. J. S. Semler (see above, p. 27) was the first to point out that the closing of the canon by the early church happened only "with respect to the clerics," and "that these may use no other books for reading and for binding instruction." He concluded therefrom that in general the investigation of the canon remains free for "all thoughtful readers." The mere fact that a book belongs to the canon is not authoritative for the Christian reader, for "the only proof which will entirely satisfy a sincere reader is the inner conviction through truths which are found in these Holy Scriptures (but not in all parts and individual books)." With this insight the strict historical investigation of the origin of the individual writings of the NT, as well as of the collection as a whole, was recognized as a theological task. For a long time scholars attempted to accomplish this task falsely either as historical criticism of the canon by testing the "apostolic" origin of its individual parts (J. D. Michaelis, F. C. Baur), or as historical defense of the canon by proving the apostolic origin of these writings (Th. Zahn). This method of historical denial or defense of the suitability of the early ecclesiastical limits of the canon was false because the justification for establishing the canonical validity of certain writings in connection with the exclusion of others cannot be *historically* tested. Thus the consequence of this false way was either the demand to abandon the dogmatic concept of the canon completely (G. Krüger, *Das Dogma vom NT*, 1896; W. Wrede, *Über Aufgabe und Methode der sogenannten Ntl. Theologie*, 1897), or the attempt to demonstrate the complete unity and equal value of the NT writings ("I possessed a unified NT," A. Schlatter; cf. WGK, NT, 539, note 238). These erroneous results, however, prove that the history of the canon exhibits the historical conditions and the motives of the origin and the establishment of the canon, but cannot give a judgment concerning the actual necessity of the formation of the canon and the correctness of its delimitation.

Nevertheless, precisely the insight achieved since Semler into the historical development and the centuries-long fluctuations in the delimitation of the canon forces us to consider the meaning and the validity of *this* canon formation. For the history of the canon shows that the two-part canon of "the gospel" and "the apostle" was formed spontaneously in the course of the second century within the life of the church, but that the delimitation of the four-Gospel canon and above all of the part of "the apostle" going beyond the Pauline epistles was carried out consciously by the church according to definite principles and in connection with elimination of other opinions. Therefore the organized church by no means only ascertained which writings *were* already canonical (Lagrange, Diem), but from the middle of the fourth century on, first determined by its judgment the disputed canonical worth of a part of the NT. Hence the existence of a NT canon rests upon the fact that the church has always been founded upon the primitive Christian proclamation of God's final eschatological act of salvation in Jesus Christ and his first witnesses, and after the generation of eyewitnesses and their hearers had died out this proclamation had to be preserved, and must be preserved, in literary form. With that it is given that the canon as preserver of the apostolic witness to Christ must be closed in principle and not be made relative by the juxtaposition with equal rights of the apostolic rule of faith (Cullmann) or by the superposition of the "sense which the Holy Mother Church has held and holds" [sensus quam tenuit et tenet sancta Mater Ecclesia] (Professio fidei Tridentinae, 1564). Yet the possibility (which only now has come to be) that newly found primitive Christian writings could be added to the traditional canon must in principle be left open. Here we must note that in connection with the delimitation of the canon from the end of the second century on the chronological factor played only an occasional role (exclusion of the Shepherd of Hermas), but in other cases was not taken into consideration (exclusion of I Clement). In the event early writings are discovered, factual agreement with the decisive witnesses of the NT should not be left out of consideration, quite apart from the question of how such an expansion of the NT could be carried out practically.

The converse question about the correctness and the abiding validity of the limits of the early church's canon is certainly no merely theoretical problem. For when the limits of the early ecclesiastical canon were established, it was presupposed that the Holy Scriptures "have God himself as their actual author and creator," which guarantees "unconditional infallibility in all their parts" (Bacht). But this view, which was later dogmatized in the doctrine of inspiration, is untenable, because not only the two Testaments, but also the individual writings of the New Testament, advocate very diverse and, in part, clearly contradictory views, as is shown by the results of the special introduction to the NT, but above all by the exegesis of individual passages and the biblical theology constructed upon that exegesis. Rather, it is "according to the course of the history of the canon, as has often been said, that the necessity of its form cannot be established abstractly. The canon in its essence is much more fact than materialization of a theological concept" (O. Weber). Hence we cannot avoid the conclusion that the early ecclesiastical limitation of the canon, which was carried out only hesitatingly in the various parts of the church, in view of all its historical fortuitousness, cannot be regarded as unconditionally binding, for "the absolutization of the limits of the canon would be the absolutization of an element of the tradition" (O. Weber). Thus the Lutheran confessions correctly have not defined the canon.

In spite of that, two reasons eliminate any serious possibility that we, by excluding particular writings, can improve upon the judgment of the early church concerning the extent of the canon. 1) The long-time favorite question, based upon the discussion in the early church and in the period of the Reformation, whether the writings which were long disputed in respect to their canonicity should yet be excluded, has rightly been given up, not only because it is unfair to raise the critical question about the apostolic origin of these writings only, a question which at any rate is inappropriate in this form, but above all because even in the writings whose belonging to the canon cannot seriously be assailed we find component parts which stand in contradiction to the central NT message. Thus already on historical grounds it would be impossible, by means of elimination of writings, to delimit a NT which would be uniform and in all of its component parts an appropriate witness to the apostolic message about Christ. 2) Of still more importance is this consideration: Such a new establishment of the NT canon would have its inception in a misunderstanding of the essence of the canon. Luther evaluated the books of the

NT according to the degree to which they "show Christ to you and teach every-thing which is necessary and blessed for you to know." In addition to that he laid down the warning: "Therefore take heed that you do not make a Moses out of Christ, or a law or a book of doctrine out of the Gospel" (Preface to the "Septembertestament," 1522). Here he makes it clear that the books of the NT are canonical insofar as they make so audible the testimony to God's his-torical act of salvation in Jesus Christ that it can be further proclaimed. With that it is given that we can recognize what rightly stands in the canon only on the basis of the apostolic witness contained in the canon, and that exegetical reflection can help to clarify the greater or lesser closeness of a writing or a section of a writing to the fundamental proclamation of Christ, but cannot yet decide in a generally valid way about the normative character of this portion of Scripture. Knowledge of the "internal limits of the canon," or of the "canon within the canon," leads to the insight that a new delimitation of the NT canon would be senseless, but it also frees us for an ever new answer to the question of what in the NT "preaches and promotes Christ." The un-protected nature of the limits of the canon corresponds to the historical nature of the revelation.

PART III

The History of the Text of the New Testament

Editions of the text, see p. 21. On introduction: EB. NESTLE, *Einführung in das Griech. NT* (1897) [4]1923, completely revised by E. v. DOBSCHÜTZ; *Introduction to the Textual Criticism of the Greek NT.* Tr. William Edie from 2nd ed. (1899), 1901; H. LIETZMANN, *Einführung in die Textgeschichte der Plsbr.*, Hdb. 8, [4]1933, 1 ff.; F. G. KENYON, *Handbook to the Textual Criticism of the NT*, [3]1926; *idem, Recent Developments in the Textual Criticism of the Greek Bible*, 1933; *idem, The Text of the Greek Bible* (1937) [3]1958, enlarged by A. W. ADAMS, German (1952) [2]1961; *idem, Our Bible and the Ancient Manuscripts*, [5]revised by A. W. ADAMS, 1958; K. and S. LAKE, *The Text of the NT*, [9]1933; H. J. VOGELS, *Handbuch der NTl. Textkritik* (1923) [2]1955, cf. *idem, Übungsbuch zur Einführung in die Textgeschichte des NT*, 1928; B. H. STREETER, *The Four Gospels* (1924) [9]1956, Part I; L. VAGANAY, *Initiation à la critique textuelle néotestamentaire*, 1934; *An Introduction to the Textual Criticism of the NT.* Tr. B. V. Miller, 1937; J. JEREMIAS, "Der gegenwärtige Stand der NTl. Textforschung," ThBl 17, 1938, 10 ff.; W. G. KÜMMEL, "Textkritik und Textgeschichte des NT 1914-37," ThRdsch, N.F. 10, 1938, 206 ff., 292 ff.; 11, 1939, 84 ff.; K. et S. LAKE, "De Westcott et Hort au Père Lagrange et au-delà," RB 48, 1939, 497 ff.; R. V. G. TASKER, "An Introduction to the Manuscripts of the NT," HarvThR 41, 1948, 71 ff.; *New Testament Manuscript Studies*, ed. M. M. PARVIS and A. P. WIKGREN, 1950; C. S. C. WILLIAMS, *Alterations to the Text of the Synoptic Gospels and Acts*, 1951 (good introduction with examples); M. M. PARVIS, "The Nature and Task of NT Textual Criticism: An Appraisal," JR 32, 1952, 165 ff.; E. C. COLWELL, *What is the Best NT?*, 1952 (good introduction); E. FASCHER, *Textgeschichte als hermeneutisches Problem*, 1953; É. MASSAUX, "État actuel de la critique textuelle du NT," NRTh 85, 1953, 703 ff. (good survey); G. ZUNTZ, *The Text of the Epistles*, 1953 (cf. thereto ThLZ 83, 1958, 765 ff.); K. W. CLARK, "Textual Criticism and Doctrine," *Studia Paulina* 1953, 52 ff.; *idem*, "The Effect of Recent Textual Criticism upon NT Studies," *The Background of the NT and its Eschatology*, 1956, 27 ff.; A. SOUTER, *The Text and Canon of the NT*, Revised by C. S. C. WILLIAMS, 1954; P. SACCHI, *Alle Origini del Nuovo Testamento*, 1956; M. KARNETZKI, "Textgeschichte als Überlieferungsgeschichte," ZNW 47, 1956, 170 ff.; J. DUPLACY, *Où en est la critique textuelle du NT?*, 1959 (comprehensive research report); *idem*, "Critique textuelle du NT I," RScR 50, 1962, 242 ff.; K. TH. SCHÄFER, "Der Ertrag der textkritischen Arbeit seit der Jahrhundertwende," BZ, N.F. 4, 1960, 1 ff.; H. GREEVEN, "Textkritik II. NT," RGG [3] VI, 716 ff. Comprehensive specialized studies: C. R. GREGORY, *Textkritik des NT* I-III, 1900-1909; HERM. v. SODEN, *Die Schriften des NT in ihrer ältesten erreichbaren Textgestalt* I, 1902-10; F. H. A. SCRIVENER, *A Plain Introduction to the Criticism of the NT*, [4]1894; M.-J. LAGRANGE, *Introduction à l'étude du NT II: Critique textuelle 2: La critique rationelle*, 1935. Survey of NT Manuscripts: C. R. GREGORY, *Die griech. Handschriften des NT*, 1908; Continuation of the manuscript list by E. v. DOBSCHÜTZ, ZNW 23, 1924, 248 ff.; 25, 1926, 298 ff.; 27, 1928, 216 ff.; 32, 1933, 185 ff.; by K. ALAND, ZNW 45, 1954, 179 ff.; 48, 1957, 141 ff. The manuscript list is being kept up-to-date by K. Aland. Cf. also K. W. CLARK, *A Descriptive Cata-*

logue of Greek NT Manuscripts in America, 1937 and B. Botte, "Manuscrits grecs du NT," DBS V, 1957, 819 ff. On the nature of ancient books and writing: V. Gardthausen, *Griechische Paläographie,* [2]1911-13; W. Schubart, *Das Buch bei den Griechen und Römern,* [3]1961; *idem,* "Griechische Paläographie" in: *Handbuch der Altertumswissenschaft,* edited by W. Otto, I 4, 1925; P. Maas, "Griechische Paläographie" in A. Gercke-E. Norden, *Einleitung in die Altertumswissenschaft* I 9, 1927; R. Devreesse, *Introduction à l'étude des manuscrits grecs,* 1954; C. H. Roberts, *The Codex,* Proceedings of the British Academy 1954, 169 ff.; *idem, Greek Literary Hands,* 1956.—On methodology P. Maas, *Textkritik,* [3]1956; S. Timpanaro, "La genesi del 'metodo del Lachmann,'" *Studi Italiani di Filologia Classica* 31, 1959, 182 ff.—The following works contain plates of NT manuscripts: H. J. Vogels, *Codicum Novi Testamenti specimina,* 1929; W. H. P. Hatch, *The Principal Uncial Manuscripts of the NT,* 1939; *idem, Facsimiles and Descriptions of Minuscule Manuscripts of the NT,* 1951; O. Paret, *Die Bibel. Ihre Überlieferung in Wort und Schrift,* [2]1950—B. M. Metzger. *Annotated Bibliography of the Textual Criticism of the NT 1914-39,* SaD 16, 1955.

§38. The Manuscript Tradition of the New Testament

No NT writing is preserved in the original. We can, however, conclude from the earliest Christian papyri that the originals of the NT writings were written on both sides of papyrus sheets ("book-form") (cf. Roberts, *The Codex* [see above]). What we possess are only more or less accurate copies and extracts by early Christian writers. To restore from these copies and extracts the original text of the NT is the task of textual criticism.

The text of modern editions is based upon 1. Greek manuscripts; 2. early versions; and 3. NT quotations of the church fathers.

1. The Manuscripts

a) General

The manuscripts are distinguished primarily according to the manner of writing employed and secondarily according to the writing material used.

The writing material was either papyrus or parchment. Papyrus (produced from the pith of the papyrus plant) was used predominantly until the beginning of the fourth century, but after that only rarely. In connection with that, all of the pre-fourth-century NT manuscripts which have been preserved are papyri codices (in contrast to the literary papyri, which customarily were published as scrolls). From the fourth to the thirteenth centuries the usual writing material was parchment (*membrana,* made from the skins of sheep, goats, calves, or other animals). Occasionally scribes wrote twice on parchment: They erased or scraped away the old writing and put on another. Such a manuscript, whose original text can be made legible again today by chemical or photographic processes, is called a palimpsest (*codex rescriptus*).

According to the manner of writing, the manuscripts fall into two groups:

manuscripts in large writing, majuscule or uncial manuscripts (letters about 1 "uncia" = 1 inch high); and manuscripts in small writing, minuscule manuscripts. In the majuscule manuscripts the text is written throughout in capital letters, without separation of words, and in earlier times also without separation of meaning at the end of lines (*scriptio continua*). In addition to this "book script," there was a more flowing majuscule cursive, in which several letters were connected with one another. Presumably the NT originals were written in such majuscule cursive (two secular examples from the first century in E. M. Thompson, *An Introduction to Greek and Latin Paleography*, 1912, 164 f.; a NT manuscript from the third century [𝔓⁵³] in *Quantulacumque, Studies Presented to K. Lake*, 1937, plates after pp. 152 and 156). From the majuscule cursive the minuscule cursive gradually developed, the latter resembling the Greek longhand used today. The majuscule manuscripts extend into the tenth century. From the ninth century on minuscule manuscripts and majuscule manuscripts held the field together. In the eleventh century the minuscule manuscripts achieved undivided sway. In the earliest manuscripts accent marks, breathing marks, and punctuation are generally missing. Not until the eighth century did they become the rule. From the second century on biblical manuscripts contain abbreviations for *nomina sacra* (e.g., $\overline{\Theta\Sigma}$ for θεός, $\overline{K\Sigma}$ for κύριος, etc.; cf. A. H. R. E. Paap, *Nomina sacra in the Greek Papyri of the First Five Centuries A.D.*, 1959).

The number of known manuscripts, according to the latest statistics, amounts to 72 papyri, 242 majuscules, 2,570 minuscules, and 1,909 lectionaries (1960, see BZ, N.F. 4, 1960, 316). The Gospels have been copied the most often. Then follow, at a considerable distance, the Pauline epistles. We have the fewest manuscripts of the Apocalypse (4 papyri, 10 majuscules, 212 minuscules; see J. Schmid, *Studien zur Geschichte des griechischen Apokalypse-Textes* II, MThSt, 1. Erg. Bd., 1955). Originally, א A B C and about fifty minuscules contained the entire NT.

The designation of the manuscripts is not uniform. Still today they are largely known by the system which J. J. Wettstein (†1754) introduced. The majuscules are designated by means of capital Latin, Greek, and Hebrew letters (A B C Ξ א, etc.), the minuscules by Arabic numbers (1 2 3, etc.). Gregory introduced a new method which alone is supposed to be used today (it lies at the basis of the official lists): The majuscule manuscripts, for which the letters of the alphabet are no longer sufficient, are designated by consecutive Arabic numerals, before which a zero (0) is placed (01 02, etc.). For the most used forty-five majuscules, however, the traditional designation by means of letters also still applies, but the letters are placed before the numerals, which are enclosed in parentheses: א (01), A(02), B(03), etc. (also the designation only with letters is used). The minuscules have the numerals 1, 2, etc. The papyri are designated by Gothic 𝔓 in bold type with an exponent in an Arabic numeral: 𝔓¹, 𝔓², etc. The lectionaries are designated by the letter l with exponents in Arabic numerals: l¹, l², etc.

Herm. v. Soden proposed other sigla and used them in his works (listed on

p. 21). He abandoned the distinction between majuscule and minuscule manuscripts and numbered the manuscripts consecutively with Arabic numerals. This system, however, is not simple and has not prevailed. A concordance of the various systems is offered by B. Kraft, *Die Zeichen für die wichtigeren Handschriften des griechischen NT*, (1926) [3]1955.

The sequence of the parts of the NT is the same in almost all the Greek manuscripts: Gospels, Acts, Catholic epistles, Pauline epistles, and Apocalypse. This same sequence is followed by a greater part of the newer editions of the NT (among others, Tischendorf, Westcott-Hort, v. Soden). But other arrangements also appear, e.g., in ℵ and A: Gospels, Pauline epistles, Acts, Catholic epistles, and the Apocalypse (followed by Weiss), or in the Muratorian canon: Gospels, Acts, Pauline epistles, Catholic epistles, Apocalypse (so also the Vulgate, Erasmus, and popular modern editions).

The manuscripts often contain all kinds of data for the orientation of the reader and for the use of the manuscript, at the beginning of the entire volume or of the individual books, also in the margin or in the text or at the end of the individual book or of the entire volume. The *Epistle of Eusebius to Carpian* and the *Canons of Eusebius*, which are synoptic tables of parallel sections in the Gospels, are often prefixed to the Gospels (Nestle, *NT Graece*, prints both in his *Prolegomena*) while section and canon numbers are then written in the margin, and refer to the appropriate canon (in Nestle these numbers appear in the inner margin). The individual books are introduced by means of prefaces (ὑποθέσεις), with information about the contents of the writing, the author, the number of chapters, etc. Then follows the *titulus*, the superscription of the book. In the margin stand chapter designations and summary-headings, information about the beginning and conclusion of pericopes, etc. In addition, there sometime appear in the margins scholia (interpretative remarks), and at times entire commentaries, as well as "chains" of comments (*catenae*). Subscriptions contain traditional information about the copyist or deliverer of the manuscript, time and place of composition, etc.

Often the manuscripts also show corrections from the hand of the scribe or later editors. In our editions of the text these later corrections are designated by means of exponents ($ℵ^2$ B^2 or $ℵ^a$ B^a, etc.), to distinguish them from the original text indicated by asterisks ($ℵ^*$ B^*). An example of such a correction is the insertion of the words ἐν Ἐφέσῳ (Eph. 1:1), by the correctors of $ℵ^*$ and B^*.

The division of chapters which is usual today came into use soon after 1200. Tradition traces it back to Stephan Langton, archbishop of Canterbury (†1228). Verse division derives from the Parisian book dealer, Robert Stephanus, and appeared for the first time in his edition of the NT in 1551.

b) The Papyrus Majuscules

The NT manuscripts on papyrus are of special significance if they are older than the preserved parchment manuscripts, and only to that extent can we justfy their special treatment and designation. On the papyri cf. generally: W. Schubart, *Einführung in die Papyruskunde*, 1918; K. Preisendanz, *Papyruskunde, Handbuch der Bibliothekswissenschaft* I, 1952, 50 ff.; K. Treu, RGG³ V, 1961, 91 ff. (lit.). Lists of NT papyri: G. Maldfeld, "Die griechischen Handschriftenbruchstücke des NT auf Papyrus," ZNW 42, 1949, 228 ff.; K. Aland, ZNW 45, 1954, 187; 48, 1957, 145 ff.; *idem*, "Neue NTl. Papyri, " NTSt 3, 1956-57, 261 ff. Also, W. G. Kümmel, ThRdsch, N.F. 10, 1938, 292 ff., and B. Botte, art., "Papyrus Bibliques," DBS VI, 1109 ff. Only the most important of the earliest papyri will be mentioned here.

𝔓⁵² Pap. Rylands Greek 457 (Manchester, John Rylands Library) is the earliest preserved fragment of the NT (early second century). The palm-sized fragment contains parts of Jn. 18:31-33, 37 f., in agreement with the Nestle text. Publication: C. H. Roberts, *An Unpublished Fragment of the Fourth Gospel in the John Rylands Library*, 1935. Also, J. Jeremias, ThBl 15, 1936, 97 ff.

𝔓⁶⁴ Pap. Magd. Greek 18 (Oxford, Magdalen College) consists of three only slightly more recent fragments of Mt. 26 (end of the second century), likewise without essential divergences from the Nestle text. Publication: C. H. Roberts, HarvThR 48, 1953, 233 ff.

From the second and third centuries, in addition to important fragments, six extensive manuscripts are preserved, which make possible a glance at the form of the Greek NT text a century before the great majuscules. Three of them (𝔓⁴⁵⁻⁴⁷) are found mostly in the possession of the English collector, A. Chester Beatty, in Dublin. Three are in the possession of the Genevan collector, M. Bodmer.

𝔓⁴⁵, 𝔓⁴⁶, 𝔓⁴⁷ (Chester Beatty Papyri) contain 126 leaves (severely mutilated, in part) from three papyrus books. 𝔓⁴⁵ (one page in Vienna) contains fragments of all four Gospels and Acts. 𝔓⁴⁶ (one part of the manuscript belongs to the University of Michigan, Ann Arbor) offers the Pauline epistles in the following sequence: Romans (from 5:7 on), Hebrews, I II Corinthians, Ephesians, Galatians, Philippians, Colossians, I Thessalonians. 𝔓⁴⁷, Rev. 6–17. 𝔓⁴⁵ and 𝔓⁴⁶ were probably written at the very beginning of the third century and offer the earliest connected text of the four-Gospel canon and of the *Corpus Paulinum*. Whereas 𝔓⁴⁵ exhibits another text-form for each Gospel, it is the earliest witness to the "short," "Egyptian" text of Acts. P⁴⁶ is a valuable witness to the unrevised Pauline text of the second century and hence to the early component parts of all later textual forms. 𝔓⁴⁷ (second half of the third century) offers the oldest, but not the best, text of the Apocalypse. Publication: F. G. Kenyon, *The Chester Beatty Biblical Papyri* II. III and III Suppl., 1933-36 (Text and Facsimile Volumes). On 𝔓⁴⁵: M.-J. Lagrange, RB 43, 1934, 1 ff., 161 ff.; C. C. Tarelli, JThSt 40, 1939, 46 ff.; 41, 1940, 253 ff.; H. W. Huston, JBL 74, 1955, 262 ff. On 𝔓⁴⁶: H. Lietzmann, SBA 1934, 25; H. Seesemann, ThBl 16, 1937, 92 ff.; K. W. Clark, *Studia Paulina*, 1953, 56 ff.; G. Zuntz, *The Text of the Epistles*, 1953. On 𝔓⁴⁷: J. Schmid, *Studien* (see above, p. 361) II, 1955, 109 ff.

$\mathfrak{P}^{66}$ (Papyrus Bodmer II) comprises all of John with few lacunae (including ch. 21). The codex, which was probably written before 200, presents a text which, like $\mathfrak{P}^{45}$ in Acts, belongs to a preliminary stage of the "Egyptian" text before the recensions. Publication: V. Martin, *Papyrus Bodmer II. Évangile de Jean chap. I-XIV,* 1956; V. Martin and J. W. B. Barns, *Papyrus Bodmer II. Supplément. Évangile de Jean chap. XVI-XXI. Nouvelle édition augmentée et corrigée avec reproduction photographique complète du manuscript,* 1962. Also, K. Aland, FuF 31, 1957, 50 ff.; *idem,* ThLZ 82, 1957, 161 ff.; H. Zimmermann, BZ, N.F. 2, 1958, 214 ff. (good lists of variants!); M.-E. Boismard, RB 64, 1957, 373 ff. (very uncertain construction!); F. Klijn, NTSt 3, 1956-57, 327 ff.

$\mathfrak{P}^{72}$ (Papyrus Bodmer VII and VIII) contains as one part of a miscellaneous collection of documents the text of Jude and both Epistles of Peter. It was written in the third century, presumably by a writer with Coptic mother tongue. The manuscript offers the earliest preserved text of these three epistles. In I Peter its textual affinities are with the "Egyptian" witnesses, in Jude partly with the "wild" text before the recensions. Publication: M. Testuz, *Papyrus Bodmer VII-IX,* 1959. Good lists of variants in F. W. Beare, JBL 80, 1961, 253 ff. (for I Peter) and É. Massaux, *Le texte de l'épître de Jude du Papyrus Bodmer VII,* ALBO III, 24, 1961.

$\mathfrak{P}^{75}$ (Papyrus Bodmer XIV-XV) comprises in a single-quire codex the Gospels of Luke and John. Lk. 4:34–18:18; 22:4–24:53 and John 1:1–13:10 are preserved with small lacunae and with the remainder of additional pages. John connects to Luke on the same page. The manuscript presumably presupposes the four-Gospel canon, and was written about the end of the second century. The text coincides most frequently with B, but also with $\mathfrak{P}^{66}$, $\mathfrak{P}^{45}$, and the Sahidic version (Jn. 10:7, ὁ ποιμήν instead of ἡ θύρα!). In any case, this text is a predecessor of the "Egyptian" text-form. Publication: V. Martin et R. Kasser, *Papyrus Bodmer XIV-XV,* 1961. Cf. B. M. Metzger, ExpT 73, 1961-62, 201 ff.; K. W. Clark, "The Text of the Gospel of John in Third-Century Egypt," NovT 5, 1962, 17 ff. (points out that $\mathfrak{P}^{75}$ offers the best text of John in the third century); J. A. Fitzmyer, "Papyrus Bodmer XIV: Some Features of our Oldest Text of Luke," CBQ 24, 1962, 170 ff.; C. L. Porter, "Papyrus Bodmer XV and the Text of Codex Vaticanus," JBL 81, 1962, 363 ff. On the text of Luke, cf. E. Haenchen, *Apg.,* Meyer III[13], 1961, 667 ff.

Two papyrus fragments from the third century are of special significance because of their text-form:

$\mathfrak{P}^{37}$, a codex page with Mt. 26:19-52 in majuscule cursive (University of Michigan, Ann Arbor), proves by its fluctuation between B and D the early existence of this mixed text ("Caesarean" text?) in Egypt. Publication: H. A. Sanders, HarvThR 19, 1926, 215 ff. Also M.-J. Lagrange, *Critique textuelle* II, 1935, 157 f.

$\mathfrak{P}^{48}$, a codex page with Acts 23:11 ff. in Florence (*Bibliotheca Mediceo-Laurentiana*), attests the broad "Western" text of Acts in the third century in

Egypt. Publication: *Papiri Greci e Latini* 10, 1932, 112 ff. Also, M.-J. Lagrange, *Critique textuelle* II, 406 ff.

And a later papyrus manuscript is significant because of its extent: $\mathfrak{P}^{74}$ (Papyrus Bodmer XVIII) consists of fragments of a papyrus codex from the sixth-seventh century, which contained Acts and the Catholic epistles. Only about half the text of Acts is well preserved. The beginning and ending of Acts are badly mutilated. Only small fragments of the Catholic epistles are extant. In Acts the text exhibits striking affinities with ℵ and to a lesser extent with A. There are no parallels to the "Western" text and the special readings from B and the Koine. Publication: R. Kasser, *Papyrus Bodmer XVII*, 1961. Cf. Ph.-H. Menoud, RThPh 12, 1962, 112 ff.

c) The Parchment Majuscules

From the third century only a very few parchment fragments are preserved, of which the most important (0220) is a Greek witness to Tatian's Diatessaron (see pp. 369 f.). From the fourth century on, we have, in addition to numerous fragments, the great majuscule manuscripts, of which the most important are:

B Vaticanus (03 Gregory), already since the end of the fifteenth century in the Vatican Library, contains the OT, with two lacunae, and the largest part of the NT. In the NT the concluding pages from Heb. 9:14*b* onward, including I II Timothy, Titus, Philemon, and the Apocalypse, are gone. B stems from the early fourth century and is thus the earliest of the great Bible manuscripts. Its home was presumably Egypt (Alexandria; according to W. H. P. Hatch, JBL 72, 1953, XVIII f., Upper Egypt). Since the ink had faded, the entire text, probably before or around 1000, was traced over afresh with new ink and supplied with accents and breathing marks. The restorer undertook at the same time a kind of recension, in that he left untouched those words and letters which appeared to him to be incorrect. Previously two correctors had already worked on the text. Photographic reproduction of the manuscript: *Bibliorum ss. Graecorum Codex Vaticanus* 1902, Pars II: *Testamentum Novum*, 1904.

ℵ Sinaiticus (01 Gregory; S in Lietzmann, Hdb., etc.), discovered by C. Tischendorf at the monastery of St. Catherine on Mt. Sinai in 1859, after a partial discovery of forty-three leaves in 1844. Tischendorf delivered up the manuscript to Czar Alexander II; whether this permanent transfer of the manuscript to Russia took place in an honest and irreproachable manner is open to question (cf. *The Mount Sinai Manuscript of the Bible*, 1934, and W. Hotzelt, ThLZ 74, 1949, 457 ff.). The manuscript was in Leningrad until 1933, when it was sold by the Soviet regime to the British Museum in London for 100,000 £ (more than $500,000 at that time). The OT is almost complete, and the entire NT has survived. At the end are the Epistle of Barnabas and a large portion of the Shepherd of Hermas. The manuscript was written not later than about the middle of the fourth century in Egypt or more probably in Palestine (Caesarea) (see M.-J. Lagrange, "L'origine médiate et immédiate du Ms. Sinaïtique," RB 35, 1926, 91 ff.). Tischendorf distinguished (probably overly sharply) six to seven different hands, who later corrected the codex. According to H. J. M. Milne-T. C. Skeat, *Scribes and Correctors of the Codex Sinaiticus*, 1938, ℵ is based upon the work of three writers and several more recent correctors. A photographic reproduction of the NT portion is presented by K. Lake, *Codex Sinaiticus Petropolitanus. The NT, the Epistle of Barnabas and the Shepherd of Hermas*, 1911.

A Alexandrinus (02 Gregory), once a complete Bible; in 1627 presented to the king of England; since 1751 in the British Museum in London. This manuscript is later than the two previous ones and was probably written in the fifth century in Egypt. It has large lacunae in Matthew, John, II Corinthians, and also contains I II Clement (−12:5). The character of its text is not uniform: In the Gospels it represents the Koine text, but otherwise the Egyptian type. Latest photographic reproduction: F. G. Kenyon, *The Codex Alexandrinus in Reduced Photographic Facsimile. NT and Clementine Epistles*, 1909. Cf. T. S. Skeat, "The Provenance of the Codex Alexandrinus," JThSt, N.S. 6, 1955, 233 ff.

C Codex Ephraemi Syri rescriptus (04 Gregory), in the National Library in Paris, the most important of the palimpsests, written in the fifth century, erased in the twelfth century and rewritten with the text of 38 treatises by the Syrian ecclesiastical teacher, Ephraem (†373). Little of the OT, but about five eighths of the NT, is preserved. Tischendorf was the first to succeed in the painstaking labor of deciphering completely the underwriting. In 1843 he published the pages of the NT in facsimile reproduction.

D designates two outstanding manuscripts of the sixth century, which once were in the possession of the friend and pupil of Calvin, Th. Beza. Since both manuscripts are bilingual (Greek text and Latin translation), they obviously stem from a region of the church where Greek was still spoken (southern Gaul, southern Italy, but also Egypt and Syria, have been proposed). The text is written in κῶλα, lines of varying length to make the pauses in sense come at the end of the lines. The first manuscript contains the Gospels (in the sequence Matthew, John, Luke, Mark) and Acts (D^{ea}), the second the Pauline epistles (D^p). D^{ea}, originally in the monastery of Irenaeus in Lyons, is called "Codex Bezae Cantabrigiensis" (05 Gregory), because it was presented by Beza in 1581 to the University of Cambridge, where it is still found. D^p is Codex Claromontanus (06 Gregory), so named after the Monastery of Clermont at Beauvais, where it was previously kept, but now it is in the National Library in Paris. D^{ea} especially offers to Luke and Acts a text which diverges remarkably from the earlier manuscripts, a text related to the Old Latin and Syriac texts, and designated as "Western" (see below, p. 384). The Latin text of D^p agrees with that of Lucifer of Calaris (fourth century). Facsimile reproduction of D^{ea}: *Codex Bezae Cantabrigiensis quattuor evangelia et actus apostolorum . . . phototypice repraesentatus*, 1899. Cf. also J. D. Yoder, *Con-*

cordance to the Distinctive Greek Text of Codex Bezae, NTTS 2, 1961. D^p only in Tischendorf's edition, *Codex Claromontanus . . . ,* 1852.

Of the remaining majuscules, the following are worthy of mention:

E^a Codex Laudianus (08 Gregory) of the Acts, a bilingual manuscript in Greek and Latin, written in Sardinia in very short κῶλα, and now in Oxford, once regarded as a Greek representative of the "Western" text, is an early representative of a mixture of text-types between "Egyptian" and "Western" texts, and hence recognized as largely unimportant for textual criticism (see J. H. Ropes, HarvThR 16, 1923, 175 ff.).

G Codex Boernerianus (012 Gregory), Greek-Latin bilingual manuscript of the ninth century from St. Gall, now in Dresden, exhibits the "Western" text of the Pauline epistles (without Hebrews). Photographic reproduction: A. Reichardt, *Der Codex Boernerianus der Briefe des Apostels Paulus,* 1909.

W Freer-Gospels (032 Gregory), manuscript of the Gospels of the fourth or fifth century from Egypt, in possession of the Freer Collection in Washington. The character of the text is curiously variegated, showing to some extent affinities with the "Western" and the "Caesarean" texts (see below, pp. 384 f.). The sequence of the Gospels (Matthew, John, Luke, Mark) corresponds to D^{ea}. A remarkable insertion, which also was known by Hieronymus, follows Mk. 16:14 (Freer Logion, see p. 71). H. A. Sanders, *The NT Manuscripts in the Freer Collection I: The Washington Manuscript of the Freer Gospels,* 1912.

Θ Koridethi (038), a manuscript of the Gospels, originally possessed by the monastery of Koridethi in the Caucasian Mountains, but now in Tiflis. This manuscript, presumably written in the ninth century on Mt. Sinai in late majuscule, exhibits in Mark affinities with the minuscule groups 1, etc. (Lake group), 13, etc. (Ferrar group), and with the minuscules 28, 565, 700, and is thus a chief witness of the so-called "Caesarean" text (see below, pp. 384 f.). G. Beermann and C. R. Gregory, *Die Koridethi-Evangelien,* 1913; B. Botte, DBS V, 1957, 192 ff. (bibl.).

d) The Minuscules

Of the minuscules as later textual witnesses (the earliest dated manuscript is from 835), only a few are of value in restoring the original text, namely, those which go back to a valuable, early "Vorlage." Most of these manuscripts are of significance only as witnesses for the history of the text of the NT during the Middle Ages. Here, however, in spite of the meritorious preliminary studies of Herm. v. Soden and numerous, especially American, works, we still know little for certain (see for the problems to be solved, K. and S. Lake, *The Byzantine Text of the Gospels,* Mémorial Lagrange, 1940, 251 ff.). Two groups of minuscules are recognized as important witnesses to the so-called "Caesarean" text: a) The Ferrar Group, identified by W. H. Ferrar, and headed by minuscule 13 (Nestle: φ; K. and S. Lake, *Family 13* [*The Ferrar Group*]. *The Text According to St. Mark,* SaD 11, 1941). b) The Lake Group (Family 1), established by K. Lake and headed by minuscule 1 (Nestle: λ; K. Lake, *Codex I of the Gospels and its Allies,* TSt 7, 2, 1902). The "Queen of the minuscules," 33 (ninth century), is a witness to the "Egyptian" text. Minuscule 1739, stemming from the tenth century, is in Romans a witness to Origen's text, and in the remaining Pauline epistles to a still earlier "Egyptian" text. 2053, a manuscript of the Apocalypse written in the thirteenth century, exhibits together with majuscules A and C the best text of the Apocalypse. Hence these and some other minuscule manuscripts cannot be neglected in the reconstruction of the original text of the NT.

e) The Lectionaries

The custom of scriptural readings in worship services led to the compilation of ecclesiastical readers or lectionaries, which present definite sections of the NT according to the order of the ecclesiastical year. Lectionaries with pericopes from the Gospels are called in the Greek Church *Euangelion* (Latin, *Evangeliarium* or *Evangelistarium*), and lectionaries whose contents were taken from Acts, Catholic and Pauline epistles, *Apostolos* or *Praxapostolos.* The greatest part of the NT, even if scattered, is contained in the lectionaries. To date we know 1,909 lectionaries. Since Gregory, they have been designated by the letter l with Arabic exponents (l^1, l^2, etc.). The earliest fragments from the ecclesiastical lectionaries probably go back to the fifth century. The lectionaries are still much less studied for purposes of textual criticism than the minuscules, yet a systematic investigation of them has begun in the *Studies in the Lectionary Text of the Greek NT* (till now have appeared I 1933, II 1 1934, II 2 1936, II 3 1944, II 4 1958). These studies have demonstrated that the individual pericopes have their own textual history and in part show points of contact with early textforms. It is still doubtful to what extent this special tradition of the text can contribute to the restoration of the original text. On the lectionaries, see H. Greeven, "Die Textgestalt der Evangelienlektionare," ThLZ 76, 1951, 513 ff., and H. Vogels, *Handbuch* (see p. 359), 69 ff.

2. The Versions

As Christianity penetrated the broad social classes in regions where the Greek world language did not prevail, there developed the necessity of translating the NT into the vernacular. Hence during the course of the spread of Christianity there arose first the Syriac, the Latin, and the Coptic translations. Among the translations of the NT, these have the greatest significance for the history of the text, because they go back to Greek "Vorlagen" which are older than the more extensive Greek manuscripts which have come down to us. The earliest extensive manuscripts of the NT which we have, $\mathfrak{P}^{45}$ and $\mathfrak{P}^{46}$ (see p. 363), stem from the beginning of the third century, and the earliest manuscript of almost the entire NT, Vaticanus (B), from the fourth century. The earliest

Syriac and Latin versions, however, originated already in the second century, and the Coptic translations reach back in part to the third century. Even the latest versions of the NT can be very valuable for textual criticism if they directly reproduce a Greek text which is only poorly, or not at all, preserved. But that is seldom the case. Mostly they are either based upon the later Greek texts which we know or they are daughter versions of the Syriac, Latin, or Coptic versions. Hence we need to mention them here but briefly. Even the earlier versions are to be used only with caution as witnesses to the Greek text: No translation is equivalent to the original, even if it is entirely word for word. The refinements and peculiarities of the Greek language (imperfect, aorist, perfect, subjunctive, optative, middle, multiplicity of prepositions, etc.) cannot at all be exactly reproduced in a translation. Often a variant in a version is only a consequence of an interpretation of the difficult Greek text. Moreover, it so happens that even the textual history of the versions themselves is full of problems. Nevertheless, the earliest versions lead us to a form of the NT text which reaches back in time toward the original form as closely as does hardly any other form, and they permit cautious inferences about the Greek text most used in their home. Cf. B. M. Metzger, "The Evidence of the Versions for the Text of the NT," in *NT Manuscript Studies* (see p. 359), 25 ff.; *idem*, "A Survey of Recent Research on the Ancient Versions of NT" NTSt 2, 1955-56, 1 ff.; A. Vööbus, *Early Versions of the NT*, 1954 (thereto, W. Nagel, ThLZ 84, 1959, 750 ff.). A. F. Klijn, "Welke waarde hebben de vertalingen voor de textkritiek van het NT?" *Nederlands Theologisch Tijdschrift* 8, 1953-54, 165 ff. (warns against inferences on the basis of versions in respect to a Greek text not otherwise attested). Additional literature: RGG³ I, 1200 f.; LThK II, 380 ff.

a) The Syriac Versions

Concerning the earliest translations into Syriac (i.e., in the language of the region of the church around Edessa in Mesopotamia), we know something through direct witnesses only in connection with the Gospels. Cf. thereto A. Vööbus, *Studies in the Gospel Text in Syriac*, CSCO 128, 1951.

1. The Diatessaron of Tatian (see p. 339), according to all probability, was the earliest Syriac text of the Gospels. To be sure, everything in this connection is sorely disputed. We know for certain that the Syrian, Tatian, who lived for a long time in Rome, was there excommunicated from the Great Church because of his extreme ascetic ("Encratitic") views, and c. 172 returned to the Orient. In the second half of the second century he composed a combination of the Gospels in one account, which, according to Eusebius (EH IV, 29, 6) was called τὸ διὰ τεσσάρων (= *Vierklang* = chord consisting of four notes?). This harmony of the Gospels as a whole has been lost, and can only be inferred from secondary and tertiary sources. A parchment fragment of the passion narrative in Greek from the beginning of the third century is presumably a piece of Tatian's original text, but because of its smallness no adequate conclusions can be based upon it (C. H. Kraeling, *A Greek Fragment of Tatian's Diatessaron from Dura*,

SaD 3, 1935). The indirect tradition divides into an eastern and a western branch. The chief witnesses of the eastern branch are as follows: a) the Syrian Ephraem's († 373) commentary on the Diatessaron. Over half of this commentary is preserved in Syriac, but all of it is available only in an Armenian translation. See L. Leloir, "L'original syriaque du commentaire de S. Éphrem sur le Diatessaron," Bb 40, 1959, 959 ff.; *idem*, "Le Diatessaron de Tatien et son commentaire par Éphrem," RechB VI, 1962, 243 ff.; *idem, Saint Éphrem, Commentaire de l'évangile concordant, Version arménienne* (with Latin translation), CSCO 137-45, 1953-54; cf. also Tj. Baarda, "A Syriac Fragment of Mar Ephraem's Commentary on the Diatessaron," NTSt 8, 1961-62, 287 ff.; b) an Arabic Diatessaron translated from the Syriac (last edition with French translation: A. S. Marmardji, *Diatessaron de Tatien*, 1935); c) a Middle Persian Diatessaron translated from the Syriac (G. Messina, "Diatessaron Persiano," BeO 14, 1951; for criticism, see B. M. Metzger, JBL 71, 1952, 47 f.); and d) quotations in the Syriac writers and lectionaries.

To the witnesses of the western branch belong the *Codex Fuldensis* of the Vulgate, which follows Tatian only in arrangement; a Middle Dutch harmony of the Gospels (*The Liège Diatessaron*, ed. D. Plooij, C. A. Phillips, A. H. A. Bakker, 1–5, 1929-38, uncompleted); several Old High German, Upper German, and Low German, Middle English, and two Old Italian harmonies (details in A. Vööbus, *Early Versions* [see above, p. 369], 6 ff.).

All of the eastern witnesses go back to a lost Syriac "Vorlage," the western witnesses to a lost Latin "Vorlage," whose texts were already assimilated to the later usual Syriac or Latin text, so that a part of the witnesses, to some extent, reproduces only Tatian's arrangement, a part only Tatian's text. Consequently, the reconstruction of Tatian's original is possible only tentatively by means of conjectures. It is even disputed whether Tatian wrote his work in Rome or Syria, whether the original language was Greek (lately Kraeling) or Syriac (so lately Vööbus, Leloir), whether Tatian's work was the source of the so-called "Western" text of the Gospels (Vogels, Herm. v. Soden) or more probably only one of its earliest witnesses, whether Tatian used, in addition to the four canonical Gospels, also the "Gospel of the Hebrews" (Baumstark, Peters), or the Childhood Gospel of James and a Hebraic Gospel (Messina), etc. But it is certain that the Syriac text of the Diatessaron was the earliest Syriac text of the Gospels and was in use in the East Syrian Church until into the fifth century. Literature to the problem of Tatian in W. G. Kümmel, ThRdsch, N.F. 11, 1939, 84 ff.; C. Peters, *Das Diatessaron Tatians*, OCA 123, 1939 (Supplement, Bb 23, 1942, 68 ff.); B. M. Metzger, "Tatian's Diatessaron and a Persian Harmony of the Gospels," JBL 69, 1950, 261 ff.; H. Vogels, "Der Einfluss Marcions und Tatians auf Text und Kanon des NT," SStW, 278 ff.; A. Wikenhauser, *Introduction*, 110 ff.; A. Vööbus (see above, p. 369), 1 ff.; J. Duplacy, *Où en est* (see p. 359), 77 ff.; L. Leloir, "Le Diatessaron de Tatien," *L'Orient Syrien* 1, 1956, 208 ff.; 313 ff.; *idem, Le Diatessaron de Tatien et son commentaire par Éphrem*, in "La venue du Messie," RechB VI, 1962, 243 ff.; A. J. B. Higgins, BhHw I, 455 f.

2. The Old Syriac Versions. Perhaps even before the end of the second century the four individual Gospels were also translated into Syriac. The Syriac designation distinguishes these "separated Gospels" (*Evangelion Da-Mepharreshe*) from the Diatessaron as the "mixed Gospel." The Old Syriac "separated Gospels," the so-called *vetus Syra*, is preserved today in a double manuscript tradition, the *Syrus Curetonianus* (syr^cur or sy^c), and the *Syrus Sinaiticus* (syr^sin or sy^s). Syr^cur was found in 1842 in a monastery in the Nitrian desert of Egypt, is now in the British Museum, and was published in 1858 by W. Cureton. The incompletely preserved manuscript stems from the fifth century. Syr^sin was discovered in 1892 by the sisters Agnes Smith Lewis and Margaret Dunlop Gibson in the Monastery of St. Catherine on Mt. Sinai, where it is still housed. It is a palimpsest manuscript from the fifth or fourth century. Publications of both texts: F. C. Burkitt, *Evangelion Da-Mepharreshe* I (Text and English Translation), II (Studies), 1904; A. S. Lewis, *The Old Syriac Gospels or Evangelion Da-Mepharreshe*, 1910. A facsimile reproduction of syr^sin was published by A. Hjelt, 1930. German translation of syr^sin: A. Merx, *Die vier kanonischen Evv. nach ihrem ältesten bekannten Text* I, 1897 (Bd. II-IV, 1902-11, offers a learned, but very one-sided, commentary). Of the two forms of the text, which probably go back to a common foundation, the form of syr^sin seems as a whole to be earlier (otherwise Lagrange, Vogels). The frequent parallels between the Old Syrian and the so-called "Western" text of the Gospels (Old Latin versions, D, etc.; see pp. 384 f.) are significant. The question of the relations between the Diatessaron and *vetus Syra* is, in spite of rare contradictions, probably to be answered by saying that the text of the "separated" Gospels, which originated around 200 or later, arose under the influence of the text of the Diatessaron, and was used in the church until the fifth century. Repressed from the sixth century on, Old Syriac readings can be found until into the twelfth century (Vööbus; an edition of all the Old Syriac materials for the Gospels has been completed by Vööbus; cf. Vööbus, "Completion of the Vetus Syra Project," BR 7, 1962, 49 ff.).

Also for Acts and the Pauline epistles the existence of an Old Syriac version can be demonstrated from quotations in Syrian writers and from the Armenian translation of Ephraem of Syria's commentary. Cf. on Acts, J. H. Ropes (see p. 107), 380 ff.; on Paul, J. Molitor, *Der Paulustext des hl. Ephraem*, MBE 4, 1938.

3. The Peshitta (syr^pesch or sy^p). Since the works of F. C. Burkitt (especially *Evangelion Da-Mepharreshe* II, 1904, 100 ff.) it was regarded as proved that this translation of the NT, which was transmitted in such a strikingly uniform manner in the later Syriac manuscripts of the NT, was the work of Bishop Rabbula of Edessa († 436), and that this Bible of the church very quickly displaced the Diatessaron and the Old Syriac versions from public use. This supposition, however, has been violently shaken by the investigations of Vööbus and Black, though no clear explanation of the new materials brought forward by Vööbus has yet been found. It is established that the revision of the Old Syriac version, which since the tenth century has been called the Peshitta

(= general [translation]), and from which the four smaller Catholic epistles and Revelation are missing (see p. 353), enjoyed increasing recognition from the end of the fifth century and has remained the ecclesiastical Bible of both the Jacobite and Nestorian branches of the Syrian Church. On the other hand, it is disputed whether the Peshitta already existed before Rabbula, arising in Antioch as the work of several revisions made to conform to the Greek text but did not succeed for centuries in Syria proper, especially among the monks (Vööbus), or whether Rabbula indeed was not the author of the revision but probably participated in its inception at the beginning of the fifth century ("Pre-Peshitta"), whereas the majority of the ecclesiastical manuscripts reproduce a later form of development of this revision (Black). Also the Greek "Vorlage" of the earliest form of the Peshitta is still unexplained. Literature: A. Vööbus, *Studies* (see p. 369), 46 ff.; *idem*, "Das Alter der Peschitta," OC 38, 1954, 1 ff.; M. Black, "The NT Peshitta and its Predecessors," SNTSB 1950, 51 ff.; *idem*, "Rabbula of Edessa and the Peshitta," BJRL 33, 1950-51, 203 ff.; *idem*, "Zur Geschichte des syr. Evangelientextes," ThLZ 77, 1952, 705 ff.; *idem*, "The Text of the Peshitta Tetraevangelium," *Studia Paulina in honorem J. de Zwaan,* 1953, 20 ff.—Critical edition of the Gospels: G. H. Gwilliam, *Tetraevangelium Sanctum juxta simplicem Syrorum versionem,* 1901. Edition of the text of the entire NT: *The NT in Syriac* (British and Foreign Bible Society), 1905-20.

4. The *Philoxeniana* and the *Harklensis.* In Monophysite circles in the year 508 a revision of the Peshitta or a new translation of the still missing writings of the NT was made, the *Philoxeniana* (sy[ph]), so called after Philoxenus, Bishop of Mabbug (Hierapolis) on the Euphrates, who had it prepared by Polycarp, one of his chorepiscopi, who used a Greek text of the Koine type (Vööbus). A century later, in 616, the *Philoxeniana* underwent a new revision in Egypt by Thomas of Harkel (Heraclea). He strove for closer agreement between the Syriac wording and the Greek Koine text, but in addition he also used good manuscripts of the so-called "Western" text (see p. 384). Thus in the marginalia of his translation, the *Harklensis* (sy[h]), we find interesting material for textual criticism, especially to Acts. The Peshitta, however, was not forced out of ecclesiastical usage by the scholarly work of the later translations, even among the Monophysites.

What J. White published as *Philoxeniana* (*Sacrorum evangeliorum* and *Actuum apostolorum et epistolarum tam catholicarum quam paulinarum versio Syriaca Philoxeniana,* 1778-1803) is correctly regarded today as the *Harklensis.* Of the *Philoxeniana* we know with certainty only the four Catholic epistles and the Apocalypse, which are wanting in the Peshitta. They are published in *The NT in Syriac* (see above under 3) after the editions of J. Gwynn, *The Apocalypse of St. John,* 1897, and *Remnants of the later syriac versions of the Bible,* 1909. See also G. Zuntz, *The Ancestry of the Harklean NT* (British Academy, Supplemental Papers 7), 1945 (also, *idem,* "Études Harkléennes," RB 57, 1950, 550 ff.); A. Vööbus, "New Dates for the Solution of the Problem Concerning the Philoxenian Version," *Spiritus et veritas,* Festschr. K. Kundsin, 1953, 169 ff.

5. The Palestinian Syriac (western Aramaic) version (sy[pal]) of the NT arose

in the fifth or sixth century and is only fragmentarily preserved. It can be classified in respect to its text critical character with just as little certainty as its origin can be explained. At any rate, it plays no important role in textual criticism. Catalog of the fragments of text in F. Schulthess, *Grammatik des christlich-palästinischen Aramäisch*, 1924, 100-102; supplements in B. M. Metzger, *NT Manuscript Studies* (see p. 359), 185, and NTSt 2, 1955-56, 9.

b) The Latin Versions

1. The Old Latin Versions. Since the seventeenth century (R. Simon), the fact was again recognized that there were Old Latin versions of the NT before the Vulgate, which was circulating from the end of the fourth century on, and which only gradually replaced the Old Latin translations. The origin and history of these Old Latin versions are, however, still inadequately clarified, because there is no extant unmixed text, and also because we do not yet have before us the material from the manuscripts and the church fathers in its entirety in a trustworthy form. But the beginning in this direction has now been made. In 1749 (new edition 1751) the Maurist, P. Sabatier, in the third volume of his work, *Ancient Latin Versions of the Sacred Books or the Old Italian Version* [*Bibliorum sacrorum Latinae versiones antiquae seu vetus Italica*], collected all of the manuscripts and quotations from the church fathers known at that time. At the end of the nineteenth century, publication of the approximately seventy Old Latin manuscripts and fragments was begun (from the fourth to the thirteenth centuries; the most important editions in H. Vogels, *Handbuch* [see p. 359], 84 ff.). A. Jülicher then prepared a complete edition of the Gospel manuscripts, which, after his death, was newly edited by W. Matzkow under the direction of the commission on church fathers of the Berlin Academy of Sciences. It offers the dependable text of all manuscripts, divided into a European and an African text-form, whereby the reconstruction of the European text remains problematic (A. Jülicher-W. Matzkow, *Itala: Matthew*, 1938; *Mark*, 1940; *Luke*, 1954). On the basis of a collection of the complete tradition in manuscripts and church fathers, begun by J. Denk, the arch-abbey of Beuron (Württemberg), under the leadership of B. Fischer, has begun an edition of the *Vetus Latina*, of whose NT part James, I II Peter, and Eph. 1:1-21 have appeared (*Vetus Latina. Die Reste der altlateinischen Bibel*. Bd. 1: *Verzeichnis der Sigel*, 1949; Bd. 24,1: *Ad Ephesios, Philippenses, Colossenses*, 1. Lieferung, 1962; Bd. 26: *Epistolae Catholicae, Apocalypsis, 1.-3*. Lieferung, 1956-60). The text is printed in two, three, or four different text forms. Under the text are found the readings of all the manuscripts and the complete quotations of all the church fathers. Although the Old Latin manuscripts are usually designated by small Latin letters, the Beuronian edition unfortunately uses a new notation.

Our judgment concerning the age of the Latin translation of the NT depends upon the still disputed question of whether Tertullian already at the end of the second century knew the Catholic, Latin text of the Bible, or (less probably) himself translated out of the Greek. It is certain that in the middle of the third century Latin texts of the NT were in use in Africa and Italy and reciprocally influenced each other. Moreover, no agreement has yet been reached as to whether one original translation (which then must have originated in Africa) became differentiated through revision according to the Greek texts, or whether from the beginning several translations arose side by side. It is also disputed whether the first Latin translation of the Gospels was a Diatessaron (Vogels, Vööbus), and whether Tertullian already had a Latin version of the Marcionite NT (Harnack, Zimmermann). Presumably the history of the separate parts of the NT has proceeded variously. It is certain, however, that we can identify at least three different forms of text (an African, a "European," and a Spanish), and that the African text-form, which is doubtless the oldest, has the strongest affinities with the witnesses to the so-called "Western" text. For the clarification of this text, which is so important for the text of the second century, the knowledge of the Old Latin version is, therefore, of great importance. The designation of the Old Latin text as "Itala" is erroneous, since Augustine doubt-less meant only one European form of the Old Latin version (*De doctrina christiana* II, 15, 2: "But among those translations the Itala is to be preferred to others" [In ipsis autem interpretationibus Itala caeteris praeferatur]; see J. Schildenberger, "Die Itala des hl. Augustinus," *Colligere Fragmenta*, Festschr. A. Dold zum 70. Geburtstag, 1952, 84 ff.). On the Latin Bible in general, see: F. Stummer, *Einführung in die lateinische Bibel*, 1928, and the bibliography in T. A. Marazuela, *La Vetus Latina Hispana I Prolegomenos*, 1953, 65-139, 530-546. On the *Vetus Latina*: K. Th. Schäfer, *Die altlateinische Bibel*, 1957, and the bibliographical reports by W. G. Kümmel, ThRdsch N.F. 10, 1938, 306 ff., and J. Klijn, *A Survey of the Researches into the Western Text of the Gospels and Acts*, 1949, 152 ff., and NovT 3, 1959, 22 ff.; also, H. Zimmermann, *Unter-suchungen zur Geschichte der altlateinischen Überlieferung des zweiten Korin-therbriefes*, BBB 16, 1960.

2. The Vulgate. Because the text of the *vetus Latina* was in hopeless con-fusion, Pope Damasus (366-84) gave Hieronymus the task of creating a uni-form translation of the Bible. In connection with the NT, which he undertook first, Hieronymus used a method different from that which he used later in the OT, which he translated almost entirely anew into Latin from the Hebrew. As he explained in his "Epistula ad Damasum," the preface with which he published his translation of the Gospels in 384 (see in Nestle's edition of the Vulgate, XIV-XVI), he used a Latin text as the basis for his revision, correcting it according to earlier Greek manuscripts. His purpose was to change only those places "which seemed to distort the sense" [quae sensum videbantur mutare], but leave all else as he found it. Thus for the Gospels the Vulgate is a revision according to the Greek text, containing many Old Latin readings (changed in about 3,500 places!). For the remainder of the NT we are not certain to what extent we have an actual revision by Hieronymus. It is also disputed as to which Latin texts and which Greek text-forms were the basis of the revision; with respect to the Gospels, Vogels has reconstructed the probable Latin "Vor-lage." For the restoration of the original Greek text of the NT, we can

cautiously use the Vulgate only as a witness to the Old Latin "Vorlagen." In the year 405 the translation of the OT and the NT was completed, but only slowly prevailed, since at first no official authority stood behind it. Not until the eighth century was the sole recognition of the Vulgate assured. This version did not receive the honorable name, "Vulgate" (in the sense of "commonly accepted"), until the end of the Middle Ages (Faber Stapulensis; cf. A. Allgeier, Bb, 1948, 353 ff.).

The text of Hieronymus, however, is not preserved in purity. The *vetus Latina* had been so thoroughly accepted that in practical usage expressions from it again infiltrated the improved text. Conversely, the Old Latin text was also assimilated to the Vulgate. Repeatedly, new recensions became necessary, in order to bring the confusion to an end. Thus Alcuin, under instructions from Charles the Great around 800, Lanfranc of Canterbury in the eleventh century, the theologians of the University of Paris in the thirteenth century, and others, more or less intensely set about making corrections. Still the text remained a mixed text. The Council of Trent determined in the fourth session on 8 April 1546 "that the old Vulgate edition, which in long use for so many centuries has been approved in the church itself is to be regarded as authentic in public reading, disputations, sermons, and expositions, and that no one dare or presume, under any pretext, to reject it" [ut haec ipsa vetus et vulgata editio, quae longo tot saeculorum usu in ipsa ecclesia probata est, in publicis lectionibus, disputationibus, praedicationibus et expositionibus pro authentica habeatur, et ut nemo illam reicere quovis praetextu audeat vel praesumat]. The authentic edition decided upon by the Council was a long time in coming. In 1590 Pope Sixtus V brought about an official edition, the so-called *Sixtina*, which contained so many errors that in 1592, upon the command of Pope Clement VIII, it was replaced by the so-called *Clementina*, which in subsequent editions had to be further improved. The text of the third edition of the *Clementina* of 1598 is till today the official Latin text of the Bible of the Roman Catholic Church.

The number of Vulgate manuscripts with NT texts is unknown. Gregory's list of 1909 comprises about 2,500 manuscripts, whereas the number of manuscripts with parts of the entire Bible is estimated at 8,000 (Vööbus). The earliest manuscript (*Sangallensis*) stems from the fifth century. The best manuscript is the *Amiatinus* from the eighth century (Florence). Publications: The official text of the Vulgate has often been published. It is most easily accessible in the edition of E. Nestle, *NT Latine* (⁸1954; with good, short apparatus). A large critical edition which attempts to restore the text of Hieronymus has appeared since 1889 in Oxford, edited by the English scholars J. Wordsworth, H. J. White, and H. F. D. Sparks: *NT Domini Nostri Jesu Christi Latine secundum editionem Sancti Hieronymi* (I: *Evv.* 1889-98; II: *Epistulae Paulinae*, 1913-41; III: *Actus apostolorum-Epistulae canonicae-Apocalypsis Iohannis*, 1954). From this large edition has been published an *Editio minor curante* H. J. White (1911; ²1920). In 1907 Pope Pius X entrusted the Benedictine Order with the same task of restoring the text of the Vulgate. From the preparatory work in the abbey S. Girolamo in Rome, which is supposed to lay the foundation for a

new revision of the Vulgate (*Biblia Sacra juxta Latinam Vulgatam versionem
. . . edita*), the OT up to the Song of Solomon has appeared thus far (11 volumes,
1926-57).

We mention the following literature on the Vulgate: S. Berger, *Histoire de
la Vulgate pendant les premiers siècles du moyen âge*, 1893; B. Fischer, *Die
Alkuin-Bibel*, 1957; H. J. Vogels, *Vulgatastudien. Die Evv. der Vulgata untersucht auf ihre lat. und griech. Vorlage*, NTA 14, 2-3, 1928; C. H. Turner, *The
Oldest Manuscript of the Vulgate Gospels*, 1931 (*Codex Sangallensis*); B.
Fischer, "Der Vulgata-Text des NT," ZNW 46, 1955, 178 ff. (criticism of the
edition of Wordsworth-White-Sparks). Additional in *NT Manuscript Studies*
(see p. 359), 55 ff.

c) The Coptic Versions

Presumably the NT has repeatedly been translated into the various dialects
of the Egyptian vernacular, collectively called "Coptic" (this designation is
derived from Αἰγύπτιος via the Arabic). Since we have only insufficient fragments of the Achmimic and Fayyumic translations (cf. A. Vööbus, *Early Versions* [see p. 369], 273 ff.), we can speak with a degree of certainty only about
the two chief versions.

1. The Sahidic (South or Upper Egypt) version (sa or sah) presumably
arose gradually in the third century, and preserves in fragments almost the entire
NT. The earliest manuscript stems from the fourth century. The text agrees
in the main with $\mathfrak{P}^{75}$ B ℵ; yet there are also "Western" readings, especially in the
Gospels and Acts. Edition of the texts as known up to 1924: G. Horner, *The
Coptic Version of the NT in the Southern Dialect, otherwise called Sahidic or
Thebaic* I-VII, 1911-24 (text with translation). Also, H. Thompson, *The Gospel of St. John According to the Earliest Coptic Manuscript*, 1924; idem, *The
Coptic Version of the Acts of the Apostles and the Pauline Epistles in the
Sahidic Dialect*, 1932.

2. The age of the Bohairic (bo or boh) (North or Lower Egypt) version
is disputed, but since we now know two manuscripts from the fourth-fifth
centuries, an origin before the end of the fourth century is certain. The Bohairic
version also is parallel in particular with the texts of B ℵ; the "Western" readings
are less frequent than in the Sahidic version. Edition of the entire NT on the
basis of the texts known till 1905: G. Horner, *The Coptic Version of the NT
in the Northern Dialect, otherwise called Memphitic and Bohairic* I-IV, 1898-
1905. Also, P. E. Kahle, "A Biblical Fragment of the IVth-Vth Century in Semi-
Bohairic," *Le Muséon* 63, 1950, 147 ff. (fragment of Philippians); *Papyrus
Bodmer III: Évangile de Jean et Genèse I-IV, 2 en bohaïrique*, édité et traduit
par R. Kasser (CSCO 177 und 178), 1958 (John from the fourth-fifth century, probably of Gnostic origin; cf. É. Massaux, NTSt 5, 1958-59, 210 ff.).

Both versions appear to have been translated directly from the Greek, but
obviously have mutually influenced each other (J. L. Koole established that for
Paul and Acts in his *Studien zum koptischen Bibeltext*, Beih. ZNW 17, 1936,

and *idem, Bulletin of the Bezan Club* 12, 1937, 65 ff.). Both versions are thus important witnesses to the "Egyptian" text.

d) Other Versions

As practically all of the remaining versions of the NT from antiquity were not translated directly from the Greek, they are not direct witnesses to the Greek text of the NT. The Gothic version of the fourth century is the only exception. Yet it is of slight value for textual criticism, because the Greek "Vorlage" basically must have belonged already to the "Koine" type (the numerous "Western" readings probably go back to later Latin influence). Of the secondary translations into Arabic, Armenian, Ethiopic, Georgian, and Sogdian, the Armenian and Georgian versions have proved important for textual criticism. For the Old Armenian version, which can be inferred only from quotations, goes back to the Old Syriac text which is close to Tatian, and the Old Georgian text, preserved in manuscript form, goes back to this Old Armenian. Yet here little agreement has been reached about details. For example, was the earliest Armenian translation of the Gospels a Diatessaron (Lyonnet) or the tetraevangelium (Vööbus)? For the restoration of the earliest Syriac text and its Greek "Vorlage," the Old Georgian and the Old Armenian versions are, in any case, important. Cf. to all of these versions A. Vööbus, *Early Versions* (see p. 369), 133 ff.; and in particular S. Lyonnet, "Les origines de la version arménienne et le Diatessaron," BeO 13, 1950; J. Molitor, "Die Bedeutung der altgeorgischen Bibel für die ntl. Textkritik," BZ, N.F. 4, 1960, 39 ff.

3. The Quotations in Early Christian Writers

There are three reasons why the quotations of portions of the NT text by the Christian writers of the first centuries are significant for textual criticism: 1. These quotations reproduce, in part, a NT text from a time from which we still have no, or only isolated, direct manuscript tradition. 2. Since the quotations by the fathers can almost all be localized geographically, we can fix the locale of manuscripts by comparing them with the quotations, and likewise determine local text groups. 3. The text-critical discussions of the fathers give an insight into the trends which at that time were influencing the formation of the text. The use of these quotations is, however, fraught with difficulties. In the first place, the quotations in the manuscripts of the works of the fathers were especially subject to modification in the course of copying, so that we should work only with critical editions of the fathers. In the second place, the fathers by no means always quoted verbatim and thus by no means always the same text.

According to some scholars, Marcion and Tatian strongly influenced the earliest text of the Gospels and Pauline epistles (Herm. v. Soden; H. Vogels,

"Der Einfluss Marcions und Tatians auf Text und Kanon des NT," SStW, 1957, 278 ff.), whereas according to the more probable supposition both fathers are only witnesses to the "Western" text which was circulating in the second century, and only scattered changes by Marcion have infiltrated the orthodox text (C. S. C. Williams, *Alterations* [see p. 359], 10 ff.; E. C. Blackman, *Marcion and His Influence,* 1948, 43 ff., 128 ff.). Doubtless Justin and Irenaeus are witnesses to the early "Western" text (cf. É. Massaux, "Le texte du Sermon sur la Montagne utilisé par S. Justin," EphThL 28, 1952, 411 ff.; K. Th. Schäfer, "Die Zitate in der lateinischen Irenäusübersetzung und ihr Wert für die Textgeschichte des NT," *Festschr. für M. Meinertz,* NTA, 1. Erg. Bd., 1951, 50 ff.), likewise Tertullian and Cyprian. Clement of Alexandria also shows affinities with this text and with that of the earliest papyri. Origen, first in Alexandria, and then in Caesarea, used alternately the "Egyptian" and the so-called "Caesarean" text (see K. W. Kim, "Origen's Text of John . . . ," JThSt, N.S. 1, 1950, 74 ff.).

The investigation of the quotations by the fathers is thus an important help in grouping the NT textual witnesses (see §40). M.-E. Boismard, however, has sought to show that from the text of the fathers before the time of the great manuscripts of the fourth century a text-form (in many cases shorter), which has been lost in the Greek manuscripts, can be reconstructed, so that the primitive text has yet to be restored from the quotations of the fathers ("À propos de Jean," 5, 39," RB 55, 1948, 5 ff.; *idem,* "Critique textuelle et citations patristiques," RB 57, 1950, 388 ff.; *idem,* "Lectio brevior, potior," RB 58, 1951, 161 ff.; *idem,* "Problèmes de critique textuelle concernant la quatrième évangile," RB 60, 1953, 347 ff.). Although Boismard's investigations, which are extremely rich in materials, have not proved that the text reconstructed from many quotations ever existed in this form and is the original text at all, they do show that we must not only use the text of the fathers considerably more, but also that we cannot simply incorporate it into the text groups recognizable in the fourth and fifth centuries (cf. M. J. Suggs, "The Use of Patristic Evidence in the Search for a Primitive NT Text," NTSt 4, 1957-58, 139 ff.). But the question is completely open whether the NT text was ever so freely handled in the manuscripts as in the quotations of the fathers (see thereto A. F. J. Klijn, NovT 3, 1959, 165).

These series, which are all incomplete, offer critical editions of the patristic literature: *Die griechischen christlichen Schriftsteller der ersten drei Jahrhunderte,* hrsg. von der Berliner Akademie, 1897 ff. (now extended to the fourth-sixth centuries); *Corpus ecclesiasticorum Latinorum,* hrsg. von der Wiener Akademie, 1866 ff.; *Corpus scriptorum christianorum orientalium,* 1903 ff.; *Patrologia orientalis,* 1903 ff. *Corpus Christianorum,* of which the *Series Latina* has first begun to appear, contains reprints of critical editions.

The publication of the NT text of the individual fathers is desirable. Here we mention especially: *The NT in the Apostolic Fathers,* 1905; A. Harnack, *Marcion,* ²1924; W. Sanday-C. H. Turner-A. Souter, *NT S. Irenaei,* 1923; H. Roensch, *Das NT Tertullians,* 1871; Hans v. Soden, *Das lateinische NT in*

Afrika zur Zeit Cyprians, TU 33, 1910; H. Vogels, *Das Corpus Paulinum des Ambrosiaster,* BBB 13, 1957; P. M. Barnard, *The Biblical Text of Clement of Alexandria,* TSt V, 5, 1899; O. Bauernfeind, *Der Römerbrieftext des Origenes,* TU 44, 3, 1923.

In addition to the writings of the fathers which have been preserved as a whole, we must also consider the fragments which are contained in catenae, i.e., the chainlike collections of the fathers' quotations written in the margins of the biblical manuscripts. Texts: K. Staab, *Pauluskommentare aus der griech. Kirche,* NTA 15, 1933; J. Reuss, *Matthäuskommentare aus der griech. Kirche,* TU 61, 1957. Literature: RGG[3] I, 1957, 1628.

§39. The Printed Text

During the fifteenth century, the century when printing was invented, no editions of the Greek NT were printed. The printed Greek NT did not appear until the beginning of the sixteenth century, in a double *Editio princeps:*

1. The Complutensian Polyglot (*Complutensis*), so named after its place of publication, Complutum = Alcalà in Spain (Latin, Greek; OT also in Hebrew). It was prepared after 1502 by qualified Spanish scholars at the instigation of Cardinal Ximenes († 1517). Which manuscripts lie behind the Greek text of the NT is still unclear. The NT was printed in 1514, but the printing of the other parts was not completed until 1517. Pope Leo X did not give his sanction to publication until 1520. The work appears not to have come to Germany before 1522. Luther did not use it in connection with his *NT Deutsch* of September 1522.

2. The edition of Erasmus. As the Basel publisher, Froben, wanted to get ahead of Ximines' work, of which he knew, he importuned Erasmus in 1515 to undertake an edition of the NT. Erasmus accepted, and already in March, 1516, he delivered to the public the first NT in the Greek language, with his own Latin translation. The over-hasty publication, which Erasmus himself later had to confess was "precipitated rather than edited" [praecipitatum verius quam editum], reproduced in the main the slightly corrected text of two minuscule manuscripts of Basle; four additional manuscripts were used only occasionally. For the Apocalypse Erasmus had one manuscript, which broke off at 22:16. He translated the missing verses imperfectly from the Vulgate back into Greek. Erasmus did improve the additional four editions, but the foundations of the text remained the same. Luther's translation of the NT was based upon a reprint of Erasmus' second edition of 1519 (cf. K. W. Clark, "Observations on the Erasmian Notes in Codex 2," StEv, 1959, 749 ff.).

The later editions of the NT from the sixteenth century are connected with Erasmus' text, into which a number of corrections were introduced, following the *Complutensis* or collated manuscripts. All four editions of the Parisian publisher, Robert Stephanus (Estienne) are famous, but especially the third edition of 1550, the *editio Regia,* which was the first Greek testament to offer a critical apparatus (printed by Stephanus on the inner margins; its siglum ϛ = Stephanus' text). The fourth edition of 1551 introduced the division of the text into verses, which is still used today. The nine editions of the Greek NT which Theodor Beza published in Geneva from 1565 to 1604 and which achieved normative significance in the domain of Calvinism, did not differ much from the text of Stephanus, though Beza used manuscript materials, but not among them, strangely enough, the two majuscules D, which he himself possessed.

In the editions of the seventeenth century the text achieved by the work of the sixteenth century finally became established. The merit of the famed editions of the Elzevier family press in Leiden, and later in Amsterdam (seven editions, 1624-78), lies basically in their exemplary printing and in their beautiful embellishments. The text is hardly distinguishable from Beza's text of 1565. In the preface to the second edition of 1633 is this sentence: "Therefore you have the text now received by all, in which we give nothing changed or corrupted" [textum ergo habes nunc ab omnibus receptum, in quo nihil immutatum aut corruptum damus]. Hence the text from Stephanus to Elzevier, which prevailed for over two centuries and which the old Protestant orthodoxy regarded as inspired, was called *textus receptus*.

The editions of the eighteenth century did not question the *textus receptus*, but they subjoined critical apparatuses and principles of scientific textual criticism according to the advancing investigation of manuscripts, versions, and quotations by the fathers, and the growing insight into the history of the NT text. In 1707 J. Mill for the first time published the readings of all the accessible manuscripts and versions under the *textus receptus*. In 1734 J. A. Bengel cited under the hardly altered *textus receptus* the readings which deserve preference over this text. J. J. Wettstein (1751-52), who introduced the sigla which are still today customary for the majuscules and minuscules (see p. 361), indicated in the text the places which should be changed. J. J. Griesbach (1774-75), upon the basis of methodical principles, very cautiously altered the text itself.

Not until the nineteenth century, however, was the predominance of the *textus receptus* broken. K. Lachmann (1831) consistently applied the tested principles of classical, philological textual criticism to the NT. As a guideline for reconstructing the NT text, he advanced the principle that scholarship is not to proceed from the *textus receptus* but from the early ecclesiastical text read around 380, which could be restored from the earliest Greek manuscripts, the Latin versions, and the quotations of the church fathers. Thus Lachmann offered for the first time a critical text of the NT, based upon the best witnesses.

C. v. Tischendorf discovered an abundance of NT manuscripts and collated and published them for the first time, thereby increasing substantially the materials available to textual critics. The first edition of his *NT graece* appeared in 1841. The eighth edition, however, contains the fullest collection of materials: *Editio octava critica major* I 1869, II 1872 (III: *Prolegomena* 1894 by C. R. Gregory). The significance of this work does not lie in its text, which is not formed according to fixed principles, and which gives too much preference to ℵ, discovered by Tischendorf himself. Rather, the incomparably rich critical apparatus makes the work an indispensable resource for every text-critical study.

A contemporary of Tischendorf, the English scholar S. P. Tregelles labored for decades upon the text of the NT, and published the mature results of his studies in one edition: *The Greek NT, ed. from Ancient Authorities with their Various Readings in Full and the Latin Version of Jerome* I-VI, 1857-72. This edition is superior to Tischendorf's in respect to the method used in restoring the text, but because its apparatus is scantier and does not use ℵ, and sometimes not B, it did not successfully compete against Tischendorf's editions.

The first Greek NT whose text was shaped according to strict, methodical principles was offered by the edition of the Cambridge professors, B. F. Westcott and F. J. A. Hort, *The NT in the Original Greek* I (text with marginal readings and special apparatus to individual passages) (1881) [2]1898, II (principles of textual criticism) (1882) [2]1896. B, as the representative of the "neutral text" is valued the most highly and is authoritative for the restoration of the text (see pp. 382 f.). The edition by B. Weiss, *Das NT. Textkritische Untersuchungen und Textherstellung*, (1894-1900) [2]1902-5, along with thorough comparison of other early majuscules, also gives preference to B.

The last monumental critical edition of the NT stems from Herm. v. Soden, *Die Schriften des NT in ihrer ältesten erreichbaren Textgestalt hergestellt auf Grund ihrer Textgeschichte* I (Untersuchungen) 1902-10, II (text with apparatus) 1913. His *Griechisches NT Handausgabe* (1913) also reproduces the text with a brief apparatus. In his large and important work von Soden went new ways, in that he especially used later manuscripts, in which he saw witnesses to early recensions. The kernel of his theory is formed by his supposition of three recensions, to which all the manuscript materials can be traced back: Lucian (Koine or Byzantine) text, Hesychian (Egyptian) text, and Pamphilian (Jerusalem [I]) text, plus his contention that the degeneration of the text of the Gospels is to be ascribed to Tatian's influence. Von Soden's results are much disputed, especially since his collations and apparatus are not unconditionally trustworthy. Von Soden's chief accomplishment was the disclosure of new materials, especially a very great number of later Greek manuscripts (for v. Soden's designation of manuscripts cf. pp. 361 f.).

C. R. Gregory (*Textkritik des NT* I-III, 1900-1909; idem, *Die griechischen Handschriften des NT*, 1908) took up carefully the contents of all manuscripts attainable till 1908 and laid the foundation for the list of NT manuscripts which is still valid today (concerning the continuation of the list cf. pp. 359 f.).

What Tischendorf created for his time in his *Editio octava*, an edition whose critical apparatus brings into view the entire textual tradition, the new, large Oxford edition of the Greek NT (*NT Graece secundum textum Westcotto-Hortianum*) intended to present from the standpoint of today's advancing knowledge of the tradition. But since the edition of Matthew and Mark by S. C. E. Legg has proved inadequate (see p. 21), a larger group of scholars is preparing on an international basis the publication of a multivolume *New Critical Apparatus of the Greek NT*, whose first volume is supposed to contain Luke (headquarters of the undertaking: Emory University, Atlanta, Georgia).

In addition, the publication of a new critical text with selected apparatus is being sponsored by the Bible Societies of America, Scotland, and Württemberg, and is now in preparation.

The *NT Graece . . . curavit* Eb. Nestle, 1898, offers no new text, but a cross-section text on the basis of a majority decision in respect to the editions of Tischendorf, Westcott-Hort, and B. Weiss. The apparatus, which since the thirteenth edition (1927) has been adapted by Erw. Nestle to the manuscripts, is always kept up-to-date by the incorporation of new discoveries, especially of the papyri (^{24}1960, edited by Erw. Nestle and K. Aland). Yet the numerous new discoveries and the new methodological insights since 1898 even here demand a new revision, which K. Aland is preparing.

Cf. to these projected editions, K. Aland, "The Present Position of NT Textual Critcism," StEv, 1959, 717 ff.; *idem,* "The New Nestle Greek NT," NTSt 6, 1959-60, 179 ff.

§40. The Present State of New Testament Textual Criticism

Lachmann, who overthrew the *textus receptus* (see p. 380), did not succumb to the illusion that he could discover the original text of the NT. Rather, he was satisfied, by means of reconstructing the text of the fourth century, to discover again the "earliest among the texts which can be proved to have circulated." The question which since then has most strongly affected textual criticism is whether, and to what extent, a closer approximation to the form of the original text is attainable by the means of historical knowledge.

The theses of Westcott and Hort (see p. 381) constitute the starting point for the modern discussion of the question. According to them, all of the materials connected with the earliest history of the Greek text of the NT fall into three chief groups and one secondary group, of which each has its own text-type. These text-types are:

1. The "Syrian" text. This text is presented by most of the majuscules and almost all minuscules, by the versions which arose after 300, and by the great bulk of the church fathers from the end of the fourth century on. The Syrian text is the basis of the *textus receptus.* It goes back to a recension of the presbyter Lucian of Antioch († 311). From Antioch it spread to Constantinople and throughout the entire East. As a mixed text which arose from other texts, it was regarded as inferior by Westcott-Hort.

2. The "Western" text. It is recognizable in D, several minuscules, the Old Latin and the Old Syriac versions, and the quotations of the earliest fathers of the West (Justin, Irenaeus, Tertullian, Cyprian, etc.). Its home, like that of the Syrian text, is Syria. Westcott-Hort, following the precedent of Semler and Griesbach, called it the "Western" text because its features were first recognized in the textual tradition of the West. It is characterized by a propensity for paraphrase, elucidation, embellishment, and harmonization in the text of the Gospels, etc. Hence Westcott-Hort also regarded it, in spite of its age (second century), as degenerate.

3. The "Neutral" text. It is represented primarily by B, and somewhat less purely by א. To this type also belong Origen and the Bohairic version, as well as some additional secondary witnesses: the majuscules A C L T X Ξ, several minuscules (especially 33), and Alexandrian fathers such as Clement and Dionysius. B and א go back, and independently of each other, to a superior text which stands close to the autographs. B offers this text quite purely, whereas א occasionally mixes with it readings of other origin. It is called "Neutral" because it has remained unchanged, and untouched by degeneration. Hence Westcott-Hort saw in it the earliest and most valuable type.

3a. The Alexandrian text is attested by manuscripts like A C L, and in part by Origen and the Bohairic version. It is really only a modification of the "Neutral" text, from which it is separated by small stylistic and factual divergences, thus indicating that in Alexandria the Neutral text underwent a slight recension.

According to their evaluation of these text-types, Westcott and Hort constructed their critical text upon the Neutral text, primarily upon B. The Syrian and Alexandrian texts were not considered, nor, on the whole, was the Western text. Only in the few places where the Western text, contrary to its usual preference for fullness, preserves a shorter reading than that of the Neutral text, was it regarded as retaining the original form of the text (so-called "Western Non-Interpolations"; see the list in A. Souter, *The Text* [2] [see p. 359], 127).

In one respect, Westcott-Hort's interpretation of the history of the text has been generally accepted: The insight into the inferiority of the Syrian text-type (most preferably called "Antiochian," "Lucian," "Byzantine," or "Reichstext," or, because of its general circulation, "Koine" text [ℜ]). This text-form, from which the *textus receptus* of the sixteenth and seventeenth centuries issued, is the artistic creation of a work of revision, which smoothed the traditional text linguistically, assimilated the divergent readings of the earlier texts to one another (cf. Rom. 6:12), and in the interest of a uniform text made emendatory additions and deletions. Yet recent investigations have shown that even Koine readings *can* be early and good, especially if the reading is not yet otherwise attested (cf. G. Zuntz, *Text* [see p. 359], 50 ff., 150; H. Greeven, "Erwägungen zur synoptischen Textkritik," NTSt 6, 1959-60, 281 ff.; B. M. Metzger, "Lucian and the Lucianic Recension of the Greek Bible," NTSt 8, 1961-62, 189 ff.). It is, however, questionable whether there ever was a homogeneous form of the Koine text which can be reconstructed (see K. and S. Lake, "The Byzantine Text of the Gospels," *Mémorial Lagrange*, 1940, 251 ff.).

Other parts of Westcott-Hort's theory have proved a failure, above all a) the exaggerated preference for B and the Neutral text, and b) the general repudiation of the Western text.

a) Besides the Koine text, there undeniably was an additional text-type, which doubtless had its home in Egypt. Its earliest representatives are 𝔓[45] (for Acts), 𝔓[46,47], B א C, and the Coptic versions. Since Hieronymus, in his letter to Damasus dedicating his translation of the Gospels (see p. 374), mentions the designation of Greek manuscripts of the NT by an Egyptian, Hesychius, it has been customary, following W. Bousset (1894), to designate this type of text as Hesychian (Nestle: $\mathfrak{H}$); but it is very questionable whether this text-type can be traced back to Hesychius (see F. G. Kenyon, "Hesychius and the Text of the NT," *Mémorial Lagrange*, 1940, 245 ff.). It is certain that this text-type was not the only type used in Egypt (see under b), but its existence in Egypt in the third and fourth centuries is assured by $\mathfrak{P}^{45,46}$ and $\mathfrak{P}^{66,75}$. Whether this text-type has extensively preserved the original text or whether it goes back to a work of recension, is disputed. In this connection, the observation is of great significance that the correctors of papyri 46 and 66 almost entirely replaced Western readings by Alexandrian readings, so that already by the end of the second century there was a work of recension which reintroduced early, good readings into the current text (see G. Zuntz, *Text* [see p. 359], 252 ff., and A. F. J. Klijn, NTSt 3, 1956-57, 333 f.). Thus the text preserved in the great manuscripts of the fourth and fifth centuries (B ℵ C) is not "neutral," but the result of a continuing purification of the text on the basis of a good philological method which had long been at home in Alexandria (cf. A. F. J. Klijn, NovT 3, 1959, 17 f.; E. C. Colwell, *The Origin* [see pp. 385 f.], 130 f.). With that it is given that perhaps there also never was a reconstructable Alexandrian text, i.e., one which once existed in one manuscript. Yet the readings of the Alexandrian text-type, without being infallible, now as before have the greatest significance for the reconstruction of the original text.

b) If the Alexandrian text in its foundation reaches back into the second century, then that doubtless also holds true for the Western text, which Justin, Marcion, Tatian, Irenaeus, Tertullian, and, in part, Clement of Alexandria, used in the second century. This text-type is attested early in Egypt ($\mathfrak{P}^{38}$ $\mathfrak{P}^{48}$, readings of the Sahidic version), but also in Syria (the Old Syriac version of the Gospels), and naturally in the West (*vetus Latina*, Irenaeus, Cyprian, etc.), whereas the geographical origin of the two chief Greek witnesses (D^{e,a} and D^{p}, sixth century [see pp. 366 f.]) is not clear. The designation "Western text" is thus incontestably erroneous, since it is a matter of a text attested from the second century on in the entire territory of the primitive Catholic Church. No better name has been found until now because the origin and the value of this text-type are not yet really understood. The view that this text-type represents the original text (so lately P. Glaue, "Der älteste Text der geschichtlichen Bücher des NT," ZNW 45, 1954, 90 ff.) is just as untenable as the view which traces it back to a revision of the primitive text in the early second century (C. C. Torrey, *Documents of the Primitive Church*, 1941, 112 ff.; W. H. P. Hatch, *The Western Text of the Gospels*, 1937). But just as little does the supposition hold true that it is simply a matter of the unrevised, "wild" text of the second century, from which all of our text-forms are derived (so, e.g., B. G. Zuntz, *The Text* [see p. 359], 263 ff.; E. C. Colwell, "The Origin" [see pp. 385 f.], 137) for there can be no doubt that an essential part of the variants of the Western text, above all in the Gospels and Acts, stems from a consciously expanded and smoothed revision (see the lists in F. G. Kenyon, *The Western Text in the Gospels and Acts*, 1939, 4 ff.). From this fact it follows that we find in the witnesses to the Western text early, even if undisciplined, traditions to be taken seriously, as well as a revision which is, on the whole, secondary; moreover, there probably never was a homogeneous Western text (especially disputed is whether the Greek "Vorlage" of the Old Syriac version of the Gospels does not belong to another tradition than the *vetus Latina* [so K. and S. Lake, RB 48, 1939, 502]).

The separation of the primary and secondary material within the witnesses of the Western text is, however, facilitated by the discovery of a third text-type which does not belong to the Koine, the "Caesarean" text. It has been established that in Mark in the majuscules Θ W (in part), the minuscules 28, 565, 700, the minuscule groups 1 and 13 (see p. 367 f.), in the Old Georgian and in part in the Old Armenian and Palestinian-Syriac versions, a special type of text is recognizable, which fluctuates between Egyptian and Western texts but also exhibits peculiar features (cf. W. G. Kümmel, ThRdsch, N.F. 11, 1939, 104, note 1; Burkitt, Lake, etc.). Streeter added the thesis that Origen, upon his emigration to Caesarea, found this text there; hence the name, "Caesarean" text. More recent investigations, however, have shown, chiefly upon the basis of papyri 37 and 45, that this text was used by Origen, in addition to the Egyptian, in Alexandria *and* in Caesarea, and that within the witnesses to the Caesarean text a development toward the Koine text took place (the earlier witnesses for Mark are 𝔓⁴⁵ W 28, minuscule groups 1 and 13). On the one hand, then, this text certainly was not used only in Caesarea. On the other hand, this text just as surely was in use in Palestine for a long time (proved for the text of the Gospels of the fourth century in Jerusalem by J. H. Greenlee, *The Gospel Text of Cyrill of Jerusalem*, SaD 17, 1955). It represents a peculiar text-type attested since the early third century, which perhaps came from Egypt to Palestine (Kenyon, Lake), and probably also was never as a whole to be found in one manuscript. Yet it is significant because of its age and helps us to recognize early readings as early, which otherwise are contained only in Western witnesses. On the Caesarean text cf.: W. G. Kümmel, ThRdsch, N.F. 11, 1939, 102 ff.; K. and S. Lake, *Family 13 (The Ferrar Group). The Text According to Mark* . . . , SaD 11, 1941; J. Geerlings, *Family 13—The Ferrar Group. The Text According to Matthew,* . . . *to Luke,* . . . *to John,* SaD 19, 20, 21, 1961-62; B. M. Metzger, "The Caesarean Text of the Gospels," JBL 64, 1945, 457 ff.; *idem,* "Recent Spanish Contributions to the Textual Criticism of the NT," JBL 66, 1947, 401 ff.; F. J. Klijn, *A Survey of the Researches into the Western Text of the Gospels and Acts,* Diss. Utrecht, 1947, 110 ff.; *idem,* "A Survey of the Researches . . . (1949-59)," NovT 3, 1959, 15 ff.

As a result of these investigations, we conclude that a strictly local text theory is untenable. Indeed, it has generally become questionable whether one original text in any text-type ever existed and could be reconstructed. Since no manuscript of a NT text has an unmixed text, we can determine only the better or poorer witnesses to a text-type, and upon the basis of such grouping, particular readings can be recognized as characteristic of this type of text (cf. especially E. C. Colwell, "The Significance of Grouping of NT Manuscripts," NTSt 4,

1957-58, 73 ff.; *idem,* "The Origin of the Text-types of NT Manuscripts," *Early Christian Origins, Studies in honor of H. R. Willoughby,* 1961, 128 ff.). The more widely a reading is attested in two or more early text-types, so much the better is the witness; thus the Egyptian text, now as before, must be regarded as the best text-type on the whole. Since, however, external evidence alone can decide the matter only in rare instances, the old rules of internal criticism must be kept in mind ("the more difficult is better than the easier reading; the shorter reading [is] preferable" [proclivi lectioni praestat arduor; brevior lectio potior]). We must note too that related texts were assimilated to one another, especially texts of Mark and Luke to Matthew (cf. H. Greeven, "Erwägungen zur synpt. Textkritik," NTSt 6, 1959-60, 281 ff.), and that intentional textual changes were made (cf. C. S. C. Williams, *Alterations* [see p. 359], 1 ff., and K. W. Clark, "Textual Criticism and Doctrine," *Studia Paulina,* 1953, 52 ff.). It is also important to observe the context of adjacent variants, which then can only be judged jointly (examples in Vogels, *Handbuch*[2] [see p. 359], 182 ff.). In view of the many uncertainties in our knowledge of the history of the text, an eclectic method is, provisionally, the only one possible (see K. W. Clark, *The Effect . . .* [see p. 359]. But even if a new edition of the text will diverge in many details from the text now customary, and even though no certain decision is possible concerning many variants, the most recent discoveries and investigations have shown that our critical text of the Greek NT must come very close to the original text of the collections taken up into the canon. If the text found by such a method should turn out to be factually untenable in particular cases, then the exegete should not shy away from a rational, intrinsically suitable conjecture, but such cases will not be very numerous.

Good surveys of the grouping of the chief witnesses: A. H. McNeile-C. S. C. Williams, *An Introduction* (see p. 28), 378 ff.; W. H. P. Hatch, *Minuscule Manuscripts* (see p. 360), 60 ff.; cf. the table by F. Hahn in F. G. Kenyon-A. W. Adams, *Der Text der griech. Bibel,* [2]1962, 191. On methodological problems cf. F. G. Kenyon-A. W. Adams, *ibid.,* 132 ff.; R. V. G. Tasker, "An Introduction to the Manuscripts of the NT," HarvThR 41, 1948, 71 ff.; M. Karnetzki, "Textgeschichte als Überlieferungsgeschichte," ZNW 47, 1956, 170 ff.; H. Greeven and E. C. Colwell (see pp. 384, 385 f.).

COMMENTARIES
on the Individual Books of the New Testament

(The last revised editions of the commentaries are cited. First, those commentaries which appear in series are listed alphabetically according to the abbreviations of the series, and then the single commentaries alphabetically according to author.)

Matthew

BNTC: F. V. Filson, 1960; Ét. bibl.: M.-J. Lagrange, [4]1927; Hdb.: E. Klostermann, [2]1927; ICC: W. C. Allen, [3]1912; IntB: S. E. Johnson, 1951; Meyer: B. Weiss, [10]1910; E. Lohmeyer, 1956 (edited by W. Schmauch; incomplete); Moffatt: T. H. Robinson, 1928; NTD: J. Schniewind, 1937; RNT: J. Schmid, [3]1956; Torch: G. E. P. Cox, 1952; Ty: R. V. G. Tasker, 1961; UB: J. Wilkens, I. II, 1934-37; Zahn: Th. Zahn, [4]1922; ZüB: W. Michaelis, I, 1948, II, 1949 (to 17:13).

A. Loisy, Les évangiles synoptiques I. II, 1907-08; C. G. Montefiore, The Synoptic Gospels II, [2]1927; A. Schlatter, Der Evangelist Matthäus, 1929; J. Wellhausen, [2]1914.

Mark

BNTC: S. E. Johnson, 1960; CGTC: C. E. B. Cranfield, 1959; Ét. bibl.: M.-J. Lagrange, [4]1929; Hdb.: E. Klostermann, [4]1950; ICC: E. P. Gould, 1896; IntB: F. C. Grant, 1951; Meyer: E. Lohmeyer, [10]1937 (with supplement, edited by G. Sass, 1953); Moffatt: B. H. Branscomb, 1937; NTD: J. Schniewind, [6]1952; RNT: J. Schmid, [3]1954; ThHK: F. Hauck, 1931; W. Grundmann, [2]1959; Torch: A. M. Hunter, 1949; Ty: A. Cole, 1961; UB: G. Dehn, [6]1953; Zahn: G. Wohlenberg, [3-4]1930.

Ph. Carrington, 1960; A. Loisy, Les évangiles synoptiques I, II, 1907-08; C. G. Montefiore, The Synoptic Gospels I, [2]1927; A. E. Rawlinson, 1925; A. Schlatter, Markus, der Evangelist für die Griechen, 1935; V. Taylor, 1952; J. Wellhausen, [2]1909.

Luke

BNTC: A. R. C. Leaney, 1958; Ét. bibl.: M.-J. Lagrange, [4]1927; Hdb.: E. Klostermann, [2]1929; ICC: A. Plummer, [5]1922; IntB: S. M. Gilmour, 1952; Meyer: B. Weiss, [9]1901; Moffatt: W. Manson, 1930; NIC: N. Geldenhuys, 1950; NTD: K. H. Rengstorf, [9]1962; RNT: J. Schmid, [3]1955; ThHK: F. Hauck, 1934; W. Grundmann, [2]1961; Torch: W. R. F. Browning, 1960; UB: L. Fendt, 1937; Zahn: Th. Zahn, [3-4]1920.

J. M. Creed, 1930; H. Gollwitzer, Die Freude Gottes, [2]1952; A. Loisy, Les évangiles synoptiques I, II, 1907-08; idem, L'évangile selon Luc, 1924; C. G. Montefiore, The Synoptic Gospels II, [2]1927; A. Schlatter, 1931; J. Wellhausen, 1904.

John

Ét. bibl.: M.-J. LAGRANGE, [5]1936; Hdb.: W. BAUER, [3]1933; ICC: J. H. BERNARD, I, II, 1928; IntB: W. F. HOWARD, 1952; Meyer: R. BULTMANN, [10]1941 (Ergänzungsheft, [2]1957); Moffatt: G. H. C. MACGREGOR, 1928; NIC: M. C. TENNEY, 1948; NTD: H. STRATHMANN, [6]1951; RNT: A. WIKENHAUSER, [3]1961; Torch: A. RICHARDSON, 1959; Ty: R. V. G. TASKER, 1960; UB: W. BRANDT, [3]1940; Zahn: TH. ZAHN, [5-6]1921; ZüB: G. SPÖRRI, I, II, 1950.

C. K. BARRETT, 1956; E. C. HOSKYNS, [2]1947; R. H. LIGHTFOOT, 1956; A. LOISY, [2]1921; H. ODEBERG, I, 1929 (incomplete); A. SCHLATTER, Der Evangelist Johannes, 1930; J. WELLHAUSEN, 1908.

Acts

BNTC: C. S. C. WILLIAMS, 1957; Ét. bibl.: E. JACQUIER, 1926; Hdb.: E. PREUSCHEN, 1912; IntB: G. H. C. MACGREGOR, 1954; Meyer: E. HAENCHEN, [13]1961; Moffatt: F. J. FOAKES-JACKSON, 1932; NIC: F. F. BRUCE, 1954; NTD: H. W. BEYER, 1932; RNT: A. WIKENHAUSER, [2]1956; ThHK: O. BAUERNFEIND, 1939; Torch: R. R. WILLIAMS, 1953; Ty: E. M. BLAIKLOCK, 1959; UB: O. DIBELIUS, [5]1951; Zahn: TH. ZAHN, I, II, [3-4]1922-27.

A. LOISY, 1920; K. LAKE and H. J. CADBURY, "English Translation and Commentary" and "Additional Notes to the Commentary," Beginnings I, 4, 5, 1933; F. STAGG, The Book of Acts. The Early Struggle for an Unhindered Gospel, 1955; L. CERFAUX and J. DUPONT, in La Sainte Bible traduite en français sous la direction de l'École Biblique de Jérusalem, [2]1958.

Romans

BNTC: C. K. BARRETT, 1957; CNT: F.-J. LEENHARDT, 1957; Eng. tr. by Harold Knight, 1961; Ét. bibl.: M.-J. LAGRANGE, [2]1930; Hdb.: H. LIETZMANN, [4]1933; ICC: W. SANDAY-A. C. HEADLAM, [5]1902; IntB: J. KNOX, 1954; Meyer: O. MICHEL, [10]1955; Moffatt: C. H. DODD, 1932; NIC: J. MURRAY, Bd. I, Kapp. 1-8, 1960; NTD: P. ALTHAUS, [9]1959; RNT: O. KUSS, 1950; Torch: A. M. HUNTER, 1955; Zahn: TH. ZAHN, [3]1925 (revised by F. HAUCK); ZüB: E. GAUGLER, I, II, 1945-52.

H. ASMUSSEN, 1952; K. BARTH, [2]1922; Eng. tr. by Edwyn C. Hoskyns from 6th ed. (1933), 1933; P. BOYLAN, 1934; E. BRUNNER, 1938 (Bibelhilfe); Eng. tr. by H. A. Kennedy of 1956 ed., 1959; TH. HAERING, 1926; J. HUBY-ST. LYONNET, [2]1957; E. KÜHL, 1913; O. KUSS, 1. und 2. Lieferung, 1957-59; A. NYGREN, Eng. tr. by Carl C. Rasmussen, 1944; A. SCHLATTER, Gottes Gerechtigkeit, 1935.

I Corinthians

CNT: J. HÉRING, 1949; Eng. tr. by A. W. HEATHCOTE and P. J. ALLCOCK from 2nd ed., 1962; Ét. bibl.: E.-B. ALLO, 1934; Hdb.: H. LIETZMANN-W. G. KÜMMEL, [4]1949; ICC: A. ROBERTSON-A. PLUMMER, [2]1914; IntB: C. T. CRAIG, 1953; Meyer: J. WEISS, [9]1910; Moffatt: J. MOFFATT, 1938; NIC: F. W. GROSHEIDE, [2]1954; NTD: H. D. WENDLAND, [6]1954; RNT: O. KUSS, 1940; Torch: W. G. H. SIMON, 1959;

Ty: L. Morris, 1958; UB: O. Schmitz, 1939; Zahn: Ph. Bachmann, [4]1936 (supplements by E. Stauffer); ZüB: W. Meyer, I, 1947, II, 1945.

K. Barth, *Die Auferstehung der Toten*, 1924; Eng. tr. by H. J. Stenning, 1933; A. Schlatter, *Paulus, der Bote Jesu*, 1934.

II Corinthians

CNT: J. Héring, 1950; Ét. bibl.: E.-B. Allo, 1936; Hdb.: H. Lietzmann-W. G. Kümmel, [4]1949; ICC: A. Plummer, 1925; IntB: F. V. Filson, 1953; Meyer: H. Windisch, [9]1924; Moffatt: R. H. Strachan, 1935; NIC: P. E. Hughes, 1962; NTD: H. D. Wendland, [8]1954; RNT: O. Kuss, 1940; Torch: R. P. C. Hanson, 1954; Ty: R. V. G. Tasker, 1958; Zahn: Ph. Bachmann, [4]1922.

A. Schlatter, *Paulus, der Bote Jesu*, 1934.

Galatians

CNT: P. Bonnard, 1953; Ét. bibl.: M.-J. Lagrange, [2]1925; Hdb.: H. Lietzmann, [3]1932; ICC: E. D. Burton, 1921; IntB: R. T. Stamm, 1953; Meyer: H. Schlier, [12]1962; Moffatt: G. S. Duncan, 1934; NIC: H. N. Ridderbos, 1953; NTD: H. W. Beyer-P. Althaus, [9]1962; RNT: O. Kuss, 1940; ThHK: A. Oepke, [2]1957; Torch: J. A. Allan, 1951; UB: G. Dehn, [3]1938; Zahn: Th. Zahn, [3]1922 (revised by F. Hauck); ZüB.: Ch. Maurer, 1943.

H. Asmussen, *Theologisch-kirchliche Erwägungen zum Gal.*, 1935; J. B. Lightfoot, [7]1881.

Ephesians

CNT: Ch. Masson, 1953; Hdb.: M. Dibelius-H. Greeven, [3]1953; ICC: T. K. Abbott, 1897; IntB: F. W. Beare, 1953; Meyer: E. Haupt, [2]1902; Moffatt: E. F. Scott, 1930; NIC: E. K. Simpson, 1957; NTD: H. Conzelmann, [9]1962; RNT: K. Staab, [3]1959; Torch: J. A. Allan, 1959; UB: K. Mittring, 1936; Zahn: P. Ewald, [2]1910.

A. Klöpper, 1891; H. Schlier, 1957.

Philippians

BNTC: F. W. Beare, 1959; CNT: P. Bonnard, 1950; Hdb.: M. Dibelius, [3]1937; ICC: M. R. Vincent, 1897; IntB: E. F. Scott, 1955; Meyer: E. Lohmeyer, [8]1930; Moffatt: J. H. Michael, 1928; NIC: J. J. Müller, 1955; NTD: G. Friedrich, [9]1962; RNT: K. Staab, [3]1959; ThHK: W. Michaelis, 1935; Torch: F. C. Synge, 1951; Ty: R. P. Martin, 1960; UB: O. Schmitz, [5]1934; Zahn: P. Ewald, [4]1923 (revised by G. Wohlenberg).

K. Barth, 1928; Eng. tr. by James W. Leitch, 1962; A. Klöpper, 1893; J. B. Lightfoot, [6]1882.

Colossians

CGTC: C. F. D. Moule, 1957; CNT: Ch. Masson, 1950; Hdb.: M. Dibelius-H. Greeven, [3]1953; ICC: T. K. Abbott, 1897; IntB.: F. W. Beare, 1955; Meyer: E.

LOHMEYER, [8]1930; Moffatt: E. F. SCOTT, 1930; NIC: F. F. BRUCE, 1957; NTD: H. CONZELMANN, [9]1962; RNT: K. STAAB, [3]1959; Torch: F. C. SYNGE, 1951; Ty: H. M. CARSON, 1960; Zahn: P. EWALD, [2]1910; ZüB.: W. BIEDER, 1943.
A. KLÖPPER, 1882; J. B. LIGHTFOOT, [6]1882.

I II Thessalonians

CNT: CH. MASSON, 1957; Ét. bibl.: B. RIGAUX, 1956; Hdb.: M. DIBELIUS, [3]1937; ICC: J. E. FRAME, 1912; IntB: J. W. BAILEY, 1955; Meyer: E. v. DOBSCHÜTZ, [7]1909; Moffatt: W. NEIL, 1950; NIC: L. MORRIS, 1959; NTD: A. OEPKE, 1933; RNT: K. STAAB, [3]1959; Torch: W. NEIL, 1957; Ty: L. MORRIS, 1956; UB: J. SCHNEIDER, I Thess., 1932, G. HELBIG, II Thess., [2]1955; Zahn: G. WOHLENBERG, [2]1909.

Philemon

CGTC: C. F. D. MOULE, 1957; Hdb.: M. DIBELIUS-H. GREEVEN, [3]1953; ICC: M. R. VINCENT, 1897; IntB: J. KNOX, 1955; Meyer: E. LOHMEYER, [8]1930; Moffatt: E. F. SCOTT, 1930; NIC: J. J. MÜLLER, 1955; NTD: G. FRIEDRICH, [9]1962; RNT: K. STAAB, [3]1959; Torch: A. R. C. LEANEY, 1960; Ty: H. M. CARSON, 1960; Zahn: P. EWALD, [2]1910; ZüB: W. BIEDER, 1944.
J. B. LIGHTFOOT, [6]1882.

Pastoral Epistles

Ét. bibl.: C. SPICQ, 1947; Hdb.: M. DIBELIUS-H. CONZELMANN, [3]1955; ICC: W. LOCK, 1924; IntB: F. D. GEALY, 1955; Meyer: B. WEISS, [7]1902; Moffatt: E. F. SCOTT, 1936; NTD: J. JEREMIAS, [6]1953; RNT: J. FREUNDORFER, [3]1959; Torch: A. R. C. LEANEY, 1960; Ty: D. GUTHRIE, 1957; UB: W. BRANDT, 1941; Zahn: G. WOHLENBERG, [3]1923.
B. S. EASTON, 1947; A. SCHLATTER, Die Kirche der Griechen im Urteil des Paulus, 1936; E. K. SIMPSON, 1954.

Hebrews

CNT: J. HÉRING, 1954; Ét. bibl.: C. SPICQ, I, II, 1952-53; Hdb.: H. WINDISCH, [2]1931; ICC: J. MOFFATT, 1924; IntB: A. C. PURDY, 1955; Meyer: O. MICHEL, [10]1957; Moffatt: T. H. ROBINSON, 1933; NTD: H. STRATHMANN, [6]1953; RNT: O. KUSS, 1953; Torch: W. NEIL, 1955; Ty: T. HEWITT, 1960; UB: W. LOEW, [3]1941; Zahn: E. RIGGENBACH, [2-3]1922.

James

Hdb.: H. WINDISCH-H. PREISKER, [3]1951; ICC: J. H. ROPES, 1916; IntB: B. S. EASTON, 1957; Meyer: M. DIBELIUS, [7]1921 (supplement by H. GREEVEN, 1956); Moffatt: J. MOFFATT, 1928; NIC: A. ROSS, 1954; NTD: J. SCHNEIDER, [9]1961;

RNT: J. Michl, 1953; Torch: E. C. Blackman, 1957; Ty: R. V. G. Tasker, 1956; UB: H. Rendtorff, 1953; Zahn: F. Hauck, 1926.

J. Marty, 1935; A. Schlatter, 1932.

I Peter

Hdb.: H. Windisch-H. Preisker, ³1951; HThK: K. H. Schelkle, 1961; ICC: Ch. Bigg, ²1910; IntB: A. M. Hunter, 1957; Meyer: R. Knopf, ⁷1912; Moffatt: J. Moffatt, 1928; NTD: J. Schneider, ⁹1961; RNT: J. Michl, 1953; Torch: C. E. B. Cranfield, 1960; Ty: A. M. Stibbs-A. F. Walls, 1959; UB: H. Rendtorff, ⁷1951; Zahn: G. Wohlenberg, ³1923; ZüB: E. Schweizer, ²1949.

F. W. Beare, ²1958 (reprint of ¹1945 with supplements); A. Schlatter, *Petrus und Paulus nach dem 1. Petrusbrief*, 1937; E. G. Selwyn, ²1947.

II Peter

Ét. bibl.: J. Chaine, 1939; Hdb.: H. Windisch-H. Preisker, ³1951; HThK: K. H. Schelkle, 1961; ICC: Ch. Bigg, ²1910; IntB: A. E. Barnett, 1957; Meyer: R. Knopf, ⁷1912; Moffatt: J. Moffatt, 1928; NTD: J. Schneider, ⁹1961; RNT: J. Michl, 1953; Torch: C. E. B. Cranfield, 1960; Zahn: G. Wohlenberg, ³1923.

Jude

Ét. bibl.: J. Chaine, 1939; Hdb.: H. Windisch-H. Preisker, ³1951; HThK: K. H. Schelkle, 1961; ICC: Ch. Bigg, ²1910; IntB: A. E. Barnett, 1957; Meyer: R. Knopf, ⁷1912; Moffatt: J. Moffatt, 1928; NTD: J. Schneider, ⁹1961; RNT: J. Michl, 1953; Torch: C. E. B. Cranfield, 1960; Zahn: G. Wohlenberg, ³1923.

I II III John

Ét. bibl.: J. Chaine, 1939; Hdb.: H. Windisch-H. Preisker, ³1951; HThK: R. Schnackenburg, 1953; ICC: A. E. Brooke, 1912; IntB: A. N. Wilder, 1957; Meyer: B. Weiss, ⁶1900; Moffatt: C. H. Dodd, 1946; NIC: A. Ross, 1954; NTD: J. Schneider, ⁹1961; RNT: J. Michl, 1953; ThHK: F. Büchsel, 1933; Torch: N. Alexander, 1962; UB: H. Asmussen, ³1957.

Apocalypse

É. bibl.: E.-B. Allo, 1933; Hdb.: E. Lohmeyer, 1926 (²1953, enlarged); ICC: R. H. Charles, I. II, 1920; IntB: M. Rist, 1957; Meyer: W. Bousset, ⁶1906; Moffatt: M. Kiddle-M. K. Ross, 1940; NTD: E. Lohse, ⁸1960; RNT: A. Wikenhauser, ³1959; ThHK: W. Hadorn, 1928; Torch: R. H. Preston-A. T. Hanson, 1949; UB: H. Lilje, ⁵1958; Eng. tr. by Olive Wyon from 4th ed. (1955), 1957; Zahn: Th. Zahn, I. II, 1924-26; ZüB: Ch. Brütsch, 1955.

A. Loisy, 1923.

BIBLIOGRAPHICAL SUPPLEMENTS

to § 1: p. 21 l. 2: now [25]1963.

p. 21 l. 8 f. b.: now I-VII, 1933-1964.

p. 22 l. 8: H. KRAFT, *Clavis Patrum Apostolicorum*, 1963.

p. 22 l. 23: Vocabulaire . . . now in German: *Wörterbuch zur biblischen Botschaft*, 1964.

p. 22 l. 25: *The Interpreter's Dictionary of the Bible*, 4 vols., 1962.

p. 23 l. 9: J. D. SMART, *Hermeneutische Probleme der Schriftauslegung*, Beiträge zur Praktischen Theologie 2, 1965.

to § 2: p. 26 l. 1: A. N. WILDER, *Early Christian Rhetoric*, 1964.

to § 3: p. 26 l. 19 f. b.: R. H. FULLER, *The NT in Current Study*, 1962; *The Cambridge History of the Bible*, ed. by S. L. GREENSLADE, 1963; S. NEIL, *The Interpretation of the NT 1861-1961*, 1964.

p. 28 l. 18: W. MARXSEN, Einleitung in das NT, 1963.

p. 28 l. 7 f. b.: C. F. D. MOULE, *The Bible of the NT*, 1962; R. M. GRANT, *A Historical Introduction to the NT*, 1963; E. F. HARRISON, *Introduction to the NT*, 1964.

p. 28 l. 3 f. b.: now read: A. F. J. KLIJN, *Inleiding tot het NT*, [2]1963.

p. 29 l. 14: B. MARIANI, *Introductio in Libros Sacros NT*, 1962; K. H. SCHELKLE, *Das NT. Seine literarische und theologische Geschichte*, 1963.

to § 4: p. 31 l. 16: R. V. G. TASKER, *The Nature and Purpose of the Gospels*, 1962.

to § 5: p. 33 l. 15 f. b.: X. LÉON-DUFOUR, *Concordance of the Synoptic Gospels in Seven Colors*, 1956 (also in French); A. BARR, *A Diagram of Synoptic Relationships*, [3]1957.

p. 34 l. 6: A. M. PERRY, "The Growth of the Gospels," IntB 7, 1951, 60 ff.

p. 34 l. 17: further L. CERFAUX, "Le problème synoptique," in *Recueil L. C.* III, 1962, 83 ff.

p. 34 l. 12 f. b.: N. B. STONEHOUSE, *Origins of the Synoptic Gospels*, 1963; R. L. LINDSEY, "A Modified Two-Document Theory of the Synoptic Dependence and Interdependence," NovT 6, 1963, 239 ff.; J. SCHMID, art. "Synoptiker," LThK IX, 1964, 1240 ff.; E. B. MARTINEX DALMAU, *A Study on the Synoptic Gospels*, 1964; F. G. DOWNING, "Towards the Rehabilitation of Q," NTSt 11, 1964-65, 169 ff.

p. 35 l. 18: R. SCHNACKENBURG, "Zur formgeschichtlichen Methode in der Evangelienforschung," ZkTh 85, 1963, 16 ff.; G. SCHILLE, "Der Mangel eines kritischen Geschichtsbildes in der ntl. Formgeschichte," ThLZ 88, 1963, 491 ff.; J. P. BROWN, "Synoptic Parallels in the Epistles and Form-History," NTSt 10, 1963-64, 27 ff.; V. TAYLOR, "Formgeschichte," ExpT 75, 1964, 356 ff.

p. 42 l. 7: cf. C. WIDENGREN, "Tradition and Literature in Early Judaism and in the Early Church," *Numen* 10, 1963, 42 ff.; further M. SMITH, JBL 82, 1963, 169 ff. Against his critics: B. GERHARDSSON, "Tradition and Transmission in Early Christianity," *Coniectanea Neotestamentica* 20, 1964.

Cf. also J. J. VINCENT, "Did Jesus Teach His Disciples to Learn by Heart?" StEv III, TU 88, 1964, 105 ff.

p. 43 l. 12: J. KÜRZINGER, art. "Papias," LThK VIII, 1963, 34 f.

p. 44 l. 2: E. STAUFFER, "Der Methurgeman des Petrus," *Ntl. Aufsätze, Festschr. J. Schmid*, 1963, 283 ff.; W. C. VAN UNNIK, "Zur Papias-Notiz über Markus," ZNW 54, 1963, 276 f.

p. 45 l. 19: cf. S. SCHULTZ, "Die Bedeutung der neueren Targumforschung für die synpt. Tradition," *Abraham unser Vater, Festschr. O. Michel*, Arbeiten zur Geschichte des Spätjudentums und Urchristentums 5, 1963, 425 ff.

p. 45 l. 22: G. M. STYLER, "The Priority of Mark," in: C. F. D. MOULE, *The Birth of the NT*, 1962, 223 ff.

p. 50 l. 21: On the origin of the symbol Q cf. C. F. D. MOULE, *The Birth of the NT*, 84 note 1.

p. 56 l. 7: E. KÄSEMANN, "Zum Thema der urchristlichen Apokalyptik," ZThK 59, 1962, 268 (= E. K., Exegetische Versuche und Besinnungen II, 1964, 115 f.); J. M. ROBINSON, "ΛΟΓΟΙ ΣΟΦΩΝ, Zur Gattung der Spruchquelle Q," *Zeit und Geschichte, Festschr. R. Bultmann*, 1964, 77 ff.

p. 57 l. 28: J. M. ROBINSON, see to p. 56 l. 7; W. SCHRAGE, *Das Verhältnis des Thomas-Ev. zur synpt. Tradition und zu den kopt. Evangelienübersetzungen*, Beih. ZNW 29, 1964 (lit.); J. B. BAUER, "The Synoptic Tradition in the Gospel of Thomas," StEv III, TU 88, 1964, 314 ff.

to § 6: p. 61 l. 4: now in W. D. DAVIES, *Christian Origins and Judaism*, 1962, 67 ff.

p. 61 l. 24: now in E. S., *Neotestamentica*, 1963, 93 ff.

p. 61 l. 25: E. TROCMÉ, *La formation de l'Évangile selon Marc*, Études d'Histoire et de Philosophie Religieuses 57, 1963; M. KARNETZKI, "Die letzte Redaktion des Mk.," *Zwischenstation, Festschr. K. Kupisch*, 1963, 161 ff.; L. W. BARNARD, "St. Mark and Alexandria," HarvThR 57, 1964, 145 ff.; S. G. F. BRANDON, "The Apologetic Factor in the Marcan Gospel," StEv II, TU 87, 1964, 34 ff.; S. SCHULZ, "Die Bedeutung des Mk. für die Theologiegeschichte des Urchristentums," *ibid.*, 135 ff.; E. SCHWEIZER, "Mark's Contribution to the Quest of the Historical Jesus," NTSt 10, 1963-64, 21 ff.; *idem*, "Die theologische Leistung des Mk.," EvTh 24, 1964, 337 ff.; T. A. BURKILL, *Mysterious Revelation*, 1963; PH. VIELHAUER, "Erwägungen zur Christologie des Mk.," *Zeit und Geschichte, Festschr. R. Bultmann*, 1964, 155 ff.; G. STRECKER, "Zur Messiasgeheimnistheorie im Mk.," StEv III, TU 88, 1964, 87 ff.

p. 63 l. 6 f. b.: Against Farrer: H. E. W. TURNER, *Historicity and the Gospels*, 1963, 45 ff.

to § 7: p. 73 l. 8: C. H. CAVE, "St. Matthew's Infancy Narrative," NTSt 9, 1962-63, 382 ff.; N. WALKER, "The Alleged Matthaean Errata," NTSt 9, 1962-63, 391 ff.; J. GNILKA, "Die Kirche des Mt. und die Gemeinde von Qumran," BZ, N.F. 7, 1963, 43 ff.; R. HUMMEL, *Die Auseinandersetzung zwischen Kirche und Judentum im Mt.*, BeTh 33, 1963; C. W. F. SMITH, "The Mixed State of the Church in Matthew's Gospel," JBL 82, 1963, 149 ff.; J. KÜRZINGER, "Irenäus und sein Zeugnis zur Sprache des Mt.," NTSt 10, 1963-64, 108 ff.; E. KÄSEMANN, "Die Anfänge christlicher Theologie," ZThK 57, 1960, 162 ff. (= E. K., Exegetische Versuche und Besinnungen II, 1964, 82 ff.); C. F. D. MOULE, "Translation Greek and Original Greek in

Matthew," in C. F. D. M., *The Birth of the NT*, 1962, 215 ff.; *idem*, "St. Matthew's Gospel: Some Neglected Features," StEv II, TU 87, 1964, 91 ff.; E. Schweizer, "Zum Mt.—Ein Kap. ntl. Redaktionsgeschichte," EvTh 23, 1963, 611 ff.

p. 84 l. 11 f. b.: Against Rengstorf cf. E. Linnemann, *Gleichnisse Jesu*, 1961, 162 f.

to § 8:   p. 87 l. 13: further H. F. D. Sparks, JThSt, N.S. 14, 1963, 457 ff.

p. 87 l. 15 f. b.: U. Wilckens, "Das Offenbarungsverständnis in der Geschichte des Urchristentums," in "Offenbarung als Geschichte," *Kerygma und Dogma* Beih. I, 1961, 73 ff.; K. Stalder, "Die Heilsbedeutung des Todes Jesu in den lukanischen Schriften," *Internationale kirchliche Zeitschrift* 52, 1962, 222 ff.; V. Taylor, "F. Rehkopf," ExpT 74, 1962-63, 262 ff.; P. Parker, "Luke and the Fourth Evangelist," NTSt 9, 1962-63, 317 ff.; H. Schürmann, "Das Thomasev. und das lukanische Sondergut," BZ, N.F. 7, 1963, 236 ff.; G. Braumann, "Das Mittel der Zeit. Erwägungen zur Theologie des Lk.," ZNW 54, 1963, 117 ff.; S. Schulz, "Gottes Vorsehung bei Lk.," ZNW 54, 1963, 104 ff.; H. H. Oliver, "The Lucan Birth Stories and the Purpose of Luke-Acts," NTSt 10, 1963-64, 202 ff.; J. H. Davies, "The Purpose of the Central Section of St. Luke's Gospel," StEv II, TU 87, 1964, 164 ff.; W. C. Robinson, *Der Weg des Herrn. Studien zur Geschichte und Eschatologie im Lk.*, Theologische Forschungen 36, 1964; V. Taylor, "Rehkopf's List of Words and Phrases Illustrative of Pre-Lukan Speech Usage," JThSt, N. S. 15, 1964, 59 ff.; D. Q. Morton, *The Structure of Luke and Acts*, 1964.

p. 90 l. 13: H. Schürmann, "Evangelienschrift und kirchliche Unterweisung. Die repräsentative Funktion der Schrift nach Lk 1:1-4," *Miscellanea Erfordiana, Erfurter Theologische Studien* 12, 1962, 48 ff.; G. Klein, "Lk. 1:1-4 als theologisches Programm," *Zeit und Geschichte, Festschr. R. Bultmann*, 1964, 193 ff.

p. 96 l. 12: H. Thyen, "ΒΑΠΤΙΣΜΑ ΜΕΤΑΝΟΙΑΣ ΕΙΣ ΑΦΕΣΙΝ ΑΜΑΡΤΙΩΝ," *Zeit und Geschichte, Festschr. R. Bultmann*, 1964, 115 ff.

p. 102 l. 12 f. b.: H. Küng, "Der Frühkatholizismus im NT als kontroverstheologisches Problem," in *"Kirche im Konzil,"* Herder-Bücherei 140, 1963, 125 ff.; L. Goppelt, "The Existence of the Church in History According to Apostolic and Early Catholic Thought," *Current Issues in NT Interpretation, Festschr. O. Piper*, 1962, 153 ff.; H. Schürmann, "Das Testament des Paulus für die Kirche," *Theologische Jahrbücher*, 1964, 23 ff.

to § 9:   p. 107 l. 6 (now in E. K., *Exegetische Versuche und Besinnungen* II, 1964, 29 f.).

p. 107 l. 7 (now in E. S. *Neotestamentica*, 1963, 418 ff.).

p. 107 l. 3 f. b.: J. Jervell, "Zur Frage der Traditionsgrundlage der Apg.," StTh 16, 1962, 25 ff.; D. Guthrie, "Recent Literature on the Acts of the Apostles," VE 2, 1963, 33 ff.; W. Schmithals, *Paulus und Jakobus*, FRLANT 85, 1963, 70 ff.; E. Haenchen, "Judentum und Christentum in der Apg.," ZNW 54, 1963, 155 ff.; F. V. Filson, *Two Crucial Decades: Studies in the Book of Acts*, 1963; J. H. Crehan, "The Purpose of Luke in Acts," StEv II, TU 87, 1964, 354 ff.; R. A. Martin, "Syntactical Evidence of Aramaic Sources in Acts I-XV," NTSt 11, 1964-65, 38 ff.; R. Glover, " 'Luke the Antiochene' and Acts," NTSt 11, 1964-65, 97 ff.; W. Schneemelcher, "Die

Apg. des Lukas und die Acta Pauli," *Apophoreta, Festschr. E. Haenchen,* Beih. ZNW 30, 1964, 236 ff.; M. D. GOULDER, *Type and History in Acts,* 1964. p. 110 l. 2 f. b.: H. ANDERSON, *Jesus and Christian Origins,* 1964, 343 f.

p. 129 l. 4: Otherwise again TH. BOMAN, "Das textkritische Problem des sog. Aposteldekrets," NovT 7, 1964, 26 ff.

p. 130 l. 11: J.-C. LEBRAM, "Der Aufbau der Areopagrede," ZNW 55, 1964, 221 ff.

p. 132 l. 3: E. HAENCHEN, "Acta 27," *Zeit und Geschichte, Festschr. R. Bultmann,* 1964, 234 ff.

p. 132 l. 11: E. SCHWEIZER, *Erniedrigung und Erhöhung bei Jesus und seinen Nachfolgern,* AThANT 28, ²1962, 53 f.

p. 133 l. 31: G. D. KILPATRICK, "An Eclectic Study of the Text of Acts," *Biblical and Patristic Studies in Memory of R. P. Casey,* 1963, 64 ff.

to §10: p. 135 l. 16 f. b. (now in E. K., Exegetische Versuche und Besinnungen II, 1964, 131 ff.).

p. 137 l. 9: on A. Guilding also: J. R. PORTER, "The Pentateuch and the Triennial Lectionary Circle: An Examination of a Recent Theory," *Promise and Fulfilment, Festschr. S. H. Hooke,* 1963, 163 ff.; L. MORRIS, *The NT and the Jewish Lectionaries,* 1964.

p. 137 l. 22: A. Feuillet, *Études Johanniques,* Museum Lessianum, Section biblique 4, 1962; J. A. T. ROBINSON, "The Relation of the Prologue to the Gospel of St. John," NTSt 9, 1962-63, 120 ff.; R. E. BROWN, "The Problem of Historicity in John," CBQ 24, 1962, 1 ff.; *idem,* "The Gospel of Thomas and St. John's Gospel," NTSt 9, 1962-63, 155 ff.; J. A. BAILEY, *The Traditions Common to the Gospels of Luke and John, Suppl.* NovT 7, 1963; R. SCHNACKENBURG, "Die Messiasfrage im Joh.," *Ntl. Aufsätze, Festschr. J. Schmid,* 1963; 240 ff.; D. M. SMITH, "John 12:12 and the Question of John's Use of Synoptics," JBL 82, 1963, 58 ff.; *idem,* "The Sources of the Gospel of John, an Assessment of the Present State of the Problem," NTSt 10, 1963-64, 336 ff.; P. PARKER, see to §8; C. H. DODD, *Historical Tradition in the Fourth Gospel,* 1963; H. BALMFORTH, "The Structure of the Fourth Gospel," StEv II, TU 87, 1964, 25 ff.; E. GRÄSSER, "Die antijüdische Polemik im Joh.," NTSt 11, 1964-65, 74 ff.; E. D. FREED, "Variations in the Language and Thought of John," ZNW 55, 1964, 167 ff.; E. HAENCHEN, "Das Joh. und sein Kommentar," ThLZ 89, 1964, 881 ff.

p. 146 l. 13 f. b.: K. ALAND, "Randbemerkung" (see to p. 359 l. 9 f. b.), 22 ff.

p. 148 l. 4: U. BECKER, *Jesus und die Ehebrecherin,* Beih. ZNW 28, 1963; K. ALAND, "Randbemerkung" (see to p. 146 l. 13 f. b.), 11 ff.

p. 153 l. 9 f. b.: (now in E. K., Exegetische Versuche und Besinnungen II, 1964, 155 ff.).

p. 153 l. 7 f. b.: E. HAENCHEN, "Probleme des joh. Prologs," ZThK 60, 1963, 305 ff.; W. ELTESTER, "Der Logos und sein Prophet. Fragen zur heutigen Erklärung des joh. Prologs," *Apophoreta, Festschr. E. Haenchen,* Beih. ZNW 30, 1964, 109 ff.

p. 159 l. 5: O. HUTH, "Das Mandäerproblem—das NT im Lichte der mandäischen und essenischen Quellen," *Symbolon* 3, 1962, 18 ff.

p. 159 l. 13: On Jewish Gnosticism cf. R. MARCUS, "The Qumran Texts and Early Judaism," BR 1, 1956, 9 ff.; J. MAIER, *Die Texte vom Toten Meer* II, 1960, 18 f.

p. 159 l. 17: Translation by W. BAUER also in E. HENNECKE-W. SCHNEE-MELCHER, Ntl. Apokryphen II, ³1964, 576 ff. Cf. also J. CARMAGNAC, "Un Qumrânien converti au Christianisme: l'auteur des Odes de Salomon," in *Qumran-Probleme*, 1963, 75 ff.; K. RUDOLPH, "War der Verf. der Oden Salomos ein Qumran-Christ?," *Revue de Qumran* 4, 1963-64, 523 ff.

p. 160 l. 9: A. D. NOCK, "Gnosticism," HarvThR 57, 1964, 255 ff.

to §11: p. 176 l. 16: T. Y. MULLINS, "Disclosure. A Literary Form in the NT," NovT 7, 1964, 44 ff.

to §12: p. 177 l. 12 f. b.: German: *Paulus und seine Briefe*, Biblische Handbibliothek 2, 1964; J. CAMBIER, art. "Paul," DBS VII, 1962, 279 ff. (esp. 329 ff.).

to §14: p. 181 l. 17: K. THIEME, "Die Struktur des I Thess.," *Festschr. O. Michel*, see to p. 45 l. 19; 1963, 450 ff.; W. SCHMITHALS, "Die Thess. als Briefkomposition," *Zeit und Geschichte, Festschr. R. Bultmann*, 1964, 295 ff.

to §15: p. 185 l. 9 f. b.: P. DAY, "The Practical Purpose of Second Thessalonians," AThR 45, 1963, 203 ff.

to §16: p. 190 l. 14 f. b.: W. FOERSTER, "Abfassungszeit und Ziel des Gal.," *Apophoreta, Festschr. E. Haenchen*, Beih. ZNW 30, 1964, 135 ff.

p. 192 l. 22: D. M. STANLEY, "Christ's Resurrection in Pauline Soteriology," *Analecta Biblica* 13, 1961, 68.

to §17: p. 198 l. 9 f. b.: C. K. BARRETT, "Cephas and Corinth," *Festschr. O. Michel*, see to p. 45 l. 19, 1963, 1 ff.; G. FRIEDRICH, "Christus, Einheit und Norm der Christen. Das Grundmotiv des I. Kor.," *Kerygma und Dogma* 9, 1963, 235 ff.

p. 202 l. 6: H. MOSBECH, "Apostolos in the NT," StTh 2, 1949-50, 196.

p. 204 l. 1: against Schmithals: P. NEUENZEIT, "Das Herrenmahl," *Studien zum A und NT* 1, 1960, 23 f.

to §18: p. 205 l. 1 f. b.: J. GNILKA, "II. Kor. 6:14–7:1 im Lichte der Qumranschriften und der Zwölfpatriarchentestamente," *Ntl. Aufsätze, Festschr. J. Schmid*, 1963, 86 ff.; G. FRIEDRICH, "Die Gegner des Paulus im II Kor.," *Festschr. O. Michel*, see on p. 45 l. 19, 1963, 181 ff. A. M. G. STEPHENSON, "Partition Theories on 2 Corinthians," StEv II, TU 87, 1964, 639 ff.; D. GEORGI, *Die Gegner des Paulus im II. Kor.*, WMANT 11, 1964.

p. 211 l. 6: L. BAECK, *Paulus, die Pharisäer und das NT*, 1961, 7 f.; L. CERFAUX, "Le Chrétien dans la théologie Paulinienne," *Lectio Divina* 33, 1962, 260 ff.

p. 211 l. 14: H. BRAUN, "Qumran und das NT," ThRdsch, N. F. 29, 1963, 221 ff.

to §19: p. 216 l. 24: A. DESCAMPS, "La structure de Rom 1-11," *Studiorum Paulinorum Congressus I, Analecta Biblica* 17, 1963, 3 ff.; F. F. BRUCE, "St. Paul in Rome," BJRL 46, 1963-64, 326 ff.; K. H. RENGSTORF, "Paulus und die römische Christenheit," StEv II, TU 87, 1964, 447 ff.; A. ROOSEN, "Le genre littéraire de l'Épître aux Romains," *ibid.*, 465 ff.; J. SCHMID, LThK IX, 1964, 28 ff.; R. C. M. RUIJS, De struktuur van de Brief aan de Romeinen, 1964.

p. 216 l. 3 f. b.: insert after Goguel: X. LÉON-DUFOUR, RScR 51, 1963, 87.

p. 222 l. 17, 32: K. ALAND, *Randbemerkung* (see to p. 359 l. 9 f. b.), 27 ff., 18 ff.

p. 223 l. 15 f. b.: add: O. KUSS, MThZ 14, 1963, 7.

to §20: p. 226, l. 4 f. b.: V. FURNISH, "The Place and Purpose of Phil III," NTSt 10, 1963-64, 80 ff.; C. O. BUCHANAN, "Epaphroditus' Sickness and the Letter to the Philippians," *Evangelical Quarterly* 36, 1964, 157 ff. (cf. NT Abstracts 9, 1964-65, 75).

p. 233 l. 15: D. M. STANLEY, see to p. 192 l. 22, 65 f.

p. 233 l. 20 f. b.: W. KRAMER, *Kyrios Christos Gottessohn*, AThANT 44, 1963, 147. 172.

to §21: p. 237 l. 16 f. b.: P. BENOIT, "Rapports littéraires entre les Épîtres aux Colossiens et aux Ephésiens," *Ntl. Aufsätze, Festschr. J. Schmid*, 1963, 11 ff.; H.-M. SCHENKE, "Der Widerstreit gnostischer und kirchlicher Christologie im Spiegel des Kol.," ZThK 61, 1964, 391 ff.

p. 240 l. 12 f. b.: E. Schweizer now in E. S., *Neotestamentica*, 1963, 299 ff.

p. 241 l. 16: now E. S., *Neotestamentica*, 1963, 429.

p. 241 l. 25: W. SCHRAGE, *Die konkreten Einzelgebote in der paulinischen Paränese*, 1961, 54 f.

p. 242 l. 16: K.-G. ECKART, "Urchristliche Tauf- und Ordinationsliturgie (Col I9-20 Act 2618)," Thv 8 1961-62, 23 ff.

to §23: p. 247 l. 21: Cerfaux now in *Recueil L. C.* III, 1962, 265 ff.

p. 247 l. 24: R. BATEY, "The Destination of Ephesians," JBL 82, 1963, 101 ff.; F. MUSSNER, "Beiträge aus Qumran zum Verständnis des Eph.," *Ntl. Aufsätze, Festschr. J. Schmid*, 1963, 185 ff.; N. A. DAHL, "Der Eph. und der verlorene 1. Brief des Paulus an die Korinther," *Festschr. O. Michel*, see to p. 45 l. 19, 1963, 65 ff.; P. BENOIT, see to p. 237 l. 16 f. b.; G. W. BARKER, HarvThR 56, 1963, 87 f.; P. N. HARRISON, "The Author of Ephesians," StEv II, TU 87, 1964, 595 ff.; R. A. WILSON, " 'We' and 'You' in the Epistle to the Ephesians," *ibid.*, 667 ff.

p. 256 l. 10: W. SCHNEEMELCHER, in E. HENNECKE-W. SCHNEEMELCHER, Ntl. Apokryphen II, ³1964, 54 f.

to §24: p. 259 l. 2: J. ALLAN, "The 'In Christ' Formula in the Pastoral Epistles," NTSt 10, 1963-64, 115 ff.; J. SCHMID, LThK VIII, 1963, 155 ff.; C. F. D. MOULE, "Luke and the Pastoral Epistles," in C. F. D. M., *The Birth of the NT*, 1961, 220 f.

p. 262 l. 28: In justification of the linguistic statistical method: M. P. BROWN, *The Authentic Writings of Ignatius. A Study of Linguistic Criteria*, 1963.

to §25: p. 273 l. 13 f. b.: Rigaux in German (see to p. 177 l. 12 f. b.), 204 ff.; R. GYLLENBERG, "Die Komposition des Hb.," Svensk Exegetisk Aarsbok 22, 3, 1957-58, 137 ff.; H. KÖSTER, " 'Outside the Camp.' Hebr. 139-14," HarvThR 55, 1962, 299 ff.; F. F. BRUCE, " 'To the Hebrews' or 'To the Essenes,' " NTSt 9, 1962-63, 217 ff.; A. VANHOYE, *La structure littéraire de l'Épître aux Hébreux*, Studia Neotestamentica 1, 1963; E. GRÄSSER, "Der Hb. 1938-63," ThRdsch, N.F. 30, 1964, 138 ff.

to §26: p. 283 l. 3: A STROBEL, "Die Kirchenbriefe in der neueren Auslegung," *Lutherische Monatshefte* 3, 1964, Literaturheft, 1 ff.

to §27: p. 284 l. 22: M. GERTNER, "Midrashim in the NT," *Journal of Semitic Studies* 7, 1962, 283 ff.; O. J. SEITZ, "James and the Law," StEv II, TU 87,

1964, 472 ff.; R. Walker, "Allein aus Werken," ZThK 61, 1964, 155 ff.; K.-G. Eckart, "Zur Terminologie des Jk.," ThLZ 89, 1964, 521 ff.; B. Noack, "Jk. wider die Reichen," StTh 18, 1964, 10 ff.

to §28:   p. 293 l. 19: J. Jeremias, *Die Kindertaufe in den ersten vier Jhdt.n,* 1958, 36; A. R. C. Leaney, "I Peter and the Passover: an Interpretation," NTSt 10, 1963-64, 238 ff.

p. 295 l. 19: C. F. D. Moule, *The Birth of the NT,* 1962, 112 ff.

to §29:   p. 299 l. 16: K. H. Schelkle, "Spätapostolische Briefe als frühkath. Zeugnis," *Ntl. Aufsätze, Festschr. J. Schmid,* 1963, 225 ff.; *idem,* "Der Judasbrief bei den Kirchenvätern," *Festschr. O. Michel,* see to p. 45 l. 19, 1963, 405 ff.

to §30:   p. 302 l. 10: E. M. B. Green, *2 Peter Reconsidered,* The Tyndale NT Lecture 1960, 1962.

to §31:   p. 306 l. 20: H.-M. Schenke, "Determination und Ethik im I Joh.," ZThK 60, 1963, 204 f.

to §33:   p. 316 l. 6 f. b.: Rowley now: ³1963.

p. 316 l. 1 f. b.: Ph. Vielhauer in E. Hennecke-W. Schneemelcher, *Ntl. Apokryphen* II, ³1964, 408 ff. 428 ff.; D. S. Russell, *The Method and Message of Jewish Apocalyptic,* 1964.

to §34:   p. 319 l. 21: J. N. Sanders, "St. John on Patmos," NTSt 9, 1962-63, 75 ff.; A. Feuillet, *L' Apocalypse. État de la question,* Studia Neotestamentica, Subsidia III, 1963 (cf. thereto S. Giet, RScR 38, 1964, 71 ff.; G. Strecker, Gn 36, 1964, 664 ff.); B. Newman, "The Fallacy of the Domitian Hypothesis: Critique of the Irenaeus Source as a Witness for the Contemporary-historical Approach to the Interpretation of the Apocalypse," NTSt 10, 1963-64, 133 ff.; Ph. Vielhauer in E. Hennecke-W. Schneemelcher, Ntl. Apokryphen II, ³1964, 437 ff.; A. Strobel, "Abfassung und Geschichtstheologie der Apk. nach Kap. 17:9-12," NTSt 10, 1963-64, 433 ff.; G. Harder, "Eschatologische Schemata in der Johannesapokalypse," Thv 9, 1963, 70 ff.

p. 331 l. 8: L. van Hartingsveld, *Die Eschatologie des Joh.,* 1962, 184 f.

to Part II: p. 334 l. 21: H. v. Campenhausen, "Die Entstehung des NT," *Heidelberger Jahrbücher* 7, 1963, 1 ff.; C. F. D. Moule, *The Birth of the NT,* 1962, 178 ff.; A. C. Sundberg, "Dependent Canonicity in Irenaeus and Tertullian," StEv III, TU 88, 1964, 403 ff.; F. E. Vokes, "The Didache and the Canon of the NT," *ibid.,* 427 ff.

to §35:   p. 334 l. 5 f. b.: H. v. Campenhausen, "Das AT als Bibel der Kirche," in H. v. C., *Aus der Frühzeit des Christentums,* 1963, 152 ff.

p. 337 l. 22 f. b.: E. Flesseman-van Leer, "Prinzipien der Sammlung und Ausscheidung bei der Bildung des Kanons," ZThK 61, 1964, 404 ff.

p. 341 l. 29: W. C. van Unnik, "The 'Gospel of Truth' and the NT," in *The Jung Codex,* ed. by F. L. Cross, 1955, 81 ff. (see thereto E. Haenchen, ThRdsch, N.F. 30, 1964, 49).

p. 342 l. 19 f. b.: H. J. Frede, "Altlat. Paulus-Handschriften," *Vetus Latina, aus der Geschichte der lat. Bibel* 4, 1964, 168 ff.

to §36:   p. 347 l. 9 f. b.: T. F. Glasson, "The Nestorian Canon and the Chinese Tablet," ExpT 74, 1962-63, 260 f.

to §37:   p. 354 l. 15 f. b.: E. Schweizer, "Scripture-Tradition-Modern Interpretation," in E. S., *Neotestamentica,* 1963, 203 ff.

to Part III: p. 359 l. 11 f. b.: J. DUPLACY, "Bulletin de Critique textuelle du NT I," 2. Teil, RScR 50, 1962, 564 ff.; 51, 1963, 432 ff.

p. 360 l. 16: G. D. KILPATRICK, "Atticism and the Text of the Greek NT," *Ntl. Aufsätze, Festschr. J. Schmid*, 1963, 125 ff.; B. M. METZGER, *Chapters in the History of NT Textual Criticism*, NTTS 4, 1963; *idem, The Text of the NT. Its Transmission, Corruption and Restoration*, 1964; K. ALAND, *Kurzgefasste Liste der griech. Handschriften des NT* I, Arbeiten zur Textforschung I, 1963; *idem*, "Glosse, Interpolation, Redaktion und Komposition in der Sicht der ntl. Textkritik. Eine Randbemerkung," *Apophoreta, Festschr. E. Haenchen*, Beih. ZNW 30, 1964, 7 ff.

to §38: p. 361 l. 21: R. C. NEVIUS, *The Divine Names in St. Mark*, SaD 25, 1964.

p. 363 l. 7: K. ALAND, "Neue Ntl. Papyri II," NTSt 9, 1962-63, 303 ff.; 10, 1963-64, 62 ff.; 11, 1964-65, 1 ff.

p. 364 l. 7: Review by M.-E. BOISMARD, RB 70, 1963, 120 ff. (list of emendations). Cf. K. ALAND, NTSt 10, 1963-64, 62 ff.

p. 364 l. 20: J. N. BIRDSALL, "The Text of Jude in $\mathfrak{P}^{72}$," JThSt, N.S. 14, 1963, 394 ff.; É. MASSAUX, "Le texte de la Iᵃ Petri du papyrus Bodmer VIII ($\mathfrak{P}^{72}$)," EphThL 39, 1963, 616 ff.

p. 368 l. 12 f. b.: A. WIKGREN, "Chicago Studies in the Greek Lectionary of the NT," *Biblical and Patristic Studies in Memory of R. P. Casey*, 1963, 96 ff.

p. 370 l. 14 f. b.: add to Baumstark: A. BAUMSTART, "Die syr. Übersetzung des Titus von Bostra und das Diatessaron," Bb 16, 1935, 257 ff.

p. 370 l. 7 f. b.: F. BOLGIANI, *Vittore di Capua e il "Diatessaron,"* 1962; B. M. METZGER's essay now in *Chapters* (see to p. 360 l. 16), 97 ff.

p. 370 l. 1 f. b.: L. LELOIR, *Le témoignage d' Éphrem sur le Diatessaron*, CSCO 227, Subsidia 19, 1962; *idem, Saint Éphrem., Commentaire de l'évangile concordant. Texte syriaque* . . . éd. et trad. par L. Leloir, Chester Beatty Monographs Nr. 8, 1963.

p. 371 l. 11 f. b.: J. KERSCHENSTEINER, "Neues zum altsyr. Paulustext," *Studiorum Paulinorum Congressus I*, Analecta Biblica 17, 1963, 531 ff.; *idem*, "Beobachtungen zum altsyr. Actatext," Bb 45, 1964, 63 ff.

p. 373 l. 6: C. PERROT, "Un fragment christo-palestinien découvert à Khirbet-Mird (Acts 10:28-29, 32-41)," RB 70, 1963, 506 ff.

p. 373 l. 15 f. b.: add to A. Jülicher-W. Matzkow: *Joh.*, 1963.

p. 373 l. 10 f. b.: add to *Vetus Latina*: Bd. 24, 1: 2.-4. Lieferung, 1963-64 (Eph.).

p. 374 l. 18 f. b.: B. FISCHER, "Ein neuer Zeuge zum westlichen Text der Apg.," *Biblical and Patristic Studies in Memory of R. P. Casey*, 1963, 33 ff.; F. H. TINNEFELD, "Untersuchungen zur altlat. Überlieferung des I. Tim.," *Klassisch-Philologische Studien* 26, 1963; H. J. FREDE, *Altlat. Paulus-Handschriften, Vetus Latina, aus der Geschichte der lat. Bibel* 4, 1964.

p. 379 l. 4: B. M. METZGER, "Explicit References in the Works of Origen to Variant Readings in NT Manuscripts," *Biblical and Patristic Studies in Memory of R. P. Casey*, 1963, 78 ff.

to §40: p. 384 l. 4: S. JELLICOE, "The Hesychian Recension Reconsidered," JBL 82, 1963, 409 ff.

p. 385 l. 6: T. C. PETERSEN, "An Early Coptic Manuscript of Acts: An Unrevised Version of the Ancient So-Called Western Text," CBQ 26, 1964, 225 ff.

p. 385 l. 12 f. b.: The essays by B. M. METZGER now in *Chapters* (see to p. 360 l. 16), 42 ff. 121 ff.

p. 386 l. 1 f. b.: E. C. COLWELL and E. W. TUNE, "The Quantitative Relationships between Ms-Text-Types," *Biblical and Patristic Studies in Memory of R. P. Casey*, 1963, 25 ff.; *idem*, "Variant Readings: Classification and Use," JBL 83, 253 ff.

Additions to List of Commentaries

Mt.: CNT: P. BONNARD, 1963; P. GAECHTER, 1963.

Mk.: to Lohmeyer: Supplement by G. SASS, [2]1963; A. LOISY, 1912.

Acts: Cancel Hdb.: E. Preuschen and add: Hdb.: H. CONZELMANN, [2]1963; NTD: G. STÄHLIN, 1963.

Rom.: Meyer: O. MICHEL, [12] 1963; ThHK: H. W. SCHMIDT, 1963; Ty: F. F. BRUCE, 1963.

Gal.: A. LOISY, 1916.

Eph: Ty: F. FOULKES, 1963.

Phil.: to Lohmeyer: Supplement by W. SCHMAUCH, 1964, 11 ff.

Col.: to Lohmeyer: Supplement by W. SCHMAUCH, 1964, 39 ff.

Phlm: to Lohmeyer: Supplement to W. SCHMAUCH, 1964, 86 ff.

Past.: BNTC: J. N. D. KELLY, 1964; C. K. BARRETT, The New Clarendon Bible (NT), 1963.

Hb.: BNTC: H. W. MONTEFIORE, 1964; Meyer: O. MICHEL, [11]1960.

Jas.: AB: B. REICKE, 1964; HThK: F. MUSSNER, 1964; Meyer: M. DIBELIUS (augmented by H. GREEVEN), [11]1964.

I-II Pet.: AB: B. REICKE, 1964.

Jude: AB: B. REICKE, 1964.

I-III Jn.: HThK: R. SCHNACKENBURG, [2]1963; Ty: J. R. W. STOTT, 1964; E. GAUGLER, *Auslegung ntl. Schriften I*, 1, 1964.

INDEXES OF PASSAGES

A. New Testament

This index does not include the passages listed in the paragraphs dealing with the contents of each book.

B. Early Church

INDEX OF PERSONS

References which can readily be located by consulting the Table of Contents
are not listed here.

INDEX OF SUBJECTS

Items which can readily be located by consulting the Table of Contents or the
Indexes of Passages are not listed here.